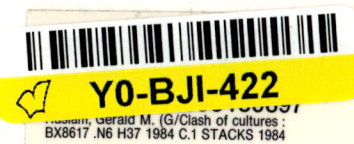

+BX8617 .N6 H37 1984

Y0-BJI-422

Haslam, Gerald M. (G/Clash of cultures :
BX8617 .N6 H37 1984 C.1 STACKS 1984

BX
8617
N6
H37
1984

Haslam, Gerald M.
Clash of cultures

DATE DUE

Clash of Cultures

American University Studies

Series IX
History

Vol. 7

PETER LANG
New York · Berne · Frankfurt am Main

Gerald Myron Haslam

Clash of Cultures

The Norwegian Experience with Mormonism, 1842–1920

PETER LANG
New York · Berne · Frankfurt am Main

Library of Congress Cataloging in Publication Data

Haslam, Gerald M.
 Clash of Cultures.

   (American University Studies. Series IX, History; vol. 7)
   Revision of thesis (PH. D.) – Brigham Young University, 1981.
   Bibliography: p.
   1. Mormon Church – Norway – History. 2. Church of Jesus Christ of Latter-Day Saints – History. 3. Norwegians – United States – Religious Life. 4. Norway – Church History. I. Title. II. Series.
BX8617.N6H37 1984   289.3'481   83-49362
ISBN 0-8204-0179-X
ISSN 0740-0462

CIP-Kurztitelaufnahme der Deutschen Bibliothek

Haslam, Gerald Myron:
Clash of Cultures: the Norwegian Experience with Mormonism, 1842–1920 / Gerald Myron Haslam. – New York; Berne; Frankfurt am Main: Lang, 1984.
   (American University Studies: Ser. 9, History; Vol. 7)
   ISBN 0-8204-0179-X

NE: American University Studies / 09

© Peter Lang Publishing, Inc., New York 1984

All rights reserved.
Reprint or reproduction, even partially, in all forms such as microfilm, xerography, microfiche, microcard, offset prohibited.

Printed by Lang Druck, Inc., Liebefeld/Berne (Switzerland)

To
Anka, Aasta, Otto,
Myron, Donna, and
"Little Donna"

PREFACE

As originally researched, this work was titled "The Norwegian Experience with Mormonism, 1842-1920" and approved as a dissertation "presented to the Department of History, Brigham Young University, in partial fulfillment of the requirements for the Degree Doctor of Philosophy" in August 1981. Dissertation committee members were: Douglas F. Tobler, chairman; James B. Allen, Department Chairman; Louis B. Cardon; Carl-Erik Johansson. Since then, the work has been thoroughly revised for publication by Peter Lang--several translations reworked with an eye toward rendering sense and meaning of the originals even more clearly and footnotes given a thorough housecleaning (redundant phrases and references removed or streamlined). I am especially indebted to Jay Wilson, Editor in Chief, Peter Lang Publishing, Inc., New York, for timely encouragement and advice; and to my beloved "Anka" who grew up in or near many historical centers of Norwegian Mormonism and has spent countless hours proofing text and footnotes, i.e., her suggestions resulted in many improvements. In summary, the present product is updated, revised and polished. Due to limitations of word processing equipment used in preparing a camera-ready manuscript, the following substitutions have been used for Scandinavian letters: "ae" for "æ" and "ä"; "oe" for "ø" and "ö"; "aa" for "å." This accords fully with Joseph Gibaldi and Walter S. Achtert, MLA Handbook (New York: Modern Language Association, 1980), p. 16.

G.M.H.

TABLE OF CONTENTS

INTRODUCTION xiii

Chapter

I. NORWEGIAN AND AMERICAN PRELUDES THROUGH
   1849 1

   Hans Nielsen Hauge and the Lay Believers
   The Sloopers and the Kendall Colony
   The Fox River Settlement and the
      Norwegian Mormons

II. FORERUNNERS AND BEGINNINGS IN
    SCANDINAVIA 7

    P. O. Hansen's History
    Beginnings in Copenhagen
    George Parker Dykes versus Erastus Snow
    Publication of Tracts and The Book of Mormon
    Beginnings in Aalborg
    The Norwegian Connection
    Svend Larsen of Risoer
    Beginnings in Risoer and Brevik
    The "Awakened" Followers of Hans Nielsen
       Hauge
    Ole P. Petersen in Fredrikstad
    Tobias Jacobsen and Methodist Fanaticism
    Mormon Beginnings in Fredrikstad
    Conclusion

III. THE SUPREME COURT DECISION OF 4 NOVEMBER
     1853 33

     The "Non-Christian" Label
     Historical Perspectives
     The Mormon Question: Pros and Cons
     "Wolves in Sheep's Clothing"
     Birch-Reichenwald's Intrigues
     The Supreme Court Case (1853)

IV. MORMONISM IN NORWAY: AN HISTORICAL OVER-
     VIEW, 1851-1919   49

          1852-1862: A Decade of Revivalism
          1860-1895: Johnsonian Orthodoxy
          1860-1895: Economic Paralysis and the
              Manpower Drain
          1875-1894: The "New Secularism"
          1890-1914: From Neo-Revivalism to the
              Doldrums
          1914-1918: "Return of the Native"

V.   MORMON RELATIONS WITH CIVIL AND ECCLESIAS-
     TICAL AUTHORITIES   67

          Mormon Relations with Civil Authorities:
            1851-1900
          Mormon Relations with Ecclesiastical
            Authorities: 1851-1906
          KUD Mormon Policy: 1851-1900
          KUD Mormon Policy versus JPD Mormon Policy:
            1880-1923
          Conclusion

VI. MORMON RELATIONS WITH THE NORWEGIAN PUBLIC:
     1851-1920   81

          Geographical and Regional Factors:
            1851-1920
          Anti-Mormon Propaganda: 1846-1920
          Violence and Persecution: 1851-1920
          Norwegian Ambivalence and Hospitality:
            1851-1920
          Popular Support of Mormonism: 1851-1920
          Conclusion

VII. THE MORMON COMMUNITY IN NORWAY, 1851-1920:
     PART I   93

          The Social Setting: 1851-1920
          Mormon Poverty, Working Conditions, Housing,
            Diet and Clothing: 1851-1920
          Communications and Transportation: 1851-1920

VIII. THE MORMON COMMUNITY IN NORWAY, 1851-1920:
      PART II   101

          The Defensive Mentality: 1851-1920
          Factors of Conversion: 1851-1920
          The Mormon World View
          Mormon Religious Practices: 1851-1920

Social Life in the Mormon Community:
1851-1920
Education in the Mormon Community:
1851-1920
Excommunication from the Mormon Community:
1851-1920
The Norwegian Experience with Mormonism:
A Retrospective Evaluation

. . . .

Appendix

1. AN ANNOTATED LIST OF THE FIRST NORWEGIAN CONVERTS TO MORMONISM 123

2. GERHARD B. NAESETH TO GERALD M. HASLAM, 4 JULY 1980 147

3. AN INVENTORY OF COURT EXTRACTS AUTHENTICATED IN CONNECTION WITH THE SUPREME COURT DECISION THAT MORMONS WERE NON-CHRISTIANS, 4 NOVEMBER 1853 149

4. BIRTHPLACES OF CONVERTS TO MORMONISM IN OSLO BRANCH 1853-1860 INCLUSIVE 153

5. BIRTHPLACES OF CONVERTS TO MORMONISM IN OSLO BRANCH 1895-1900 INCLUSIVE 157

6. MORMON PLACES OF WORSHIP IN NORWAY BEFORE 1920 161

Notes

    CHAPTER I 169

    CHAPTER II 177

    CHAPTER III 193

    CHAPTER IV 215

    CHAPTER V 237

    CHAPTER VI 261

    CHAPTER VII 283

    CHAPTER VIII 299

SELECTED BIBLIOGRAPHY 327

LIST OF TABLES

1. Mormonism in Norway: Statistical Overview, 1851-1919 51
2. Mormonism in Norway: Five-Year Totals, 1851-1919 52
3. Mormonism in Norway: Five-Year Averages, 1851-1919 53
4. Mormonism in Norway: Missionary Work Statistics, 1896-1918 60
5. Age of Mormons at Baptism: Oslo Branch, 1853-1860 64
6. Age of Mormons at Baptism: Oslo Branch, 1895-1900 65
7. Oslo Branch Membership Male and Female Totals, 1851-1907 66

INTRODUCTION

In his history of the Norwegian Mission of the Church of Jesus Christ of Latter-day Saints, <u>Den norske misjons historie</u>, published under Mormon auspices in 1966, Hilmar Freidel briefly discussed dossiers on Mormonism in collections of Norway's Royal Justice and Police Department (Det kongelige Justis- og Politidepartement) and the Royal Church and Education Department (Det kongelige Kirke- og Undervisningsdepartement). Freidel had earlier perused documents in the Justice Department's dossier, but decided against including them in his history since "I personally find no reason to make public more differences of opinion, verbiage and vexation than what I have already noted."[1] The Church and Education Department, meanwhile, ignored his request to examine their dossier, but Freidel was unruffled, i.e., ". . . the papers this department has concerning the Latter-day Saints can hardly contain anything which I would desire to include in my account of the Mission."[2] Freidel fashioned his history around "that truth which is positively informative, which promotes or induces constructive reflection," and excluded any discussion of "weaknesses and character flaws" among Norwegian Mormons since they "had no effect on the common goal."[3]

Freidel's was one of several histories which discussed Mormonism in Norway in rather glowing terms. In 1927, Assistant Church Historian Andrew Jenson published his pioneering <u>History of the Scandinavian Mission</u> based on printed sources, diaries, interviews and personal recollections. Jenson considered the history "a labor of love" and "the author's tribute to his race--the stalwart sons and daughters of the North."[4] Strictly chronological in format, the work soon became the standard account of Mormonism's early history in Scandinavia and served as "a primary source" for Albert L. Zobell Jr.'s <u>Under the Midnight Sun: Centennial History of Scandinavian Missions</u> (1950).[5] Other works were Carl M. Hagberg's <u>Den Norske Misjons Historie</u> published in 1928--a fifty-six-page pamphlet which celebrated seventy-five years of Mormonism in Norway--and <u>Jubileum aaret 1850-1950</u> (The Jubilee Year 1850-1950) published by the Norwegian Mission of the Church of Jesus Christ of Latter-day Saints as a commemorative volume. Unpublished studies included Curtis B. Hunsaker's "History of the Norwegian Mission from 1851 to 1960" (M.A. thesis, Brigham Young University, 1965) which rather abruptly concluded "the Lord was the power behind any [Mormon] success . . . in the land of the 'midnight sun.'"[6]

Most of the accounts relied almost entirely on secondary Mormon sources--mission and branch histories, mission publications and periodicals or journals--deposited in Library-Archives of the Church of Jesus Christ of Latter-day Saints in Salt Lake City, Utah, but Freidel based his work on printed Norwegian materials to the general exclusion of primary or manuscript sources. Freidel, Jenson, Zobell, Hagberg, Hunsaker and officials of the Norwegian Mission could quite accurately be termed Mormon apologists--authors fired by a certain missionary zeal somewhat incompatible with serious scholarship. In addition, their histories were largely administrative--histories of the various administrations of Mormon mission presidents in Norway--and paid little or no attention to long-range developments (historical evolution). That said, we cannot simply ignore inestimable contributions of Freidel, Jenson, and Hagberg in preserving anecdotes, personal and/or secondhand remembrances and biographical details for future generations.

Historical works by non-Mormons included Knut Rygnestad's excellent overview of laws and resolutions which affected Mormons and other religious dissenters during the late 1800s, <u>Dissentarspoersmaalet i Noreg fraa 1845 til 1891: Lovgjeving og Administrativ Praksis</u> (The Dissenter Question in Norway from 1845 to 1891: Legislation and Administrative Practice), published in 1955, and Karl Sandvin's "Mormonisma i Noreg med utsyn over samfunnet si amerikanske historie" (Mormonism in Norway with an Overview of the Sect's American History)--University of Oslo, 1946--a valuable exposition of theory and practice as regards Mormon relations with religious and civil authorities. But neither study addressed social history of the Mormon community in Norway, religious and social backgrounds of Mormon converts, and divergent policies of government and religious bodies vis-a-vis Mormons. Furthermore, both studies were largely written without any reference to Mormon sources.

Justification for the current study largely resided in the fact that none of the above-mentioned writers had attempted to integrate Mormon and non-Mormon sources into a unified whole. Nor did they, with the possible exception of Rygnestad, rely to any great extent on unpublished or manuscript sources--sources which are often hard to locate, time-consuming and (depending on the handwriting) very difficult to read, and, in a few cases, restricted to all but a few bonafide researchers: (1) no historian had previously attempted to present the history of Mormonism in Norway in a work which incorporated primary Norwegian sources--- documents created by the Lutheran or State Church, the Justice Department, the Church and Education Department, the inferior and superior courts, the Parliament or <u>Storting</u>, and Norwegian civil and religious authorities; (2) Mormonism had never been discussed in its full Norwegian context--the Norwegian background of converts to Mormonism, the history of Mormon relations with Norwegian religious and civil authorities, and Mormon relations with the general Norwegian public; (3) no one had read each of the over eighty manuscript journals, the numerous mission and branch manuscript histories, and manuscript correspondence in Mormon archives for purposes of determining the social, religious and educational backgrounds; the diet, clothing and means of transportation; and factors of conversion, social and recreational activities, and religious practices of resident Norwegian Mormons.

The fact that the hundreds of manuscripts in the Justice and Church and Education Department dossiers on Mormonism, together with diaries and journals written by Norwegian Mormons and their leaders, form the backbone of the study which follows, is indicative of the new direction and change of emphasis which this work will hopefully disclose. Serious students could also very profitably read Arne Hassing's "Methodism and Society in Norway: 1853-1918" (Northwestern University, 1974) for purposes of comparing the Mormon experience with its Methodist counterpart and to gain a more comprehensive understanding of Norwegian religious and social crosscurrents during the seven decades before 1920.

NOTES

[1] "Personlig finner jeg ingen grunn til aa offentliggjoere flere meningsbrytninger, ordgytelser og harme enn hva jeg alt har notert." Hilmar Freidel, <u>Jesu Kristi Kirke i Norge: Den norske misjons historie, 1851-1966</u> (Oslo: Jesu Kristi Kirke av Siste Dagers Hellige Misjonskontoret, 1966), p. 44.

[2] ". . . men de papirer dette departement har vedroerende De siste dagers hellige inneholder neppe noe som jeg kunne oenske aa taa med i min misjonsberetning." Ibid.

[3] ". . . den sannhet som er positivt opplysende, som gavner eller gir en belaerende ettertanke. . . . Svakheter og brister innenfor soeskenflokken, og som ingen virkning har hat paa det felles maal, er gjemt i den guddommelige sentens: Kjaerligheten skjuler en mangfoldighet av synder!" Ibid., p. 5.

[4] Andrew Jenson, Preface to <u>History of the Scandinavian Mission</u>, by Andrew Jenson (Salt Lake City, Utah: Deseret News Press, 1927), p. iv.

[5] Albert L. Zobell, Jr., Acknowledgements to <u>Under the Midnight Sun: Centennial History of the Scandinavian Missions</u>, by Albert L. Zobell, Jr. (Salt Lake City, Utah: Deseret Book Company, 1950), n.p.

[6] Curtis B. Hunsaker, "History of the Norwegian Mission from 1851 to 1960" (M.A. thesis, Brigham Young University, 1965), p. 116. More scholarly works included Helge Seljaas, "The Mormon Migration from Norway" (M.A. thesis, University of Utah, 1972), and William Mulder, <u>Homeward to Zion: The Mormon Migration from Scandinavia</u> (Minneapolis: University of Minnesota Press, 1957). Seljaas examined antecedents of Mormon emigration from Norway, the emigration experience, and the history of Norwegian immigrants in the Utah setting, whereas Mulder treated many of the same subjects with special emphasis on the Danish Mormons.

CHAPTER I

NORWEGIAN AND AMERICAN PRELUDES

<u>Hans Nielsen Hauge and
the Lay Believers</u>

The fires of religious dissent in Norway did not originate outside the country or with religious sects outside the State or Lutheran Church. Instead, seeds of apostasy were nurtured in a revivalist movement which was internal, both in its germination within the framework of the orthodox church, and in its conception and leadership under lay preacher and martyr, Hans Nielsen Hauge (1771-1824).

Born 3 April 1771 in Tune, Oestfold, Norway, Hauge was the son of a prosperous farmer and grew up, along with three brothers and four sisters, in a happy, God-fearing home well stocked with pietistic and other religious writings.[1] Sunday activity in the parish centered around the church where young Hauge attended sermons of parish priest Gerhard Seeberg for over fifteen years. Seeberg had earlier served as pastor to the Danish Royal Family, and his preaching, peppered with pietistic doctrines, angered orthodox local officials. Late in 1795, he was stripped of his priestly office by the Norwegian Supreme Court, but he and a few select friends continued to preach and succeeded in spawning a minor religious revival in Tune and vicinity.

Hauge did not support Seeberg and led a rather uneventful life until that fateful spring day of 5 April 1796 when, while plowing in his father's fields and singing an old gospel hymn, his thoughts were so lifted up to God

> . . . that I stood transfixed . . . my soul experienced something supernatural, divine, and blessed . . . a joy which no tongue can describe. . . . No one can convince me otherwise; for I know the spiritual fruits of this experience, especially the deep burning love for God and my neighbor, that I experienced a change of mind, a sorrow for all sin, a desire that all men should partake with me of the same grace; a keen desire to read the Word of God as contained in Holy Writ, especially the teachings of Jesus, coupled with an increased power to understand, and to direct all religious instruction toward the one basic truth,

that Christ has come as our Savior, that we can be born again through His Spirit. . . . It was as if I saw the world wallowing in evil, which occasioned in me great sorrow, and I prayed God would stay His Punishment, so that some could repent. My whole desire now was to serve God, and I asked Him to reveal to me what I should do? A voice echoed in my soul: Thou shalt make known My Name for mankind, warn them to repent and seek me while I can be found, call on Me when I am near and touch their hearts, so they will repent from darkness and enter into Light.[2]

In direct opposition to ecclesiastical law, Hauge interpreted his experience as a personal call to preach, and preach he did to the great dismay of regularly ordained clergymen and civil authorities whose forefathers had watched over parish life for generations. At Graalum Farm where Hauge preached soon after his conversion, parish priest and local sheriff combined to warn him his gatherings were forbidden by <u>Konventikkelplakaten</u> [the Conventicle Ordinance] of 13 January 1741 which protected the ordained clergy's preaching monopoly, and thus began a prolonged conflict which was, in fact, "a clash between civil authorities and farmers."[3]

Initially bolstered by contacts with scattered pietistic groups,[4] Hauge's movement attracted most of its converts in farming communities where workers and unschooled farmers gathered in parish churchyards to hear Hauge preach after regular Lutheran services had concluded. In contrast to the dry rationalism of parish priests, Hague illustrated his sermons with actual examples from daily life: his preaching was down-to-earth; it was believable and understandable.[5]

From 1796-1803, Hauge preached throughout Norway,[6] winds of revivalism accelerated apace, and, although he insisted his teachings were purely Lutheran and orthodox, there was a subtle difference: Hauge stressed obedience to God[7] and called for repentance and a return to the ethical life;[8] he also taught that the law of God should be preached in order to awaken the sinner to necessary repentance and (since he feared ethical consequences of the State Church doctrine of salvation by faith) claimed "works are the evidence of faith."[9] In effect, his preaching "reflected a general yearning for personal salvation and sanctification."[10]

Hauge also preached an economic gospel (Believers should pool financial resources to improve living conditions and become increasingly independent of the rich)[11] and solicited contributions for a fund held in common. It was this so-called "Holy Fund" which brought about his demise. Enemies could now attack him on civil (as well as ecclesiastical) grounds, and immediately accused him of swindling ignorant and unsuspecting persons[12] in order to enrich himself under the mask of righteousness.[13] Hauge was subsequently arrested and charged with: (1) indoctrinating gullible people with "fantastic theories" which caused them to disregard civic duties; (2) creating a "Holy Fund" to enrich himself under the guise of piety and of religion; (3) deceiving children into leaving parents; (4) heaping abuse on State Church priests; and (5) openly disobeying the Conventicle Ordinance of 1741 by refusing to cease holding revivals and prayer gatherings.[14]

Despite the great number of charges, a speedy judgment in Hauge's case was difficult to arrive at: the hackneyed Coventicle Ordinance of 13 January 1741 contained no punishment clauses, and another ordinance dated 5 March 1745 also lacked a punishment clause and was aimed at foreign sects in Denmark-Norway. Hauge was not a foreigner, and had not formally established a sect or congregation. With Hauge languishing in prison (1804-1811), years of laborious investigation and court hearings commenced, surveys and questionaires were compiled, and debate raged back and forth. The result was Hauge's conviction on charges of fraud and having tried to establish "a state within the State."[15]

Throughout history, men have resorted to persecution and imprisonment to rid the world of "dangerous" ideas or movements. Hauge left prison a broken man, his health shattered, his writings confiscated and destroyed. His attempt to infuse soul-searching and moral purpose into Norwegian religious life had been repulsed, but his ideas would continue to inspire other men and women, and would find new root and expression, not only in the rocky substratum of old Norway, but in richer, more exotic soil of the American Frontier.

<u>The Sloopers and the Kendall Colony</u>

In 1821, a Norwegian adventurer, Kleng Peerson, arrived in America and traveled extensively in New York State.[16] Thrilled with what he saw as a unique opportunity for Norwegian settlement in America, he hurried back to Norway to promote a Norwegian colony in Murray (now Kendall) Township, Orleans County, New York.[17] In Stavanger, Norway, Peerson succeeded in convincing a group of Norwegian Quakers[18] and Haugians[19] to purchase a tiny sloop. This sloop, dubbed the <u>Restoration</u>, sailed from Stavanger on 4 July 1825; aboard were fifty-two persons who "came to be known as 'sloopers' or 'sloop folk,'" whereas "their ship, the 'Restoration,' is often referred to as the 'Norwegian Mayflower.'"[20]

On arriving in Orleans County, New York, twenty-four of the "Sloopers" lived together in a venture where all things were shared in common. No doubt "driven to this step by sundry privation, all twenty-four persons lived--or at least survived-- in a tiny log house twelve by twelve feet with a garret, which Peerson had apparently built for the group in 1824."[21]

From the start, however, the experiment was doomed to failure: "Peerson and his followers simply did not have the religious zeal that Hans Nielsen Hauge had displayed, back in Norway, in leading his followers over equally difficult obstacles toward communal cooperation; and Peerson . . . was too restless to organize anything he started."[22] Peerson, in fact, had already left New York State for greener pastures.

The Fox River Settlement and the Norwegian Mormons

By 1833, Peerson was casting about for another "promised land" where his fellow Norwegians could settle. He had heard rumors of better farmland in regions west of New York, consequently traveled on foot to an area west and south of Lake Michigan, and finally decided on a spot near the Fox River in what is now La Salle County, Illinois.[23] In 1834, Peerson and five families--"those of Endre Dahl, Jacob Anderson Slogvig, Gudmund Haugaas, Nels Thompson, and Thorstein Olson Bjaadland"--left the Kendall Settlement and traveled to La Salle County where they established the Fox River Settlement.[24]

Knud Slogvig, one of the Fox River settlers, returned to Norway the next year (1835) and persuaded about two hundred persons to emigrate in the summer of 1836. This was the first group to leave Norway for the Fox River Settlement. In 1837, about 215 additional emigrants left Norway for the Fox River Settlement,[25] and in the next few years a steady stream of immigrants founded new Norwegian settlements in: (1) Rock County, Wisconsin (Jefferson Prairie); (2) Waukesha and Racine Counties, Wisconsin (Muskego); (3) Dane County, Wisconsin (Koshkonong); and (4) Lee County, Iowa (Sugar Creek).[26]

Many of the immigrants were Haugians who envisioned a cluster of Haugian colonies in the New World, and indeed it began to look as if this dream might be realized in a broad area of the new settlements where religious life was characterized by Haugian "lay preaching and home devotions."[27] But by 1842, the settlements had become nesting grounds for a major frontier revival mounted by numerous religions and characterized by heightened "fervor and missionary zeal."[28] Haugian lay preachers were thus forced to contend with Presbyterians, Methodist circuit riders, Baptists and American Quakers[29] in an area where "American churches were reaching out to the frontier with contagious enthusiasm and organized power."[30]

Greatly adding to the confusion was the arrival in Fox River Settlement of the Mormon missionary, George Parker Dykes, (1814-1888), in March 1842. Dykes hailed from Nauvoo, the Mormon headquarters two hundred miles to the southwest,[31] and his relentless zeal soon swayed two pillars of the Settlement, Gudmund Haugaas and Ole Heier, who, along with their wives, accepted Mormon baptism late in April 1842.[32] Dykes soon organized a Mormon congregation called the La Salle Branch of the Church of Jesus Christ of Latter-day Saints,[33] and contemporaries soon described a congregation of over a hundred converts in 1844 who enjoyed such "spiritual gifts" as "Prophecy, healing, speaking in tongues, and the interpretation in a very remarkable degree."[34]

On 27 June 1844, the Mormon Prophet, Joseph Smith, was murdered. A short time later, several Mormon Apostles, including Brigham Young, Heber C. Kimball and Parley P. Pratt, visited the La Salle Branch and purchased 160 acres of land from Sloopers Gudmund Haugaas and Jacob Anderson Slogvik. On this land they laid out a city called "Norway" and selected ten acres on the Haugaas Farm for a temple site. Sites for other public buildings, including a tabernacle and tithing house, were also selected,[35] and many Norwegians, including Canute Peterson, heard Brigham Young say that the new settlement "would be a gathering place for the Scandinavian people and that they would build the temple on the site selected . . . that in this temple they would have the privilege of giving and receiving the Endowments in their own language."[36] Haugaas had been ordained a High Priest in the Melchizedek Priesthood, and was preparing a missionary journey to Europe to bring Scandinavians to the new Zion.[37]

But the Scandinavian Zion proved stillborn. Dissension soon rocked the La Salle Branch and men such as Gudmund Haugaas, Endre Dahl and Ole Heier joined with the disaffected James J. Strang of Voree, Wisconsin. Brigham Young, in an effort to win back some of the Norwegians, sent out George W. Bratton in January 1848 with instructions to reorganize the branch and soothe some of the bad feelings. Bratton succeeded in part and obtained pledges from twenty-five Norwegians to support Young and the Apostles and go west to Utah with the main body of the Saints.[38] Most of those who pledged carried through (a notable exception was Gudmund Haugaas who died of cholera at Fox River on 28 July 1849)[39] and a company of twenty-two Norwegians left Fox River on 18 April 1849 in six wagons.[40]

At Winter Quarters, Nebraska, they joined with the Ezra T. Benson Company which headed west on 14 July 1849.[41] On 2 October 1849, the Company encountered a violent snowstorm which killed about seventy horses and cattle,[42] and on 23 October the Weber River in Utah Territory was sighted. There the Company crossed paths with several Mormon Apostles and missionaries bound for Europe[43] including Apostle Erastus Snow enroute to Europe to open up Denmark for the preaching of Mormonism. Snow spent a night and part of a day with the Company, and observed that "they were near their Journeys end, while we were launching out upon a Journey of some eight or ten thousand miles and upon a mission of years."[44]

In the meeting with Snow on the banks of the Weber we note both an end and a beginning. Snow was heading to Denmark to open the Scandinavian Mission. A tiny caravan of about twenty-five Norwegians was once again ready to settle down in a community inspired by a religious dream[45] where five or six of them would marry polygamous wives and die surrounded by a numerous progeny. Canute Peterson, for example, died in Ephraim, Sanpete, Utah, in his late seventies having fathered twenty children by three wives;[46] Erik Hogan died at age seventy-three in 1876 leaving behind seventeen children by three wives;[47] Goudy Hogan fathered twenty-five children by polygamous wives before his death in 1898;[48] John Jacobs had twenty children by two polygamous wives;[49] Christian Hyer had sixteen by three wives;[50] and Swen Jacobs, though not a polygamist, had thirteen children by his wife Sarah.[51]

    Canute Peterson--President of the Mormon Sanpete Stake for twenty-five years,[52] and Christian Hyer--President of the Richmond, Utah Cooperative Mercantile Institution,[53] died as pillars of their Utah communities. Others, such as Shure Olson who helped build the famous Tabernacle Organ in Salt Lake City,[54] or John Jacobs, Christopher Jacobs and Swen Jacobs who founded a new settlement in what is now Cedar City, Utah,[55] were unsung heroes whose only legacy was an honorable name. Nor must we forget Norwegian women--some of them such as sisters Lovina and Caroline Hogan,[56] or Harriet and Ellen Sanders, polygamous wives of the same man.[57] All were builders--pioneers whose Mormon descendants number today in the thousands.

    Three of the group--Canute Peterson, and father and son, Erik G. M. and Goudy Hogan--stand out for yet another reason; they personally took the "glad tidings" of their Mormon faith to relatives and countrymen in far-off Norway[58] thereby completing the cycle of events leading from Hans Nielsen Hauge to Norwegian-American settlements where Mormons first preached before groups of non-English-speaking Europeans. It is this preaching of Mormonism to Norwegians in Norway which we will next examine against its Scandinavian and American background.

CHAPTER II

FORERUNNERS AND BEGINNINGS IN SCANDINAVIA

P. O. Hansen's History

Mormon beginnings in Scandinavia revolved largely around lives of key men or forerunners. Chief among these was P. O. (Peter Olsen) Hansen (1818-1894). A native of Copenhagen and son of a Danish naval officer, Hansen was entitled to free government schooling. This, however, was against wishes of his father who, fearing the public schools would expose his son to "bad habits,"[1] decided to teach him at home. Hansen's father taught him from "good books, not romance or such like," and acquainted him with "pictures imported from Leipsick or Nurnberg in Germany which were cheap and yet well done," and "were calculated," said Hansen, "to awaken my ideas and increase my understanding." The older Hansen's library was also open for his son's perusal: "My father," said Hansen, "rather blaimed me a little for not using the previlege more than I did."[2]

Hansen's mother died of consumption in 1832, and her death transformed her husband, ever a man of deep sentiment and emotion, into a despairing and possessive drunkard who spent his lonely days "filing away on his fiddle early and late to drive off his troublesome thougts [sic]."[3] Hans Christian Hansen (1806-1890), Hansen's older brother, escaped the gloomy household by going to sea in 1835, whereas Hansen, more of an introvert and as yet unsure of himself, remained at home. But conditions there grew worse and worse, and Hansen began making frequent trips to the harbor to watch incoming ships from all over the world, especially America: "And now whenever I could get the chance of seeing an american vessel, I thought them the nicest in the world, and even the sight of the american flag was a feast to my longing soul."[4]

In 1842, Hansen happened on "a mere statement in a news-paper . . . that some Norwegian had wrote from America to his friends in Norway, that an ancient book called Mormon's Book, had been found in a miraculous way by a young man whose name was Joseph Smith."[5] Probably written by a Norwegian in the Fox River Settlement, this account filled Hansen with a strange excitement further heightened in June 1842 when his seafaring brother wrote "that he had become a member of the true church of Christ, which now had been restored by the power of God &c &c naming the prophet Joseph Smith, speaking of the apostacy of the ancient church, and pointing to the 29 Chapter of Isaiah with out mentioning the books name."[6]

Hansen's brother was by this time sailing on an American line which used Boston, Massachussetts, as its home port, and with this in mind, Hansen made secret arrangements with friends of his father for passage to America. On 1 November 1843, he arrived in Boston and spent the winter there working odd jobs; on 7 March 1844, his brother baptized him into the Mormon Church.[7]

P. O. Hansen's enthusiasm for Mormonism was boundless, and after paying an apostate named Phellps a dollar for a copy of the Book of Mormon, he hit on the idea of translating it into Danish:

> I commenced to translate a little every evening by the light of a lamp, and continued till I got to about the middle of the third chapter in the book when I had to quit because the evenings were getting too short and the days were growing longer and warmer and consequently I was too tired when the evening came.[8]

By year's end, Hansen had traveled west to Mormon headquarters at Nauvoo, Illinois, where he communicated his interest in translating to Apostle Brigham Young:

> The president [Young] being pleased therewith put it upon me as a binding duty to do it. But now I was perswaded to go with three others to New Orleans to spend the winter there working for to obtain some money. On asking the President wether I should work at the translation whilest down there, he said: no, not in that wicked place. While there I was sick for a long time, and came back to Nauvoo in the month of May 1845, moneyles. As soon as Prest. Young found that I had got back he urged me on to the task he had put upon me, and sent me to ask Elder Orson Pratt for information how to proseed. Bro. Pratt however was called away to England, and I worked at it alone steadily for about six months. Some of the last was done in the Vestry of the temple were I was door keeper. Then came the time for the church to leave Illinois and for want of paper I had to quit translating, when I wrapped the manuscript in a piece of calico and laid it on the bottom of my chest ready for the long journey. Being with Elder Heber C. Kimball's folks,[9] I left Nauvoo with them on the 12th of February 1846. After wintering on the Missouri we sent our Pioneers ahead in April 1847.

> I came to the valley [Great Salt Lake Valley, Utah] on the 29th of September that year.[10]

During his first year in Salt Lake Valley, Hansen lived in the old Mormon Fort--a structure which "had no openings on the outside but the big gates and shooting holes, doors and windows being on the inside."[11] With the other pioneers he endured privations of the harsh winter, i.e., "a little wolfs flesh we would not refuse, neither that of a calf which had perished in a snow storm," and early in the spring helped gather snipe eggs which were mixed with raw daisies.[12]

Summer came, winter snows in the mountain passes had melted, and Hansen headed east with a provisioning caravan sent to meet Mormons at Winter Quarters, Nebraska, preparing for the trek west. On this trip Hansen met the famous Oliver Cowdery who at one time had been Joseph Smith's right-hand man. Cowdery was one of three witnesses who claimed not only to have seen the "golden plates" from which Smith had translated the Book of Mormon, but also the Angel Moroni who had given Smith the plates. Of his visit with Cowdery, Hansen noted simply "an interesting conversation on the translation of the book of Mormon."[13]

Hansen's outfitting duties kept him away nearly seventeen months during which time "it was several times revealed to me that now I would be sent to my native land with the gospel. Not in words, nor by hearing a voice. But I sensed that the information was imparted to me and yet I could not account for it. But as often as it came it made me glad."[14]

Hansen's feelings persisted following his return to Salt Lake City, and he shared them with his adoptive father, Heber C. Kimball, counselor to the famous Mormon Prophet and colonizer, Brigham Young. Never a man of inaction, Kimball immediately informed Young who agreed the time was at hand to open Scandinavia for the preaching of Mormonism, and stated "he had understood by the spirit for some time that the time had come for preaching of the Gospel to be extended to other nations as well." Young suggested Hansen travel to Denmark with Apostle Erastus Snow since it was the calling of apostles "to open the Gospel door (dispensation) to the nations."[15]

Beginnings in Copenhagen

Snow and Hansen were sustained as missionaries to Scandinavia at a General Conference on 6 October 1849, and this prompted the Swede, John Erik Forsgren (1816-1890), to ask Brigham Young if he too could be sent along to preach Mormonism in Scandinavia. Forsgren was accordingly called "to go to Sweden to preach the Gospel, under the direction of Elder E. Snow."[16]

Although it was late in the season, Snow, Hansen, and Forsgren made hasty preparations, and left Salt Lake Valley on 19 October in a company of thirty-five men. Traveling together as far as Kanesville, Iowa, the men then split into small groups.

Hansen crossed the Atlantic with a group which arrived in Liverpool on 8 April 1850, and pushed on ahead from there to Scotland where Mormons supplied him with money and clothing. Not wishing to wait for Snow who was still in England, he then boarded a steamer for Copenhagen.

Hansen disembarked in the Danish Capital on 12 May 1850--a Sunday--and visited a Baptist meeting whose preacher, a certain Peter C. Moenster,[17] asked if he were a Baptist. "No," replied Hansen, "but I am not far from it." Later that day, Hansen joined two Baptist sailors for an afternoon of reading about "the way of salvation," and rejoicing "much together in the Lord."[18]

Snow, meanwhile, was still in England, and traveled in early May to Bradford, Yorkshire, where he met none other than George Parker Dykes, the same Dykes who first preached Mormonism to Norwegians at Fox River, Illinois. Snow knew Dykes spoke Norwegian, and, having previously "consulted with Brother Pratt when I met him in Boston, as also with brothers L. Snow and F. D. Richards," decided Dykes should accompany him to Denmark. Snow, Dykes, and Forsgren accordingly booked passage on the *Victoria* which departed Hull 11 June 1850 and arrived 14 June in Copenhagen.[19]

Copenhagen in 1850 had a population of 135,000 and was completely surrounded by old earthen walls.[20] There was no telegraph; a solitary railroad, sixteen miles long, ran out from the Capital into the countryside; and the city was lit at night by dingy old oil lamps posted along the streets.[21] Under provisions of the new Danish Constitution of 1849, freedom of religion, although allowed, was hemmed in by vague and poorly defined laws and restrictions,[22] and the 1840s had seen widespread grass roots revivalism among many Lutherans in rural areas combined with severe persecution, physical abuse, and imprisonment of nonconformists, especially Baptists.[23]

Snow soon found himself greatly disheartened by "an almighty power of darkness, unbelief and wickedness in the land, love of pleasure and the lusts of the flesh and a total disregard of spiritual things with the great mass of the people"; Lutheran priests "fatning upon the tithings of the people," who controlled "all the meetinghouses, and all the schools and schoolhouses," and "a national police all pety tyrants to do the dirty work of the Priests."[24] Snow, in fact, considered Mormonism's prospects in Denmark so dim he compared himself and companions to "a few grains of powder placed in a mountain of rock to burst it."[25] Snow spoke no Danish considering it a language "chewd all up and swallowed and then spit out of the throat," P. O. Hansen had "so far forgotten his native tongue that he could scarcely make himself understood," and Dykes "could read Danish a little But could not speak it."[26]

In light of Snow's feelings of gloom, it was Hansen's association with Moenster's Baptist congregation which saved the day for Mormonism. Snow wisely continued the relationship, and Mormons soon became regular Sunday visitors at Baptist meetings in the old Hotel Scandinavia in downtown Copenhagen.[27] Snow and companions made no mention of the word "Mormon," and at first attempted only to make friends with individual members of the congregation. Soon they were accepting invitations to private homes where they discussed the true nature of their visits "in a comparitively unobserved manner,"[28] declaring that

> . . . our Lord Jesus Christ's arrival was near, that God had restored his Church to the earth and appointed Apostles and Prophets in it, etc. that he had raised up a young man named Joseph Smith to be an instrument in his hand to carry out his purposes and allow the Gospel to spread in its purity to the inhabitants of the earth.[29]

John Aahmanson, one of the Copenhagen Baptists who later converted to Mormonism and served as one of the first Mormon missionaries to Norway, later recalled that many of his co-believers were attracted to Mormonism because of curiosity and interest in America, and because the Mormons possessed "an extraordinary knowledge of the Bible and knew just how to use it."[30] Snow and company exhibited no trace of fanaticism, their approach was practical, and their preaching was down-to-earth.[31]

Peter C. Moenster, the Baptist leader, was nearly fifty years old, a man whose "countenance and bearing bespoke intelegence meekness and sincerity." As the first to preach baptism by immersion in Denmark, he had often endured fines and imprisonment (The length of his imprisonments totaled over three years), "yet he had continued to teach his faith and some 350 had been baptised. Had he been a foreigner he would have been expelled from the country, but being a native they could only fine or imprisson him." Moenster spoke English, a factor which facilitated a friendship with Snow and resulted in his acceptance of an invitation to accompany Moenster to a Baptist gathering ten miles from Copenhagen. Moenster introduced him as a missionary, and Snow told the group the Lord had sent him "not to undo any good that he (Moenster) had done but that he and his people and all others that would hear us might receive more and obtain power to do a much greater work in the land." At these words, the congregation rejoiced "exceedingly," and, said Snow, "flocked around me as if I were an Angel."[32]

By early August, Moenster finally realized his leadership and authority were being undermined, and began condemning Mormons and their doctrine. But Snow refused to answer any call to arms: "I urged none to be baptized but rather held them back myself untill the Lord should [showed] me in a Dream that I should do so no longer For the Spirit of the Lord was stiring them up to obey the word that we had given them."[33] Eight men and seven women, all former members of Moenster's congregation, were subsequently baptized by Snow in waters of Oeresund near

Copenhagen on the evening of 12 August 1850.[34] The first to be baptized was Ole C. U. Moenster--one of two Baptist sailors who first invited P. O. Hansen to dinner.[35]

Convert baptisms continued during the following weeks, and on 15 September Snow organized fifty converts into a branch (Mormon congregation)--the first on the European Continent.[36] Up to this time, Snow had not allowed members to hold public meetings, but after Danish citizens were formally organized into a Mormon congregation in Copenhagen, the meeting ban was relaxed and Snow felt confident that now the government "could not legally forbid them to worsh[ip] according to their faith."[37] That decision was further buttressed by a meeting with the government minister for church and education where P. O. Hansen asked if Mormons might preach and organize and was told to "hold your meetings in the name of God, and if you are carefull none can forbid you."[38]

George Parker Dykes versus Erastus Snow

With organization of the Copenhagen Branch, a personal rift between Snow and Dykes reached sour proportions. Newly appointed president of the branch, Dykes asked Snow for funds to pay hall rent, and described what ensued:

> Unpleasant feelings arose betwen us 3-Br Hanson & I wanted it [the money] to be given for the purpose for which it was appropriated in England & Br Snow wanted it to go as a loan to be paid back to <u>him</u> as soon as the church was able, & as I did not put it out in that way before the Congregation, he [Snow] <u>call</u> on Br Hanson to give an explanation, in which also he Br H. caried the Idea that the money was given in England for the mision to Denmak [sic], after which we dismissed & also I by Br Snow's request dedicated the hall for the meeting of the saints & for preaching the word, after which I asked Br Snow if he would go with me & the comittee to see the owner of the house but, he turned & went home, . . . before dismission I asked Br Snow if he would have meeting at night & I with a few would go to the watters [of baptism] but he said not, unless I could be there) so I went to the watter & by the way Br & Sister Malling come up with us & I asked them if Br Snow was coming & they said now he had lay down upon the sofa for a sleep.[39]

The Snow-Dykes rivalry had been brewing several weeks, primarily aggravated by what Dykes felt was Snow's stinginess with funds obtained from Mormons in England to finance the work in Scandinavia, and also Dykes's independent and headstrong nature. Dykes, furthermore, was financially destitute, was entirely at Snow's mercy for food and clothing, and often found himself going to bed hungry. Said Dykes: ". . . yet, I can say that I found that promise in the book of covenants true that the Elder if faithful should not go hungry, although it does not say that they will find something to eat all the time but the[y] shall not go hungry."[40] Dykes did receive winter slippers and gloves from Sister Malling,

> . . . which was a present to me as I had not any money, for Br Snow had all the money that was given for the mision & I had not any to help myself with & when Br Hanson found out that I was under the necesity of going some times for thirty six hours without eating more than one meal he gave me a few marks he had in his trunk.[41]

That the problem was not one-sided is evidenced by recollections of Chr. Christiansen who noted that about September 1850, Dykes "began . . . to tell us, that he was every bit as great an Apostle as Erastus Snow."[42] No doubt it was this direct threat to his authority which moved Snow on 24 September to call Dykes on a mission to, of all places, Aalborg in Jutland (about as far away from Copenhagen as Dykes could go and yet remain in Denmark).

Informed of Snow's decision, members of the tiny branch in Copenhagen expressed great dissatisfaction, wept openly and voiced strong feelings of dislike for Snow "because, as they believed, he was so hard on Dykes."[43] According to Snow, "Br Dykes also became the willing tool of the Devil in this rebellion against what we felt constrained by the Holy Ghost to do,"[44] although Dykes contended Snow was sending him to Jutland because of jealousy over his success in winning converts and "that he heard Br. Snow & Br Forsgren talking in which Br Snow said if I did not go way, that soon I would have all the _influence_ here & he would be Looked upon as Nothing."[45]

Despite the furor among the members, Snow rebuked Dykes as "a team of himself <u>and himself</u> the driver,"[46] and stood firm in his decision. Late in September, he called Dykes, Forsgren and Hansen to a meeting in a grove of trees near Copenhagen where:

> We counciled & prayed together & the word of the Lord came unto us by the Power of the Holy Ghost chastening us for our folies & causing Bro. Dykes to tremble & quake before the Lord. He confesd how the adversary had influenced him for a long time. We

all worshiped & asked forgiveness and after this felt the approbation & blessing of God upon us & all the Saints and we persued our labours with Joy.[47]

Dykes accordingly traveled to Aalborg in early October.

Publication of Tracts and The Book of Mormon

Soon after arriving in Copenhagen, P. O. Hansen wrote and published three hundred copies of a "small sheet pamphlet" entitled <u>En Advarsel til Folket</u> [A Warning to the People]--the first Mormon tract published in Denmark.[48] When Snow arrived in June 1850, he worked with Hansen to revise the manuscript translation of the Book of Mormon, and encouraged him to translate several revelations from the Mormon Doctrine and Covenants.[49] With work progressing well on the Book of Mormon, Snow began writing a small tract entitled "A Voice of Truth" in which he briefly sketched the history of Mormonism and described basic tenets of Mormon doctrine. Hansen translated it in September 1850, and two thousand copies were printed that same month with the title <u>En Sandheds Roest.</u> In March 1851, the Mormon "Articles of Faith" and several Mormon revelations were published "for the instruction and government of the Saints," followed by publication of a hymnbook containing hymns "put into Danish, and adapted to the tunes used in Zion."[50]

With funds running low in October 1850, Snow left for Liverpool where he convinced Mormon Apostles Pratt and Richards to loan him two hundred pounds Sterling "from the book funds in the 'Star' office" for the purpose of publishing the Book of Mormon in Danish;[51] he also obtained funding from two Liverpool merchants.[52] Snow returned to Copenhagen with renewed enthusiasm for getting the Book of Mormon completely translated and published, and worked with Hansen seven months revising and correcting the translations, preparing manuscripts, and reading proof sheets, often until 2:00 or 3:00 A.M.[53] In addition, Snow employed two other compositors, besides Hansen, to speed the work along, but lamented on 16 April 1851 that "we have worked upon it [the Book of Mormon] all winter and shall probably not get through with it before the 20th of May. It is double the work I expected."[54] The first few pages of the Danish Book of Mormon had come off the press in January 1851, and were distributed to subscribers in Copenhagen, Aalborg and vicinities "as they issued from the press by the sheet."[55] By 20 May, the completed manuscript was submitted to the printers, and on 22 May "the last sheet was issued from the press and turnd over to the binders. . . ."[56] "The book was printed by Mr. F. E. Bording, for 1,000 'rigsdaler' (about $500)" in an edition of three thousand copies.[57]

Publication of the Book of Mormon in such a large first edition was indication of new optimism and growth among the

Danish membership which by mid-1851 numbered approximately 260 Saints.[58] Earlier that year, Snow received word from the King of Denmark stating he was not prepared to grant Mormons special privileges, but was "nevertheless resolved not to throw obstacles" in their way,[59] and Snow presented English Books of Mormon to the Royal Family and several government ministers a few weeks later.[60]

The greatest evidence of Mormon optimism and growth, however, was a conference resolution adopted on 15 August 1851 to publish a "monthly periodical in the Danish language as the organ of the Church." The first number of that publication, Skandinaviens Stjerne [Scandinavia's Star], was printed on 1 October 1851, and contained sixteen medium octavo pages.[61]

Beginnings in Aalborg

Of all the forerunners described in this chapter, George Parker Dykes possessed the most interesting and striking personality. Arrived in Aalborg on 10 October 1850 after his "exile" from Copenhagen, Dykes found he was short of money as usual, and took lodgings in an "exceedingly dirty" room where spider webs filled almost every corner and a "woman spread a cloth over a chair to have it fit for me to set in. . . ." In looking about the room, and at the floor which had not been swept for days, Dykes was filled with self pity, and reflected on the difference between lodgings for which he paid "10 1/2 cents a week," and "Br [Brother] Snows room for which he was paying 5 Dollars a month, being well furnished & kept in the nicest stile. . . ."[62]

Acting on prior experience with Baptists in Copenhagen, Dykes soon hunted up members of the local Baptist congregation and began preaching to them privately in their homes. On Sunday, 27 October, he preached in the Baptist meeting hall itself before most of the Baptists in Aalborg, and, directly following the general meeting, took aside those who "now believed," gave them instructions on the nature of the "New Covenant," and immediately repaired to waters of the fjord where he baptized four men and their wives. The first convert was Hans Peter Jensen, who, along with two other men, O. C. Nielsen and Niels Christian Skou, was a former teacher in the Baptist Church.[63] Jensen owned an iron foundry in the suburb of Noerre Sundby, having started out in business for himself about 1840 as an ordinary blacksmith and working up in the course of a decade to develop a foundry employing over a hundred men. His conversion to Mormonism caused widespread consternation among his employees, his Baptist Brethren, and business associates. Community leaders, thinking it incredible a men of Jensen's stature would join the Mormons, circulated rumors that Mormons planned to undermine the Danish nation itself and bring on a state of war and confusion. A pillar of society had been "swallowed up" by Mormon propaganda, and forces of reaction rushed to repair the hole in the dike.[64]

By 2 December 1850, a Mormon congregation was meeting in Aalborg, and mob violence and reprisals grew as the number of converts increased. On Christmas Day, Dykes called the faithful together for a secret meeting, but word leaked out, and the streets surrounding the hall were soon crowded with unruly and noisy boys who exploded a lighted rocket into the hall near the front door.[65] Dykes, meanwhile, decided not only to step up proselyting efforts in Aalborg, but to expand the scope of Mormon activity in the surrounding countryside. He accordingly traveled to nearby Hals where he told frightened listeners the Almighty God would soon burn the ungodly as stubble:

> . . . for yea, the Day is near and the time soon at hand when God's voice will be heard from Heaven and it will be a voice of earthquakes, wars, pestilence, hunger, lightning and the rumble of thunder, and Angels shall fly through the Heavens sounding trumpets so loudly they will be heard by all the inhabitants of the Earth. . . . if you could see with prophetic vision the true nature of the times in which we live, then you would humble yourselves and enter into prayer calling on the Name of the Lord to spare you from the great plagues which will soon envelop the Earth. . . . Take heed to yourselves . . . before the evil day arrives; for it will come and will be horrible, but blessed are they who hold themselves unspotted from the world and are prepared. . . .[66]

Meanwhile, Dykes was in great danger of starving to death. Propelled by a fanatic missionary zeal, he took little care of his physical needs, and traveled from place to place like a half-crazed Savonarola. Those looking out their windows that winter saw Dykes, his long hair and even longer beard blowing in the wind like a prophet of doom, plowing through snowdrifts "so high that it was imposible . . . to keep the road," or climbing up on stone walls in order to inch along over the snow while maintaining a precarious balance.[67] When hunger pangs became too severe, Dykes scrounged up cabbage leaves and bits of hay which had fallen onto roads from passing carts, or, like a wild boar, went grubbing around in snowy forests for frozen leaves.[68] Such a figure could not help but attract attention, and Dykes was soon preaching before large crowds both in Hals and Aalborg. On 24 January 1851, at the home of a Mormon surnamed Domgaard in Hals, Dykes preached so fervently that people entered the house by scores. Spurred on by the size of the crowd, Dykes lashed out against his enemies among the Lutheran clergy and Baptist teachers. Verbal exchanges between supporters and detractors subsequently erupted, and a group of drunken fishermen began pushing into the room with the object of giving Dykes a severe beating. Dykes, however, found himself protected by a group of women who formed a human ring around him, which, in his own words,

> . . . [was] so thick that the [fishermen] could not get to me, at first but the[y] pressed so hard upon them that they [the women] began to give way, & one of the mob got hold of my hand but I jerked it from him & stood a little further back & the woman of the house (who was a baptist) goot between me & the mob & said to them that she did not want them to do so in her house, but they were now so drunk with rage & whiskey that they would not hear to reason, but in this critical state of affairs the priest with who I had had the debate [a Baptist priest surnamed Foeltved] came & the people were some what under his influence, but the mob would not hear him, he ordered every body out of the house but the mob would not go, so he said to them that if they would go out in the streets he would preach for them so he got them all out (there was about 30 of the mob & perhaps 150 that stood & looked on) & when they all went out the man of the house (br Dumgaard) bared the doors so they could not come in, & the priest stood there & talked with them till dark but he could not have them leave, so he left & they began to stone the house, & they broke in windows, & the few women in the house was fearful they would brake in & take my life so they put a petty coat on me & a shawl & awhite hankerchief on my head & thought to eskort me out at the back door but in that moment there was some of the mob that come there to brake in & as the door was open, but fill up with women the[y] jerked some of them out & I, stept back & shut the door & boulted it with the help of some of the women that was on the insid, but the mob pressed hard upon it & there [w]as a ladder there that led up to the loft so I went up that by the suggestion of some that was there & hid my [sic] under some straw & things that was there but the mob did not come in, so I took of the petticoat &c came down & when the[y] had dispurst a little I went out to an other house at about 10 o'clack at night where they hid me in the loft under some hay wher I remained

till 5 A.M. when the man came & led me down & conducted me out a back way to the main road so I left the city. . . ."[69]

Mormon membership in Aalborg increased to sixty persons in the space of four months, and that success did not go unnoticed as witness a letter on 24 February 1851 from the Mayor of Aalborg directing Dykes to change his time of preaching on Sundays because "they did not want us to have meeting the same hour of the Established Church. . . ."[70] Further evidences of Mormon growth were the ordination on 3 March of Hans Peter Jensen, a native Dane, to the office of Mormon Elder, and compilation and printing of one thousand copies of a tract authored by Dykes describing "Mormon Articles of Faith."[71] Public agitation also intensified as per a scene on 13 March when Dykes, enroute to visit H. P. Jensen in Sundby, was clobbered with snowballs by roughnecks at the ferry landing, and anti-Mormon lectures delivered by a Baptist leader from Hamburg, Herr Kobner, on the three consecutive nights of 26-28 March.[72] Mormon children were so severely persecuted by peers at school that a Mormon school was established early in April 1851--the first in Continental Europe[73]--and Dykes reported by mid-April that ninety-one persons had joined the Mormons in Aalborg since his arrival the previous October.[74]

Dykes's efforts were also bearing new fruit not restricted to Denmark per se. On the evening of 9 April 1851, shortly before going south to Schleswig as the first Mormon emissary to the German-speaking Duchies, Dykes preached before a large group of people crowded into a tiny house. Next day, he recorded "an interesting interview with a man that was to meeting the night before he was a ship captian [sic] & was from Norway & he come to see that we had the truth & so he purchased some of our workes & promised to come again if he could. . . ."[75]

The Norwegian Connection

On arriving in Copenhagen in the Summer of 1850, Apostle Erastus Snow wrote the Mormon First Presidency in Utah about Norway, observing that the Norwegians had their own Constitution, even though under Swedish dominion, and enjoyed greater political freedom than either Swedes or Danes.[76] Snow, although concentrating on establishing a mission in Denmark, did not discount the possibility of sending missionaries to Norway, and as early as August 1850 was informing the First Presidency that he had decided to bring George Parker Dykes to Scandinavia since Dykes had previously preached to Norwegians at Fox River, Illinois, and "my intention was, if the Lord opened the way, to send him to Norway to usher in the Gospel Dispensation there."[77]

Popular accounts of Mormon beginnings in Norway claim a Norwegian skipper, Svend Larsen, first heard about Mormonism from a Norwegian tailor surnamed Olsen who lived in Aalborg.[78] Larsen himself stated that in August 1851 he sailed with a load of lumber to Aalborg where Herr Olsen came aboard the sloop and said his wife had left the Baptists, joined the Mormons, and been baptized for the remission of sins. Later that afternoon, two of Olsen's sons escorted Larsen to H. P. Jensen's home in Sundby and introduced him to Apostle Erastus Snow. Larsen described their meeting:

> I was meanwhile asked very politely to take a seat, which I did, and on request stated who I was and where I was from. Brother Snow sat down beside me in front of a dining table on the other side of which stood a sofa right under the windows. He asked if I understood English to which I answered Yes, but I did not understand religious terms in the English language; he explained the first principles of the Gospel to me therefore in the Danish language. I mentioned several times that I believed what he said. I must here observe that an inner voice whispered to me the words "this is a Man of God." I was every bit as convinced on that occasion that Brother Snow was a Man of God as I am today and I believed every word he told me, and remarked now and then, "I believe it." Brother Snow rose to his feet and sat down on the sofa so that he could look me squarely in the eyes in order to better determine if I was sincere or not. He gave me a good introduction and told me how Joseph Smith received the Plates from which the Book of Mormon is translated among other things, and showed me from the Book the Pearl of Great Price characters similar to those which were engraved on the plates. Our conversation lasted about two hours and in that time I gained a knowledge of completely new events which I believed just as completely as if I had been an eyewitness to them all. Brother Snow asked if we enjoyed freedom of religion in Norway to which I replied Yes, since the Dissenter Law allows all Christian sects freedom to worship according to their beliefs, but prohibits Jesuits and monasterial orders from entering the country. Brother Snow asked if I would take a Brother with me to Norway to preach the Gospel which I agreed to do provided said Brother could get his belongings on board and get his passport arranged since according to the Skipper Oath I could only bring a person

possessing a valid passport into the country or else risk a fine.[79]

As described above, Larsen first heard Mormon doctrine preached by Apostle Snow in August 1851, but this claim is questionable. The Snow-Larsen meeting undoubtedly took place, and Snow even wrote about it in his journal: "A Mr Swend Larsen from Norway master of a vesel came in search of me saying that he had heard of me and my religion and had come to enquire and learn for himself."[80] The fact remains, however, that George Parker Dykes recorded a meeting with a Norwegian "ship captain" on 10 April 1851, and that said captain attended a sermon the previous evening where Dykes preached in a tiny, crowded room. According to Dykes, the captain believed Mormonism was true "& so he purchased some of our workes and promised to come again if he could. . . ."[81] There is a strong possibility the captain mentioned by Dykes was Svend Larsen, and that Larsen's introduction to Mormonism preceded by a good four months his meeting with Snow. This is further indicated by P. O. Hansen's statement that "a Norwegian skipper was baptized by Bro. Dykes in Aalborg, which opened the door to the Land of Norway, and missionaries were subsequently sent over to preach the Gospel."[82] Hansen was mistaken in stating Larsen was baptized by Dykes,[83] but his account does indicate some knowledge of a Dykes-Larsen connection.

If indeed Larsen first heard Mormonism preached by Dykes and not by Snow, the question remains as to why he did not acknowledge the fact in his autobiography. There are several possibilities. In the first place, Dykes was a fanatic who went around delivering fiery diatribes, poverty had reduced him to a diet of leaves and hay droppings with a wardrobe to match, and he was not well-groomed or what better folk might call "respectable." Snow, on the other hand, was well-dressed and well-groomed, possessed an even temperament, and was a member of the select Quorum of Twelve Apostles in the Mormon hierarchy. Snow was "respectable." Certainly an account claiming Mormonism was introduced into Norway after a quiet conversation in a private home between a Norwegian sea captain and an Apostle of the Lord Jesus Christ reads a lot better than one stating Mormonism's real genesis in Norway was sparked when a Norwegian sea captain attended a crowded gathering where a dirty, half-starved religious fanatic preached hell and damnation. Further, Larsen's autobiography was written about 1882, and by that time Dykes had long been in disfavor with the main body of the Mormon Church in Utah because of his baptism into the Reorganized Church of Jesus Christ of Latter Day Saints and his criticism of Brigham Young, as also his anti-polygamy views.[84] Larsen probably decided giving credit to an apostate was something he did not want to do. Whatever the sequence of events, Larsen was indebted to Dykes for his introduction to Mormonism, at least indirectly, since the Herr Olsen who arranged his meeting with Snow was motivated by a wife whom Dykes had converted.

If Larsen first became acquainted with Mormonism in April 1851, a further question remains as to why he waited until August before reestablishing contact with the Mormons. Probably Larsen's "wait and see" attitude stemmed from events following Dykes's departure from Aalborg. On Sunday, 22 June 1851, Hans Peter Jensen and other Mormons in Aalborg performed several baptisms by immersion at a public beach before a large and hostile crowd. Jensen and a Mormon named Larsen bore their testimonies, and then, much as Dykes had done earlier that year in Hals, criticized the Lutheran clergy and warned the people to flee from the Church of the Devil and from "those priests they had in those high steepled temples." At this, several in the crowd became infuriated, marched on the Mormon meeting hall,[85] smashed out all the windows,

> . . . broke up all the benches and destroyed alle the furniture in the house . . . shamefully abused the brethren casting them down & treading on their necks & women were insulted by them & when the[y] could not accomplish thir Lustful desires upon them they were cast out of the window, & the womman that was in the house was confined with a young child & the mob entere[d] her room & sham[e]fully beat her man in her presence & threw her mother on the floor & shamefully abused her, & broke up all the dishes in the room but one cup & stoled all the money they had, but there was one more merciful than the others took the wife & young babe to a family that Lived upstairs & the man with some others of the saints hid themselves in the garden & there remained all night in the rain for there was a great rain with thunder & Lightning & while alle these things were going on the city authorities seemed to be quite indifferent & the mayor himself visited the place . . . & saw the work of destruction but after remaining a few moments on the spot he went hom[e] & on leaving said at denne folk kunne gjerne blive der nu that is, that that company (meaning the mob) could remain there if they chose but there was some of the more honorable citizens went to him & said he must call out the soldires [sic] and stop the work of destruction so he did for the soldiers were quartered near there & the rain, thunder, & Lightnig helped them & thus was the work of destruction stopt for that night, but continued about every night efter [after] for a week to a Limited extent,

mostly destroying private property such as breaking in of vindows &c. . . .[86]

On 30 June 1851, Dykes returned to Aalborg from Schleswig to find the Mormon meeting hall "all nailed up & the doors Locked," and received a summons from the mayor who "sent for me & told me to leave the town forthwith as he would not promise me protection to myself or any of the saints if I remained & said he would not have mormonism in the Land for he could not afford to have such disturbance for our sakes & I should leave the city immediately saa [so] I left according to his orders. . . ."[87] A week later, P. O. Hansen traveled to Aalborg disguised in "a seaman's overcoat & a broad brimmed strawhat," and saw soldiers patrolling the area around the Mormon meetinghouse. Hansen visited Mormons secretly, and "in the house of Thomsen the farrier in a back room" ordained H. F. Petersen an Elder in the Mormon Priesthood (13 July 1851), setting him apart to preside over the Branch, and also ordained five priests and four teachers.[88]

Svend Larsen of Risoer

The export and import trade was long the livelihood of countless Norwegian skippers who sought release from the tedium of life ashore in direct confrontation with the winds, rains and restless sea. Such a man was Svend Larsen (1816-1886), the first resident Norwegian to join the Mormons, and the first to bring Mormon missionaries to Norway itself.

Larsen's hometown, Oester Risoer, was a shipbuilding and trading center on the southern Norwegian coast with a population in 1850 of nearly two thousand people.[89] The town itself was wedged between low-lying mountains on one side, and a bay dotted with small islands which sheltered the town from ocean winds.[90] Skippers like Larsen lived in a part of town called "Tangen" crisscrossed by narrow footpaths between the houses; the houses were perched directly atop steep cliffs down which wooden steps led to the harbor waters.[91]

Although large sailing vessels from Sweden, Denmark, Great Britain, Prussia, Portugal, Italy, Russia and Holland frequently docked in Risoer, Larsen and other skippers made a good living hauling supplies to and from England, Holland, France, and Denmark in small sloops. The trading season usually started in March when the first loads of the season--lumber and lumber products-- were hauled to Denmark. About Eastertime, the boats returned laden with milk and dairy products, especially butter. Trips to Holland, France and England followed in due course--to Holland with beams and cords of dried oak; from Holland with green vegetables, cheeses, cakes and Dutch gin; to France with fir beams; to Scotland with beams and birchwood, and to England with iron from the Egeland Ironworks; from England with porcelain, foundry castings and coal.[92]

An only child, Larsen first attended a school in Risoer where more than two hundred pupils clamored for the attention of a solitary schoolmaster;[93] at age ten he joined his seafaring father on a coastal barge, and in February 1829 shipped as cabin boy on the brig <u>Edward</u> which sailed for London. Although a powerful storm enroute nearly capsized the ship, it also occasioned a "conversion experience":

> [The storm] forced me to think about Jesus and the Disciples when they were apparently facing a watery grave in the Sea of Galilee and Jesus was evidently asleep, though when the Disciples asked Him to, He arose and calmed the wind and the seas and all was still again. I therefore prayed quietly to Jesus with complete faith, asking Him to calm the winds and the waves and give us a favorable wind. I had not learned to pray on my knees to the Father in the Name of Jesus Christ . . . but to my great astonishment, and even before I finished praying, my prayer was answered and I saw that the waves suddenly diminished and the wind began to moderate, and before the night was over the wind was coming from the east (fair breeze) . . . I mention this occurrence in order to praise the Name of the Lord and show that He is merciful and hears the prayers of those who pray in faith and confidence.[94]

Larsen found life on the sea exhilarating, and for the next twenty years sailed his own sloop to every major European port. As per the custom among sailors, he initially visited a Lutheran priest once each autumn for purposes of communion, but gradually perceived the priest a liar "because he said, I grant you merciful forgiveness of your sins in the name of the Father, the Son and the Holy Ghost." Larsen thought to himself: "How do you dare take upon yourself to lie in the name of the Lord, for here is probably not one who has had thoughts of repenting and certainly not one who has prayed for forgiveness."[95] "From that time on," said Larsen, "I avoided the priest and never visited the church again."[96]

The picture emerges of a basically serious, sober and steady individual who had faced the elements and met their challenge, but yet was not entirely self-sufficient. Larsen filled his navigation log with detailed charts and drawings, nautical puzzles and their solutions, and a variety of notes and observations on seamanship. The log also comprised a sailor's manual which he co-edited with a man named Brown in 1833 "for the purpose of gathering together that which could prove beneficial both for the young and the more experienced sailor."[97] Brown and

Larsen included such varied topics as: the approximate length and weight of sea cannon; rules for determining the weight of rigging, anchor, ropes and chains; and ship measurements and how to determine the ship's burden. Eighteen assorted tables detailed weight of anchor ropes in relationship to their length and thickness; strength of ropes and rope contraction; anchor and rope size compared with tonnage; rope strands and their weights; commodity weights; and cannon and musket powder.[98]

The manual also evidenced Larsen's analytical skills. His introductory notes to the section "Anchors, Ropes and Chains," for example, reads in part: "A look at Tables 7, 8 and 9 will show how varied the opinions are about the weight of anchors with relation to the ship's breadth, the ship's tonnage and the thickness of the ropes. In my opinion, the [sizes of] chain anchors in Table 9 are overcalculated with relationship to . . . tonnage." Larsen further illustrated his points of divergence with computations and diagrams. If the handwritten year of 1833 on the title page is correct, he analyzed the tables and compiled his notes when only seventeen years old.[99]

Beginnings in Risoer and Brevik

Svend Larsen was baptized a Mormon on 23 September 1851 by Ole Christian Nielsen in Aalborg,[100] but before being baptized, made a hurried trip to Norway accompanied by Hans F. Petersen, a Mormon missionary. On arriving in Risoer on 11 September 1851, Petersen began distributing Mormon tracts,[101] but was cut short by civil officials who declared his passport invalid. Larsen and Petersen returned to Aalborg on 20 September,[102] and sailed once again for Risoer on 7 October accompanied by another missionary, Johan August Aahmanson.[103]

On 26 November, Petersen baptized master blacksmith, John Olsen, and Olsen's assistant, Peter Adamsen.[104] Enraged that Olsen would join such a sect, his relatives immediately stirred up groups of troublemakers who marched on Larsen's home in hopes of giving Petersen a thrashing. Petersen, however, escaped by hiding in the fireplace.[105] On 7 December, Svend Larsen, Peter Adamsen, John Olsen and Hans F. Petersen met in an upper room of Larsen's home and Adamsen and Olsen were confirmed members of the Church of Jesus Christ of Latter-day Saints "by the laying on of hands for the Gift of the Holy Ghost"; they also observed the sacrament of the Lord's Supper for the first time in Norway. Said Petersen: " . . . I thanked and praised my Heavenly Father for this day and this blessed hour. The Lord be praised! for [sic] He has heard and answered my prayer."[106]

By August 1852, Mormon proselyting campaigns had spread to Brevik and Fredrikstad, and ensuing months marked sporadic mob activity against the Mormons, the arrival of additional missionaries from Denmark, and several hearings where civil authorities warned missionaries and members that further baptisms would not be tolerated until Mormonism's "dissenter" status was established. Hans P. Jensen, the wealthy foundry owner from Aalborg, and Larsen further advertised the Mormon presence by purchasing a small sailing sloop in July 1852 for transporting members and missionaries to meetings and conferences. Christened Zions Loeve [Zion's Lion] by Larsen, the sloop was decked out with a white banner flying from the masthead "whereon was painted a lion holding in the loop of a bent golden halberd a beaming eye, and under the same the letter 'Z' painted in blue."[107]

In Brevik, Mormonism encountered its first serious opposition from inhabitants of the town and civil and religious authorities. Mormons had begun proselyting there as early as 10 June 1852, and succeeded in renting a large hall for preaching meetings. Larsen's periodic comings and goings in Zions Loeve further aroused public interest, as did the fact that Mormon missionaries were Danish and preached in the Danish tongue.[108]

In a stream of articles, the editor of the local newspaper, Adresse-Tidende for Brevig, attacked Mormons, accused them of sexual excesses,[109] and claimed the Mormon Prophet, Brigham Young, had ninety wives, and had recently been seen riding around with sixteen of them, of whom about fourteen had suckling babies at their breasts. Other articles declared every man in Utah could take as many wives as he pleased.[110]

Matters climaxed late in August 1852 at a "mission meeting" where the Lutheran Dean railed against the Mormon menace "in such a manner to the already deeply moved congregation that the eyes of many were bathed with tears, occasioned by sorrow and worry over the dangers to which several of their respectable fellow citizens have been exposed...."[111] Following the imprisonment of Mormon missionaries Aahmanson and Folkmann on 7 September, mobs several times threatened to kill on sight any Mormon found entering Brevik, but resident Mormons averted confrontation by rowing up the sound in a tiny boat and diverting Svend Larsen and several missionaries aboard Zions Loeve at the mouth of Brevik Fjord.[112]

"Awakened" Followers of Hans Nielsen Hauge

Although Hans Nielsen Hauge died in 1824, his disciples continued preaching his doctrines to "believers" who gathered for group singing and group prayer.[113] These Haugians had not formally broken with the State Church but formed a church apart in many ways: Haugian elders--those recognized as leaders because of exemplary lives and spiritual maturity--watched over the flocks, chastized "sinners," and rebuffed preachers of any false doctrine; Haugians were intimately acquainted with fellow believers and considered themselves members of a common movement; and Haugian preachers in all parts of Norway kept in touch via correspondence or personal visits.[114]

Many Haugians were important people in their individual communities: members of Parliament, merchants, traders, skilled artisans, progressive farmers--persons whose religious puritanism went hand in hand with upward social mobility.[115] They considered themselves "awakened" to a knowledge of their sinful state, but differed from ordinary sinners in claiming they had recognized their "ungodliness," humbled themselves before God, and received spiritual regeneration through worship and prayer with others of a like mind.

Sermons about frightful conditions in Hell awaiting the unrepentant--flames consuming the Devil and his wicked angels, eternal self-reproach, and self-loathing after a sinner was told by Christ to join the goats and depart His presence forever--often triggered a personal "awakening," usually traumatic and accompanied by deep personal anguish and feelings of guilt. Thus the Haugian Christian Hallesby described a period of extreme sorrow over sin leading to the day when, reeling under a burden of guilt so heavy he felt himself forever damned, he fell to his knees, confessed his sins before the Lord, and asked forgiveness. Comforting words immediately filled his mind: "You are now completely clean; there is no longer any sin in you."[116]

But Hallesby's experience was unusual in that most Haugians, although "awakened," received no immediate confirmation relieving them of guilt and anxiety. Repentance in the Haugian mold was more often viewed as a lengthy process; its requirement was a life of sober good works where loud laughter and laziness were abhorred:[117]

> Christianity remained somber, humorless, pietistic, and legalistic among Haugian groups. . . . So strong was the emphasis on the necessity of a thorough conversion that the assurance of actually being converted could drag on for months and even years. Even when a modicum of assurance was granted, it was not to be spoken of in tones other than those that emphasized the total depravity of man, even of the saved man, and an attitude of complete abjection before the Throne of God. God alone was to be glorified among Haugians, and that was its strength, but it was done entirely at man's expense.[118]

Ole P. Petersen in Fredrikstad

It is against this backdrop, where awakened sinners felt only partially relieved of guilt, that we must view the work of Ole P. Petersen (1822-1901)--the first preacher to disseminate Methodist doctrines in Norway. A native of Fredrikstad, Petersen read the Bible as a young man--especially the accounts of Christ's Life--and was deeply touched by the sufferings Christ had endured. But reading was not enough:

> I had no one to take me by the hand and lead
> me to Christ; there was no one to speak with
> me about experimental religion. But on
> the othere hand, Ministers and schoolteachers
> told me, that none could live up to the
> requirment of the Scriptures.[119]

Because of "a strange love" for America and "people called Americans," Petersen took work as a sailor on American ships in 1843.[120] Feelings of severe guilt over personal sins--remorse which he first experienced as a teenager--intensified during lonely days at sea, and Petersen finally sought out a private room and kneeled to pray:

> I felt, as if a person stood behind me,
> trying to lift me up from my knes [sic], at
> the same time suggestion was made, God will
> not hear you, you are a hypocrite, give it
> up. . . . I knelt down agian, saying Lord
> help me. After a few strugle, the good
> Lord mercyfully come to my help, the heavens
> opened around my [sic], and I could talk
> with God as a child with a dear Father.[121]

Petersen subsequently joined the Methodist Episcopal Church's Bethel Ship Congregation in New York,[122] and on 28 January 1849, while aboard a ship anchored near Mobile, Alabama, felt a refreshing "cleansing power" come over him which filled him with "great love" for the Lord and witnessed that his sins were washed completely away.[123] He later heard a Methodist sermon which suggested that each person, individually, is the temple of the Holy Ghost: ". . . I said to my self, if this body is the temple of the holy Ghost, o how carefull we ought to live, how clean and neet we ought to keep our self."[124]

Returning to Fredrikstad in 1849, Petersen found his fiancee living in the home of her uncle--a merchant named Tobias Jacobsen.[125] Jacobsen and family were Haugians with whom Petersen immediately shared his conversion experience: "First thing I tall [tell] them, was that the Lord had converted my soul, they all wept like children, and some said, that they felt that it was not right with them. I exhorted them to seek Jesus the only savior of menkind."[126]

Petersen next preached in the Fredrikstad suburbs where on 5 July an old woman threw herself down at his feet. "I tried," said Petersen, "to get her to stand up, but she would not." A week later, he and Jacobsen sailed to Egersund where they met a Captain Jensen [Johan Andreas Jensen]. Jensen, a Haugian, said he hoped God would grant him forgiveness of sins "when the time is right," to which Petersen countered God did not require long-term agonizing over sin, and that Jensen could experience forgiveness in a matter of days.[127] At a Haugian meeting Petersen and Jensen attended the following Sunday, Jensen interrupted the singing with a flood of joyful exclamations: "I could never have believed such peace and happiness were obtainable on this earth! This experience surpasses all human understanding! Praise the Lord!"[128]

Petersen preached "repentance, faith and justification"[129] to numerous Haugians during ensuing months. But despite numerous requests, and despite his own belief that Haugians were "sheep without a shepherd," he refused to organize a Methodist congregation. He was not an ordained minister and his heart was set on returning to America. He and his bride of a few weeks soon sailed for New York to rejoin the Bethel Ship Mission of the Methodist Episcopal Church.[130]

When Petersen returned to Norway four years later (December 1853), he did so as a regularly ordained minister with formal instructions to win converts and establish Methodist congregations. But wolves had entered the little flock: Petersen's "converts" confronted him with the "greater light" of Mormonism and urged him to immigrate with them to Utah. When the Lutheran priest blamed the "Mormon abomination" on Petersen's "heresies," he could only respond in kind: "They felt themselves as sheep without a shepherd, and as a result, were receptive to doctrine from other quarters than those which showed them coldness and opposition."[131]

Tobias Jacobsen and Methodist Fanaticism

After Petersen left for New York in 1850, de facto leadership over "Methodists" in Fredrikstad devolved on Tobias Jacobsen. Jacobsen had long contemplated leaving the State Church, adamantly refused to allow his sons or stepsons to proceed to Lutheran confirmation, and took his new role as "Methodist leader" so seriously it soon went to his head. On 2 May 1852, he stood up in church and told Lutheran priest Arup to go to Hell; later that evening he sang a lusty sea chanty and openly castigated Arup and "other servants of Satan" at a religious meeting in city hall: the crowd screamed and spit; swearing was heavy on every side; and others whistled and jeered. Jacobsen stood in the middle of the room, arms upraised, bellowing like a demon.[132]

On 29 May, Jacobsen and stepsons, Svend Peter Larsen and Niels Theodor Emil Larsen, attracted a crowd of rowdies near walls of the old city. Jacobsen called the Lutheran Church a "whorehouse," and the mob egged him on until Colonel Jens Christian Blich, Commander of Fredrikstad Fortress, rode up on horseback, slashed him across the lips with a whip, and ordered him arrested. Seeing his stepfather abused, Svend Peter Larsen commanded the rabble to "repent, or the Lord will destroy you!" Two soldiers immediately dragged him to jail and bashed in his mouth with rifle butts.

Jacobsen and Larsen were released a few hours later, and Jacobsen demanded a court hearing to press formal charges against

Colonel Blich. That request was denied, and on 26 May, he again caused a scene by deriding civil and ecclesiastical authorities from a boat in mid-river before scores of curious onlookers who thronged the banks.[133]

Jacobsen, meanwhile, was not the only "Methodist" in the limelight. On 29 April 1852, another of Petersen's followers, Jens Andreas Jensen, announced the following in a Fredrikstad newspaper:

> By the grace of God, I hereby declare to all the world that I, J. A. Jensen, skipper and citizen of Fredrikstad, have, through the boundless grace [of God], received the spirit of truth in my heart, which witnesses with my spirit that I . . . am the true and only Son of God united with the Father.[134]

Jensen's advertisement merited a twenty-dollar fine for slander, plus a court hearing where he charged the judge was unfair and all Norwegian officials--both ecclesiastical and civil--were corrupt.[135] Jensen was now treading a fine line: he had only directly criticized a minor judge; indirectly, he had denounced all government and ecclesiastical officials, but not by name. Niels Larsen, Jacobsen's stepson, further vexed official tempers by declaring in court that he, Jacobsen and Jensen were "of God" making it "impossible for us to lie."[136]

At this juncture, one of the more interesting figures in the drama--Christian Birch-Reichenwald (1814-1891), district governor of Oestfold--became involved. "Birch," as he was known to associates, was an administrator of the old school--the son of a general, a man who demanded respect, and a governor who equated governance with "order." Word soon reached him that Jacobsen and Jensen had marched through streets of Fredrikstad singing revivalist hymns and that--horror of horrors--children had deserted the schoolhouse en masse to follow the Methodist "pied pipers."[137] Birch immediately summoned both men to appear in court.

At the hearing on 15 June, Jensen defiantly told the court he would preach repentance and sing in the streets "whenever the spirit of God should so move and inspire a desire thereto. . . ."[138] Both he and Jacobsen pounded on tables with their Bibles, called the judge dirty names, cowed witnesses by yelling at them full in the face, and paced up and down like wild horses.[139] There were no such antics, however, at the follow-up hearing three days later when the judge confronted Jensen with an article from <u>Christianiaposten</u> written by Jensen himself. That article described a letter Jensen had written to King Oscar of Sweden-Norway two years earlier decrying moral laxity, and also insinuated the King was a liar because he had supposedly reneged on a promise to meet personally with Jensen.[140]

Jensen swallowed the bait. Caught up in the drama of confrontation, and undoubtedly surprised by the new evidence, he called King Oscar "the biggest liar of all the liars in our Country."[141] That, and not the street disorders, was sufficient to sway the court, and he was sentenced to a year in jail.[142]

With one pillar of dissent out of the picture, Birch-Reichenwald went after Jacobsen, and despite the fact Judge Berg had pronounced him quite rational "on all subjects except religion," insisted he be examined by a psychiatrist.[143] Jacobsen was summarily hauled away to the Oslo Madhouse for observation, but escaped early in the spring of 1853 after being doused repeatedly with ice water. Policemen apprehended him near Fredrikstad and incarcerated him in Fredrikstad Jail where he "amused himself" by "tearing apart one iron stove after another, smashing windows and whatever else fell into his hands, and, were he capable of so doing, would, like another Sampson," have brought "the entire jail crashing down upon himself."[144] Jacobsen's stepsons, meanwhile, received minor sentences for their parts in the disturbances: Emil Larsen spent fifteen days in prison on bread and water; Svend Peter Larsen paid an eight-dollar fine.[145]

Mormon Beginnings in Fredrikstad

Soon after bringing the first Mormons to Risoer in 1851, Svend Larsen made a business trip to Fredrikstad where he evidently contacted Svend Peter Larsen, Tobias Jacobsen's stepson. Larsen of Risoer was possibly interested in Methodist doctrines, or else his association with Larsen of Fredrikstad stemmed from business ties. But there is little doubt he told his fellow skipper about the Mormons, and that Larsen of Fredrikstad accordingly visited Mormon missionary, Hans F. Petersen, in Risoer on 14 December 1851. Larsen of Fredrikstad was enroute to Bergen in his sloop Den gode Hensigt [The Goodly Purpose], and Petersen, in constant danger from prowling mobs, was only too happy to travel along.[146]

Larsen of Fredrikstad subsequently visited Mormons in Copenhagen and accepted Mormon baptism there on 2 April 1852; his wife, Berthine Randine, was baptized four days later.[147] Larsen and wife returned to Fredrikstad, but chose not to advertise their Mormon conversion; there is no indication Larsen preached or alluded to Mormonism when he joined his stepfather, Tobias Jacobsen, in preaching repentance outside the old fortress walls on 20 May 1852.

Not until 9 July 1852, in fact, was there any indication Larsen in Fredrikstad had plans to preach Mormonism: on that date, Willard Snow, President of the Scandinavian Mission, wrote his brother, Erastus, about "an influential man [Svend Peter Larsen] and his wife from Norway"--recent converts baptized in Copenhagen. Snow reported Larsen had "written an excellent letter back [from Fredrikstad] . . . and there seems to be quite an opening there and he is all alive in the spirit of the work."[148]

Jeppe J. Folkmann, a Mormon missionary who had earlier preached on the Island of Bornholm, arrived in Fredrikstad about mid-July to a warm welcome from both Svend Peter Larsen and his brother, Niels--stepsons of the old Methodist, Tobais Jacobsen. Both brothers had withdrawn from the Lutheran Church earlier that summer, and Niels and wife were embroiled in controversy with Lutheran priest, L. Chr: Arup, over their refusal to allow him to christen their infant twins. Arup informed his brother, Bishop of Oslo, about the matter on 4 July, having warned Niels's wife, Maren Lovise, "that her children, if necessary, would be christened by resorting to the full force of the law."[149]

Hans Peter Jensen of Aalborg and skipper Svend Larsen of Risoer arrived in Fredrikstad on 23 July. The first Mormon to begin serious proselyting in the Fredrikstad area, Jensen visited a meeting of so-called "Kirketroende" [Church-believers] the following Sunday afternoon (25 July) and induced Johan Johansen, leader of the group, and several members of the congregation, to follow him to the home of a Guttorm Baardsen where he "proved" from the Bible the State Church was false. Jeppe J. Folkmann baptized five persons (including three Church-believers) "near the Island of Krakeroey in a bay fronting Fuglevig Farm" later that night.[150]

Conclusion

Mormon beginnings in Scandinavia centered largely around personalities and lives of key forerunners: P. O. Hansen's rather cursory decision to visit a Baptist meeting proved the vital "plug-in" Mormons needed to establish a bridgehead in Copenhagen; only because of personal rivalry with Erastus Snow, as heightened by his own restless and headstrong nature, did George Parker Dykes go to Aalborg where his proselyting efforts sparked Mormon beginnings there and in Norway, and where the preaching zeal and lack of tact displayed by men such as H. P. Jensen and Dykes himself served from the start to brand Mormons "fanatics"-a label relayed to credulous populations of Scandinavia via the popular press.

Mormon beginnings in Norway were closely aligned with the history of men "who went to the sea in ships"--Svend Larsen, Ole P. Petersen, Svend Peter Larsen, Jens Andreas Jensen and Tobias Jacobsen. As sailors and skippers, they had seen some of the world and its great diversity, and were generally more receptive to new ideas and philosophies than those who were homebound in the traditional and rather static Norwegian society. Closely related to the "seafaring aspect" were ties to "American" religion displayed in lives of key figures: George Parker Dykes preached Mormonism to Norwegians at Fox River, Illinois, in 1842; P. O. Hansen translated parts of the Book of Mormon in the Mormon temple at Nauvoo; Ole P. Petersen felt a "strange Love" for America and propounded American Methodist doctrines in Fredrikstad in 1849; Svend Larsen of Risoer wanted to meet the "Apostle from America" at Aalborg in 1851. It was in America the first Scandinavian connections with Mormonism were forged and plans for Mormon missionary efforts in Scandianvia conceived;

it was to America Mormon Scandinavians would "flee by the thousands in their headlong rush to the New Zion.

Svend Larsen of Risoer was the man directly responsible for bringing Mormonism to Risoer and Fredrikstad, but in the latter case the seed grew in soil already harrowed by Haugian and Methodist initiatives. Inhabitants of Fredrikstad could not help but dub Mormons "fanatics," largely because some of the first Mormon converts were relatives of the infamous Tobias Jacobsen, or were rabble-rousers themselves. And civil and religious authorities made the same connection with long-term consequences for Mormonism in Norway for generations to come.

CHAPTER III

THE SUPREME COURT DECISION OF 4 NOVEMBER 1853

The "Non-Christian" Label

In his thesis, "Mormonisma i Noreg" [Mormonism in Norway], Karl Sandvin described Mormonism's history in Norway as one of controversy over a single point of argument:

> As we time after time have seen, that point has been whether Mormons could be considered Christians. As soon as they came to this country, that was [the question] which engendered debate, both from a theological and juridical standpoint, and the doubt has continued unabated ever since.[1]

Sandvin was referring to debate before and after the Supreme Court Decision of 4 November 1853 which labeled Mormons in Norway "non-Christians" who could not, therefore, enjoy protection under the Dissenter Law of 1845. That law defined "dissenters" as "those who confess the Christian Religion without being members of the State Church."[2]

Public opinion accepted the Decision as "proof" Mormons were reprobates who did not believe in Christ or the Christian ethic. The Decision became a convenient prop for blanket indictments, and the rationale for treating Mormons in Norway as second-class citizens. A confrontation between the Mormon, A. S. Schou, and a Lutheran schoolteacher aboard a steamer in 1878 was typical: the teacher told Schou Mormonism was of the Devil, and when Schou refuted his arguments with help from a passenger who had lived several years in America, "sought a way out" by damning Mormons and "telling us that Mormons were not considered Christians."[3] Likewise, Mormons in Sandnes who tried to rent a meeting hall in 1896 were told by the owner he did not rent to non-Christians,[4] and a Methodist at a Mormon "magic lantern show" in 1906 expressed surprise at seeing "christ on the first pictures for sead [said] he he had always herd we did not beleve in a christ but worshiped Adam for our god. . . ."[5]

Parliamentarians frequently referred to the 1853 Decision, and such politicians as Jakob Sverdrup used it to buttress charges Mormonism was immoral, corrosive of society, and not to be tolerated in a civilized country.[6] Lutheran priests and bishops, newspaper editors, lawyers, and civil authorities followed suit: the Supreme Court had declared Mormons and Mormonism "non-Christian," and surely that decision was based on evidence of pernicious doctrines.

It was the bedrock upon which opinions of Mormonism must rest--the point of reference for debate on the Mormon Question.

Not surprisingly, perhaps, Mormons themselves attributed the Decision solely to official censure of their religious beliefs, and as recently as 1977 referenced their contention that Mormons were Christians with Mormon scriptures about Christ. "A Christian," they said, "is commonly defined as one who accepts the New Testament Christ and His teachings as the norm for conduct and doctrine." They then asked: "Who decides if another person is Christian? To whom does one go to find out if a Latter-day Saint [Mormon] is Christian; to a Lutheran or a Latter-day Saint?"[7]

Historical Perspectives

The Supreme Court Decision of 4 November 1853 was part and parcel of ideological and class conflicts in Norwegian society beginning with events in the early 1830s when a new generation of students came on the scene--a generation with no experiential ties to the Napoleonic Wars or events surrounding Norwegian Independence in 1814. These students were generally divided into opposing groups or flanks revolving around two young poets-- Henrik Arnold Wergeland (1808-1845) and Johan Sebastian Cammermeyer Welhaven (1807-1873).

Wergeland's group--so-called "patriots"--was by far the most numerous and displayed a boisterous patriotism coupled with romanticized interest in Norwegian folklore and peasant tradition. They despised despots, aristocrats and Swedish overlords, and supported increased farmer representation in Parliament, general education for the masses, free lending libraries and other programs. Welhaven and company--"Intelligenspartiet" [The Intelligence Party]--favored a more cosmopolitan policy of moderation, cutural accommodation with other nations, especially Denmark, and government by an elite.

Although the most bitter contentions between the two groups stemmed from personal jealousies and rivalries, the conflict mirrored widespread antagonisms between the lower classes and the ruling civil servant estate.[8] Members of that estate [embetsmandsstanden]-- cabinet ministers, government functionaries, jurists, clerics, university professors and military officers--filled most public posts during the approximate years 1814-1870, were heavily concentrated in cities or towns, spoke a language more akin to Danish than Norwegian, and were quite isolated from Norwegian society at large.[9]

Next on the social totem pole were merchants and well-to-do artisans in urban areas, and so-called storboender [large farmers] in rural areas. Storboender owned large tracts of land, employed numerous cotters and laborers, and were nearly the social equals of civil servants, especially in parts of Oestlandet and the Province of Troendelag.[10] They had the vote in accordance with the Constitution of 1814, comprised a majority in Parliament, and were locked in a decades-long power struggle with the King and his ministers who insisted cabinet posts remain the domain of civil servants. That struggle was not effectively resolved until 1884.[11]

More ominous, however, was the virtual explosion in the number of cotters, day laborers and servants; the number of cotters alone rose from 39,400 in 1801 to over 67,000 in 1855.[12] Norway's total population of about 1,238,000 in 1850 included an urban total of 162,000; the number of cotters, however, was 67,000 (350,000 including families)--nearly double the population of all the cities combined.[13] For cotters and children of cotters this meant there was not enough land to go around. Those without land (or without enough land) had to accept "help" from *storboender* which bound them even more hopelessly than before to years of *pliktarbeid* [duty work]. Body and soul, they were hardly better off than slaves or indentured servants.[14]

If farmers posed no direct threat to the civil servant estate by 1850, growing numbers of cotters and landless laborers did. In 1849, well-known radical, painter, poet and agitator, Harro Harring, arrived in Norway and founded a revolutionary journal in Oslo. Harring had fought in the Greek Wars of Liberation, and was well-acquainted with both Mazzini and Garibaldi. His political agitations soon alarmed government officials, and Vice-Regent Loevenskioeld hurriedly convinced a cabinet majority to deport him; Harring's summary expulsion in May 1850 generated storms of protest from members of Parliament who felt they should have been consulted beforehand.[15]

Concurrently with Harring's arrival, the Norwegian Marcus Thrane published the first number of a newspaper for workingmen-- *Arbeiderforeningernes Blad* [The Workers' Associations Newspaper]. Thrane agitated for universal suffrage, general military conscription, and repeal of restrictive wheat tariffs;[16] he also lectured to groups of small farmers, landless cotters and apprentices throughout Norway, and organized workingmen's associations in areas of favorable response. Results were phenomenal: More than a hundred local associations were functioning by February 1850; by July 1851, membership in four hundred local associations exceeded thirty thousand, with heaviest membership concentrations in population centers around Oslo and Drammen.[17]

Leaders of Thrane's associations gathered at Ladegaardsoeen near Oslo in the Summer of 1850, and presented the King a petition seeking government aid to cotters, judicial and tariff reforms, and implementation of universal suffrage. Despite some thirteen thousand signatures, the King rejected the petition out of hand. Events then took a more radical turn. In Stjoerdalen early in 1851, a Thranite named Carl Johan Michelsen advocated unlawful depletion of timberlands. Michelsen was arrested on 7 February 1851 in Levanger, but his cohorts disrupted court proceedings and pelted the sheriff with stones until the Army quelled the disturbance. The Supreme Court sentenced Michelsen to seven years' hard labor.[18]

Thranites gathered once again in Oslo on 11 June 1851 at a central meeting dubbed by detractors *Lilletinget* [The Little

Parliament]. The big question was whether workers' associations would threaten full-scale rebellion. Confusion reigned and delegates bantered about lots of daring talk about revolution, but the result was compromise: delegates restated worker demands in a petition to Parliament. Nothing happened.

When violence again erupted in early July, worried members of the upper classes demanded immediate action. Government authorities arrested Thrane and other leaders--a total of 149 persons--in a mass cleanup operation on 7 July 1851, and the Supreme Court eventually sentenced Thrane and his assistant, Abildgaard, to four years' imprisonment (One Thranite got nine years with a chance for clemency after six years' good behavior).[19] According to the jurist, Frede Castberg:

> In the days of the Thranite Movement, leaders in [Norwegian] society and large segments of the population felt themselves threatened by civil disobedience and revolution. It was a threat--no matter how vague and exaggerated--which condoned both violence and infringement of property rights. The drama was acted out against the background of bloody revolutions in Europe a few years before. And the sentences meted out reflected that fact.[20]

The Mormon Question: Pros and Cons

It was against the backdrop of Thranite uprisings that the first Mormons arrived in Norway in 1851. In March 1852, master blacksmith John Olsen, a former Thranite,[21] wrote Sheriff Engebreth Finne requesting official recognition as Mormon leader in Risoer according to provisions of the Dissenter Law of 1845.[22] Olsen would not swear an oath as stipulated by the Dissenter Law, but was willing to "promise" or "affirm" in accordance with paragraph ten of said Law which directed that:

> Those whose religion does not allow the swearing of oaths in any form, shall give, in those circumstances where an oath is required, promises or affirmation in a manner or form prescribed by the King, which shall be accepted in place of an oath.[23]

Finne forwarded Olsen's request to District Governor Iver Steen Thomle, who in turn sent it to the Ecclesiastical Department [KUD] in Oslo on 31 March. A Mormon in Risoer, meanwhile, refused to swear an oath at a court case, and Thomle wrote again to Oslo--this time to the Justice Department [JPD]--asking for advice and referring to his earlier letter.[24] The JPD noted Thomle's request on 17 April, and asked the KUD to formulate a decision on the matter of Mormons and oaths.[25] The KUD, meanwhile, had written members of the Theological Faculty at the University of Oslo seeking their advice.[26] What we see in the above exchanges is a classic case of "passing the buck": Sheriff Finne in Risoer did not want personal responsibility for deciding whether Mormons could formally organize, and the same was true of Governor Thomle, the KUD and JPD.

But the Theological Faculty stood firm in a decision dated 17 May 1852 that blacksmith John Olsen of Risoer should be recognized as leader of a Mormon group or congregation,

> . . . since the Law [Dissenter Law of 1845] itself shows how liberally it would define "those who confess the Christian religion," by including among such those who renounce baptism . . . an extension to which the State in practice lends validity with reference to the Quakers, and since the [Mormon] Articles of Faith submitted to the Faculty contain nothing contrary to law or decency.[27]

The Faculty also suggested Mormons make promises, in lieu of oaths, in the manner stipulated for Quakers by Royal Decree of 19 May 1847.[28]

As reiterated by the Faculty, debate over the question of "Christian" dissenters prior to passage of the Dissenter Law clearly showed Parliament wanted the law left as open-ended as possible--the less control by King and clerics, the better. But Hans Riddervold, head of the KUD, had other ideas. A former Lutheran bishop,[29] Riddervold "governed more in accordance with the old bureaucratic state-church view than with the developing thoughts of freedom," and "was constantly on guard against every development which could be suspected of 'robbing the Church Administration of power to exercise that control which was presumably its due.'"[30] Dressed in his "Quaker hat, his strange cape, his calot," and "his glossy boots," "Father Riddervold" wielded power absolutely in the mold of an "aging cardinal."[31] In the case of the Mormon petition, Riddervold was sure he smelled a rat. Rumors about Mormon harems and a "political Zion" were even then sweeping the Capital, and he was no doubt informed increasing numbers of missionaries--Mormon missionaries who ignored orders to stop preaching and baptizing--were being arrested by local authorities. Despite the Theological Faculty's pro-Mormon pronouncement, therefore, Riddervold solicited opinions from Lutheran bishops in a move to delay any pro-Mormon decision.

Riddervold's circular to the bishops in July 1852 described Olsen's request to head a Mormon congregation in Risoer, and asked whether Mormons should be considered Christians under the Dissenter Law of 1845; Riddervold discussed the Theological Faculty's liberal interpretation of the phrase "those who profess the Christian religion," but disagreed with the Faculty's pro-Mormon decision since Mormons "accept a different historical basis for their profession of religious belief, and namely believe in revelation outside that contained in Holy Scripture . . . which is evidently not the case with any other religious group heretofore defined as Christian."[32] (Riddervold also wrote the Theological Faculty asking it to reconsider its earlier verdict.)[33]

The Theological Faculty and Lutheran bishops expressed no unanimous decision in replying to Riddervold's circular, and indeed, their answers compounded the growing indecision and vacillation surrounding the case. Daniel Bremer Juell, Bishop of Tromsoe, noted Mormons looked to the Book of Mormon more than the Bible, and therefore stood outside the normal range of Christian dissent. On the other hand, the Dissenter Law applied to sects which, even though they supposedly based their theology on the Bible, denigrated the sacraments of baptism and the Lord's Supper. Mormons should, therefore, enjoy protection under the law.[34]

In much the same vein, the Theological Faculty in Oslo wrote that Mormon reliance on the Book of Mormon disqualified them as "a Christian sect" in any traditional sense. But since sects which rejected baptism--the only means provided by Christ for entrance into His Church--still enjoyed dissenter status, Mormons should also be considered Christians so long as they recognized Christ as their Savior. The Faculty noted Mormon history in America paralleled that of Anabaptists during the Reformation who believed in a hierarchical, secular kingdom-- a "state within the State." Mormons might, therefore, only obey civil authorities long enough to establish a power base.[35]

Hans Joergen Darre, Bishop of Trondheim, basically agreed that Mormons should enjoy dissenter status. The State should, as far as possible, allow all individuals freedom of belief and conscience since history itself showed that persecution of particular sects usually resulted in their winning more converts than would have otherwise been the case.[36] Jacob von der Lippe, Bishop of Kristiansand, detailed his opinions in two letters. His first dated 14 August 1852 declared for allowing Mormons religious freedom, but a subsequent letter on 17 November expressed serious doubts Mormon tracts and books painted a true picture of Mormon beliefs and purposes.[37]

Johan Balthasar Flottmann, acting Bishop of Bergen, described Mormons as "opportunists" who attempted to win proselytes on the sly; Mormons should not enjoy protection of the law because they based their theology on the Book of Mormon instead of New Testament Christianity.[38] Oslo Bishop, Jens Laurits Arup, agreed with Flottmann that Mormons could not be formally recognized as Christian dissenters since they placed the Book of Mormon on an equal footing with the Bible. Arup mentioned such "indecent practices" as polygamy and baptism of naked women in oceans and streams attributed to Mormons in America, and advocated "careful and thorough" examination of Mormon doctrines.[39]

"Wolves in Sheep's Clothing"

As intimated by Bishops Arup, von der Lippe, and Flottmann, and detailed by the Theological Faculty, Mormonism was increasingly considered an insurrectionary movement. Thranite uprisings had only recently been put down, and it was that fact which moved Arup and others to pour forth fears about Mormonism. In subsequent years, Arup would complain that Thranite uprisings had created "great divisions" in Norwegian society,[40] would envision the fire of anarchy as "still smoldering under the ashes, waiting for the breath of wind which will cause it to flare up,"[41] and in 1855, at the height of court proceedings against Thrane and cohorts, would particularize Mormonism a seedbed of revolution:

> Religious aberration generally unites with political; since the essence of truth must needs be corrupted when used to adorn the unashamed and dissolute forward march of evil. _There is no little common ground between communism and Mormonism; and it is therefore not surprising if this [Mormonism] wins supporters._[42] (Italics mine.)

Arup was certainly not the first to allege Mormon-Thranite connections. Governor of Smaalenenes County, Christian Birch-Reichenwald, worried about Mormonism's "subversive" tendencies as early as 1852, and, unlike ecclesiastical authorities, was prepared to attack the problem head-on. "Birch," as he was known to contemporaries, was a phenomenon by any standard: foreman of the Oslo Student Association at age eighteen where he belonged to "Intelligenspartiet"; bureau chief of the Ecclesiastical Department at twenty-three; secretary of the Ecclesiastical Department at age twenty-seven; Mayor of Oslo at thirty-two; District Governor of Smaalenenes County at thirty-three.[43] Son of a general, Birch inherited a strong sense of discipline, a perfectionist's eye for precision, an overriding sense of command, and a love of power.

Birch's behavior was never easy to predict: he considered political defeats or setbacks shameful losses of face,[44] and his manic-depressive personality exhibited wide fluctuations in mood accompanied by frequent bouts of depression lasting weeks and even months. His friends, however, were numerous and influential. (Not a few were blood relatives or related through marriage):

> Birch-Reichenwald's strength was his friends. He had a rare talent for friendship. . . . Motzfeldt and Sibbern, Dunker and Welhaven, were among those who stood closest to him right from the days of his youth. His circle

of friends permeated all branches of the civil servant and merchant estates in the Capital City. Frederik Stang, who himself lacked the ability to win friends, was well aware of Birch-Reichenwald's following, and feared the strength which it gave him. Birch-Reichenwald, he wrote, "has more special political friends than any other public official I know in the country."[45]

Birch's enemies called him a power-hungry tyrant:

> For him, power is the goal; . . . he is more power-hungry than ambitious. This personality quirk is tied . . . to the thoroughly negative character of his being. The only positive thing he has ever wanted and desired is power; if one asked him what he planned to do with that power, he would be unable to answer, or more probably, would not understand the question. There is nothing for which he works, no goal for which he strives -- except power.[46]

Birch and his peers were deeply committed to preserving traditions and values of their class.[47] As conservative power brokers, they weighed every development and event in society at large in much the same way an autocratic judge might assess facts of a case: "They would have the entire country--and every situation therein--firmly within their grasp and imbued with their ideals."[48]

On 6 October 1852, the Justice Department in Oslo advised Birch of Governor Aall's decision to imprison Mormon missionaries who baptized or preached, and recommended he do the same.[49] Birch accordingly declared in a circular on 8 October that so-called Mormon priests in the County were not recognized or authorized under the Dissenter Law, some of them were under arrest for having broken laws of the land, and their "Letters of Authority," supposedly signed by Mormon officials in Copenhagen, were of doubtful validity.[50] Four days later, Birch confided his fears about Mormon emissaries to JPD officials in Oslo: "Today [12 October 1852], I have, by pure chance, come across what I have every reason to believe will lead to complete vindication of my suspicion that these fellows, the Mormons, or in any case some of them, are good "Soerflationists,"[51] _just as they, in all probability, are dyed-in-the-wool Thranites._"[52] (Italics mine.)

On 14 October--two days after writing about Mormon Thranites--Birch personally confronted four Mormons--Svend Larsen, Jeppe G. Folkmann, Niels Hansen and Christian J. Larsen--in the countryside near Fredrikstad. Christian J. Larsen gave the following account:

> When I, in company with Brothers Svend Larsen, Jeppe G. Folkmann and Niels Hansen . . .

> (14 October) were heading toward Ingolsrud to visit some of the Saints, we met Birch-Reichenwaldt, the Governor of Smaalenenes County, who arrested us and addressed us in a very brutal manner, yea, even hurled insults at us when he heard that we belonged to the Church of Jesus Christ of Latter-day Saints, or "the Mormons." He told us to go with him back to Fredriksstad to be imprisoned, which we refused to do, since we had not transgressed any law. . . . We bid farewell to the Governor and continued our journey to Ingolsrud.[53]

Svend Larsen also gave an eyewitness account:

> Brothers Folkman, C. Larsen, Hansen and I were enroute to Ingolsrud when we were arrested by District Governor Birch Reichenwald. Since I did not know the man, I asked for proof of his authority to arrest [us], whereupon he tore open his coat in a rage and displayed a badge of office and ordered us to accompany him to Frederikstad to be booked, which we refused to do and bid him farewell and continued on our way to Ingolsrud where, shortly after arriving, we were arrested by Sheriff Ytter's son accompanied by a group of farmers.[54]

Civil authorities soon rounded up all Mormon missionaries in Fredrikstad and vicinity: Christian J. Larsen, Mormon leader in Norway; Svend Larsen of Risoer; and missionaries Johan F. F. Dorius, Peter Beckstrom, and Johan A. Aahmanson were locked up in Fredrikstad Jail; whereas missionaries Ole Olsen, Niels Hansen, Christen Knudsen, and Jeppe G. Folkmann were imprisoned at nearby Elverhoei. Citizens of Fredrikstad, Johan Johansen and Niels Theodor Emil Larsen, were accused of preaching and baptizing, but not imprisoned.[55]

Birch initially made several visits to the imprisoned missionaries and, according to Christian J. Larsen, "treated us in a very impolite manner, as if we were criminals, and when we made any reply, would roughly tell us to 'shut up.'"[56] There is little doubt most of those arrested had baptized and preached Mormonism in direct opposition to strictures laid down by local and county officials. Svend Larsen of Risoer, however, had not baptized or officiated in the sacrament of the Lord's Supper. Larsen was a Norwegian citizen, a homeowner in Risoer, and a registered skipper; his arrest and imprisonment, in the absence of formal charges, were flagrant violations of his rights as a citizen.[57]

Birch-Reichenwald's Intrigues

Birch soon uncovered enough from court hearings to conclude Mormon doctrine diverged markedly from that of Lutherans, and all other Christian sects as well. That said, the question remained as to which laws Mormons had broken since laws which seemingly applied had fallen into general disuse.[58] Rather than prosecute, therefore, he recommended the JPD deport the missionaries en masse.[59] The JPD rejected Birch's recommendation, however, probably because one prisoner--Svend Larsen--was a Norwegian citizen, and because Harro Harring's deportation in 1850 had evoked screams of protest from Parliament. In lieu of deportation proceedings, the JPD issued a Government Resolution on 25 January 1853 stating "no decision possible" in the matter of Mormons and oaths. The Resolution strongly implied Mormons were not Christian dissenters by suggesting they could not be trusted in a court of law; it also underlined JPD hesitancy to formulate Mormon policy tied to the Dissenter Law.[60]

Armed with the JPD Resolution, Birch immediately interjected the issue of Mormons and Christianity into proceedings of Fredrikstad City Court in an effort to divert attention from antiquated laws to the more general question of Mormon dissenter status--a question, incidentally, above and beyond the lower court's jurisdictional authority,[61] and one it had not previously considered in connection with the imprisoned Mormons. On 1 March 1853, the lower court found Mormon prisoners guilty of breaking Norwegian Law 6-1-4, and assessed each of them a fine of eight dollars. More importantly, the court ruled that Mormons, generally, were not Christian dissenters.[62]

Mormons immediately appealed the decision to Oslo Superior Court,[63] and that court decreed on 4 April 1853 that Mormon prisoners should be fined because they had preached and baptized before Mormonism's status was determined by law. The court described as invalid, however, the lower court ruling that Mormons were not Christian dissenters:

> . . . the Court fails to see that there is any meaningful difference between those who accept an addition [the Book of Mormon] to the original foundation of the [Christian] faith, and those [Quakers] who deny an essential part of that foundation. Under these circumstances, it must be concluded that Mormon doctrine, no matter how corrupt it may be, describes Christ as the Savior of Mankind and the Holy Scriptures as divine revelation.[64]

The Superior Court ruling left Birch with egg on his face. His singlehanded decision to corral Mormon missionaries and force a decision on "Mormon Christianity" had backfired, and the results were twofold: severe depression and a frantic effort to appeal the decision. Not until 21 April did Birch learn his "remonstrance" to the JPD had been favorably considered: he was forthwith given permission to appeal the Superior Court's decision to the Norwegian Supreme Court.[65]

The Superior Court's decision was dated 4 April 1853, and compliance therewith mandated Birch release Mormons imprisoned since October, or, at very least, inform them of the court's decision. But Birch felt himself above the law in this respect. Only after receiving permission from the JPD to appeal the case--a full eighteen days after the Superior Court announced its decision--did he instruct the Sheriff of Fredrikstad to inform Mormons of "the Superior Court Decision and the appeal to the Supreme Court in connection therewith. . . ."[66]

On 24 April, Birch's brother-in-law, Carl Motzfeldt, wrote him from Oslo as follows:

> You have by now hopefully recovered from the disagreeable state of mind occasioned by the Superior Court Decision in the Mormon case? No one mentions the case here, and I have no reason to believe that anyone in the Department [JPD] will view your connection therewith in any unfavorable light whatsoever.[67]

Motzfeldt's assurances aside, Birch was already working to effect a favorable decision by the Supreme Court. His hope, and indeed his most trusted mentor throughout his political career, was the renowned Supreme Court attorney, Carl Christian Henrik Bernhard Dunker (1809-1870), with whom he conspired to prosecute the Mormon case late in April 1853. Dunker's reply of 25 April left no doubt of willingness to bestow a personal favor:

> I just this moment received your letter . . . . I will confidentially inform the Secretary of the Supreme Court that I would like to serve as prosecutor against the Mormons because the question interests me. The secretary will think this reasonable, which it is, and since the persons [Mormons] are now at large [this was not the case; the prisoners were released on 5 May], I look upon it as a foregone conclusion that this case will not inconvenience you in any way whatsoever.[68]

Dunker was a somewhat paradoxical figure. His friendship with Birch stemmed from student days when, with other Welhaven devotees, they immersed themselves in Hegelian writings about "Philosopher Kings";[69] he was also deeply emotional--an incurable romanticist who rejoiced in Nature's beauty, and savored ocean breezes or journeys by boat on the open sea.[70] His life was not a happy one. "Discord," he once observed, "is my daily bread, in the house and out of the house; with my wife, my sister and my brother...."[71] Although independently wealthy, his upper-class pleasures were decidedly low-key: George Sand novels; private lunches with Lutheran priests; after-dinner smokes with the Mayor; or travels south to remote German spas.[72]

Dunker had long been Norway's most sought-after lawyer, and, in the words of G. Hallager,

> ... was the lawyer most respected by the general public. He was therefore entrusted with the most difficult and important cases, cases where the verdict was a matter of life and death, of public honor or humiliation, or where powerful interests were at stake. Throughout the country there grew up an almost superstitious conviction that if one could get Dunker to plead one's case, victory was virtually assured.[73]

The Supreme Court Case

On 7 July 1853, Brevik Conference President, Christian J. Larsen, and other Mormons visited their attorney in the pending Supreme Court case, a Mr. Jorgensen, who, according to Larsen, was "not at all freindly [sic] disposed to us or our cause, but . . . became more civil towards us before we left him, and . . . even asked us to pray for him."[74] The Mormons also visited Bernhard Dunker who told them the case would come before the court in September.[75]

The case did not, in fact, come before the court until 2 November 1853 on which date Dunker argued for the prosecution by detailing Mormon history in Denmark and Norway, confusion over the question of Mormons and oaths, restrictions on Mormon missionaries by District Governor Aal in Bratsberg County, and--in great detail--Birch-Reichenwald's part in bringing Mormons to trial for their crimes.[76] Dunker then turned from criminal to purely religious aspects of the case--aspects which concerned not only a few Mormon missionaries, but all Mormons in Norway, including unborn generations:

> That to be decided is whether Mormon doctrine can be classified as belonging to the Christian religion. The question is one of worldwide dimensions. I shall not further belabor what is contained in the extracts. We have declarations by the Bishops, the Theological Faculty, [and] the Ecclesiastical Department, as well as the Government Resolution of 25 January 1853. Three of the Bishops as also the Theological Faculty have classified Mormons as Christians. The other authorities

have pointed out that since the Mormons have their own Bible compiled by Joseph Smith in accordance with divine revelation to him, they cannot be considered Christians. The State's intention in [formulating] the Dissenter Law must assuredly not have been that dissenters themselves could decide whether they should be considered Christians or not. That the Bible is interpreted in different ways is something very different from acceptance of an entirely different Bible which, in cases of divergence, is given precedence over our Bible.[77]

Arguing for the defense was Mathias Andreas Rye who contended the court should concern itself only with criminal charges:

The Supreme Court cannot entertain the question of whether a sect is Christian or not. In order to do that, the relevant [Mormon] scriptures would have to be authenticated, but that has not been done and cannot be done in connection with this case. The accused have evidently made a better case for their faith and belief than the majority [Lutherans] in general have been able to do. We have the testimony of the best authorities in the country that the Mormon Sect must be considered a Christian [sect]. It would be strange indeed if the Supreme Court should determine that the Mormon Sect is not Christian and thereby preclude all future examination of [the question] by theologians. I will not, therefore, engage in any investigation of the theological question.[78]

Justices hearing the case formally registered opinions on 4 November 1853, and by a vote of seven to one determined Mormons had broken the law by preaching and baptizing before their dissenter status was determined; and that Mormons were not Christian dissenters protected or recognized under the Dissenter Law of 1845.[79] <u>Justice Jacob Aall</u> summarized the majority opinion that Mormons were guilty of baptizing, preaching, and administering the Lord's Supper before their dissenter status was determined. The chief question, however, was whether Mormons were Christians. Although none of the defendants denied the Bible, they did put more credence in the Book of Mormon. A line must be drawn: the Dissenter Law, although allowing differing interpretations of the Bible, did not countenance a sect built on an entirely different historical foundation than other Christian sects. "Mormons cannot be considered a Christian sect," declared Aall, since "the acceptance of a new Christ, in direct opposition to the Holy Scriptures, constitutes a denial of the true Christ . . . ."[80]

Justice Ulrik Anton Motzfeldt, Birch-Reichenwald's brother-in-law, and one of those who formulated the Dissenter Law of 1845, declared that "discussions preceding the Dissenter Law were essentially made with reference to sects which were at the time recognized in this Country as being Christian," but this did not imply that "one should also define as Christian all other sects" which subsequently arrived on the scene. Mormons were not Christians.[81] Professor Fredrik Christian Stoud Platou, a substitute who was not a regularly appointed Supreme Court Justice, charged that belief in the Book of Mormon and continuing revelation "must necessarily lead to doctrines and dogmas which differ very little in their conception of Christianity from that of the Mohammedans . . . ," and that Mormons, therefore, were not Christians. Despite such strong pronouncements, however, Platou admitted "great uncertainty" ["megen Uvished"] about the case in general.[82]

While basically agreeing that Mormons were not Christians, Justice Anton Wilhelm Manthey complained about "insufficient information on their [Mormon] baptism and communion to decide whether these can be considered Christian ordinances,"[83] and Justice Claus Moerch charged Dunker with taking up "the Court's valuable time in an unwarranted manner," i.e., ". . . the greatest part of what he has authenticated was unnecessary since those accused have admitted the fact. . . . His review of opinions . . . by the relevant authorities, on the other hand, has been all too short. . . . His conclusion[s], therefore, were extremely weak and of little help."[84] Both Moerch and Justice Eskild Bruun, although agreeing Mormons were not Christians, moved that Dunker's salary be reduced by two-thirds, from thirty dollars to ten.[85] Chief Justice Georg Jacob Bull concluded the majority opinion by terming Mormonism "an insult to the State Religion."[86]

The only dissenting opinion was that of Justice Claus Winter-Hjelm who agreed with three Lutheran Bishops and the Theological Faculty that Mormons were Christians. "It is well known," he said, "that Catholics and Quakers are considered Christians despite the fact that they, along with several other sects, do not consider the Bible the source of all revelation." Winter-Hjelm continued:

> The Catholics build on a tradition in addition to the Bible. . . . The Quakers accept a great deal which diverges from the fundamental doctrine of our Church. . . . The Mormons do not, like the Socinians, deny the divinity of Christ, and the Book of Mormon contains, in spite of its many untruths, nothing which conflicts more with Christianity than the Catholics and Quakers.[87]

Conclusion

Opinions buttressing the Supreme Court Decision of 4 November 1853 accord well with observations of the historian, Jens Arup Seip, that Supreme Court justices in the years 1840-1870 "seem to have a surprisingly marked ability to preserve their faith in their own objectivity, even though political or religious passions break forth like baying bloodhounds in their argumentation."[88] That does not mean, however, that justices deliberated in a vacuum: the Mormon Decision was passed down against the backdrop of Thranite uprisings, comments by bishops and civil authorities about Mormonism's "subversive tendencies," and repeated Mormon pronouncements (cited at length in appendix 3) that it was "better to obey God than man."

Most of all, the Decision was a victory and "exoneration" for Christian Birch-Reichenwald: victory over those who threatened the religious status quo in his county, and personal exoneration from political embarrassment--real or imagined--occasioned by the Oslo Superior Court Decision of 4 April 1853. Carl Motzfeldt's note to Birch on 8 November 1853 put it as well as anyone could: "I congratulate you," he wrote, "on the Supreme Court decision in the Mormon Case."[89] In the minds of friends and foes, there was never any doubt the "Mormon Case" was Birch's and Birch's alone.

CHAPTER IV

MORMONISM IN NORWAY: AN HISTORICAL
OVERVIEW, 1851-1919

1852-1862: A Decade of Revivalism

As described in Chapter II, initial Mormon successes in Norway came on the heels of a religious revival sparked by Haugian and Methodist preaching to so-called "awakened" Christians. Mormon missionaries described a revivalist climate in Fredrikstad (August 1852) "so great that even some of the policemen requested baptism";[1] President Willard Snow reported (24 July 1852) a "friendly feeling" and "widespread religious excitement" in Norway;[2] and Hans Peter Jensen cited "a very great revival" in Brevik to support predictions half the city would convert to Mormonism.[3]

Brevik's *Adresse-Tidende* compared Mormon preaching meetings in 1853 to Haugian gatherings where sinners were called to repentance,[4] and there was little doubt Mormon sermons, with warnings of impending destruction and denigration of Lutheran priests, complimented certain points of Haugian sermonizing--complaints the State Church did not emphasize individual repentance and a true Christian life, a dissatisfaction with "passive" State Church priests, and charges the Church was no longer a people's church.[5]

Mormons also capitalized on the fact that most itinerant preachers were Haugians.[6] Munitions laborer, Andreas Berg, for example, opened his home in Kongsberg to the Mormon Hans Olsen Magleby in September 1858, and was subsequently called into court to answer charges of "unlawful participation" in religious activities. Berg testified Magleby and companion, when requesting permission to hold a meeting in his home, "did not say that they wanted to hold a meeting for any particular religion, but said instead that they wanted to hold a Christian revival or a Christina gathering."[7]

In Roeken, Lutheran priest F. Dybdahl described revivalism generated by the Haugian lay preacher Erlandsen in 1862 which awakened "a Christian gravity" in many parishioners, but also set the stage for "Mormon missionaries seeking to take advantage of the revival for their own purposes." Fourteen of Dybdahl's parishioners joined the Mormons, and "several were favorably inclined."[8]

Similar Mormon-Haugian connections emerged in Trondheim Diocese where Bishop Darre described "unusual excitement about religion" ["meer en almindelig religioes Gjaering"] in 1858:[9] a full-scale revival was underway, people exhibited a "veritable hunger" to hear the Word of God preached privately in their homes, and the burning question everywhere was "What must I do to inherit and be assured of Eternal Life?" ["Hvad skal jeg gjoere, at jeg kan arve og bevare et evigt Liv?"]. Areas most affected were Ageroe and Boersen Clerical Districts, and "Bynaeset" in Trondheim City--the very places Mormonism suddenly reared its head in 1861.[10]

1860-1895: Johnsonian Orthodoxy

But Mormonism had not generated the revivalist climate, and the result was a Mormon harvest of overripe plums--a series of Mormon brushfires in "burned over" Haugian districts. Mormons herded away "strays" to sanctification in Zion, but established no meaningful bridgehead in Norway itself.[11] C. C. A. Christensen described a definite slump in Mormon fortunes as early as 1855 when he visited the once-thriving congregation in Brevik and found only a remnant--most members had emigrated or fallen away.[12] Lutheran Bishop, Jens L. Arup, informed the KUD in 1856 that Mormonism was on the wane in districts around Fredrikstad,[13] and Lutheran Dean, P. F. Bassoee, verified Arup's observations in January 1857: "Mormon activity in the Deanery [Vestre Borgesyssel] must be described as suspended; only a few such [Mormons] remain in Onsoe."[14]

Replies by Lutheran priests to a KUD circular in 1859 also noted, with few exceptions, a "decreasing number" of Mormons throughout Norway,[15] and Mormon Conference President G. M. Brown observed in 1865 that "in Langesune [Langesund], Brevig, Porsgrund, and Skien the gospel has been preached for many years and hundreds have been obedient to its requirements and emigrated to Zion and I think that the greater portion of the honest in heart are gathered out from the towns. . . ."[16] In Risoer, once the epicenter of Mormonism in Norway, missionaries found "all as dead as it can be" in 1866:

> The few saints are without employment and the strangers will not have anything with Mormonism to do. Is that so wonderful [strange]? There have been baptized in this little place since 1851 something like 165 persons and of these 63 have emigrated.[17]

Tables 1, 2 and 3 (see following pages) show long-range developments: the baptism rate leveled off in the early 1860s, and registered marked declines from 1865-1869, whereas emigration rates accelerated steeply during the same period (see especially table 2).[18] "Average annual decrease" (emigration, excommunications and deaths) as a percentage of baptisms leaped from fifty-three percent in the late 1850s to approximately one hundred percent during the late 1860s, and "average annual decrease" as a percentage of "average annual membership" stagnated at about fourteen percent by 1865 (see table 3),[19] i.e., a steady decline in the baptismal

Table 1

Mormonism in Norway: Statistical Overview, 1851-1919

Years	Total Baptisms per Decade	Percent Increase or Decrease in Total Baptisms per Decade	Average Annual Number of Baptisms	Average Annual Membership (Number of Mormons in Norway)	Percent Increase or Decrease in Average Annual Membership per Decade	Average Annual Baptisms as a Percentage of Average Annual Membership	Total Emigration per Decade	Percent Increase or Decrease in Total Emigration per Decade	Total Excommunications per Decade	Total Deaths per Decade	Total Decrease (Emigration, Excommunications & Deaths) per Decade	Percent Change in Total Decrease per Decade
1851-1859	982	---	109	249	---	44	146	---	320	25	535	---
1860-1869	1538	+57	154	860	+245	18	526	+260	591	95	1301	+143
1870-1879	1178	-23	118	872	+2	14	617	+17	361	84	1128	-13
1880-1889	1041	-12	104	820	-6	13	664	+8	305	109	1090	-3
1890-1899	836	-20	84	726	-12	12	359	-46	114	90	563	-48
1900-1909	1436	+72	144	1086	+50	13	538	+50	151	164	810	+44
1910-1919	896	-38	90	1268	+17	7	442	-18	149	165	614	-24
Totals	7907	---	---	---	---	---	3292	---	1991	732	6014	---

Source: Andrew Jenson, History of the Scandinavian Mission, (Salt Lake City, Utah: Deseret News Press, 1927), p. 536.

Table 2

Mormonism in Norway: Five-Year Totals, 1851-1919

Years	Total Baptisms per Five-Year Period	Percent Increase or Decrease in Total Baptisms per Five-Year Period	Total Emigration per Five-Year Period	Percent Increase or Decrease in Total Emigration per Five-Year Period	Total Decrease (Emigration, Excommunications and Deaths) per Five-Year Period	Percent Change in Total Decrease per Five-Year Period
1851-1854	309	---	62	---	133	---
1855-1859	673	+118	84	+36	358	+169
1860-1864	902	+34	245	+192	578	+61
1865-1869	636	-30	281	+15	634	+10
1870-1874	667	+5	277	-1	556	-12
1875-1879	511	-23	340	+23	506	-9
1880-1884	628	+23	378	+11	637	+26
1885-1889	413	-34	286	-24	441	-31
1890-1894	283	-32	208	-27	301	-32
1895-1899	553	+95	151	-27	262	-13
1900-1904	756	+37	244	+62	434	+66
1905-1909	680	-10	294	+21	419	-3
1910-1914	624	-8	252	-14	423	+1
1915-1919	272	-56	190	-25	348	-18
Total	7907	---	3292	---	6030	---

Source: Andrew Jenson, History of the Scandinavian Mission, (Salt Lake City, Utah: Deseret News Press, 1927), p. 536.

Table 3

Mormonism in Norway: Five-Year Averages, 1851-1919

Years	Average Annual Number of Baptisms	Average Annual Membership (Number of Mormons in Norway)	Average Annual Emigration	Average Annual Decrease (Emigration, Excommunications and Deaths)	Average Annual Number of Baptisms as a Percentage of Average Annual Membership	Average Annual Decrease as a Percentage of Average Annual Membership	Average Annual Emigration as a Percentage of Average Annual Number of Baptisms
1851-1854	77	108	16	33	71	31	20
1855-1859	135	362	17	72	37	20	12
1860-1864	180	863	49	116	21	13	27
1865-1869	127	856	56	127	15	15	44
1870-1874	133	850	55	111	16	13	42
1875-1879	102	894	68	101	11	11	67
1880-1884	126	883	76	127	14	14	60
1885-1889	83	756	57	88	11	12	69
1890-1894	57	628	42	60	9	10	73
1895-1899	111	823	30	52	13	6	27
1900-1904	151	1064	49	87	14	8	32
1905-1909	136	1108	59	84	12	8	43
1910-1914	125	1253	50	85	10	7	40
1915-1919	55	1283	38	70	4	5	70

Source: Andrew Jenson, History of the Scandinavian Mission, (Salt Lake City, Utah: Deseret News Press, 1927), p. 536.

rate combined with consistently heavy emigration to calcify the residual membership base.

As baptismal rates plummeted, Mormons themselves attributed the decline to heavy emigration rates which drained congregations of needed manpower, persecution by non-Mormons, and economic discrimination, i.e., "the saints here [Risoer] have to work under very adverse circumstances as regards temporal affairs for the people here have tried to force them to forsake the truth by taking their means of subsistance from them."[20] Somewhat different were views expressed by Lutheran clerics like Anton Wilhelm Fangen in Aker who pegged the decline to general popular disgust (1859):

> There are two principle reasons as to why Mormonism does not gain a foothold in the rural districts. The first is that its immoral and blasphemous doctrine meets opposition, yea, even loathing, in the moral consciousness of the general populace . . . whereupon they [the people] go to the priest to obtain sound advice; and the second reason is the financial burden which Mormon priests occasion. They lodge where they will and pay nothing for board and room, and collect . . . tithing. The paradox of having to pay 1/10 of their weekly income, [as opposed to] the prospect of inheriting the earth, is obvious to many.[21]

But the underlying reason for Mormon (and Haugian) quiescence by 1865 revolved around Norwegian Lutheranism's most able and charismatic spokesman, Professor Gisle Johnson (1822-1894).[22] Johnson understood the masses, knew that parish priests were not generally respected, and sensed crying needs for individual repentance and internalized commitment.[23] His forceful and influential sermons marked a new chapter in Haugian-State Church relations, bridged in large part the gap between what was rightly seen as one religion for an educated elite and another for the masses,[24] and testified "of sin and grace, of salvation or damnation . . . so intensely, with such deep inner feeling, with such heartfelt intensity," that it "led many to an awakening and repentance."[25]

Johnson "applied the yardstick of The Law to inanimate 'Name-Christianity' to the godless, worldly life; but . . . also pointed to the Seat of Mercy personified in Jesus our Redeemer. It was the great 'Either-Or' which he expounded with a seriousness and clarity which touched the hearts of all who listened. One was forced to make a choice; there was no room here for vacillation."[26] Johnson also elevated "The Word" as a primary means of grace, described baptism and the Lord's Supper as "secondary," and envisioned "an essential Church" of true believers--a living inner kernel within the framework of the temporal Church. That did not, however, exclude passive believers: the "Church in the world" could not hope for perfection, and was of necessity a "mixed" denomination.[27]

Johnsonianism was institutionalized in two ways. The first was establishment of "Indre Mission" [Inner Mission] societies--societies aimed at combating the spread of dissenter sects in the parishes and promoting "a more systematic effort for revivalism and spiritual rejuvenation among the people"[28]--beginning in Skien in 1853, and spreading from there throughout the entire country.[29] Of greater importance, however, was the seminal role of the University of Oslo's Theological Faculty in educating a new generation of Lutheral priests. Johnson's central position as Professor of Theology enabled him to inspire hundreds of disciples-- young "Johnson Priests" imbued with a strong sense of duty to preach the gospel of personal commitment and involve themselves with the spiritual and temporal welfare of parishioners.[30]

Johnson priests "were sufficiently presbyterian to establish a rapport with conservative laymen [mostly Haugians]," and "sufficiently confessional to combat advancing separatism [including Mormonism]."[31] "Mass Christianity, Christian institutions and practices. . . meant little or nothing" to them, and they scarcely mentioned the sacraments except to declare infant baptism was no guarantee of salvation, and that each man must examine himself and beware of eating the Lord's Supper unworthily, lest he eat and drink damnation to his soul.[32]

Above all, "they saw themselves as revivalists, as missionaries."[33] In their eagerness--their abundant missionary zeal--they established close ties with voluntary religious organizations under the umbrella of mother church, took active part in meetings and celebrations arranged by laymen, developed personal friendships with parishioners, and "sought to give their sermons a more practical emphasis."[34] They were "pietistic, approachable, . . . eager revivalist preacher[s] . . . with troubled conscience[s]"[35] who gradually replaced the old generation of priests who had lived quietly as intellectual aristocrats apart from the soul-searching of the Haugian "awakened."[36]

In the wake of Johnsonian domination over Norwegian religious life by the early 1860s--and for thirty years thereafter[37]-- Mormonism, attuned as it was to growth in areas of Haugian discontent, gradually found itself outflanked by a State Church which had partially accommodated itself to Haugian demands, and by a new generation of priests who combined crusading zeal with evangelical populism. Whereas the climate of revivalism emanating from a divided State Church nurtured Mormon growth, the gradual shift, especially during the 1860s, to a more harmonious relationship between Lutheran clerics and Haugians, diminished Mormonism's attraction as a viable theological and denominational alternative.

1860-1895: Economic Paralysis and the Manpower Drain

There were also economic factors. Whereas the 1850s were years of economic expansion, the following decades marked economic stagnation.[38] Mormons and non-Mormons experienced years of struggle, "especially in those crushing years 1860-1865, when the great American war caused the whole wor[l]d to suffer," "no cotton" or "bread stuff was sent over from the west," and "factories . . . were closed up" bringing "business . . . to . . . a stand still."[39] The decades after 1860 found Mormons and Mormon congregations "in sorry shape." "Poverty and oppression" were "everywhere," members were "poor and dispersed," and some congregations could not afford hall rent.[40] Reports from Stavanger (1877) described all fifty members as "impoverished,"[41] members in Halden--about twenty in the 1880s--were "all very pore [sic],"[42] and members in Eidsvold Branch "were very pore and fare [sic] between."[43] Oslo Conference President Andrew Israelsen described "most of the saints" in Oslo as "so poor [1893]" he "did not feel justified in asking them for dinner, as I knew that often they had to go without meals themselves."[44]

Conditions on the conference and mission levels were hardly better. Mission President Nils C. Flygare felt himself "run to death for money" (1879) since "every boddy wants to borrow, and no prospect for paying";[45] even those with collateral could not borrow as per Christian Hogensen's report to mission headquarters (1881) that Norway's Hypothek Bank would no longer loan the Church money, or accept Church-owned buildings and grounds in Oslo as security;[46] and leaders could do little more than observe "the cashbox was empty" when faced with the impending physical collapse of Oslo's dilapidated meetinghouse.[47]

The most reliable barometer of economic paralysis, however, was Mormon emigration from Norway which registered dramatic increases during the approximate years 1860-1895.[48] Emigration in the years 1875-1879 was up twenty-three percent over the previous five-year period (corresponding to a twenty-three percent decline in the baptismal rate); the next five-year period, 1880-1884, saw a further eleven percent increase (see table 2).[49] "Average annual emigration" as a percentage of "average annual baptisms" increased from a little over forty percent in the early 1870s, to over sixty percent in the years 1875-1889, and to seventy-three percent in the years 1890-1894. More shocking, however, was the rise in "average annual decrease" (emigration, excommunications and deaths) as a percentage of "average annual baptisms" to nearly one hundred percent in the late 1870s, and to 106 percent in the late 1880s and early 1890s (see table 3)![50]

Heavy emigration triggered numerous administrative and morale problems, the most pressing of which was insufficient manpower to staff branch leadership and auxiliary positions. Mission leaders attempted to fill the gap by pulling in missionaries[51]--those previously occupied with winning new converts--but even that did not always mean branches were fully staffed. "Trondheim Branch," wrote Conference President Christian Hogensen in 1881, "which comprises [geographically] about half of the total land mass of Norway, has been left to itself as sheep without a shepherd . . . for there are not enough men who can assume leadership of the congregation."[52] Members in Bergen, Stavanger and Namsos also reported "no branch leaders" during the early 1880s.[53]

Manpower shortages and inadequate or nonexistant grass roots leadership also spawned member apathy and instability--this plus the fact that those too aged or infirm to emigrate could hardly be expected to consistently attend branch functions, or provide needed financial and moral support.[54] Of 340 members in Oslo in 1873, "not more than half" were regular attenders,[55] and Stjerne articles as late as 1891 warned Priesthood holders that nonattendance at meetings was especially harmful, "for if the head [Priesthood] is dead, what can be said about the rest of the body [general membership]?"[56] Other leaders, such as Mission President Nils C. Flygare, described a general malaise, i.e., members felt "it does not matter whether or not I perform any work in the Church. The work will go forward in any case without my help. Mostly I feel too weak to do anything, and besides, the missionaries are those who are especially called to be Messengers of the Gospel."[57]

1875-1895: The "New Secularism"

Declining conversion rates--especially after 1875--also reflected the "new secularism" in Norwegian intellectual circles which soon spilled over into society at large.[58] Despite widespread conservative opposition, for example, directors of the University of Oslo seated Ernst Sars, an advocate of historical positivism, as Professor of History in 1874; Sars's brother, Ossian, a proponent of Darwinism, became Professor of Zoology that same year.[59] Two years later--1876--the Danish literary critic, Georg Brandes, gave a series of lectures in Oslo which cited Kirkegaard's philosophy to prove Christianity's "utter impossibility" for the common man, i.e., Christianity was riddled with too many dark superstitions to provide any practical help for people preoccupied with day-to-day problems.[60]

Brandes was hardly a voice in the wilderness: Bjoernstjerne Bjoernson, the great poet and political activist, broke with Christianity--also in 1876--and publicly declared his disbelief in an eternal Hell;[61] the novelist, Arne Garborg, revealed (1878) he had given up Christianity entirely, and would henceforth be a "Free Thinker"; Alexander Kielland poked fun at "hypocritical clerics" in several novels of the 1880s; more subtle in his criticism of religion, Henrik Ibsen questioned traditional mores and probed dark regions of the human psyche; and Hans Jaeger declared (1885) in Fra Kristiania-Bohemen [From the Christiania-Bohemian] that marriage destroyed the essence of men's souls.[62]

On the labor front, the Kristiania Oestre Arbeidersamfunn [Oslo East Workers' Association] adopted an anti-clerical resolution in December 1888:

> . . . priests are avowed enemies of education and thought, and the doctrine they preach is a corruption of Christ's teachings. . . . The priests are the greatest hindrance to the success of the labor movement because they are trained to passively accept exploitation by the power mongers.[63]

Lutheran bishops and deans also monitored significant changes: the Bishop of Trondheim quoted parishioners (1872) who told priests, "We are now well enough informed that we no longer pay attention to what the priests say";[64] the Bishop of Oslo cited (1875) large numbers of nonattenders who avoided all church meetings, widespread alcoholism and prostitution, especially in Oslo suburbs;[65] and Lutheran deans complained (1876) that more people read political journals than the Bible, i.e., the masses were primarily interested in political and material concerns.[66]

More radical changes followed in the 1880s: most of those withdrawing from the State Church called themselves "Free Thinkers"[67] and had cut all ties to organized religion;[68] "thoughts and views subversive to morality" had "crept in among certain circles of young people of both sexes who belonged to the educated classes";[69] "threatening dark clouds," including skepticism, moral laxity and popular literature, loomed on the horizon;[70] and young people were leaving the State Church to obtain civil marriages free of Church control and "uncluttered" by religious ceremony.[71]

Mormons described growing secularism as a "dullness" or "deafness": J. F. F. Dorius, for example, complained in 1876 about "a dull spirit over the whole Country";[72] A. S. Schou expressed (1877) "great disappointment" over "the apathy of the people in regards to the Latter-day revealed Gospel. . . .";[73] and Goudy Hogan lamented (1879) that "people here [Drammen] . . . seem to be deaf to Mormonism."[74] "Very few indeed" were willing to learn about Mormonism, few of those who listened were "willing to receive," and "not few" of those who received fell "by the wayside."[75] Conference President Hans J. Christiansen put it even more succinctly in 1886: "It appears," he said, "as if the harvest is over and we are now gathering up the ears."[76]

1890-1914: From Neo-Revivalism to the Doldrums

"Prospects for mission activity were . . . becoming rosy in most sections of Norway" by 1890, and there were indications "a new and milder era of mission work" had begun.[77] 1890 also marked two major policy shifts. On 24 September 1890, the Mormon Prophet Wilford Woodruff issued a "Manifesto" announcing Mormons would no longer sanction polygamous marriages; Mormons approved the "revelation" at the General Conference of the Church on 6 October 1890.[78]

More importantly, a <u>New York Times</u> article quoted George Q. Cannon of the Mormon First Presidency as saying, "Our converts are made abroad by missionaries just like those of any other Church, but instead of inducing them to come to this Country, <u>we really urge our missionaries to dissuade them in any way they can</u>."[79] (Italics mine.) By 1894, mission leaders were instructing missionaries in Norway not to encourage members to emigrate,[80] and Mission President Christian N. Lund reemphasized the new policy in 1898 by observing that "Saints who live their religion and are setting good examples, are the very best missionaries we have."[81] Members were henceforth "to remain in these [Scandinavian] lands, so that people can learn to recognize the fruits of the Gospel through the example of a good life."[82]

Mormon emigration from Norway actually began tapering off in the late 1880s, and continued to fall throughout the 1890s.[83] "Average annual emigration" as a percentage of baptisms dropped nearly two-thirds in the decade 1894-1904, and "average annual decrease" (emigration, excommunications and deaths) as a percentage of baptisms was more than halved. Membership totals increased markedly during the same period.[84]

Decreasing emigration rates paralleled an economic upturn attended by increasing member donations. Conference President Andrew Israelsen reported in 1893 that Oslo Conference was out of debt "which it had not been for many years,"[85] and Mission President Christian N. Lund described Oslo Branch in 1896 as "the most substantial and thriving branch in the Mission," including branches in Denmark.[86] Other leaders noted most members were paying tithing and other offerings,[87] and described numerous new converts from the "respectable" classes.[88]

The 1890s also marked a dramatic increase in the number of Utah missionaries. Whereas approximately three Utah missionaries arrived each year during the 1880s, the 1890s witnessed an average of ten to fifteen arrivals per year. By 1900, there were forty-two missionaries from Zion, and the total nearly doubled by 1907.[89] More missionaries meant more Norwegians hearing about the Mormons, and missionary statistics after 1896 showed unheard-of intensification of proselyting efforts (see table 4).[90] The fact remains, however, that all the missionaries in the world could not significantly increase convert baptisms if people themselves were not interested in doctrinal and denominational alternatives. Like Mormon successes during the 1850s, Mormonism's resurgence in Norway during the late 1890s--the number of baptisms shot up a dramatic ninety-five percent-- was directly related to schism in the State Church and a new wave of religious revivalism.

Schism in the State Church was tied to theological, organizational and political questions in the 1880s and 1890s. "New rationalists"--priests who encouraged historical criticism of the Bible and more moderate, culturally open approaches to theological questions--were locked in bitter debate with their more conservative brethren,[91] and the Church was also racked by dissension over

Table 4

Mormonism in Norway: Missionary Work Statistics, 1896-1918

Year	Number of Local Priesthood Holders	Number of Utah Missionaries	Number of Mormon Branches	Number of Norwegian Households Visited by Missionaries	Number of Gospel Discussions Presented by Missionaries	Number of Mormon Tracts Distributed by Missionaries	Number of Books Distributed by Missionaries	Number of Mormon Meetings Held (All Types)
1896	110	23	11	17,562	6,168	16,024	150	1,318
1897	112	27	11	21,688	7,646	24,349	123	1,156
1898	91	36	13	44,922	10,997	43,263	627	1,371
1899	115	40	19	44,127	11,209	44,189	1,098	1,347
1900	123	42	18	61,349	12,330	77,418	2,429	1,651
1901	146	44	17	76,164	14,403	93,229	5,156	2,261
1902	156	51	19	73,705	19,728	88,420	17,937	2,771
1903	114	63	25	73,696	19,430	88,907	27,543	1,563
1904	126	67	26	56,542	21,261	65,416	25,072	2,616
1905	138	61	18	51,097	19,264	69,670	21,334	2,690
1906	131	70	22	102,264	28,113	144,270	29,497	2,474
1907	122	71	23	154,830	28,047	216,634	37,090	2,254
1908	134	65	21	179,154	28,688	270,780	25,224	4,311
1909	124	58	21	167,888	19,022	350,186	10,255	3,013
1910	138	64	18	191,423	13,852	479,578	9,115	3,199
1911	140	60	15	201,101	17,897	399,862	7,587	3,381
1912	142	41	15	100,310	21,967	298,818	12,356	1,990
1913	150	42	12	95,163	14,523	227,335	6,026	1,670
1914	143	45	12	42,359	10,839	142,545	10,584	1,137
1915	130	9	12	---	1,516	6,197	1,303	771
1916	139	10	14	---	2,173	11,997	356	1,348
1917	152	10	14	156	1,612	31,058	359	1,586
1918	161	4	14	10,499	1,036	31,118	473	2,499
Total	---	---	---	1,765,999	331,841	3,221,563	251,694	---

Source: "Statistisk Rapport over Jesu Kristi Kirke af Sidste Dages Hellige i Skandinavien," Skandinaviens Stjerne vol. 46, 1 February 1897 to vol. 58, 15 March 1919.

administrative and organizational procedures. The virtual flowering of "free organizations"--Bible societies, mission lecture series, prayer groups, orphanages, youth clubs, poorhouses, and Sunday schools--in the latter part of the nineteenth century led to increasing and forceful agitation by such groups for more official-- as opposed to lay--recognition,[92] and "free organizations" also pushed for separation of Church and State, parish councils empowered to appoint parish priests,[93] and revision of rules prohibiting laymen from distributing the Lord's Supper.[94]

On the political front, conservatives convinced Gisle Johnson in 1883 to issue an "Appeal to the Friends of Christianity"[95] they hoped would muffle liberal demands for true parliamentary government. Johnson attacked liberal politicians and their political programs, claimed political "radicalism" threatened Christianity's very existence, and called on true Christians to close ranks against the obvious menace. But the appeal fell on deaf ears. Most active church-goers--tenant farmers, fishermen, artisans, tradesmen and apprentices--refused to support Johnson in political matters, despite their great respect for him as a sincere Christian, because "they primarily belonged to those groups in society which were dissatisfied with social and political conditions in the country and were agitating for wide-ranging reforms."[96]

Johnson was also outflanked on another front. Whereas his disciples strongly emphasized the importance of "the individual will," an increasing number of lay and official preachers in the 1880s and 1890s described the Gospel as a free invitation to come unto Christ. Claims that "Jesus has done everything for you," "the price has been paid," and "you can come as you are," heralded the dawn of a new revivalism administered by a new generation of activist priests.[97]

A leader in revivalist circles was the Swede, Fredrik Franson (1852-1908), a student of the American evangelist, Dwight L. Moody. Franson preached the Gospel as an invitation to the sinner--"Come unto Jesus and be saved"--and deplored discussion of controversial doctrinal questions. As the guest of "free congregations" in Oslo in 1883, he initiated a new type of revivalist gathering by inviting members of the congregation who believed they were "God's Children" to pray with him, and read scriptures as watchwords along life's way. Franson's approach paved the way for basic changes in the confessional consciousness of many Lutherans whose ties to a definite, formal creed were essentially broken.[98]

Contemporary Mormon accounts showed definite connections with "new revivalism." Missionaries in Tromsoe, for example, held two preaching meetings a week in 1892--meetings so well-attended many were turned away--but felt Mormon doctrine was "too strong" for those attending since it appeared "people . . . had concluded that they do not need to do as much as before in order to be saved and inherit a reward with the faithful in the Kingdom of God."[99] Mormon meetings in the open-air tradition of 1850s' Revivalism were also making a comeback: missionaries preached to over three hundred persons in a field at Bredebygden (Guldbrandsdalen) in 1893;[100] open-air meetings in Stavanger attracted such large crowds

(1899) that the chief of police banned all Mormon gatherings, indoors or out;[101] and meetings (1899) in Kopervik--in competition with Salvation Army revivals--drew crowds of over two hundred persons, some of whom stood nearly two hours in pouring rain.[102]

Those flocking to Mormon meetings were accustomed to the ecstatic, gladsome nature of "Come to Jesus" revivalism, and missionaries described meetings where "people would remain and request that we sing another hymn or two,"[103] or where people "showed no signs of leaving" until missionaries "sang songs and otherwise entertained them till a late hour."[104] Other missionaries, such as Milton H. Knudsen in Bodoe (1903), claimed to have "touched off a strong revival" themselves, i.e., "every evening we held meetings for packed houses. We baptized five persons. . . . I am nearly tempted to say that we experienced a real Pentecost."[105]

Mormon rejuvenation on the heels of neo-revivalism, however, was tragically short-lived. An economic slump in the years 1899-1905 forced mission leaders (1904) to assess missionaries large sums to pay monthly hall rent, and leaders complained of insufficient funds to "meet the expences of our long, dark, cold nights."[106] Mission President Andrew Jenson described financial conditions in Oslo Branch as "not at all satisfactory on general principles" in 1909, and branch reports showed "Saints did not pay their tithing."[107]

There were other signs of renewed stagnation: Mission President Hans J. Christiansen discovered in 1914 that branch leaders in Oslo knew the whereabouts of only half--about 350--of the members (The rest had "disappeared");[108] some member girls were prowling the streets as prostitutes; several Oslo members were living in adultery without censure by branch leaders; Oslo Branch Choir, once the largest Mormon choir in Europe, was demoralized and without an organist; and none of the native Priesthood holders were qualified to serve as district teachers.[109]

Leadership in the branches was increasingly concentrated in the hands of "young, inexperienced [Utah] missionaries" who spoke little Norwegian, knew "little about the Gospel,"[110] and "were generally unacquainted with Norwegian habits and customs."[111] Some missionaries, moreover, had little desire to serve: "I am trying to read norsk [Norwegian]," lamented E. C. Ekman of Erda, Utah, in 1905, "but it is all the same Dutch to me . . . and if I have got to Stay in norway untill I Learn to talk and preach in this Language my Little wife will be Gray and my baby married and have a family so good by all that is near and Dear to me."[112]

Disharmony was also rife: nineteen of twenty-two missionaries voted "no confidence" in Oslo Conference President Albert Hagen (1904);[113] Andrew Jenson, Scandinavian Mission President, reported (1910) that "Elders in Christiania were not united enough to eat together," i.e., "I never saw such a 'mess' before among missionaries";[114] and mission leaders discovered (1910) "that John H. Berg [Oslo Conference President] had placed a girl's name on the list for emigrating without paying the money with the evident intention of defrauding the Scandinavian mission or the Church for her emigration money."[115]

1914-1918: "Return of the Native"

"The Guns of August"--the outbreak of World War I on 1 August 1914--further disrupted the demoralized Mormon community. President Hans J. Christiansen instructed conference presidents on 7 September 1914 to set branch finances and accounts in order, and leadership of the branches reverted--theoretically--to local members when American missionaries left Norway in mid-October.[116] Post-missionary leadership in many branches, however, was either nonexistent, or devolved on a few feeble old men, and Mormons meeting (18 October) in Oslo Branch--the largest Mormon congregation in Norway--failed to muster a quorum large enough to sustain General Authorities of the Church.[117]

The picture gradually stabilized, however, as native Mormons discovered long-hidden leadership talents--indication some member "inactivity" during pre-War years was simply "noninterference" in administrative affairs of a non-acculturated Utah elite. By early 1915, "good local Elders who are enthusiastic men" were leading branches in Drammen, Larvik, and Fredrikstad;[118] local elders were presiding in Haugesund and Stavanger by midsummer 1915;[119] and leaders in Oslo Conference reported at year's end "that, despite the loss of Elders from Zion to work in the branches, all of the branches [in Oslo Conference] are in extremely good condition, and many sincere persons are investigating Gospel teachings."[120]

But glowing reports were somewhat misleading: Halden Branch, once a thriving congregation, was dead to Mormonism by June 1916, the few elderly members who remained "suffering spiritual hunger since they are left to themselves";[121] Arendal Branch (1916) had only one male member--a priest "wholly incapable of leading a meeting";[122] and leaders in some branches faced increasing criticism from members who asked the same question ad nauseam: "When will the missionaries return?"[123]

The final War Years (1916-1918) marked cessation of postal and telegraphic communications with England and the United States (1916); dwindling financial resources; hundreds of unemployed members--a result of the German blockade of coal shipments; and astronomical prices for bread and other basic commodities.[124] Through it all, Mormons continued to meet in the larger branches--Oslo, Drammen, Fredrikstad, Larvik, Stavanger, Haugesund, Bergen and Trondheim[125]--and War's end revealed congregations largely intact, i.e., Norwegian Mormons could "survive" under local--as versus "Utah"--leadership, and Mormonism, although far from institutionalized, was a viable "Norwegian" entity.[126]

Table 5

Age of Mormons at Baptism: Oslo Branch, 1853-1860

Number of Mormons at Age of Baptism Who Were:

Year	Under Age 15 Male	Under Age 15 Female	Age 15-19 Male	Age 15-19 Female	Age 20-29 Male	Age 20-29 Female	Age 30-39 Male	Age 30-39 Female	Age 40-49 Male	Age 40-49 Female	Age 50-59 Male	Age 50-59 Female	Over Age 60 Male	Over Age 60 Female
1853	--	--	--	4	7	3	4	3	--	--	--	--	--	--
1854	--	1	3	5	6	10	16	6	4	5	1	1	--	1
1855	1	1	--	2	3	3	5	7	2	3	--	--	--	--
1856	4	2	2	2	19	12	13	14	4	7	6	2	1	1
1857	1	1	3	2	15	13	12	12	6	3	--	2	1	--
1858	--	2	--	2	17	24	24	13	5	8	4	5	1	1
1859	--	1	1	4	15	12	13	9	5	9	1	--	3	2
1860	--	1	4	6	14	12	7	11	6	3	--	--	--	1
Total	6	9	13	27	96	89	94	75	32	38	12	10	6	5

Source: Christiania Branch, Record of Members, 1853-1907, Christiania Conference, Scandinavian Mission, LDS Church Archives, Salt Lake City, Utah.

Table 6

Age of Mormons at Baptism: Oslo Branch, 1895-1900

Number of Mormons at Age of Baptism Who Were:

Year	Under Age 15 Male	Under Age 15 Female	Age 15-19 Male	Age 15-19 Female	Age 20-29 Male	Age 20-29 Female	Age 30-39 Male	Age 30-39 Female	Age 40-49 Male	Age 40-49 Female	Age 50-59 Male	Age 50-59 Female	Over Age 60 Male	Over Age 60 Female
1895	12	14	1	2	4	3	1	5	1	6	1	1	1	2
1896	10	13	3	1	--	11	2	1	2	5	--	3	--	--
1897	3	4	1	6	3	7	3	5	--	1	--	--	1	--
1898	3	10	5	6	8	14	3	1	2	3	1	1	2	2
1899	7	7	1	6	9	15	1	6	2	1	--	--	--	1
1900	1	--	--	1	3	6	1	1	--	--	--	--	--	1
Total	36	48	11	22	27	56	11	19	7	16	2	5	4	6

Source: Christiania Branch, Record of Members, 1853-1907, Christiania Conference, Scandinavian Mission, LDS Church Archives, Salt Lake City, Utah.

Table 7

Oslo Branch Membership Male and Female Totals: 1851-1907

Years	Female Converts - Total Number of Female Converts	Female Percentage of Total Number of Converts	Male Converts - Total Number of Male Converts	Male Percentage of Total Number of Converts
1851-1859	236	50.86	228	49.13
1860-1869	549	59.60	372	40.39
1870-1879	380	57.66	279	42.33
1880-1889	298	60.08	198	39.91
1890-1899	261	66.24	133	33.75
1900-1907	318	72.10	123	27.89
Total	2042	60.50	1333	39.49

SOURCE: Christiania Branch, Record of Members, 1853-1907, Christiania Conference, Scandinavian Mission, LDS Church Archives, Salt Lake City, Utah.

CHAPTER V

MORMON RELATIONS WITH CIVIL AND
ECCLESIASTICAL AUTHORITIES,
1851-1923

Mormon Relations with Civil
Authorities: 1851-1900

Armed with the Supreme Court Decision of 4 November 1853, the Government Department for Church and Education (KUD) expressed no qualms over enlisting police and parliamentary support to contain the "Mormon menace"; arrest, imprisonment, and threats of deportation--all were deemed justifiable by Lutheran clerics out to stop Mormon proselyting activities once and for all. Authorities zeroed in specifically on missionaries--"Mormonism's visible arm in Norway"--since few if any were permanent residents, most were not Norwegians or Norwegian citizens, few had close relatives in cities where they were proselyting, and most were unversed in legal procedures. Their impoverished circumstances, furthermore, precluded successful court battles or vindication campaigns.
    Hans Olsen Magleby's experience was typical. A native Dane, he first served five weeks and three days in jail early in 1857 for having baptized (including five days on bread and water).[1] Far from discouraging him, however, the experience augmented his missionary zeal, and late November 1857 found him imprisoned once again, but expressing no regrets: "[I] rejoiced in suffering for the Name of Jesus or the cause of truth and may it be to my good, Amen."[2]
    Court officials meted out prison sentences when missionaries could not pay court-assessed fines: a missionary named Petersen in Boersen (near Trondheim), for example, could not pay an eighty-dollar fine in October 1857, and was accordingly imprisoned thirteen days on bread and water for "having consigned the people to Hell with his false beliefs."[3] There were also arbitrary arrests such as that of Svend Larsen at Halden in 1867. Police Chief Froelik personally warned Larsen preaching Mormonism would lead to arrest, and exclaimed "I am the Law!" when challenged to cite a specific punishment clause. Froelik--assisted by three deputies--then arrested Larsen, and kept him imprisoned fifteen days on bread and water before sentencing him to a further twenty days' imprisonment.[4]
    In Molde in 1859, police arrested missionary C. S. Winge for preaching Mormonism, and detained him "for several weeks in the dark prison . . . waiting for sentence to be passed." "I was given three small pieces of poor bread," said Winge,

"and one crock of water every 24 hours on which diet I became very hungry. I still remember very well that particular Christmas eve, I was so hungry I cried as a little child. . . . My prison cell was full of filth and lice."[5] Winge spent eight weeks in prison, and was again imprisoned the following year:

> Inside of these thick walls it was dark and dismal. One small window high up on the wall, with thick iron bars, a large oak door heavily reinforced with iron and a strong lock on it, made escape impossible. In one corner were some old carpets which were intended for a bed, and in another corner an old barrel for necessary use. There was neither table nor chairs. Food was shoved to me through a hole in the door, and I had to sit down on the floor to eat it. Books were refused, not even a Bible was allowed for me to read.[6]

There were also cases where civil authorities fined or imprisoned resident Mormons who were Norwegian citizens: a judge fined Amund Dahle eight dollars plus court costs in 1854 for having preached, baptized, and opened his home to Mormon meetings in Drammen--Dahle protested the sentence in a "Memorial" to the King claiming infringement of "the unrestricted privacy of his home which is enjoyed by every Norwegian subject";[7] officials in Fredrikstad imprisoned Mons Pedersen, a former schoolteacher, in November 1854, and denied him wood to build a fire.[8] "Marith Greslie, Madame Olsen," and "Lina Christensen" were imprisoned five days on bread and water in Trondheim in 1855 for proclaiming Mormon doctrines;[9] and officials--again in Trondheim--fined Mormon women four dollars each in 1861 for partaking of the Mormon communion.[10]

"It is no uncommon thing in the Country [Norway] for both the servants of God and those who recieve [sic] them to suffer imprisonment, on bread and water," declared Oslo Conference President G. M. Brown in 1863. "Oh, God, thou who has all power in thine hand, hasten the day when the honest in heart can be free. When no longer the yoke of tyrrany shall bend down the fair necks of millions of thy fair creation."[11] Melodramatics aside, however, inhumane treatment of Mormon missionaries and members--even those placed in prison--was the exception, and not the rule. Whereas police and local authorities took a strict stand against Mormon activities immediately following the Supreme Court Decision of 1853, missionaries, such as C. C. A. Christensen, noted a change in police attitudes as early as 1854, i.e.,

> . . . our hearings had given the police authorities a better understanding of us and our religion. Several of our Brethren had changed their earlier lifestyles to

such a degree that the police were forced to recognize the worthy fruits of repentance [in the lives] of these men. Despite the fact that the letter of the law was against us, the civil authorities had now become our friends and occasioned us no inconvenience except when forced to do so by priests and other egoists. . . . The police teased the priests in return, and during the Winter [of] 1854-1855 there ensued a series of public debates in which the priests came out second best. Elder Knud Peterson and I were the Mormon representatives, and Eilert Sundt, Ole Vig and [Caspar Holten] Jensenius, supported by several priests, were our opponents. Those Sunday debates were repeated on a large scale, and the foremost officials of the City, including Herr Morgenstjerne [the Oslo Chief of Police], were in attendance.[12]

Nor were authorities, especially those in Oslo, terribly concerned with forcing missionaries to pay court-imposed fines: although sentenced to pay a small fine in September 1854, C. C. A. Christensen was only imprisoned after "several unsuccessful attempts" to serve a prison sentence in lieu of the fine. Newly released from prison, he preached a lively sermon in Oslo--the very offense for which he was fined in the first place--and picked up his passport from police authorities who knew full well he had preached again.[13]

There were other examples of police forbearance: District Sheriff Utsing asked missionaries in Sigdal (1855) if they had preached Mormonism, but made no arrests although answered in the affirmative;[14] a rural magistrate and the district sheriff at Hof near Soloer (1871) "were very tolerant," and simply asked missionary Jonas Johansen to leave their area of jurisdiction when they learned he had baptized;[15] Emil Noekleby was called before police authorities in Drammen (1871) and forbidden to baptize, but "on the other hand . . . was allowed to preach to his heart's content";[16] and police authorities in Larvik (1874) released C. S. Winge without further adieu when he produced papers attesting to his American citizenship.[17]

There was, in short, ample evidence police officials throughout Norway were "going easy" on Mormon missionaries by the mid-1860s, and that, far from being persecuted, Mormons were actually receiving police assistance. Reports from Porsgrunn in 1865, for example, described mob disturbances at Mormon meetings, but police officials had "punished a number of rowdies," and issued "a strong warning to others who were rather young."[18] Again in Oslo (1866), a constable called in to restore order at a Mormon meeting declared "he would have been on hand to keep order" since he "had orders to that effect," but did not know Mormons had changed their meeting time.[19]

Mormon Relations with Ecclesiastical Authorities: 1851-1906

Whereas Mormon relations with police and civil authorities gradually improved during the decades before 1900, such was hardly the case with priests and officials of the State or Lutheran Church. Priests feared Mormonism would undermine their positions of authority in community life--as also income from officiation at christenings, marriages and burials--and attempted to counter the threat via head-on confrontation. "Priest Dedriksen" of Stavanger, for example, engaged Canute Peterson in a five-hour debate in 1854, gave Peterson anti-Mormon pamphlets, and commanded him to speak according to their precepts;[20] Priest Stenstru [sic] stormed into a Mormon meeting in Oslo in 1855 and charged that Mormons "were not only deceivers, but were dishonest deceivers as well [and] knew better than what [they] taught";[21] and Priest Noimand interrupted Mormon preachers at Roervik in 1857, read anti-Mormon pronouncements, and called Mormons liars.[22]

Such heavy-handedness, however, often turned parishioners against their own priests: Pastor Steensrud in Oslo, for example, launched stiff attacks on Mormons in 1856, but missionary N. C. Poulsen noted "the people were on our side, and stood forth and defended our Doctrine."[23] Priest Holter of Ekerstrand likewise engaged Mormons in debate for over three hours in 1857, but finally departed to jeers from the crowd.[24] There were other factors: Lutheran priests did not speak the earthy vernacular of ignorant parishioners, and generally employed logic and formal rules of debate; Mormon preachers, conversely, were generally unschooled, and relied on heavy sarcasm and criticism, i.e., the masses identified with Mormon derision and folksy humor, but failed to comprehend well-reasoned arguments by a parish priest. Lutheran priests fared so badly, in fact, the Bishop of Oslo finally directed in 1855 that priests avoid debates with Mormon preachers whenever possible:

> . . . the reason for this being that the Mormon emissaries generally display great volubility and extensive acquaintance with the obscure, seldom-used Scriptures, especially of the Old Testament, which they without hesitation distort and misconstrue according to their own purposes; that a Priest can be a very capable man and work to good purpose in his calling, without possessing to any marked degree the presence of mind, the quickness of perception, the ability to easily come up with the right words and expressions, the ability to improvise, which would enable him to get right to the point in an ofttimes chaotic exchange of words, and to clearly, convincingly and

> fluently point out and refute the heresies; that it would be very damaging should the Priest, though he have ever so much truth and the victory on his side, appear to the onlookers to come out second best; that those, who are most easily duped and ensnared by Mormonism's appetizing, ingratiating doctrine, have in general their own yardstick by which they judge what they hear . . . and are incapable of differentiating between what is proof and what is not proof; yea, comprehending what is said rather aphoristically, not being able to follow an extended, logically connected and thorough argument such that they could digest the essentials. . . . Thus it is my opinion that it requires a conscious and burning inner conviction and a singular, well-informed competency in order to contend successfully as a defender of our Church against Mormonism.[25]

Lutheran priests generally abandoned direct confrontation with Mormon preachers by the 1860s, and opted instead for pressurizing individual parishioners who felt inclined to attend Mormon meetings, allow Mormons to preach in their homes, or provide Mormons food and shelter. At Kongsvinger in 1865, Oslo Conference President G. M. Brown obtained permission to preach at a private home, but several Lutheran ministers

> . . . went to the Madame of the house and scolded and threatened to have her arrested for renting us the hall. She replied that if they wished to arrest her for letting people preach who preached from the Bible which she lent us, that they would have to do it; and if they wished to stop people from reading the Bible she did not know what they pretended to be ministers for.[26]

Several ministers entered the house after Brown began preaching and tried to induce those present to leave, "but they were not all willing to go. One man stood up and thanked us [Mormons] and said it was very good. The poor ministers, many as they were, did not have courage to say a word, but just tried to drag the people away with them."[27]

Lutheran Dean in Aalesund, Knudsen, employed similar tactics in 1866 against Mormon missionary Anthon L. Skanchy who was lodging with master shoemaker Nielsen. Knudsen visited Nielsen, ordered him to kick Skanchy out of the house, and

> . . . later . . . wrote to Mr. Nielsen and hammered away, since Nielsen was indeed

> a respected man in the community, and, if
> he was to protect his good name, there was
> no way he could let me [Skanchy] stay.
> Mr. Nielsen laid the facts before me, he
> was now in a frightful predicament. On
> the one hand he did not have the callousness
> to turn me out, but it was also a terrible
> thing to be in disfavor with the Dean [and]
> so he wept.[28]

The decades after 1880 marked even more concentrated attempts to curtail Mormon proselyting: housewives in Bergen told missionaries (1884) they could not allow Mormons into their homes unless they (Mormons) produced written permission from Lutheran priests; missionaries in Halden reported similar responses;[29] and missionary E. C. Ekman reported from Hedrum in 1906 as follows:

> Everry one that I would meet and talk to
> would first want to know if I had talked
> to the preist as much as to say if I had
> and the preist had taken tracts and belived
> me that thay would do the same. I promised
> them that I would call on the preist which
> I did but low when I told him who I was
> he jest turned on his heal and left me standing
> in the dore I tryed to holler to him through
> the dores, but he bid me go so . . . I followed
> his advise and went. . . .[30]

KUD Mormon Policy: 1851-1900

On the administrative level, the KUD issued a steady stream of anti-Mormon pronouncements and directives to priests during the years 1851-1910;[31] the KUD also sought Department of Justice (JPD) support for its Mormon policy, and pushed openly for issuance of anti-Mormon pronouncements under JPD auspices alone.

The most burning issue in the 1850s and early 1860s was the question of Mormons and marriage. A KUD pronouncement in 1853 that Mormons, as non-Christians, could not be married by a Lutheran priest, amounted to de facto disallowance of legal marriage for Mormons since Norwegian Law dictated marriages be celebrated in the State Church.[32] A second pronouncement on 6 August 1858 further underlined that policy: "There is no permission for Mormons to be married by a State Church priest."[33]

Mormons circumvented the law in several ways: couples lived together without marriage; others pretended they were Lutherans in order to be married by unsuspecting priests; and Mormon leaders performed marriage ceremonies they felt would be recognized, if not by civil authorities, at least by God. A missionary named Olsen, for example, married "Brother Brynild Isaksen and Sister Lovise Halvorsdatter, both members of the Church of [Jesus]

Christ of Latter-day Saints," at Brevik on 3 August 1853 "in a gathering assembled for that purpose," and "in accordance with Church custom";[34] on 6 November 1862, Conference President C. C. N. Dorius--"Submitting . . . to pressing necessity, and after repeated urgings"--married "Brother Gunde and his sweetheart Ane" at Hadseloeen in Nordland.[35]

Increasing numbers of surreptitious Mormon marriages finally prompted Oslo Bishop Jens L. Arup to urge formation of an advisory council to review the question of Mormons and marriages in 1858. A Royal Decree on 27 January 1859 subsequently established a parliamentary committee to investigate the "Mormons [who] employed deception to obtain Lutheran marriage or [who] lived in concubinage,"[36] and committee findings led to passage of a law on 22 June 1863 prescribing marriage for Mormons and other non-Christians by a registered notary public.[37]

Another sore point was the question of Mormon burials. KUD pronouncements in 1866 and 1881 prohibited any graveside ceremony, prayer, song, speech or dedication by Mormons, and Lutheran burial chapels were also off-limits. Mormons were therefore forced to hold funeral ceremonies (including dedicatory prayers) in the private home of the deceased, followed by perfunctory transportation of the body to the churchyard and immediate burial.[38] Despite restrictions, however, run-ins with Lutheran priests were rare, and only one of note occurred in 1885 at Thistedalen when a Mormon "had the misfortune to loose one of his children, [and] the Preist showing the utmost contempt, . . . would intirely had prevented the child being buried on the grave yard had it not happened to have been baptized [a Lutheran] before the parents joined the [Mormon] church."[39]

During the 1890s and beyond, Lutheran authorities increasingly allowed Mormon graveside ceremonies, although technically against the law: the Deacon of Drammen granted missionary Andrew Israelsen "the privilege of saying a few words and of dedicating the grave" at the funeral of Oscar Nielsen's infant son in 1892;[40] clerics allowed Mormons "to sing at the grave" of Christen Nyborg's son, Gustave Adolph, in Oslo in 1893;[41] and churchwardens in Nordre Gravlund, Oslo, accorded Mormons use of the Lutheran chapel for the funeral of Pauli Larsen in 1894.[42] Mormons in Bergen, conversely, obeyed the letter of the law in 1897 by "paying the priest 4 crowns and the sexton 2 crowns in order to be free of their services" in connection with the funeral of a Sister Olsen.[43]

KUD versus JPD Mormon Policy: 1880-1923

Mormon missionaries coming to Norway in the early 1880s were no longer native-born Scandinavians: the "new" missionaries--mostly Utah-born and educated with little or no knowledge of Norwegian--could not help but attract attention, especially in light of antipolygamy fever raging in the United States. Alarmists in church and government dubbed missionaries "Mormon agents" in search of unsuspecting young women, and prominent politicians, such as Jakob Sverdrup, described conditions "worse than slavery" awaiting girls in Utah.[44]

Agitation climaxed in Bergen on 21 August 1887 when police broke up a Mormon meeting and abused a defenseless cripple. When Mormons called the meeting "a private gathering" against which police had no right to move in,[45] Bergen officials cited the Supreme Court Decision of 1853--Mormons did not have freedom to practice their religion under conditions of the Dissenter Law, and the meeting was a public, not private, gathering.[46] JPD officials in Oslo generally concurred,[47] and some even considered "clean up" operations, especially in Oslo where Mormons had met openly for decades. Other JPD personnel disapproved of such action, however, especially in light of "the increased tolerance which is everywhere evident at this time with reference to such questions."[48]

There the matter was shelved for nearly twenty years, only to be resparked by a heavy influx of Utah missionaries during the early 1900s, intensive saturation tracting by Mormon missionaries and members, and inflammatory letters from non-Mormon priests in America, such as H. S. Waaler, Pastor of the Presbyterian Church in Preston, Idaho, who advised Norwegian officials in 1904 that

> . . . Mormons . . . are sending a large number of, so called, Missionaries to your country every year. . . . I blieve [sic] that your govrnment [sic] should look into this matter, and . . . Expel evry Mormon Missionary from the Land, It is the most dangerous sect that ever invaded any country, they are Anarchists of the worst type. . . . I doubt if you, the high officials of the State-Church, the God-sent teachers of the true doctrine of Christianity, have any adequate Idea, as to the great extent of evil propagated in your beloved Country by the agents of the Mormon Church.[49]

A KUD-employed lawyer, meanwhile, reviewed the whole gamut of questions relating to Mormons and Norwegian Law, and affirmed in 1905 that Mormons "have no right to free practice of their religion or to establish congregations with their own priests or leaders."[50] Members of the Reorganized Church of Jesus Christ of Latter Day Saints were likewise not protected by the Dissenter Law since "this new version of the sect and its 'new' doctrine is like a new patch on an old garment; the purpose is to gain acceptance for Mormonism--under a new name and new form--among unsuspecting persons."[51]

Law such as Norwegian Laws 6-1-4-and 2-1 under which Mormons had earlier been prosecuted, however, no longer applied: the new Criminal Law of 1902 specifically invalidated Law 6-1-4 and the Decree of 22 October 1701, section II, chapter 2. The lawyer concluded as follows:

> In light of the above observations, there . . . is at present full freedom to assemble for religious purposes, and . . . it is not possible to stop Mormons from practicing their religion and spreading their propaganda. If, on the other hand, they perform baptisms, distribute the Lord's Supper, perform marriages or conduct burial ceremonies--rites which can only be performed by State Church priests or ministers of Christian dissenting faiths--they can be punished in accordance with . . . paragraph 328, item 3 of the new Criminal Law [1902]. . . . Elders from Utah who come here cannot be summarily deported (cf. paragraph 38 of the new Criminal Law and Law Number One of 4 May 1901, paragraph 6).[52]

Given their own lawyer's conclusion it was "not possible to stop Mormons from practicing their religion and spreading their propaganda," KUD officials immediately petitioned the JPD on 4 January 1905 to enforce existing laws against Mormons, and cited the Supreme Court Decision of 4 November 1853 and paragraph one of the Dissenter Law of 1891 which stated that only "Christian dissenters" could establish congregations. Resolutions by Kristiania Presteforening [Kristiania Association of Ministers] and Dissenterthinget [The Dissenter Assembly] calling for "enforcement of the Law's stipulations" against Mormons, accompanied the Petition.[53]

JPD authorities, however, were in no hurry to climb aboard the KUD bandwagon; their own investigations in 1904 had elicited reports from police stations throughout Norway on Mormon activities, and the general consensus was that Mormons, "despite the fact that they are not recognized as Christian dissenters, should be tolerated" as a religious sect.[54] Oslo's Chief of Police described Mormons as "sober, law-abiding, industrious and generally decent people such that one could only wish there were as many good citizens in the population at large,"[55] and police colleagues in Trondheim, Stavanger and Drammen generally concurred.[56]

The JPD underlined its reluctance to tackle the Mormon question by letting a full year elapse before it answered the KUD petition: the actual reply cited responses from chiefs of police throughout Norway, and counseled moderation, i.e., "there is no reason to clamp down on Mormon activities at the present time."[57] That response hardly satisfied the KUD, and on 20 January 1906, a second KUD petition charged Mormons in Oslo, Trondheim and Arendal with sponsoring offensive propaganda campaigns. The KUD again insisted the JPD forbid all public Mormon meetings and implement tighter controls on "Mormon agents" and Mormon emigration.[58]

The JPD's reply--two years later--acknowledged the KUD petition (plus follow-up letters from the KUD on 12 and 22 February, 17 March and 21 June 1906), and restated JPD policy: "It does not appear possible, under existing law, to publicly curtail Mormon activities here in Norway."[59] The JPD did cite paragraphs in the Dissenter Law which described punishments for those who attempted to win converts through threats, force, or promises of material advantage; the JPD would alert police departments of those provisions, but that would hardly hinder Mormonism since proof of wrongdoing in such cases was extremely difficult to obtain.[60]

The JPD also noted a decision by the Trondheim Appellate Court on 19 April 1906 which, in effect, marked the death knell for prosecution of practicing Mormons under Norwegian Law. That judgment concerned three Mormons--missionary Nils Evensen and two resident Norwegians, Hans J. Karlsen and Gerhard M. Andresen--accused of running afoul of paragraph 328 of the Criminal Law[61] which prescribed punishment for anyone who "performs any rite appertaining to an official calling which he does not have."[62] Highly significant arguments in that case provided unforseen and radically different interpretations of the Supreme Court Decision of 4 November 1853:

> It appears, meanwhile, that the defendants cannot be punished under provisions of this paragraph [paragraph 328] for having baptized and distributed the Lord's Supper, inasmuch as the sect to which they belong is not considered a Christian sect. It is the Christian baptism and the Christian communion which is here entrusted to Christian priests (dissenting ministers), and which others are allegedly forbidden to be concerned with; . . . that a non-Christian religious organization . . . employs ceremonies, which to a greater or lesser degree resemble the Christian sacraments, does not constitute the sect a Christian sect nor its ceremonies Christian symbols or expressions of the Christian Confession. As long as there is no question of blasphemy, there is, presumably, nothing to restrict a non-Christian organization from using the water--for purposes of sprinkling or immersion--as the sign of a certain individual's admittance to membership in the organization, and none who confess the Christian religion would therefore contend that the individual had truly been baptized a Christian; yea, it is acknowledged that no Christian baptism has been performed under such circumstances, and that it is only this [Christian baptism] which none other than Christian priests can perform, and that the same must apply to the communion; accordingly, the accused have not performed "any rite appertaining to an official calling which he does not have," since they have only performed something which Christians consider to be completely

meaningless, and which, with like justification and like result, could be performed by anybody at all. . . . The accused are, therefore, not guilty. It is obvious, and the court is fully aware of the fact, that many will consider this verdict extremely unfortunate, and that it can strike some as very peculiar that a Christian dissenter, who baptizes a person who has not officially withdrawn from the State Church, will be punished, whereas the non-Christian Mormon who baptizes, will not be punished; but in connection herewith it should be pointed out that: (1) the first example has to do with arrangements decreed by law between the State Church and those Christian dissenters recognized by the State, where the State has, of necessity, drawn a line, whereas the latter example concerns actions which the State, from its standpoint, considers meaningless as they relate to Christian congregations; (2) the above-described "gaps" in the law. . . can only be remedied by new legislation. The verdict is unanimous.[63]

Faced with an appellate court judgment that Mormons who preached, baptized, or distributed the Lord's Supper could not be prosecuted, and a Justice Department which was obviously stalling in hopes KUD officials would drop the issue entirely, the KUD next pressed for passage of an entirely new law aimed at counteracting Mormon activities, and forwarded main points of the proposed law to Lutheran Bishops on 19 December 1908. Among other things, the KUD recommended a total ban on public Mormon meetings; stiff fines and/or imprisonment for those (including Norwegian citizens) attending such meetings; and expedited court proceedings against accused Mormons "in the swiftest and simplest manner, such that, among other things, the court have immediate access to unappealable opinions by trained theologians as to the nature of the [religious] doctrine which the accused might cite in defending himself."[64] (Italics mine.)

The Lutheran Bishops generally supported the new KUD proposals. Bishops in Trondheim and Bergen were especially interested in clauses aimed at house-to-house visits by Mormon missionaries and distribution of Mormon tracts,[65] whereas the Bishop of Tromsoe, Peter Wilhelm Kreydahl Boeckman, considered a "general ban" on Mormons seeking to enter Norway a la similar restrictions on Jesuits:

Events will possibly show that there is only one method which can achieve the desired result, and that is a general ban on Mormons entering the Kingdom. Such a measure would no doubt be draconian, but would possibly be equally justifiable against Mormons as against Jesuits, who at any rate must be considered solely religious agitators, whereas Mormons are something more besides.[66]

Criticism of the proposed law, however, came from an unexpected source--the Bishop of Hamar, Christen Brun. Brun's letter of 18 January 1909 marked a new milestone: the first time a Lutheran bishop disagreed with KUD Mormon Policy:

> In my opinion all religions ought to have freedom to practice within the bounds of law and decency. This is rightly a consequence of the principle of religious freedom which is so strongly emphasized in our time. Non-Christians and also heathen religions ought to benefit from such freedom. Accordingly, the question of whether Mormons are to be accounted Christian dissenters has nothing to do with the question of free practice of religion. And if one points to the doctrine of plural marriage as comprising an integral part of their system, and as justification for placing them in a special category, one must also observe that they, as far as we know, have made no effort to actualize said doctrine in our country.[67]

Brun did agree Mormon propaganda was harmful,

> . . . but the means of combating Mormonism's pernicious activities must first and . . . foremost be found in more comprehensive Christian instruction. The fact that Mormons can lure away young girls, who have attended our schools and have been confirmed in our Church, is ample testimony that the situation [with reference to Christian instruction] is not as good as one would like to believe.[68]

Brun advised modification of KUD proposals "to a high degree," and removal of clauses advocating stiff fines and imprisonment.[69]

JPD criticism of KUD proposals was also direct, i.e., "to protect a single Church organization [the State Church] by combating differing religious philosophies and their dissemination with punishment and police regulations seems to fly in the face of what is generally perceived as being the responsibility of the State in our time."[70] The JPD strongly recommended the KUD discard the proposed law, and described as "reprehensible" efforts to direct punishment clauses "against members of a specifically named religious society without naming specific charges."[71] Despite numerous complaints about Mormon activities, the JPD still believed "these charges, at least partly, are blown all out of proportion and are not always based on a completely reliable knowledge of contemporary Mormon behavior and doctrine."[72] The JPD further stated that a law prescribing "unappealable opinions by trained theologians" ["inappellabelt skjoen av teologisk utdannede maend"] "would directly contravene the principles of our criminal law procedure, and is . . . an objectionable provision."[73]

Conclusion

Mormon relations with civil authorities and Lutheran clerics from 1851-1923--both on the grass roots and administrative levels--revealed steadily diverging methodologies by secular and ecclesiastical functionaries in a nation which, however paradoxically, was becoming increasingly democratic while continuing to support a State Church. As originally conceived, a State Church presupposed "religious unity" as "a necessary prerequisite for political [unity]" ["at religioes enhed var en noedvendig forudsaetning for den politiske"], such that every deviation from official State Church doctrines was, *ipso facto*, "a civil offense" ["en borgerlig forbrydelse"].[74] That was the justification for Norwegian Laws 2-1 and 6-1-4;[75] the Resolution of 22 October 1701; and decrees by King Christian VI on 12 February, 5 March, and 2 April 1745 forbidding all "new and unknown sects," and prescribing immediate deportation of foreign separatists.[76] The fallacy in KUD Mormon policy was its attempt to actualize prosecution of nineteenth and twentieth-century Mormons--Mormons who practiced their religion in a nation and an age where liberal philosophies were in the ascendancy--under provisions of antiquated laws formulated by absolute monarchs during the seventeenth and eighteenth centuries. In addition, the growing secularization and democratization of nineteenth-century Norwegians made it progressively more difficult to mount successful public relations campaigns in support of KUD-sponsored schemes increasingly perceived as violations of the freedom of religion concept.

CHAPTER VI

MORMON RELATIONS WITH THE NORWEGIAN
PUBLIC, 1851-1920

Geographical and Regional
Factors, 1851-1920

Vestlandet (western Norway), including Rogaland, Hordaland, Sogn og Fjordane, Sunnmoere, and parts of Romsdal and Vest-Agder Counties, is physically separated from Oestlandet (eastern Norway) by a north-south mountain range--the most prominent geographical barrier in Norway, and one which generally precluded cultural contact with broader plains and valleys of the east (especially the southeast) during the period before 1910. Social distinctions in Oestlandet, where stor boender [well-to-do farmers] subjected the population of tenants and cotters to conditions little short of slavery during most of the nineteenth century, were much more pronounced than in Vestlandet where the soil was poorer, terrain more rugged, population more sparse, and distinctions between "farmer" and "cotter" less pronounced; cotters and their class in Oestlandet were generally dissatisfied with their lot in the decades after 1850--in Marxian terms, Oestlandet was birthing a proletariat, whereas Vestlandet was yet wrapped in swaddling clothes of hoary tradition.[1]

Regional and cultural differences, including "the almost morbid suspicion between east and west" ["den nesten sykelige mistenkelig-gjoerelse mellom Oest-og Vest-Norge"],[2] and a language in Vestlandet based on "speech forms" that "differed widely from those of the urban upper class thoughout the country, and even from those of the rural and lower class urban population in southeastern Norway,"[3] were at least partly responsible for Mormonism's dismal showing in Vestlandet where the only Mormon missionaries to visit the area in the 1850s were either Danes or Oestlendinger, and the only Mormon foothold worth mentioning was carved out in Bergen--an urban center in the midst of rural surroundings--over thirty years after initial successes in Oestlandet.

When Mormon missionaries, therefore, described residents of Mandal in Vest-Agder in 1855 as "just as hard and unreceptive to the Gospel as the unyielding and naked cliffs which surround them on all sides,"[4] or stated in 1862 that "people here in Vestlandet, both in town and country, are generally very narrow of heart,"[5] they were not saying people in those areas disliked Mormonism per se. What they were saying was that very different "mentalities and differences in character and thought processes . . . existed between the different population groups" in Norway[6] such as those delineated by Christiansand Bishop Johan Christian Heuch:

> The further east, the more excitement, the more individualism in religious beliefs and uncertainty in doctrine, the more indifference and all the easier opportunity for sects [dissenters]; in the western regions, conversely, a uniformity in faith and doctrine which easily becomes rote servitude, a fear of not quite measuring up as a Christian, which occasions considerable [reliance on] formulary as also hypocrisy, and an almost complete absence of sects. . . .[7]

Anti-Mormon Propaganda, 1846-1920

More important than regional or cultural differences in shaping Mormon relations with the general Norwegian public, however, were hundreds of anti-Mormon articles in newspapers and magazines,[8] anti-Mormon books and pamphlets. Up through the 1860s, and again in the 1890s and early 1900s when the number of Mormon missionaries increased dramatically, papers and journals devoted inordinate space to Mormonism:

> . . . there was no question here of a "pro and con" . . . they all aligned themselves from the very beginning on one side, i.e., against the Mormons and their activity. Nor does it appear the newspaper people required a long time to orient their view after the Mormons arrived. Immediately they could report the first meeting in this town or that, they had already made up their minds about the whole thing, that Mormonism was not worth much, and that people, therefore, ought to leave it alone.[9]

J. W. C. Dietrichson, a Lutheran minister in Illinois and avowed foe of Mormonism, wrote the first Norwegian book to openly castigate Mormon preachers and their doctrines--<u>Reise blandt de norske emigranter i "de Forenede Nordamerikanske Fristater"</u> [Travels among the Norwegian Emigrants in "the North American Free States"]--in 1846,[10] and the next seventy years witnessed a flood of books and pamphlets calling Mormons--especially Mormon missionaries--the very "wolves in sheep's clothing" Jesus Himself had warned about.[11]

"Most of the . . . anti-Mormon pamphlets . . . originated in newspapers and periodicals" packed with "accusations over and over that Mormonism was unchristian, an imperium in imperio, its followers ignorant, its leaders scheming, the whole movement a foul hypocrisy, <u>with polygamy its crowning abomination</u>."[12] (Italics mine.) Like newspaper articles of the same ilk, they were "intensely polemical, self-righteous," and filled with "meaningless rumors and assertions. . . ."[13]

Folk songs,[14] public debates, lectures,[15] and, beginning about 1910, motion pictures, also called attention to Mormons and Mormonism. The most famous debates were those in Oslo between Ole Vig, the famous and rather acerbic Grundtvigian educator, and Mormon missionaries in 1855, "which, combined with the fact that the newspapers took sides for and against the missionaries," led to increased attendance at Mormon meetings, and several convert baptisms.[16] Lectures included spoofs in Oslo in 1903 by "Mr. Daniels, the Turk," who stood before audiences in a Turkish soldier's uniform and declared "Joseph Smith was born in England but driven out and then went to Utah,"[17] and lectures in 1911 by Norwegian author, Joergen Jansen-Fuhr, who cited personal experiences in Utah to buttress contentions Mormons were "non-Christians."[18]

"Mormonens Offer" [A Victim of the Mormons], a film portraying Mormon missionaries as white slave traffickers, played to packed houses throughout Norway and Denmark in 1911. Scandinavian Mission President Andrew Jenson termed it "one of the most profitable plays ever put on films," and attributed its success to "the people's taste for sensational matters."[19] Produced in Denmark by Det Danske Filmkompagni [The Danish Film Company], and billed as "a Drama of Love and Sectarian Fanaticism," the film was banned in the United States after strong protests by Utah's Governor William Spry.[20]

Violence and Persecution, 1851-1920

In The Church of England, The Methodists and Society 1700-1850, Anthony Armstrong isolated factors of anti-Methodist violence in England during the 1740s and 1750s: "The sympathy of the Church of England clergy towards the violence" was "certainly evident from time to time"; but most outbursts could be described as "the horseplay of an ignorant crowd in search of sport, a crowd inadequately controlled by the creaking machinery of law and order."[21] There were strong indications anti-Mormon violence in Norway was cast in the same mold,[22] i.e., public invective and catchpenny rumor converged on star-crossed Mormon missionaries[23]-- Mormonism's "visible arm" and the personification, at least in the public mind, of multiple evils, dangers and sins of commission[24]--and led to confrontations perpetrated by rowdies "out on the town for a good time."

"The man who goes on a mission in Norway," said Canute Peterson in 1853, "must take his life in one hand and the Bible in the other. Every time he leaves the Saints [Mormons], his life is in danger."[25] Although Peterson was probably exaggerating, mobs frequently spilt Mormon blood in the 1850s: street gangs in Fredrikstad in 1853 pelted Mormons with stones, "and Brother, Niels Mauritsen (Brake) was hit in the head, causing blood to flow freely, and others were also hit, but not seriously hurt";[26] mobsters in Christiansand in 1856 nearly crushed missionaries Samuel Gudmundson and his companion against a wall--"the mood of the people got uglier and uglier and their cries were that they would spit in our faces, chase us from the town, throw us in the river, etc.";[27] and a sailor broke into a Mormon meeting in Fredrikstad in 1857 and struck a "Brother Torger" and another man denoted "our friend Lunde."[28]

Not infrequently, mob incidents were also connected with imbibing of whisky or brandy: "a drunken mob" chased Hans Olsen Magleby and other Mormons in Roeyken in 1858, "and threatened," said Magleby, "to spill our blood";[29] four or five intoxicated bullies jumped Mons Pedersen, a Mormon in Fredrikstad (1860), and tried to force brandy down his throat;[30] a mob of about two hundred persons, "a part of them drunk," threatened to tear down the Mormon meetinghouse in Larvik (1906), and missionary E. C. Ekman noted that "to see them one would come to the concludsion that hell had turned its self loos and that the Devel and all his imps were present. . . ."[31]

Eviction of Mormons from rented meeting halls was also common practice,[32] but much more serious was eviction of Mormons from their own homes or apartments. Olaf Henrik Nielsen recounted the eviction of his parents after they joined the Mormons in Olso in 1859:

> My parents heard the Gospel [Mormonism] in and around Kristiania [Oslo] and accepted it because they felt and understood that it was true; at that time we children were all small and I [was] about 1 1/2 years old. Now the Devil began to rage; my parents lived at that time in Maridalen 1 [Norwegian] mile north of the Capital City; and a few days before they joined the Church, the landlord arrived with a whip in his hand [and] with this warning: that "if my parents became Mormons today they must leave the house in the morning and father would lose his employment." Fate could not be stayed: we had to leave the house and employment for the sake of the Gospel; and my father was unemployed for a long time; none would give him work "because he was Mormon."[33]

The plight of the Olaus Johnsen Family in Ytteroeen was even more severe: they could not obtain work, shopowners refused to sell to them, civil authorities openly interrogated them, their landlord threatened eviction from a house Johnsen had built himself, and before Johnsen and family could load their possessions into a sailboat, the people of Ytteroeen started tearing down their house.[34]

Not all Mormons, however, refused to fight back: when mobs chased Mormons to Svend Larsen's yard in Risoer (1853), and threatened to storm the house, Larsen "stood just inside of the door on one side with an Ax in his hands . . . and promised to give them the Ax if they ventured to come in";[35] Canute Peterson chased "Sven Eiesand and schoolteacher Sten . . . from the house and pursued them until they left the place," after the two disrupted a Mormon meeting in Knud Luraas's home at Grave in 1854";[36] and missionary E. C. Ekman confronted "one of the worst Devels

[sic] in Town" who tried to break up a Mormon meeting in Larvik in 1906: "[The troublemaker] wanted to fight me," said Ekman, "because I wanted to keep him locked up in the hall untill the police came but we had to let him go as the police was to long in coming and when he got out you Aught [ought] to of herd him cuss."[37]

Mission President Andrew Jenson countered mob violence at Trondheim in 1911 as follows:

> We had taken all precautions to protection against any possible attacks from mobs, having stationed some of our physically strong Utah or Idaho giants at the door and posted the police on the outside. And one of our local brethren (Bro. Oejen) sat by the window to watch for any demonstration on the outside, and had a mob rushed upstairs (our hall being in the second story with an outdoor stairway leading up to it) our boys would immediately have received the signal and there would have been lively fighting. Our boys would from the top of the stairway [have] had the advantage and could have stood off a great number of men. This was no doubt apparent to the mob leaders, the worst of whom (a shoemaker by the name of Staalsmo) confined his efforts to walking to and fro in the yard cursing and swearing as we poured forth the word of the Lord on the inside.[38]

Overt physical violence was only one side of the coin: much more common were vague threats, verbal abuse, and blind intolerance, such as the public burning of Mormon "books and tracts" in Setesdal in 1866 because "people discovered that they contained new and strange doctrines";[39] or the case of C. S. Winge, a missionary from Drammen, who baptized girls from Stavanger in 1860, and confronted "a group of elderly women"-- mothers of the girls--"who were so embittered at me that they spit on me, and pointed their fingers at me [and] used all the unpleasant words they could think of."[40]

Tied up with all of this were elements of prejudgment and inconsistency. People who believed "if it's printed it must be true" about anti-Mormon literature,[41] did not, of course, apply the same yardstick to Mormon literature itself: after O. H. Nielsen sold Mormon tracts to a woman in Arendal in 1877, the woman's little girl chased after him with the tracts and the excuse her mother "dared not read it because it was a Mormon tract." "Immediately thereafter," said Nielsen, "a woman came & called after me; she had also bought a tract; but dared not read it."[42] A. S. Schou observed in 1878 that "the people [near Namsos] were so full of prejudgment against Mormonism that it was impossible to get them to believe that there was anything good about the people that call themselves Mormons, either in teachings or in life,"[43] and also described people who "admitted that that which they heard [Mormon doctrine] was the truth, but were very much afraid to accept the message of salvation, as the world would soon call them Mormons. . . ."[44]

Norwegian Ambivalence and Hospitality, 1851-1920

We cannot, however, typify Norwegians as basically mean or hateful. Harangues by prelates, newspaper and magazine editors, and self-styled protectors of public morality were often ancillary to deep-seated personal revulsion: Mormons induced a son to emigrate leaving "old folks" to man the family farm; Mormons converted single girls whose parents feared they were being sexually exploited or dreaded the heartbreak of permanent separation; some parents considered the "loss" of a son or daughter to Mormonism, or worse yet, that child's marriage to a "heathen Mormon," a social slap in the face. There was also the matter of tradition: Mormon converts were usually the first in their communities to challenge clerics and civil authorities in religious and political matters. Mormon teachings about polygamy, though never actualized in Norway, were deemed particularly serious challenges to traditional sexual mores and monogamous family life.

There was abundant indication much "anti-Mormonism" was skin-deep or tied to Norwegian ambivalence, i.e., "when you think you just about have them then there is something that com [sic] up that change ther [their] mind. . . ."[45] There was obviously little malice, for example, in farmer Petter Stavsaet's criticism of Mormon doctrine near Aalesund in 1894. Stavsaet engaged two missionaries in debate, soon admitted he was over his head, and asked the name of the Mormon prophet. "Wilford Woodruff," was the reply, whereupon Stavsaet "began to clap his hands and look up at the clouds and laugh as hard as he could and all of those standing nearby did likewise, for there was a large crowd gathered from the neighboring farms."[46]

Missionary Carl Kjaer "tracted a biter [sic] enemy at Vaage" in 1909, but noted

> . . . her datters were on my side, [and] on [one] snatched [the] tract out of there mother's hand while she was in [the] act of giving it back to me, they said they'd read it, if she would'nt. Finally she [the mother] invited me to eat supper. I told her about my partner out on [the] rd [road]; she told me to get him too. . . . Rec'd hot milk with poteter Kager [potato cakes] and broed [bread] for supper, free of charge."[47]

Kjaer also visited a lady at Langaaker (south of Haugesund),

> . . . & because it rained so hard she invited me inside, her husband was in bed (Kviling middag) he woke up but started at once calling me down, he said he'd rec'd some of our tracts before but said they were some of the worst tracts he'd ever read, he then told me to sit down while he read this one thru, this I did of course. He read the first side and 2 pages of a Sandheds Roest ["A Voice of Truth"] out loud then said, thats the truth every word of it then he told his wife to make me some hot coffee. I said I'd rather have milk, so I got it, he was very friendly and took me in the hand, so did his wife, when I went.[48]

There were also numerous occasions where residents in remote districts treated Mormon missionaries with respect, and exhibited, as it were, true Norwegian hospitality with layers of rumor and suspicion peeled off. Probably the first Mormon to visit remote regions of Telemark, for example, was O. H. Nielsen who preached for a group of "mountain people" at Folkestad (Boeherred) in 1877:

> The men wore short, white vests & jackets, long or knee-length black trousers and red caps; the women [wore] long black skirts which extended up under their arms, belts around the waist, short black jackets, breast pins & rings, and large embroidered head scarves. It was truly a Norwegian setting and very interesting to observe. . . . I . . . declared our belief & teaching as based on Biblical proofs, and all present listened with rapt attention. . . . As far as I know this was the first gathering which was held in this area under Latter-day Saint auspices.[49]

Missionary and native Norwegian, Anthon L. Skanchy, recounted a classic example of Norwegian hospitality near Godfjord, northern Norway, in 1864 after losing his way in a severe snowstorm, and floundering all day in knee-deep snow:

> I stopped . . . [at a hut] to ask for lodging, but was so exhausted I could barely speak. The man of the house understood this, said not a word to me, but took a

chair and sat me by the warm stove - and took off my boots [and] went down into his cellar and brought up a bowl of home-brewed malt beer - and gave me to drink, asked me to sit at the table to eat. This was done in all haste. He then began asking if I had come over the isthmus, and why I hadn't hollered when I got to the beach--then he would have come and fetched me in his boat, for he said he had done it before, for those who had come over the isthmus. This was a poor fisherman's home, the only house on that side of the island. After I had eaten and was somewhat revived the [fisherman's] wife began getting the bed ready . . . (put on clean sheets and pillowslips [and] then brought in straw mats and [a] boat sail and laid them in a corner (There was only one room in the house) Then had a prayer. They knew who I was [i.e., a Mormon]. I was then told to sleep in the bed, which I didn't want to do but would [have been] grateful to sleep on the straw which had been brought in, but no! that didn't matter-I must sleep in the bed. In the morning after we had eaten our humble breakfast the man transported me over the sound to Langoeen. He would not accept any money.[50]

Popular Support of Mormonism, 1851-1920

In direct contrast to violence or persecution, popular grass roots support for Mormonism often bubbled just beneath the surface. George M. Brown, for example, observed in Gran Clerical District in 1866 that "in this place there are no people who belong to the [Mormon] Church but we have many good friends here who receive us and administer to our wants with great kindness and warmness of heart."[51] Many "friends" were so-called Troende [Believers] who did not request baptism, but understood and respected Mormon beliefs: Trondheim Branch President A. S. Schou, for example, visited a non-Mormon man from Nordland in 1878 who "had a good understanding of the Plan of Salvation, and desired to live among the Latter-day Saints";[52] missionary O. H. Berg noted the baptism of a nineteen-year-old girl at Roervik (1864) "in the presence of her Mother and a Sister as also the man of the house who were believers";[53] and Conference President Hans J. Christiansen visited Mormons and other "friends" in Oslo in 1895, and discovered "that the Spirit had been working to our advantage such that several have complete faith in the Gospel."[54]

Mormon celebrations and social events frequently attracted large numbers of "friends": more than a hundred non-Mormon well-wishers, including an officer of the civil court, attended missionary N. C. Poulsen's farewell party in Trondheim 26 November 1857, ate assorted refreshments, and drank coffee and red wine;[55] over two hundred persons--"Saints and strangers"--honored departing Mission President Andrew Jenson at a feast in Bergen on 22 April 1912, and heard him sing his Hawaiian song, "Aloha oe";[56] nearly a hundred persons in Bergen, including about fifty non-Mormons, rented a steamboat for a day's excursion during the Easter holidays in 1920;[57] and E. C. Ekman described a Mormon outing on Bygdoey on 22 May 1907 where "ther [sic] was many with us that did not belong to the Church," members and guests played ball games, and "we had lunch and lemonad [sic]. . . ."[58]

Beginning in 1872, Oslo Branch Mormon Choir held regular public concerts--J. C. A. Weibye described a "song concert" on 11 February 1872 for 145 persons including "many strangers,"[59] and "a midlen good Concert" on 29 December 1872 for two hundred persons.[60] Concerts were held at Mormon headquarters, Oesterhausgade 27, Oslo, such as one on 2 May 1907 where approximately six hundred persons heard eleven selections, including choir renditions of "Norsk Faedrelandshymne" [Norwegian Patriotic Hymn] by Sven Ulsaker, and "Let the Mountains Shout for Joy" by Stephens; "Troldtoget" [The Parade of the Trolls], a Grieg piano solo, played by Kitty Berg; and violin solo, "Ave Maria," performed by Otto Bruun--all for a few pennies![61]

Though hardly conclusive, attendance figures at Mormon preaching meetings, especially during the approximate years 1893-1910, also evidenced a Mormon influence on rather large groups of non-Mormons. A Mormon meeting on "Temples and what Temples are used for" attracted nearly two hundred people--half of them non-Mormons--in Oslo on 16 April 1893.[62] Mormon meetings in Aalesund--a town of nearly nine thousand inhabitants in the late 1890s--attracted crowds of over a hundred non-Mormons in 1894, and Hans J. Christiansen observed that "the greatest part of the town has been tracted out and there are many who believe in the [Mormon] gospel including the leading police deputy."[63] A meeting in Oslo on 25 October 1903 where J. A. Hendricksen spoke on "Utah and its People" to over four hundred people, roughly half non-Mormons, was likewise typical of non-Mormon attendance at Mormon preaching meetings during early years of the twentieth century.[64]

More revealing than sporadic attendance figures, however, were Mormon Sunday school tallies which showed sizeable numbers of non-Mormon children attending Bible classes during the approximate years 1900-1910. Schools in Oslo Conference at Oslo, Vaalerengen, Drammen, Halden, Fredrikstad, Larvik, and Roeken, had a total enrollment of 395 pupils, including eighty-five children of non-Mormons (twenty percent of total enrollment), in 1906,[65] and non-Mormon enrollment climbed to twenty-seven percent (113 of 414 pupils) in 1907.[66]

Totals from some areas were surprisingly lopsided: thirty-six (eighty percent) of forty-five pupils in the Mormon Sunday school at Arendal in 1910 were children of non-Mormons--"gratifying testimony," according to a <u>Skandinaviens Stjerne</u> editorial, "of the trust and good graces which our doctrine and our Sunday school system win among conservative and right-thinking parents";[67] and non-Mormon enrollment in Trondheim Conference Sunday schools in 1902 was an amazing eighty-eight percent of total membership (seventy-five of eighty-five pupils).[68] Although non-Mormon attendance decreased somewhat in the years after 1910, leaders described "many strangers" ["mange fremmede"] at Mormon Sunday schools as late as 1917.[69]

Conclusion

The story of Mormon relations with the Norwegian public was one of violence, propaganda campaigns, suspicion and rumor;[70] it also encompassed enduring and meaningful friendships, generous hospitality, and non-Mormon participation in Mormon social and religious functions. Unfortunately, the onus of polygamy clouded Mormon-Norwegian relations to an inordinate degree during the years before 1920, and, not suprisingly, Mormons often criticized the opposing camp's "double standard," and complained they were "surrounded by the children of the world, who wander in darkness and ignorance, and know not Thy way which leads to salvation."[71]

F. F. Hintze's report from Oslo in 1885 was typical of Mormon appraisals. A polygamist with four wives, Hintze reported that

> . . . nearly all the [Norwegian] males [on a Saturday night] were more or less drunk, a pityfull sight indeed walking arm in arm with young ladies in such a condition. A person will ask. Why will the young ladies do so? Why not seek better company? But the answer will invariable [sic] be: were [where] is it[?] The whole nation seemed to be sleeped [steeped] in sin. But that here described is not all but these same women have perhap[s] been betrayed of their virtue that same evening and been the victim of some low deprived being that perhaps refuse to be in their company if they will not be subject to them. O what a pity! Indeed, it is anough [enough] to make a person weep all day long. . . .[72]

The greatest tragedy--and deepest irony--was the fact that were Hintze's account recast as "a description of immoral conditions in Utah," it would have found a ready printer, and a believing, censorious public. In all likelihood, it would have then become "a matter of record" in Norwegian parliamentary proceedings or courts of law.

CHAPTER VII

THE MORMON COMMUNITY IN NORWAY,
1851-1920: PART I

The Social Setting, 1851-1920

The story of Mormonism in nineteenth-century Norway was part and parcel of that of Norwegian industrialization, especially after 1845. The setting was the cities--especially Oslo and Fredrikstad--with poor and unplanned housing, water troughs on the streets, inadequate sewage control, and shanty towns which sprang up almost overnight.[1] "Bit players" were the hordes of new arrivals:

> The picture emerges of a society in upheaval. The old, established community life was broken to bits. People became like Abraham, uprooted from "his country, from his kindred and from his father's house," and like him, many set out for parts unknown. Among all these rootless persons now emerged a renewed desire for community, for uniting themselves with others of a like mind. That was true in the social and political arenas as well as the religious.[2]

Mormons won most of their early converts in "low, ill-drained, and dirty" Oslo neighborhoods of Piperviken and Ruseloekbakken[3] which social historian Eilert Sundt described in 1858 filled with "crooked and narrow . . . and filthy streets" ["krumme og smale . . . og soelede gader"].[4] Another Mormon stronghold was "Forstaden" [Suburb] District of Fredrikstad where a surge of economic activity tied to export of beams to Holland attracted large numbers of workers in the late 1840s: two steampowered saw works were operational by 1851, and Fredrikstad emerged in the 1850s as center of Norway's wood products industry populated by newcomers who "had moved in from places far enough away that they lost the regular contact with their home communities; . . . [and] had torn themselves loose from the roots of tradition."[5]

Mormonism's connection with members of the working class in Norway began when skipper Svend Larsen visited John Olsen's smithy in Risoer in September 1851: Larsen explained Mormonism to Olsen and his co-workers, and Olsen and another blacksmith, Petter Adamsen, subsequently joined the sect.[6] Mormon beginnings in Oslo sprang from similar roots after Carl J. E. Fjeld, a foundryman in Drammen, read newspaper accounts of court proceedings against Mormons in Fredrikstad in 1852:

> My interest was particularly aroused by foundry laborer, H. P. Jensen's [Hans Peter Jensen's of Noerre Sundby, Denmark] powerful testimony about the validity of Mormonism. As a laboring man, I felt proud that a foundry worker could pick to pieces [the] arguments of priests and police authorities, and I now felt that the foundry workers had amounted to something.[7]

Fjeld subsequently traveled to Denmark, converted to Mormonism in Copenhagen in 1853, and obtained work at Akers Mekaniske Verksted [the Aker Machine Works] in Oslo (1853). "Here I met many old friends," said he, "and passed around various small [Mormon] tracts and my little psalm book which I had brought with me from Denmark, together with the New Testament, to the foundry workers and smiths until these volumes were every bit as black as we ourselves were."[8] When Mormon missionaries, Canute Peterson and Mathias Olson, arrived in Oslo on 8 October 1853, Fjeld invited them to preach for his workmates--"the first time that the Gospel [Mormonism] was ever offered to the good people of Christiania."[9] Although "the men were black and dusty from their work," and "came to the meeting without washing," fifteen soon joined the Mormons and constituted the nucleus of a congregation in Oslo.[10]

Reports from Lutheran priests in 1859 further underlined Mormon success in working-class strongholds. Anton Wilhelm Fangen, parish priest in Aker, wrote about Mormon activity "in the so-called [Oslo] suburbs" ["i de saakaldte Forstaeder"] inhabited by "large groups from other clerical districts here in the Country and several Swedish laborers" ["en stor Maengde fra andre Praestegjaeld her i Landet og flere svenske arbejdsfolk"]:

> They are very obscure persons and, though baptized as Mormons, do not formally withdraw from the State Church. . . . In addition to the opportunity [for proselyting] provided by the large influx of workers into the City [Oslo], the people from all places, not least from Oslo, gathered near the large factory operations at Saugene, provide ample opportunity for [Mormon] initiatives.[11]

Alexander Lange, parish priest in Asker, Tanum, and Haslum--areas adjoining Oslo City proper--reported well-attended Mormon meetings "at the nail factory near the Aker River,"[12] and Paul Irgens Dybdahl, parish priest in Roeken, noted Mormon successes among workers in the lumber industry.[13]

Although Mormons often called themselves "church members [who] belonged to the working class and were always busy,"[14] and although "joining the Mormon Church in Norway was almost always a step down the social ladder" since Mormonism "was the religion at the very lowest end of the prestige scale,"[15] we cannot characterize Mormons in Norway--although members of the "working class"--as "unskilled day laborers."[16] Helge Seljaas's study[17] of Mormon emigrants from Norway before 1914 revealed that:

> . . . housekeepers or servants [made] up the largest single group with 112 (16.8 per cent). Other occupational groups arranged according to size included ninety-two (13.8 per cent) seamstresses, followed by . . . fifty-nine (8.8 per cent) laborers, fifty-two (7.8 per cent) farmers, fifty (7.5 per cent) carpenters, twenty-six (3.9 per cent) clerks, twenty each (3.0 per cent) tailors and shoe-makers, eighteen (2.7 per cent) smiths, seventeen (2.5 per cent) masons, sixteen (2.4 per cent) sailors, fifteen (2.2 per cent) painters, nine each (1.3 per cent) machinists, eight each (1.2 per cent) printers and [petty] merchants, seven each (1.0 per cent) laundresses and bakers, six each (0.9 per cent) cooks, weavers and factory girls. [There were] five: rope makers and hewers; three: drivers, book binders, sales ladies, photographers, teachers and millers; two: milliners, glovemakers, knitteresses, mechanics, coopers, watchmakers and founderers. Occupations of which there was only one were: miner, plumber, mail carrier, barber, steward, presser, musician, railroad man, instrument maker, auctioneer, trunk maker, goldsmith, manufacturer, stenographer, office boy, dentist, telephone employee, midwife, umberella [sic] maker, china decorator, saw master, harness maker, brazier, builder, gardener, carver, florist, lawyer and dyer.[18]

Although most converts were poor, "so were the great majority of Norwegians," such that Mormonism in Norway, although it "appealed to very few of the upper class, . . . otherwise represented a fairly accurate cross section" of the urban, working-class population.[19] There were two major qualifiers: "the vast majority of the converts were won from among that part of the population which was just barely removed from the farm and not yet fully adapted to city life"; "there were comparatively few converts from among the agricultural population . . . probably due . . . to the State church's having a stronger hold in the rural areas. . . ."[20]

Mormon Poverty, Working Conditions,
Housing, Diet and Clothing,
1851-1920

By "Mormon Community" we do not mean a community physically separated from other Norwegians during the years 1851-1920: most Mormons lived in poverty, bent their backs to the same menial jobs which employed most of their countrymen, lived in the same run-down apartments, and ate the same fish and potatoes. Scandinavian Mission President Canute Peterson described "over 5000 Poor saints in this Mission looking and Baging [begging] for help" in 1872,[21] A. S. Schou reported in 1877 that nearly all fifty Mormons in Stavanger were poor,[22] and F. F. Hintze described Mormons in Thistedalen in 1885 as "more like slaves than free people."[23] John Johnson visited twenty Saints in Halden Branch--"all very pore"--in 1889,[24] and Oslo Conference President Andrew Israelsen admitted in 1893 that "most of the Saints were so poor that I did not feel justified in asking them for dinner, as I knew that often they had to go without meals themselves."[25]

Sometimes poverty had cruel antecedents: Anders Olsen, a Mormon in Oslo, served twenty days in prison in the 1850s for having baptized, and returned home to find his wife and eight children "sitting on the floor eating food from a kettle" with only two spoons "which they passed around amongst themselves." Police "had confiscated the furniture and taken it to an auction in order to enforce a ten-dollar fine Olsen was sentenced to pay."[26] More tragic was the death of Ole Nielsen who fell through thin ice and drowned while skating home from a Mormon meeting at Roervik in 1858; his pregnant widow was forced to "farm out" six small children.[27]

Poverty of another sort haunted a Sister Gustavsen who turned to drink after her husband deserted her and "6 hungry small" ["6 Broedloese Smaa"] children in 1901;[28] a Sister Eriksen's drunken husband forced liquor down her throat in full view of their twelve children (1902);[29] and poverty even occasioned "tragedy of the macabre" in the case of Brother Christoffersen whose wife died in Oslo in 1916, and whose family circumstances--he had six children--were described by Hans J. Christiansen the next day: "The dead woman still lay in the bed after her death yesterday, and since they only had one room besides a very tiny kitchen, they had slept in the same room during the night, where the mother lay as a corpse."[30]

In the decades before 1900, laborers and artisans worked eleven-hour days, tailors and shoemakers twelve- or thirteen-hour days, and bakers fifteen-hour days if we include night work.[31] Until enactment of social legislation in the 1890s and early 1900s, workers could be arbitrarily dismissed, insurance and pension schemes were nonexistent, and employers could pay in kind as per Mons Pedersen's lament just before Christmas in

1857, that "we could not receive money for our work, but we could receive rye & butter."[32]

Like other children, Mormon youngsters worked graveyard shifts in the 1860s for "as much as 10 cents" a night,[33] put in twelve-hour days at a mill, or, like Ole Harmon Olsen (born 1847), worked as a nail sorter in Oslo for "twelve cents a day": "My work as a 'nail boy' was tiresome as I was tied to the stool from six o'clock in the morning until seven o'clock at night five days per week. . . . On winter mornings the nails were cold as ice, and the iron table at which I worked seemed colder still."[34] Nor was serving an apprenticeship thirty years later in the 1890s any guarantee of improved working conditions, as witness woes of baker's apprentice, C. J. Zahl Hansen, whose boss "generally carried a hatchet in his hand and pointed it, and if annoyed . . . would, without hesitation, fling it at the offender." Hansen soon learned "apprentices could not expect decent treatment."[35]

Working-class housing was uniformly poor. A cellar full of stagnant water, "rotting cat, mouse and rat cadavers and pieces of a horse's skeleton" ["raatne kadaver av mus, rotter og katter og stykker av et hesteskjelett"] spawned a serious cholera epidemic in Oslo in 1850--four adults and seven children lived in an apartment directly over the cellar[36]--and Eilert Sundt's study of housing conditions in Oslo's Ruseloekbakken--the area where most Mormons lived--showed an average of five persons per rented room in the mid-1850s, with numerous pigs "under the table or bed."[37] Dr. Axel Holst's surveys of Oslo neighborhoods in the 1890s also revealed widespread privation: fifteen thousand working-class people in poorly built, drafty, damp, overcrowded dwellings, who shared kitchens (and communal toilets) with several neighbors.[38]

Although hardly that of beggars, Mormon diet also reflected humble circumstances of members. Bread, potatoes, coffee, and herring were working-class staples well into the 1870s,[39] and poor man's fare described by O. C. Larsen in 1858 at Sandsvaer was hardly atypical:

> It was a little one-room house, black and sooty on the inside from the smoke of the fireplace. My companion addressing the old lady said, "Mother have you anything to eat? We are hungry and tired." The old lady answering, "God help you we having nothing in the house." Yet while so saying, she reached up on a shelf under the sooty mud and straw roof, took down an earthen bowl with some mush in it, covered with a hard dry crust as black as the chimney, saying, "this is all we have." It was soon devoured and we felt relieved.[40]

Fresh berries, especially raspberries, supplemented Mormon diets in season,[41] and George M. Brown observed (1865) that goat's cheese was "a delicious and nourishing article of food . . . produced and consumed in abundance in this country."[42] Breakfast on more prosperous farms included "flat broed [flatbread], waffler [waffles], butter, cheese," and "oel ost [eggs mixed with hot beer],"[43] and milk was a common ingredient in many popular dishes: rice pudding (made from water, butter, skim milk, sugar and cinnamon);[44] thick, sour milk [tykk melk] resembling yogurt;[45] and milk pudding--"a thick mixture of boiled cows milk; the 1st milk after the cow had had a calf."[46]

Mormon diarists frequently mentioned "fish and potato" meals: herring and potatoes;[47] fried halibut, potatoes, bread and coffee;[48] boiled cod, potatoes and gravy;[49] or boiled fish and potatoes with sweet soup.[50] Other potato dinners included: potatoes, coffee and meatballs;[51] cream porridge, sausages, potatoes and cake;[52] and sour milk and potato cakes served "out of [the] same big bowl."[53] Rare "special occasion" dinners featured: "rice and boiled eider eggs" in northern Norway;[54] sweet soup, pickled pork, sweet cake [voerterkake], coffee and jam in Odalen;[55] "boiled fresh Salmon & Mackrel, fish soup, vegetables, coffee & cakes" in Oslo;[56] roast beef, gravy, potatoes, pickles, cranberries and cloudberry pudding in Trondheim;[57] and mutton, cabbage and whortleberries in Halden.[58]

Oslo Conference President George M. Brown observed in 1864 that "the country people make nearly all their own clothing," and that "it is rather pleasant than otherwise to sit by a country fireside of a winter's evening and see the old woman and the girls as busy at their wheels as a lot of bees making honey. They spin all their wool on small wheels which are turned by the foot, and the cloth is all woven by hand."[59]

Workingmen in town and country generally wore leather or sheepskin trousers, a work apron, and leather shoes, whereas Oestlendinger preferred wooden clogs.[60] Most members of the working class, both adults and children, did not wear underwear.[61] Country boys and girls went barefooted from early May to October, jackets--pea coats--and scarves were standard outerwear in wintertime,[62] and a few, like Ole Harmon Olsen in Oslo, even owned Sunday clothes: "The Sabbath day, my well earned Sabbath, was always a treat to me. I could dress in my better clothes and feel contented and free. I shall not try to describe my common daily apparel, it is not worth while mentioning."[63]

Communications and Transportation, 1851-1920

The first government-funded telegraph lines were strung in 1851, and mission leaders in Copenhagen enjoyed twenty-four-hour reply service to Liverpool dispatches after 1861.[64] Telephone service was operational in Oslo by 1895,[65] and mission leaders heralded another telephone milestone in 1910 on completion of a "wireless" connection between the Eiffel Tower in Paris and New York offices of Mutual Life.[66]

Steamboat service between Norwegian coastal towns commenced in the 1820s, and the 1840s and 1850s marked extensive construction of new roads, improvement of existing roadbeds, and wide-ranging canal-dredging projects which opened remote regions of the country.[67] In the 1850s and 1860s, "railroad fever" impelled construction of three new branch lines near Oslo, and plans for the important Drammen-Randsfjord and Oslo-Drammen lines.[68]

The first Mormons in Risoer, Brevik and Fredrikstad traveled to conferences and other meetings on a former whaling sloop which Hans Peter Jensen of Aalborg and Svend Larsen of Risoer purchased at Stavern for 150 dollars in 1852. Larsen converted the craft to a pleasure yacht he dubbed <u>Zions Loeve</u> [Zion's Lion]: "It was a good sailer, and floated a white ensign from the masthead whereon was painted a lion holding in the loop of a bent golden halberd a beaming eye, and under the same the letter 'Z' painted in blue."[69] Most Mormons, however, simply traveled on foot during summer months, and relied on ice skates, skis, and horsedrawn sleds during wintertime.[70]

Members in rural districts--especially Tromsoe Branch which "comprised all the territory north of the Arctic circle"[71]--were very spread out, and foul weather, such as "the verry rough and stormy weather" which kept "the brethren and sisters from the country" away from meetings at Stavanger during the winter of 1867,[72] played havoc with branch administration, meeting attendance, and proselyting activities. Oslo Conference President Andrew Israelsen logged over ten thousand travel miles in routine visits to branches during 1892-1893,[73] Oslo Conference President Hans J. Christiansen reported in 1894 that "proselyting can only be carried out during summer months in the fjord districts since it is very difficult to travel around in the darkness since in the winter there is one continuous night";[74] and missionary Christian Knudsen "was travling and tracking the most of my time" at Tromsoe during the Winter of 1897, "and that to [sic] by moonlight and with out enny [any] Roads. . . ."[75]

Travelers approaching Oslo by sea during winter months could only make part of the journey by boat since icebreakers could not clear paths through the ice before late March or early April. Slow-moving steamers from Arendal, Brevik, Fredrikstad, and other coastal towns puffed up fog-filled Oslo Fjord until they reached the ice shelf itself--about fifteen miles downfjord from Oslo[76]--and left disembarking passengers to dicker with a waiting army of drivers in horsedrawn sleighs eager to whisk travelers over the ice to Oslo.[77] Summer travel was also "greatly hindered" ["hindrede meget"] because "the never-ending number of fjords, bays and inlets" made "sailing a necessity, and the [Mormon] Brethren, in general," seldom had "sufficient travel monies."[78]

CHAPTER VIII

THE MORMON COMMUNITY IN NORWAY,
1851-1920: PART II

The Defensive Mentality, 1851-1920

Scarred not only by negative confrontations with fellow countrymen (see chapters V and VI), but by acrimonious exchanges with non-Mormon family members and near relatives, many Mormons in Norway comprised a group on the defensive. Olena Olsen's father ranted at her in an Oslo street in 1865 after she decided to immigrate to Utah, called Mormon missionaries "a degenerate group from America with only one purpose in mind, to get more wives, such as she," and--after she immigrated--"bitterly disowned her and forbade her name being mentioned in the home."[1] Marie Carlsen's father forcibly removed her from a Mormon meeting at Larvik in 1906, and stirred up a mob of two hundred rowdies who threatened to destroy the Mormon meetinghouse. Branch leader E. C. Ekman later reported Marie "was going to apostatize that is She dont know what to do in the matter pore girl is between to [two] fires and she dont realy know what to do."[2]
 A Mormon named Anders Svendsen cut short a visit to his parents' home in Soerum in 1861 when "his oldest brother and sister came home from work, pounded on the table" ["thi hans Aeldste Broder, og Soester kom hjem fra Arbeidet, slog i Bordet"], and threatened to throw him out the door.[3] Torkel Torkelson, a native of Stavanger, visited relatives in 1880 who "would not contaminate themselves and their houses by allowing a Mormon missionary to come inside" ["vilde ikke besmitte sig og sine Huser og lade en Mormon Missionaer ind i dem"], and a cousin only gave him food on condition he eat it out in the yard.[4]
 Mormon "defensiveness" was especially evident in dreams such as Svend Larsen's in 1853 where he "saw a serpent, about six feet long, ready to spit poison on me, but I pulled out my jackknife and stuck it through the serpent's head, and afterwards I skinned it."[5] Larsen also dreamed

> . . . that I was on a Norwegian schooner and . . . left the boat and made for the shore, After I had visited various houses, the people began persecuting me from all sides, some came rowing in and others came on foot until a large crowd was gathered, and I stood in their midst. . . . The Lord gave me presence of mind and power and I

> preached for them, all stood still and listened to my talk, and when I had concluded they all went away peacefully.[6]

Other Mormons escaped raging waterfalls in their dreams,[7] passed through vaporous fires,[8] or, like Oslo Conference President George M. Brown, confronted murderous beasts:

> I was wandering in a forest when I spied an animal which looked much like a wolf, though it was larger and of a more ferocious nature. Whether it attacked me or I attacked it I don't remember. Anyhow I came in collision with it, and took it by the jaws and turned them asunder like Sampson did with the lion. I cast the animal on the ground at my feet, the blood ran from it where I had torn the jaws apart. I felt sorry, but yet justified as I had the impression and belief that I did it in self-defense.[9]

Events and conditions surrounding the act of Mormon initiation itself--"baptism by immersion for the remission of sins"[10]--further buttressed the defensive mentality. Before construction of indoor fonts in the 1890s,[11] Mormons were forced to baptize in rivers, small streams, and the ocean itself, and this in turn meant trouble from Lutheran authorities who considered Mormon baptism "a blasphemous horror" and pressured civil authorities to impose fines and imprisonment, even as late as 1910.[12]

Mormons, accordingly, developed refined methods of evasion. "I had been counseled not to baptize any one into the Church, for this would surely put me into prison," declared Canute Peterson in 1853:

> . . . I therefore sent for my friend, Brother Mathias Olson from Fredrikstad, and he came and baptized nine persons. These were the first baptisms in Christiania. Brother Mathias Olson had made arrangements to emigrate to Utah, and we planned to have the baptisms performed the day he was to leave. He baptized these people between 9 and 10 o'clock at night, And left on the steamer Nord-Cap, at about 11 o'clock P.M. Some of the new converts and I accompanied him to the docks.[13]

In lieu of contrived escapes, Mormons generally avoided detection by baptizing late at night: court minutes and Mormon diaries abound with accounts of midnight baptisms followed by confirmation--"the laying on of hands for the Gift of the Holy Ghost"--on remote beaches or peninsulas.[14] Other ploys included "decoy parties" which led would-be spies a merry chase while baptisms were in process,[15] and "fishing excursions" where baptizer and baptismal candidate were dropped off on a lonely island while the rest of the group continued fishing from the boat.[16]

Those who happened on Mormon baptisms were often out on strange errands themselves, such as Morten Iversen, forty-two-year-old servant in Fredrikstad, who, riding along the beach near Vaterland "on a sick horse belonging to his master" shortly after midnight in April 1853, heard

> . . . loud voices coming from the Krageroe end of Fuglevig Bay as if a sermon were being preached. It was very dark at the time such that the deponent could not see what was taking place over there. The deponent cannot say what was taking place. About 2 A.M. of the same night a boat containing about five or six persons came gliding out of Fuglevig Bay and docked at Vaterland.[17]

Factors of Conversion, 1851-1920

Why did Norwegians convert to Mormonism?[18] Detractors, such as Eilert Sundt, charged gross ignorance:

> If the inhabitants of Piperviken and Ruseloekbakken, who have shown themselves so indifferent when it comes to reading secular materials, had displayed a countervailing interest in sensible and soberminded reading of their [Lutheran] religious tracts, then Ruseloekbakken would assuredly not have become the very place where the Mormons have made the biggest inroads. In my opinion, it is a fact worth noting as far as concerns our country, that Mormonism's absurdities have found any credence at all only among such as have not only been little occupied with religion, but who have done extremely little reading and [been] largely denied an education.[19]

Sundt's arguments, however, fly in the face of Seljaas's contention that "the ability of even the lowest socio-economic classes to read and write was probably a factor in their conversion to Mormonism,"[20] and Mulder's observation that "the Norwegian proselytes, largely from Christiania . . . proved a highly articulate minority [in Utah], producing an intelligentsia easily distinguished among the Scandinavian converts."[21]

Most converts to Mormonism had earlier undergone Lutheran confirmation--evidence in itself of literacy since confirmation presupposed reading knowledge of the Bible and Catechism,[22] and Mormons themselves frequently emphasized the primary role "reading" played throughout the conversion process. Torkel Torkelson, for example, joined the Mormons in 1880, and recalled that reading the Bible at school during the 1860s first made him aware of "inconsistencies" between Biblical acounts and practices in the State Church,[23] and Anthon L. Skanchy, one of the first to preach Mormonism in northern Norway, read incessantly before his Mormon baptism: "I had my own room in our home and spent all my spare time in the study of the Bible and the 'Mormon' books."[24] In weeks preceding his Mormon baptism in 1856, O. C. Larsen (born 1836) described himself as reading so much "people thought I was going crazy,"[25] and Carl J. E. Fjeld from Drammen visited Mormons in Copenhagen in 1852, "as I had read considerable about these people in the papers during the summer before I left home, [and] I was very anxious to meet one of them."[26]

Ole Ellingsen, a twenty-two-year-old servant man at Kjaevelsroed Farm, declared at a court hearing at Onsoe on 1 October 1852 that his attendance at Mormon meetings at Kjoelbergbroe and Kjaevelsroed "resulted in his reading in the Bible [where he] discovered that such baptism [baptism by immersion] corresponded with what occurred in the time of Christ, wherefore he determined to let himself be rebaptized [accept Mormon baptism]."[27] Karen Helene Andersdatter, age twenty-eight, a servant in Doctor Larsen's employ, testified at Fredrikstad on 11 October 1852 that she "had never been prevailed upon to be baptized [a Mormon] . . . but had instead become convinced that it [Mormonism] was true through reading the New Testament";[28] and Christian Hansen, age sixteen, testified about his conversion process in 1853 as follows:

> The Deponent was persuaded to accept the Mormon faith the first time upon hearing a conversation in the jail between the district governor [Christian Birch-Reichenwald] and Olsen [Mormon missionary Ole Olsen imprisoned at Elverhoei in 1852] during which the latter declared that there was not a fraction of God's Word [the Word of God as preached by Lutheran priests] which agreed with [descriptions of] baptism and the Sacrament of the Lord's Supper in the Bible, and [Hansen] found this [to be] true after perusal of the Bible.[29]

There were other factors of conversion. Mormon preachers, especially during the 1850s and 1860s, preached hell and damnation sermons which often catalyzed persons already preoccupied with sin, or caught up in remorse over personal sins, to opt for repentance and complete immersion in "cleansing waters of baptism." Hearings at Fredrikstad and Onsoe in 1852, for example, revealed great anxiety and feelings of guilt over personal sin: farmer Niels Eriksen Ingulsroed, age fifty-two, felt his sins were "far away" ["langt borte"] after being baptized, and servant girl Karen Andrea Nielsdatter, age seventeen, "felt an inner urgency . . . to accept [Mormon] baptism, without which she did not feel she could be saved."[30] Anders Nielsen, age thirteen, was baptized "with the view that it would benefit him as a sinner";[31] and the widow, Berthe Jacobsdatter Kjaevelsroed, age sixty-six, said she was baptized because she believed "if a man is not born again, he cannot receive remission of [his] sins."[32] Ole Ellingsen, age twenty-two, felt baptism had "relieved his mind" ["lettet hans Sind"],[33] and Emilie Halvorsen, age twenty-five, was baptized "because she did not see any other way by which she could obtain peace, since she felt restless both night and day."[34]

Some converts described personal loneliness or feelings of apartness from Norwegian society in general. C. S. Winge (born 1835), shoemaker's apprentice in Drammen from 1849-1854, "pondered over the fallen condition of the world" to such an extent before meeting the Mormons, that he completely withdrew from society:

> I had no desire to attend [the Lutheran] church, because I did not believe in their teachings. As I read in the Acts of the Apostles of the wanderings of these holy men and their faithfulness, I thought, "Oh, that I might have lived in their day, then could I also have been faithful in proclaiming the Gospel of Jesus Christ, and even though I were brought before a judge and thrown in prison, I would have stood fast."[35]

Others described a "conversion experience" (usually tied to personal prayer) prior to joining the Mormons. Carl J. E. Fjeld, for example, was addicted to alcohol, which he knew he "must repent of in order to become a member of the [Mormon] Church." Fjeld asked "the Lord in secret to give me strength to overcome this great weakness," and no sooner raised himself to his feet after praying in a private garden, "than the spirit of the Lord came upon me in power and I felt happy and full of courage and determination."[36] O. C. Larsen studied Mormonism in Drammen in 1856, finally summoned courage to pray vocally, "and kneeled down . . . humbly and earnestly asking God in a few words to be with me and help me understand what was right for me to do." "After this I found quite a relief," said Larsen, "and became more and more convinced that Mormonism was true. No matter what should become of me or what I should have to pass through, I felt that I should have to embrace it; though the struggle it was for me by day and night nobody but myself knew."[37]

Others, such as Tellef John Israelsen (born 1826 at Kasfjord), claimed visitation by an angelic personage in a dream,[38] or, like Nils Evensen's father at Ringsaker about 1870, alleged religious instruction from a heavenly voice.[39] C. J. Zahl Hansen, a young apprentice in Bodoe, was awakened by a voice saying

"Conrad! It is seven o'clock!" just before his Mormon baptismal appointment in 1905--"the first supernatural phenomenon which I had experienced."[40]

A few claimed "instant conversion": Anna Helena Dyresen attended a Mormon meeting near Drammen in 1860, and "as soon as I heard them sing the first song: 'Come Therefore Come all and make no delay, our Saviors gone the same road we may, that road leads to life Eternal,' etc. . . . it seemed to me I had heard that message before, and I was only too glad to receive it."[41] Merchant Lars Iverson invited Torkel Torkelson to a Mormon meeting in Stavanger in 1880, "and the first psalm which was sung," said Torkelson, "filled my breast with the conviction that they were Children of God. The Spirit accompanied them."[42]

The Mormon World View

Mormon doctrine contained several other drawing cards, not least of which were promises to the righteous of a bliss-filled "life eternal" in the world to come, and economic security in the temporal Mormon Zion. Mormonism provided a "world view" akin to that defined by sociologist Thomas Luckmann as a "hierarchy of meaning through which everyday reality is linked with a universal order or moral universe [and which provides] meaning for the individual's life cycle, his internal conversations with himself, and for his death."[43] The Mormon "hierarchy of meaning" was tied to the basic tenet of "personal salvation by works," i.e., "after man is raised from the dead he will be judged according to his works, and will receive the reward, and be consigned to the [heavenly] sphere, exactly corresponding to his former [earthly] deeds, and the preparations or qualifications which he possesses."[44]

Good works included "paying tithing" (defined as "a tenth part of one's annual increase"); "living a respectable life"; "refusing to engage in gossip or support it"; and "helping with rent payments for meeting halls."[45] Joining the Mormons also required a "general reformation . . . which would have the converts, human beings by birth, become Saints by adoption, legalizing their common law marriages, ceasing card playing, abstaining from tobacco and strong drink, and paying their debts."[46]

As visualized by Mormon Apostle Parley P. Pratt in 1860, "resurrection and eternal life" in the Mormon heaven also "meant more than flipping the strings of a harp":[47]

> To contemplate man in his true light, we must as it were, forget that death is in his path; we must look upon him as an eternal, ever living being, possessing spirit, flesh and bones, with all the mental and physical organs, and all the affections and sympathies which characterize him in this world. Or rather, all his natural affections and sympathies

will be purified, exalted, and immeasurably increased.

Let the candidate for celestial glory forget, for a moment, the groveling sphere of this present existence, and make the effort to contemplate himself in the light of eternity, in the higher spheres of his progressive existence, beyond the grave--a pure spirit, free from sin and guile, enlightened in the school of heaven, by observation and experience, and association with the highest order of intelligences, for thousands of years; and clothed with immortal flesh, in all the vigour, freshness and beauty of eternal youth; alike free from pain, disease, death, and the corroding effects of time; looking back through the vista of far distant years, and contemplating his former sojourn amid the sorrows and pains of mortal life, his passage through the dark valleys of death, and his sojourn in the spirit world, as we now contemplate a transient dream, or a night of sleep, from which we have awakened, renewed and refreshed, to enter again upon the realities of life.

Let us contemplate, for a moment, such a being, clothed in the finest robes of linen, pure and white, adorned with precious stones and gold; a countenance radiant with the effulgence of light, intelligence and love; a bosom glowing with all the confidence of conscious innocence; dwelling in the palaces of precious stones and gold; bathing in the crystal waters of life; promenading or sitting 'neath the evergreen bowers and trees of Eden; inhaling the healthful breezes, perfumed with odours, wafted from the roses and pinks of Paradise.[48]

Mormonism was also an economic gospel with wide-ranging social and political implications, i.e., ". . . in the Church of Jesus Christ the spiritual and the so-called temporal cannot be separated, and the one is neglected at the peril of the other, but both parts must be attended to with equal conscientiousness."[49] Such a synthesis presupposed specific "means to combat the evils of this life" ["Midler mod dette Livs Onder"],[50] and Mormon leaders in Scandinavia perceived the two most pressing evils as poverty and tyranny.[51] As early as 1851, Scandinavian Mission President Erastus Snow decried "the misery and wretchedness of Europe," especially "the groanings of the masses under their almost insupportable burdens,"[52] and Mission President John

Van Cott described the "oppresson of the labouring classes" in 1855 under appalling conditions "worse than American slavery." "My desire," said Van Cott, "is that those bonds which now bind them may be broken."[53]

Against this necessitous backdrop, Mormons preached "The Gathering" to Utah or Zion--"to the land of Joseph, the land of inheritance."[54] "'The Gathering,' not polygamy, was Mormonism's oldest and most influential doctrine . . . the signature of the 'new and everlasting covenant' which the Lord had made with his elect in this last of all gospel dispensations." Gathering became synonymous with conversion, and "the convert who did not feel the pull was considered a queer fish in the Gospel Net."[55]

An early *Stjerne* editorial described the Gathering's purpose as emancipation of "the poor and enslaved who accept the Gospel," thereby providing them with "both temporal and eternal salvation,"[56] and President Brigham Young promised prospective immigrants a place "where honest work and diligence are rewarded with a just wage, where avenues for advancement are open to the lowborn and impoverished," and where faithful Saints could "erect the foundation of an indissoluble union between themselves and their children in the eternal scheme of human progression. . . ."[57]

Once in Utah, Saints could help build up the "Kingdom of God," whereby, "if we build it up, we shall be built up,"[58] and look as well to the Second Coming of Christ which would "bring no more than a change in administration . . . the benevolent monarchy of the King of Kings. The Kingdom, already established, would go right on, and its yeomanry would keep their inheritances, tilling their fields and tending their shops as they had done the day before."[59] In the words of William Mulder: "The materialism of this vision filled the Saints with security and made them eager to plant their vines and fig trees."[60]

Mormon Religious Practices, 1851-1920

Mormonism filled a variety of social and spiritual needs endemic to the "rootless urban poor" imbued with a "renewed desire for community," and of "uniting themselves with others of a like mind."[61] Mormons frequently expressed feelings of "spiritual union" with fellows members ("bonafide relatives in the Spirit" with whom they shared "feelings and sympathies to a much greater degree than with those related . . . by blood");[62] described "great happiness and encouragement, both temporal and spiritual" ["megen Glaede og Opmunttring [sic], saavel Timlig [sic] som Aandelig"], in the company of fellow Mormons;[63] and observed "that we [Mormons] soon become acquainted one with another, because we possess the same spirit, namely the spirit of unity and peace. . . ."[64] Englebrecht Olsen spoke in 1862 about "the hostility he had endured from friends and relatives at the time he left the society of the world," and summed up feelings of Mormon acculturation as follows: ". . . he felt, that the friends he had acquired in his [Mormon] brothers and sisters completely made up for his earlier loss; he felt as happy as he could possibly be."[65]

Basic to such feelings were a variety of spiritual experiences in conjunction with religious ceremonies or ordinances, social and recreational activities,[66] and numerous educational opportunities in the group setting. When combined with "factors of conversion" discussed earlier, these activities did much to insure that many Mormons, although unable to emigrate, remained faithful Latter-day Saints in Norway.

The most important observance for believers was the sacrament of the Lord's Supper, sometimes called "the holy sacrament." Because of persecution, the ceremony, at least before 1920, was confined to one meeting each month[67] where members ate bread and drank juice or wine in remembrance of the body and blood of Christ.[68] As revealed by depositions at court proceedings in Onsoe in 1852, Mormons based sacramental procedure on Biblical accounts of the Last Supper (I Corinthians 11:23-30):

> [Deposition of Niels Eriksen Ingulsroed on 15 October 1852]: Distribution of the Lord's Supper proceeded such that those who wished to partake fell down on their knees, together with the preacher, who held a prayer, and therein declared, that if there were any present who harbored bad feelings against any of their fellows, they were not worthy to receive the sacrament, whereupon he broke some common rye bread into pieces in accordance with Holy Writ, and put them on a plate, which was then passed around to those [who wished to partake], and from which they each took one piece. Thereafter, the cup containing the wine was likewise passed around, from which they drank.[69]

> [Deposition of Caroline Knudsdatter on 19 October 1852]: Dorius, who as priest administered the sacrament, took a common loaf of rye bread which he broke into pieces and placed on a plate, afterwhich he fell to his knees together with all who planned to partake of the sacrament, blessed the bread and thereafter walked around with the plate from which each one took a piece of bread. Likewise with the cup which held wine or fruit juice mixed with water, and distribution of the bread and the wine was accompanied by the same words used by Christ when he distributed the Lord's Supper to his disciples.[70]

A second common observance was so-called "fast day" where members went without food and drink for two or three meals, and contributed "money saved" to the poor. As early as 2 June 1853, Christian J. Larsen, Brevik Conference President, instituted fast day observances at Risoer "according to the rules of the Church, on the first Thursday in each month,"[71] and an article in *Stjerne* in 1859 urged members to observe regular monthly fast day, including "conscientious" payment of "fast offerings to the poor fund."[72]

Members also combined "special fasts" with group and individual prayer during times of difficulty, or when seeking special blessings from God. Mormons in Drammen, for example, fasted and prayed on 23 December 1855--the day before a court hearing against Mormon missionaries;[73] Mormons, such as Hans Olsen Magleby, fasted frequently while serving prison sentences;[74] and male priesthood holders often fasted and prayed for seriously-ill members, such as a special fast for Oslo YMMIA President Pauli Larsen who lay bedridden in 1894.[75]

Mormon "love feasts"--occasions featuring a simple meal, scripture reading, and the bearing of testimonies, were commonplace in the 1850s and 1860s, probably served more of a social than religious function, and gradually gave way to private parties and group outings. Typical was a love feast on 4 January 1862 at Brother Haarbye's in Halden where members "rejoiced in song and conversation until midnight, . . . it being highly gratifying to see the many young people who attended, which made for a pleasant get-together."[76]

Prayer meetings or "prayer circles" were another feature of Mormon religious life which disappeared before 1900, probably because fast meetings, including bearing of testimonies, served much the same function as "prayers which exhibited religious convictions." Mormons first attended meetings where "those present fell down and prayed aloud, one after another,"[77] at Fredrikstad in 1852, and the practice continued well into the 1890s.

Christian J. Larsen characterized Saints at prayer meetings in 1852 as exhibiting "much zeal in their prayers for themselves as also for those who had opposed us,"[78] and C. C. N. Dorius observed that members at prayer meetings in Oslo in 1861 "stood up" and expressed their feelings, whereas "others prayed to the Lord."[79] Prayer meetings evolved by the mid-1860s into revivalist gatherings encompassing both "praying and preaching,"[80] members in the 1870s habitually referred to "common prayer and testimony meetings,"[81] and Hans J. Christiansen described weekly prayer meetings in 1893 "well-attended by Mormons and non-Mormons of which some of the latter were deeply touched by the prayers as well as the testimonies which were borne."[82]

Special ordinances, such as "naming and blessing" young children, or administering to the sick, were performed in private homes, although children were also blessed in connection with prayer meetings, or after celebration of the Lord's Supper.

The priesthood holder giving a child a blessing audibly intoned the infant's Christian name, usually consecrated it to a life of good works, and conferred ancillary blessings of physical and mental health.[83]

Annointing and blessing the sick was the most widely practiced of all Mormon religious ordinances with the possible exception of baptism itself. As with baptism, celebration of the Lord's Supper, and blessing of infants, only properly ordained priesthood bearers could perform the ordinance, but whereas only baptized Mormons could partake of the Lord's Supper, or as a general rule have children blessed, annointment of the sick was available to Mormons and non-Mormons alike.

Mormon elders paired up to bless the sick: one elder annointed the subject's head with consecrated or holy oil, and the other "sealed" the annointing and pronounced a blessing "by the laying on of hands."[84] Elders also pronounced blessings not preceded by annointing with oil if oil was not available,[85] or if the person being blessed was non-Mormon.[86] Elders pronounced blessings for numerous indispositions, including bleeding during pregnancy,[87] toothache,[88] "possession by evil spirits,"[89] convulsions,[90] sorrow occasioned by death of a loved one,[91] and heart ailments.[92]

Confronted as early as 1854 by rumors Mormons possessed "supernatural powers" for healing all sicknesses and disease,[93] Mormon leaders described healing as conditional, i.e., only those who exercised faith could be healed.[94] A. S. Schou declared in 1878, for example, that the blessing of healing "is always present when the necessary faith is present,"[95] and missionary Goudy E. Hogan praised the Norwegian people in general in 1880 for having "a great deal of faith" so that "in administrations and in cases of sickness many times our administrations were rewarded with immediate recovery."[96]

Social Life in the Mormon Community, 1851-1920

Formalized observance aside, Mormons could hardly be accused of sabbatarianism, especially in light of "after-meeting" eating, drinking, dancing, singing, and speech-making lasting well into the night.[97] On Sunday, 16 December 1860, at Groenneloekken, for example, members "ate, drank, danced, sang and played with happy abandon until 2 A.M.,"[98] and Svend Larsen attended festivities at Kjoerven on Sunday, 4 November 1866, where members "played all night. . . ."[99] Popular Sunday amusements also included tours "in the . . . green fresh forest" where members "sang, played and prayed to God,"[100] long overland hikes combined with rowboating excursions,[101] and steamboat trips to remote islands where members "plucked blueberries, sang and played, ate, and drank coffee . . . under the shade of the trees in the delightful and free surroundings of nature."[102]

Sunday merrymaking did not fully accord with Church directives or wishes of mission leaders, however, and C. C. N. Christensen complained in 1865 about "dance and other games . . . sponsored by the [Oslo] Congregation" ["Dands og andre Lege som . . . foretages af Menigheden"], and the detrimental effect on investigators (non-Mormons interested in Mormon doctrine) who "on Sunday morning see us preach repentance and faith in this work with a loud voice, urging preparation for the Coming of The Lord and the Judgment of the World, and in the afternoon see us, young and old, priests and elders, whirling 'round in the dance hall manner in full public view."[103]

Mission leaders subsequently curtailed Sunday festivities in a directive published 1 December 1865 to Mormons throughout Scandinavia advising abstinence from "dance and other noisy entertainments" ["Dands og andre larmende Forlystelser"] viewed offensive to serious investigators who believed "that a holy and God-fearing life does not accord with such amusements."[104] Other pronouncements included Oslo Conference President Weibye's statement (1871) that "President A. Carrington in England, and President Canute Peterson in Copenhagen do not want us to dance when abroad among the Outsiders,"[105] and Andrew Jenson's explication in 1877:

> God-fearing and righteous persons can engage in dancing and other innocent pleasures without sinning or experiencing harmful results. Past experience has meanwhile convinced the presiding brethren in Scandinavia that gatherings of the Saints to which young people are invited occasion greater risks, and young brothers and sisters [are] tempted to take greater liberties, than is the case among the Youth in Zion. Thus, it has been deemed necessary from time to time to deny the Saints at large certain amusements which would have been completely permissible were it not for the fact that the participants were adversely influenced by the sinful and ungodly ways of the world before they accepted the Gospel.[106]

Confronted with these and other pro forma proscriptions, most Mormons stopped dancing altogether, but continued Sunday afternoon picnicking, group singing, and games in forests or parklands. A few younger Mormons circumvented restrictions on "public dancing" by gravitating to "private birthday parties" where violin music and dance groups were de riguer,[107] or by wheedling special concessions from sympathetic branch leaders.[108] Others attended "gentile dance halls"[109]--an aberration which prompted partial modification of anti-dance policy a la Oslo Conference President Hans J. Christiansen's vouchsafement of "light dancing" ["let Dans"] in private homes early in 1894.[110]

Although requirements of the work week relegated most Mormon outings to Sunday afternoons, there was no dearth of weekday activities: early morning field trips at 4:00 A.M.;[111] "midnight flower-picking excursions" against a backdrop of "beautiful weather, dead calm sea and midnight sun";[112] sailboat rides;[113] formal evening dinners;[114] and birthday parties.[115] Christmas tree festivals highlighted Christmas observances with dances around the tree, "bread [and] butter with sandwich Cake and Chocklate," songs and recitations, "more dance around the tree," and "harvesting" of the tree (distribution of presents) "to old and young."[116]

Special occasions included celebrations of silver or golden wedding anniversaries;[117] special mission and branch jubilees;[118] special birthday festivals;[119] and "going away" parties like that for Oslo Conference President Hans J. Christiansen in 1895:

> . . . it was a genuine surprise to him [President Christiansen] when we entered the beautiful decorated Hall which was embellished with green birches flowers and roses all over till it more resembled a fairy ground than a plain meeting House. When we were all seated the choir sang. Prayer, and singing again. after which 31 girls from the age of 7-11 years old dressed in white marched in a circle in front of President, (or Father) Christiansen, for they all loved him like a father, and placed each one of them a fine boquet of flowers in his lap till he got more of them than he could hold and they had to be placed on a table. a [sic] lot of young boys were also circled around the girls. Parents and Saints in general stepped forth greeting Bro. Christiansen. After the situation was fully taken in Prest. C. arose and spoke & gave expression of thanks while he was moved to tears. His remarks lasted about 45 minutes. Then the whole assembly, children in center, marched around the Hall singing for about one hour. A general chat was the next thing on the programme and a pleasant separation.[120]

Education in the Mormon Community, 1851-1920

"[Mormonism] craves and gives a full and complete scholastical education," declared F. F. Hintze at Fredrikstad in 1885. "In a few words it elavates it [its] followers from ignorance to the highest degree of perfection and places them in time above all. . . ."[121] Hintze further claimed "the Gospel of Jesus Christ comprised all truth and that its adherents was expected to become learned men and not as some supposed, that to be a Christian a man must be an ignoramous."[122]

Other sermons urged Mormons in Norway to "seek wisdom and education,"[123] advised women to "educate their spirit through reading good and useful books,"[124] and counseled young people "to study the good books of the church and historical and scientific works."[125] Leaders also imparted "counsel, instruction and advice in both temporal and spiritual affairs" in issues of the mission periodical, Stjerne.[126]

"Mormon schools" in Norway usually operated under touch-and-go circumstances, i.e., school populations or teaching staffs vanished overnight during periods of heavy emigration; missionaries sandwiched English instruction between pressing administrative duties; and civil and religious authorities expressed open skepticism. But the diversity of instruction at Mormon day schools, Sunday schools, English schools, choral societies, Young Men's and Women's Mutual Improvement Association (YMMIA and YWMIA) discussion groups, sewing circles, and industrial courses, was nevertheless little short of amazing.[127]

Ex-schoolteacher Mons Pedersen founded the first "writing & arithmetic school" under Mormon auspices 31 August 1856 at Fredrikstad.[128] Pedersen's school soon floundered--as did one taught by Brother Oerstad in Oslo in 1861--[129] but Oslo Conference President George M. Brown revived the schooling tradition in 1865 by moving "that Elder Isaackson's wife hold school for the children of the Saints in this place [Oslo]," and proposing a "Sunday School for all the Saints to come on every Sunday morning before meeting, so that all could have a privilege to learn to read, write and cipher as those things would be learned."[130]

Mormons could not legally establish day schools before 1867 when Oslo Bishop Jens L. Arup used his post as foreman of the School Commission to flaunt widespread opposition and allow Mormons full licensing privileges "on condition that officers of the School Commission conduct annual investigations for accreditation purposes." All Mormon children, meanwhile, were "exempted" from religious instruction.[131]

Mormon Sunday school teachers in Oslo supplemented day school instruction with "spelling, reading [and] interpretation" classes for children in the early 1870s, and boasted a Sunday school enrollment of more than forty pupils in 1872 who regularly competed for such "scholarship prizes" as "writingbooks, penholders, Slates and Slate Pencils."[132] Mormon leaders also encouraged adult participation in "Sunday & Writing school," but enrollment never exceeded a high of thirteen registrants in 1872;[133] theological classes for adults, and Bible or Book of Mormon history classes for children, entirely replaced secular instruction in Mormon Sunday schools in the late 1870s, a result of increasing secularization of the curriculum and new mandatory attendance statutes in government schools during the 1860s and 1870s, inability of Mormon day schools to keep pace with constantly changing government regulations, and resulting demise of Mormon day schools as children returned en masse to government institutions.[134]

Mormon English schools (missionary night schools) consistently attracted an average of thirty to forty pupils in Oslo during the 1860s, 1870s, and early years of the twentieth century.[135] Ole Harmon Olsen, a regular attender during the 1860s, described his brother John's achievement as class valedictorian about 1869:

> My first English lesson was the song, "O Ye Mountains High," which had just been composed by Penrose. My brother John and I learned it together. We were both eager, painstaking students. The L.D.S. missionary night school now offered a prize to the student who could define the greatest number of English words. There were forty pupils ranged against one another in two groups. John and I remained standing to the last, he on one side and I on the other. The contest was very, very close. Finally John defined the word "admirable" just a little more accurately than I had defined it. He won the Norwegian-English Dictionary. We had it in the family anyway and it proved very helpful to us.[136]

Mormon singing instruction dated from 1855 when members in Oslo organized a choir at Ruseloekbakken,[137] and several "large choirs" were holding forth in branches by 1860, including a "choral society" organized in 1859 at Fredrikstad by Mons Pedersen "who understood music and could play the violin."[138] Pedersen also reorganized the Oslo Branch Choir in 1861 after a brief revival in 1860 when "a few brothers began singing again" under "Chorister Johnsen from Bergen" who was paid five dollars a month to rehearse the choir once a week for two hours at a time.[139] Chorister Andreas Weihe led approximately forty vocalists in weekly rehearsals at Munkedamsveien 17, Oslo, during the mid-1860s.[140] Weihe's assistant, Ole Harmon Olsen, described "many choice friends . . . and much joy in my musical endeavors,"[141] further enhanced in 1871 when Oslo Mormons purchased an organ to accompany the choir and heighten "religious animation" at branch meetings.[142]

Excommunication from the Mormon Community, 1851-1920

Ex-members of the Mormon community included the disaffected, "sinners," and "religious cranks"--persons consigned to "spiritual death" ["aandelig Doed"][143] in accordance with "God's Law" ["Guds Lov"].[144] As noted in chapter V, about a third of all excommunicants returned to the Mormon fold,[145] but that still left about one in four permanently expelled from "the fellowship of the Saints" in the years before 1920.[146] Excommunication rates as a percentage

of convert baptisms were highest during the early decades--
33 percent in the 1850s; 38 in the 1860s; 31 in the 1870s; 29
in the 1880s. Later years marked declining rates: 14 percent
in the 1890s; 11 in the years 1900-1909; and 17 in the period
1910-1919.[147]
    There were several reasons for the decline: the revivalist
fervor of Mormon preaching in the 1850s and early 1860s often
attracted fanatics "carried about by every wind of doctrine"
whose zeal offended more sober members, and challenged the authority
of branch leaders; branch leaders in the early decades--usually
natives of Norway--frequently acted on their own authority unlike
"Utah" branch leaders of the 1870s and later decades who served
in an increasingly centralized organization, and conferred with
conference and mission leaders before initiating excommunication
proceedings; centralization of mission organization generated more
formalized and stringent baptismal procedures including "screening"
and "pre-baptismal" interviews; some embittered members opted
voluntarily for excommunication during periods of heavy persecution;
until a pronouncement by the First Presidency in 1897 discouraged
the common practice of "rebaptizing" already baptized members,
some leaders in Norway considered excommunication "temporary
censure" easily nullified by rebaptism.[148]
    While offenses diverse as adultery,[149] addiction to alcohol,[150]
"lying and backbiting,"[151] worldliness,[152] obfuscation,[153] "disobedience to counsel,"[154] "fighting . . . and hollering and
noice [sic] in the street,"[155] "lack of attendance to duties,"[156]
"disrespect for the preesthood [sic],"[157] and theft[158] merited
excommunication, at least according to some leaders, others
urged compassion and pragmatism. Mission President Canute Peterson,
for example, when asked whether a young couple guilty of adultery
should be excommunicated from Drammen Branch in 1872, replied
"our mode of procedure here in such cases . . . is to let the
parties get married, after first taking away the Priesthood
from the male transgressor then after the marriage of the two,
permitting them to be rebaptized. . . ."[159] Oslo Conference
President J. C. A. Weibye likewise decided against extreme punishment
in the case of an unmarried couple caught in adultery in 1872:
". . . we concluded in as much that he [the offender] is young
in the Church (9 months old) and a young talented man to let
him keep his standing and them both to be Rebaptized, and keep
it secret if it can be secret? if she not is in familyway."[160]
    Scandinavian Mission President Anthon H. Lund told a Priesthood council in 1884 to "act as men" by forgiving a married
adulterer, since revealing the man's sin to his wife "might
ruin their happiness forever," and the council could "keep it
a secret so that it never need come to his wife's knowledge."[161]
Daniel H. Wells, President of the the European Mission, responded
similarly in 1885 when asked whether a Norwegian woman who "had
murdered her child before she came into the church" should remain
a Mormon in good standing. As reported by Anthon H. Lund: "Bro
Wells wanted us to not make a scandal in the Church but when

transgression was not known to more than one or two to let such renew their covenant and keep it quiet."[162]

The Norwegian Experience with Mormonism: A Retrospective Evaluation

In concluding <u>The Church of England, the Methodists and Society 1700-1850</u>, Anthony Armstrong emphasized twin elements of social change and individual attainment: ". . . social change could only take place by the use of the machinery that was there, and much of the machinery was religious. The process of rising in society was one which the sects--and particularly Methodism--facilitated. It provided the experience of oratory and business, the wherewithal for self-education. . . ."[163]

Much the same could be said of Mormonism in Norway. Mormonism posed a threat to the civil servant estate by reintroducing elements of religious nonconformity and civil "disobedience" authorities believed had long since been quashed with the imprisonment of Hans Nielsen Hauge. As the first American religionists in Norway, Mormon emissaries decried political and religious tyranny, and spread a gospel of economic, political, and religious sanctuary in a Zion built on pillars of hard work and social equality.

Mormons could take credit for numerous "social changes": Norwegian authorities enacted civil marriage statutes only after Mormon "common-law" marriage became sufficiently problematic in the 1860s; de facto title to Norwegian real estate vested in the Trustee in Trust of the Mormon Church, the Mormon Prophet in Utah, challenged Norwegian laws prohibiting ownership by non-residents; and Mormon insistence their children be exempted from Lutheran religious instruction in public schools prompted new legislation with implications for non-Mormon dissenter groups and ethnic minorities.

Burials according with Mormon custom and belief received de facto recognition from ecclesiastics despite contrary official missives; Mormon worship services--despite legal injunctions and the "non Christian" label--revealed the limits of jurisprudential fiat in a nation and age increasingly receptive to liberal ideas; efforts by Utah missionaries to enter Norway after World War I eventually led to an admissions policy based on law instead of religious bias.

But the real yardstick of Mormon success or failure ("actualization of the message of salvation") lay in thousands of individual lives Mormonism affected for bad or good. Lutheran priests themselves often cited "visible improvements" in lives of Mormon converts, such as observations by Sven Brun, parish priest of Oslo's Trinity Congregation in 1859, that Mormons were generally law-abiding citizens and that,

> . . . while it is certainly true that none are more <u>internally</u> detached from the civil

> society in which they live, than [the Mormons],
> and that in the event of difficult circumstances,
> they, least of all, could be depended upon
> to rally to the cause of city and country,
> I have, nevertheless, heard from reputable
> persons, that a great change has taken place
> in many homes since the husband or *wife*
> or both joined with this sect [the Mormons].[164]
> (Italics mine.)

Authorities also noted Mormon abstinence from alcohol,[165] described "a certain morality" exhibited by a Mormon cottager who "truly improved his life in several categories and clearly displays a good deportment,"[166] and "confidentially" described Mormons as "sober, law-abiding, industrious and generally decent people such that one could only wish there were as many good citizens in the population at large."[167]

Mormons willing to pay the price through "legalizing their common-law marriages, ceasing card playing, abstaining from tobacco and strong drink," and "paying their debts,"[168] reaped tangible rewards in healthy lives free of addiction and governed by a strong moral ethic. Their religion also provided spiritual and social community, and opportunities for individual betterment

> . . . by serving as missionaries and singing in
> choirs, and by entering Sunday-school work, Young
> people's organizations, and other activities.
> In addition, they took . . . active part in
> picnics, dances, and many other forms of social
> life, . . . studied English, [and] learned
> personal and household cleanliness. . . .[169]

There is little doubt many Mormon immigrants shaped new lives for themselves and children on the Utah Frontier qualitatively all out of proportion to the sordid, bleak existence in Oslo slums or the impoverished Norwegian countryside plagued by over-population and traditional social stratification. Utah also afforded an environment largely free of persecution and social ostracism.

Most immigrants believed with Canute Peterson that Norway was "a good Country to be boren [sic] in, but a better one to Emigrat [sic] from,"[170] and, like Andrew Amundsen's mother, "shed tears of joy" as they sailed out Oslo Harbor forever away from the land of their birth.[171] George M. Brown's description of Mormons departing Oslo by steamer on 25 April 1865 was typical:

> . . . we glided out of the harbor amid the cheers
> of our brethren and sisters who stood on the
> shore. No tears were shed; no murmurings were
> heard from any one that they had to leave
> relatives and friends behind, but every one
> appeared cheerful and happy as becomes Latter

Day Saints who are starting to the promised land. We were sixty four souls in all and we all took deck passage as we did not like to be one above the other, but have all things in common. As we passed down the fjord the weather was fine and all felt well and to thank God for their deliverance from Babylon.[172]

Mormonism in Norway meant other things. It meant, for example, places of special historical attachment like Rostad Farm near Drammen "situated in a very romantic little vale among or surrounded on three sides by cliffs and forest and bounded on the other side by the Christiania Fjord . . . the scene of many persecutions, though none of a very serious character," and a place where "elders have had a home and an asylum . . . for many years when they have preached in these parts."[173] Mormonism meant a lonely devotion by twenty-four-year-old Samuel [Saamund] Gudmundsen, Mormon lumberjack, who climbed a hill near Christiansand one morning in 1856, prayed, sang, and "rejoiced exceedingly over God's goodness to mankind."[174]

Mormonism meant the evening baptism of Herr Tharde Sensen of "Fredrikshavn ved Jorde Moelle [Larvik]" described by J. L. G. Johnson in 1897:

> . . . we walked down to the beach to perform the ordinance . . . and performed it on his [Sensen's] own property, off the shoreline of Larvik Fjord, a very beautiful place, and Gundersen performed the baptism and I confirmed him by the laying on of hands. . . . The man's cat followed us down to the beach, which was quite a distance from the house, and sat on a stone there until we were finished and them accompanied us on our return journey . . . .[175]

There were numerous standards of success against which Mormonism in Norway could never measure up: the number of converts--approximately eight thousand in the years 1851-1920--was a drop in the bucket compared with total Norwegian population; the Mormon presence in Norway occasioned widespread rancor and suspicion, and was far from a public-relations coup; Mormonism often meant permanent separation of husband and wife as in the case of "a flock of five children ranging in age from 4 1/2 to 15 years" who boarded an emigrant steamer in Oslo in 1916. "Their father," observed Hans J. Christiansen, "went to Utah about two years ago, and since that time their mother had died in Fredrikstad, and now they were leaving to be with their father."[176]

Mormonism also meant divided families such as the hauntingly symbolic scene on an Oslo pier in 1885 when

> . . . a boy that Bro. Klinger [a missionary
> from Utah] was sending home [to Utah] started
> to cry violently when he was to say goodby
> with his Mother & Grandmother, so Brother
> Klinger took and carried him down in the
> ship by force and tried to passify [sic]
> the boy, which he also succeeded in doing.
> as [sic] the boy wanted to go all the time
> the worst kind, but just at the moment he
> was to say good by he gave away, as did
> also the mother, making a very unpleasent
> [sic] scene. A Stranger tryed to take the
> boy away from Brother Klinger and when he
> could not do it he fetched the police and
> upon investigation it was found the police
> could not hinder the boy from going as it
> was a mutual agreement with all parties
> concerned that the [sic] should go and be
> adopted into brother Klingers family.[177]

For Norwegian Mormons, classifying Mormonism in Norway as "successful" or not would hinge on qualifiers of personal experience, and the mix of psychological scars, intangibles like testimony, rigors of pioneer life, and physical and emotional effects of persecution, imprisonment or disownment. Perhaps the genial intermingling of these "factors of success" was best personified by Canute Peterson, the old <u>harding</u> whose Norwegian experience with Mormonism spanned the gamut of conversion in a Haugian settlement at Fox River, Illinois; crossing the plains to Utah; pioneering missionary work and imprisonment in Norway; leadership of the Scandinavian Mission; and retirement in "Ephraim's peaceful vales" (Sanpete County, Utah). While returning home from a mission to Norway in 1856, Peterson wrote his wife Sarah Ann as follows:

> I must tell you one thing I have not told you
> before, And that is about myself. I am very
> much plagued with rheumitism in my hips, so that
> I limp considerable when I walk. I can say that
> I am broke down in my body, but not in Spirit.
> <u>I am glad to tell you that I am broke down for
> the Kingdom's Sake</u>.[178] (Italics mine.)

On 1 April 1920, August Severin Schow assumed leadership of the newly created Norwegian Mission of the Church of Jesus Christ of Latter-day Saints. To the casual observer, it might well have seemed Norway had formally come of age in the ranks of Mormon missions worldwide. But far from being a change which conferred mission status on a country Mormon authorities in

Utah deemed a promising missionary field, the change was motivated by necessity and was effected amidst rather gloomy prospects.

During the final year of War hostilities (1918), Scandinavian Mission President Hans J. Christiansen faced increasing difficulty in obtaining permission to visit members in Norway. Norwegian passport authorities held up visa permission for weeks at a time, Christiansen had an equally difficult time obtaining re-entry permission to Denmark, and his last visit to Norway in 1919 was a fiasco--in order to visit Mormon leaders and carry out other duties, Christiansen overstayed his visa and became an illegal resident whose nighttime forays marked the only time he came out of hiding.[179]

The problem stemmed from the Norwegian Law of 13 July 1917 which established passport requirements for Americans. Passport authorities in Oslo bent the letter and intent of the law by denying resident visas to American Mormons or Norwegian-born American citizens who professed Mormonism. Creation of a separate Norwegian Mission was therefore a move by Mormon authorities to ease administrative duties of the mission president in Copenhagen, but, more importantly, an effort to avoid travel and visa entanglements by making inter-Scandinavian travel by a mission president unnecessary.[180] In light of visa and other restrictions, newly appointed Mission President Schow, a resident of Richmond, Utah, evidently entered Norway on 21 March 1920 by posing as a tourist. This assumption is further buttressed by the fact that nearly all Utah Norwegians called as Mormon missionaries through 1923--passport restrictions were eased late in 1923--<u>were called after arrival in Norway as tourists</u>![181]

As described in chapter IV, most larger Mormon branches in Norway remained intact throughout World War I although forced to rely on local as versus Utah leadership, and despite the fact few if any Utah Mormons remained to carry on proselyting activities. By 1920, only one Utah missionary remained in Norway; larger branches, with the exception of Oslo, were incompletely organized--there were not enough leaders to staff branch and auxiliary positions; and branches like Arendal were completely staffed by women who conducted meetings and performed administrative and leadership duties. President Schow, however, did describe "viable organizations" in many branches, and also declared "there was no lack of spiritual nourishment" among the membership.[182]

In some ways, the situation of Mormonism in Norway in 1920 resembled that in the 1850s--civil authorities were attempting to restrict arrival of missionaries from Utah and harass and deport Mormon emissaries who attempted to work in the Country; nearly all branch administrative affairs were in the hands of local, native-born members; and prospects for missionary work and future growth were extremely uncertain. But there were also meaningful differences: unlike the 1850s, the Church in 1920 could look back on a seventy-year tradition of ever-increasing accommodation with civil authorities--at least before 1917; there was room for optimism in the fact that by 1920, Catholics, Jews and other religious minorities had gained numerous freedoms denied them throughout the

1800s; Mormonism's residual membership base in 1920 was much more stable and less threatened by impending waves of emigration than at any time in the past; the number of Mormon priesthood holders in 1920 compared favorably with earlier years; the total number of members--1,287--was the highest in history with the exception of the years 1917-1919;[183] and Mormon auxiliary organizations--Sunday schools and young men's and women's organizations--were firmly established in larger branches.

Very importantly, mission president, August S. Schow, was himself willing to implement approaches to preserve the status quo and forge new links with a most important resource--the youth of the Church:

> President August S. Schow did much to involve young people in the Church; his work consisted primarily of shoring up the residual base, strengthening the internal chain of command and encouraging an independent approach. He needed the enthusiasm and energy of youth and accordingly gave them [young people] responsibility and assignments.[184]

The situation somewhat resembled events in 1852 when a group of seven or eight blond, blue-eyed Danes in their early twenties set out to win the Land of the Midnight Sun for Mormonism. They won instead months-long stints in prison, hatred of various Lutheran clerics and their parishioners, and the undying admiration of a few converts heartened by the courage of their younger brethren. It was much the same spirit which moved Mormon youth under President Schow in 1920 to reset sails of an idealism and sense of mission which had somewhat flagged until billowed again by bracing winds of persecution and a renewed call to arms.

APPENDIX 1

AN ANNOTATED LIST OF THE FIRST NORWEGIAN
CONVERTS TO MORMONISM

Who were the Norwegian converts to Mormonism during the Nauvoo Period? Of approximately 150 converts, we know the names of sixty-two (forty-one men and twenty-one women) gathered from Nauvoo Temple Endowment Rolls, the Mormon "Early Church Information File" (ECIF), private journals, Mormon pioneer company lists and the 1850 Federal Census of Utah Territory. Of those we know about, six were "Sloopers" (passengers on the sloop Restoration in 1825). The majority emigrated from the area around Stavanger City (twenty-five) or Tinn in Telemark (twenty). Thirty can be positively identified as children of farmers (gaardmenn) compared with six identified as children of cotters (husmenn). Most joined the Mormons while in their twenties or thirties. After the martyrdom of Joseph Smith in 1844, most of the Norwegian Mormons appear to have cut their ties to organized religion, and approximately ten percent joined the Reorganized Church of Jesus Christ of Latter Day Saints; only a remnant came west to the Salt Lake Valley. Following is an annotated list of some of the first Norwegian converts to Mormonism. Wherever possible, the date of birth, place of birth, and parentage of the members have been verified from Lutheran (Norwegian) parish registers or histories. This marks the first time reliable dates and places of birth have been ascertained for many of those on the list, and the first time names of these early Norwegian members have been compiled. The Norwegian name of the person is given first (if the person involved went by more than one farm or place name, other names are given in parenthesis) followed by the name the person used in America (Americanized name) in brackets. In some cases, the name the immigrant used in America is entirely different from the Norwegian name. Some of the members have never been located in Norwegian parish or clerical district registers, and, in such cases, only the Americanized form of the name is given even though it is obviously a common corruption of a Norwegian name and spelling. Names are listed alphabetically by first given name.

AAGAAT OEYSTEINSDATTER BAKKA [Ellen Augusta Sanders Kimball]: Born 11 April, christened 27 April 1823 Atraa, Telemark, Norway (PR Atraa); daughter of Oeystein Sondresen Bakka and Aase Olsdatter Rommeraasen (Svalestuen 317). Came to America with her parents 1837. Left an orphan when malaria struck the Beaver Creek Settlement in Illinois 1838 and killed both parents (Rosdail 498) (FGS Gealta). Joined the Mormons at La Salle County, Illinois, 1842.

Married Brigham Young's counselor, Heber C. Kimball, at the Mormon Temple in Nauvoo, Illinois, 7 January 1846 and bore him five children (FGS Hodges). One of three pioneer women to arrive in the Great Salt Lake Valley with the original company of Mormon Pioneers 24 July 1847; the first Norwegian to set foot on Utah Territory (Ulvestad 204) (Jenson II:772). Died Salt Lake City, Salt Lake, Utah, 22 November 1871 (Jenson II:772).

ANDERS LARSEN MOELI (HEIER) [Andrew Hayer]: Born 20 November, christened 3 December 1815 Mael, Telemark, Norway; son of Lars Andersen Heier (Moeli) (Folseland) and Ane Olsdatter Sandveien (PR Mael). Came to America with his parents 1842 (Hayer 5), and married a fellow immigrant named Oloug [Olena] Olsdatter Oedegaard on the boat while crossing the Atlantic (Quamme 459) (Hayer 14). Married his second wife, Ellen Danielson, late 1840s at Miller, La Salle, Illinois. No children. "He was a man of very decided opinions. He had many friends and of course some enemies. He was outspoken; if he did not like a man he very soon told him so. However, he was very benevolent, helpful, and kindhearted to those who were sick or were in need of assistance. When the Elders of the Church of Jesus Christ of Latter-day Saints had converted and baptized his brothers, Christian and Oliver, he not knowing anything of their doctrine, declared he would kill the Elders on first sight. But after learning more of their claims he cooled down and after a time united with the order and never in after life would he listen to any other doctrine. He was an Elder and did some preaching. He is kindly remembered by many of the poorer people" (Ibid.). Was a Seventy in the Mormon Priesthood and endowed at Nauvoo Temple 6 February 1846 (NR 306). Died 26 February 1899 Miller, La Salle, Illinois (Hayer 10).

ANDREAS OLSEN: Christened 6 March 1808 Mandal, Vest-Agder, Norway; son of Ole Bergesen and Marthe Elene Torgiesdatter (PR Mandal). Already a Mormon 25 October 1841 when he received a patriarchal blessing from Hyrum Smith, brother of the Mormon Prophet Joseph Smith, at Nauvoo, Illinois (ECIF). Probably the first Norwegian Mormon since the main group of Norwegians at Fox River Settlement was first visited in March 1842 by the Mormon missionary, George Parker Dykes.

ANNE LARSDATTER FOLSELAND (HEIER) [Ann Hayer Elefson]: Born 7 August, christened 9 October 1831 Gransherred, Telemark, Norway; daughter of Lars Andersen Heier (Moeli) (Folseland) and Ane Olsdatter Sandveien (PR Gransherred). Came to America with her parents in 1842 (Hayer 5). Was baptized a Mormon late 1844 or early 1845 (Peterson 15). Married Elef H. Elefson in 1853 and had eleven children (Hayer 20). Died 12 October 1910 Miller Township, La Salle, Illinois (Ibid. 10).

ANNA JOHANNA JONSDATTER HELLAND (HERVIK) [Hannah Dahl]: Christened 22 October 1793 Rennesoey, Rogaland, Norway; daughter of Jon

Jonson Helland (Hervik) and Anna Kjeldsdatter Varaberg (PR Rennesoey) (Sunnanaa 207-08). Married (1) 21 July 1822 Svend Jacobsen Nordre-Aasen at Tysvaer, Rogaland, Norway (PR Tysvaer), and had two sons by him (FGS Johnson). Came to America 1830 with her husband and children on the second emigrant ship from Norway and after a six-month ocean journey, went straight to Kendall Colony, New York (FGS Johnson) (Rosdail 54). [Svend Jacobsen Nordre-Aasen died about 1832 and Anna married Endre Salvesen Dahl--Andrew Dahl--May 1832 at Kendall and bore him two children (Rosdail 57).] Baptized a Mormon along with three of her sons by William Levet 12 August 1842 (FGS Johnson) and endowed at Nauvoo Temple 27 January 1846 (NR 206). Arrived with her husband in Great Salt Lake Valley 31 October 1849 and appears on the 1850 Census of Davis County, Utah (Census 21). Died at the home of her son, John, 17 December 1878 aged 86 Lehi, Utah, Utah (Rosdail 177, 182).

CHRISTIAN LARSEN MOELI (HEIER) [Christian Hayer or Hyer]: Born 8 September, christened 4 October 1817 Mael, Telemark, Norway; son of Lars Andersen Heier (Moeli) (Folseland) and Ane Olsdatter Sandveien (PR Mael). Immigrated with parents 1842 (Hayer 5) (Quamme 459) and baptized a Mormon by Ole Olsen Omdal (Heier) 15 June 1843 (ECIF). Was a Seventy in the Mormon Priesthood (Ibid.) and received his endowment at Nauvoo Temple 6 February 1846 (NR 290). Personally met Brigham Young, Heber C. Kimball, and Parley P. Pratt, Mormon Apostles, in the fall of 1844. Arrived Great Salt Lake Valley 25 October 1849 in Ezra T. Benson's Company and moved to Davis County, Utah, 1850 where he appears on the 1850 Census (Census 31). A polygamist; his three wives (Kari Ericsdatter Haugen, Liv Ericsdatter Haugen and Rozina Shephard) bore him sixteen children (Hayer 15-16). Settled Richmond, Cache, Utah, 1860 and served many years as president of the Richmond Cooperative Mercantile Institution. Served as counselor in a Mormon bishopric (Ibid. 16-17). Died 20 September 1901 Richmond, Cache, Utah (FGS Kemp IV).

CHRISTOPHER CHRISTOPHERSEN HERVIK [Christopher Jacobs]: Born 4 January, christened 16 February 1820 Tysvaer, Rogaland, Norway, the illegitimate son of Christopher Christophersen Hervik and Anna Johanna Jonsdatter Helland (Hervik) [Hannah Dahl] (PR Tysvaer) (FGS Johnson) (FGS Little). Immigrated to Kendall Colony, New York, with his stepfather and mother 1830 (Rosdail 54). Baptized a Mormon 12 September 1842 (FGS Little) and was a Seventy in the Mormon Priesthood (ECIF). Wrote the Reverend Yance Jacobs 6 April 1846 while prospecting in Wisconsin Territory as follows: "I have had many hard and terble times with the gentilz here but that has not shaekend my feith the least. Iff the church goes to California my foot shall trod the soyl on California iff god lets me live. Give my best respect to all the saints at Norway" (Rosdail 125). Journeyed to Salt Lake Valley 1849 and married Mary Margaret Dodge 24 December 1849 Salt Lake City, Salt Lake, Utah. Settled Lehi, Utah, Utah, shortly thereafter

(FGS Little). Called by Brigham Young to go 300 miles south of Lehi and start a new settlement in Cedar City (Cedar City, Iron, Utah) 1853. Returned to Lehi 1857 (Rosdail 178) and by December 1858 was in Toquerville, Washington, Utah, where he lived until ca. 1870. Was the father of ten children and died 17 August 1907 Alton, Kane, Utah (FGS Little).

ELIZABETH JACOBS: Born 10 June 1823 Bergen Diocese, Norway; daughter of Jacob Jacobsen and wife Maulina (ECIF) (FGS Nielsen). Supposedly sister to Jens Jacobsen Boerke [Yance Jacobs] of Aardal, Rogaland, Norway, but this not confirmed by the Aardal Parish Register. [Jens Jacobsen Boerke did have a sister born 28 September 1823 at Aardal named Giertrud and it is possible this Giertrud changed her name to Elizabeth upon arrival in America. Jens Jacobsen Boerke was the son of Jacob Knudsen Eggeboe and Magla Jensdatter Boerke, and his parents supposedly died of cholera soon after emigrating from Norway in 1836 (Rosdail 510) (Eikeland 57).] Married Shure Olsen 18 May 1847 Illinois and bore him six children. (Both she and her sister, Ellen Sophia [Sarah Ellen] Jacobs, were polygamous wives of Shure Olson) (FGS Nielsen). Among members of La Salle Branch who voted to sustain the Twelve Apostles and go west 1848 (JH 26 February 1848, pp. 3-5), and appears on 1850 Census Salt Lake County, Utah (Census 77). Died 10 June 1891 Bridge, Cassia, Idaho (FGS Nielsen).

ELEAS or ELI JOHNSON: Born 14 November 1807 "Bergen, Bergen, Norway"; son of "Yan Olson" (ECIF). A Seventy in the Mormon Priesthood and endowed at Nauvoo Temple 27 January 1846 (NR 306).

ELLEN SOPHIA or SARAH ELLEN JACOBS: Born 11 February 1830, "Bergen County, Norway"; daughter of Jacob Jacobsen and wife Maline (ECIF). Supposedly sister to Jens Jacobsen Boerke [Yance Jacobs] of Aardal, Rogaland, Norway, but this relationship not confirmed by the Aardal Parish Register. [Jens Jacobsen Boerke did have a sister born 15 June 1830 at Aardal named Ragnilda (PR Aardal), and it is possible that this Ragnilda changed her name after arriving in America. Jens Jacobsen Boerke was the son of Jacob Knudsen Eggeboe and Magla Jensdatter Boerke, and his parents supposedly died of cholera soon after coming to American in 1836 (Rosdail 510) (Eikeland 57).] Came to Utah with the Norwegian Company 1849 (Rosdail 176-77) and lived with her brother-in-law, Shure Olson, and family (Census 77). Married Shure Olson 30 November 1851 Salt Lake City, Salt Lake, Utah, as a polygamous wife. (Her sister, Elizabeth, was Olson's other wife) (IGI). The mother of five children born in Salt Lake City; died 2 August 1919 (FGS Jensen).

ENDRE SALVESEN LINDLAND (DAHL) [Andrew Dahl]: Christened 25 April 1784 Sogndal, Rogaland, Norway; son of Salve Endresen Lindland and Siri Abrahamsdatter (Rosdail 176). Left his farm, Lindland,

1821 and brought his wife, Bertha Mortensdatter Eikeland, and five children to Stavanger. Probably had connections with Quakers in Stavanger. One of the "Sloopers" on the ship <u>Restoration</u> 1825. (His wife was eight months pregnant and decided to remain behind with the agreement that she and children would come to America at a later date.) Served as ship's cook (Ibid. 10, 28). [According to family tradition, his first wife, Bertha, remarried in Norway as per information brought by Endre's son, Salve, who came to New York about 1828 (Ibid. 97).] Married the widow, Anna Johanna Johnsdatter Helland (Hervik), 1832 Kendall, New York (Ibid. 57), and had two children by her (Ibid. 199-200). Joined five other families for the move to Fox River, Illinois, 1834 (Ibid. 66) and was converted a Mormon by George P. Dykes about March 1842 as were his stepsons, Svend and John. Traveled to Nauvoo after his conversion to give Joseph Smith one hundred sheep and cattle and money from Norwegian Mormons for building the Nauvoo Temple. Was a guest in Nauvoo of the Prophet Joseph Smith and held a lengthy conversation with him (Ibid. 105). Received a patriarchal blessing 27 May 1845 Nauvoo (ECIF) and was a High Priest in the Mormon Priesthood when he took out his endowment at Nauvoo Temple 27 January 1846 (NR 205). Decided to follow the apostate, James J. Strang, of Voree, Wisconsin, April 1846 (Rosdail 125), but reconsidered and pledged to follow Brigham Young to Utah January 1848. Arrived Great Salt Lake Valley 31 October 1849 with the Norwegian Company and moved to Dry Creek (Lehi), Utah County, 1851. Died and buried Lehi, Utah, Utah, about 1860 (Ibid. 125-26, 175, 177-78, 181).

<u>ENOCH DANIELSEN NEDREBOE</u> [Enoch Daniels]: Born 7 June, christened 17 June 1821 Fossand, Rogaland, Norway; son of Daniel Gitlesen Nedreboe and Ingebor Pedersdatter (PR Fossand). Baptized a Mormon December 1843 by Gudmund Haugaas (ECIF) and was a Seventy in the Mormon Priesthood (ECIF). A brother to "Mr. Danielson" [Gitle Danielson?] visited by Canute Peterson and Gudmund Haugaas at Muskego, Wisconsin Territory, late 1844 (Peterson 15). Appears in 1850 Census of Salt Lake County, Utah, along with Jerusha who was evidently his first wife (Census 121). Married Rebecca Jane Brinkley 1872 at Thistle, Utah, Utah, and they had four children. Died 15 April 1894 Payson, Utah, Utah (FGS Rammell).

<u>ERICH GAUTESEN RAMBERG (MIDTBOEEN) (HAUGEN)</u> [Erik Goudason Midboen Hogan]: Christened 25 July 1802 Aal, Buskerud, Norway; son of Gaute Erichsen Ramberg (Midtboeen) and Margit Knudsdatter Svenningsgaard (PR Aal) (Svalestuen 317). Married (1) 6 June 1827 Tinn, Telemark, Norway, Kari Sondresdatter Bakka; she was forty-two and he was twenty-five. After his first wife died, married (2) Helga Knudsdatter Noersteboe 26 March 1829, Austbygdi, Telemark, Norway; she was twenty years old and he twenty-seven (PR Austbygdi) (Svalestuen 317). Sold his farm, Haugen, to his brother, Knud Gautesen, 1836 and led a company of three families to Fox River Settlement, Illinois (Einung 231, 233, 280) (Svalestuen 317). "How they got information about America is nowhere stated, but

the fact that they went directly to the Fox River Settlement is evidence that they had been in communication with the earlier emigrants from Stavanger" (Anderson 231-32). Lost two of his children on the journey to America. About 1841, moved his family from La Salle County, Illinois, to Lee County, Iowa, about ten miles west of Nauvoo. Was baptized a Mormon 23 January 1843 after listening to the preaching of Gudmund Haugaas (Hogan 1-4) (FGS Hogan). Journeyed to Utah 1848 and, while crossing the plains, buried one of his tiny children. Settled Bountiful, Davis, Utah, and his son, Charles Peter, died there 1850--the first person to die in Bountiful (FGS Hogan) (Jenson III:409-10). Was a Mormon missionary along with Canute Peterson in Norway 1853-1855 where he suffered physical abuse and severe persecution (Peterson 46). A polygamist and had three wives who bore him seventeen children. Died Woods Cross, Davis, Utah, 29 June 1876 (Jenson III:410) (FGS Hogan) (Census 31) (ECIF).

ERICH HENDRICHSEN SAEBOE [Ira Saby]: Born 2 March, christened 28 March 1830 Hjelmeland, Rogaland, Norway; son of Hendrick Erichsen Riveland (Saeboe) and Magla Jonasdatter Oesthus (PR Hjelmeland). Promised to support the Twelve Apostles and go west in January 1848 (JH 26 February 1848, pp. 3-4). Appears with parents in the 1850 Census Salt Lake County, Utah (Census 122).

EVER AFTERDAHL: Born 1 May 1823; endowed at Nauvoo Temple 27 January 1846 (NR 207).

GAUTE ERICHSEN HAUGEN [Goudy Hogan]: Born 16 September, christened 11 October 1829 Austbygdi, Telemark, Norway; son of Erich Gautesen Ramberg (Midtbocen) (Haugen) and Helga Knudsdatter Noersteboe (PR Austbygdi). Came to Fox River, Illinois, with parents 1837 and baptized a Mormon 12 February 1843. Heard Joseph Smith, the Mormon Prophet, preach. ["I remember," said he, "that he [Joseph Smith] had on a light colored linen coat with a small hole in each elbow of his coat sleeve. I remember thinking that he was not a proud man and that his [this] very noble experience inspired me with great confidence and faith that he was a great prophet of the Lord" (Hogan 1,6) (Jenson IV:593).] Arrived Great Salt Lake Valley with his parents 22 September 1848 (Hogan 14). A Mormon bishop. Mormon missionary to Norway 1877-1879. A polygamist with twenty-five children (at the time of his death had forty-eight grandchildren). Died 30 January 1898 Richmond, Cache, Utah (Jenson IV:593) (Adair 59) (JH 30 January 1898, p. 6) (FGS Hatch).

[GITLE?] DANIELSEN Mentioned in Canute Peterson's Autobiography: "We began our labors in Muskego among the Norwegians there. Here we met the Danielson's and Lars Heier. . . . Brother Danielson, his wife, and his brother Enoch [Enoch Danielsen Nedreboe] . . . joined the church. Here we organized a Branch of the Church, and Brother Danielson was called to preside over the Branch [November 1844 in Muskego, Wisconsin Territory]" (Peterson 15). Probably the Gitle Danielsen Nedreboe born 20 August and christened 28 August 1808 Fossand, Rogaland, Norway; son of Daniel Gitlesen Nedreboe and Ingebore Pedersdatter (Ellingsen 342). Evidently the same Gitle Danielsen who lived at Rennesoey, Rogaland, Norway, as a stock and dairy farmer (immigrated 1839) (Anderson 306, 309, 313).

MRS. [GITLE?] DANIELSEN: Converted to Mormonism about November 1844 (Peterson 15).

GUDMUND DANIELSEN HAUGAAS [Goodman Hougas]: Christened 8 March 1800 Tysvaer, Rogaland, Norway; son of Daniel Johannesen Haugaas and Brethe Hansdatter Fjon (Rosdail 408). Went to Rennesoey, Rogaland, Norway, as a young man and then to Stavanger 1820 where he worked as a servant. A wheelwright (Ibid. 10). Fond of books and loved to read (Anderson 105). One of the "Sloopers" who emigrated on the sloop Restoration 1825. Married Guri Thormodsdatter Foss-Eigeland (Madland) [Julia Madland] 15 June 1826 Kendall, New York (Rosdail 445); she bore him seven children (Ibid. 467). Arrived La Salle County, Illinois, with the first Norwegian settlers 1834 (Anderson 105) and served as a frontier doctor although he had no medical training of a professional nature (Ibid. 95-96). Helped establish the first Norwegian-language newspaper in America, Nordlyset, 1846. The paper's motto was: "Liberty and Equality without regard to rank or nationality" (Rosdail 123-24). One of Haugaas's main objectives in founding the paper was to "in every respect befriend, and so far as possible, assist the oppressed" (Ibid. 124). Among the first Norwegians in Fox River Settlement to accept Mormon doctrine preached by George P. Dykes March 1842 and baptized late April 1842 (Peterson 12). Dykes described Haugaas as "a man of strong mind, and well skilled in the scriptures," and ordained him an Elder in the Mormon Priesthood and set him apart as president of the La Salle Branch. By January 1843, had spent three weeks in Sugar Creek Settlement, Iowa, and baptized ten Norwegians into the Mormon faith. Accompanied Ole Heier on missionary journey to Wisconsin Territory and met with some success among Norwegians in area southwest of Milwaukee (now Rock County, Wisconsin) (Rosdail 105) (Hayer 6). Endowed at Nauvoo Temple 7 February 1846 (NR 347). Married Kari Christophersdatter Hervik 26 June 1847 La Salle County (Rosdail 129) and had one child by her (Ibid. 467). [Following the murder of Joseph Smith 27 June 1844, Brigham Young and other Mormon leaders came to Fox River Settlement and purchased land from Haugaas and Jacob Andersen Slogvig (Rosdail 106) and laid out a city called Norway located about "three miles southwest of the present town of Norway which it preceded by many years" (Ibid.). The two main streets were named Young and Hougas and here the Mormons hoped to build a temple. Haugaas, who by this time was a Mormon High Priest, was to be sent to Scandinavia to gather converts to the new Zion (Ibid. 108). Dissension soon entered the Norwegian camp and several, including Haugaas, joined with the apostate James J. Strang of Voree, Wisconsin, in April 1846. By July 1846, the Strangites were in disarray, and by 1848, Haugaas was back in the Mormon fold with plans to journey west with the main body of Mormons (Ibid. 124-26).] Grew ill with cholera while serving as community doctor and died on his farm between Ottawa and Norway, La Salle, Illinois, 28 July 1849 (Ibid. 131) (Anderson 106). [His oldest son, Thomas, joined the Reorganized Church of Jesus Christ of Latter Day Saints in Fox River and served as pastor of that church in La Salle County, Illinois, for fifty years (1868-1918) (Rosdail 419).]

GURI THORMODSDATTER FOSS-EIGELAND (MADLAND) [Julia Madland Hougas]: Christened 29 October 1809 Hoeyland, Rogaland, Norway; daughter of Thormod Jensen Madland (Foss-Eigeland) and Siri Iversdatter Seldal (PR Hoeyland). Accompanied parents to America on the <u>Restoration</u> 1825. Married "Slooper" Gudmund Danielsen Haugaas 15 June 1826 Kendall, New York, when sixteen years old (Rosdail 445). Was endowed at Nauvoo Temple 7 February 1846 (NR 347) and died La Salle County, Illinois, 24 December 1846 (Anderson 105).

HALVOR LARSEN MOELI (HEIER) [Oliver Hayer]: Born 24 March, christened 3 April 1820 Mael, Telemark, Norway; son of Lars Andersen Heier (Moeli) (Folseland) and Ane Olsdatter Sandveien (PR Mael). Baptized a Mormon by Ole Olsen Omdal (Heier), a relative, 15 June 1843. (He [Halvor] had come to America with his parents in 1842.) A Seventy in the Mormon Priesthood and received his endowment at Nauvoo Temple 6 February 1846 (NR 306) (Hayer 5) (ECIF) (Quamme 459). Worked as a shoemaker in Norway, but in America preferred to farm. Married Julia Elefson April 1845 and had eight children. Was greatly afflicted by asthma and slept sitting in a chair. Joined the Reorganized Church of Jesus Christ of Latter Day Saints 1860 and was made a priest in that Church (Hayer 18). Lived many years at Danway, La Salle, Illinois. Owned two hundred acres in Miller, La Salle, Illinois, 1877 and as a young man carted wheat to Chicago with ox teams and sold it for fifty cents a bushel. Served as school director in Miller, Illinois (La Salle 647) and died 31 October 1886 (FGS Kemp III).

HANS LARSEN FOLSELAND (HEIER) [Hans Hayer]: Born 28 July, christened 8 September 1822 Gransherred, Telemark, Norway; son of Lars Andersen Heier (Moeli) (Folseland) and Ane Olsdatter Sandveien (PR Gransherred). Came to America with parents 1845 (Hayer 5) (Quamme 459). Baptized a Mormon 25 December 1844 or 1845 by Canute Peterson. A Seventy in the Mormon Priesthood (ECIF) and endowed at Nauvoo Temple 6 February 1846 (NR 290). Married Sarah Elefson 17 March 1849 Miller, La Salle, Illinois, and she bore him nine children (FGS Kemp I). Had blue eyes, dark hair and was five feet, ten inches tall. Lived forty years on a comfortable farm in Miller, La Salle, Illinois, and then moved to Sheridan, La Salle, Illinois, 1886. Moved to Lamoni,

Decatur, Iowa, 1894 and died there 17 or 21 April 1905 (Hayer 19) (FGS Kemp I).

HELGA OEYSTEINSDATTER BAKKA [Harriet Sanders Kimball]: Born 7 December 1824, christened 2 January 1825 Atraa, Telemark, Norway; daughter of Oeystein Sondresen Bakka and Aase Olsdatter Rommeraasen (PR Atraa) (Svalestuen 317). Came to America with parents 1837 and lived at Beaver Creek Settlement, Illinois. (The Beaver Creek Settlement was east of Fox River Settlement near the Indiana Border.) [The area of the Beaver Creek Settlement was very swampy, and when malaria struck in 1838, most of the settlers died including Helga's parents (Rosdail 498) (Anderson 184) (FGS Hambleton).] Escaped to Fox River Settlement where she joined the Mormons in 1842. Endowed at Nauvoo Temple 3 January 1846 (NR 94) and, like her sister, married Brigham Young's counselor, Heber C. Kimball (married 4 November 1850) (FGS Hambleton). Died 5 September 1896 Meadowville, Rich, Utah (JH 5 September 1896, p. 3).

HELGA KNUDSDATTER NOERSTEBOE [Helga Hogan]: Christened 15 March 1809 Atraa, Telemark, Norway; daughter of Knud Olsen Noersteboe and Helga Toresdatter (PR Atraa) (Svalestuen 317). Married Erich Gautesen Ramberg (Midtboeen) (Haugen) 26 March 1829 Austbygdi, Telemark, Norway, and came to America 1837 (PR Austbygdi) (Svalestuen 317). Baptized a Mormon 30 January 1843 Lee County, Iowa (ECIF), and came to Utah 1848 (Jenson III: 410). Died 21 February 1884 Woods Cross, Davis, Utah (FGS Hogan).

HENDRICH ERICHSEN RIVELAND (SAEBOE) [Henry Saby]: Born 18 June, christened 21 June 1792 Aardal, Rogaland, Norway; son of Erich Sivertsen (Sjursen) Bratthetland and Anna Hendrichsdatter Ytreneset (PR Aardal) (Eikeland 440). Married Magla Jonasdatter Oesthus 12 June 1822 Hjelmeland, Rogaland, Norway (PR Hjelmeland). Came to America 1836 and settled at Fox River with his family. (His daughter, Anna, came to America many years later as a widow from Hjelmeland, Rogaland, Norway, and resided in Strand, Adams, Iowa, in 1895) (Anderson 152). A Seventy in the Mormon Priesthood (ECIF) and endowed at Nauvoo Temple 27 January 1846 (NR 208). Appointed president of the La Salle [Norway] Branch January 1848 and one of those who pledged to support the Twelve Apostles and go west to Utah in 1848 (JH 26 February 1843, pp. 3-4). Came to Utah with the Norwegian Company 1849 (had three wagons, three horses and ten oxen) (Rosdail 176). Appears on the 1850 Census Salt Lake County, Utah, with wife and five dependents (Census 122) and died Utah (place and date not known) (Anderson 152).

HERBORG KNUDSDATTER GAREN [Herborg Peterson]: Born 20 March, christened 22 March 1792 Eidfjord, Hordaland, Norway; daughter of Knud Oestensen Tveite (Garen) (Sysendal) and Helga Nilsdatter Garen (PR Eidfjord). Married Peder Jonsen Maurset 16 May 1815 Eidfjord, Hordaland, Norway (PR Eidfjord), and was the mother of the famous Knud Pedersen Maurset (Canute Peterson) (1824-1902)

(Kolltveit 98-101). Immigrated to America with husband and son 1837. Widowed soon after arrival in Fox River Settlement (Peterson 10-11). Baptized into the Mormon Church 12 August 1842 (Ibid. 12). Lived with Johanna Dahl as an invalid many years and died June 1848 at Fox River Settlement, La Salle, Illinois (Ibid. 17).

INGABOR JOHNSON: Born January 1818. Endowed at Nauvoo Temple 27 January 1846 (NR 206). Probably the wife of Eleas (Eli) Johnson.

JACOB ANDERSEN SLOGVIK [Jacob Anderson Slogvig]: Born 15 June, christened 21 June 1807 Tysvaer, Rogaland, Norway; son of Anders Knudsen Slogvik and Anna Jacobsdatter Fikstvedt (Rosdail 410) (NR 82). A file maker and carpenter and brought files and tools with him on the sloop Restoration 1825. [While the Restoration was being unloaded in New York Harbor, Slogvik's tools slipped out and fell into the harbor waters (Rosdail 30).] Evidently a Quaker (Ibid. 9); married Serine Thormodsdatter Foss-Eigeland (Madland) [Serena Madland] 1 March 1831 Kendall, New York, in the woods near Lake Ontario (Ibid. 468) (Anderson 101) and had ten children (Rosdail 473). One of the original settlers of Fox River Settlement 1834 (Ibid. 66). Moved to Kleng Peerson's new settlement about sixty miles west of Hannibal in Shelby County, Missouri, March 1837, but by December 1837, was back in Fox River Settlement (Ibid 92). [On 24 December 1837, a destitute immigrant, Osmund Guttormson Meling, arrived with his wife and family in Fox River Settlement. Gudmund Haugaas was away at the time, and Julia, Gudmund's wife, admitted the Meling Family into her home. Gudmund Haugaas was upset to find the family in his home upon his return and took them to his brother-in-law, Jacob Andersen Slogvik: "Gudmund was so glad to get rid of this 'trash' that he grabbed the bundles they carried and went in Slogvig's door ahead of the immigrants. Slogvig who was fond of a joke, pretended to be very angry with him for bringing these foreigners into his house, and threatened to have him arrested. This quite frightened Gudmund...." (Ibid. 89).] Joined the Mormons at Fox River and took out endowment at Nauvoo Temple 1 January 1846. (By this time he was a Mormon High Priest) (NR 82). Started west 1848 and made it as far as Council Bluffs, Pottawattamie, Iowa, where he entered a claim on six hundred acres. Never did continue the journey west with the other Mormons (Rosdail 126). He and family made the long trek to California in a covered wagon pulled by oxen and settled at a place called Soscol in Napa County just north of San Francisco Bay 1854. Acquired 555 71/100 acres of swamp and other marshlands as well as fifty acres of ranchland. Raised grain and livestock. Died there 5 May 1865 (Ibid. 425) (Anderson 101).

JENS JACOBSEN BOERKE [Yance Jacobs]: Born 11 May, christened 18 May 1821 Aardal, Rogaland, Norway; son of Jacob Knudsen Eggeboe (Boerke) and Magla Jensdatter Boerke (PR Aardal). Came to America with parents about 1836, and when they died of the cholera, was raised by a pioneer family named Green in the area of Danway, La Salle, Illinois (Rosdail 510, 539). Married Caroline Rossedal [Rosdail], daughter of "Sloopers" Daniel Stensen Rossedal and Britha Johanne Ovesdatter Rossedal, 20 May 1847 La Salle County, Illinois, and had six children (Ibid. 539-43). Endowed at Nauvoo Temple 27 January 1846 (NR 207). Started out to follow Brigham Young's trail west in a wagon 1847, but soon turned back (Rosdail 125). Moved to Livingston County, Illinois, 1864 and settled about a mile south of Emington. ["This was all wide prairie and Jens' house was the first" (Ibid. 510).] Died Livingston County, Illinois, 28 October 1865 (Anderson 99).

JOHANNES LARSEN LANDENES [John Larson]: Born 15 October, christened 16 October 1831 Avaldsnes, Rogaland, Norway; son of Lars Larsen Landenes and Marthe Tostensdatter (PR Avaldsnes) (FGS Thompson). Baptized a Mormon 8 November 1843 by John Rillion (ECIF) and appears on 1850 Census of Salt Lake County, Utah (Census 191). Married Amelia Weight 8 October 1855 Salt Lake City, Salt Lake, Utah, and had seven children. Died 6 August 1871 South Cottonwood, Salt Lake, Utah (FGS Thompson) (FGS Shipley).

JOHN SVENDSEN NORDRE-AASEN [John Jacobs]: Born 7 December, christened 11 December 1825 Tysvaer, Rogaland, Norway, son of Svend Jacobsen Nordre-Aasen and Anna Johanna Jonsdatter Helland (Hervik) [Hannah Dahl] (PR Tysvaer). Came to America with parents 1830 and settled in Kendall, New York (Rosdail 54). Baptized a Mormon 12 August 1842 by William Levet (FGS Johnson) (ECIF) and crossed the plains to Utah 1849 (Rosdail 175). Headed for California and the goldfields with two of his brothers 10 November 1849 (Ibid. 177); returned to Utah 1851 and lived in Lehi, Utah, Utah (Ibid. 178). Called by Brigham Young to help establish a settlement in what is now Cedar City, Iron, Utah, 1853 and remained there four years (Ibid.). Married Elizabeth Coleman 27 October 1852. Married Harriet Austin 23 March 1867 Salt Lake City, Salt Lake, Utah. (Both wives were from Bedfordshire, England) (FGS Rolfe) (FGS Sales). Had ten children by each wife for a total of twenty children. (Eight died young.) Died 17 January 1919 Lehi, Utah, Utah, aged ninety-four years (Ibid.).

JONAS HENDRICHSEN SAEBOE [Jonas Saby]: Born 7 January, christened 9 January 1827 Hjelmeland, Rogaland, Norway; son of Hendrich Erichsen Riveland (Saeboe) and Magla Jonasdatter Oesthus (PR Hjelmeland). Immigrated to Fox River Settlement 1836 with parents (Anderson 152). Endowed at Nauvoo Temple 27 January 1846 (NR 208) and one of those in La Salle Branch who promised to support the Twelve Apostles and go west (January 1848) (JH 26 February 1848, pp. 3-4) (ECIF).

JOERGEN PEDERSON: A Norwegian schoolteacher chosen by Haugians in Fox River Settlement to administer the Lord's Supper. (He also administered the Lord's Supper in the Indian Creek Settlement near Leland, Illinois.) Heard about the Mormons about the time he intended to become a Lutheran minister, and joined the Mormons soon thereafter (Anderson 399).

KARI ERICHSDATTER HAUGEN [Caroline Hogan Hyer]: Born 21 July, christened 9 October 1831 Austbygdi, Telemark, Norway; daughter of Erich Gautesen Ramberg (Midtboeen) (Haugen) and Helga Knudsdatter Noersteboe (PR Austbygdi). Came to Fox River Settlement with parents 1837 (Svalestuen 317) and baptized a Mormon either November 1844 (FGS Hogan) or 1 May 1845 (FGS Kemp IV). Married Christian Larsen Moeli (Heier) [Christian Hayer or Hyer] 23 November 1850 Salt Lake City, Salt Lake, Utah, and bore him eleven children (Ibid.). One of Christian Hyer's three polygamous wives. Another of the wives was her sister Liv [Lovina] (Ibid.). Appears in 1850 Census of Davis County, Utah (Census 31), and lived in Bountiful, Davis, Utah, until 1860 when she moved with her husband to Richmond, Cache, Utah (FGS Kemp IV). A good cook and housekeeper noted for her skill in making straw hats. ("She always prided herself on having the whitest front porch, which could be done by scrubbing the native lumber flooring with lye, which made the boards very white") (Hayer 15). Died 8 December 1917 Cove, Cache, Utah (FGS Kemp IV).

KARI LARSDATTER MOELI (HEIER) [Caroline Hayer Anderson]: Born 27 October, christened 7 November 1812 Mael, Telemark, Norway; daughter of Lars Andersen Heier (Moeli) (Folseland) and Ane Olsdatter Sandveien (PR Mael). Married (1) Oestein Olsen Bakka 1833 (Quamme 459). Came to America 1842 (Hayer 5) and settled in what is now Rock County, Wisconsin (Ibid. 6). After the death of her first husband married (2) Anders B. Andersen (Andrew B. Anderson) (Ibid. 5). The mother of six children by her first marriage (Ibid. 13) and four by her second marriage (Ibid. 5). Died "suddenly while calling on one of her neighbors," 5 February 1856 Illinois (Ibid. 10, 13). Baptized a Mormon late 1844 or early 1845 (Peterson 15).

KNUD PEDERSEN MAURSET [Canute Peterson]: Born 7 May, christened 9 May 1824 Eidfjord, Hordaland, Norway; son of Peder Jonsen Maurset and Herborg Knudsdatter Garen (PR Eidfjord) (Jenson I:362) (Peterson 7). Did not attend school, but his mother taught him religious hymns, The Lord's Prayer and The Ten Commandments (Peterson 9). Came to America with parents 1837 and settled at Fox River Settlement, La Salle, Illinois. First heard Mormonism preached by George P. Dykes March 1842 (Ibid. 12) and baptized a Mormon 12 August 1842 La Salle County, Illinois. Ordained a Seventy in the Mormon Priesthood Nauvoo 1844 and filled a mission with Gudmund Haugaas among Norwegians in Muskego (Wisconsin) in the Winter of 1844-1845 (Jenson I:362). Endowed at Nauvoo Temple 27 January 1846 (NR 208). Married Sarah Ann Nelson, daughter of "Sloopers" Cornelius Nilsen Hersdal and Kari Pedersdatter Hesthammer, five miles east of Kanesville, Iowa, 2 July 1849. [They were married by Apostle Orson Hyde (Peterson 21) (Anderson

106). Sarah Ann (Nelson) Peterson was a niece of the famous Cleng Peerson (Anderson 182), and was reportedly the second Norwegian child born in America (Ibid. 407).] Came to Utah 1849, and his first child, Peter Cornelius Peterson, was born in Old Salt Lake Fort, Salt Lake City, Salt Lake, Utah, 22 June 1850--the first Norwegian male child born in Utah (Peterson 21). Called to settle Lehi, Utah, Utah, 1850. Mormon missionary in Norway 1853-1855 and helped establish Mormon congregation in Oslo 8 December 1853. Called as Mormon Bishop in Ephraim, Sanpete, Utah, 1867 and was so effective in gaining the trust of rampaging Indians he became known as the "White Father." President of the Scandinavian Mission of the Mormon Church (comprising Denmark, Sweden and Norway) 1871-1873. President of the Mormon Sanpete Stake 1877-1902 (Jenson I:362-63). Had twenty children by three polygamous wives (Peterson 131). Died 14 October 1903 Ephraim, Sanpete, Utah (Jenson I:362-63) (Kolltveit 98-101) (FGS Christiansen) (FGS Peterson) (FGS Peterson I) (FGS Willcox).

LARS ANDERSEN HEIER (MOELI) (FOLSELAND) [Lars Hayer]: Christened 19 October 1785 Gransherred, Telemark, Norway; son of Anders Erichsen Heier and Karen Malene Marcusdatter (FGS Van Orden). Came to America 1842 (Hayer 5) (Quamme 459) and settled in what is now Rock County, Wisconsin. Lived in crude log cabin where he was visited by two Mormon Elders, Ole Olsen Omdal (Heier) and Gumund Haugaas. (Ole Olsen Omdal [Heier] was a son of Lars Hayer's niece) (Hayer 6). Joined the Mormons, as did most of his children, about 1843, and by 1845 had moved to Fox River Settlement, La Salle, Illinois (Ibid. 6). About five feet six inches tall and weighed about 150 pounds. Died April 1863 Lamoni, Decatur, Iowa (Ibid 7, 10). [It is not known whether Lars Hayer's wife, Ane Olsdatter Sandveien, ever joined the Mormons. He married her 3 January 1812 at Tinn, Telemark, Norway (PR Tinn), and she died in 1843 at Rock County, Wisconsin (FGS Van Orden).]

LARS LARSEN STEKKEN [Lars Larson]: Born 10 January, christened 14 January 1825 Kvam, Hordaland, Norway; son of Lars Larsen Stekken and Martha Tostensdatter (PR Kvam). Baptized a Mormon 23 January 1843 or February 1843 (FGS Baker) (ECIF). Married Mary Adelphia Bellows 1848 (FGS Baker), and appears on 1850 Census Salt Lake County, Utah (Census 191). A Seventy in the Mormon Priesthood having been ordained 9 April 1845 (ECIF), and father of ten children; died 7 February 1903 St. George, Washington, Utah (FGS Baker).

LARS OLSON: Born 29 September 1807 Norway. A Seventy in the Mormon Priesthood and endowed at Nauvoo Temple 27 January 1846 (ECIF) (NR 207). May be the Lars Olson Dugstad born Voss 1807, immigrated 1839, and died Albion, Dane, Wisconsin, 1863 (Anderson 329-30).

LIV ERICHSDATTER HAUGEN [Lovina Hogan Hyer]: Born 14 July, christened 14 August 1836 Austbygdi, Telemark, Norway; daughter of

Erich Gautesen Ramberg (Midtboeen) (Haugen) and Helga Knudsdatter Noersteboe (PR Austbygdi). Came to Fox River Settlement, La Salle, Illinois, with parents 1837 (Svalestuen 317), and baptized a Mormon April 1845 (FGS Hogan). Appears in 1850 Census Davis County, Utah (Census 31), and was polygamous wife (along with her sister, Kari [Caroline]) of Christian Larsen Moeli (Heier) [Christian Hayer or Hyer] whom she married 7 March 1854 Salt Lake City, Salt Lake, Utah (FGS Ovard). The mother of three children. Lived Richmond, Cache, Utah, most of her married life and died there 16 September 1862 (Ibid.).

MADDE (MADDY) MADISON: Born 10 or 12 September 1812 Norway (ECIF) (NR 207). A Seventy in the Mormon Church and endowed at Nauvoo Temple 27 January 1846 (NR 207). Earlier ordained a priest in the Mormon Priesthood along with several others from La Salle County, Illinois, at meeting at Newark, Kendall, Illinois, 18 May 1844 (Smith VI:400). One of those in La Salle Branch in January 1848 who promised to support Brigham Young and go west to Utah (JH 26 February 1848, pp. 3-4), but does not appear in 1850 Census of Utah.

MAGLA JONASDATTER OESTHUS [Melinda Saby]: Christened 4 August 1798 Hjelmeland, Rogaland, Norway; daughter of Jonas Johnsen Oesthus and Walborg Olsdatter (PR Hjelmeland) (Berge 26). Married Hendrich Erichsen Riveland (Saeboe) 12 June 1822 Hjelmeland, Rogaland, Norway (PR Hjelmeland), and came to America with husband 1836 (Anderson 152). Appears in 1850 Census Salt Lake County, Utah (Census 122).

MARGITH BJOERNSDATTER MIDGAARD (FLAATEN) [Martha Anderson Heier]: Born 18 September, christened 27 September 1812 Hovin, Telemark, Norway; daughter of Bjoern Andresen Lyngflaat and Margit Olsdatter Flaaten (PR Hovin) (Svalestuen 318). Immigrated to America 1837 (Anderson 236-37) and married Ole Olsen Omdal (Heier) about 1838 (Hayer 21). Mother of seven children (FGS Kemp II) and joined the Mormons with her husband at Fox River late April 1842 (Peterson 12) (ECIF). Took out endowment 6 February 1846 at Nauvoo Temple along with her husband (NR 290). Died before 1868 near Danway, La Salle, Illinois (FGS Kemp II).

MARIA SOPHIA HENDRICKSON [Mary Simpson]: Born 7 March, 18 March or 13 May 1818 "Tronyon [sic], Norway" (may be Trondheim, but a check of Trondheim parish registers reveals no christening entry for her); daughter of Christian Henderson or Hendrixon and Martha or Maret (ECIF). Married Tosten Sebioernsen Tronrud [Thorsten Simpson] and bore him at least four children (FGS Nielson) (Census 88). Was endowed at Nauvoo Temple 6 February 1846 (NR 305) and is listed on 1850 Census Salt Lake County, Utah (Census 88).

NILS or NELSON HANSON: Born 26 March 1800 or 1805 "Bergen, Bergen, Norway" (may be Bergen Diocese); son of "Hans Allison" and Ellen

(ECIF). Endowed at Nauvoo Temple 17 January 1846 (NR 149) and evidently married Marilla Terry (she born 2 July 1823 in Albion, Canada) (Ibid.). A Seventy in the Mormon Priesthood (ECIF).

ODEN or ADEN JACOBS: Born 1 December 1809 or 1820 "Luning, Norway" (may be Loening, Loenning or Loeining even though parish registers or parishes which contain such a farm or place name have been searched for his christening without result); son of "Goodman" and "Betsy" (ECIF). A Seventy in the Mormon Priesthood and endowed at Nauvoo Temple 29 January 1846 (NR 227). One of those in La Salle Branch who promised to support the Twelve Apostles and go west 1848 (JH February 1848, pp. 3-4).

OLE JOERGENSEN SOERBOE [Ola or Oley Johnson]: Born 7 May, christened 10 May 1816 Rennesoey, Rogaland, Norway; son of Joergen Joergensen Soerboe and Kisti Tostensdatter Boe (PR Rennesoey) (Sunnanaa 389). Immigrated to America 1839 (Sunnanaa 389) and endowed at Nauvoo Temple 27 January 1846 (NR 207) (ECIF).

OLE OLSEN OMDAL (HEIER) [Ole Heier]: Born 1 June, christened 20 June 1813 Hovin, Telemark, Norway; son of Ole Olsen Maarvik (Omdal) and Kari Christiansdatter Heier (PR Hovin) (Svalestuen 318). Came to America 1837 and lived La Salle County, Illinois (Anderson 236-37). ["In Thelemarken he was regarded as a pious Reader, and had conducted Haugian meetings, and when he first came to the Fox River settlement he was active in holding gospel meetings in the interest of the Haugians. He is said to have been of a most winning personality and to have possessed remarkable gifts as a speaker" (Ibid. 400).] Was married to Margith Bjoernsdatter Midgaard (Flaaten) [Martha Anderson] about 1838 (Hayer 21) and she bore him seven children (FGS Kemp II). The first Norwegian converted by Mormon missionary, George P. Dykes, at Fox River, La Salle County, Illinois, and baptized late April 1842 (Peterson 12). Served "first as an elder and later as a bishop" (Rosdail 102). A Seventy in the Mormon Priesthood and was endowed at Nauvoo Temple 6 February 1846 with his wife (NR 290). Chosen to preside over La Salle Branch of Norwegian Mormons about 1843 (Smith V:395). Accompanied Gudmund Haugaas to Wisconsin Territory as Mormon Elder (in what is now Rock County, Wisconsin) in Winter of 1842-1843, and converted Lars Andersen Heier (Moeli) (Folseland) [Lars Hayer] and several of his children (Hayer 6). Went by the title "Preacher Ole Hayer." Left the Mormons and joined the Baptists after the murder of the Mormon Prophet, Joseph Smith, 1844 (Ibid. 21) (Anderson 237). Left Illinois 1868 and traveled to Boone, Boone, Iowa (Hayer 21). Died 16 November 1873 Danway, La Salle, Illinois (FGS Kemp II).

OLOUG OLSDATTER OEDEGAARD [Olena Hayer]: Born 16 September, christened 4 November 1820 Hovin, Telemark, Norway; daughter of Ole Hansen Oedegaard and Sigrid Jonsdatter (PR Hovin). Married Anders Larsen Moeli (Heier) [Andrew Hayer] on the brig Washington while crossing the Atlantic 1842 (Quamme 459) (Hayer 14). Endowed 6 February 1846 Nauvoo Temple (NR 305); died late 1840s, probably Miller, La Salle, Illinois (Hayer 14).

PEDER HENDRICHSEN SAEBOE [Peter Saby]: Born 6 September, christened 20 September 1835 Hjelmeland, Rogaland, Norway; son of Hendrich Erichsen Riveland (Saeboe) and Magla Jonasdatter Oesthus (PR Hjelmeland). Came to America 1836 with parents (Anderson 152). One of those in La Salle Branch 1848 who promised to go west and support the Twelve Apostles (JH 26 February 1848, pp. 3-4). Appears in 1850 Census Salt Lake County, Utah (Census 122).

SERINE THORMODSDATTER FOSS-EIGELAND (MADLAND) [Serena Madland Anderson]: Born 1 January 1814 evidently at Hoegsfjord, Rogaland, Norway; daughter of Thormod Jensen Madland (Foss-Eigeland) and Siri Iversdatter Seldal (Rosdail 468-69) (NR 82). Was eleven when she and parents immigrated on the sloop Restoration to Kendall Colony, Orleans County, New York, 1825 (Rosdail 29). Married the "Slooper" Jacob Andersen Slogvik 1 March 1831 Kendall, New York (Anderson 100-01), and was the mother of ten children (Rosdail 473). Received endowment at Nauvoo Temple 1 January 1846 with her husband (NR 82). Accompanied her husband to California 1854 (Rosdail 425). After death of husband in 1865, ran a roadhouse called Soscol House (just north of San Francisco Bay in Soscol, Napa County, California, with her son, Andrew J.) (Ibid. 425-26). Moved to Pottawattamie County, Iowa, 1867 and moved with her son to Carson, Pottawattamie, Iowa, about 1880. Returned to California about 1888 and died Fruto, Glenn, California, 7 January 1895. Buried in Troucalay Cemetery, Napa County, California, beside her husband (Ibid. 426).

SEVERT OLSON: Ordained a priest at Mormon Conference at Newark, Kendall, Illinois, 18 May 1844 (Smith VI:400).

SHURE OLSON: Born 23 June or 18 July 1818 Skudeneshavn, Rogaland, Norway (parish registers before 1841 burned); son of Ole Dedricson [sic] and Maria Anderson (ECIF) (FGS Jensen) (FGS Nielsen). Baptized a Mormon 1842 by Gordon Dewal and ordained a Mormon High Priest 21 October 1845 by George P. Dykes in Nauvoo (ECIF). Endowed at Nauvoo Temple 27 January 1846 (NR 207). Married Elizabeth Jacobs 18 May 1847 Illinois and among those who promised to support the Twelve Apostles and go west 1848 (JH 26 February 1848, pp. 3-4). Appears on 1850 Census Salt Lake County, Utah, as a "joiner" (Census 77). Married his wife's sister (Sarah Ellen Jacobs) 30 November 1851 Salt Lake City, Salt Lake, Utah (IGI), and by his two polygamous wives had eleven children (FGS Jensen) (FGS Nielsen). A skilled maker of cabinets, and helped build the Tabernacle Organ, Salt Lake City (Mulder 57). Died Salt Lake City, Salt Lake, Utah, 8 January 1901 (FGS Nielsen).

SONDRE OEYSTEINSEN BAKKA [Sondra Sanders, Sr.]: Born 6 February, christened 8 March 1829 Atraa, Telemark, Norway; son of Oeystein

Sondresen Bakka and wife Aase Olsdatter Rommeraasen (PR Atraa) (Svalestuen 317). Came to America with parents 1837; orphaned when malaria struck Beaver Creek Settlement, Illinois, 1838 (Rosdail 498) (FGS Gealta). Baptized a Mormon 1842 (probably at Fox River, La Salle, Illinois) (FGS Haslam). Married Anna Jorgensen 1 December 1857 Salt Lake City, Salt Lake, Utah, and she bore him eleven children (Ibid.). Married Anna Marie Larson 1 December 1881 Salt Lake City after his first wife died, and she bore him two children (FGS Knell). Both wives were natives of Sweden (FGS Haslam) (FGS Knell). Died 21 September 1894 South Cottonwood, Salt Lake, Utah (FGS Knell).

SUSAN ANNE CORNELIUSDATTER HERSDAL [Anne Nelson Lightfoot]: Born 15 November 1814 Tysvaer, Rogaland, Norway; daughter of "Sloopers" Cornelius Nilsen Hersdal and Kari Pedersdatter Hesthammer (ECIF) (Anderson 93) (Rosdail 293). Came to America 1825 with parents on the sloop Restoration (Anderson 93). Married (1) Jerome Lake by whom she had one child; married (2) Levi Lightfoot (1816-1900) and bore him four children (Rosdail 293). Washed and annointed at Nauvoo Temple 24 January 1846 (NR appendix "A", p. 1). [Her husband, Levi Lightfoot, was one of those who promised to support the Twelve Apostles and go west in 1848 (JH 26 February 1848, pp. 3-4), but this promise was never fulfilled.] Died 1858 Illinois (Anderson 94). [Her husband was later a member of the Reorganized Church of Jesus Christ of Latter Day Saints (Rosdail 227).]

SVEND SVENDSEN NORDRE-AASEN [Swen Jacobs]: Born 17 December 1823, christened 1 January 1824 Tysvaer, Rogaland, Norway; son of Svend Jacobsen Nordre-Aasen and Anna Johanna Jonsdatter Helland (Hervik) [Hannah Dahl] (PR Tysvaer). Came to America 1830 with parents (Rosdail 54) and baptized a Mormon 12 August or 21 September 1842 (ECIF) (FGS Jacobs). Endowed at Nauvoo Temple 27 January 1846 (NR 207) and was a Seventy in the Mormon Priesthood (ECIF). Came to Utah 1849 with stepfather, Andrew Dahl, and family (Rosdail 175), and during the trek west was appointed huntsman to obtain food for the wagon company. "On one occasion he killed a deer, and while skinning it was accosted by a big Indian. From the latter's belt hung a long hunting knife. He made motions to let Swen know he wanted the deer's liver, and when this was given him, he ate it raw. That did not seem to satisfy him so he motioned for the kidneys, which he proceeded to eat with relish. When he finished he pounded his broad chest with his hands and looked very pleased. By this time a pack of wolves had smelled the fresh kill, and hovered near by. Among them was a pure white one. Swen raised his gun and fired and the wolf dropped to the ground. The Indian immediately ran over to it but it had just been stunned and jumped up and ran away barely missing the Indian. The last Swen saw of the latter, he was still chasing the wolf" (Ibid. 176-77). Left Salt Lake Valley 10 November 1849 for the California goldfields (Ibid. 177); returned to Utah about 1851 (Rosdail 178). Called by Brigham

Young to help found a settlement where Cedar City, Iron, Utah, now stands 1853, and was there until 1858 (Ibid. 178). Married Sarah Sophia Hopkins 2 November 1853 Lehi, Utah, Utah, and she bore him thirteen children (five died young) (FGS Jacobs). Lived in Lehi, Utah, Utah, from about 1860-1868 and in Newton, Cache, Utah, from 1871 to about 1880. Died 3 January 1891 Salem, Madison, Idaho (Ibid.).

TORBUR IVERSON: One of those in La Salle Branch who said he would support the Twelve Apostles and go west to Utah 1848 (JH 26 February 1848, pp. 3-4).

THORE TOSTENSEN AARVELTA [Tora or Tory Thurston]: Born 20 July, christened 25 July 1819 Veggli, Buskerud, Norway; son of Tosten Tostensen Aarvelta and Ingeboer Thoresdatter (PR Veggli). Baptized a Mormon 10 December 1842 by Ole Heier and ordained a Seventy in the Mormon Priesthood 8 October 1844 (ECIF). Endowed at Nauvoo Temple 6 February 1846 (NR 342). By three polygamous wives had at least twenty children (FGS Hobbs) (FGS Redd) (FGS Thurston). Appears on 1850 Census Salt Lake County, Utah (Census 121), and died 14 November 1896 Annabella, Sevier, Utah (FGS Hobbs).

TOSTEN SEBIOERNSEN TRONRUD [Thorsten, Thorsen or Thurston Simpson]: Born 11 December, christened 30 December 1808 Nore, Buskerud, Norway; son of Sebioern Knudsen Tronrud and Gunil Gunulsdatter Murugaard (PR Nore) (PR Opdal) (ECIF). Baptized a Mormon 25 January 1843 Lee County, Iowa, by Gudmund Haugaas (Ibid.). Married Maria Sophia Hendrickson and had at least four children (FGS Nielson). Married a total of four wives (FGS Hall). Endowed at Nauvoo Temple 6 February 1846 (NR 305) and was a Seventy in the Mormon Priesthood (ECIF). Appears in 1850 Census Salt Lake County, Utah, with wife, Maria Sophia (Mary), and four children (Census 88). Died Salt Lake City, Salt Lake, Utah, 23 October 1859 (FGS Hall).

VALBORG HENDRICHSDATTER SAEBOE [Walber or Walbur Saby]: Born 4 June, christened 9 June 1833 Hjelmeland, Rogaland, Norway; daughter of Hendrich Erichsen Riveland (Saeboe) and Magla Jonasdatter Oesthus (PR Hjelmeland). Came to America 1836 with parents (Anderson 152). One of those in La Salle Branch 1848 who promised to go west and support the Twelve Apostles (JH 26 February 1848, pp. 3-4). Appears in 1850 Census Salt Lake County, Utah (Census 122).

OESTEN LARSEN FOLSELAND (HEIER) [Austin Hayer]: Born 17 June, christened 23 July 1826 Gransherred, Telemark, Norway; son of Lars Andersen Heier (Moeli) (Folseland) and Ane Olsdatter Sandveien (PR Gransherred). Came to America with parents 1842 (Hayer 5) (Quamme 459) and baptized a Mormon about 1843 by Ole Heier (ECIF). A Seventy in the Mormon Priesthood (Ibid.) and endowed at Nauvoo Temple (under the name Orson Hayer) along with his father and brothers 6 February 1846 (NR 304). A large man about six feet high and weighed 225 pounds; a Republican. Left the Church of Jesus Christ of Latter-day Saints (Mormon) and joined the Reorganized Church of Jesus Christ of Latter Day Saints where he was a member of the Aaronic Priesthood and served as chorister (Hayer 19-20). Twice married and had eight children-- two by his first wife, Elizabeth Jacobs, who died 1850, and six by his second wife, Ann Danielson (Ibid. 19) (FGS Kemp). Served as Assessor and Collector for several years in Miller, La Salle, Illinois, and as Constable four years (La Salle 647). Died on his farm at Miller, La Salle, Illinois, 9 March 1896 (Hayer 19).

Appendix 1: Key to Abbreviations

Adair	Salt Lake City, Utah. The Church of Jesus Christ of Latter-day Saints. Library-Archives [hereinafter cited as LDS Church Archives]. Josephine H. Adair and Goudy E. Hogan, "Biography of Goudy E. Hogan by himself and daughter Mrs. Josephine H. Adair." (Microfilm of typescript.)
Anderson	Anderson, Rasmus B. *The First Chapter of Norwegian Immigration, (1821-1840): Its Causes and Results.* Madison, Wisconsin: By the Author, 1906.
Berge	Berge, Olav, ed. "Manntal for Ryfylke 1801." *Rogaland Aettesogelag* 3 (1943):3-67.
IGI	Salt Lake City, Utah. The Church of Jesus Christ of Latter-day Saints. Genealogical Department. Library Services Division [hereinafter cited as GS]. International Genealogical Index.
Census	Burns, Annie Walker, and Miller, J. Emerson, eds. *First Families of Utah as Taken from the 1850 Census of Utah.* Washington, D.C.: By the Editors, P.O. Box 6183 Apex Station, 1949.
ECIF	GS. LDS Reference. Early Church Information File.
Eikeland	Eikeland, Sigurd. *Aardal: Gardane og folket.* Vol. 2. Sandnes: Bygdeboknemda for Aardal, 1969.

Einung	Einung, H. H. <u>Tinn Soga</u>. Vol. 2. Krageroe: Eigi Forlag, 1953.
Ellingsen	Ellingsen, A., ed. "Kyrkjebok for Hoele og Fossand 1702-1854." Transcript prepared for Rogland Historie- og Aettesogelag, [Stavanger?], 1965 (Mimeographed.)
FGS Baker	GS. Family Group Record Archives [all family group sheets listed below are from the same repository]. William Baker, Patron Family Group Sheet [hereinafter cited as PFGS] "Lars Larson and Mary Adelphia Bellows."
FGS Christiansen	Edith P. Christiansen, PFGS "Canute Peterson and Sarah Ann Nelson."
FGS Gealta	Francis A. Gealta, PFGS "Osten or Ysten Sondresen and Aase Olsen."
FGS Hall	Elna Ann Simonsen Hall, Main FGS "Thurston Simpson and Anne Sophie Pedersen."
FGS Hambleton	Hilda Hambleton, PFGS "Osten Sondresen and Aase Olsen."
FGS Haslam	Mary Angeline Berg Haslam, PFGS "Sondra Sanders, Sr. and Anna Jorgansson (Jorgenson) (Yorganson)."
FGS Hatch	Olive H. Hatch, PFGS "Goudy Hogan and Ann Nelson."
FGS Hobbs	Florence Hobbs, PFGS "Tore Torstensen Thurston and Margaret Ann Hansen."
FGS Hodges	Mrs. Heber Morris Hodges, PFGS "Heber Chase Kimball and Ellen Sanders."
FGS Hogan	Lawrence M. Hogan, PFGS "Eric Gautesen (Midboen) Hogan (Haugen) and Helge Knudsen."
FGS Jacobs	Elizabeth Jacobs, PFGS "Swen Johnson Jacobs and Sarah Sophia Hopkins."
FGS Jensen	Florence Langford Jensen, PFGS "Shuredale Olson and Sarah Ellen Jacobs."
FGS Johnson	Arvilla Johnson, PFGS "Svend (Sven) Jakobson and Anna Johanne Johnson or (Johnsdatter)."

FGS Kemp	Annie Eliza Hyer Kemp, Main FGS "Austin Larsen Hayer and Ann Danielson."
FGS Kemp I	Annie Hyer Kemp, Main FGS "Hans Larsen Hayer and Sarah Elefson."
FGS Kemp II	Annie Eliza Hyer Kemp, Main FGS "Ole Olsen Hayer and Martha Anderson."
FGS Kemp III	Annie Hyer Kemp, Main FGS "Oliver Larsen Hayer and Julie Elefson."
FGS Kemp IV	Annie Hyer Kemp, PFGS "Christian Larsen Hyer (or Christian Larsen Hejer) and Caroline Hogan (or Kari Ericsen Haugen)."
FGS Knell	Virginia Pearl Sanders Knell, PFGS "Sondra Sanders, Sr. and Anna Marie Larson."
FGS Little	Irene Little, PFGS "Christopher Jacobs and Mary Margaret Dodge."
FGS Nielsen	Ethel P. Nielsen, PFGS "Shure Olson and Elizabeth Jacobs."
FGS Nielson	Eva May Galloway Nielson, PFGS "Thorsen (Thurston) Simpson and Maria Sophia Hendricks."
FGS Ovard	Helen Farnsworth Ovard, PFGS "Christian Larsen Hyer and Lovina Hogan."
FGS Peterson	Antone L. Peterson, PFGS "Canute Peterson (Knut Pedersen Maursether) and Sarah Ann Nelson."
FGS Peterson I	Ferdinand Euray Peterson, PFGS, "Canute Peterson and Gerturde Maria Rolfson."
FGS Rammell	Arthur Leon Rammell, PFGS "Enoch Daniels and Rebecca Jane Brinkley."
FGS Redd	Afton N. Redd, PFGS "Tore or Torstensen Thurston and Margaret Ann Hansen."
FGS Rolfe	Melba Rolfe, PFGS "John Jacobs and Elizabeth Coleman."
FGS Sales	Margaret Sales, PFGS "John Jacobs and Harriet Austin."

FGS Shipley	Brenda H. Shipley, PFGS "John Larson and Amelia Weight."
FGS Thompson	Sharon Reber Thompson, PFGS "John Larson and Amelia Weight."
FGS Thurston	Leslie M. Thurston, PFGS "Tora Thurston and Lodica Abelina Marsh."
FGS Van Orden	Eunice Hyer Van Orden, PFGS "Lars Andersen Hejer and Anne Olsen."
FGS Willcox	Daisy Amelia Beal Willcox, PFGS "Canute or Knud Peterson and Sara Ann Nelson."
Hayer	Kemp, Annie Hyer. _What We Know About The Hayer (Hyer) Family_. Logan, Utah: By the Author, 1954.
Hogan	LDS Church Archives. Dr. Joel E. Ricks Collection. Goudy E. Hogan Autobiography. (Microfilm of typescript.)
JH	LDS Church Archives. Journal History of the Church.
Jenson	Jenson, Andrew. _Latter-day Saint Biographical Encyclopedia: A Compilation of Biographical Sketches of Prominent Men and Women in the Church of Jesus Christ of Latter-day Saints_. 4 vols. Salt Lake City, Utah: Andrew Jenson History Company et al., 1901-36; reprint ed., Salt Lake City, Utah: Western Epics, 1971.
Kolltveit	Kolltveit, Olav. _Granvin, Ulvik og Eidfjord i Gamal og ny tid: Bygdesoga_. Vol. 2. Granvin: Granvin, Ulvik og Eidfjord Bygdeboknemnd, 1977.
La Salle	_The Past and Present of La Salle County, Illinois, containing a History of the County--its Cities, Towns, &c., a Biographical Directory of its Citizens, War Record of its Volunteers in the Late Rebellion, Portraits of Early Settlers and Prominent Men, General and Local Statistics, Map of La Salle County, History of Illinois, Constitution of the United States, Miscellaneous Matters, Etc. Etc._ Chicago: H. F. Kett & Co., 1877.

Mulder	Mulder, William. "Norwegian Forerunners Among the Early Mormons." *Norwegian-American Studies and Records* 19 (1956):46-61.
NR	GS. LDS Reference. Nauvoo Temple Endowment Register.
PR Aal	GS. European Reference [all parish registers listed below are from the same repository]. Aal, Buskerud, Norway Parish Register [PR]. Microfilm [MF] of original.
PR Atraa	Atraa, Telemark, Norway PR. MF.
PR Austbygdi	Austbygdi, Telemark, Norway PR. MF.
PR Avaldsnes	Avaldsnes, Rogaland, Norway PR. MF.
PR Eidfjord	Eidfjord, Hordaland, Norway PR. MF.
PR Fossand	Fossand, Rogaland, Norway PR. MF.
PR Gransherred	Gransherred, Telemark, Norway PR. MF.
PR Hjelmeland	Hjelmeland, Rogaland, Norway PR. MF.
PR Hovin	Hovin, Telemark, Norway PR. MF.
PR Hoeyland	Hoeyland, Rogaland, Norway PR. MF.
PR Kvam	Kvam, Hordaland, Norway PR. MF.
PR Mandal	Mandal, Vest-Agder, Norway PR. MF.
PR Mael	Mael, Telemark, Norway PR. MF.
PR Nore	Nore, Buskerud, Norway PR. MF.
PR Opdal	Opdal, Buskerud, Norway PR. MF.
PR Rennesoey	Rennesoey, Rogaland, Norway PR. MF.
PR Tinn	Tinn, Telemark, Norway PR. MF.
PR Tysvaer	Tysvaer, Rogaland, Norway PR. MF.
PR Veggli	Veggli, Buskerud, Norway PR. MF.
PR Aardal	Aardal, Rogaland, Norway PR. MF.

Peterson	LDS Church Archives. Canute Peterson et al., "Story of the Life of Canute Peterson as Given by Himself and by Some Members of His Family." (Xerox of MS.)
Quamme	Quamme, O. A., and Tjoennaas, Ketil. *Gransheradsoga*. Pt. 1: *Aettar, Gardar og Plasser*. Notodden: Notodden Kommune, 1977.
Rosdail	Rosdail, J. Hart. *The Sloopers: Their Ancestry and Posterity--The Story of the People on the Norwegian Mayflower -- The Sloop, "Restoration."* Broadview, Illinois: Norwegian Slooper Society of America, 1961.
Smith	Smith, Joseph. *History of the Church of Jesus Christ of Latter-day Saints*. 2 ed. 6 vols. Salt Lake City, Utah: Deseret Book Company, 1971.
Sunnanaa	Sunnanaa, Vilhelm, and Vetrhus, Haavard. *Rennesoey Gards- og Aettesoge*. Rennesoey: Rennesoey Kommune, 1974.
Svalestuen	Svalestuen, Andres A. *Tinns Emigrasjons Historie 1837-1907: En undersoekelse med saerlig vekt paa den demografiske, oekonomiske og sosiale bakgrunn for Amerika-farten, og en statistisk analyse av selve utvandringen*. Oslo: Universitetsforlaget, 1972.
Ulvestad	Ulvestad, Martin. *Nordmaendene i Amerika: deres Historie og Rekord*. Minneapolis, Minnesota: History Book Company's Forlag, 1907.

APPENDIX 2

GERHARD B. NAESETH TO GERALD M.
HASLAM, 4 JULY 1980

"4909 Sherwood Road
Madison, Wis., 53711
July 4, 1980

"Mr. Gerald M. Haslam
   3520 South 660 East
   Salt Lake City, Utah   84106

"Dear Mr. Haslam:

"Thank you for your letter of June 30, enclosing a copy of your paper on the first Norwegian converts to Mormonism. And for your generosity in suggesting that make [sic] free use of your article.

"I realize that you are interested especially in my input on the biographies. However, as I read your preliminary papers -- with interest -- I noticed on page 6 a discrepancy. Line 8 'to the southeast' should be 'to the southwest.'

"One piece of my methodology has been to go (as far as my time and energy permitted) to the original Norwegian parish books, and to copy the names and other data of all those going to America. Thus, for the approximately 18,000 Norwegians who came in the years 1825-1850, I am sure that I have more than 17,000 working cards. Perhaps closer to 18,000.

"I can tell you no more now than that Iver Iversen Oeftedahl, born about 1823?, emigrated in 1844 from Haaland. This is a Haaland in Rogaland. Looking back at my notes, I see that I have: Oeftedahl a Molde.

"Gitle Danielsen, according to the grave marker in the Muskego (now called Norway) Lutheran Cemetery, died Feb. 11, 1855. His wife was Ellen Knudsdatter, born 1813, died Oct. 23, 1866, buried same cemetery.

"Joergen Pedersen. I have four in my file. This first is doubtful. He was Joergen Pedersen Axelrud, born Oct. 29, 1843, in Soendeled, emigrated 1850. The second, too, is not very hopeful. Joergen And. Pedersen Haave, born 1830?, emigrated from Landvik in 1846; I know that in 1850 he was living in Washington Township, Buchanan County, Missouri.

"Joergen Pedersen Nesthus, born 1814, emigrated in 1842 from Voss, coming first to Muskego, later to Chicago, served in the Mexican War.

"Most likely is Joergen Pedersen Tvet, son of Peder Joergensen Tveit [sic], and Asbaer Johnsdatter Tveit, baptized in Drangedal, May 11, 1800. Emigrated in 1839 to Freedom Township, LaSalle County, Illinois. He was married, May 31, 1830, to Maria Larsdatter Vaagsland. I know of eight children. Maria was baptized, May 13, 1808, the daughter of Lars Olesen Vaagsland and Aslau Knudsdatter Tveit. My sources are the Drangedal parish records; Olav Sannes, Drangedal med Toerdal, 620, 639; the 1850 Illinois census.

"You realize, I am sure, that I have not examined any Mormon original sources. In this (hopefully first response), I have been looking at those names which offered identification problems.

"On Elias and Ingabor Johnson, you might try Helje Johnsen Osvaag, son of John Olsen Gjerde, born about 1807 in Etne, emigrated in 1843. He was married, July 13, 1838, to Ingebor Abrahamsdatter Vee, daughter of Abraham Pedersen Vee and wife Anna, born January 23, 1818. They emigrated with two children. My sources are the Etne parish records; the passenger list of the Haabet; and an article in Haugesunds avis, April 3, 1970. In fact, I think it likely that this is the couple.

"The most frustrating name is Ira Thompson, since both names are not Norwegian. I do not regard him, however, as a lost cause, especially in view of the birth date you have. I tried Erik, with a patronymic of T----; no luck.

"Well, I believe that this is all I can produce on a first round. I am not sure how much more I can find, although I certainly would like to identify Ira Thompson. I have a great many projects -- all genealogical -- going at the present time, thus cannot give priority to your article. However, I will nibble at it from time to time; if I find anything at all, adding to what you already have, I will write.

"After your article has been published, you should hear from some of the subscribers, perhaps opening some new name mysteries. Again, I would be willing to try to help to identify them.

"Yours very sincerely,

"Gerhard B. Naeseth"

APPENDIX 3

AN INVENTORY OF COURT EXTRACTS AUTHENTICATED
IN CONNECTION WITH THE SUPREME COURT
DECISION THAT MORMONS WERE
NON-CHRISTIANS, 4 NOVEMBER
1853

Court extracts for the Supreme Court Decision of 4 November 1853 are in two bundles--one numbering 106, and a second numbering 116 pages. The first bundle contains the following items:

(pp. 1-6) copies of Mormon letters of authority for all missionaries accused of breaking the law; (pp. 7-10) citations from *Skandinaviens Stjerne*, vol. 12, describing a Mormon conference in Copenhagen where H. P. Jensen said he and Aahmansson had baptized twenty persons in Norway with "authority from God in spite of secular law" ["Myndighed fra Gud trods verdslig Love"] and had organized a branch in Fredrikstad; (pp. 10-11) abstracts of passports, certificates of ordination, and letters of authority pertaining to the accused Mormons; (p. 12) copy of a city court judgment dated 30 August 1852 sentencing dyer Emil Larsen to imprisonment on bread and water for fifteen days for having broken Criminal Law 8-1 (ridiculing the State religion); (pp. 13-17) copy of a letter 26 September 1852 from the Rural Sheriff of Onsoe to the Sheriff of Moss on Mormon baptisms in the middle of the night and claiming that those baptized had on scanty clothing and that their health had been endangered; (pp. 17-21) copy of letter 28 September 1852 from Sheriff Ytter to Rural Judge Bing describing Mormon baptisms near Ingulsroed Farm in Onsoe Clerical District and Ole Olsen's claim that he was called of God to baptize and would continue doing so as long as physical restraints were not placed in his way; (Deputy Colberg had warned missionaries to cease baptizing, but when missionaries continued to baptize, Sheriff Ytter ordered Ole Olsen's arrest); (pp. 21-37) minutes of a hearing 29 September 1852 at Thunoe against Mormon missionary, Ole Olsen; (pp. 37-48) minutes of a hearing 1 October 1852 against Ole Olsen; (pp. 48-49) extract from Moss Police Journal 1 October 1852 describing a meeting between Birch-Reichenwald and Mormon missionaries, Christen Knudsen and Niels Hansen, during which Birch read them pertinent paragraphs from the Dissenter Law (pars. 1, 5 and 17) and said he believed their letters of authority were invalid; he also told them he felt obligated to retain their papers and warned them against breaking laws of the land; (pp. 49-52) copy of a letter 1 October 1852 from Birch to the JPD describing Mormon activities in his county; (pp. 52-58) minutes of a hearing in Fredrikstad 4 October 1852--

further testimony about baptisms performed by Ole Olsen as also shoemaker Johan Johansen's description of efforts to seek dissenter status for Mormons in Fredrikstad; (pp. 58-60) copy of letter 6 October 1852 from JPD to Birch-Reichenwald describing the Governor of Bratsberg County's warning to Mormons there to cease all practice of their religion until their legal status was decided; the JPD advised Birch-Reichenwald to follow the same procedure in his County; (pp. 60-63) copy of Birch-Reichenwald's Circular of 8 October 1852 about the Mormons in Norway; (pp. 63-64) two Mormon letters of authority dated 11 October 1852; (p. 64) copy of Superior Court Judgment 11 October 1852 against dyer Emil Larsen, ratifying the lower court decision of 30 August; (pp. 64-83) minutes of a hearing 11 October 1852 in Fredrikstad describing Mormon baptisms and celebration of the Lord's Supper in the vicinity of Fredrikstad; (pp. 83-89) minutes of a hearing in the City of Fredrikstad 15 October 1852 containing testimony by Svend Larsen of Risoer about his conversion to Mormonism and activities in Norway; (pp. 89-96) minutes of hearing 15 October 1852 in Thunoee regarding baptisms performed by Ole Olsen and others; (pp. 96-106) minutes of hearing 19 October 1852 against the Mormons.

The second bundle of court extracts in connection with the Decision of 4 November 1853 contains the following items:

(pp. 1-3) copy of a declaration by sexton Berlund in Moss on 25 October 1852 on Mormon attempts to rent a hall in Moss and other Mormon activites there; (pp. 3-4) minutes of a hearing on 25 October 1852 at Moss describing Mormon proselyting efforts in Moss; (pp. 4-5) minutes of a court hearing in Moss on 26 October 1852 describing proselyting efforts by Mormons; (pp. 5-20) minutes of a hearing in Thunoe on 9 November 1852 detailing Mormon teachings about "Zion" and describing Mormon baptisms by Ole Olsen, dyer Larsen and others; (pp. 20-49) minutes of a hearing on 12 November 1852--continuation of hearing in Thunoe on 9 November 1852; (pp. 49-55) minutes of a hearing on 13 November 1852 in Fredrikstad describing Mormon doctrine about "Zion" and Mormon activities in Risoer and the City of Fredrikstad; (pp. 55-63) minutes of hearings on 16 and 17 November 1852 in Fredrikstad--continuation of hearings on 13 November 1852; (pp. 63-81) materials sent by Pastor Buch to Birch-Reichenwald on 26 November 1852; (Buch had prepared a summary of Mormon doctrine from issues of Skandinaviens Stjerne and Mormon tracts including various citations about the Mormon Zion, the Apostacy, Joseph Smith's revelations, the incompletenesss of biblical revelation and The Book of Mormon); the summary quoted such Mormon expressions as "The Book of Mormon, the most important of all books for this generation" ["Mormons Bog, den aller vigtigste af alle Boeger for den nuvaerende Slaegt"]-- p. 77--and detailed Mormon claims that God had again spoken to a prophet, that angels had again visited the earth, and that infant baptism was a wicked practice; (Buch further observed that Mormons were all things to all men and opportunists who

focused on points of doctrine which their listeners were sure
to accept, "and this with only one ultimate and crowning goal--to
establish a temporal Kingdom" ["og dette kun i grunden for som
sidste og hoeieste Formaal at stifte et Rige af denne Verden"]--
pp. 67-68); (pp. 81-83) copy of letter 7 December 1852 from
JPD to Birch-Reichenwald referring to Birch's letters of 22
and 27 November and instructing Birch to institute proceedings
against the Mormons if he so desired, and referring to a KUD
opinion of 30 November 1852 stating that Mormons could not be
considered Christians; (pp. 83-84) copy of an order from Birch-
Reichenwald dated 10 December 1852 directing that eleven Mormons
be charged with breaking Norwegian Law 6-1-4 and 5; (pp. 84-87)
court minutes of a hearing 22 December 1852 which noted the
KUD's opinion that Mormons were not Christians, as also detailed
descriptions of a lower court's opinion that Mormons could not
be put under oath when testifying in a court of law as per a
letter from the JPD of 7 December; (pp. 87-94) minutes of a
hearing on 4 January 1853 about a blessing given by missionary
Ole Olsen to a sick woman during which event he "stroked her
on the arm" ["da Olsen stroeg hende paa Armen"]--p. 92; (pp. 94-95)
minutes of a court session on 14 January 1853; (pp. 95-107)
minutes of a court session on 19 January 1853 containing testimony
by accused Mormons: Ole Olsen noted that his letter of authority
was signed by Aahmansson who also signed the mission president's
signature to the document with said president's permission and
in his presence; Jeppe Joergensen Folkmann said he was told
by the sheriff's deputy in Moss that he could hold meetings,
but only on condition he tell the police where said meetings
were to be held; Christian Larsen said polygamy was strictly
forbidden among Mormons, and that those involved in it were
cut off from the Mormon Church; Johan August Aahmansson said
he had permission from the Mormon mission president in Copenhagen
to sign the president's name to letters of authority in the
branch of the Church where he was presiding, but no longer had
in his possession the letter from the president granting him
permission; Niels Theodor Emil Larsen said the Sheriff of Fredrikstad
attended a Mormon gathering at his house on 13 October 1852
and did nothing to stop the meeting, and Larsen further said
he had never been told not to baptize or administer the Lord's
Supper before being called into court; (The court recorder introduced
an extract from a Supreme Court Case dated 17 December 1852
where Niels Theodor Emil Larsen was sentenced to 15 days' imprisonment
on bread and water for having ridiculed the State Church--this
in reference to Larsen's part in disturbances initiated by the
infamous Methodist rabble-rouser Tobias Jacobsen in Fredrikstad
early in 1852); (p. 107) copy of a Government resolution
dated 25 January 1853 stating that no rules were to be adopted
regarding Mormons and oaths; (pp. 107-08) copy of a letter dated
15 February 1853 from the acting sheriff in Moss describing
conversations with Mormon missionary, Jeppe Folkmann, and instructions
given to Folkmann about holding meetings; (pp. 108-09)
minutes of court sessions 17 and 21 February 1853; (pp. 109-10)

copy of sentence decreed against eleven Mormons by the District Judge of Tunoe, Herr Bing, fining Mormons for unlawful practice of their religion; (pp. 110-11) abstract of the Superior Court Decision--1st division--Oslo, 4 April 1853, stating Mormon missionaries were to pay fines; (pp. 111) copy of Birch-Reichenwald's appeal dated 22 April 1853 of the Oslo Superior Court's decision; (pp. 111-16) copy of a document dated Fredrikstad, 26 April 1853, signed by the acting president of Mormons in Norway--and in their behalf--Christian J. Larsen stating that Mormons were pleased with that part of the Superior Court Decision which stated they were Christians, but still pleaded not guilty to criminal charges; (Larsen traced the history of Mormonism in Norway and said that Mormon petitions seeking recognition as Christian dissenters were sent to the civil authorities before any sacraments were performed, but when petitions were neither accepted nor rejected, Mormons decided it was better "to obey God than to obey men" ["vi agtede det bedre 'at adlyde Gud mere end Menneskene,' hvorledes end Foelgerne vilde blive"]--p. 113--and baptisms were carried out and sacraments administered--[Larsen asked the Supreme Court to consider moral as well as juridical aspects of the case. All the accused Mormons, both those who had performed baptisms and administered other sacraments, and those who had not done so, had received the same sentences. Mormons considered this unfair since it was a well-known fact that numerous unordained laymen spoke in religious gatherings in Norway without punishment therefore; Mormons had most assuredly not preached any doctrine other than that which could be read in the Bible. Larsen enclosed a copy of the pamphlet "A Voice of Truth" ["En Sandheds-Roest"] for perusal by Supreme Court justices and reiterated that Mormons were Christians who believed in baptism for the remission of sins; the Mormon sacrament of the Lord's Supper commemorated the death and Atonement of Christ and His sacrifice for the sins of the world. Mormons believed the Bible was the Holy Scripture of the Asian Jews and the Book of Mormon was the Holy Scripture of the American Israelites, each of which substantiated and confirmed the other. Since Mormons did not have funds to hire an attorney and were not learned in the law, they put their trust in God and the Supreme Court]); (p. 116) copy of letter of 28 May 1853 from Birch-Reichenwald to JPD stating that none of the accused Mormons were still imprisoned; (p. 116) Dunker's recommendation dated 22 October 1853 that the lower court decision against the Mormons be augmented or upheld, and that he be paid his salary. "Udtog af Justitssagene mod 1/ Ole Olsen 2/ Jeppe Joergen Folkmann 3/ Christian Larsen 4/ Johan Frederik Ferdinand Dorius 5/ Johan August Aahmanson 6/ Peter Beckstroem 7/ Niels Hansen 8/ Christen Knudsen 9/ Svend Larsen 10/ Niels Theodor Emil Larsen og 11/ Johan Johansen," pakke 79, Utdrag i muntlige saker, 5L. no. 172, 2s 1853, Hoeiesterett, Riksarkivet, Oslo, Norway.

APPENDIX 4

BIRTHPLACES OF CONVERTS TO MORMONISM IN OSLO BRANCH 1853-1860 INCLUSIVE

	Birthplace	Totals	Percent of 469
I.	**Denmark**		
	A. Denmark (nonspecific)	5	
	B. Sjaelland (nonspecific)	1	
	C. Aalborg County		
	1. Aars	4	
	D. Copenhagen County		
	1. Copenhagen City	5	
	[DENMARK TOTAL	15]	3.19
II.	**Germany**		
	A. Germany (nonspecific)	1	0.21
III.	**Iceland**		
	A. Iceland (nonspecific)	1	0.21
IV.	**Norway**		
	A. Akershus County		
	1. Asker	5	
	2. Blaker	1	
	3. Baerum	11	
	4. Droebak	2	
	5. Eidsvoll	3	
	6. Enebakk	2	
	7. Fet	6	
	8. Fossum Jaernverk	1	
	9. Frogn	3	
	10. Gjerdrum	1	
	11. Hakadal	1	
	12. Hoeland	3	
	13. Lysaker	2	
	14. Loerenskog	3	
	15. Nannestad	1	
	16. Nittedalen	1	
	17. Nordby	17	
	18. Oppegaard	3	
	19. Romerike	2	
	20. Rustad	1	
	21. Skedsmo	8	
	22. Son	2	

Birthplace	Totals	Percent of 469

IV. Norway (continued)
- A. Akershus County (continued)
  - 23. Soerum — 3
  - 24. Troegstad — 2
  - 25. Ullensaker — 2
  - 26. Vennersborg — 1
  - [AKERSHUS TOTAL — 71] — 15.13
- B. Aust-Agder County
  - 1. Lillesand — 1 — 0.21
- C. Bergen County
  - 1. Bergen City — 1 — 0.21
- D. Buskerud County
  - 1. Drammen — 11
  - 2. Eiker — 2
  - 3. Hallingdal — 4
  - 4. Helgeland — 1
  - 5. Hurum — 3
  - 6. Hoenefoss — 1
  - 7. Kongsberg — 4
  - 8. Lier — 2
  - 9. Modum — 2
  - 10. Nes i Hallingdal — 1
  - 11. Numedal — 1
  - 12. Ringerike — 18
  - 13. Roeyken — 1
  - 14. Sigdal — 1
  - [BUSKERUD TOTAL — 52] — 11.08
- E. Hedmark County
  - 1. Elverum — 1
  - 2. Grue — 5
  - 3. Hedemarken (non-specific) — 23
  - 4. Loeiten — 1
  - 5. Nes — 16
  - 6. Odalen — 1
  - 7. Ringsaker — 6
  - 8. Soloer — 3
  - 9. Vang — 2
  - 10. Vinger — 2
  - [HEDMARK TOTAL — 60] — 12.79
- F. Hordaland County
  - 1. Hardanger — 1 — 0.21
- G. Nordland County
  - 1. Vesteraalen — 1 — 0.21
- H. Oppland County
  - 1. Fron — 1
  - 2. Faaberg — 2
  - 3. Gausdal — 1
  - 4. Gudbrandsdalen — 8
  - 5. Hadeland — 3

	Birthplace	Totals	Percent of 469

IV. Norway (continued)
- H. Oppland County (continued)
  - 6. Jevnaker — 1
  - 7. Toten — 10
  - 8. Valdres — 1
  - 9. Vardal — 4
  - 10. Oeyer — 1
  - [OPPLAND TOTAL — 32] — 6.82
- I. Oslo County
  - 1. Aker — 66
  - 2. Maridalen — 1
  - 3. Oslo City — 57
  - [OSLO TOTAL — 124] — 26.43
- J. Soer-Troendelag County
  - 1. Trondheim City — 3
  - 2. Oerland — 1
  - [SOER-TROENDELAG TOTAL — 4] — 0.85
- K. Telemark County
  - 1. Bamble — 1
  - 2. Holden — 5
  - 3. Skien — 4
  - 4. Telemarken (non-specific) — 1
  - [TELEMARK TOTAL — 11] — 2.34
- L. Tromsoe County
  - 1. Kvaefjord — 1 — 0.21
- M. Vest-Agder County
  - 1. Flekkefjord — 1
  - 2. Kristiansand — 1
  - 3. Mandal — 1
  - 4. Soendre Undal — 3
  - [VEST-AGDER TOTAL — 6] — 1.27
- N. Vestfold County
  - 1. Borre — 1
  - 2. Eidsfoss — 4
  - 3. Holmestrand — 3
  - 4. Sande — 1
  - 5. Sandefjord — 1
  - 6. Skoger — 2
  - [VESTFOLD TOTAL — 12] — 2.55
- O. Oestfold County
  - 1. Fredrikstad — 2
  - 2. Halden — 5
  - 3. Hoelen — 2
  - 4. Krogstad — 1
  - 5. Moss — 2
  - 6. Onsoey — 1
  - 7. Rakkestad — 1
  - 8. Raade — 4
  - 9. Spydeberg — 3

	Birthplace	Totals	Percent of 469
IV.	Norway (continued)		
	O. Oestfold County (continued)		
	[OESTFOLD TOTAL	21]	4.47
	[NORWAY TOTAL	398]	84.86
V.	Sweden		
	A. Sweden (nonspecific)	39	8.31
	B. Gaevleborg County		
	1. Gaevle	1	0.21
	C. Goeteborg och Bohus County		
	1. Faagelvik	1	
	2. Goeteborg	2	
	[GOETEBORG OCH BOHUS TOTAL	3]	0.63
	D. Halland County		
	1. Oexared	1	0.21
	E. Joenkoeping County		
	1. Joenkoeping (nonspecific)	1	0.21
	F. Kalmar County		
	1. Vaestervik	1	0.21
	G. Stockholm County		
	1. Stockholm City	2	0.42
	H. Vaermland County		
	1. Holmedal	1	
	2. Toecksmark	2	
	[VAERMLAND TOTAL	3]	0.63
	I. Vaermland Province (nonspecific)	3	0.63
	[SWEDEN TOTAL	54]	11.51

GRAND TOTAL FOR ALL COUNTRIES   *469

NOTE: The total sample size was 601. The number of members for whom no place of birth could be determined was 132; thus birthplaces could be determined for seventy-eight percent of the members enumerated on Oslo Branch membership lists for the years 1853-1860 inclusive. Record of Members, 1853-1867, microfilm of MS, Christiania Branch, Christiania Conference, Scandinavian Mission, Library-Archives, The Church of Jesus Christ of Latter-day Saints, Salt Lake City, Utah.

APPENDIX 5

BIRTHPLACES OF CONVERTS TO MORMONISM
IN OSLO BRANCH 1895-1900 INCLUSIVE

	Birthplace	Totals	Percent of 244
I.	**Denmark**		
	A. Denmark (nonspecific)	2	
	B. Copenhagen County		
	1. Copenhagen City	1	
	C. Ringkoebing County		
	1. "Houn" [Hoven]	1	
	2. Tjoerring	1	
	[DENMARK TOTAL	5]	2.04
II.	**Norway**		
	A. Akershus County		
	1. Asker	4	
	2. Baerum	1	
	3. Droebak	2	
	4. Eidsvoll	6	
	5. Enebakk	2	
	6. Fet	1	
	7. Fetsund	1	
	8. Frogn	2	
	9. Hoeland	1	
	10. Lillestroem	1	
	11. Lysdal	1	
	12. Nesodden	6	
	13. Oppegaard	2	
	14. Skedsmo	1	
	15. Son	1	
	16. Ullensaker	1	
	[AKERSHUS TOTAL	33]	13.52
	B. Aust-Agder County		
	1. Arendal	4	1.63
	C. Bergen County		
	1. Bergen City	4	1.63
	D. Buskerud County		
	1. Drammen	4	
	2. Hurum	3	
	3. Hoenefoss	3	
	4. Lier	2	
	5. Modum	1	
	6. Ringerike	1	
	7. Roeyken	2	

	Birthplace	Totals	Percent of 244

II. <u>Norway</u> (continued)
   D. Buskerud County (continued)
       8. Aadal   1
           [BUSKERUD TOTAL   17]   6.96
   E. Hedmark County
       1. Eidskog   1
       2. Grue   1
       3. Hof   1
       4. Odalen   5
       5. Romedal   2
       6. Soloer   5
       7. Storhamar   1
       8. Aasnes   2
           [HEDMARK TOTAL   18]   7.37
   F. Hordaland County
       1. Roeldal   1   0.40
   G. Moere og Romsdal County
       1. Kristiansund   1   0.40
   H. Nord-Troendelag County
       1. Levanger   1   0.40
   I. Oppland County
       1. Gran   2
       2. Hadeland   5
       3. Lillehammer   1
       4. Oestre Toten   1
           [OPPLAND TOTAL   9]   3.68
   J. Oslo County
       1. Aker   1
       2. Oslo City   82
           [OSLO TOTAL   83]   34.01
   K. Telemark County
       1. Brevik   1
       2. Eidanger   1
       3. Krageroe   2
       4. Langesund   1
       5. Porsgrunn   1
       6. Skien   1
           [TELEMARK TOTAL   7]   2.86
   L. Tromsoe County
       1. Tromsoe City   1
       2. Trondenes   1
           [TROMSOE TOTAL   2]   0.81
   M. Vest-Agder County
       1. Mandal   1   0.40
   N. Vestfold County
       1. Holmestrand   1
       2. Sandefjord   2
       3. Stavern   1
       4. Svelvik   2
           [VESTFOLD TOTAL   6]   2.45

	Birthplace	Totals	Percent of 244
II.	Norway (continued)		
	O. Oestfold County		
	1. Borge	1	
	2. Fredrikstad	6	
	3. Halden	3	
	4. Krogstad	1	
	5. Moss	5	
	6. Rakkestad	1	
	7. Skjeberg	2	
	8. Troegstad	1	
	[OESTFOLD TOTAL	20]	8.19
	[NORWAY TOTAL	207]	84.83
III.	Sweden		
	A. Sweden (nonspecific)	5	2.04
	B. Bohuslaen Province (nonspecific)	4	1.63
	C. Dalsland Province (nonspecific)	1	0.40
	D. Goeteborg och Bohus County		
	1. Goeteborg	2	0.81
	E. Skaraborg County		
	1. "Udvang" [Utvaengstorp]	1	0.40
	F. Vaermland County		
	1. Holmedal	2	
	2. Jaernskog	1	
	3. "Segestad" [Segerstad]	1	
	4. Silbodal	2	
	[VAERMLAND TOTAL	6]	2.45
	G. Vaermland Province (nonspecific)	13	5.32
	[SWEDEN TOTAL	32]	13.11

GRAND TOTAL FOR ALL COUNTRIES   *244

NOTE: The total sample size was 327. The number of members for whom no place of birth could be determined was eighty-three; thus birthplaces could be determined for seventy-five percent of the members enumerated on Oslo Branch membership lists for the years 1895-1900 inclusive. Record of Members, 1853-1900, microfilm of MS, Christiania Branch, Christiania Conference, Scandinavian Mission, Library-Archives, The Church of Jesus Christ of Latter-day Saints, Salt Lake City, Utah.

APPENDIX 6

MORMON PLACES OF WORSHIP IN NORWAY BEFORE 1920

The first Mormons in Oslo held meetings in Carl Fjeld's rented home "at a place called 'Skarpsno' near the lower waterfall of the Aker River" ["paa et Sted, kaldet 'Skarpsno' i Naerheden af Akers-Elvens nedre Fald"] in the Winter of 1853-1854, and Oslo Branch was organized there on 8 December 1853 with nine members. Beginning in the summer of 1854, Oslo members met in Gustav Andersen's home at "Egeberg"; Andersen sold his home late in 1854, and Mormons rented a hall on Ruseloekkbakken (now Victoria Terrasse)--one of Oslo's worst slum districts. Andrew Jenson, "De Sidste-Dages Helliges Forsamlingslokaler i Christiania," Skandinaviens Stjerne 52 (15 November 1903):345; Lars Jakob Holt, Norges historie med hovedlinjer i de andre nordiske lands historie ([Oslo]: H. Aschehoug & Co., 1974), p. 221. The hall on Russeloekkbakken adjoined or fronted Drammensveien ["like ved Drammensveien hvor det vakre parkanlegg nu er anlagt"], and housed the offices of Oslo Branch for six years. Non-Mormons called it "The Mormon Temple" ["mormonernes tempel"]. Carl M. Hagberg, Den Norske Misjons Historie (Oslo: Universal-trykkeriet, 1928), p. 24. According to branch leader C. Andersen, members rented the hall for a few shillings per month, and the hall itself was "a room a little larger than that of an average man on Rusloekbakken. The room was small and located on the top floor right under the house rafters. The window was small and let in only a few of the sun's rays; the stairway up was narrow and inconvenient, such that hardly more than one at a time could come up or down" [". . . et Rum af en lidt mere end almindelig liberal Mand paa Rusloekbakken. Vaerelset var lille og oeverst oppe ved Taget af Huset; Vinduet var lille og sendte kun sparsomt Dagens Lys derind; Opgangen var snever og ubekvem, saa neppe meer end En ad Gangen kunde komme op eller ned"]. Skandinaviens Stjerne 20 (15 August 1871):339-40. On 16 October 1860, Mormons rented a new hall on Storgaden (on the corner of Storgaden and Youngsgade) for which they paid two hundred dollars annually. Carl C. N. Dorius, "Dagbog: Carl C. N. Dorius's Missionsforretninger i Skandinavia, samt en kort Beretning om det tidligere Levnetsloeb," p. 27, 16 October 1860, holograph, Library-Archives, The Church of Jesus Christ of Latter-day Saints, Salt Lake City, Utah [hereinafter cited as LDS Church Archives]; Jenson, "Forsamlingslokaler," p. 346. Oslo Conference President George M. Brown wrote on 19 April 1864: "We moved the office from Ponvit's Goard [Gaard] to No. 27 Young's Gode [Gade] in the same building and in the story above our meeting hall. Here we obtained two very suitable rooms for the purpose." George Mortimer Brown Autobiography, p. 62, 19 April 1864, typescript, Library Services Division, Genealogical Department, The Church of Jesus Christ of Latter-day Saints, Salt Lake City, Utah. On 17 October 1864, Mormons in Oslo rented the entire fourth floor "in master mason C. Jacobsen's quadrangle, Munkedamsvejen Nr. 17" ["i Murermester C. Jacobsens Gaard, Munkedamsvejen Nr. 17"] for which they paid 300 dollars annually. Jenson, "Forsamlingslokaler," p. 346. Oslo Conference President George M. Brown had Jacobsen sign a contract stipulating that "Herr Jacobsen is to construct a certain portion of the building into a meeting hall and the remaining rooms he is to fit up for dwellings, and we expect to have a nice place prepared for an office. . . . We have three hundred spd. to pay in advance which will make one year's rent, and then we shall have to furnish our own benches, etc., as well as bringing gas into the building. It is indeed very expensive for us but we can not do any better. As we are what the world calls 'Mormons' we can not get a meeting room cheaper in this place." Brown Autobiography, p. 82, 7 October 1864. On 31 October 1864, Brown described a debt of "400 spd." [four hundred dollars], "the entire sum of which we have paid out to the meeting house, three hundred to one year's rent which we had to pay in advance, and the other hundred to benches, pulpit and bringing the gas in as we had to bring it from the street and it was a long way. We have contracted to take the house for five years at 300 spde. per year. It is a large sum and will doubtless be a burden to the people. I think that we could have done much better by purchasing, but the brethren in England and Copenhagen did not like the idea as they did not and could not understand the matter as well as they could if they were here." Ibid., p. 85, 31 October 1864. On 2 November 1864, Brown reported: "We moved things into our new office rooms as they were now ready--two small rooms adjoining the meeting hall, one to do the conference business in and the other to be occupied by a servant girl who will take care of and keep in order both the office and meeting room." Ibid., p. 85, 2 November 1864. The new meeting hall was dedicated on 13 November 1864; the afternoon meeting later that day was "disturbed by a mob of a considerable number, who, although afraid to injure anyone, made considerable disturbance, and we were obliged," said Brown, "to put some of them out." Ibid., p. 85, 13 November 1864. On 1 November 1870, Mormon leaders met and decided to erect a building at Oesterhausgade 27 in Oslo. The contractor, a Mormon named Engebregt Olsen, decided that the third floor would be a meeting hall, and the first and second floors would be family apartments to be rented out. Work on the foundation commenced on 9 November 1870, and construction continued, with brief pauses, during the winter. On 22 July 1871, the building was insured with the General Norwegian Fire Insurance Society ["det almindelige norske Brandforsikringsselskab"] for 6,530 dollars, and was dedicated on 23 July 1871. <u>Skandinaviens Stjerne</u> 30 (15 August 1871):337. Voluntary contributions for the building totaled 125 dollars. Ibid. Lorin Farr described the building on 17 April 1871:

"De Hellige lade et nyt Forsamlingshuus opfoere, hvilket er 70 Fod lang, 40 Fod bredt og tre Etager hoeit. Forsamlingssalen er i tredie Etage (2den Sal), medens det Meste af Stuen, foerste Sal og Kjaelderleiligheden agtes udleiet. Det vil indeholde 18 Vaerelser og er beliggende midt i Byen." Lorin Farr to H. S. Eldredge, 17 April 1871, in Skandinaviens Stjerne 20 (1 May 1871):236. J. C. A. Weibye described the meeting hall on 22 July 1871 as "a nice room 30 by 43 feet for meeting-room, with a stand 8 by 16 1/2 feet and pulpit, and a gallary [sic] ___ [sic] by ____ [sic] feet for the sing-coir [choir], in the room are place for 12 gass [sic] flames, the room is nicely finnished, painted (even the floor is painted) and the Pulpit, and some on the stand are gilt; 6 big windows in each two sides of the Hall, which makes it very light." Jens Christian Andersen Weibye Diary, vol. 4, p. 2, 22 July 1871, holograph, LDS Church Archives. Weibye made the following description in a letter dated 24 July 1871: "Salen er stor og rummelig, med 12 Fag Vinduer (6 paa hver Side), et Galleri for Sangchoret, der bestaaer af omtrent 40 Medlemmer, en Forhoeining for endeel af Praestedoemmet samt en praegtig Talestol. . . . Tredie Sal indeholder Forsamlingssalen, Contoir og Sove-kammer for Conference-Praesidenten." J. C. A. Weibye to K. Peterson, 24 July 1871, in Skandinaviens Stjerne 20 (1 August 1871):336. By 8 October 1871, eleven families were living in the building. Andrew Jenson, "J. C. A. Weibyes Biografi," Morgenstjernen 3 (15 May 1884):157. In a letter on 17 June 1878, Mission President Nils C. Flygare reported the property at Oesterhausgade 27 was insured for 26,120 crowns, but was worth at least 30,000 crowns. Mortgages on the property were held by: the Oslo Hypothek Bank (8,200 crowns at 4 3/4 percent interest); merchant N. O. Young (2,056.76 crowns at 5 1/2 percent); lawyer J. Bruun (4,800 crowns at 5 percent). Annual income from the property in 1877 included 1,944 crowns in rent from sundry families and 720 crowns in hall and office rent, or 2,664 crowns total; annual expenses were 1,544.59 crowns (one crown in 1878 being equal to $0.26). Flygare also noted that "Peter Brown of Coalville [Coalville, Utah] holds the deeds of the [Oslo] property, under the pretention that our church cannot hold property in Norway, but that is not the case. I inquired of a firstclass lawyer in regard to that matter, and were [sic] informed, that there were nothing to hinder our Church from holding the deeds of the property, either in the name of the Trustee in Trust or in the name of our church here in Scandinavia." Flygare also noted that "if the Council [Quorum of the Twelve Apostles] should deside [sic] that the Church should assume the property, then Peter Brown should imediately [sic] deed it over, as it stand [sic] we might lose it all. The deeds to be lawful, must be sent here to be read in court or 'Tinglaest' in Christiania [Oslo], which is the same as recording it. The amount of 'Kroner' 5200.00 that Hacon [Haakon] Olsen, of Salt Lake City claims, is an amount that his father Ingelbrekt Olsen, deseased [sic], who sold the property to the Church, intended to give to the Church, and for that purpose wrote to Weibye

[J. C. A. Weibye] in 1872. . . ." Nils C. Flygare to Jos. F. Smith, 17 June 1878, carbon copy, "Letter Book of Niels [sic] C. Flygare, President of the Scandinavian Mission, 1878-1879," p. 27, LDS Church Archives. By 22 November 1878, Flygare could report that Peter Brown had deeded the Oslo property over to the Trustee in Trust of the Mormon Church. Nils C. Flygare to J. Rolfsen, 22 November 1878, carbon copy, "Letter Book of Flygare," p. 66. Flygare later wrote Oslo Conference President Rolfsen on 5 February 1879: "I send you now the Deeds and other papers conected [sic] with the Christiania property. The [they] have now to be recorded (Tinglaest) in the court of Christiania." Nils C. Flygare to J. Rolfsen, 5 February 1879, carbon copy, "Letter Book of Flygare," p. 84. On 16 November 1887, missionary J. A. Hendricksen noted that Oslo Conference President Hans J. Christiansen had his office and dwelling at Oesterhausgade 27. Said Hendricksen: "The first two [stories] is devided [sic] into small roomes [sic] used for dwellings and there are fifteen families renting in the house. The upper story is utalized [sic] as follows. One office about 14 X 15 ft. and bedroom 9 X 15 and one end, and the remainder is for meetings. Its nicely decorated." John Anthon Hendricksen Diary, vol. 1, pp. 43-44, 16 November 1887, microfilm of holograph, LDS Church Archives. President A. L. Skanchy traveled to Oslo on 9 August 1903 and made arrangements for tearing down the building at Oesterhausgade 27. One of Oslo's foremost architects, and a member of the State Building Committee, Mr. Olaf Boeje, drew up plans for a new building on the same site; the new hall would have three floors and a cellar: the two lower floors would be divided into rental units, and the top floor would be a meeting hall. A three-story side building was planned for office purposes comprising six rooms--two rooms per floor--as well as two main stairways leading up to the meeting hall. Skandinaviens Stjerne 51 (1 September 1903):264. The new building cost 60,000 crowns, of which 18,500 crowns were contributed from a general church building fund under auspices of the First Presidency in Utah. Professor Evan Stephens, director of the Mormon Tabernacle Choir, offered to pay for all inside decorations in the meeting hall. The building was also equipped with electric lights, and was dedicated by Mormon Apostle Francis M. Lyman on 24 July 1903. Hendricksen Diary, vol. 2, p. 6, 24 July 1903; Skandinaviens Stjerne 52 (15 August 1903):243-44. On 22 October 1909, Andrew Jenson, President of the Scandinavian Mission, "called on the chief of the equalization board [Oslo] . . . and entered a complaint against the high taxation of the Oesterhausgade 27 property." Andrew Jenson Diary, bk. J, p. 140, 22 October 1909, holograph and typescript, LDS Church Archives. In spite of persecution, Mormons in Brevik rented a hall in 1852 according to Christian J. Larsen Journal, vol. 2, p. 122, holograph and MS, LDS Church Archives. Members in Drammen evidently met at a place called "Hjardalsplassen" outside the city limits in 1857 according to Hans Olsen Magleby Journal, 11 February, 3 March 1857, holograph, LDS Church Archives; in 1862, Mormons in Drammen were meeting in private homes as per H. P. Lund to Jesse N. Smith, 18 June

1862, quoted in <u>Skandinaviens Stjerne</u> 11 (1 July 1862):296-97. Reports from Drammen Branch in 1885 mentioned three halls rented by Mormons--one each in Drammen, Hurum and Roeken. <u>Skandinaviens Stjerne</u> 35 (15 October 1885):29. Andrew Israelsen described the Mormon office in Drammen on 20 November 1891 as follows: "It was a little side room on the second floor. It contained a bed, table, stove, writing desk, a book case and a book shelf, one wash stand, a few dishes, two lamps, two looking glasses . . . this place and the things it contained must have been used by the elders for over 15 years. It was very shabby, the paper loose and dirty. . . . The main room on the second story was the meeting hall. A fairly nice room it was, big enough to seat about a hundred persons. The place had been rented by the branch for 15 years for 30 kroner [crowns] per quarter. The location was fine, on a slope near the Lutheran church." Andrew M. Israelsen, <u>Utah Pioneering: An Autobiography</u> (Salt Lake City, Utah: Deseret News Press, 1938), pp. 94-96. Israelsen gave the address of the meetinghouse as "Taylor Nielsen's Hall, 'Cappelens Gada.'" Ibid. According to Hilmar Freidel, <u>Gren og Misjon: Jesu Kristi Kirke av Siste dagers hellige Norske misjon</u> (Oslo: Skrivestua A/S, 1971), pp. 162-63, Mormons in Drammen met in private homes during the early years; "det foerste mer faste leie-sted var i Cappelens gate 19, siden til Gjaetergaten, til Forbergsalen, Ruuds Auksjonslokale, og i 1921 i Thornegaten hvor det gamle Folkets hus laa. I 1921 kjoepte Kirken Vebergs gate 4 for 30 000 kroner, og for aa beholde det ble Ingvald Johansen insatt som 'gaardeier.'" Mormons in <u>Fredrikstad</u> met at a place called Berggaard in the suburbs of Fredrikstad in 1857 according to Mons Pedersen Journal, pp. 36, 38, 21 April, 29 May 1857, holograph, LDS Church Archives. In 1892, A. Madson reported that a Brother Hansen in Fredrikstad had built a two-story home and rented a room on the top floor to Mormons as a meeting hall. A. Madson to Mission Headquarters in Copenhagen, 18 April 1892, in <u>Skandinaviens Stjerne</u> 41 (1 June 1892):265. Mormons in <u>Halden</u> and <u>Tistedalen</u> met in a rented hall in 1862. H. P. Lund to Jesse N. Smith, 18 June 1862, in <u>Skandinaviens Stjerne</u> 11 (1 July 1862):296. F. F. Hintze reported from Halden in 1885 that "[Mormons] have a nice little hall just out side of the city limits as the municple [sic] authoritys will not alow [sic] the saints to hold meeting with in the city limits. So we have hired a hall just outside, but here a Methodist priest has been to the owner twice and tryed to get us out. . . ." Ferdinand Friis Hintze Diary, vol. 1, pp. 434-35, 2 August 1885, holograph, LDS Church Archives. In 1864, Mormons in <u>Stavanger</u> were meeting in a room at carpenter Lars Johnsen Nesse's quadrangle on Verket Gaden according to Brown Autobiography, p. 73, 23-24 June 1864. According to Hilmar Freidel, <u>Jesu Kristi Kirke i Norge: Den norske misjons historie, 1851-1966</u> (Oslo: Jesu Kristi Kirke av Siste Dagers Hellige Misjonskontoret, 1966), pp. 94-95, members of Stavanger Branch met for many years in a hall at Nygata 15 and later at Ostervaag 20. On 29 July 1909, missionaries in <u>Haugesund</u> moved to new quarters evidently used for the Mormon meeting hall as described by Carl Kjaer: ". . . in eve. [sic] we moved from Groenhauggade 5 til Strandgaden 147. Bro. Johan Sjursen had loaned a hand car with which he helped us move. Sisters Samsonsen and Kolstoe, Fru M. were also in the moving gang. . . ." Carl Kjaer Diary, p. 231, 29 July 1909, holograph, LDS Church Archives. On 30 July 1909, Kjaer noted that "Alfilde Samsonsen was here with supper. . . . Sister M. put up our curtains for us in nye lokale [new headquarters]." Ibid. Mormons in Arendal met in a large building called "Arken" [The Ark], so-named because of the numerous poor people who lived there in 1867. Arendal Mormons also met in Johan Olsen's home--referred to by neighbors as "Mormontemplet" [The Mormon Temple]--in 1867. John S. Hansen, ed., Mindeudgave C. C. A. Christensen: Poetiske Arbejder, Artikler og Afhandlinger tilligemed hans Levnedsloeb (Salt Lake City, Utah: Bikubens Bibliotek, 1921), p. 443. In 1877, members in Arendal met frequently at Terje Andersen's home in Kolbjoernsvig which neighbors referred to as "Slotta" [The Castle]. Olaf Hendrik Nielsen Journal, vol. 2, 15 July, 19 August 1877, holograph, LDS Church Archives. Mormon congregations assembled in private homes in Hedemarken Branch throughout the 1880s according to Skandinaviens Stjerne 35 (15 June 1886):282. In 1891, missionary A. Ericksen visited Brother Groenn at Stavnaes Lighthouse near Trondheim and held four meetings there. A. Ericksen to Mission Headquarters in Copenhagen, 26 January 1891, in Skandinaviens Stjerne 40 (15 February 1891):153. At Larvik in 1906, missionaries decided to find a new meeting hall for the members, i.e., E. C. Ekman reported that "the place we have here is full of Devels [sic] as we have just discovered that ther [sic] is a place of ilfame [ill fame] in one part of the house and a Drunken lot in another part." Edward C. Ekman Diary, 31 January 1906, holograph, LDS Church Archives. On 11 February 1906, Ekman reported: ". . . we held Sunday School and meeting for the Last time in this hell hole. . . . Elder Johansen in his remarkes [sic] to night sead [said] at the close that we were going to move from here and that thay [sic] wouldent [sic] be so many hudlums [hoodlums] premited [permitted] to come to the meeting as ther had ben here then you aught [ought] to of herd [sic] them hoot." Ibid., 11 February 1906. J. C. A. Weibye and companion "slept in the Later [sic] Day Saintes meeting hall in Bro. Gunner Bergs house on Indre Bakkelandet here in Throndhjem [Trondheim]" on 5 August 1871. Weibye Diary, vol. 4, pp. 8-9, 5 August 1871. Conference reports in 1913 noted that Mormons in Trondheim "had no hall to assemble in," but on 1-2 November 1913, a Mormon conference convened in Trondheim in "Arbeiderpartiets Lokale" [Labor Party headquarters]. Skandinaviens Stjerne 62 (15 December 1913):376-77. A Mormon-owned meeting hall at Gamle Kongevei 6 in Trondheim was dedicated on 8 February 1914 according to Skandinaviens Stjerne 63 (15 March 1914):90. According to Hilmar Freidel, Gren og Misjon, p. 170: "Lokaler til bruk for moeter [i Trondheim] var til en begynnelse vanskelig aa skaffe, det foerste mer faste var en stor stue hos Anthon L. Skanchy paa Lademoen. Siden fikk misjonaerene leid et lokale i Moellenberg nr. 25, siden i nr. 79, inntil man i begynnelsen av aarhundreskiftet fikk leid brukbare rom i Gamle Kongevei 6. Hele denne bygningen ble kjoept av Kirken den 1. desember 1913, og ble innviet den 8. februar 1914 av misjons-president Martin Christophersen." As late as 1885, police in Bergen refused to allow anyone to rent a meeting hall to Mormons according to Skandinaviens Stjerne 35 (15 October 1885):29. Mormons in Bergen held meetings at Nye Sandvigsvei 16 in 1899, but District President Peter N. Garff obtained a larger hall at Kong Oscars gate 5 in March 1901; members met there until 1912. Freidel, Gren og Misjon, pp. 173-74. By 15 April 1912, Mormons had purchased a hall in Bergen from members of "Bergens Totalafholdsforening" [Bergen Temperance Society] prompting "fearful agitation in Bergen over the Mormons who 'had now become so strong and numerous that they could purchase a property worth 50,000 kroner.'" According to Mission President Andrew Jenson: "The priests had tried to influence the 'Totalafholdsforening' to break their bargain and not sell us the property, and the newspapers had teemed with lies and misrepresentations against us. Even the Bergen City Council had decided by a unanimous vote to advise the Government not to grant the concession that we had petitioned for to permit the property we had bought to be deeded to Prest. Joseph F. Smith. There is a new law in Norway which makes it unlawful for a foreigner to hold property (real estate) in Norway except by special permission from the King." Jenson Diary, bk. J, pp. 883-84, 15 April 1912. On 16 April 1912, Jenson proposed that members in Bergen form "a board of directors (5 in number) . . . to receive the deed, and that I step in personally as the money lender, so that the name of Prest. Smith should not be known in the transaction. With that view I went to a lawyer (John Stabell) . . . and he at once coincided with my views. . . ." Ibid., p. 884, 16 April 1912. Jenson then "organized the branch committee . . . of three local Saints (Ingvald Hoeiem, Henrik Henriksen and Andreas Fosse) and two American Elders (Martin Christophersen and Hyrum D. Jensen). We then proceeded to Kong Oscarsgade 44 and met with the 'Afholds' directors and two lawyers, Mr. Stabell representing our side. I paid the sum stipulated, Kr. 19,000 and the deed was made out to 'Bergens Menighed af Jesu Kristi Kirke af Sidste-Dages Hellige' [the Bergen Congregation of the Church of Jesus Christ of Latter-day Saints]. I then had the five directors representing the 'Bergens Menighed' [Bergen Congregation or Branch] make out a mortgage to me for 25,000 kroner, so that the Church as a whole was not known in the transaction; the mortgage I took I can transfer to the Trustee-in-Trust at any time." Ibid., p. 885, 16 April 1912. "We rejoiced exceedingly," continued Jenson, "that we had thwarted the plans of our enemies; for while they were guarding 'one gate' we went quietly in through the other and took possession." Ibid., p. 886. The Bergen property was situated at Kong Oskarsgade 44, also known as "Jury-Lokalet" since it "for quite a period was used as a court building." Ibid., pp. 885-86. Jenson described the property as follows: "The purchased property contains a two-story rock building. . . . There are ____ [sic] rooms and a number of closets in the first story and a large hall . . . and three other good sized rooms and a hallway in the second story, and besides three rooms in the attic. . . . I consider this property the best for the money the Church has bought in Scandinavia." Ibid., p. 887. Jenson dedicated the building on 21 April 1912. Ibid., p. 891, 21 April 1912. By 31 May 1914, Mormons had bowed to public pressure and sold the Kong Oskarsgade property to the State Church. Mormons then purchased a new building at Store Markevej 36 for fifteen thousand crowns; a Mormon from Aalesund, Niels Andersen, was named owner of the property in order to avoid legal problems, but Mission President Hans J. Christiansen had Andersen sign over a thirty-five-thousand-crown bond to Anthon H. Lund to protect Mormon interests. Hans Jacob Christiansen Journal, vol. 8, p. 45, 31 May 1914, holograph, LDS Church Archives. On 2 June 1914, Christiansen received word from Bergen Branch President Anderson that a lawyer in Bergen warned of renewed persecution from the State Church if the deed of property and the bond to Anthon H. Lund were registered in court "since they [State Church priests] would soon understand that the whole thing was arranged to go around the law, which prohibits foreigners from owning real estate in Norway" ["da man af samme straks kunde forstaae, at det Hele var udfoert for at undgaa Loven, som forbyder Udlaendinger at holde fast Ejendom i Norge"]. Christiansen followed the lawyer's advice, and noted that "we must now depend entirely on that Brother's [Niels Andersen's] honesty, who now holds the property in his name" ["vi maa da fuld ud stole paa den Broders Aerlighed, som nu holder Ejendommen i sit Navn"]. (The lawyer had further advised that Mormons wait about a year before registering the deed.) Ibid., pp. 49-50, 2 June 1914. In order not to attract attention, Mormons did not meet in the new meeting hall; a Mormon conference convened in "Folkets Hus" [the People's Hall] on 19 June 1914, and priesthood brethren met that afternoon in a band pavilion in Bergen City Park. Ibid., pp. 65-66, 19 June 1914. On 29 June 1914, Christiansen met with a lawyer named Egedius who gave him the deed to the property (Store Markevej 36) along with other papers connected with the transaction. Since Christiansen was not a Norwegian citizen, he turned over administration of the property to Egedius. Ibid., p. 73, 29 June 1914. City officials in Bergen refused to let Mormons renovate the building according to Ibid., p. 87, 15 July 1914, and the property was eventually sold. Mormons in Bergen purchased a new hall at Vaskerelvgaten 1 from "Bergens Sjoemandsforbund" [Bergen Seamen's Society] for sixty thousand crowns in April 1915; Hans J. Christiansen dedicated the building on 18 July 1915. Freidel, <u>Gren og Misjon</u>, p. 174.

NOTES

CHAPTER I

[1] Included were works by Luther, Pontoppidan, Johan Arndt and Heinrich Mueller.

[2] ". . . nu blev mit Sind saa oploeftet til Gud, at jeg ikke sandsede mig . . . min Sjel foelte noget Overnaturligt, Guddommeligt og Saligt . . . en Herlighed, som ingen Tunge kan udsige. . . . Ingen kan heller fradisputere mig dette; thi jeg veed alt det gode i min Aand, som fulgte paa fra denne Stund, isaer den inderlige braendende Kjaerlighed til Gud og min Naeste, at jeg havde et ganske forandret Sind, en Sorg over alle Synder, en Begjaerlighed at Menneskene skulde blive deelagtige med mig i samme Naade; en saerdeles Lyst til at laese i den hellige Skrift, isaer Jesu egen Laere, samt nyt Lys at forstaae den, og sammenbinde alle Guds Maends Laerdomme til det ene Maal, at Christus er kommen til vor Frelser, at vi skulle ved hans Aand foedes paany. . . Det var da ligesom jeg saae Verden ligge nedsaenket i det Onde, hvilket jeg soergede meget over, og bad Gud skulde forhalde med Straffen, saa kunde Nogle omvende sig. Jeg vilde nu gjerne tjene Gud, bad han vilde aabenbare mig hvad jeg skulde gjoere? Det gjenloed i mit Indre: Du skal bekjende mit Navn for Menneskene, formane dem at omvende sig og soege mig medens jeg findes, kalde paa mig naar jeg er naer og roerer ved deres Hjerter, saa kunde de omvende sig fra Moerket til Lyset." Andreas Aarflot, <u>Tro og Lydighet</u> (Oslo: Universitetsforlaget, 1969), p. 94.

[3] Johannes Gulbranson, "Hans Nielsen Hauge og Christiania," <u>St. Hallvard</u> 49 (1971):150-53.

[4] Ibid., p. 154.

[5] Ibid., p. 158.

[6] Oscar Albert Johnsen, <u>Norges Boender: Utsyn over den Norske Bondestands Historie</u>, 2nd ed. (Oslo: H. Aschehoug & Co., 1936), p. 342.

[7] Einar Molland, <u>Fra Hans Nielsen Hauge til Eivind Berggrav: Hovedlinjer i Norges Kirkehistorie i det 19. og 20. Aarhundre</u> (Oslo: Gyldendal Norsk Forlag, 1972), p. 21.

[8] Johs. Lavik, <u>Spenningen i Norsk Kirkeliv: Kirkehistoriske konturtegninger</u> (Oslo: Gyldendal Norsk Forlag, 1946), p. 36.

[9] J. L. Balling and P. G. Lindhardt, <u>Den Nordiske Kirkes Historie</u> (Copenhagen: Nyt Nordisk Forlag [Arnold Busck], 1973), p. 287.

[10] Arlow W. Andersen, <u>The Norwegian-Americans</u> (Boston: Twayne Publishers, 1975), p. 16.

[11] Einar Molland, "Kristen Tro og Oekonomisk Aktivitet hos Hans Nielsen Hauge," <u>Norsk Teologisk Tidsskrift</u> 59 (1958):196, 201.

[12] Halvdan Koht and Johan Schreiner, "Aarsakene til at Regjeringen grep inn mot Hans Nielsen Hauge," <u>Historisk Tidsskrift</u> 30 (1934-1936):63.

[13] Johnsen, <u>Boender</u>, p. 343.

[14] Gulbranson, "Hauge," p. 164.

[15] Ibid., 165-66.

[16] Peerson was born in Tysvaer, Rogaland, Norway, in 1783 according to Mario S. De Pillis, "Cleng Peerson and the Communitarian Background of Norwegian Immigration," <u>Norwegian-American Studies</u> 21 (1962):137. J. Hart Rosdail in <u>The Sloopers, Their Ancestry and Posterity: The Story of the People on the Norwegian Mayflower-- The Sloop, "Restoration"</u> (Broadview, Illinois: Norwegian Slooper Society of America, 1961), p. 137, notes that Peerson "had been out of sympathy with the State church as early as 1818" having "influenced others to refrain from church attendance and taking part in the Lord's Supper."

[17] De Pillis, "Peerson," 138.

[18] Norwegian sailors who had been imprisoned on English jail barges during the Napoleonic Wars (1807-1814) brought Quakerism to Norway in 1814. Enoch Jacobsen, the Quaker leader in Oslo, had been imprisoned on a British ship in Chatham Harbor where he obtained a copy of <u>Apologia</u> written by the Quaker, Robert Barclay. Barclay's work had been translated into Danish and Jacobsen used it to convert several other Norwegian prisoners. By War's end, nineteen Norwegians had become Quakers on the prison boats (most of those who joined the Quakers had been followers of Hans Nielsen Hauge in Norway), and in the fall of 1814 they returned to Norway where they formed the nucleus of a small congregation in the area around Stavanger. By 1816, a congregation of Quakers numbering about twenty men and women was meeting at Tollbugata in Oslo. In that year, two Quakers, Knud Halvorsen and Anne Olsdatter, were married according to Quaker custom, but this the Deacon of Oslo, Lumholtz, could not allow, and demanded that Knud and Anne be deported. A Royal Commission decreed on 27 December 1819 that Halvorsen and wife

could remain in Norway as Quakers if they abided by strict controls. Anti-Quaker sentiment grew over the next two decades climaxing in a Supreme Court decision on 14 December 1839 against the Quaker, Soeren Eriksen Stakkland, who was stripped of his horse, seven cows, two rams, three sheep and two lambs because he would not allow his two youngest children to be christened in the State Church. He was left with one calf. Andreas Seierstad, <u>Kyrkjelegt Reformarbeid i Norig i Nittande Hundreaaret</u> (Bergen: A/S Lunde & Co.s Forlag, 1923, pp. 220-22, 227, 243.

[19] Rosdail in <u>Sloopers</u> (p. 9) cites claims that as many as twenty-seven of the "Sloopers" were Quakers or had Quaker sympathies, although only one, Lars Larsen Jeilane, appears on Quaker records in Norway. Others, such as De Pillis in "Peerson" (p. 139), say that only a handful were Quakers and the rest Haugians. According to Theodore C. Blegen in his <u>Norwegian Migration to America</u> (Northfield, Minnesota: The Norwegian-American Historical Association, 1940), pp. 100-01, the "Sloopers" and those who followed after them "had a stubborn belief in the rightness of lay preaching," were critical of high church and aristocratic practices, and "came out of a Norway that was seething with interest in religion and in which the spirit engendered by Hauge was broadening from a matter purely of Godly zeal to a broad-gauged struggle of the common people against the aristocracy." According to De Pillis in "Peerson" (pp. 154-55), religious dissent in Norway at that time "usually expressed itself in Haugean Lutheranism or in Quakerism," and "both . . . sects were then still very close to the pietistic communitarian traditions of northern Europe."

[20] De Pillis, "Peerson," p. 138. The "Sloopers" of 1825 were the first Norwegians to immigrate to America as a group. Conversely, the first Norwegians to come to America for religious reasons were a scattered lot, did not emigrate in groups, and were almost exclusively unmarried males. Through travel and individual study they had become acquainted with the pietism espoused by Unitas Fratrum (The United or Moravian Brethren), and some were original settlers of the Moravian Colony "Wachovia" founded in North Carolina in 1753. These Norwegians pietists numbered only eight or nine souls, none were famous, and most died without heirs. For purposes of this study, their importance lies in their acceptance of pietistic ideas while engaged in such varied pursuits as studying at the University of Copenhagen, traveling as merchants to London, learning a trade in Holland, or serving as sailors on ships which docked in the Americas. Their initial introduction to pietism did not take place in Norway, and most left Norway never to return. Almost to the man, they and their fellow believers found an outlet and growing space in the far reaches of Georgia, Pennsylvania, North Carolina or some other American frontier. Martin Ulvestad, <u>Nordmaendene i Amerika: deres Historie og Rekord</u> (Minneapolis, Minnesota: History Book Company's Forlag, 1907), pp. 8-9.

[21] De Pillis, "Peerson," p. 151.

[22] Ibid., p. 153.

[23] De Pillis in "Peerson," p. 137, records a folk myth about Peerson's journey as follows: "One day in Illinois, Peerson lay down under a tree, and, falling asleep, beheld the wild prairie transformed into a great fruitful garden with herds of fat cattle peacefully grazing between splendid fields of waving grain. This vision he took as a sign from God that the Fox River Valley was to be the Norwegian Land of Promise and he its Moses. His hunger and sufferings were then forgotten."

[24] Carlton C. Qualey, Norwegian Settlement in the United States (Northfield, Minnesota: Norwegian-American Historical Association, 1938), p. 25. Qualey further notes on p. 29 that "although the Fox River settlement, properly speaking, consisted only of the townships of Mission, Rutland, Miller, Manlius, Adams, Earl, Freedom, and portions of adjacent townships in La Salle County, it came in time to include a much larger area. The immigrants of 1836 and 1837 settled not only on lands near the farms of the 1834 settlers, but they also took land in Adams Township to the northwest. This part of the Fox River settlement expanded into Earl Township and centered in the village of Leland."

[25] One of the emigrants was Erich Gautesen Ramberg (Midtboeen) (Haugen) from Tinn, Telemark, Norway. His son, Gaute Haugen [Goudy Hogan], related that his father was the first one in that part of Norway to emigrate, and the departure of the Haugen Family occasioned "great mourning that was done by all our relations, at a funeral there could not have been more mourning manifested." Goudy E. Hogan Journal, 1837, p. 2, microfilm of typescript, Library-Archives, The Church of Jesus Christ of Latter-day Saints, Salt Lake City, Utah [hereinafter cited as LDS Church Archives].

[26] Rasmus B. Anderson, The First Chapter of Norwegian Immigration, (1821-1840): Its Causes and Results (Madison, Wisconsin: By the Author, 1906), pp. 112, 237, 326.

[27] Blegen, Migration, p. 102.

[28] Ibid., p. 104.

[29] Rosdail, Sloopers, p. 105.

[30] Blegen, Migration, p. 104.

[31] Rosdail, Sloopers, p. 105.

[32] Joseph Smith, History of the Church of Jesus Christ of Latter-day Saints, 2nd ed., vol. 5: Period I: History of Joseph

Smith, the Prophet, 1842-43 (Salt Lake City, Utah: Deseret Book Company, 1973), p. 395.

[33]Mormon activity in the Fox River Settlement was centered in an area about nine miles northeast of the town of Ottawa in La Salle County. Canute Peterson et al., in "Story of the life of Canute Peterson as given by himself and by some members of his family," p. 15, xerox of MS, LDS Church Archives, relates that he and Gudmund Haugaas traveled to the Wisconsin Territory as Mormon missionaries in November 1844. They began their proselyting work in Muskego where they "met the Danielson's and Lars Heier who had a large family. Brother Heier, five of his son's and two of his daughters joined the church. Here we organized a Branch of the Church, and Brother Danielson was called to preside over the Branch." From Muskego, Haugaas and Peterson went to Koshkonong Settlement where they held several meetings, "but the people were very indifferent." Haugaas and Peterson headed home in the Spring of 1845, and arrived at the Fox River to find it full of floating ice. There was no bridge or ferry, and Peterson recorded: "We undrest, tied up our clothes into bundles, tied the bundles on our heads, and waded and swam until we reached the other shore."

[34]Peterson, "Story," p. 12. Rosdail in Sloopers, p. 109, quotes a letter to Norway sent by the Lutheran minister, J. W. C. Dietrichson, describing conditions in Fox River Settlement on 10 May 1845: "The confusion here is terrible. Our dear countrymen, baptized and confirmed in the faith of our fathers, are here divided into seven or eight different sects. About 80 belong to the Mormon sect. Others are Methodists, Presbyterians, Baptists, Quakers, and followers of Elling Eielsen." Another Lutheran minister, Ole Andrewson, wrote that Mormonism had left the Fox River region "like a prairie swept by fire." Ibid. According to William Mulder in "Norwegian Forerunners Among the Early Mormons," Norwegian-American Studies and Records 19 (1956):50, nearly 150 Norwegians in the western settlements (including eighty in Fox River) had accepted the "Mormon delusion" by late 1845. Why did Mormonism appeal to so many of the Fox River Norwegians? According to Blegen in Migration, pp. 113, 115, the Mormons rejected infant baptism, predicted Christ's imminent return, warned of "the coming destruction of the world," and pointed to "a thousand-year rule by Christ in the New Jerusalem surrounded by the Mormon faithful." Mormon doctrine, with its emphasis on adult baptism and promises of "a special sanctuary to true believers after the anticipated second coming of Christ," appealed very strongly "to many pietistic pioneers torn loose from their old environment and facing frontier difficulties."

[35]Peterson, "Story," p. 14.

[36]Rosdail, Sloopers, p. 108.

[37]Ibid., p. 106, notes that the city laid out by the Apostles about 23 October 1844 was just over three miles southwest of the present town of Norway.

[38]Rosdail, *Sloopers*, pp. 124-26; Journal History of the Church, 26 February 1848, pp. 3-4, LDS Church Archives.

[39]Rosdail, *Sloopers*, p. 131.

[40]Mulder, "Forerunners," p. 59. General Files of the Perpetual Emigrating Fund Company, 1849-1898, box 1, folder 2, pp. 3-4, LDS Church Archives, list the following members of the Norwegian Company of Mormons and their ages: Hannah Doll 57, Andrew Doll 16 [sic], Sven Jacobs 25, John Jacobs 23, Elen Jacobs 18, Shure Cleson 30, Elizabeth Oleson 24, Ola Oleson 11 months, C. Peterson 24, Sarah A. Peterson 22, Rosmas Rosmason 28 [possibly a Dane], Henry Saby 57, Magla Saby 51, Ira Saby 19, Jones Saby 22, Walber Saby 16, Peter Saby 14, Betsy Saby 8, Christian Hyer 32.

[41]The Introduction to a typescript volume entitled, "Church Emigration," 1849-1857, vol. 2, p. 16, LDS Church Archives, records the following: "Saturday, July 14th, 1849, a large company left Winter Quarters under the direction of Apostle George A. Smith and Ezra T. Benson. After reaching the Platte liberty pole, the company was divided into camps denominated George A. Smith's camp (including the Welsh Company under Captain Dan Jones, consisting of about 25 wagons) and Ezra T. Benson's camp (including a company of Norwegians.) This division was made for convenience sake, but the two camps kept close together in traveling and camping. Both camps contained 467 souls, 129 wagons, 514 oxen, 243 cows, 70 loose cattle. . . ."

[42]Erastus Snow Journal, vol. 5, 19 October 1849, microfilm of holograph, Erastus Snow Collection, LDS Church Archives.

[43]William I. Appleby Journal, p. 18, 23 October 1849, in "Emigration," n.p.

[44]Ibid.; Snow Journal, vol. 5, 23-24 October 1849.

[45]According to Blegen in *Migration* (p. 118), Norwegian settlement in the Mormon Zion would in turn have a direct impact upon Norway "through missionaries sent to that country after the great Mormon trek to Utah. . . . Mormon lines of sequence and of influence can be drawn from the Fox River and Sugar Creek Norwegian settlements to the Old World by way of Utah." Mormon propaganda in Norway would naturally be more effective because it was voiced by native Norwegian sons.

[46]Edith P. Christiansen, Patron Family Group Sheet [hereinafter cited as PFGS] "Canute Peterson and Sarah Ann Nelson," Family Group Record Archives, Library Services Division, Genealogical

Department, The Church of Jesus Christ of Latter-day Saints, Salt Lake City, Utah [hereinafter cited as GS]; Antone L. Peterson, PFGS "Canute Peterson (Knut Pedersen Maursether) and Sarah Ann Nelson," GS; Ferdinand Euray Peterson, PFGS "Canute Peterson and Gertrude Maria Rolfson," GS; Daisy Amelia Beal Willcox, PFGS "Canute or Knud Peterson and Sarah Ann Nelson," GS.

[47] Andrew Jenson, <u>Latter-day Saint Biographical Encyclopedia: A Compilation of Biographical Sketches of Prominent Men and Women in the Church of Jesus Christ of Latter-day Saints</u>, vol. 3 (Salt Lake City, Utah: Andrew Jenson History Company, 1920; reprint ed., Salt Lake City, Utah: Western Epics, 1971), p. 410; Lawrence M. Hogan, PFGS "Eric Gautesen (Midboen) Hogan (Haugen) and Helge Knudsen," GS.

[48] Jenson, <u>Encyclopedia</u>, vol. 4 ([Salt Lake City, Utah:] Andrew Jensen Memorial Association, 1936; reprint ed., Salt Lake City, Utah: Western Epics, 1971), p. 593; Josephine H. Adair and Goudy E. Hogan, "Biography of Goudy E. Hogan by himself and daughter, Mrs. Josephine H. Adair," p. 59, microfilm of typescript, LDS Church Archives; Olive H. Hatch, PFGS "Goudy Hogan and Ann Nelson," GS.

[49] Melba Rolfe, PFGS "John Jacobs and Elizabeth Coleman," GS; Margaret Sales, PFGS "John Jacobs and Harriet Austin," GS.

[50] Annie Hyer Kemp, <u>What We Know About the Hayer (Hyer) Family</u> (Logan, Utah: By the Author, 1954), pp. 15-16.

[51] Elizabeth Jacobs, PFGS "Swen Johnson Jacobs and Sarah Sophia Hopkins," GS.

[52] Andrew Jenson, <u>History of the Scandinavian Mission</u> (Salt Lake City, Utah: Deseret News Press, 1927), p. 208.

[53] Kemp, <u>Hayer Family</u>, pp. 16-17.

[54] Mulder, "Forerunners," p. 57.

[55] Rosdail, <u>Sloopers</u>, p. 178.

[56] Helen Farnsworth Ovard, PFGS "Christian Larsen Hyer and Lovina Hogan," GS; Annie Hyer Kemp, PFGS "Christian Larsen Hyer (or Christian Larsen Hejer) and Caroline Hogan (or Kari Ericsen Haugen)," GS.

[57] Hilda Hambleton, PFGS "Osten Sondresen and Aase Olsen," GS; Mrs. Heber Morris Hodges, PFGS "Heber Chase Kimball and Ellen Sanders," GS.

[58] Jenson, <u>Scandinavian Mission</u>, pp. 76, 208, 235-36.

CHAPTER II

[1] Andrew Jenson, <u>Latter-day Saint Biographical Encyclopedia: A Compilation of Biographical Sketches of Prominent Men and Women in the Church of Jesus Christ of Latter-day Saints</u>, vol. 2 (Salt Lake City, Utah: Andrew Jenson History Company, 1914; reprint ed., Salt Lake City Utah: Western Epics, 1971), p. 766; Peter Olsen Hansen Autobiography and Journal, p. 17, holograph, Peter Olsen Hansen Collection, Library-Archives, The Church of Jesus Christ of Latter-day Saints, Salt Lake City, Utah [hereinafter cited as LDS Church Archives].

[2] Hansen Autobiography, p. 22.

[3] Ibid., p. 29.

[4] Ibid., p. 24.

[5] Peter Olsen Hansen, "How the Danish translation of the Book of Mormon originated," p. 1, holograph, Peter Olsen Hansen Collection, LDS Church Archives.

[6] Hansen Autobiography, p. 45. Hans Christian Hansen was one of the Mormon Pioneers of 1847 and was born on 23 November 1806 in Copenhagen, Denmark. Jenson, <u>Encyclopedia</u>, vol. 2, p. 766. Before joining the Mormons, he belonged for a time to the Baptist Church. He first heard about the Mormons from the first Danish member of the Church, Peter Clemensen. Clemensen lived in Boston, Massachusetts, and told Hansen that God had raised up a latter-day prophet. After a trip to Liverpool, England, Hansen returned to Boston where he listened to the sermons of a Mormon named "Father Nickerson," and joined the Mormons in the summer of 1842. H. C. Hansen, "H. C. Hansens Beretning," <u>Morgenstjernen</u> 2 (1 January 1883):9. Hansen was one of the first fiddlers in Utah, and died at Salina, Sevier, Utah, on 10 October 1890. Jenson, <u>Encyclopedia</u>, vol. 2, p. 766. We know very little about the first Danish Mormon, Peter Clemensen. P. O. Hansen recorded that in the summer of 1845, Clemensen came to Nauvoo shortly after his wife had died in childbed in St. Louis. Some of Clemensen's children had also died, but he brought those who survived to Nauvoo. "Being acquainted with father Nickerson he found shelder [sic] at his house; but there he heard old Mother N. swearing, and that tried his faith a little; his 15 year old daughter took sick & died; that shick [shook] him still worse; and on hearing how the Saints were persecuted he took fright & went away saying, if this was the people God [sic], he would not suffer them thus to be ill-treated." Hansen Autobiography, pp. 60-61. Clemensen was the first native

Dane to join the Mormons, Hans Christian Hansen was the second, and Peter Olsen Hansen was the third. Jenson, **Encyclopedia**, vol. 2, pp. 766-67.

[7] Hansen Autobiography, pp. 49, 51, 331.

[8] Ibid., p. 52.

[9] Hansen and his brother were adopted by the Mormon Apostle Heber C. Kimball in February 1846 before leaving Nauvoo. Hansen Autobiography, p. 62.

[10] Hansen, "Book of Mormon," pp. 3-4.

[11] Hansen Autobiography, p. 69.

[12] Ibid., p. 70.

[13] Ibid., p. 74.

[14] Ibid., p. 76.

[15] Ibid., p. 77. Erastus Snow (1818-1888) was ordained a Mormon Apostle on 12 February 1849 in Salt Lake City, Utah. At that time, he was told by Brigham Young to "henceforth drop the axe, the shovel and the hoe and let your labors be in Building up the Kingdom of God in all the world." Erastus Snow Journal, vol. 5, 12 February 1849, microfilm of holograph, Erastus Snow Collection, LDS Church Archives. At the time he was called on his mission to Scandinavia, Snow recorded the promise made to him by Brigham Young that "the Angels of the Lord should go before my face to prepare the way whethersoever I went." Ibid.

[16] Hansen Autobiography, p. 77.

[17] Ibid., p. 84; Andrew Jenson, **History of the Scandinavian Mission** (Salt Lake City, Utah: Deseret News Press, 1927), p. 4-5.

[18] Hansen Autobiography, p. 84.

[19] Snow Journal, vol. 5, n.d.; Andrew Jenson, "Erindringer fra Missionen i Skandinavien," **Morgenstjernen** 1 (January 1882):5.

[20] Andrew Jenson, "For tredsindstyve Aar siden," **Scandinaviens Stjerne** 59 (1 August 1910):225-31.

[21] Erastus Snow, **One Year in Scandinavia: Results of the Gospel in Denmark and Sweden - Sketches and Observations on the Country and People - Remarkable Events - Late Persecutions and Present Aspect of Affairs** (Liverpool: F. D. Richards, 1851;

reprint ed., Dallas, Texas: S. K. Taylor Publishing Co., 1973), p. 19.

[22] Snow Journal, vol. 5, n.d.

[23] John Ahmanson, Vor Tids Muhamed: En historisk og kritisk fremstilling af mormonismens fremkomst og udbredelse, samt skildringer af Utahs hemmelige historie (Omaha, Nebraska: Den Danske Pioneer's Trykkeri, 1876), p. 5.

[24] Erastus Snow to his family in Utah, 4, 7 July 1850, Erastus Snow Letter File, Erastus Snow Collection, LDS Church Archives.

[25] Erastus Snow to his wife, [?] February 1851, Erastus Snow Letter File, Erastus Snow Collection, LDS Church Archives.

[26] Snow to family, 4, 7 July 1850.

[27] Ahmanson, Muhamed, p. 6.

[28] Erastus Snow Reminiscences, 1818-1854, p. 2, holograph, Erastus Snow Collection, LDS Church Archives.

[29] Samme Sommer var fra Amerika ankommen til Kjoebenhavn 4 Misionnaerer [sic], for at forkynde et meget besynderligt Budskab, nemlig at Gud havde atter Aabenbaret sig, og sendt Engle som i gamle Dage, at Tiden for vor Herre Jesu Christi Tilkommelse var naer, at Gud havde optrykket sin Kirke paa Jorden og i den indsat Apostler og Propheter o.s.v. at han havde opreist en ung Mand ved Navn Joseph Smith til at udfoere hans Besluttninger og lade Evangeliet udgaa i sin Renhed til Jordens Beboere o.s.v." John F. Ferdinand Dorius, "No. 1 Dagbog for J. F. Ferdinand Dorius tilligemed et kort Udtog af hans tidligere Levnetsloeb," p. 2, holograph, LDS Church Archives.

[30] Ahmanson, Muhamed, p. 8.

[31] Ibid.

[32] Snow Journal, vol. 5, n.d.

[33] Snow Journal, vol. 5, n.d. Snow's hesitancy and caution are well-illustrated by George Parker Dykes in his diary. On 1 September 1850, Dykes went to a private Mormon meeting, but "bro Snow did not come. . . ." On 3 September, some people who wanted to hear Mormonism preached sent for Snow, "but it being late Br Snow declined. . . ." On 4 September, Dykes wrote a letter to John E. Forsgren in Sweden, "& I took the Letter to Br Snow to read it to him but as he was not yet up I took it to the post office. . . ." On 5 September, Dykes was enroute to visit an investigator and "called on Br Snow to have him go with me but he was not up yet so I went alone. . . ." Dykes

stopped at the home of a Brother Malling on 6 September "to read a letter to Br Snow that I had received from my wife but as he was not up I went on. . . ." On 7 September, Dykes "went after breakfast to see Br Snow but as he was not yet up I went into other [sic] room where I talked with the family. . . ." Next morning (8 September), Dykes went to visit Snow after breakfast, "but he was not yet up but after waiting some time I found he would not be ready in time so I went alone and at ten oppend meeting. . . ." Dykes continued: ". . . thus passed a week of hard labor of hunger & wearisomeness, while (I think) except to the meetings Br Show was at home evry day through the week though I asked him to to [sic] go out & assist me to fill the many calls on the wright [sic] hand & the Left but he said he would stay at home & write, & brother H told me on Saturday evening he had written but 4 pages foolscap of common hand." George Parker Dykes Diary, 1, 3-8 September 1850, holograph, LDS Church Archives. On 27 August, Snow had received word of the death of his eldest son, James, and was going through a period of depression and grief. Snow Journal, vol. 5, 27 August 1850.

[34]Jenson, "Erindringer," pp. 1-7; Snow Journal, vol. 5, n.d.

[35]Hansen Autobiography, p. 86.

[36]Snow Journal, vol. 5, n.d.

[37]Snow Reminiscences, p. 3.

[38]Peter Olsen Hansen, "Elder P. O. Hanson's [sic] account of his mission to Denmark," 29 September 1855, pp. 3-4, holograph, Peter Olsen Hansen Collection, LDS Church Archives. Following the organization of the Copenhagen Branch and the more visible nature of Mormon meetings thereafter, Danish newspapers began running anti-Mormon articles "teeming with Old English & American lies, translated & newvamped, in which dirty work the Baptists made themselves conspicuous." Snow Journal, vol. 6, p. 14. In addition, the Bishop of Copenhagen issued a pamphlet urging the Government to protect the people against the Mormons--"that dangerous sect." Ibid. By December, disturbances and rowdyism at Mormon meetings were commonplace, and Snow was forced to discontinue all evening meetings. This did not prevent mobs from beating in the meetinghouse door, however, and venting "their fury upon the building and each other, while the Saints were praying at home." Ibid., p. 15. Snow described difficulties confronting Mormonism as follows: "The novelty of a new religion in the country, the excitability of the people, the control of the priests, over churches and school-houses; the fear of violence and damage, that deters men from leasing us houses; the restrictions of law upon street preaching and promiscuous assemblages; the spleen and jealousy of a well organized national

police, are all no small obstacles in the way of getting truth before the people." Snow, *Scandinavia*, p. 20.

[39] Dykes Diary, 15 September 1850.

[40] Ibid., 11 September 1850.

[41] Ibid., 13 September 1850. Other sore points were Dykes's impatience with Snow's apparent lack of missionary zeal and Snow's refusal to go with Dykes to visit the Government Minister of Education. Ibid., 16 September 1850. Dykes was forced to wait two hours for Snow to get out of bed and give him "fine paper" on which to write a petition to the Government on the morning of 20 September. Snow, in fact, never did give Dykes the paper, and Dykes felt "a little agrivated that Br Snow should be so dillatory in all his movements." Ibid., 20 September 1850. In addition, Snow had reproved both P. O. Hansen and Dykes "in a high tone of voice" saying they were "not doing right," and when Dykes spoke with Brother Malling, Snow's landlord, he found him "so tired of Br Snows oppression that he wanted my permission to have him Leave his home for he said it would not be so great a trail [trial] to him if he did not see it so much." Ibid., 24 September 1850.

[42] Chr. Christiansen to Andrew Jenson, 15 February 1882, in *Morgenstjernen* 1 (February 1882):26-27.

[43] Ibid.

[44] Snow Journal, vol. 6, p. 6.

[45] Dykes Diary, 25 September 1850.

[46] Erastus Snow to Willard Snow, 25 September 1851, Erastus Snow Letter File, Erastus Snow Collection, LDS Church Archives.

[47] Snow Journal, vol. 6, p. 7.

[48] Hansen Autobiography, 11 May 1850.

[49] Snow Journal, vol. 5, n.d.; Hansen, "Book of Mormon," p. 5.

[50] Snow, *Scandinavia*, p. 13.

[51] Snow Journal, vol. 6, p. 9.

[52] Snow to wife, [?] February 1851.

[53] Andrew Karl Larson, *Erastus Snow: The Life of a Missionary and Pioneer for the Early Mormon Church* (Dugway, Utah: Pioneer Press, 1971), p. 228.

⁵⁴Ibid.

⁵⁵Snow Journal, vol. 6, p. 19.

⁵⁶Ibid., p. 21.

⁵⁷Jenson, Scandinavian Mission, p. 25. Snow summarized his publishing ventures on 4 March 1852: "The publications which I have issued in the Danish Language are as follows viz: 3,000 copies of the Book of Mormon, 800 copies of the Book of Doctrine and covents [sic]--three small editions of Hymns makeing 2,500 cipies [sic] in all. 'Skandinaviens Sjerne' [sic] organ of de sidste Dages Hellege [sic]. 1000 copies monthly during the last six months of which between five and six hundred has been circulated among the people. Besides these I have issued seven different tracts and pamplets [sic] of different sizes from 4 to 24 pages Octavo amounting to about 10,700 copies among which was a translation of Elder O. Pratts 'Remarkable visions' and 'Divine Authority.' The greatest portion of these pamplets have been circulated among the people." Erastus Snow, "A Summary of the Danish Mission by Erastus Snow to the Presidency of the Church of Jesus Christ of Latter Day Saints," pp. 1-2, microfilm of holograph, Erastus Snow Collection, LDS Church Archives.

⁵⁸Snow Journal, vol. 6, p. 21.

⁵⁹Ibid., p. 16.

⁶⁰Snow to wife, [?] February 1851.

⁶¹Snow Journal, vol. 6, pp. 30, 32.

⁶²Dykes Diary, 10 October 1850.

⁶³Ibid., 27 October 1850.

⁶⁴Ibid., 2 December 1850; Jenson, Scandinavian Mission, p. 17.

⁶⁵Dykes Diary, 2, 25 December 1850.

⁶⁶". . . thi see, den Dag er naer og den Tid er snart ved Haanden, naar Guds Roest skal hoeres fra Himmelen og Roesten af Jordskjaelv, Svaerd Pestilentse, Hunger, Lynild og Tordens Roest, og Engle skal flyve midt igjennem Himmelen og basune med hoei Roest og det skal hoeres af alle Nationer, Stammer, Tungemaal og Folk, . . . om I kunne see med prophetisk Aand igjennem den Tid hvilken vi leve [sic], da vilde de ydmyge sig selv enhver i Sagtmodighed og blive i Boen og Paakaldelse paa Herrens Navn, til at bevare dem fra de store Plager, som vil komme over Jorden; . . . Giv noeie Agt paa Eder selv . . . foerend

den onde Dag kommer; thi den vil komme og den vil vaere stor og salige ville de vaere, som har holdet sig selv rene og er beredt for den." George Parker Dykes, <u>Mindeblad efter Aeldste Parker Dykes til Jesu Christi Kirke af Sidste Dages Hellige i Aalborg</u> ([Aalborg?]: n.p., 1851), pp. 1-4.

[67] Dykes Diary, 9 January 1851.

[68] Ibid., 19 December 1850.

[69] Ibid., 24 January 1851.

[70] Ibid., 24 February 1851.

[71] Ibid., 19 February, 3, 30 March 1851.

[72] Ibid., 13, 26-28 March 1851.

[73] Ibid., 12 April 1851.

[74] Ibid., 14 April 1851.

[75] Ibid., 9-10 April 1851.

[76] Jenson, "Erindringer," pp. 1-7.

[77] Ibid.

[78] Jenson, <u>Scandinavian Mission</u>, p. 33; Hilmar Freidel, <u>Jesu Kristi Kirke i Norge: Den norske misjons historie, 1851-1966</u> (Oslo: Jesu Kristi Kirke av Siste Dagers Hellige Misjonskontoret, 1966), pp. 26-27.

[79] "Jeg var imedlirted [sic] anmodet meget artig at tage Saede hvelket jeg gjorde, og paa spoergsmaal, fortalte hvem jeg aer og hvor jeg hoerte hjemme. Brother Snow satte sig ved min Side foran et Spisebord paa hvis anden Side stod en Sopha lige under Vinduerne. Han spurgte om jeg fotod [forstod] Engelsk til hvilket jeg sagde Ja, men jeg forstod dog ikke Evangeliets Sprog i det Engelske; han fortalte mig derpaa Evangeliets foerste Principper i det Danske Sprog. Jeg ytred ved enkelte leiligheder at jeg troede hvad han sagde. Jeg maa her bemerke at en indre Stemme tilvesket mig disse ord, denne er en Guds Mand. Jeg var ligesaa overbevist dengang om at Br. Snow er en Guds Mand som jeg er i dag og jeg troede hvert Ord han fortalte mig, hvorfor jeg bemerket nu og da, jeg troer det. Broder Snow reiste sig op og satte sig paa Sophaen, sagtenes for at see mig lige i Oeinerne for desto bedre at bedoemme om jeg var aerlig eller ikke. Han gav mig en god Underviisning og fortalte blandt andet om hvorledes Joseph Smith fik Pladerne som Mormons Bog er oversat efter og viste mig ved, The Perl [Pearl] of great prise [Price], lignende karakterer af de som var indgravet paa Pladerne.

Conversationen varede omtrent 2 Timer og i den tid fik jeg Kundskab om aldeles nye Ting som jeg troede ligesaa fulkommen som om jeg havde vaeret Oeienvidne til alt. Broder Snow spurgte om man har fri Religions-oevelse i Norge, hvortil jeg sagde ja, thi Decenterloven giver alle Chrestne sekter frihed til at pragtisere efter deres Tro, men udelukker Jesuiter og Munkeordener fra adgang til Riget. Br Snow spurgte om jeg vilde tage en Broder med til Norge for at praedikke Evangeliet hvilket jeg samtykede, saa fremt den Broder kunde faa sit toei ombord samme Aften, og faa sit Pas med thi ifoelge Skippereden maa man ingen pasloes Person bringe ind i Landet under Mulkt." Svend Larsen, "Uddrag af min Biographi (1816-1867)," pp. 5-7, holograph, LDS Church Archives.

[80] Snow Journal, vol. 6, p. 34.

[81] Dykes Diary, 9-10 April 1851.

[82] Peter O. Hansen, "Evangeliets Indfoerelse i disse Lande," Skandinaviens Stjerne 32 (1 October 1882):14.

[83] Larsen was baptized a Mormon at Aalborg on 23 September 1851 by O. C. Nielsen. Larsen, "Uddrag," p. 10.

[84] George Parker Dykes to Mrs. King, 8 August 1864, LDS Church Archives.

[85] J. E. Forssgren to Erastus Snow, 1 July 1851, quoted in Snow, Scandinavia, pp. 16-17.

[86] Dykes Diary, 30 June 1851.

[87] Ibid.

[88] Hansen Autobiography, 13 July 1851.

[89] Tallak Lindstoel, Risoer gjennem 200 Aar: 1723-1923 (Risoer: I Hovedkommission hos Erik Gunleikson for Risoer kommune, 1923), p. 464.

[90] Hans Jacob Christiansen Journal, vol. 3, pp. 11-12, holograph, LDS Church Archives.

[91] Lindstoel, Risoer, p. 209.

[92] Ibid., pp. 82, 87.

[93] Ibid., p. 385; Larsen, "Uddrag," p. 1.

[94] "[Stormen] bragte mig til at tenke paa Jesus og Deseplerne da de (Deseplerne) syntes at vaere i Havsnoed paa Geneserets Soee og Jesus lod til at sove, dog paa Deseplernes Boen stod

han op og truede Vinden og Havet og det blev ganske stille. Dette bevirket at jeg i al stilhed med fulkommen Tillid ogsaa bad til Jesus at han veld [sic] stille Vinden og Havet og give os foeielig Vind. Jeg havde ikke laert at bede knaelende til Faderen i Jesu Chresti Navn . . . dog blev jeg boenhoert til min egen forundring endog foeren jeg havde endt Boennen, jeg saa at Boelgerne med et aftog og Vinden begyndte at loeie, og inden Aftenen gik Vinden Oesterlig (god Vind). . . . Jeg bemerker denne Tildragelse for at aere Herrens Navn og vise at Herren er naadig og boenhoerer den som med tillid eller Troe beder til Ham. . . ." Larsen, "Uddrag," pp. 1-2.

[95]". . . jeg tilgiver eder alle eders Synders naadige forladelse i Navnet Faderens og Soennens og den Hellig Aands. . . . Jeg tenkte da hvorledes toer du paatage dig at lyve i Herrens Navn, thi her maaske ikken [sic] en som haver tenkt paa at omvende sig og sletikke bedet om tilgivelse. . . ." Ibid., p. 3.

[96]". . . jeg betragted Praesten fra den tid af med afsky og kom ikke mere til Kirke." Ibid.

[97]". . . for at samle, Hvad baade kunde vaere den unge og den mere moderne Soeemand til Gavn." M. F. Brovn [Brown] and Svend Larsen, eds., "Journal of Navigation," 1833, MS, LDS Church Archives.

[98]Ibid., tables 3-5, 15-17.

[99]"Hvor forskillige Meninger er om Ankernes Vaegt i Forhold til Skibets Brede, til Skibets Draegtighed, eller til Taugets Tykkelse vil sees af Tabellerne 7, 8 og 9. Min meninger [sic] at Kjaetting-Ankerne i Tabellen 9, er anfoert forsvaere i forhold til Skibets Dregtighed. . . ." Ibid., p. 15. Larsen's eye for detail is well-illustrated by an entry in his diary under date of 4 August 1866 near Halden: "Besaa en Moellejul Axel sat sammen af 4 Stykker Tapperne af Stoebt Jaern 6 tommer Tyk og havde 4 Vinger som gik ind i Axelen til enden af Tappen og paset til Axelens Tykkelse saa at 4 Ringer holdt den fast. Mandagen foerhen havde jeg beseet Valseverket, hvor der blev arbeidet Jaernstenger. Ligeledes besaa jeg Bomulds Spinneriet, og blev vist af Mesteren alle operationer fra de foerste Karemaskiner lige til den fine Traad for Vaevning kommer ud og bliver Hespet og lagt i Pakker. . . . Besaa derpaa en Savemoelle som havde 8 Blade i en Ramme og 14 Blade i en anden, og et Sirkelsageblad som alt kunde gaa paa en gang - Saa paa samme Tid, en Moelle Flom, som var omtrent 12 Fod Bred og 5 Fod dyb ganske ful af Vand fordelt til 5 Brysthjul i et Moellehuus." Svend Larsen Diary, 4 August 1866, holograph, LDS Church Archives. On 26 July 1866, Larsen described a bridge in Sarpsborg: ". . . besaa Sarpebroen, som er bygget efter den samme Stil som Niagara Broen. Er 100 Skrit Lang og 51 Skrit mellem Steen Pillarerne over hvilke 8 Jaernstaenge paa hver side af Broen er dragen og hviler paa

Ruller, disse Jaernstenger er 4 Tomer brede 5/8 Tomme tykke og omtrent 8 Fod lange og Sammenfoeiet med Bolte der tjaener som Lede - Dette baerer Brostykket mellem Pillarerne." Larsen Diary, 26 July 1866.

[100] Svend Larsen said he requested Mormon baptism because he felt he could not come unto God without repenting and promising God with his heart and soul that he would not sin again. To seal his promise, Larsen was baptized a Mormon for the remission of sins. Afskrift av Extraret paa Fredrikstads Byfogedscontor, 15 October 1852, Fredrikstads Byes Politiprotokol, Mormonpakken, Trossamfunn Samling [hereinafter cited as TS], Det kongelige Justis- og Politidepartement, Oslo, Norway [hereinafter cited as JPD].

[101] Jenson, *Scandinavian Mission*, p. 33.

[102] Ibid., p. 34.

[103] Ibid., p. 35.

[104] John E. Christiansen, "H. F. Petersens Biografi," *Morgenstjernen* 3 (1 September 1884):270.

[105] Larsen, "Uddrag," p. 11.

[106] Christiansen, "Petersens Biografi," p. 271.

[107] Svend Larsen, "Extracts from my Autobiography," p. 6, typescript translation, LDS Church Archives.

[108] J. A. Aahmansen, "Beretning om Missionens Begyndelse i Brevig," pp. 1-2, in Historical Record and Record of Members, 1852-1862, Brevik Branch, Christiania Conference, Scandinavian Mission, LDS Church Archives.

[109] *Adresse-Tidende for Brevig*, 1 November 1851.

[110] Ibid., 21 February 1852, p. 4.

[111] "[Provsten snakket slik] til den allerede dybt bevaegede Menighed, at Manges Oeine Vaededes med Taarer, fremkaldte af Sorg og Bekymring over de Farer, hvorfor flere haederlige Medmennesker . . . have vaeret udsatte. . . ." Ibid., 25 August 1852, p. 2.

[112] Aahmansen, "Beretning," pp. 1-2; Christian J. Larsen Journal, vol. 2, p. 113, 12 September 1852, holograph and MS, LDS Church Archives. On 30 September, about twenty Mormons met in John Olsen's home while a mob outside heckled and disturbed the meeting until midnight. Larsen Journal, vol. 2, p. 122,

30 September 1852. Svend Larsen and a few missionaries ventured back to Brevik in October, but not for long. While preparing to leave Brevik on 5 October 1852, Larsen and the missionaries were threatened by a mob which "made some noisy demonstrations . . . without doing any harm." Ibid., p. 124, 5 October 1852.

[113] Andreas Aarflot, *Norsk Kirkehistorie*, vol. 2 (Oslo: Lutherstiftelsen, 1967), p. 261.

[114] Ola Rudvin, *Indremisjonsselskapets Historie*, vol. 1: *Den Norske Lutherstiftelse 1868-1891* (Oslo: Lutherstiftelsens Forlag, 1967), pp. 174-75. In a letter to the Bishop of Oslo on 26 January 1857, the Dean of Tune, P. F. Bassoee, described major differences between Lutheran and Haugian conceptions of justification: "It is obvious that in this Deanery no real harmony can exist between true Christian priests and lay preachers [Haugians] . . . . What we have here are two interpretations of Christianity . . . one advocated by clerics; the other by the lay preachers. The former believe that the essence of Christianity is grace; human action means nothing; grace is obtained through faith in the Father, Son, and Holy Ghost . . . such grace is only available through the Church and its sacraments, namely through Baptism, the Word and the Lord's Supper, and all three of these sacraments are of equal worth and meaning. The other [Haugian] school of thought . . . declares that because 'I have repented I am therefore sanctified.' They also claim . . . that faith in Christ is faith in Him as the Redeemer of Mankind, and when describing the life of a true Christian (one united with Christ), do not stress the fact that such a life should be a life in Christ imbued with His Mind and Spirit, but, in direct opposition thereto, fall back upon the Law . . . as interpreted in Old Testament times. . . . They overemphasize the Word whereas baptism and the Lord's Supper are pushed into the background. When one of them, through the preaching of the Word by a lay preacher, is what they call awakened, he views this as a rebirth without attributing any great importance to whether or not he is baptized; the Lord's Supper is considered as simply a symbol and as nourishment for the spiritual life, not as the impartation of Christ Himself, of His death for the sins of the world. As a result, the Church does not have the importance for them that it should have. . . ." ["Her i Provstiet, som vel overalt i vort Land, har det viist sig, at ingen sand Harmoni har kunnet finde Sted mellem de i Sandhed christelige Praester og Laegpraedikanterne. . . . Der er nemlig to Hovedretninger i Opfattelsen af Christendommen hvoraf den ene i Almindelighed hyldes af Praesterne, den anden af Laegpraedikanterne. De som ere af den ene Retning antage, at Alt i Christendommen er Naade; den menneskelige Gjerning har Intet at betyde, Naaden gribes ved at modtage ved Troen Faderen, Soennen og den Helligaand . . . at denne Naade meddeles gjennem Kirken ved dens Midler, nemlig ved Daaben, Ordet og Alterets Sacramente, og at alle disse tre Midler have lige vaerd og Betydning. Den anden Retning . . . siger,

at fordi jeg er omvendt, derfor faaer jeg Salighed. De som ere af denne Retning, paastaa ogsaa . . . at Troen paa Christus er Troen paa ham som Menneskehedens Forsoner, men naar det kommer til Skildringen af, hvorledes dens Liv skal vaere, som ved Troen er forenet med Christus, da laegges ikke den tilboerlige Vegt paa, at Livet skal vaere Livet i Christo, gjennemtraengt af hans Sind og Aand, men derimod gaaer man tilbage til Loven . . . [og] opfatter den i dens gammel testamentlige Betydning. . . . Orden . . . faaer en overveiende Betydning, hvorved Daabens og Alterens Sacramente traeder i Skyggen. Naar nemlig Nogen ved en Laegpraedikants Forkyndelse af Ordet blive, hvad han kalder, vakt, da ansees han dette for Gjenfoedelse, uden at laegge nogen saerdeles Betydning i, enten han er doebt eller ikke; Alterens Sacramente betragtes fast blot som et Pant og som Naering for det aandelige Liv, ikke som en Meddelelse af Christus selv, af hans Doed for Verdens Synder. Deraf foelger, at Kirken for dem ikke har den Betydning, den skulde have. . ."] P. F. Bassoee to Jens L. Arup, 26 January 1857, Visitasberetninger, 1856-1860, pakke 1856, Kristiania Stift, Kontor A [hereinafter cited as "A"], Det kongelige Kirke- og Undervisningsdepartement [hereinafter cited as KUD], Riksarkivet, Oslo, Norway [hereinafter cited as RA]. In the same vein, Jens L. Arup, the Lutheran Bishop of Oslo, observed (1857) that certain Haugians were thinking of leaving the State Church "because they could not agree with the practice of making a confession of belief on behalf of a child at its christening--the child itself having no opinion or belief whatsoever." Arup described such a view as "the rationalistic interpretation of the sacraments." [". . . af en agtvaerdig Praest har jeg nylig medtaged Underretning om, at Visse iblandt Haugianerne taenke paa Udtraedelse, fordi de ikke kunne finde sig i, at der paa Barnets Vegne, som jo selv ingen Mening kan have, aflaegges i Daaben Troesloefte--en consaeqvent Foelge af den rationalistiske Opfatning af Sacramenterne."] Jens L. Arup to KUD, 21 March 1857, Visitasberetninger, 1856-1860, pakke 1856, Kristiania Stift, A, KUD, RA.

[115]Johs. Lavik, Spenningen i Norsk Kirkeliv: Kirkehistoriske konturtegninger (Oslo: Gyldendal Norsk Forlag, 1946), p. 36.

[116]H. Mustorp, Haugianere i Oestfold (Oslo: Lutherstiftelsens Forlag, 1930), pp. 17-18.

[117]Aage Skullerud, Bondeopposisjonen og religionsfriheten i 1840-aarene (Bergen, Oslo, and Tromsoe: Universitetsforlaget, 1971), p. 62.

[118]Arne Hassing, "Methodism and Society in Norway: 1853-1918" (Ph.D. dissertation, Northwestern University, 1974), p. 29.

[119]Ole Peter Petersen, "Short and imperfect sketches of my expiriance. and labor," holograph, Metodisme-historisk Selskap Archives, Oslo, Norway [hereinafter cited as MHSA].

[120] Hassing, "Methodism," p. 26.

[121] Petersen, "sketches."

[122] Hassing, "Methodism," pp. 24, 27.

[123] Ibid., p. 28.

[124] Petersen, "sketches."

[125] Hassing, "Methodism," p. 28.

[126] Petersen, "sketches."

[127] Ibid.

[128] Ibid. Jensen claimed a cleansing witness which relieved all feelings of guilt, i.e., "Christ crucified [was] a complete and free Savior from all sin for all who would take upon themselves His name" [". . . at fremsaette Christus og ham Korsfaestet, som en fuld og fri Frelser fra al Synd, for alle som vilde annamme ham"]. Ibid.

[129] Ole Peter Petersen, "Nogle Erindringer om mine Oplevelser og Religions Erfaringer," p. 65, holograph, MHSA.

[130] Hassing, "Methodism," p. 31.

[131] ". . . de foelte sig selv som Faar uden Hyrde, og som en Foelge deraf, var de aabne til Modtagelse af Laerdom fra andre Kilder, end fra dem, som viste dem Koldhed og Modstand." Petersen, "Erindringer," pp. 146, 167. The Dean of Tune, P. F. Bassoee, lamented Mormon successes in Fredrikstad in 1857: "That such a non-Christian sect and reprehensible group as the Mormons could gain a foothold shows the sorry state of affairs that existed in many congregations. They [the Mormons] first gained a foothold among the so-called 'Awakened,' who were earlier influenced by the Methodists and lay preachers; that such a thing could happen showed how counterfeit this revival [the revival spawned by Haugian lay preachers and Ole P. Petersen] was." ["At et saa uchristeligt, ja bespotteligt Parti som Mormonerne kunne finde Indgang, var et Beviis paa, hvor slet det stod til med Mange i Menighederne. De vandt foerst Indgang hos de saakaldte Opvakte, der i Forveien vare paavirkede af Methodister og Laegpraedikanter; at Saadant kunde ske, viste, hvor falsk denne Opvaekkelse var."] P. F. Bassoee to Jens L. Arup, 26 January 1857, Visitasberetninger, 1856-1860, pakke 1856, Kristiania Stift, A, KUD, RA.

[132] Martin Dehli, Fredrikstad bys historie, vol. 2: Fra festningsby til trelastsentrum, 1767-1860 (Fredrikstad: Fredrikstad Kommune, 1965), pp. 457-58.

[133] Ibid., pp. 459-60. Svend Peter Larsen had formally withdrawn from the State Church on 14 May; Jacobsen followed suit on 29 May, and his other stepson, Niels, withdrew on 16 June. Avskrift av dokument nr. 10, Forhoeret under Tune Sorenskriverie, 9, 12 November 1852, Mormonpakken, TS, JPD.

[134] "Ved Guds Naade bekjendes herved for den ganske verdens Kreds, at jeg, Skipperborger til Fredrikstad, J. A. Jensen har ved denne i hans ubegrundelige Naade Erholdt en Sandheds Aand i mit hjerte, som vidner med min Aand, at jeg . . . er den sande og eneste Guds Soen forenet med Faderen." "Udtog i Justitssag mod 1. Johan Andreas Jensen og 2, Emil Larsen," pp. 1-2, Utdrag i muntlige saker for Hoeiesteret, 2s. 1852, pakke nr. 74, L. nr. 234/2, Hoeiesteret, RA.

[135] Ibid.

[136] "Yder mere stadfaester jeg Alt, hvad der af Tobias Jacobsen, J. A. Jensen og Svend Larsen bliver indfoert med Ja og Amen, da jeg og Dem ere af Gud og umulig kan lyve." Ibid., p. 3.

[137] Ibid., pp. 3-4; Dehli, trelastsentrum, p. 460.

[138] ". . . han erklaerer, at han fremdeles agter at gaae frem paa samme Maade, naar Guds Aand drive ham dertil og opvaekker Lysten, da han i saafald gjoer det paa hvilketsomhelst Sted. . . ." "Justitssag," pp. 5, 7.

[139] Dehli, trelastsentrum, p. 461.

[140] "Justitssag," pp. 5-9.

[141] ". . . Kong Oscar er en Loegner og den stoerste Loegner af alle Loegnere i vort Land." Ibid., p. 16.

[142] Ibid., pp. 17-18; Dehli, trelastsentrum, p. 462.

[143] Dehli, trelastsentrum, p. 462

[144] "Den forhen i dette Blad omtalte Methodistgalning, Tobias Jacobsen, . . . har i Sommer sat i Arresten her i Byen, hvor han muntrer sig med at nedrive den ene Kakkelovn efter den anden, slaa ud Vinduerne og ellers hvad der falder ham i Haenderne, og formaaede han det, rev han som en anden Samson hele Raadstuen ned over sig." Fredrikstad Smaalehnenes Amtstidende, 17 November 1853, p. 4; Hassing, "Methodism," pp. 34-35.

[145] Dehli, trelastsentrum, p. 426.

[146] Andrew Jenson, "Scandinavian Reminiscences," Contributor, March 1895, pp. 301-02.

[147] Historical Record and Record of Members, 1852-1858, Fredrikstad Branch, Christiania Conference, Scandinavian Mission, LDS Church Archives; Kenneth O. Bjork, West of the Great Divide: Norwegian Migration to the Pacific Coast, 1847-1893 (Northfield, Minnesota: Norwegian-American Historical Association, 1958), p. 86.

[148] Willard Snow to Erastus Snow, 9 July 1852, Erastus Snow Collection, LDS Church Archives.

[149] Chr: Arup to Jens L. Arup, 3 December 1852, Visitasberetninger, 1851-1855, pakke 1852, Kristiania Stift, A, KUD, RA.

[150] ". . . paa Krageroeen i en til Gaarden Fuglevig henhoerende Bugt 'Bedhuusbugten kaldet'. . . ." Avskrift av Extraret paa Fredrikstads Byfogedcontor, 4 October 1852, Fredrikstads Byes Politiprotokol, Mormonpakken, TS, JPD. Those baptized were: Niels Theodor Emil Larsen (born 13 March 1826 at Fredrikstad; a dyer by trade; married with one child; Tobias Jacobsen's stepson); Maren Lovise Poulsdatter (born 7 March 1825 at Fredrikstad; Larsen's wife); Johan Johansen (born 12 August 1821 at Vinger; a master shoemaker and married man with four children; ex-leader of the so-called group of "Church-believers" in Fredrikstad); Inger Kirstine Thoresdatter (born 29 September 1823 at Fredrikstad; Johansen's wife); Randine Larsdatter (born 14 January 1822 at Glemminge; unmarried servant girl in Captain Scheel's employ). Ibid. Johan Johansen was ordained to the Mormon Priesthood and set apart as leader of Mormons in the Fredrikstad area on 25 July 1852. Three more persons were baptized the following night, 26 July: Anne Marie Jacobsdatter (born about 1792; shoemaker Johansen's mother-in-law); Karen Helena Andersdatter (born 5 May 1823 at Borge; servant girl in Doctor Larsen's employ); Emilie Olsdatter Halvorsen (born 29 May 1827 at Halden; unmarried). Ibid.; Andrew Jenson, "Biografiske Skizzer: Hans Peter Jensen," Morgenstjernen 1 (July 1882):106; Record of Members, 1852-1858, Fredrikstad Branch; Bjork, Divide, p. 88.

CHAPTER III

[1]"Dette Hovedpunkt har, som vi gong etter gong har set, vore kor vidt mormonane kunne reknast som kristne, eller ikkje. Straks dei kom hit til landet, var det dette eine det reiste seg tvil om, baade fraa religioes og juridisk synstad, og tvilen har halde seg like til dei siste aara." Karl Sandvin, "Mormonisma i Noreg med utsyn over samfunnet si amerikanske historie" (Hovedoppgave, University of Oslo, 1946), p. 100.

[2]". . . Saadanne, som bekjende sig til den christelige Religion, uden at vaere Medlemmer af Statskirken." Knut Rygnestad, *Dissenterspoersmaalet i Noreg fraa 1845 til 1891: Lovgjeving og Administrativ Praksis* (Oslo: Lutherstiftelsens Forlag, 1955), p. 13.

[3]August Severin Schou Diary, vol. 1, p. 40, 29 March 1878, xerox of typescript, Library-Archives, The Church of Jesus Christ of Latter-day Saints, Salt Lake City, Utah [hereinafter cited as LDS Church Archives]. Parents, in turn, passed on circumscribed interpretations to their chidren as witness cries of "Gentile, gentile, there goes a gentile!" ["Hedning, hedning, der gaar en Hedningen!"] from children who pursued Carl Kjaer through the streets of Haugesund in 1910. Carl Kjaer Diary, p. 293, 7 February 1910, holograph, LDS Church Archives.

[4]Peter Olsen Diary, 31 July 1896, microfilm of holograph, LDS Church Archives.

[5]Edward C. Ekman Diary, 5 November 1906, holograph, LDS Church Archives.

[6]Norway, Storting, *Storthingstidende indeholdende to og tredivte ordentlige Storthings Forhandlinger* (Odelsthinget), 1883, "Forhandlinger i Odelsthinget," p. 602.

[7]"En vanlig definisjon av en kristen er at det er en som tror paa Nytestamentets Kristus som Frelser og Forloeser og anerkjenner hans budskap som norm for liv og laere. . . . Hvem avgjoer om en annen person er kristen? Hvem gaar man til for aa faa vite hva en katolikk tror, til en katolikk eller en lutheraner? Hvem gaar man til for aa faa vite om de siste-dagers-hellige er kristne, til en lutheraner eller til en siste-dagers-hellig?" Ole Podhorny and Petter Svanevik, "Noen Kommentarer Omkring et 'Ikke-Kristent' Trossamfunn," Oslo, 1977, pp. 3-4, typescript, Norway Office, Translation Services Department, The Church of Jesus Christ of Latter-day Saints, Moss, Norway [hereinafter cited as Norway TSD].

[8] Edv. Bull et al., eds., <u>Norsk Biografisk Leksikon</u>, vol. 18 (Oslo: H. Aschehoug & Co. [W. Nygaard], 1977), p. 405. Ideological and social divisions were still very much in evidence on 17 May 1881 when the famous poet, Bjoernstjerne Bjoernson (1832-1910), presided at an unveiling ceremony for a newly completed statue of Henrik Wergeland. The choice of Bjoernson as speaker for the occasion had unleashed a stream of polemics between his friends and enemies. It was obvious, however, that most of the working-class population wanted Bjoernson as speaker for the ceremony. Wergeland--the great champion of the common man--had been dead for a generation, but the working classes still revered his name. The big day arrived, and a ceremony began at the poet's grave. Next came a parade of about seven hundred students with banners; fifty artists; and groups of painters, mechanics, printers, carpenters, masons, tinsmiths, farmers and labor leaders with their flags. Every window looking onto Karl Johansgate (Oslo's main street) was jammed, and the street itself was packed with onlookers. But no representatives from the Government, the Supreme Court, the Parliament or the Oslo City Council were to be seen, and no memorial wreath was presented by parliamentary or city officials. Events of the day showed quite clearly that divisions in Norwegian society revealed during the student conflicts of the 1830s were still very much a part of Norwegian life. S. C. Hammer, <u>Kristianias Historie</u>, vol. 5: <u>1874-1924</u> (Oslo: J. W. Cappelen for Hovedkommission, 1928), pp. 40-45, 47.

[9] Jens Arup Seip, <u>Utsikt over Norges historie</u>, vol. 1: <u>Tidsrommet 1814-ca. 1860</u> (Oslo: Gyldendal Norsk Forlag, 1974), pp. 65, 67. Power exercised by the civil servant estate was that of life and death as witness the arrest on 19 April 1846 of a young man and two women who were wandering around "preaching God's will on earth." District Sheriff Klykken of Skogn arrested the trio because they would not reveal their names. At a hearing several days later, they still refused to supply any information about themselves except to say "they were the Children of God and had no passport or letter of passage. Their passport was Christ." At this, Sheriff Klykken angrily ordered all three imprisoned on bread and water until they would cooperate. Two itinerant women preachers visited those in prison, and were themselves imprisoned when they declined to say who they were. In addition to bread so stale they could not keep it down, the prisoners were fed decaying fish. All five were confined in a tiny cubicle with air so foul they nearly suffocated; this in large part because the latrine was in the middle of the cell. Two of the five finally agreed to tell who they were, and were placed in another room. The others remained in the first cell and received only water five days of each week. One of the women soon died of starvation. The others were released after Klykken was charged with "maltreatment." He was, however, never convicted of a crime. Arnet Olafsen, <u>Vaare Sorenskrivere: Sorenskriverinstitusjonen og Sorenskrivere i Norge (Et Bidrag til den Norske Dommerstands Historie)</u>, vol. 2: <u>1814-1927</u> ([Oslo]: A/S O. Fredr. Arnesen Bok og Akcidenstrykkeri, 1945), p. 88.

[10] Dagfinn Mannsaaker, *Det Norske Presteskapet i det 19. Hundreaaret* (Oslo: Det Norske Samlaget, 1954), p. 169.

[11] Edvard Bull, *Arbeiderklassen i Norsk Historie* ([Oslo]: Tiden Norsk Forlag, 1947), p. 124.

[12] Ingrid Semmingsen, ed., *Husmannsminner* (Oslo: Tiden Norsk Forlag, 1961), p. 1.

[13] Arne Bergsgaard, *Norsk Historie 1814-1880* (Oslo: Det Norske Samlaget, 1964), p. 157.

[14] Seip, *1814-ca. 1860*, p. 184. Crime was increasing: in 1815, there was one convict per 1,846 Norwegians; by 1840, there was one convict for every 694 Norwegians. Sverre Steen, gen. ed., *Norges Historie*, 2 vols. (Oslo: Gyldendal Norsk Forlag, 1938), vol. 2: *Fra 1660 til Vaare Dager*, by Magnus Jensen, p. 203.

[15] Seip, *1814-ca. 1860*, pp. 185-86.

[16] Frede Castberg, *Rett og revolusjon i Norge* (Oslo, Bergen, and Tromsoe: Universitetsforlaget, 1974), p. 28. Thrane called for recognition of human worth, and wanted the upper classes to treat workers with respect. Birger Steiro, *marcus thranes politiske agitasjon 1849-1855* (Melhus, Norway: snoefugl forlag, 1974), p. 22. He did not attack Christianity, but did attack priests whom he felt ignored the essentials of Christian doctrine. Thrane accused the priests of trying to preserve the status quo with its social inequities, and of living in the lap of luxury while their parishioners barely subsisted on near-starvation diets. Ibid., pp. 65, 68. Thrane claimed the priests used their priestly offices as forums for defending social injustice. Thrane also advocated religious freedom, and condemned use of force against religious dissenters, i.e., "if a religion, in and of itself, does not have power to convince men, that religion must be false" ["thi hvis en Religion ikke har Overbevisningens Kraft i sig selv, saa maa den vaere falsk"]. Ibid., pp. 69-70. Thrane's newspaper advised Norwegians to escape miserable conditions in Norway by fleeing to America where treasure hunters in California plucked up diamonds from the ground like eggs. As early as 1848, Thrane wrote: "All my thinking, day and night, is directed toward America, and especially California . . . California is the Garden of Eden." ["Al min Tanke, Dag og Nat, staar til Amerika, og isaer Californien . . . Californien er Edens Land."] Sigmund Skard, *USA i Norsk Historie: 1000-1776-1976* (Oslo: Det Norske Samlaget, 1976), p. 131. In calling for judicial reforms, universal suffrage, easier credit laws, and religious and trade freedoms, Thrane constantly pointed to conditions in America as the great standard worthy of emulation. Ibid.

[17] Seip, *1814-ca. 1860*, pp. 188, 190.

[18] Castberg, *Rett*, pp. 31-32. The prosecutor in the case was the famous lawyer, Bernhard Dunker. Ibid.

[19] Ibid., pp. 32-36, 41.

[20] "I thraniter-bevegelsens dager foelte statssamfunnets ledere og store kretser i folket seg truet av opproer og revolusjon. Det var en trusel--saa ubestemt den enn var og saa overdrevet den enn ble oppfattet--som innebar baade vold og eiendomsinngrep. Den ble opplevet paa bakgrunn av de blodige revolusjoner i Europa faa aar i forveien. --Og rettsoppgjoeret ble preget av det." Ibid., p. 42.

[21] Olsen was a very prominent Thranite in Risoer where he served as foreman of a workers' benefit fund committee. "Fortegnelse over den hervaerende [Risoers] Arbeiderforenings faste og contribuerende Medlemmer," Medlemsfortegnelser, pakke Thrane-saken, Det kongelige Justis- og Politidepartement [hereinafter cited as JPD], Riksarkivet, Oslo, Norway [hereinafter cited as RA]. Olsen signed a Thranite petition in 1850 seeking redress for worker grievances. Thranite petitions and membership rolls were filed with the JPD in 1850 and 1851, so it is possible, therefore, the JPD knew of Olsen and his Thranite connections before he submitted his Mormon petition. Petition no. 92 from Oesterriisoeers Arbeiderforening, Petisjoner, pakke Thrane-saken, JPD, RA.

[22] Hilmar Freidel, "Historiske dokumentasjoner: Edsavleggelse," pp. 1-2, xerox of typescript, Norway TSD.

[23] "De hvis trosbekjennelse ikke tillater ed under noen form, avgir i de tilfelder hvori ed kreves, loefte eller bekreftelse paa den maaten som Kongen bestemmer, hvilket skal tas til foelge som om ed av dem var avlagt." Ibid.

[24] I. S. Thomle to JPD, 6 April 1852, Mormonpakken, Trossamfunn Samling [hereinafter cited as TS], JPD, Oslo, Norway [hereinafter also cited as JPD].

[25] JPD to Det kongelige Kirke- og Undervisningsdepartement [hereinafter cited as KUD], 17 April 1852, pakke "Mormonerne 1851-1920," Kontor A [hereinafter cited as "A"], KUD, RA.

[26] KUD to det theologiske Facultet [hereinafter cited as DTF], 15 April 1852, carbon copy, A, KUD, RA; KUD to DTF 23 April 1852, carbon copy, A, KUD, RA.

[27] ". . . da nysnaevnte Lov selv viser, hvor overordentlig vidt den vil have udstrakt Begrebet af 'dem, der bekjende sig til den christelige Religion,' idet den blandt disse ogsaa regner

saadanne, der forkaste Daaben . . ., en Udstraekning, som derfor ogsaa Staten in praxi gjoer gjaeldende med Hensyn til Qvaekerne, og da den her omhandlede Sekts, Fakultetet forelagt Bekjendelse Intet indeholder, der overskrider Lovs og Aerbarheds Graendser." DTF to KUD, 17 May 1852, Mormonpakken, TS, JPD. In 1814, members of the Eidsvoll Constitutional Convention recognized full freedom of religion for all Christian sects, but through an oversight never afterwards explained, did not include a paragraph on religious freedom in the final draft of the Norwegian Constitution. Bergsgaard, <u>Historie</u>, p. 153. Not until 1833, when a Supreme Court attorney named Soerensen proposed a law on religious freedom for all Christian sects, and asked the Theological Faculty for comments and suggestions, did the question come up again. On that occasion, the Faculty focused on the expression "Christian sects" which it felt was unclear. By "Christian sects" did one mean only sects already operating in Norway, or sects which might be established? Who should decide if a sect was Christian? The Faculty chose to define a "Christian sect" as one which accepted the sacraments of baptism and the Lord's Supper, as also the Apostolic Creed. But opponents quickly pointed out that such a definition was too narrow--it would lock out the Quakers. Ragnhild Marthins, "Synet paa religions-frihet i Norge i foerste halvdel av det 19. aarhundre slik det kommer fram i debatten om paragraf 2 i grunnloven" (Hovedoppgave, University of Oslo, 1963), p. 18. Debate continued until 13 November 1843 when a commission was formally established to draft a dissenter law. Andreas Seierstad, <u>Kyrkjelegt Reformarbeid i Norig i Nittande Hundreaaret</u>, vol. 1 (Bergen, Norway: A/S Lunde & Co.s Forlag, 1923), p. 326. The resulting document referred only to "Christian sects," later amended to "those who confess the Christian religion." A Church committee next reviewed the Commission's proposals, and decided that more conservative wording was necessary--the King should decide if a religious sect was Christian or not. The proposals were accordingly amended and submitted to Parliament where the Farmers' Party sought to strip religious minorities of any power to define themselves as Christians by recommending yet another restrictive clause: "Only those Dissenters who accept the Apostolic Symbol [Creed] are defined as Christians." Ibid., pp. 330-34; Aage Skullerud, <u>Bondeopposisjonen og religionsfriheten i 1840-aarene</u> (Bergen, Oslo, and Tromsoe: Universitetsforlaget, 1971), pp. 68-70. Supporters of the original wording proposed by the Royal Commission carried the day, however, and the more restrictive clauses were dropped. Seierstad, <u>Reformarbeid</u>, p. 334. On 16 July 1845, the Dissenter Law received Royal sanction, and paragraph one read as follows in its final form: "Dissenters, or those who profess the Christian Religion, without being members of the State Church, shall enjoy free public practice of their religion within the bounds of law and decency, and can establish congregations under the direction of their own priests or leaders." ["Dissentere, eller Saadanne, som bekjende sig til den christelige Religion, uden at vaere Medlemmer af Statskirken, have fri offentlig Religionsoevelse inden Lovs og Aerbarheds Graendser, og kunne danne Menigheder under Ledelse af egne Praester eller Forstandere."] Rygnestad, Dissenterspoersmaalet, p. 13.

[28]DTF to KUD, 17 May 1852.

[29]Edv. Bull et al., eds., Norsk Biografisk Leksikon, vol. 11 (Oslo: H. Aschehoug & Co. [W. Nygaard], 1852), p. 435.

[30]"Han styrte mer i pakt med det gamle byraakratiske statskirkesyn enn etter de voksende frihetstankene i samtiden. Enhver utvikling som kunne tenkes aa 'beroeve Kirkestyrelsen Adgang til at udoeve den Control som formenes at maatte tilkomme den' var han paa vakt mot." Einar Engoey, "Kirkeforfatningsdebaten i 1850-aarene: Om bakgrunnen for kirkekommisjonen av 1859" (Hovedoppgave, University of Oslo, 1968), p. 3.

[31]"Han 'egnede sig til Praeses for et Collegium i Rom,' sa Vinje som tegner et bilde av ham i 'hans Kvaekerhat, hans rare Kappe, hans Kalot, hans blanke Stoevler.'" Seip, 1814-ca. 1860, pp. 35-36.

[32]"[Mormonerne] antage en anden historisk Grundvold for deres Religionsbekjendelse og navnlig troer paa en aabenbaring der ligger udenfor den, der indeholdes i den hellige Skrift . . . hvilket ikke vides at vaere Tilfaeldet med noget andet Religionsparti, der er blevet betragtet som christeligt. . . ." KUD to Tromsoe Biskop, 3 July 1852, carbon copy, A, KUD, RA; KUD to samtlige biskoper, 10 July 1852, carbon copy, A, KUD, RA. In connection with Riddervold's circular, it is interesting to compare a prior or rough draft of that document filed in the KUD's dossier on the Mormons: the rough draft details the Theological Faculty's pro-Mormon decision on Mormons and oaths (a section omitted in the final draft), and does not contain a paragraph about Mormon revelation. Konsept av KUD to samtlige biskoper, 10 July 1852, "Mormonerne," A, KUD, RA.

[33]DTF to KUD, 14 October 1852, Mormonpakken, TS, JPD.

[34]J. C. Collett, L. Kyhn, and C. Motzfeldt, eds., Departements-Tidende for 1853 (Christiania: Chr. Schibsted, n.d.), pp. 87-88.

[35]Ibid., pp. 84-87.

[36]Ibid., pp. 88-89.

[37]Jacob von der Lippe to KUD, 14 August, 17 November 1852, "Mormonerne," A, KUD, RA.

[38]Johan Balthasar Flottmann to KUD, 21 July 1852, "Mormonerne," A, KUD, RA; Collett et al., eds., 1853, p. 92.

[39] Jens Laurits Arup to KUD, 21 July 1852, "Mormonerne," A, KUD, RA; Collett et al., eds., 1853, pp. 89-92. The JPD, meanwhile, was fielding a steady stream of petitions and letters demanding resolution of the Mormon question as follows: <u>a letter 26 August 1852 from Hans Joergen Christian Aall, District Governor in Bratsberg County, reporting that two so-called Mormon priests had reportedly baptized six adults in Brevik</u> and held public lectures there on Mormonism; Aall believed Mormon preachers had transgressed the Criminal Law (chapter eight, paragraph one) which stated that ridiculing the official religion of the State was a punishable offense, as also paragraph seventeen of the Dissenter Law which prescribed punishment for those who sought to win converts to a religion through use of false promises and use of force or threats (Hans Joergen Aall to JPD, 26 August 1852, Mormonpakken, TS, JPD); <u>a letter 2 September 1852 from Aall in Bratsberg County describing a hearing in Brevik on 25-28 August regarding Mormon activities there</u>, and asking if Mormons were considered a Christian sect since Aall had serious doubts that Mormons should be allowed freedom to practice their religion, and had notified the Sheriff of Brevik to instruct Mormon priests Aahmansson and Folkmann that they must cease all practice of their religion until the Mormon question was decided, or else be arrested (Hans Joergen Aall to JPD, 2 September 1852, "Mormonerne," A, KUD, RA); <u>a letter 4 September 1852 from Mormon missionary Joh. Aug. Aahmansson in Brevik to the KUD which traced the history of Mormonism in Norway</u> and noted a petition sent by Mormons in Risoer to the KUD asking for recognition as Christian dissenters since they were currently threatened with imprisonment if they practiced their religion (Joh. Aug. Aahmansson to KUD, 4 September 1852, Mormonpakken, TS, JPD); <u>a letter 9 September 1852 from Governor Aall in Bratsberg County to the JPD reporting that on 7 September, Mormon missionaries Aahmansson and Folkmann were arrested in Brevik</u> for disobeying orders not to proselyte or baptize, and asking the JPD to make a decision soon on the status of Mormons in Norway "since I do not dare assume responsibility for allowing them [Mormons] the possibility of winning converts to a doctrine which possibly will be defined as non-Christian" [". . . jeg ikke toer paatage mig Ansvaret for, at de gives Adgang til at forlede Landets Indvaanere til en Laere, som muligens ikke vil blive Anseet som christelig"] (Hans Joergen Aall to JPD, 9 September 1852, Mormonpakken, TS, JPD); <u>a letter 13 September 1852 from Aall to the JPD saying he deemed it unnecessary to retain the two Mormons in custody any longer</u>, and had released them on 11 September on condition they not hold public religious services, administer the sacrament of the Lord's Supper, perform baptisms or ordain priests until Mormonism's status in Norway was decided (Hans Joergen Aall to JPD, 13 September 1852, Mormonpakken, TS, JPD); <u>a letter 27 September 1852 from Aall to the JPD noting the arrival in Brevik of a Mormon named Dorius from Denmark</u> who was informed by the Sheriff of Brevik that he could not hold public meetings or baptize in the county until the status of Mormonism was determined (Hans Joergen Aall

to JPD, 27 September 1852, Mormonpakken, TS, JPD); a letter 1 October 1852 from the District Governor in Smaalenenes County, Christian Birch-Reichenwald, to the JPD submitting transcripts of hearings against Mormons in Moss, and stating that he could not recognize as valid so-called "letters of authority" submitted by Mormon missionaries; Birch-Reichenwald asked whether Mormons were considered Christians, and reported that in the region between Moss and Fredrikstad, various Mormon baptisms had supposedly taken place, and a so-called Mormon priest had been arrested and would soon be tried (Christian Birch-Reichenwald to JPD, 1 October 1852, MS copy, "Mormonerne," A, KUD, RA).

[40]Jens L. Arup to KUD, 24 February 1852, Visitasberetninger, 1851-1855, pakke 1851, Kristiania Stift, A, KUD, RA.

[41]"Ilden ulmer vistnok fremdeles under Asken, ventende paa Vindpusten, der skal bringe den til at flamme op." Jens L. Arup to KUD, 10 April 1854, Visitasberetninger, 1851-1855, pakke 1853, Kristiania Stift, A, KUD, RA.

[42]"Med politiske Forvildelsen forene sig gjerne religioese; thi Sandheden i sit Vaesen maa forvanskes, naar den skal anvendes til Besmykkelse for det ondes aabenbare og udskeiende Fremtredden. Der er ikke liden Overeenstemmelse imellem Kommunismen og Mormonismen; og det er derfor ikke underligt, om denne vinder Tilhaengere." Jens L. Arup to KUD, 14 April 1855, Visitasberetninger, 1851-1855, pakke 1854, Kristiania Stift, A, KUD, RA.

[43]Andreas Hjelm, Christian Birch-Reichenwald: En Studie i Norsk Konservatisme (Oslo: Gyldendal Norsk Forlag, 1950), p. 114; Edv. Bull et al., eds., Norsk Biografisk Leksikon, vol. 1 (Oslo: H. Aschehoug & Co. [W. Nygaard], 1923), pp. 528-30.

[44]Hjelm, Birch-Reichenwald, pp. 84-85.

[45]"Birch-Reichenwalds styrke var hans venner. Han hadde et sjeldent talent for Vennskap. Megen hengivenhet stroemmet ham i moete. . . . Motzfeldt og Sibbern, Dunker og Welhavn var blant dem som stod ham naer like fra ungdommen av. Han hadde vennskapsforgreninger langt inn i hovedstadens embetsmanns-og grosserer-sosietet. Fredrik Stang, som selv manglet evnen til hengivelse, kjente godt til Birch-Reichenwalds foelge, og fryktet den styrke det gav ham. Birch-Reichenwald, skrev han, 'har flere specielle politiske Venner end nogen anden mig bekjendt offentlig Mand her i Landet.'" Seip, 1814-ca. 1860, p. 77.

[46]"For ham er Magten Oeiemedet; . . . han er mere herskesyg end aergjerrig. Denne saeregne Sjaelsretning har netop sin Forklaringsgrund . . . i Forbindelse med hans Charakters helt igjennom negative Vaesen. Det eneste Positive, han nogensinde har villet og vil, det er at have Magten; spurgte man ham, hvortil han agtede at bruge den, vilde han vistnok blive forlegen for

Svaret, eller maaske snarere ikke forstaa Spoergsmaalet. --Der er ingen Sag, hvorfor han arbeider, intet Maal, hvortil han straeber, --undtagen det at have Magten." Fr. Brandt, Morgenbladet (Oslo), 24 January 1861, quoted in Hjelm, Birch-Reichenwald, p. 121.

[47]Hjelm, Birch-Reichenwald, p. 143.

[48]"De skal ha hele landet - og dermed alle saker - i sin haand og i sin aand." Ibid., p. 42.

[49]JPD to Christian Birch-Reichenwald, 6 October 1852, MS copy, "Mormonerne," A, KUD, RA.

[50]Christian Birch-Reichenwald, circular 8 October 1852, "Mormonerne," A, KUD, RA. Mormons named in the circular were shoemaker Johan Johansen of Fredrikstad; and the following Danes and Swedes: master smith Ole Olsen, Peter Beckstroem, Christen Knudsen, J. A. Aahmansson, Jeppe Folkmann, and Nils Hansen. Ibid.

[51]Followers of Ole Soerflaten who believed in the imminent destruction of the world, and claimed they were free of sin. Soerflaten's mesmeric sermons gained him numerous female disciples who supposedly became his concubines. He was sentenced to eighteen months of hard labor in 1843. Andreas Aarflot, Norsk Kirkehistorie, vol. 2 (Oslo: Lutherstiftelsen, 1967), p. 277.

[52]". . . jeg [skal] tillige oplyse, at jeg ganske tilfaeldigvis idag er kommen paa et, efter havd jeg har al Grund til at antage, fuldkommen sikkert Spor til at faae godtgiort Rigtigheden af min Formodning om, at DHere Mormonere, eller i al Fald en Deel af dem, er ligesaa gode 'Soerflationere' som de efter all Anledning ere grundige 'Thraniter.'" Christian Birch-Reichenwald to JPD, 12 October 1852, Mormonpakken, TS, JPD. In late September 1852, civil authorities arrested a Mormon named Ole Olsen for preaching in Onsoe Parish near Fredrikstad. Olsen, a blacksmith and native Dane, admitted to having baptized as well, and declared with zealous bravado that he would continue "as long as physical restraints were not laid in his way, since he . . . was called of God and had a letter of authority signed by the Mormon leader, shoemaker Johannessen, in Fredriksstad" [". . . saalenge ikke physiske Hindringer lagdes ham i Veien, da han, havde Befaling fra Gud og en Fuldmagt fra Mormonernes Forstander hersteds en Skomager Johannessen i Fredriksstad"]. Olsen's letter of authority contained the following declaration: "Our intent is to comply with all laws of the land, to the extent they do not conflict with the salvation of our souls." (Italics mine.) [". . . vaares fremgangsmaade, er at opfylde all Lov i Landet, saae vidt det ikke strider mod vaar sjaels Frelse."] Avskrift av Forhoeret under Tune Sorenskriverie paa Gjaestgiverstedet Kjoelberglesoe [sic] i Onsoee Sogn, 29 September 1852, Mormonpakken, TS, JPD. When Birch-Reichenwald wrote to the JPD on 12 October claiming

a connection between Mormons and Thranites, he was probably referring to Olsen's statements about obedience to laws of the land, and the above-quoted passage from the "Letter of Authority," both of which were by then matters of record in a court of law. The number of Thranites who later joined the Mormons was never very great, but a few can be positively identified from workers' association lists and petitions sent to the JPD in 1851. They included: "Bjelkehugger, <u>Hans Amundsen</u>, i Arbeide paa Konsul Gutzeits Lastetomt" (no. 19 on list entitled "Arbeiderforeningen i Drammen," Medlemsfortegnelser, pakke Thrane-saken, JPD, RA); "<u>Elen Andersen</u> Bjelkehugger" and <u>Anders Andersen</u>, Bjelkehugger" (on list dated 12 August 1851 of members of <u>Arbeiderforeningen i Drammen</u>, Medlemsfortegnelser, pakke Thrane-saken, JPD, RA); <u>Andreas Hansen Gjerdahl</u>, a cotter (no. 26 on list entitled "Fortegnelse over Medlemmerne af Arbeiderforeningen i Roegens Praestegjeld," Medlemsfortegnelser, pakke Thrane-saken, JPD, RA); <u>Johannes Svenske</u>, "Arbeidsmand som boer i Svelvig" (no. 50 on list entitled "Fortegnelse over Medlemmer af de i Hurum Thinglag vaerende Arbeiderforeninger," Medlemsfortegnelser, pakke Thrane-saken, JPD, RA); "<u>Anders Madsen</u>--Toemmermand, Korstved i Soendeled Sogn" (no. 50 on list entitled "Udenbyes Medlemmer, som tillige ere Medlemmer af Understoettelsescassen" appended to list of Thranites in Risoer, Medlemsfortegnelser, pakke Thrane-saken, JPD, RA); "<u>Peter Adamsen</u>, Arbeidsmand" (no. 43 on ibid.); <u>John Olsen</u>, "Smedemester"; and <u>Lars Johnson</u>, "Arbeidsmand" (nos. 1 and 23 on list entitled "Fortegnelse over den hervaerende [Risoers] Arbeiderforenings faste og contribuerende Medlemmer, Medlemsfortegnelser, pakke Thrane-saken, JPD, RA). A petition to the king in 1850 by Thranites in Risoer contained signatures of three men--Peter Adamsen, Lars Johnsen, and John Olsen--who later became Mormons. Petition no. 92 from Oesterriisoeers Arbeiderforening, Petisjoner, pakke Thrane-saken, JPD, RA.

[53]"Da jeg i Forening med Broedrene Svend Larsen, Jeppe G. Folkmann og Niels Hansen . . . (14de Oktbr.) gik for at Besoege Soeskende paa Gaarden Ingolsrud, moedte vi undervejs Birch Reichenwaldt, Amtmanden over Smaalenenes Amt, der anholdt og tiltalte os i en meget brutal Tone, ja brugte endog Skjaeldsord, da han hoerte at vi tilhoerte Jesu Kristi Kirke af Sidste-Dages Hellige eller 'Mormonerne.' Han boed os at foelge med ham tilbage til Frederiksstad for at faengsles, hvilket vi naegtede at gjoere, eftersom vi ikke havde overtraadt nogen Lov. . . . Vi boede Farvel til Amtmanden og fortsatte vor Gang til Ingolsrud. . . ." Christian J. Larsen to Willard Snow, n.d., quoted in Andrew Jensen, "Erindringer fra Missionen i Skandinavien," <u>Morgenstjernen</u> 1 (November 1882):164-66.

[54]"Brodrene [sic] Folkman, C. Larsen, Hansen og jeg paa en Visittuer til Gaarden Ingolsrud blev anholdt af Amtmanden Birch Reichenwald. Da jeg ikke kjaendte manden spurgte jeg om hans Autoritet til at anholde os hvorpaa han i Vrede rev Overfrakken op i Brystet og viste frem et Embedstegn samt befalede

os at foelge med til Frederikstad for at aresteres, hvilket vi nektet bad farvel og fortsatte vor Vei til Ingolsrud hvor vi kort efter vor ankomst atter blev anholdt af Fogd Ytters Soen som var eskorteret af endeel Boender." Svend Larsen, "Uddrag af min Biographi," p. 15, holograph, LDS Church Archives. Christian J. Larsen recorded a confrontation with a posse of ten men at Ingolsrud, and his subsequent arrest and imprisonment. Christian J. Larsen Journal, vol. 2, p. 130, 14 October 1852, holograph and MS, LDS Church Archives.

[55] Andrew Jenson, History of the Scandinavian Mission (Salt Lake City, Utah: Deseret News Press, 1927), p. 66; Larsen, "Uddrag," p. 16; Christian Birch-Reichenwald to JPD, 27 November 1852, Mormonpakken, TS, JPD. Document abstracts taken from assorted minutes of hearings in the Mormon case contain abstracts of the following passports: Danish passport dated 1 September 1852 at Copenhagen for Niels Hansen, unmarried, age 20, born on Fyen, of average height and weight, blond-haired, blue-eyed; Swedish passport dated 18 October 1851 in Malmoe Province for shoemaker Per Baeckstroem, noting that he was going to Copenhagen to seek employment; Danish passport dated 18 August 1852 at Copenhagen for servant Christian Laursen, age 21, born on Jylland, of medium weight and height, blond-haired, blue-eyed; Danish passport dated 31 August 1852 at Copenhagen for shoemaker's apprentice Johan Frederik Ferdenand Dorius, age 20, born in Copenhagen, below-average weight, average height, blond-haired, blue-eyed; Danish passport dated 30 August 1852 at Aalborg for Christen Knudsen, age 20, born at Kjeldgaard, of average height and weight, light-haired, blue-eyed. Avskrift av dokumenter 15a, 16a, 16b, 16c og 16d, Forhoeret under Tune Sorenskriverie, 9, 12 November 1852, Mormonpakken, TS, JPD. Court minutes also contain the abstract of a Swedish attestation dated 29 August 1849 at Joenkoeping for journeyman bookbinder Johan August Aahmansson, born 7 April 1827 "uti Joenkoepings Stad och Laen," son of N. N. and Johanne Aahman, noting that he was moving to Copenhagen. Avskrift av "De under Forhoeret den 13^e. d. 16^e. og 17^e. november 1852 fremlagte Documenter," Forhoeret paa Fredrikstad, 13, 16-17 November 1852, Mormonpakken, TS, JPD.

[56] Larsen Journal, vol. 2, p. 133, 10 November 1852.

[57] Willard Snow to S. W. Richards, 13 April 1853, quoted in Andrew Jenson, "Erindringer fra Missionen i Skandinavien," Morgenstjernen 2 (2 February 1883):17. Mormon missionary Johan A. Aahmansson was in Risoer on 14 October. The Sheriff of Risoer informed Aahmansson of the arrests in Fredrikstad, and said "he had received orders from the Governor of Smaalehnene to arrest me and bring me to Fredrikstad with the steamship 'Constitutionen'. . . . The Sheriff . . . was just as surprised with the instructions as I was." [". . . han havde faaet Ordre fra Amtmanden i Smaalehnene til at lade mig arrestere og bringe til Frederikstad med Dampskibet 'Constitutionen'. . . . Byfogden . . . forundrede sig lige saa

meget over denne ordre som jeg."] John Ahmanson, <u>Vor Tids Muhamed: en Historisk og kritisk fremstilling af mormonismens fremkomst og udbredelse, samt skildringer af Utahs hemmelige historie</u> (Omaha, Nebraska: Den Danske Pioneer's Trykkeri, 1876), p. 11. Aahmansson was accordingly transported to Fredrikstad and imprisoned--proof that Birch was overstepping his jurisdictional authority. Ibid. Svend Larsen was released from prison on 16 March 1853 after writing several letters to Birch-Reichenwald decrying his unjust imprisonment. Larsen, "Uddrag," pp. 17-18; Svend Larsen Diary, p. 3, 16 March 1853, holograph, LDS Church Archives.

[58]Laws which Birch-Reichenwald considered included: Norwegian laws 6-1-4 and 6-1-5 which prohibited members of religious sects not recognized by the State from preaching publicly, baptizing and administering the Lord's Supper; Norwegian Law 2-1 which stipulated (1687) that the only religion allowed in the Kingdom was that which accorded with the Bible, the Nicene Creed, and the Augsburg Confession [see P. I. Paulsen, ed., <u>Kong Christian den Femtes Norske Lov af 15de April 1687</u> (Kristiania: H. Aschehoug & Co., W. Nygaard, 1904), pp. 60, 225]; a Royal Decree dated 22 October 1701, section II, chapter I, stating that chiefs of police were to prevent the practice of any unrecognized religion in the Kingdom, and that children of parents, of which one was not a Lutheran, were to be christened in the Lutheran Church and brought up in the Lutheran Faith, as also prescribing punishment for those who preached doctrine which advocated vice or promiscuity or was critical of the State Church or the State [see <u>Kong Friderich den Fierdes Allernaadigste Forordninger og Aabne Breve for Aar 1701 til 1702</u> (Copenhagen: Hans Kongel. Majests. privilegerede Bogtrykkeri, n.d.), pp. 76-77]; Criminal Law 1-2 which decreed that foreigners were to be punished according to Norwegian Laws for crimes prosecuted before a Norwegian court of law [see Julius August S. Schmidt, ed., <u>Love, Anordninger, Tractater, Resolutioner, Kundgjoerelser, Departementsskrivelser, Circulaerer m. m. for Kongeriget Norge i Tidsrummet fra 1814-1848</u>, vol. 2: <u>1832-1843</u> (Christiania: Chr. Toensbergs Forlag, 1850), p. 538]; Criminal Law 8-1 which prescribed fines and punishment for those who ridiculed the State Religion, the Bible or the holy sacraments, and declared that if such ridicule appeared in print, the guilty party was to be sentenced to hard labor in the fifth degree (see Ibid., p. 547); Criminal Law 21-29 which prescribed punishment for those who used documents which they knew were false or forged (see Ibid., p. 569). Christian Birch-Reichenwald to JPD, 27 November 1852, Mormonpakken, TS, JPD.

[59]Birch's quandary was well-illustrated by his own reflections on the Mormon question: "I first became involved with this case after Ole Olsen had already been arrested and after several irritating incidents had transpired in Onsoe and the vicinity of F[redrik]stad of which I was previously unaware. But just at the very time that investigations were proceeding against

Olsen, more and more foreign M[ormon] p[reachers] started appearing in the district in open violation of restrictions placed upon some of them after their release from custody in Bratsberg County (see circul[ar] 8 October), and when they were accordingly arrested, some of them would not promise to cease their activities (O. Olsen, Sv. Larsen), and indeed such a promise, in view of the circumstances of the case and in connection with such a large movement as that here, would not have been reliable. After the investigations were concluded and material brought to light which conclusively showed that M[ormons] could not be considered Christian Dissenters, recommendation was made to the Justice Department that they be deported (6-1-4 and also Ord. 1702 and 1706 etc.); this however was not carried out due to insufficient cause. At that juncture, prosecution under existing laws could not be avoided, especially since the Ecclesiastical Department under date of November 30th had declared its opinion that they [Mormons] were not Christians. Despite the fact that it was doubtful whether the harsher punishments were applicable, it was nevertheless obvious that they could not simply be set free thereby negating the injunction [the restriction placed on the Mormons by Governor Aall of Bratsberg County]; this however was the case with one of them who was released on his own recognizance [Paer Beckstroem]. To single-handedly send those who were agreeable thereto out of the country would also have resulted in inequities, especially since those who were natives of the Country (Johannesen and Larsen) would have to be prosecuted at any rate for having performed baptisms, etc." ["Jeg fik foerst at gjoere med denne Sag, efter at Ole Olsen allerede var arresteret, og megen Forargelse havde fundet Sted i Onsoe og ved Fstad, hvorom jeg tidligere ikke havde faaet Knudskab. Men netop medens Undersoegelsen mod Olsen gik frem, traadte flere og flere fremmede M. Praed. paa eengang op omkring i Districtet med aabenbar Trods mod det Forbud, som Enkelte havde faaet ved deres Frigiorelse i Bratsb. Amt (jfr. Circul 8/10) og da de derfor bleve anholdte, vilde de dels bestemt ikke indgaae paa at holde sig rolige (O. Olsen, Sv. Larsen), dels vilde et saadant Loefte efter Forholdets Natur under en saa stor Bevaegelse, som her var, ikke vaeret at sto[le paa]. Efter at Undersoegelserne vare endte og derunder Data tilveiebragtes der maatte ansees aldeles afgj. for at M. ikke kunde betragtes som christne Dissenter, henstilledes det til Just Dept at bevirke dem udfoerte af Landet (6-1-4 jfr Rescr. 1702 og 1706 m. fl.) hvortil der dog ikke fandtes Grund. Holde [sic] dem i Arrest uden Tiltale, gik ikke an. Tiltale efter de gjaeldende Love kunde da ikke undgaaes, isaer efterat ogsaa Kdpt under 30/11 havde afgivet sin Betaenkning derhen, at de ikke erkjendtes for Christne. Foruden at det i al Fald maatte agtes tvivlsomt, om ikke de strenger Straffebud skulde komme til Anvendelse, kunde det ikke gaae an at lade Forbudet uhaevdet [sic] ved at loeslade dem uden Videre, hvilket derimod skede med en af dem efter hans Oenske og paa Betingelser. Paa egen Haand at sende de Enkelte, som dertil vare villige, ud af Landet, vilde have laedet til Ulighed i Behandlingen, isaer da de her i Landet

Hjemmehoerende (Johannesen og Larsen) alligevel maatte tiltales for at have forrettet Daab m.V."] Christian Birch-Reichenwald, ". . . [a]fgivet sin Betaenk" [The document is damaged along the top margin], Chr. Birch-Reichenwald arkiv, Private arkiv [hereinafter cited as PA], RA. Paer Beckstroem was released from prison on 5 December 1852. John F. Ferdinand Dorius, "No. 1 Dagbog for J. F. Ferdinand Dorius tilligemed et kort Udtog af hans tidligere Levnetsloeb," p. 88, 5 December 1852, holograph, LDS Church Archives. Most of the remaining prisoners were released on 5 May 1853 after more than six months in prison. Ibid., p. 94, 5 May 1853.

[60]Otto Mejlaender, ed., Love, Anordninger, Traktater, Resolutioner, Kundgjoerelser, Departementsskrivelser, Cirkulaerer m. m. for Kongeriget Norge, vol. 4: 1851-1855 (Christiania: Chr. Toensbergs Forlag, 1857), p. 234.

[61]Ahmanson, Muhamed, pp. 1-11.

[62]Notes by Sheriff Berg of Fredrikstad 27 April 1853 affixed to a petition dated 19 April 1853 from Mormons in Fredrikstad, Brevik and Risoer to the King, "Mormonerne," A, KUD, RA.

[63]Dorius, "Dagbog," p. 90, 4 March 1853; Larsen Journal, vol. 2, p. 155, 4 March 1853.

[64]"Det maa nemlig bemaerkes, at den yderligere Aabenbaring, hvortil Mormonerne bekjende sig, ikke er i Strid med den foregaaende, men angives at slutte sig til den som fuldstaendiggjoerende, og dette forudsat, formaaer Retten ikke at indsee, at der er nogen vaesentlig Forskjel mellem dem, som antage et Tillaeg til den oprindelige Grundvold for sin Troesbekjendelse, og dem, som fornegte en vaesentlig Deel af denne Grundvold. Under saadanne Omstaendigheder ansees det at maatte vaere afgjoerende, at Mormonerne i deres Bekjendelse, hvor forvandsket denne end er, saette Christus som Menneskenes Frelser, og den hellige Skrift som guddommelig Aabenbaring." "Sager, paakjendte i Hoeiesterets 2den Session 1853," Norsk Retstidende 46 (14 November 1853):735-36.

[65]JPD to Christian Birch-Reichenwald, 20 April 1853, "Inkomne brev fra JPD 1853-1857," Smaalenenes Amt, Statsarkivet, Oslo, Norway [hereinafter cited as SA].

[66]". . . at lade Overretsdommen og den paa samme lignede Indankning til Hoeiesteret forkynde for de i Frstad." Christian Birch-Reichenwald to Byfogden i Fredrikstad, 22 April 1853, carbon copy, "Kopibok 1851-1854," Smaalenenes Amt, SA. See also Dorius, "Dagbog," 23 April, 5 May 1853.

[67]"Du har vel nu forhaabentlig forvundet den ubehagelige Stemning, hvori Overretsdommen i Mormonsagen satte dig? Her taler Ingen om den Sag, og jeg har ingen Grund til at troe,

at man i dept. skulde see Dit Forhold til samme paa minste Maade i noget ufordelaktigt Lys." Carl Motzfeldt to Christian Birch-Reichenwald, 24 April 1853, "Brev til Birch-Reichenwald K-M," Birch-Reichenwald arkiv, PA, RA.

[68]"I dette Oeieblik modtog jeg Dit Brev. . . . Jeg skal sige Secretairen i Hoeiesteret underhaanden, at jeg gjerne vilde vaere Actor mod Mormonerne, fordi Qvaestionen interesserer mig. Dette vil Secretairen finde meget rimeligt, som det ogsaa er, og da Personene nu ere paa fri Fod, saa anseer jeg det for afgjort, at Du ikke vil faae nogensomhelst Ubehagelighed af denne Sag." Bernhard Dunker to Christian Birch-Reichenwald, 25 April 1853, "Brev til Birch-Reichenwald A-F," Birch-Reichenwald arkiv, PA, RA.

[69]"Welhaven," said Dunker, "overpowered me with his youthful maturity and commanding presence, and I was simply his slave. But he possessed my whole heart, and I was always ready to go into the fire for him." ["Welh. kuede mig ved sin tidlige Modenhed og overmaegtige Fremtraeden, og jeg var kun hans Drabant. Men han eiede mit hele Hjerte, og jeg var altid rede til at gaae i Ilden for ham."] Bernhard Dunker to A. F. Krieger, 11 December 1866, quoted in Bernhard Dunker, <u>Breve til A. F. Krieger</u>, ed. Oeyvind Anker (Oslo: J. W. Cappelens Forlag, 1957), p. 30. In a letter from Malmoeen dated 4 May 1855, Dunker discussed a matter of State and observed: "I have conferred with my own friends of any political consequence, Birch-Reichenwald and others. . . ." ["Med mine egne Venner af nogen politisk Betydenhed, Birch-Reichenwald og flere, har jeg endog raadfoert mig. . . ."] Bernhard Dunker to Conradine Dunker, 4 May 1855, Brev fra Bernhard Dunker til Conradine Dunker, Brevsamling [hereinafter cited as BS], Universitetsbiblioteket, Oslo, Norway [hereinafter cited as UB].

[70]Bernhard Dunker, <u>Reise til Tellemarken og til Arendal Sommeren 1852</u> (Kristiania, Copenhagen, London, and Berlin: Gyldendalske Bokhandel, 1922).

[71]Solveig Tunold, Introduction to <u>Breve til Julie Winther</u>, by Bernhard Dunker (Oslo: J. W. Cappelens Forlag, 1954), p. 16.

[72]Brev fra Bernhard Dunker til Conradine Dunker, BS, UB. Dunker's mother, Conradine, was a "daughter of the Enlightenment" --a Deist for whom organized religion had the same purpose as a social club. Dunker, <u>Winther</u>, p. 7. Conversant in German and French, she spent her declining years in Trondheim reading works by Rousseau, Goethe, Holberg, and Voltaire. Brev fra Conradine Dunker til Bernhard Dunker, 1850-1857, BS, UB. Her frequent letters to her son exuded an air of open disdain for the lower classes, combined with thinly veiled fears of revolution. "A new chapel for sectarians," she wrote on 24 September 1850, "--whether Haugians, Swedenborgians, Zinzendorfians, or Mormons,

I know not--has just been erected right before our eyes. The priest or leader is said to reside in the building; his name is Volter and he is a missionary. One could probably acquiesce in such doings if they did no more damage than rob us of our view. Years ago, when they confined themselves to their metaphysical mumblings, the most damage effected by such types was the commitment from time to time of some poor fool to the madhouse, but now they have become demagogues and I believe they are dangerous. They have all but taken over public instruction of the youth--and are pure Jesuits. I often had to rub shoulders with some of these despicable persons when I was with Blom, but I never meet them anymore." [Lige for vore Oeine er nu opfoert et Capel for nogle Secterere, om Haugianere, Svedenborgianere, Zinzendorfianere, eller Mormoner veed jeg ikke - Praesten eller Forstanderen skal boe i Bygningen, han heder Volter og er en Missionaer. Dersom dette Vaerk ikke gjorde anden Skade end Betage os Udsigten, da kunde man let finde sig heri. Foer gjorde disse Mennesker, saalaenge de holdt sig til deres metaphysiske Sludder, ingen anden Ulykke, end at imellem en Stakkel maatte saettes i Daarekisten, men nu ere de blevne Demagoger og synes mig nu farlige - De have bemaegtiget sig naesten gandske ungdommens Underviisning - og ere rene Jesuiter. Hos Blom stoedte jeg ofte paa nogle af disse modbydelige mennesker, nu traeffer jeg dem ikke mere."] Conradine Dunker to Bernhard Dunker, 24 September 1850, Conradine Dunker til Bernhard Dunker, 1850-1857, BS, UB.

[73]"Dunker var i en aarraekke den advokat, som noed stoerst tillid hos den store almenhet. Han blev derfor betrodd de stoerste og vanskeligste saker, saker, hvor det dreiet sig om liv eller doed, borgerlig aere eller vanaere, eller hvor store interesser stod paa spil. Ut over landet dannet der sig en naesten overtroisk forvissning om, at kunde man faa Dunker til at foere sin sak, var man sikker paa at seire." G. Hallager, <u>Norges Hoeiesteret 1815-1915</u>, vol. 1: <u>1815-1863</u> (Kristiania: H. Aschehoug & Co., W. Nygaard, 1915), p. 275.

[74]Larsen Journal, vol. 3, pp. 42-43, 7 July 1853.

[75]Ibid., vol. 1, p. 70, 8 July 1853. In connection with the case against the Mormons, it is interesting to review various Supreme Court cases before November 1853, and the judgments meted out: (1) 11 December 1850, a decision against student, Marcus Thrane, convicted of blaspheming the name of God; (2) 19 March 1852, a decision against Carl Johan Michelsen, one of Thrane's emissaries in Troendelag, sentenced to seven years of hard labor for having threatened Parliament with "bloody revolution" if workers' demands were not met; (3) 15 May 1852, a decision against fifty-nine members of a workers' association in Romedal (Hedemarken) sentenced to varying degrees of imprisonment on bread and water for threatening a rural sheriff and preventing his holding an auction; (4) 30 October 1852, a decision against twenty-one persons from Meldalen sentenced to hard labor of

varying degrees for threatening officials of a rural court; (5) 25 November 1852, a decision against thirty-five Thranites in Nedre Stjoerdal, sentenced to imprisonment on bread and water--the ringleader was sentenced to hard labor--for unlawful depletion of forest timberlands; (6) 18 July 1853, a decision against twenty-nine persons in various parts of Troendelag convicted of bashing in a courthouse door, pelting a sheriff with stones, breaking windows in several buildings, and bombarding army troops with stones and blocks; several were sentenced to hard labor varying in degree from one month to six and a half years, whereas a few were set free. Hallager, 1815-1863, pp. 308-09, 315-18.

[76] Defendants were Ole Olsen, Jeppe Joergen Folkmann, Christian Larsen, Johan Frederik Ferdinand Dorius, Johan Aahmansson, Paer Beckstroem, Niels Hansen, Christen Knudsen, Svend Larsen, Niels Theodor Emil Larsen, and Johan Johansen. Extract-Protocol for Hoeiesteret, Rekke B, no. 80, L. no. 171, 13/10 1853-29/4 1854, fol. 18, Hoeiesteret, RA.

[77] "Hvad der skal afgjoeres er altsaa om Mormonernes Laere gaaer ind under den christelige Religion. Spoergsmaalet er et Verdens Spoergsmaal. Jeg veed ei at tillaegge Noget til hvad der er indtaget paa Udtoget. Man har Biskoppernes, det theologiske Facultets, Kirke Deptets. og Justits-Deptets Erklaeringer og Regjeringens Resl. 25/1 53. Tre af Biskopperne have antaget Mormonerne for Christne, ligesom og det Theol. Facultet. De oevr. Autoriteter have antaget at da Mormonerne have en egen Bibel, sammenskrevet af Joseph Smith efter guddommelig Aabenbaring for ham, kunne Mormonerne ei ansees Christne. Statens Mening med Dissenterloven maa dog have vaeret en Anden end den, at det skulde beroe paa vedk. Dissenter selv om de ere at ansee som Christne eller ikke. At Bibelen fortolkes paa forkjellige Maader er dog noget ganske Andet, end at antage en ganske anden Bibel ved Siden og i collisionstilfaelde altsaa at give den Fortrin for vor Bibel." Ibid., fols. 18-19.

[78] "Hoeiesteret kan ei gaae ind paa det Spoergsmaal om en Sect er christelig eller ikke. For at indlade sig herpaa maatte vedkommende Bekjendelsesskrifter vaere documenterede, men dette er ikke og kunde ikke vel skee i naervaerende Sag. De Angld. have formeentl. gjort bedre Rede for deres Tro og Boernslaerdom, en Pluraliteten i Alm. er i stand til. Man har de bedste Autoriteter, som her i Landet kan haves, for at Mormonerenes Sect maa betragtes som en christelig. Det vilde vaere besynderlig om Hret. nu skulde doemme, at Mormonernes Sect ikke er christelig og derved afskjaere enhver senere Undersoegelse af Theologerne herom. Jeg vil derfor aldeles ikke indlade mig paa nogen Undersoegelse om den theologiske Qvaestion." Ibid., fol. 19.

[79] Dom-protocol for Hoeiesteret, 1853, fol. 127, Hoeiesteretsarkiv, Oslo, Norway.

[80]"Jeg antager saal. at Mormonerne ikke kan betragtes som en christen Sect. Antagelse af en ny Christus, tvertimod Skriftens Ord, indeholder en Fornaegtelse af den sande Christus. . . ." Voterings-Protocol for Hoeiesteret, Rekke B, no. 91, L. no. 171, 6/7 1853-11/1 1854, fol. 113, Hoeiesteret, RA.

[81]". . . det framgaaer at alle Forhandl. som gik forud for Dissenterloven, vaesentl. kun havde for Oeie de Secter, der da kjendtes som christelige her i Landet; men heri ligger dog ei, at man skal antage alle Secter som senere maate opstaae, ogsaa som Christne." Ibid., fol. 115.

[82]"Men at en saadan Sect, hvis Grundlag og Princip i sin forsatte Udvikling noedvend. maa foere til Doctriner og Dogmer, hvis Anskuelse af Christendommen ikke kan fjerne sig synderlig fra Mohamedanernes, ikke kan benaevnes christelig i Dissenterlovens Forstand, forekommer mig klart." Ibid., fols. 115-16.

[83]"M.H.t. Mormonernes Religionshandlinger har jeg ei fundet tilstraekl. Oplysning om deres Daab og Communion kan ansees som christelige Handlinger, og jeg vil i dette Stykke have mig reserveret." Ibid., fol. 115.

[84]"I selve Sagen enig med Aall idet jeg tiltraeder Mantheys Bemaerkn. Derimod formener jeg, at Actor, paa en mindre forsvarlig Maade har udfoert sit Hverv i denne Sag. Han har paa en utilboerlig Maade opholdt Rettens Tid, da den stoerste Deel af hvad han documenterede var ufornoedent, eftersom de Angld. havde tilstaaet Factum. Paa den anden Side har han vaeret altfor kort og ei paa Udtoget indfoert vedk. Autoriteters Erklaeringer, hvorpaa det isaer kom an. Hans Deduction var derhos yderst Mangelfuld og til liden Veilede." Ibid. In view of his prosecution of the Mormon Case, it is interesting to note that Dunker was chief lawyer for the defense in the 1855 trial of Marcus Thrane and his cohort Abildgaard, leaders of the Thranite Workingmen's Movement. (Their case did not come to trial until four years after the uprisings of 1851.) Although he lost the case, and Thrane, Abildgaard, and others were given harsh prison sentences, Dunker was nevertheless hailed by the working classes as a great friend of the common man; the workers in Oslo formed a procession and sang a song in his honor. Hallager, <u>1815-1863</u>, p. 338. Dunker had earlier told Thrane that he could expect no sympathy from the Supreme Court, and that all the Supreme Court justices were his (Thrane's) sworn enemies. Dunker therefore advised Thrane to escape before sentence was passed, but Thrane had no money, and escape proved out of the question. Berhard Dunker to Conradine Dunker, 22 June 1855, Bernhard Dunker til Conradine Dunker, BS, UB. Dunker claimed no interest in Thrane personally, and only took the case because certain aspects of it interested him--especially "the difference between theory and practice. . . . Whereas the law . . . is liberal to the utmost degree, and allows a right and freedom, which possibly could prove dangerous, the

adjudicators are just as highly fanatic as the law itself is liberal, and thus the tolerance of the law is of no consequence. . . ." ["Hvad der egentlig har interesseret mig ved denne Sag, det er de Betragtninger over Forskjellen mellem Theorie og Praxis. . . . Medens Loven, som er given i Forveien, er i hoeieste Grad liberal og mild, og indroemmer en Ret og Frihed, som muligens kunde vaere farlig, saa ere Lovens Anvendere ligesaa fanatiske, som Loven er liberal, og Lovens Mildhed nytter derfor ikke til nogen Ting. . . ."] In the case against Thrane and Abildgaard, Dunker felt "the judgement seats have not been occupied by judges, but by revengeful and skulking conquerors hovering over a defeated foe." ["Lig[e]overfor Thrane og Abildgaard have efter mine Tanker Domstolene ikke vaeret Dommere, men haevngjerrige og frygtsomme Seierherrer ligeoverfor en overvunden Fiende."] Bernhard Dunker to Conradine Dunker, 17 August 1855, Bernhard Dunker til Conradine Dunker, BS, UB. Referring to the Supreme Court justices, Dunker noted that "every one of those esteemed fellows listens only to that which accords with his own opinions; anything else they simply ignore. . . . It makes no difference that the law is lenient and tolerant when the disposition of the judges is not." ["Enhver af de hoeie Herrer hoerer kun efter det, det stemmer med hans egne Meninger, det andet bryder han sig ikke om. . . . Det nytter lidet, at Loven er mild og overbaerende, naar Dommernes Sind ikke er det."] Bernhard Dunker to Conradine Dunker, 22 June 1855. Dunker had a great dislike for Chief Justice Bull, and described him in 1854 as "a complete dunce." ["Blandt de sidste er Justitarius Bull, der er et complet Fae."] Bernhard Dunker to Conradine Dunker, n.d. 1854, Bernhard Dunker til Conradine Dunker, BS, UB. The historian, Edvard Bull, described the judgment against the Thranites in 1855 as "the most typical 'class judgment' handed down by a Norwegian court of law in modern times." ["Den harde dommen -den mest typiske 'klassedom' som nyere norsk rettsvesen noen gang har felt- knekte arbeiderforeningene fullstendig."] Bull, Arbeiderklassen, p. 81.

[85] Voterings-Protocol, fol. 115.

[86] "Efter min Anskuelse er Mormonismen ligefrem en Forhaanelse af Statens Religion." Ibid., fol. 116.

[87] "Det er bekjendt nok at Catholiker og Qvaeker henregnes til Christne uagtet det er bekjendt nok, at ingen af disse eller flere andre Secter betragte Bibelen som en afsluttet Aabenbaring. Catholikerne bygge paa en Tradition ved Siden af Bibelen. . . . Qvaekerne antage Meget, der strider mod vor Kirkes Grundlaerdomme. . . . Mormonerne naegte ei, som soc[in]ianerne Christi Guddommelighed, og Mormon-Bogen indeholder, trods dens mange Urigtigheder, dog Intet der strider mere mod Christendommen end Catholikerne og Qvaekerne." Ibid., fols. 114-15. Historian Jens Arup Seip describes the Norwegian Supreme Court of the 1850s as a "political organ," and observes that at times, judges pass judgments which

contradict the law. Jens Arup Seip, <u>Tanke og handling i norsk historie</u> (Oslo: Gyldendal Norsk Forlag, 1968), p. 90. Seip states that the Supreme Court during the years 1840-1870 was a political organ to a very marked degree. Ibid., p. 91. In the period 1840-1870, the two centers of political power were the Council appointed by the King on the one side, and the Parliament on the other; the Supreme Court had to find its place somewhere in between. Ibid., p. 92. "In the final years of this period, the Supreme Court edged completely over to the side of the Council; the judges became partners with members of the King's Council in matters of political consequence. This development took place during a time when the civil servant estate's power in Parliament was waning and its power base was increasingly concentrated in the King's Council." ["I siste del av den delte statsmakts periode gled hoeyesterett helt over til regjeringens side; dommerne ble statsraadenes partnere i saker av politisk rekkevidde. Denne utvikling falt sammen med at embedsstandens posisjon i stortinget sviktet, og dens maktgrunnlag ble konsentrert i regjeringen."] Ibid., p. 93. According to Seip, the Supreme Court decision against Thrane and cohorts in 1855 was an expression of the hand-in-glove relationship between the Supreme Court and the Council. Seip describes the decision as a clear miscarriage of justice--a textbook example showing that "moral indignation shapes its own law." ["Denne sak er et skoleeksempel paa at rettsanvendelse kan vaere kamuflert maktanvendelse, eller -om man vil- et eksempel paa hvorledes nettopp den gode samvittighet gjoer mordet mulig, fordi moralsk indignasjon skaper sin egen lov."] Ibid., p. 94. Seip's analysis of Supreme Court decisions in the period 1840-1870 shows the Supreme Court was politically involved to a very high degree; this involvement was evidenced by two tendencies: (1) a tendency to interpret the "spirit of the Law" ["<u>Lovens aand</u>"] rather than the actual written laws; (2) a tendency to assert the autonomy of juridical argument. Ibid., pp. 109-11. Seip concludes as follows: "The foremost Norwegian jurists--district governors, professors, department heads, justices--comprised the kernel in a civil servant elite which occupied the basic position of power, especially in the government. They were not simply an estate within the State; they were themselves the State." ["De norske toppjurister- amtmenn, professorer, ekspedisjonssjefer, dommere-utgjorde kjernen i en embedsmannselite som rekrutterte de vesentlige politiske maktstillinger, saerlig paa regjeringsplanet. De var ikke bare en stat i staten, de var selv staten."] Ibid., p. 119.

[88]"Overhodet synes advokater og dommere aa ha overraskende stor evne til aa bevare troen paa sin objektivitet, selv naar politisk eller religioes lidenskap bryter frem som halsende hunder i deres resonnement." Ibid., p. 111. The Supreme Court Decision in 1853 meant that Mormons in Norway could not legally hold general meetings, perform baptisms, perform marriages, conduct burials, administer the Lord's Supper, or proselyte for converts. A detailed discussion of laws and decrees relating to Mormons in Norway is found in subsequent chapters. In 1883, Mormons

petitioned the Government for recognition as Christian dissenters; their petition was denied, not because they accepted the Book of Mormon, but because they preached the doctrine of polygamy. Hilmar Freidel, "Historiske dokumentasjoner: Dissentersaken," p. 4, typescript, Norway TSD. It should be noted that the Dissenter Law of 1891, paragraph 24, granted dissenter rights and recognition to Unitarians and Orthodox Jews despite the fact that neither group was considered Christian. <u>Arbeiderbladet</u> (Oslo), 10 December 1955. In 1955, Mormons again sought official recognition as a Christian sect, but without result. Freidel, "Dissentersaken," p. 5. Meanwhile, the Law on Registered Religious Groups [<u>Loven om registrert trossamfunn</u>] of 13 June 1969 stated the following: "All have the right to practice their religion alone or in company with others and to establish religious congregations within the bounds of decorum and law." ["Alle har ret til aa drive religioes verksemd aleine eller saman med andre, og til aa skipa trudomssamfunn naar ret og soemd ikkje vert krenkt."] Ibid. With the law of 1969, the question of Mormons and the Dissenter Law was essentially moot; Mormons could now decide whether to register as dissenters under the law. Despite that fact, Mormons have not (1981) been granted admission to the Norwegian Association of the Boy Scouts, and are not recognized as a Christian sect by the Norwegian State Church. Podhorny and Svanevik, "Trossamfunn," p. 2. The Decision of 1853 also had consequences for the Reorganized Church of Jesus Christ of Latter Day Saints in Norway. As early as 1902, members of the Reorganized Church petitioned the District Governor of Nedenes County for recognition as Christian dissenters. In a chain of correspondence reminiscent of action on the Mormon petition of 1852, the Governor forwarded the petition to the JPD which sent it in turn to the KUD; the KUD referred the question to the Theological Faculty. The result was a letter to the District Governor of Nedenes County from the JPD on 14 November 1903 stating that the Reorganized Church of Jesus Christ of Latter Day Saints could not be recognized as a Christan sect. Sandvin, "Mormonisma," p. 89. Not until 1915 did Reorganites again seek recognition as a Christian sect in Norway. In that year, the President of the Church in Independence, Missouri, submitted a petition to the Norwegian Ministry of Foreign Affairs through the American Legation in Oslo. The case was officially tabled. In 1922, the KUD sent letters to the Theological Faculty and the Congregational Faculty [<u>Menighets Fakultet</u>] asking their opinions on the question. Lutheran bishops in Norway also discussed the matter at a conference in 1923. The result was the same: the Reorganized Church was not to be considered a Christian sect. In 1932, the Reorganized Church again petitioned for recognition-- this time in a letter to the JPD. That petition also stated that the Reorganized Church should in no way be considered part of the regular Mormon Church. The result was again negative: the Reorganites were not Christians. Ibid., pp. 91-92. In connection with the above efforts, it is interesting to review opinions by the Theological Faculty in 1903, 1922, and 1932. In 1903, the Faculty, in opposition to opinions by that body in 1852 that Mormons were Christian dissenters, stated that the Reorganized Church was not Christian, and backed up this decision by citing the Supreme Court Decision of 1853 which stated that Mormons accept revelation not contained in the Bible. On 14 June 1922, however, the Faculty reversed its position in an opinion which declared the Supreme Court Decision of 1853 invalid. According to the Faculty, revelation outside of that in the Bible was an integral part of Christianity and Christian history; such revelation was found among Anabaptists in Luther's time, as also later among Independents, Quakers, Pietists and the like. The Faculty also mentioned Catholic traditions and the Catholic doctrine of papal infallibility. The Faculty concluded as follows: "As far as can be determined from materials at our disposal, the Reorganized Church of Jesus Christ of Latter Day Saints must be considered a Christian dissenter sect. Due to lack of information, however, the Faculty cannot express an opinion on whether said sect fulfills the other requirements set forth in the Dissenter Law." ["Saavidt man kan doemme av det materiale som staar til raadighet, maa 'den gjenorganiserede Jesu Kristi kirke av de siste dagers hellige' bli aa betrakte som et kristent dissentersamfunn. Hvorvidt den i andre henseender tilfredsstiller de krav som ifoelge dissenterloven maa stilles til et offentlig anerkjent dissentersamfunn, kan fakultetet paa grunn av manglende opplysninger ikke uttale noget om."] Ibid., pp. 94-95. In 1933, the Faculty refused to decide whether Reorganites were Christians. Ibid.

[89] "Jeg gratulerer med Hoeisteretsdommen i Mormonsagen." Carl Motzfeldt to Christian Birch-Reichenwald, 8 November 1853, "Brev K-M," Birch-Reichenwald arkiv, PA, RA.

CHAPTER IV

[1] "Opvaekkelsen var stor dersteds, saa endog nogle af Politiet bejaerede Daab." *Skandinaviens Stjerne* 1 (1 September 1852):188.

[2] Willard Snow Diary, 24 July 1852, holograph, Library-Archives, The Church of Jesus Christ of Latter-day Saints, Salt Lake City, Utah [hereinafter cited as LDS Church Archives].

[3] "I Brevig, den foerste Stad, . . . var en saare stor Opvaekkelse saavel blandt Rige som Fattige, og han [H. P. Jensen] ventede at Halvdelen af Byen ville blive kaldede." *Skandinaviens Stjerne* 1 (1 September 1852):188.

[4] *Adresse-Tidende for Brevig, Stathelle og Langesund*, 23 March 1853, p. 1. While preaching near Risoer in 1853, Canute Peterson noticed that "more than half of those present were weeping." Canute Peterson et al., "Story of the life of Canute Peterson as given by himself and by some members of his family," p. 44, xerox of MS, LDS Church Archives.

[5] Ola Rudvin, *Indremisjonsselskapets Historie*, vol. 1: *Den Norske Lutherstiftelse 1868-1891* (Oslo: Lutherstiftelsens Forlag, 1967), pp. 180, 209.

[6] Events in Bergen in October 1852 also underlined Mormon-Haugian connections: Svend Peter Larsen of Fredrikstad arrived there on 16 October, and engaged the Haugian preacher, Erik Toennesen, in heated debate which ended with Larsen standing upright--arms stretched high above his head--imploring God to strike Toennesen dead on the spot! Bergens Politikammer to Bergens Stift Herr Schydtz, 30 October 1852, Mormonpakken, Trossamfunn Samling [hereinafter cited as TS], Det kongelige Justis- og Politidepartement, Oslo, Norway [hereinafter cited as JPD]. Mormon missionary, Carl Christian Nicolai Dorius, arrived in Eker in November 1853 to find a large crowd gathered in Anders Boedker's yard. Those assembled begged Dorius to preach to them. When he refused, the crowd pushed into Boedker's parlor uninvited and forced Dorius to preach before they dispersed. Forhoersprotokoll no. 4, 28/8 1851-3/8 1861, fol. 100, Lier, Roeyken og Hurum sorenskriveri, Statsarkivet, Oslo [hereinafter cited as SA].

[7] ". . . sagde de ikke at de vilde holde religioes Forsamling men de sagde at de vilde holde en christelig Opbyggelse eller en christelig Forsamling." Ekstrarettsprotokoll no. 4, 22/10 1857-2/10 1862, fol. 60, 28 September 1858, SA.

[8]"Mormonerne have . . . soekt at foere sig Bevaegelsen tilgode; 14 Individuer antages at have underkastet sig Mormondaab, medens Flere ere staemte for Vildfarelsen. . . ." F. Dybdahl to Jens L. Arup, 17 October 1862, Visitasberetninger, 1861-1872, pakke 1862, Kristiania Stift, Kontor A [hereinafter cited as "A"], Det kongelige Kirke- og Undervisningsdepartement [hereinafter cited as KUD], Riksarkivet, Oslo, Norway [hereinafter cited as RA]. By 1865, over thirty persons had joined the Mormons in Roeken. "Afskrift af Drammens Provsties Visitatsprotocol, saavidt vedkommer i 1865 afholdte Visitatser," 27 June 1865, Visitasberetninger, 1861-1872, pakke 1865, Kristiania Stift, A, KUD, RA.

[9]Trondheim Biskop Darre to Den kongelige Norske Regjering, 24 March 1858, Visitasberetninger, 1851-1860, pakke 1857, Trondheim Stift, A, KUD, RA.

[10]Trondheim Biskop Grimelund to KUD, 15 January 1863, Visitasberetninger, 1861-1877, pakke 1862, Trondheim Stift, A, KUD, RA. Andrew M. Israelsen's parents joined the Mormons at Kasfjord (near Harstad) in the early 1860s, and Israelsen traced their conversion to events about 1855 "and for several years later" when great religious revivals swept northern Norway and many people "left the Lutheran Church, which was the dominant or State Church, and formed a society called Dissenters." Andrew M. Israelsen, Utah Pioneering: An Autobiography (Salt Lake City, Utah: Deseret News Press, 1938), p. 17. Israelsen was referring to Den frie apostolisk-christelige Menighed [the Free Apostolic Christian Congregation] founded by Gustav Adolph Lammers (1802-1878), a Lutheran priest who left the State Church in 1856 over the Lutheran practice of granting indiscriminate absolution from sin, as also infant baptism which he termed "a pernicious abuse." Lammers's "Free Church" was especially strong in northern Norway with ten congregations in 1860, of which two were located in areas of Mormon activity--Kvaefjord and Harstad (Trondenes). Tromsoe Biskop Essendrop to KUD, 25 March 1862, Visitasberetninger, 1857-1864, pakke 1861, Tromsoe Stift, A, KUD, RA. The Mormon branch at Kvaefjord numbered about fourteen members in 1862. Carl C. N. Dorius, "Dagbog: Carl C. N. Dorius's Missionsforretninger i Skandinavia, samt en kort Beretning om det tidligere Levenetsloeb," 24 October 1862, holograph, LDS Church Archives.

[11]Analysis of early Mormon branch records bears this out. During the years 1851-1853 inclusive, sixty-six persons joined the Mormons in Risoer. Of these, forty-three emigrated, two died, eleven were excommunicated, and seven moved--all during the 1850s--so that by 1860, fifty-eight (eighty-eight percent) of the converts from 1851-1853 no longer lived in Risoer. "Protocol for Oesterriisoeers Green i Jesu Christi Kirke af Siste Dages Hellige opretet i Oesterriisoeer i October 1851," Oester Risoer Branch, Brevik Conference, Scandinavian Mission, LDS Church Archives. Of forty-four persons who joined the Mormons in Brevik

during the years 1852-1853 inclusive, eight had emigrated, twenty had been excommunicated, and ten had moved by 1860, i.e., eighty-nine percent of those baptized in Brevik during the period 1852-1853 were no longer active Mormons there in 1860. Historical Record and Record of Members, 1852-1862, Brevik Branch, Christiania Conference, Scandinavian Mission, LDS Church Archives. One hundred and two persons joined the Mormons at Fredrikstad in the years 1852-1853; by 1860, twelve had moved, forty-two had emigrated, twenty-one had been excommunicated, and four had died--a total of seventy-nine persons or more that three-fourths (seventy-seven percent) of the 1852-1853 membership. Historical Record and Record of Members, 1852-1858, Fredrikstad Branch, Christiania Conference, Scandinavian Mission, LDS Church Archives.

[12]John S. Hansen, ed., Mindeudgave C. C. A. Christensen: Poetiske Arbejder, Artikler og Afhandlinger tilligemed hans Levnedsloeb (Salt Lake City, Utah: Bikubens Bibliotek, 1921), p. 423.

[13]Jens L. Arup to KUD, 2 April 1856, Visitasberetninger, 1851-1855, pakke 1855, Kristiania Stift, A, KUD, RA.

[14]"Mormonernes Virksomhed i dette Provsti maa ansees som ophoert; kun nogle faa saadanne ere tilbage i Onsoe." P. F. Bassoee, "Bemaerkninger ved Provstevisitats i Vestre Borgesyssels Provstie i Aaret 1856," Visitasberetninger, 1856-1860, pakke 1856, Kristiania Stift, A, KUD, RA. Mormon leaders scheduled a meeting in Brevik on 3 June 1864, but Conference President G. M. Brown observed that "none came to meeting so we could not testify for them." Brown "felt that nearly all the honest in heart were gathered out of this place [Brevik]." George Mortimer Brown Autobiography and Diary, pp. 69-70, 3 June 1864, typescript, Library Services Division, Genealogical Department, The Church of Jesus Christ of Latter-day Saints, Salt Lake City, Utah.

[15]Hilmar Freidel, Jesu Kristi Kirke i Norge: Den norske misjons historie, 1851-1966 (Oslo: Jesu Kristi Kirke av Siste Dagers Hellige Misjonskontoret, 1966), pp. 62-63.

[16]Brown Autobiography, p. 98, 23 June 1865.

[17]Theodore M. Samuelsen to George M. Brown, 23 February 1866, quoted in Brown Autobiography, p. 142. Convert baptisms began falling off in the 1860s, dropped twenty-three percent in the 1870s, and dropped a further twelve percent in the 1880s (see table 1). Baptisms in the period 1885-1889 were down thirty-four percent from the previous five-year period, and plunged thirty-two percentage points in the years 1890-1894 (see table 2). Stavanger District in 1862 comprised eighty-nine members in two branches according to Dorius, "Dagbog," (9 September 1862); in 1889, conversely, President J. A. Hendricksen reported only one branch in Stavanger District with an average attendance of only four

persons at meetings including "one apostate and one stranger." John Anthon Hendricksen Diary, 16 March 1889, microfilm of holograph, LDS Church Archives. Oslo Conference President Andrew Israelsen bypassed Stavanger while touring in 1893 because members there "had no place at which . . . to hold meeting." Israelsen, Utah, p. 138. Brevik Branch--Mormon headquarters in Norway in the 1850s--numbered only two members in 1884. M. Christophersen to Anthon H. Lund, 5 December 1884, quoted in Skandinaviens Stjerne 34 (15 December 1884):86. Lutheran priests meeting in Trondheim on 18 November 1885 described Mormonism in Trondheim Deanery as "without any consequence whatsoever." ["Mormonerne har ingen Betydning."] "Udskrift af Visitasprotokollen for Trondhjems Stiftsprovsti," 18 November 1885, Visitasberetninger, 1878-1893, pakke 1885, Trondheim Stift, A, KUD, RA.

[18] An attempt to explain the ups, downs, peaks and dips is risky at best: Mormon statistics during the period under consideration do not uniformly differentiate between children and adults, not all Mormon congregations submitted regular reports to mission leaders in Copenhagen, and the total number of baptisms is further distorted because of the practice of rebaptizing (although infrequently) those who were already members. Another problem with baptism and excommunication totals is illustrated by the journal of Mormon missionary, J. A. Hendricksen, who on 16 September 1888 baptized a Peter Fredricksen "who had been Severet [sic] from the Church 3 or 4 times for Drunkenness, but who has now evidently repented. . . . Also Loura Pehrsen who was cut off shortly before my arrival, for lack of attending to her duties, but is now a good member." Hendricksen Diary, vol. 1, p. 207, 16 September 1888. In the early decades of Mormonism in Norway, it was not unheard of for a member to be excommunicated as many as three different times during a single year--this meant the member was rebaptized at least twice in one year. Given their drawbacks, it is still useful to compare membership and other statistics for various decades and five-year periods since they add additional insights not readily apparent from journals and mission publications. Certain groups of statistics are more reliable than others: i.e., emigration tallies are generally more reliable than those for baptisms or excommunications since a person did not usually emigrate more than once.

[19] Andrew Jenson, History of the Scandinavian Mission (Salt Lake City, Utah: Deseret News Press, 1927), p. 536.

[20] Samuelsen to Brown, 23 February 1866.

[21] "Der er tvende Grunde, der afgjort tale mod at Mormonismen vinder fast Fod i Landdistrictet; den ene er, at dens usaedelige og gudsbespottelige Laere finder Modstand, ja ofte Afsky i Folkets moralske Bevidsthed . . . hvortil kommer, at Mange henvende sig til Praesten, for at erholde sund Oplysning; ---og den anden Grund er det materielle Tryk, som Mormonpraesterne udoeve.

De indlogere sig hvor de ville og betale Intet for Underholdning og Ophold, og tage i egentligste Forstand Tiende. Modsaetningen i hver Uge at betale 1/10 af deres Fortjeneste og Udsigten til at arve Jorden synes Mange ikke vel om." Anton Wilhelm Fangen to Jens L. Arup, 5 July 1859, pakke "Mormonerne 1851-1920," A, KUD, RA. The Doctrine of Celestial Marriage was publicly announced in Scandinavia on 1 October 1853 when a revelation on polygamy was published in Copenhagen. Andrew Jenson, "Erindringer fra missionen i Skandinavien," Morgenstjernen 2 (April 1883): 49-55. Willard Snow, President of the Scandinavian Mission, received a letter from his brother, Erastus, on 1 December 1852 (The letter was dated 1 October 1852) stating "that the revelation which was given Joseph [Joseph Smith] 1842 was reat [sic] and published in pamphlet form togathe [sic] witt [sic] the minutes of the conference and severel sermons preached publickelly by President B Young & others which shewed that the cat was out of the bag head first." Said Willard: "I can truly say my heart leaped for joy heaven knows I am thankful that I have not got to drag the old cat by the tail any longer for I have been tail sick long ago I am now ready for the storm . . . thank God I am not ashamed of the Gospel of christ [sic] nor afraid to preach it defend it and live by it and practise what I preach both in time and eternity let the heaven the earth the sea and the dry land praise the Lord and let all the saints say amen whether in life or death." Snow Diary, pp. 113-14, 1 December 1852. On 13 April 1853, Willard Snow recorded that "Br Hougan [Erik G. M. Hogan] & Petersen [Canute Peterson] left for Norway Br H P Jensen for Sleshwig and Holsten and the Presidents of confrences and presiding Elders of branches to their several missions But not till I had called a private council of the Presidents togather and read them the revelation on marriage. . . ." Ibid., p. 155, 13 April 1853. Brevik Conference President Christian J. Larsen denied that Mormons practiced polygamy in America or anywhere else in 1852. Avskrift av dokument no. 12, Avskrift av Forhoeret under Tune Sorenskriverie, 9, 12 November 1852, Mormonpakken, TS, JPD. Larsen changed his tune, however, on 28 May 1853 at Risoer when he and five other missionaries first learned about polygamy from Erik G. M. Hogan and Canute Peterson. "At that place," said Larsen, "the brethren made known to me for the first time, that God had given a revelation to the Prophet Joseph Smith, commanding him to take some more wives, and the Spirit of God, at once gave me a testemony, that it was the Truth." Christian J. Larsen Journal, vol. 3, p. 28, 28 May 1853, holograph and MS, LDS Church Archives. Missionary Canute Peterson added his account: "On one of the high hills near Risor [sic], I explained to the Brethern [sic] for the first time the 'revelation On Plural Marriage.' which I read and interpreted to them from the Deseret News. This paper I carried with me. They asked if they were to preach this Doctrine. I told them 'No,' not even to talk of it privately before they were better informed concerning it. This gave them new light and also satisfied them." Peterson et al., "Story," p. 45.

22 Rudvin, Lutherstiftelse, p. 204.

23 Godvin Ousland, En Kirkehoevding: Professor Gisle Johnson som Teolog og Kirkemann (Oslo: Lutherstiftelsens Forlag, 1950), p. 44.

24 Einar Molland, Fra Hans Nielsen Hauge til Eivind Berggrav: Hovedlinjer i Norges Kirkehistorie i det 19. og 20. aarhundre (Oslo: Gyldendal Norsk Forlag, 1972), pp. 33-34.

25 "Det var Vidnesbyrdet om Synd og Naade, om Frelse eller Fortabelse, han frembar med en saa gribende Inderlighed, med en saa indtraengende Styrke, at hans Tale blev Mangfoldige til Vaekkelse og Omvendelse." Rudvin, Lutherstiftelse, p. 205.

26 "Han svang Lovens Hammer over den doede Navnkristendom, over det gudloese, verdslige Liv, men han viste ogsaa hen til den Naadestol, som er opreist i Jesus vor Frelser. Det var det store 'Enten-eller,' han holdt frem med et Alvor og en Klarhed, som ikke kunde lade nogen Tilhoerer blive uberoert deraf. Man maatte traeffe et Valg, her duede ikke de delte Hjerter." Ibid.

27 Ousland, Johnson, pp. 132, 149.

28 ". . . et mere planmessig arbeide for vekkelse og aandelig oppbyggelse blant folket." Fridtjof O. Valton, De Norske Vekkelsers Historie: Et Kortfattet Overblikk over det Kristelige Liv i Norge fra Begynnelsen inntil vaare Dager (Oslo: Filadelfiaforlaget A/S, 1942), p. 131. Historians such as Rudvin in Lutherstiftelse (p. 217), and Sigmund Skard, USA i Norsk Historie: 1000-1776-1976 (Oslo: Det Norske Samlaget, 1976), (p. 193), point to Mormon successes as a prime reason for establishment of the Inner Mission Society in Oslo in 1855; Rudvin describes the Inner Mission as "a Lutheran and ecclesiastical alternative" ["et luthersk og kirkelig alternativ"] to the activity of dissenting religions. Rudvin, Lutherstiftelse, p. 217. Others, such as Gunnar Jaeger, describe Mormon convert totals in Norway as somewhat meaningless; what was important was the strong Lutheran backlash--"greater than for any other dissenter group" ["stoerre enn for noen annen dissenter menighet"]--occasioned by Mormon proselyting. Gunnar Jaeger, "Kirken, dissenterne og Lekmannsbevegelsen i Bergen 1850-1880," in Bergens Historiske Forening: Skrifter (Bergen: J. D. Beyer A. S. Boktrykkeri, 1971), p. 46.

29 J. L. Balling and P. G. Lindhardt, Den Nordiske Kirkes Historie (Copenhagen: Nyt Nordisk Forlag, Arnold Busck, 1973), p. 292. The Movement was consolidated in 1868 with establishment of Den norske Lutherstiftelse [The Norwegian Lutheran Foundation]-- essentially a functioning synod. Ibid.

30 Rudvin, Lutherstiftelse, pp. 205-06.

[31]"Dei var laagkyrkjelege nok til aa koma paa god fot med det konservative lekfolket, dei var tilstrekkeleg Lutherskkonfesjonelle til aa gjera front mod framand separatisme. . . ." Dagfinn Mannsaaker, Det Norske Presteskapet i det 19. Hundreaaret (Oslo: Det Norske Samlaget, 1954), p. 120.

[32]"Massekristendom, kristne institusjoner og skikker . . . veide i deres oeyne meget lett. . . ." Molland, Berggrav, pp. 38-39.

[33]". . . dei kjende seg som vekkjarar, som misjonaerar." Mannsaaker, Presteskapet, p. 120.

[34]". . . de soekte aa gi sine prekener et mer aktuelt tilsnitt." Andreas Aarflot, Norsk Kirkehistorie, vol. 2 (Oslo: Lutherstiftelsen, 1967), p. 441.

[35]". . . pietistisk, omgjengelig overfor de vakte, nidkjaer vekkelsespredikant og statskirkelig embetsmann med daarlig samvittighet." Molland, Berggrav, p. 38.

[36]Ibid.

[37]Mannsaaker, Presteskapet, p. 120.

[38]The downturn reflected an agrarian crisis triggered when cheap American wheat began flooding European markets. The number of factory workers in Norway dropped from 51,000 in 1879 to under 46,000 in 1885. The urban population, meanwhile, increased. The result was widespread unemployment and privation, especially among city workers whose wages were further undercut by an influx of cheap labor from the farms. Edvard Bull, Arbeiderklassen i Norsk Historie ([Oslo]: Tiden Norsk Forlag, 1947), p. 119; Jostein Nerboevik, Norsk Historie 1870-1905 (Oslo: Det Norske Samlaget, 1973), p. 28.

[39]Johann August Olsen Journal, pp. 47-48, typescript, Special Collections, Harold B. Lee Library, Brigham Young University, Provo, Utah.

[40]Dorius, "Dagbog," p. 30, ca. 18 September 1862. A serious economic downturn commenced in 1875, and the next twenty years--until 1895--were years of economic stagnation. Nerboevik, Historie, p. 28.

[41]August Severin Schou Diary, vol. 1, 3 January 1877, xerox of typescript, LDS Church Archives.

[42]John Johnson Reminiscences, p. 31, ca. November 1889, xerox of holograph, LDS Church Archives.

[43]Ibid., p. 33, ca. August 1890.

[44]Israelsen, Utah, p. 148.

[45]Nils C. Flygare to A. W. Carlson, 21 February 1879, carbon copy, "Letter Book of Niels C. Flygare, President of the Scandinavian Mission, 1878-1879," p. 87, LDS Church Archives. Canute Peterson, President of the Scandinavian Mission, observed in 1872, that despite sizeable cash contributions from Scandinavians who had already immigrated to Utah, there were "over 5000 Poor saints in this Mission looking and Baging [begging] for help." Canute Peterson to Wives and Children in Utah, 13 June 1872, Canute Peterson Collection, LDS Church Archives. Missionary John F. F. Dorius complained in 1876 that "the mission in 'Scandinavia' is not as it used to be years ago . . . especially in financialy matters, we are poor, and tied up, all Thiting [tithing] shall be sent home, must not be used only by orders from 'Zion' and we the missionaires [sic], are cut down so close, that we have to think twice, before we dare bring a shirt to the washerwomman I have sold my blankets and my watch, and if I had more to sell I would do it, in order to defray some expenses with. . . ." John F. F. Dorius to John Frantsen, 3 September 1876, pp. 2-3, Canute Peterson Collection, LDS Church Archives. Dorius, in fact, was unable to survive without dipping into funds deposited by members for emigration purposes. Dorius, who returned to Utah in 1878 after serving as President of the Oslo Conference, was informed by Nils C. Flygare, Scandinavian Mission President, in a letter dated 19 November 1878 that he owed the Mission 911.83 crowns or 250 dollars--"the means you borrowed and did not pay back as also the means you recived [sic] of individuals to put in the Saving Deposit, which you failed to do." Flygare continued: "[I] would, if I had the means . . . pay those amounts due individuals in Norway, for it is a crying sin to take the means the poor saints, through starving themself [sic], are able to put in the Saving Deposit, but I am not able, and this mission has no fund for that purpose, so I have to give you an other chance before any more stringent mesures [sic] are taken to colect [sic] the same, for I have promised the Saints in Norway that they shall not loose [sic] a cent." Nils C. Flygare to John F. F. Dorius, 19 November 1878, carbon copy, "Letter Book of Flygare," pp. 54-55, 64-65, LDS Church Archives. Flygare was not averse to using some tithing monies for missionary expenses as witness a letter on 25 February 1879 to Oslo Conference President J. Rolfsen where he directed that tithing could be used to help with hall rental and clothing needs for various missionaries. But missionaries were not to use tithing for everyday needs, especially housekeeping expenses. Members would have to help with most missionary expenses, i.e., "those who are benefitted of the labor of the Elders must support them, and the Elders going out in the field should not depend on the tithing for support, but trust in God and they will find friends who will administer to their wants." Nils C. Flygare to J. Rolfsen, 25 February 1879, carbon copy, "Letter Book of Flygare," pp. 88-89, LDS Church Archives.

[46]Christian Hogensen to N. Wilhelmsen, 19 February 1881, carbon copy, Letter-Copy-Book, bk. B, 1880-1905, Christiania Conference, Scandinavian Mission, LDS Church Archives.

[47]Hans Jacob Christiansen Journal, vol. 2, 16 October 1893, holograph, LDS Church Archives. Little financial help was forthcoming from Zion during the troubled years of the 1880s and early 1890s. In 1887, Congress passed the Edmunds-Tucker Act designed to destroy the Church as an economic and political entity. The Law dissolved the Church as a legal corporation and required it to forfeit to the United States Government all property in excess of $50,000. James B. Allen and Glen M. Leonard, The Story of the Latter-day Saints (Salt Lake City, Utah: Deseret Book Company, 1976), p. 406. By the early 1890s, most of the Church's marketable property was in the hands of receivers. Ronald W. Walker, "Crisis in Zion: Heber J. Grant and the Panic of 1893," Sunstone 5 (January-February 1980):27. Total Church debt in 1898 was $1,250,000. Allen and Leonard, Story, p. 427.

[48]Mormon emigration from Norway peaked in the years 1875-1884. The average number of members remaining in Norway was fairly constant during the years 1860-1884, and then dipped abruptly until basic member strength began building up once again near the turn of the century (see tables 1-3).

[49]Oslo Conference President George M. Brown observed in 1865 that "Elder Sprague and I now turn nearly all of our attention to the coming emigration, as we desire to get as many of the honest Saints off as possible, that they may be freed from the pestilence and punishments which are caused them." Brown Autobiography, p. 87, 3 January 1865. Brown also described "much poverty among the people of this country who are not saints and in general feeling [sic] of dissatisfaction appears to prevail and the cry is, 'Let us emigrant [sic] to America!' The America fever appears to be general and thousands are preparing to go this season. Things are conducted on such a principle here that it is hardly possible for the working class to live. Thousands are without employment all winter and it takes them all summer to pay up their debts again." Brown Autobiography, p. 143, 5 March 1866. Zion, in this context, was described as "a place of freedom and rehabilitation" ["et Befrielses - og Opreisningssted"]. Mons Andersen to W. W. Cluff, 3 December 1870, quoted in Skandinaviens Stjerne 20 (1 January 1871):109.

[50]Jenson, Scandinavian Mission, p. 536.

[51]The few missionaries who continued to proselyte found themselves horribly overworked. John Johnson's account of labors in Hedemarken from 23 October 1890 to 2 May 1891 gives some idea: "I destributed or sold 450 Gosple tracts allso some books, held 24 meetings baptised four taylor Nilsen and wife, Johan Flink, and a lady by the name of Marie. I walked 1400 miles

traveled by railroad 455 miles and 7 miles on a steamboat. I sleped [slept] in 130 deferent beds and traveled through 23 deferent distrects (Praestejel) or Counties, my helth being very good except a slight cold now and then." Johnson Reminiscences, p. 35, 2 May 1891.

[52]"Throndhjems Gren, der indeholder omtrent Halvdelen af Norges Land, er nu efter Br. Skanchy's afreise, overladt til sig selv som Faar uden Hyrde-, thi der findes ikke en Mand der kan tage Ledelsen af Forsamling. . . ." C. Hogensen to Andrew Jenson, 22 August 1881, carbon copy, Letter-Copy-Book, bk. B, 1880-1905, Christiania Conference, Scandinavian Mission, LDS Church Archives.

[53]Chr. Hogensen to C. D. Fjeldsted, 8 November 1881, carbon copy, Letter-Copy-Book, bk. B, 1880-1905, Christiania Conference, Scandinavian Mission, LDS Church Archives. Reports at a missionary meeting in Oslo on 17 October 1891 showed that leaders had been pulled out of the Hedemarken and Eidsvold Branches because of a shortage of missionaries. Skandinaviens Stjerne 41 (1 November 1891):44. "We need men with means," said Conference President H. J. Christiansen in 1894, "who could go out to various places of labor such as Toenesberg, Sandefjord, Skien, Oevre and nedre Tellemarken, Langesund, Riisoe [Risoer], Krageroed, Christiansand, Mandal and several places. These places have been without missionaries for many years. . . ." Christiansen Journal, vol. 3, pp. 10-11, [?] June 1894.

[54]"It is the same here as it is everywhere," lamented L. P. Borg from Norway in 1869, "the financially able have emigrated and have left the poor behind." ["Det er her som overalt, de Bemidlede ere reiste og have efterladt de Fattige."] L. P. Borg to J. N. Smith, 29 December 1869, quoted in Skandinaviens Stjerne 19 (15 January 1870):122.

[55]Jens Christian Andersen Weibye Diary, vol. 5, p. 2, 1 January 1873, holograph, LDS Church Archives.

[56]"I Saerdeleshed skulde Praestedoemmet vaere flittig i denne Henseende, thi dersom Hovedet ikke er levende, hvad kan da siges om Legemet?" Skandinaviens Stjerne 40 (15 February 1891):153.

[57]"Det gjoer mindre til Sagen, enten jeg udretter noget eller ej. Vaerket gaar sin Gang fremad alligevel foruden min Hjaelp. Ioevrigt foeler jeg mig saa svag til at kunne gjoere noget, og det er jo desuden ogsaa Missionaererne, som isaer ere kaldede til at vaere Evangeliets Budbaerere." Skandinaviens Stjerne 37 (1 January 1884):104.

[58]Declining conversion rates were also tied to social and political changes. O. C. Larsen, a native of Drammen, returned

to his native city in 1881 (Larsen had immigrated to Utah in 1862) to find "a great change in Drammen, socially, politically and religiously. The older population had mostly died. The old spirit of aristocracy had also gone. The younger class had a more liberal democratic spirit. The servants, male and female were much more respected. Politically, the common people were much better informed and all took a great interest in politics. There were two parties known as the right and the left and I saw that the common people agitated their principles just as much as the higher-ups. This gave the people a chance to think for themselves and they were nearly as far advanced as the people of America. I also found a great improvement in their school system, especially among the poorer classes. In the country places it was more like former days. Religiously, there was more freedom. It seemed the state religion had entirely lost its power. During my youth [Larsen was born in 1836] the priest seemingly had entire dominion over mind and body as well as the soul. To oppose the priest and talk against him was considered worse than to talk against God himself. To oppose his ideas or to offend him would surely bring his retaliation in one way or another whether the offenders were rich or poor." Oluf Christian Larsen, "A Biographical Sketch of the life of Oluf Christian Larsen dictated by himself and written by his son Oluf Larsen dedicated to his posterity who might desire to read it," p. 61, xerox of typescript, LDS Church Archives.

[59]Carl Fr. Wisloeff, Norsk Kirkehistorie, vol. 3 (Oslo: Lutherstiftelsens Forlag, 1971), pp. 12-13.

[60]Ibid., p. 13.

[61]Ibid., p. 14.

[62]Ibid., pp. 14-15.

[63]"I, at prestene er avgjorte fiender av opplysning og tenkning, samt at den laere de forkynner er et vrengebilde av Kristi laere, II. at prestenes virksomhet er den verste hindring for arbeidernes frigjoerelse, da de opplaeres til rolig aa finne seg i makthavernes utsugelse." Ibid., p. 108.

[64]"Vi ere nu blevne saa vel oplyste, at vi ikke mere hoerer paa det, som Presterne sige." A. Grimelund to KUD, 1 February 1873, Visitasberetninger, 1861-1877, pakke 1872, Trondheim Stift, A, KUD, RA.

[65]"Visitation for Kristiania By," 21 October 1875, Visitasberetninger, 1873-1885, pakke 1875, Kristiania Stift, A, KUD, RA.

[66]A. Grimelund to KUD, 27 February 1877, Visitasberetninger, 1861-1877, pakke 1876, Trondheim Stift, A, KUD, RA.

[67] Oslo Biskop to KUD, 28 February 1885, Visitasberetninger, 1873-1885, pakke 1884, Kristiania Stift, A, KUD, RA.

[68] Oslo Biskop to KUD, 6 March 1888, Visitasberetninger, 1886-1894, pakke 1887, Kristiania Stift, A, KUD, RA.

[69] ". . . inden visse Kredse af Unge af begge Kjoen, som hoere til den dannede Klasse, er indtraengt en Aand, der har affoedt Tanker og Anskuelser, som maa undergrave Saedeligheden." Gjenpart av "Visitation for Oslo Stiftsprovsti 1886," 15 April 1886, Visitasberetninger, 1886-1894, pakke 1886, Kristiania Stift, A, KUD, RA.

[70] N. J. Laache to KUD, 20 February 1890, Visitasberetninger, 1878-1893, pakke 1889, Trondheim Stift, A, KUD, RA.

[71] Oslo Biskop to KUD, 24 February 1891, Visitasberetninger, 1886-1894, pakke 1890, Kristiania Stift, A, KUD, RA; Trondheim Biskop to KUD, 28 February 1894, Visitasberetninger, 1878-1893, pakke 1893, Trondheim Stift, A, KUD, RA.

[72] Dorius to Frantsen, 3 September 1876, p. 2.

[73] Schou Diary, vol. 1, p. 25, 18 July 1877.

[74] Gaudy Hougan to N. Wilhelmsen, 29 November 1879, quoted in *Skandinaviens Stjerne* 29 (1 January 1880):106-07. Articles in *Skandinaviens Stjerne*--especially during the 1880s--decried the growing secularism: "Herskende Vantro" ["Prevailing Skepticism"], *Skandinaviens Stjerne* 32 (15 August 1883):344-45; "Atheisme og Mormonisme" ["Atheism and Mormonism"], *Skandinaviens Stjerne* 33 (15 April 1884):222-24; "Betragtninger over fritaenkeriske Indvendinger" ["A Look at Objections Posed by Free Thinkers"], *Skandinaviens Stjerne* 33 (1 September 1884):363-66, and 33 (15 September 1884):378-80. These and similar articles sounded calls to arms in the wake of reports from the branches complaining about dim prospects and general disinterest in religion. Oslo Conference President Hans J. Christiansen described Mormons in Oslo Branch in 1894 who "live wicked lives," young people who "seem to be more passive," leaders who were "apathetic and worldly," and "apathy and dissipation . . . in many places." ["En deel Ubehageligt var i Menigheden, flere som levede et daarligt Liv, og de Unge synes at blive mere ligegyldige og tillader sig selv at gaa paa den brede vei. Den Unge Soesterforening trued med oploesning. Presidentinden Josefine Johnsen gav op, og den ene af Raadgiverne viser sloev og lader sig drage af Verden; dette haver alt sammen vist sin Frugt, saaledes at slovhed [sic], og Udesvaevelser spores paa flere Steder. . . . Iblandt de Gamle Soestre viser sig ogsaa en Sloevhed. . . ."] Christiansen Journal, vol. 3, p. 53, 29 August 1894.

[75] Ferdinand Friis Hintze Diary, vol. 1, pp. 472-73, 26 August 1885, holograph, LDS Church Archives.

[76] H. J. Christiansen to N. C. Flygare, 24 September 1886, quoted in Skandinaviens Stjerne 36 (15 October 1886):26-27.

[77] Kenneth O. Bjork, West of the Great Divide: Norwegian Migration to the Pacific Coast, 1847-1893 (Northfield, Minnesota: Norwegian-American Historical Association, 1958), p. 129.

[78] Allen and Leonard, Story, pp. 414-15. At a meeting in Liverpool on 4 November 1887, Apostle George Teasdale, President of the European Mission, told new missionaries they "were not sent to preach polygamy." Hendricksen Diary, vol. 1, p. 23, 4 November 1887.

[79] Leonard J. Arrington and Davis Bitton, The Mormon Experience: A History of the Latter-day Saints (New York: Alfred A. Knopf, 1979), p. 140.

[80] Christiansen Journal, vol. 3, p. 55, 29 August 1894; and p. 68, 26 September 1894.

[81] Christian N. Lund to the Mormon First Presidency, 24 June 1898, typescript copy in Christian N. Lund, "Diary of Christian N. Lund, 1846-1921," p. 137, xerox of typescript, LDS Church Archives.

[82] Hilmar Freidel, "Historiske dokumentasjoner: er Innsamlingen og Emigrasjon To Ting?", p. 3, xerox of typescript, Norway Office, Translation Services Department, The Church of Jesus Christ of Latter-day Saints, Moss, Norway. "The fact that Emigration is not incouraged [sic] but rather discouraged has proven a benefit to the work," wrote Mission President Christian N. Lund in 1898, "inasmuch as it has served to strengthen the Branches and Conferences and been an aid to missionary work." Lund to First Presidency, 24 June 1898.

[83] The American Government urged Sweden-Norway to clamp down on Mormon emigration in 1879. Skard, USA, p. 192. No uniform measures were enacted in the United States until 1887, however, when Congress passed the Edmunds-Tucker Act which dissolved the Mormon Perpetual Emigrating Fund Company--the Church's chief agency for immigration comprising the "financial and organizational machinery that had assisted the immigration process." Arrington and Bitton, Experience, pp. 138-39.

[84] Jenson, Scandinavian Mission, p. 536.

[85] Israelsen, Utah, p. 149.

[86] Lund, "Diary," p. 109, 9 April 1889.

[87] *Skandinaviens Stjerne* 47 (15 February 1898):59.

[88] *Skandinaviens Stjerne* 45 (1 June 1896):266.

[89] Jenson, *Scandinavian Mission*, p. 536.

[90] In the years 1900-1905, Mormon missionaries visited over 50,000 Norwegian households per year; that jumped to over 100,000 households in 1906, and exceeded 201,000 in 1911. Such totals are staggering in light of a total Norwegian population of 2.3 million. Lars Jakob Holt, *Norges historie med hovedlinjer i de andre nordiske lands historie* (Oslo: H. Aschehoug & Co., 1974), p. 228. Distribution of Mormon tracts was just as phenomenal: from a low of 16,024 tracts distributed in 1896, the number rose to over 200,000 in 1907, and reached an incredible 479,578 in 1910. The number of books distributed and meetings held also rose dramatically, especially from 1900-1910. "Statistisk Rapport over Jesu Kristi Kirke af Sidste Dages Hellige i Skandinavien," *Skandinaviens Stjerne* 46 (1 February 1897) to 58 (15 March 1919). ". . . by 1890, almost every Norwegian home contained some type of Mormon literature." Curtis B. Hunsaker, "History of the Norwegian Mission from 1851 to 1960" (M.A. thesis, Brigham Young University, 1965), p. 111. After 1900, missionaries began tracting in remote parishes and islands. Mormon "saturation tracting" is illustrated by the fact that in the course of one year (1901-1902), Haugesund City had been completely tracted out (Each home had been visited by Mormon elders) at least four times. *Skandinaviens Stjerne* 51 (15 November 1902):347. Missionary Johann A. Olsen noted on 22 March 1907 in Stavanger that he "gave away 42 [tracts] in 21 families and sold and loaned away 7 books and had 4 gospel conversations." Olsen Journal, p. 195, 22 March 1907. Missionary E. C. Ekman visited sixty-five houses, distributed 108 tracts, and held four gospel conversations in Drammen on 4 February 1907. Edward C. Ekman Diary, 4 February 1907, holograph, LDS Church Archives. On 30 August 1909 at Skudesneshavn, four Mormon missionaries distributed about four hundred tracts. According to missionary Carl Kjaer, "the tracts that Pres. Keller ordered last winter, that had sunk with a ship out in [the] ocean, had drifted part of them into Skudesnaes and an old lady had them in her house quite a number of them, she'd been distributing them to many of the people in her town but did'nt [sic] know, they were Mormon tracts. . . ." Carl Kjaer Diary, pp. 243-44, 30 August 1909, holograph, LDS Church Archives. On 1 September 1909, missionaries Nephi Hansen and a "Brother Olsen" visited Kvalavaag near Haugesund, and "gave out 128 tracts after tracting 16 hours." Nephi Hansen Diary, 1 September 1909, holograph, LDS Church Archives. On another occasion (24 February 1910), Hansen and companion traveled by boat to a small island near Egersund. "We tracted 9 hours," said Hansen. "I gave out 180 tracts and had a very fine time." Ibid., 24 February 1910. On 3 November 1910, missionary Carl P. Lind visited the

little town of Aasgaardstrand (near Toensberg) where he distributed 108 tracts and held eight gospel conversations. Carl P. Lind Journal, p. 35, 3 November 1910, holograph, LDS Church Archives. As early as 1895, missionaries Heber C. Christensen and Nephi Andersen began preaching Mormonism in remote towns and villages of northern Norway, including Vardoe, Vadsoe, Jacobselv, Mortenaes, Kiby and Kiberg. In a period of eight weeks, Christensen and Andersen held ten meetings, visited 194 families, had 108 gospel conversations, and distributed 325 tracts. Nephi Andersen and Heber C. Christensen to Peter Sundwall, 5 June 1895, quoted in Skandinaviens Stjerne 44 (15 July 1895):315. In August 1905, missionaries J. C. Jensen and Ephraim Petersen obtained lodgings in Vardoe, northern Norway, and from there visited several Russian border towns. Returning to Vardoe, they traveled throughout the surrounding countryside. Said Jensen: "We was gone eight days. Visited 80 famlies [sic] most of wich [sic] was Fines [Finns] and Lapes [Lapps]. The distance we walked was 95. Eng. miles." James Christian Jensen, "Record Book," p. 5, holograph, LDS Church Archives.

[91] Molland, Berggrav, p. 67

[92] "Afskrift af Drammens Provstis Visitatsprotokol 1887, Bragernaes Praestegjeld," 18 June 1887, Visitasberetninger, 1886-1894, pakke 1887, Kristiania Stift, A, KUD, RA.

[93] Helge Hov, "Bakgrunnen for og Nedsettelsen av Kirkekommisjonen av 1908" (Hovedoppgave, University of Oslo, 1973), pp. 71, 76, 117.

[94] Ibid., pp. 172-73.

[95] Prominent conservatives and approximately three hundred priests and laymen backed the appeal which was published in several newspapers on 27 January 1883, and later reissued in brochure form over the names of 450 supporters and the Lutheran Bishops. Wisloeff, Kirkehistorie, pp. 29-30, 32-33.

[96] ". . . de gjennomgaaende hoerte til de grupper i samfunnet som naa var misfornoeyet med de politiske og sociale forhold i landet, og som naa var i bevegelse for aa gjennomfoere vidtgaaende reformer." Ibid., p. 33.

[97] One such was Lars Oftedal, parish priest of St. Peter's in Stavanger, whose restless energy led to the founding of an orphanage, construction of several prayer houses, including the famous "Betania Chapel," establishment of the newspaper, Vestlandsposten, and support of moderate liberal political programs. Ibid., pp. 41-42, 47-48. Sermons by another priest, Marius Giverholt, were so anti-confessional that Dean Lassen of Kristiansand accused him of "denying that baptism is a covenant" and deprecating the Church, the school system, and the civil

servant estate. ["Stiftsprost Lassen i Kristiansand beskylder ham for aa 'overspringer saliggjoerelsens orden og fornekte daapen som en pakt.'"] Ibid., p. 46. New revivalism penetrated almost all corners of Norway by 1900. The high point came in the years 1905-1906 when a sweeping revivalist movement shook Oslo, and old-timers described "a spiritual dawn, the likes of which had not been seen in years" [". . . en aandelig vaartid, som man ikke hadde hatt maken til paa lenge"]. Hov, "Kirkekommisjonen," pp. 29-30.

[98] Wisloeff, Kirkehistorie, pp. 51-52. "It is obvious in many areas," wrote the Bishop of Oslo in 1890, "that the people, in their desire for edification through the Word of God, exhibit a deplorable disregard for doctrinal purity and likewise seek to satisfy their yearnings [by listening to] dissenting preachers or to men with nonconformist sympathies." ["Det viser sig paa mange Steder, at Folket under sin Trang til Opbyggelse af Guds Ord viser en soerlig Ligegyldighed for Bekjendelsens Renhed og ligesaa snart soeger sin Trang tilfredsstillet hos Dissenterpraedikanter eller Maend, som ialfald staar Dissentere naer."] Oslo Bishop to KUD, 27 February 1890, Visitasberetninger, 1886-1894, pakke 1889, Kristiania Stift, A, KUD, RA. The number of dissenter sects was mushrooming as per the Bishop of Olso's report in 1891 that of 1,086 persons in the Diocese who had withdrawn from the State Church in 1890, "187 had not stated which dissenter group they planned to join, 358 had withdrawn in order to obtain civil marriage, 230 had joined the Methodists, 158 to various Lutheran Free Churches (including 46 to the Jarlsbergian Free Church), 51 to the Baptists, 21 to the so-called 'Free Mission Association,' 17 to the Adventists, 16 to avoid swearing oaths in court, 13 to 'The Association of God's Children,' 10 to the Catholic-Apostolic Congregation, 8 to the Roman Catholics, 6 to 'Communion with the Father and the Son,' 2 to 'The Christian Congregation,' 2 to the Salvation Army, 2 to the Mormons and 2 as 'non-Christians.'" ["Af de i forrige Aar Udtraadte have 187 ikke opgivet, til hvilket Samfund de vilde slutte sig, 358 have erklaeret at udtraede for at opnaa borgerlig Aegteskabsstiftelse, 230 have sluttet sig til Methodisterne, 158 til lutherske Frimenigheder (deraf 46 til den jarlsbergske Frimenighed), 51 til Baptisterne, 21 til den saakaldte 'fri Missionsforening,' 17 til Adventisterne, 16 for at undgaa Edsaflaeggelse, 13 til 'Guds Boerns Forsamling,' 10 til den Katholsk-apostoliske Menighed, 8 til de Romersk-Katholske, 6 til 'Samfund med Faderen og Soennen,' 2 til 'Kristi Menighed,' 2 til Fraelseshaeren, 2 til Mormonerne og 2 som 'Ikke-Kristne.'"] Oslo Biskop to KUD, 24 February 1891, Visitasberetninger, 1886-1894, pakke 1890, Kristiania Stift, A, KUD, RA. The Bishop of Trondheim decried dissenter activity in his Diocese in 1891: "The more sectarians who come with their new doctrines . . . the more the one preaches against the other and cries: 'Here is Christ!' the greater the resulting confusion, the greater the chance that the Word of God will be despised by the masses, and the greater probability that

skepticism will increase." ["Og jo flere Sekterere der kommer med sine nye Laerdomme . . . jo mere den Ene praediker imod den Anden og raaber: 'Her er Kristus!' jo stoerre Forviring man derved afstedkommer, desto mere vil selvfoelgelig Guds ord ringeagtes af Maengden, og desto bedre Fremgang vil Vantroen have."] Biskop Laache to KUD, 10 March 1891, Visitasberetninger, 1878-1893, pakke 1890, Trondheim Stift, A, KUD, RA.

[99]" . . . at Menneskene alle Vegne ere komne til den Slutning, at de ikke behoeve at gjoere saa meget nu som foer for at blive frelste og modtage en Ophoejelse med de Trofaste i Guds Rige." H. A. Pedersen to Joseph Christiansen, 27 December 1892, quoted in Skandinaviens Stjerne 42 (15 January 1893):124.

[100]Ole Sorensen to Scandinavian Mission Headquarters, 7 July 1893, quoted in Skandinaviens Stjerne 42 (1 August 1893):329.

[101]Christopher Kempe to Scandinavian Mission Headquarters, 18 August 1899, quoted in Skandinaviens Stjerne 48 (1 September 1899):262.

[102]Ibid.

[103]Historical Record, bk. A, 1886-1908, p. 41, Tromsoe Branch, Trondheim Conference, Scandinavian Mission, LDS Church Archives.

[104]Andrew Jenson Diary, bk. J, p. 426, 6 November 1910, holograph and typescript, LDS Church Archives.

[105]" . . . vi fremkaldte en staerk Opvaekkelse. . . . Hver Aften afholdt vi Moeder, der alle vare besoegte indtil Traengsel. Vi doebte fem Personer. . . . Jeg kan naesten fristes til at sige, at det var en virkelig Pintsefest, vi oplevede. . . ." Milton H. Knudsen to Anthon L. Skanchy, 24 February 1903, quoted in Skandinaviens Stjerne 52 (15 March 1903):93. Attendance at Mormon member meetings and Mormon lectures reflected the revivalist fervor of the 1890s and early 1900s. On 16 April 1893, over two hundred persons attended a Mormon meeting in Oslo on "Temples and what Temples are used for" in honor of the dedication of the Salt Lake City Temple. Over half of those attending were non-Mormons. Israelsen, Utah, pp. 127-28. At a Mormon gathering in Drammen in 1894, over half of those assembled were non-Mormons. Christofer Iversen Diary, 21 October 1894, microfilm of holograph, LDS Church Archives. A Mormon meeting that year in Aalesund attracted over a hundred curious onlookers. Christiansen Journal, vol. 3, pp. 22-24, [?] June 1894. Approximately one hundred of those attending a Mormon meeting in Oslo on 27 September 1903 were not Mormons. Hendricksen Diary, vol. 2, p. 34, 27 September 1903. Over two hundred non-Mormons attended a lecture in Oslo by J. A. Hendricksen on "Utah and its People" on 25 October 1903. Ibid., p. 45, 25 October 1903. On 8 November

1903, over six hundred persons--most of them non-Mormons--attended another Hendricksen lecture in Oslo entitled "The Apostacy," (see Ibid., p. 49, 8 November 1903), and Johann A. Olsen described a Mormon meeting in Aalesund on 11 February 1906 "crowded full of honest listeners, mostly strangers. . . ." Olsen Journal, p. 115, 11 February 1906. Revivalism had also penetrated the back country as witness Mormon missionary Carl Kjaer's account of a visit he and companion made to Skjolden on Lusterfjord on 23 October 1908: "Many asked us if we would'nt [sic] hold 'opbygelse Moede' ['revivalist meeting']." Kjaer Diary, p. 110, 23 October 1908. On 27 June 1909, Kjaer spoke about "Faith and Works and the Organization of the Church of Jesus Christ" at a Mormon meeting in Haugesund. Fourteen Mormons and twenty strangers (including a Methodist, three members of the Salvation Army, and various Lutherans) attended. Ibid., p. 216, 27 June 1909.

[106]J. A. Hendricksen to Joseph Mortensen, 13 January 1904, carbon copy, Letter-Copy-Book, bk. B, 1880-1905, Christiania Conference, Scandinavian Mission, LDS Church Archives.

[107]Jenson Diary, bk. J, p. 166, 31 December 1909. Financial hardship was especially acute in the Trondheim Conference. Most members there did not pay tithing according to Hans J. Christiansen. Christiansen Journal, vol. 8, p. 157, 30 October 1914. President A. M. Andreasen reported on 13 April 1915 that members in Trondheim Conference contributed an average of about thirty-seven crowns per month compared with monthly Conference expenses in excess of one hundred crowns. Ibid., vol. 9, p. 84, 13 April 1915.

[108]Ibid., vol. 8, p. 35, 19 May 1914, and pp. 48-49, 2 June 1914.

[109]Ibid., pp. 48-49, 2 June 1914.

[110]Ibid.

[111]Robert Brookman Cushman, "American Religious Societies in Norway" (Ph.D. dissertation, Northwestern University, 1942), p. 61.

[112]Ekman Diary, 6 December 1905.

[113]Nils Evensen Autobiography, p. 14, microfilm of typescript, LDS Church Archives.

[114]Jenson Diary, bk. J, p. 293, 15 January 1910.

[115]Ibid., p. 296, 23 January 1910. The years 1906-1912 marked the high point of anti-Mormon campaigns by Lutheran and other religious organizations; Norway was flooded with anti-Mormon

books, tracts, newspaper articles, cartoons, songs and jokes. But the effect on Mormonism was probably negligible. President Andrew Jenson asserted that anti-Mormon efforts had a positive effect in stirring up public interest and serving as free advertisement of Mormon doctrine. Andrew Jenson, "Praesident Andrew Jensons Afskedshilsen," Skandinaviens Stjerne 61 (15 May 1912): 152-55. Reports from the branches described a "more friendly and liberal" attitude toward the Mormons among the people at large by 1907. Skandinaviens Stjerne 56 (1 October 1907):301.

[116] Christiansen Journal, vol. 8, p. 112, 7 September 1914.

[117] Ibid., p. 156, 30 October 1914. Members of the female Relief Societies were guiding branch affairs throughout Trondheim Conference. Ibid., p. 156, 30 October 1914. Mormons in Bergen found their hall appropriated by the Bergen City Fire Commission in March 1915. Ibid., vol. 9, p. 46, 4 March 1915.

[118] Ibid., p. 87, 17 April 1915.

[119] Ibid., pp. 166-67, 20-21 July 1915.

[120] ". . . skjoendt ingen Aeldster fra Zion virke i Grenene, saa vare de dog alle i saerdeles god Forfatning, og mange oprigtige Mennesker undersoege Evangeliets Laere." Skandinaviens Stjerne 64 (15 November 1915):348.

[121] ". . . nogle stakkels oprigtige Soeskende, som lider aandelig Hunger, idet de er overladt til dem selv." Christiansen Journal, vol. 11, p. 55, 28 June 1916.

[122] ". . . en god Mand, men har ingen Evne til at lede. . . ." Ibid., pp. 73-74, 14 July 1916.

[123] Hans J. Christiansen, "Min Foraarsrejse i Missionen," Skandinaviens Stjerne 65 (1 June 1916):168-70.

[124] Christiansen Journal, vol. 11, pp. 210-12, 2 February 1917; p. 214, 6 February 1917; p. 218, 13 February 1917; p. 221, 16 February 1917; pp. 237-38, 14-15 March 1917; pp. 239-40, 17-18 March 1917; p. 262, 15 April 1917; Hans J. Christiansen, "Naervaerende vanskelige Tider," Skandinaviens Stjerne 66 (15 February 1917):56-57.

[125] Mission President Hans J. Christiansen visited Norway for the last time in July 1917 and blessed a Sister Olsen's little boy in Oslo "whose Father died when a boat was torpedoed in the North Sea" ["hvis Fader omkom ved at Skibet blev torpederet i Nordsoeen"]. Christiansen Journal, vol. 12, p. 37, 16 July 1917. Christiansen found branch finances in good shape--Trondheim Branch had a nine-hundred-crown surplus. But disharmony--"[idle] talk, selfishness," and "the local Priesthood's disinclination

to work" ["Snak, Egenkjaerlighed; det lokale Praestedoemmes liden Interesse for at virke"]--clouded the picture. Ibid., p. 38, 17 July 1917; p. 78, 22 September 1917; pp. 80-81, 24 September 1917. Conditions--spiritually and financially--in Bergen, however, were "excellent." Ibid., p. 92, 3 October 1917. Christiansen also preached to large crowds in Oslo. Ibid., p. 96, 7 October 1917.

[126]The history of Mormonism in Norway through April 1920 when Norway was made an independent Mormon mission was one of increasing consolidation and systematization. Mormons organized teaching districts in Oslo Branch in the late 1850s. Mons Pedersen Journal, p. 74, 17 April 1859, holograph, LDS Church Archives. In 1888, Mormons divided Oslo Branch into ten districts, each of which had a teacher and assistant who regularly visited members in their homes. Skandinaviens Stjerne 38 (15 October 1888):26. Mormons attended their first general conference in Norway on 6 April 1853 near Fredrikstad. Svend Larsen Diary, pp. 11-12, 6 April 1853, holograph, LDS Church Archives. The first district meeting for Priesthood leaders was held in Fredrikstad on 17 April 1859. Pedersen Journal, p. 74, 17 April 1859; p. 80, 4 May 1860. Conferences and district meetings were subsequently held on a regular basis. Mormons in Oslo dedicated the first Church-owned and constructed meetinghouse in Scandinavia (Oesterhausgade 27) on 23 July 1871. Skandinaviens Stjerne 20 (15 August 1871):337. The structure was described in 1885 as "a three story building, with about 20 rooms" including "a fine hall and office." Hintze Diary, vol. 1, p. 393, 4 July 1885. Members dedicated a new Oslo meetinghouse (on the site of the old hall) on 24 July 1903. Hendricksen Diary, vol. 2, p. 6, 24 July 1903. A Church-owned meetinghouse in Trondheim was dedicated on 8 February 1914. Skandinaviens Stjerne 63 (15 March 1914):90. Another church-owned meetinghouse was dedicated at Bergen on 18 July 1915. Christiansen Journal, vol. 9, p. 64, 18 July 1915. On 8 May 1899, mission leaders divided Norway into three conferences--Oslo, Bergen and Trondheim-for purposes of administration with conference headquarters in all three cities. Skandinaviens Stjerne 48 (15 June 1899):190. Oslo Conference in 1903 comprised branches in Oslo, Moss, Fredrikstad, Halden, Odalen, Eidsvold, Roeken, Drammen, Toensberg, Larvik, Arendal and Christiansand. Skandinaviens Stjerne 52 (1 December 1903):366. Bergen Conference in 1903 comprised branches in Bergen, Aalesund, Stavanger, Egersund, Voss and Nordfjord. Ibid., p. 368. Trondheim Conference in 1904 comprised branches in Trondheim, Christiansund, Roeros, Mosjoeen, Bodoe, Harstad, Tromsoe, and Vardoe. Skandinaviens Stjerne 53 (15 June 1904):191. The semimonthly mission periodical, Skandinaviens Stjerne, first issued in October 1851, informed members of organizational developments and doctrinal pronouncements. Other Danish-language publications issued by the Scandinavian Mission (1851-1884) included the following books and tracts: Mormons Bog, Laere og Pagter, a hymnbook, "En Advarselsens Roest," "Er Mormonismen en Vranglaere?", "Sammenligninger mellem Beviserne,"

"Maerkvaerdige Syner," "Sanhedsroest," "Israels Indsamling," "Guddomelig Fuldmagt," "Patriarkalske Ordener," "Aegteskab og Saeder i Utah," "Anskuelser om Aegteskab," "Indbydelser til Guds Rige," and "Eneste Vej til Salighed." "Statement of Publications issued by the Scandinavian 'Stjerne' Office 1851-1884," in Anthon Hendrik Lund Diary following entry for 30 March 1884, microfilm of holograph, LDS Church Archives. Mormon women belonged to a <u>women's charitable organization</u> in Oslo as early as 1870. It was originally a sewing school where women sewed clothes for the needy, but on 22 October 1877, the "sewing school" was phased out and reorganized as a "special women's association"; a further reorganization in 1879 established the <u>"Oslo Branch Relief Society</u>"--part of the worldwide Mormon Relief Society Organization. The Norwegian Mission, <u>Jubileum aaret 1850-1950</u> (Oslo: Haraldssoen A.S., [1950]), p. 27. By 1 October 1882, eleven branch relief societies were functioning in Norway. <u>Skandinaviens Stjerne</u> 32 (1 November 1882):44. Mormons organized their first <u>Sunday school</u> in Norway in Oslo Branch on 27 November 1870. Freidel, <u>historie</u>, p. 86. Other Sunday schools were organized in the larger branches soon thereafter, and by 1904, seven Sunday schools in Oslo Conference comprised 388 members. Hendricksen Diary, vol. 2, p. 103, 3 April 1904. The Oslo Sunday School in 1903 had "one theological class and five other classes." Ibid., p. 33, 20 September 1903. A new Sunday School Handbook in 1913 diagrammed classes and lesson plans for an eight-year period with the purpose of "making the Sunday School work more systematic. . ." <u>Skandinaviens Stjerne</u> 62 (15 April 1913):121. Members established a <u>Young Men's Part-time Mission</u> [Unge menns leilighets-misjon] in Oslo Branch in 1874 which was formally incorporated on 29 January 1879 as a "Young Men's Association." That organization was superseded in turn by organization of the "Young Men's Mutual Improvement Association"--part of the worldwide <u>YMMIA</u> of the Mormon Church--on 20 January 1880. A similar organization for young women--the <u>YWMIA</u>--was founded on 10 January 1881 in Oslo. The Norwegian Mission, <u>Jubileum</u>, p. 27. Mutual Improvement Associations were subsequently organized in larger branches throughout Norway. Mormon <u>General Authorities</u> first visited Norway in 1860 when Mission President John Van Cott and Apostles Amasa M. Lyman and Charles C. Rich conducted a conference in Oslo. John Van Cott Diary, vol. 3, 17, 19-20 October 1860, xerox of holograph, LDS Church Archives. Mormon Apostle Heber J. Grant visited Norway in 1906. Ekman Diary, 8 July 1906. Joseph F. Smith, the first President of the Mormon Church to visit Norway, arrived in Oslo in July 1910 accompanied by Charles W. Nibley, Presiding Bishop of the Church. Jenson Diary, bk. J, pp. 372-73, 29 July 1910. In 1915, Norwegian Mormons were instructed to hold <u>family home evenings</u> at least once a month in accordance with desires of the First Presidency in Utah. <u>Skandinaviens Stjerne</u> 65 (1 January 1916):11. <u>Mormons who did not immigrate to Utah and who remained active for long periods</u>, exerted a stabilizing influence on congregations in Norway, as per comments by O. C. Larsen who returned to Oslo in May 1881 after an absence of twenty years: "I felt as though I had never been away from Norway and even met several old people who were in the church before I left." Larsen, "Sketch," p. 56. A "Brother and Sister Simonsen," Mormons in Bergen since 1853, assisted Andrew Amundsen in 1883--the first Mormon to visit Bergen in nearly thirty years. Andrew Amundsen Journal, p. 54, 13, 16, 20 September 1883, typescript, LDS Church Archives. Missionaries also mentioned other members of long-standing, some of whom were all that remained of once-thriving congregations. Andrew Israelsen described the family of "Chris Weeding and his two sons"--the only Mormon family in the vicinity of Kvaefjord, northern Norway, in July 1892. Weeding "had been a Mormon for thirty-five years." Israelsen, Utah, p. 109. President Hans J. Christiansen visited an "old Bro. Ekstroem and his wife" in Christiansand (June 1894) who had been members more than thirty years. Christiansen Journal, vol. 3, pp. 13-14, [?] June 1894. A report in Skandinaviens Stjerne in 1894 described a Brother Groen at "Stavnes Fyr ved Christiansund." Groen was a lighthouse keeper who figured prominently in annals of Trondheim Branch for over thirty years. Skandinaviens Stjerne 43 (1 August 1894):330. Peter Olsen visited an old sister (not named) in Stavanger in 1896 who had been a Mormon thirty years. Peter Olsen Diary, 15 June 1896, microfilm of holograph, LDS Church Archives. Missionary Johan Johnson described Brother Brynhild Isaksen of Brevik in 1897 who at that time had been a faithful Mormon for forty-five years. Johan L. George Johnson Diary, 4 July 1897, holograph, LDS Church Archives. Isaksen was still going strong in 1910 when Mission President Andrew Jenson described him as "an old veteran who joined the Church in 1852 . . . undoubtedly the oldest member of the Church in Scandinavia." Jenson Diary, bk. J, p. 427, 7 November 1910. A "Brother Christensen" who joined the Mormons in 1853 was still living in Skien in 1897. Johnson Diary, 20 July 1897. A Pioneer Day Celebration in Oslo on 24 July 1904 honored the two oldest Mormons in Oslo Branch--Lars Andersen baptized on 21 January 1867, and Marthe Pedersen baptized on 8 June 1859. Skandinaviens Stjerne 53 (15 August 1904):250. E. C. Ekman visited a bedridden eighty-six-year-old man in Skien in 1906 who had been a faithful member for fifty years (possibly the "Brother Christensen" J. L. G. Johnson visited in 1897). Ekman Diary, 24 July 1906. James Jensen visited a Sister Hansen in Oslo in 1908 who had been a Mormon for fifty years. James Jensen Journal, p. 57, 16 September 1908, xerox of holograph, LDS Church Archives.

CHAPTER V

[1] Hans Olsen Magleby Journal, 18-19, 22, 24 February, 1, 6, 10, 13, 20-21, 23, 28 March 1857, holograph, Library-Archives, The Church of Jesus Christ of Latter-day Saints, Salt Lake City, Utah [hereinafter cited as LDS Church Archives].

[2] ". . . [jeg] foelte gleede ved at lide for Jesu Navn eller Sandhedenskyl [sic] og maa det tjenne mig til gode Amen." Ibid., 28 November, 2 December 1857.

[3] Niels Christian Poulsen Journal, 15 October 1857, holograph, LDS Church Archives.

[4] Svend Larsen Diary, 19 April, 11 June 1867, holograph, LDS Church Archives.

[5] Christopher Sigvarth Winge Autobiography, p. 5, microfilm of typescript, LDS Church Archives.

[6] Ibid., p. 6.

[7] ". . . den uindskraenskede [sic] Husret som enhve [enhver] norsk Undersat nyder." Minute Book and Record of Members, bk. A, 1854-1873, pp. 4-5, Drammen Branch, Christiania Conference, Scandinavian Mission, LDS Church Archives.

[8] Mons Pedersen Journal, 30 October-9 November 1854, p. 1, holograph, LDS Church Archives.

[9] *Skandinaviens Stjerne* 26 (1 February 1877):141; Anthon L. Skanchy Autobiography, p. 7, holograph, Anthon L. Skanchy Collection, LDS Church Archives.

[10] Carl C. N. Dorius, "Dagbog: Carl C. N. Dorius's Missionsforretninger i Skandinavia, samt en kort Beretning om det tidligere Levnetsloeb," p. 95, 26 January 1861, holograph, LDS Church Archives.

[11] George Mortimer Brown Autobiography and Diary, p. 47, 12 December 1863, typescript, Library Services Division, Genealogical Department, The Church of Jesus Christ of Latter-day Saints, Salt Lake City, Utah.

[12] ". . . vore Forhoer havde givet Politioevrigheden bedre Begreber om os og vor Religion. Flere af vore Broedre havde forandret sin tidligere Levemaade i den Grad, at Politiet noedtes til at anerkjende Omvendelsens vaerdige Frugter hos disse Maend.

Skjoendt Lovens Bogstav var imod os, vare Oevrighedspersonerne nu blevne vore Venner og gjorde os ingen Ulejlighed, uden naar Praester eller andre Egoister, noedte dem dertil. . . . Politiet tirrede Praesterne til Gjengjaeld, og om Vinteren 1854-55 kom saaledes en Raekke offentlige Debatter i Stand, i hvilke Praesterne bleve meget medtagne. Aeldste Knud Peterson og jeg vare Evangeliets Repraesentanter, og Eilert Sundt, Ole Vig og Jensenius, understoettede af flere Praester, vare vore Modstandere. Hin Soendags Kamp gjentoges i stor Maalestok, og Byens fornemste Embedsmaend, indbefattende Hr. Morgenstjerne, var tilstede." C. C. A. Christensen, "C. C. A. Christensens Beretning," Morgenstjernen 3 (1 July 1884):203-04. Sheriff Torbjoernsen in Kil (Sannidal) treated Mormon prisoner, Canute Peterson, very kindly in 1854, and when confronted by a woman who demanded that Peterson be placed in the worst cell possible, replied: "I will not; he shall have the Bast [best] Plase [place] I have!" Canute Peterson Journal, 31 March 1854, holograph, LDS Church Archives.

[13] John S. Hansen, ed., Mindeudgave C. C. A. Christensen: Poetiske Arbejder, Artikler og Afhandlinger tilligemed hans Levnedsloeb (Salt Lake City, Utah: Bikubens Bibliotek, 1921), pp. 421-22. Many Mormons, especially missionaries, were guilty of deception and outright lying. Mormon preachers often posed as "Readers" or Lutheran lay preachers. Avskrift av "Extraret paa Raadhuset i Moss under ledelsen af Byfoged Lorentz Juhl Vogt," 25 October 1852, Mormonpakken, Trossamfunn Samling [hereinafter cited as TS], Det kongelige Justis- og Politidepartement, Oslo, Norway [hereinafter cited as JPD]. After the Supreme Court Decision of 4 November 1853, many Mormon missionaries stopped using the term "Mormon" altogether. Canute Peterson, a missionary in Oslo in 1854, promised the Chief of Police "that no baptisms should be performed within the City limits of Christiania," and signed a contract to that effect. Thereafter, Peterson baptized in a stream about forty rods outside the Oslo City limits. Canute Peterson et al., "Story of the life of Canute Peterson as given by himself and by some members of his family," pp. 66-67, xerox of MS, LDS Church Archives. Missionaries were still using Peterson's ploy as late as 1865 when missionary L. L. Olson in Lillehammer held meetings "outside the city" in a shoemaker's house and bragged that the police could not arrest him since his preaching took place "outside the city limits." Lars Larson Olson Journal and Notebook, 26-27 August 1865, holograph, LDS Church Archives. In 1854, the Mayor of Oslo asked Canute Peterson and Carl Widerborg if they held meetings and baptized; both Peterson and Widerborg answered that they did not--a bold lie! Peterson Journal, 1, 3 March 1854. Missionary O. C. Larsen prevaricated even further in 1858, i.e., "finding there was no escape from the officers who had been notified in various cities to arrest me whereever I was found I concluded to give myself up. By so doing we were generally liberated by promising to perform no ordinances of the gospel. I then gave myself up to the city [Drammen] authorities and was indited [sic] and liberated to

Appear at a stated time on the usual promises. I, however, continued to preach the gospel on another pretext, as if I were entirely free." Oluf Christian Larsen, "A Biographical Sketch of the life of Oluf Christian Larsen dictated by himself and written by his son Oluf Larsen dedicated to his posterity who might desire to read it," p. 18, xerox of typescript, LDS Church Archives. Larsen was arrested a second time, but told the magistrate "that I had not preached a sermon in public, but that it was a private gathering and I only sat on a chair and read the Bible to the people." Ibid., p. 19. Missionary C. S. Winge was fined ten dollars in 1858 for preaching, and was warned to stop proselyting. "This last order I didn't take much notice of," said Winge, "for thereafter I preached early and late to all who would hear." Christopher Sigvarth Winge Autobiography, p. 3, microfilm of typescript, LDS Church Archives. In Kongsberg in 1860, missionary C. C. N. Dorius held a prayer meeting and avoided the letter of the law by sitting down as he preached. Dorius, "Dagbog," p. 78, 5, 8 November 1860. G. M. Brown declared in 1863 that since "the authorities were so strict we were obliged to sit down and preach." Brown Autobiography, 13 December 1863. Brothers C. C. N. and J. F. F. Dorius served missions in Norway to avoid military conscription in Denmark. Dorius, "Dagbog," 14 April 1862. Frants Christian Grundvig, a young Mormon in Denmark, followed suit, i.e., "the time had come that I had to be a soldier as every young man had to be in Denmark at that time [1863]. Brothers Carl and Fredinaent Dorices [Carl and Ferdinand Dorius] came over from Norway, they had been back their [sic] on a Mission from Utah, they told me to ask the President of the Scandinavian Mission to send me to Norway thats what they had done to get out of being a soldier before they Emigrated." Frants Christian Grundvig Autobiography, p. 6, holograph, LDS Church Archives. This also worked the other way as witness the case of C. S. Winge, a native Norwegian, who headed for Denmark in 1861 to avoid the Norwegian draft. While traveling to Denmark via Sweden, Winge posed as a traveling journeyman, but observed "that the people did not believe me and many times took me for a deserter, which as a matter of fact I was." Winge Autobiography, pp. 6-7. Other missionaries, such as O. H. Berg, went to ridiculous lengths to avoid the draft. Berg left Norway in 1864 for a Mormon mission to Denmark after consulting with Mission President S. L. Sprague, and avoided detection by assuming an alias--the name of his grandfather, O. H. Andersen! Ole Hendriksen Berg Diary, vol. 1, 23-24, 26-27 April 1864, holograph, LDS Church Archives. Other Norwegians who avoided the draft by serving missions in Denmark included Anton Olsen in 1872 and A. S. Schou in 1880. Jens Christian Andersen Weibye Diary, vol. 4, p. 127, 16 July 1872, holograph, LDS Church Archives; August Severin Schou Diary, vol. 3, p. 8, 22 May 1880, xerox of typescript, LDS Church Archives.

[14]Poulsen Journal, 6 December 1855.

[15] Jonas Johansen Diary, pp. 35-38, 11 January 1871, holograph, LDS Church Archives.

[16] "Br. Emil Noekleby var indkaldt for Politiet i Drammen den 17de Decbr. og blev forbudt at doebe der i Byen; derimod tillod man ham at praedike saa meget han lyster." Skandinaviens Stjerne 21 (15 January 1872):124.

[17] Andrew Jenson, "Erindringer fra Missionen i Skandinavien," Morgenstjernen 3 (1 October 1884):290.

[18] Brown Autobiography, p. 126, 24 December 1865.

[19] Ibid., p. 144, 18 March 1866. A Mormon survey of police attitudes throughout Norway in 1873 reported the following: Oslo--"humane"; Fredrikstad--"kind"; Trondheim--"humane"; Hadeland--"humane"; Drammen--"kind"; Arendal--"peaceful"; Stavanger--"humane"; Odalen--"good." Historical Record, bk. B, 1873-1895, p. 12, Christiania Conference, Scandinavian Mission, LDS Church Archives. Bergen was the glaring exception. Missionary Andrew Amundsen was imprisoned there in 1883, and police disruption of Mormon meetings was commonplace during the 1880s. John Anthon Hendricksen Diary, vol. 1, p. 102, 18 March 1888, microfilm of holograph, LDS Church Archives. Mormons in Bergen met privately behind locked doors as late as 1889 according to Skandinaviens Stjerne 39 (15 October 1889):27, but all signs of persecution were over by 1892, and "the People and civil authorities" were described as "very humane." Skandinaviens Stjerne 42 (15 January 1892):122-23. "The Brethren," said Conference President Hans J. Christiansen in 1894, "now have full freedom to preach [in Bergen] without being disturbed." ["Broedrene haver nu sin fulde Frihed til at praedike uden at blive forstyrret."] Hans Jacob Christiansen Journal, vol. 3, p. 21, [June] 1894, holograph, LDS Church Archives. Mormon relations with the Norwegian Parliament [Storting] were somewhat worse than those with civil and police authorities generally. Mormon petitions to Parliament in 1852, 1854, 1856, 1862, 1865, and 1882 for recognition under the Dissenter Law fell on deaf ears or were tabled in committee. William Mulder, Homeward to Zion: The Mormon Migration from Scandinavia (Minneapolis: University of Minnesota Press, 1957), p. 45. The petition of 1854 was signed by at least sixty-five non Mormons. John Van Cott to the Presidency of the European Mission in Liverpool, 3 May 1854, quoted in Andrew Jenson, "Erindringer fra Missionen i Skandinavien," Morgenstjernen 2 (May 1883):67. The petition of 1865 was personally presented to Storting President Harbitz by Ivar Isaacksson, an influential Mormon who owned a large mechanical workshop in Oslo. Conference President G. M. Brown reported that Isaacsson visited Harbitz "to consult the president in regard to the best course for us [Mormons] to pursue in order to obtain freedom of religion and the right to preach, teach, and organize branches of the church in different parts of the Country without living in danger of fine and imprisonment. . . .

Herr Harbitz was very kind and gave some good council in the matter and spoke very well of our religion. He said that there was a law which was enacted in the year 1863 which was principally meant for us. It gave us the privilege of having our members united in matrimony by the magistrates and that in his opinion was acknowledging our freedom to organize our church in the land, though it was in an indirect way. He said that he thought that a petition from us to that effect would be heard and in all probabilities granted. He further said that if we would have those whom we baptized first have their names stricken from the records of the Church of the state that we would meet with no difficulty whatever." Brown Autobiography, pp. 93-94, 121, 9 October 1865. The Mormons accordingly drew up a petition seeking "the privilege of preaching the Gospel and performing the ordinances of the same as written in the books of the New Testament, without being thereby subject to imprisonment or other persecutions," but made the fatal mistake of including the catchall phrase: "We should obey God rather than man." Ibid., p. 122, 22 October 1865. Over six hundred Mormons petitioned Parliament in 1883 stating that they paid regular taxes and fulfilled military duties, and sought only the privilege of worshiping God as they pleased without fear of reprisal. Skandinaviens Stjerne 32 (1 April 1883):199. In the ensuing parliamentary debate, MP Hagbard E. Berner cited a "law of history" to the effect that religious controversy could only be resolved by appeals to truth, and not by reliance on force. Berner expressed disappointment that Norway was so far behind the times with regard to the principle of religious freedom, and noted the religious freedoms granted by the American Constitution; Berner further pointed out that nothing in the Norwegian Constitution could be construed as restricting religious freedom. Berner also stated that Mormons were meeting openly in Oslo without hindrance from police authorities, and called the Supreme Court Decision of 1853 against the Mormons a decision based on fear. Norway, Storting, Storthingstidende indeholdende to og tredivte ordentlige Storthings Forhandlinger (Odelsthinget), 1883, "Forhandlinger i Odelsthinget," pp. 605-06. Jacob L. R. Sverdrup, Chairman of the Parliamentary Committee for Church Affairs, agreed in part with Berner that freedom of religion was desireable, but added his opinion that such freedom was not boundless and did not include opening the doors to wolves (in this case, Mormons). Sverdrup referred to Mormon political theory--the concept of a political Zion--and the Mormon doctrine of polygamy as beliefs detrimental to society at large, and refuted Berner's praise of the Constitution of the United States by pointing out that the U.S. Government was currently waging war against the Mormons (cf. Edmunds-Tucker Bill, etc.). Sverdrup also accused Mormons of luring unsuspecting young women ("white slaves") to Utah with false promises. Ibid., pp. 608, 611; Norway, Storting, Storthings Indstillinger og Beslutninger 1883, B, "Odelsthingets og Lagthingets Indstillinger og Beslutninger," pp. 18-19; Andrew Amundsen Journal, p. 39, 16 January 1883; p. 50, 4 May 1883;

typescript, LDS Church Archives; Hilmar Freidel, <u>Jesu Kristi Kirke i Norge: Den norske misjons historie, 1851-1966</u> (Oslo: Jesu Kristi Kirke av Siste Dagers Hellige Misjonskontoret, 1966), pp. 52-55. Parliamentary debates on the Mormon question in 1891 and 1912 were likewise characterized by emotionally charged references to polygamy and the "white slave traffic." Norway, Storting, <u>Storthings Forhandlinger i Aaret 1891</u>, pt. 8, "Forhandlinger i Odelsthinget," pp. 590, 604, 608, 634-35; Norway, Storting, <u>Storthings Forhandlinger i Aaret 1891</u>, B, "Indstillinger til og Beslutninger af Odelsthinget og Lagthinget," pp. 4-5; Norway, Storting, <u>Stortings Forhandlinger 1912</u>, pt. 7, "Forhandlinger i Stortinget," B, pp. 2718-28. Debate in 1891 was tied to proposals for a new Dissenter Law; minority proposals would have granted all non-Christians, including Mormons who did not propound polygamy, protection under the law. In the words of the minority proposition: "To put these people [non-Christians] in a position--as would occur under terms of the [majority] proposal--which robs them of religious rights, to pretend that they do not exist, while in fact their numbers are increasing year by year, seems a deplorable contradiction of the proposed Law's intent and the spirit of our times." ["At stille disse Mennesker saaledes, som Propositionen gjoer det, religioest talt retsloese, at lade, som om de ikke er til, medens deres Tal dog Aar for Aar vokser, synes at staa i en besynderlig Uoverenstemmelse med hele Tidens og ikke mindst med naervaerende Lovforslags Tankegang."] Storting, <u>Forhandlinger 1891</u>, B, "Indstillinger," p. 4. Minority spokesmen also pointed out that the proposed law would grant freedom of religion to Jews--a group much further removed from Christian beliefs than, for example, Unitarians. Ibid., p. 5. MP Haegstad added further insights: "If our goal is freedom of religion, the State Church must be dissolved, and we must arrange it such that all in this country who profess belief in a religion have the same civil rights, such that material advantages do not accrue to those who belong to a certain religion. . . . If it was freedom of religion we were talking about, the word 'Dissenters' would have to be stricken from Norwegian Law; for in a country which enjoys religious freedom, there can be no talk of dissenters, i.e., there would be no dissenters." ["Vil vi have Religionsfrihed, saa maa Statskirken oploeses, og da maa vi indrette det saaledes for alle Religionsbekjendere i dette Land, at de har de samme borgerlige Rettigheder, saaledes at der ikke foelger materielle Fordele ved at tilhoere en vis Religionsbekjendelse. . . . Hvis det var Religionsfrihed der var Tale om, saa maatte Ordet 'Dissentere' ud af den norske Lov; thi i et Land, hvor der er Religionsfrihed, kan der ikke vaere Tale om Dissentere, for der bliver der ikke Dissentere." Storting, <u>Forhandlinger 1891</u>, pt. 8, "Odelsthinget," p. 634. The upshot of the debate was passage of the majority proposal including (by a vote of fifty-seven to twenty-five) the majority proposal barring non-Christians from protection under the Law. Ibid., p. 635. Mormon petitions to Parliament were sometimes accompanied by appeals to the King of Sweden-Norway. Thus, when Mormons met at Fredrikstad in 1852 to decide on a program to counter official harassment, they not only "decided to write and present a petition to the Government [Parliament]," but also sought, "if possible, to see and speak with the King, who, at that time was in Christiania, and thus, verbally present him with a statement of the wrongs, which some of our people had suffered on account of their religion." Christian J. Larsen Journal, vol. 2, p. 128, 11 October 1852, holograph and MS, LDS Church Archives. The resulting petition to the King was dated 19 April 1853 and signed by 125 Mormons in Brevik, Fredrikstad, and Risoer, but was never acknowledged by the King or the Government. Petition by members of the Church of Jesus Christ of Latter-day Saints in Brevik, Fredrikstad and Risoer to the King of Sweden-Norway, 19 April 1853, pakke "Mormonerne 1851-1920," Kontor A [hereinafter cited as "A"], Det kongelige Kirke- og Undervisningsdepartement [hereinafter cited as KUD], Riksarkivet, Oslo, Norway [hereinafter cited as RA]. On 17 December 1855, Scandinavian Mission President John Van Cott "wrote petion [petition] to the King of Sweden asking for religious liberty," and on 18 December it was "translated into Swedish and Posted to Norways and Swedens Kong [King]." John Van Cott Diary, vol. 1, p. 17, 18 December 1855, xerox of holograph, LDS Church Archives. Nothing came of that petition either. In connection with Mormon petitions to Parliament in 1865, Ivar Isaacksson, a wealthy Mormon who owned a machine shop in Oslo, sought an interview with the King to request that he use his influence with the Storting on behalf of Mormon requests; Isaacksson "was informed that his majesty could not have anything to do with the subject." Brown Autobiography, p. 129, 11 January 1866. In 1897, Mormon authorities in Utah commissioned J. M. Sjoedahl "to go to Sweden and there in behalf of the Scandinavien [sic] people in Utah present to the King and Queen, on the occasion of their Jubelee [sic] of the 25th Anniversary of their reign, a copy of the book of Mormon beautifully bound and put in an elegant box of Utah Onyx." Sjoedahl was accordingly "favored with a personal audience with his Majesty King Oscar on Sep 19th [1897] . . . and presented him with this beautiful treasure - The King recieved [sic] him Kindly and thanked him in a few well chosen words, and bade him bring his greeting to his Countrymen in far off Utah." Christian N. Lund, "Diary of Christian N. Lund, 1846-1921," p. 91, xerox of typescript, LDS Church Archives. On 23 July 1904, Oslo Conference President, Gilbert Torgersen, missionaries Otto J. Monsen, Charles W. Larsen, John M. Thorup, Finn H. Berg, Georg T. Larsen, and Lars Olsen, together with Sister Anna Burgon and her two daughters, Rosa and Lillian, obtained an audience with King Oscar II of Sweden-Norway. "At the close of their meeting, President Torgersen called down the blessings of the Lord on the King, his family and the inhabitants of the Country," to which the King responded, "God bless you and all of your people!" ["Ved audiensens slutning nedbad president Torgersen Herrens Velsignelse over kongen med familie og landets befolkning. Med hjertelig foelelse svarte kongen: 'Gud velsigne eder og eders hele folk.'" Carl M. Hagberg, Den Norske Misjons Historie (Oslo: Universal-trykkeriet, 1928), p. 37. John Halvorsen, Vice-consul for Norway in Utah, and Judge C. M. Nielsen of Salt Lake City, obtained separate interviews with King Haakon VII of Norway on 28 September 1911. Halvorsen described the King as "a tall, athletic, handsome man." "What I appreciated most," he continued, "was the democracy of his manner. He made me feel at home at once." Halvorsen and the King discussed economic and commercial conditions in Utah, whereas Nielsen discussed Mormonism, tried to refute various anti-Mormon rumors then circulating in Norway, and described visits to Utah by Roald Amundsen and Erling Bjoernson. John Halvorsen, "An Interview with King Haakon VII of Norway," Improvement Era, December 1911, pp. 146-48. United States Secretary of State Evart sent a circular to the governments of England, Prussia, Denmark and Sweden-Norway in 1879 seeking their help in controlling or halting Mormon emigration, and claiming that most Mormons who emigrated from Europe intended to practice bigamy in Utah. Skandinaviens Stjerne 29 (1 October 1879):9; Udenrigs Departementet to den Norske Statsraads-Afdeling, 14 January 1880, MS copy, Mormonpakken, TS, JPD; JPD Circular, 6 July 1880, Mormonpakken TS, JPD; Carl F. Eltzholtz, Et Vaaben mod Mormonismen (Copenhagen: Andr. Fred. Hoest & Soen, [1884]), p. 6.

[20] Peterson Journal, 21 October 1854.

[21] Ibid., 26 March 1855.

[22] Magleby Journal, 24 May 1857.

[23] Poulsen Journal, 24 February 1856.

[24] Magleby Journal, 1-2 April 1857.

[25] "Hertil kommer endnu, at Mormonismens Emissairer i Almindelighed udmaerke sig ved stor Tungefaerdighed og stort Bekjendskab isaer med de dunklere, sjeldnere benyttede Skriftsteder fornemmelig af det gamle Testamente, hvilke de uden Betaenkning forvanske og fordreie efter deres egne Hensigter; at en Praest kan vaere en meget dygtig Mand og i sit Kald virke med Velsignelse, uden i hoei Grad at besidde den Aandsnaervaerelse, den Sikkerhed i at opfatte, den Lethed for strax at finde de rette Ord og Udtryk, den improvisoriske Svade, der kunde saette ham istand til strax i en ofte chaotisk Ordstroem at udfinde, hvorom det egentlig gjaelder, og klart, overbevisende og derhos flydende at udhaeve og imoedegaae Vildfarelserne; at det vilde vaere til stor Skade, om Praesten, han have i Virkeligheden nok saa meget Sandheden og Seieren paa sin Side, skulde for de Tilstedevaerende synes at ligge under; at de, der ere meest udsatte for at lade sig lokke og bedaare af Mormonernes kjoedet smigrend Laere, i Almindelighed have en egen Maalestok, hvorefter de bedoemme hvad de hoere; . . . ere ud af Stand til at skjelne

imellem hvad der er Beviis og hvad ikke er det; ja opfattende hvad der siges ganske aphoristisk, ikke engang formaae at foelge et laengere, sammenhaengende og grundigt Foredrag saaledes, at de der af kunne samle og tilegne sig det Vaesentlige. . . . Min Mening er saaledes, at der skall haves et bevidst, levende foelt Kald og en saeregen af Sagen og Forholdene Betinget Dygtighed for at kunne med Held i offentlig Forsamling indlade sig paa at optraede som vor Kirkes Forsvarer imod Mormonismen." Jens L. Arup to KUD, 14 April 1855, Visitasberetninger, 1851-1855, pakke 1854, Kristiania Stift, A, KUD, RA.

[26] Brown Autobiography, p. 106, 6 August 1865.

[27] Ibid. Missionary O. H. Nielsen described a similar incident on 10 March 1879 at the home of Christian Hansen in Stange: "Shortly before we began, the parish priest arrived dressed in: large woolen greatcoat, [a] red scarf about the neck and the waist, large riding boots, woolen hat and gloves, glasses, short beard and a whip in his hand. He took off his spectacles, polished them and returned them to his nose, took off his riding clothes and walked right up to me and asked if it was I who traveled around in his parish and preached for his sheep. I had now preached so often and walked such long distances in the snow, cold, and wet that I was hardly able to talk. My strength was nearly gone due to a cold. But I summoned all my powers to defend our belief and teachings. We entered into a lively discussion. He said he would chase me away from the place; for I was an emissary [from] the Devil. He held a speech outside the house and warned the people about our doctrine, and prayed to his God that he would protect them from the Mormons. When the priest had gone, I started the meeting and good testimonies were borne." ["Lidt foer vi begyndte, kom Sognepresten ifoert: stor lodden tullup [sic], roedt skjaerf om halsen og livet, store reisestoevler, lodden lue, og vanter, briller, sort skjaeg og en svoebe i haanden. Han tog sine briller af, pussede dem og satte den paa naesen, tog sit reisetoei af og kom lige hen til mig og spurgte om det var mig som reiste om i hans sognekald og predikede for hans faar. Jeg havde nu prediket saameget og gaaet lange [sic] strekninger i sne, kulde og vede at jeg nesten ikke var istand til at tale -- mit holvemele var mig beroevet af forkjoelelse. Dog brugte jeg alle mine krefter forat forsvare vor tro og laere. Vi kom i en livlig samtale. Han sagde han vilde jage mig fra stedet; thi jeg var en udsending Djevlen [sic], sagde han. Han holdt en tale udenfore huset og advarede folket fra vor laere, og bad en boen til sin Gud at han maatte bevare dem fra Mormonerne. Da presten var reist begynte jeg forsamlingen og gode vidnesbyrd blev aflagte."] Olaf Henrik Nielsen Journal, 10 March 1879, holograph, LDS Church Archives.

[28] "Siden skrev han til Mr. Nielsen og pressede paa, thi Nielsen var jo en anset man i Samfundet, og for at beholde sit

gode navn, maatte han aldeles ikke logere mig. Mr. Nielsen lagde det for mig, Nu var han i en farlig Knibe. Ikke havde han Samvittighed til at vise mig ud, og det var ogsa [sic] haardt at staa i Ugunst hos Prosten saa han graed." Skanchy Autobiography, p. 32. O. H. Nielsen discovered that the parish priest of Grue (1879) "had visited the houses, frightened and warned the people about our [Mormon] teachings, and sent a notice to the schoolmaster that he, on behalf of the pastor, should instruct the children to tell their parents not to allow Mormons entrance to their homes, since the Mormons do not believe in God, etc. The priest himself had visited the residents of 'Kongsgaarden' and told them not to give lodging to any Mormon priest." ["Stedets prest havde veret i husene, skremt og advaret folket fra vor laere, og sendt skrivelse til skolelaereren at denne paa pastorens vegne skulde sige til boernene at de maatte fortelle sine foraeldre at de ei maatte tage nogen mormon i sine huse; thi mormonerne tro ikke paa Gud, o.s.v. Presten havde selv vaeret paa 'Kongsgaarden,' og budt folkene ikke at huse nogen mormonprest."] Nielsen Journal, 5 May 1879.

[29] Skandinaviens Stjerne 34 (15 October 1884):30-31.

[30] Edward C. Ekman Diary, 8 August 1906, holograph, LDS Church Archives. Not all priests were intolerant as witness C. N. Dorius's statement in 1856 that priests in Trondheim allowed him to preach in a schoolhouse. C. N. Dorius to Jesse N. Smith, 13 January 1863, quoted in Skandinaviens Stjerne 12 (15 February 1863):155-57. Missionary O. H. Berg had a lengthy discussion in 1864 with the Lutheran Deacon and organist at Holmestrand, and noted that "we parted as good friends." Berg Diary, vol. 1, pp. 11-12, 25-26 January 1864. Berg and companion also visited Lutheran priest Foss, his wife, and two sons at Hoff in 1864; Foss invited the Mormons into his home, and his wife fixed them a meal. Foss said that Mormonism had many good points. Ibid., pp. 13-15, 27 January 1864. In Setesdal in 1866, missionary Theodore M. Samuelsen and companion visited the Lutheran priest "and contrary to expectation . . . were kindly received and invited to remain and take dinner and coffee which with [sic] thankful hearts accepted. After a rest of some three hours at the Priests [sic] habitations, we departed." Theodore M. Samuelsen to George M. Brown, 23 February 1866, copied in Brown Autobiography, pp. 140-41. Missionaries Niels Jensen and Willard R. Smith reported from Alta in 1906 that "the Priest was friendly and a real gentleman and before we left said he had nothing against us." Historical Record, bk. A, 1886-1908, p. 50, Tromsoe Branch, Trondheim Conference, Scandinavian Mission, LDS Church Archives. In 1910, the Lutheran priest in Haugesund visited missionary Carl Kjaer who was in prison for having baptized. Said Kjaer: "The Priest comes up and takes me in the hand and says well, well, I didn't expect to find you here . . . he took me in the hand and said adjoe but first he looked at my rations

[bread and water] & shook his head." Carl Kjaer Diary, pp. 310-11, 11 March 1910, holograph, LDS Church Archives.

³¹Major prouncements included the following: 15 April 1857: Births of Mormon children were to be recorded in Lutheran parish registers in columns reserved for dissenters, and it was not the responsibility of the Lutheran priest to inform civil authorities about Mormons who did not allow their children to be christened in the Lutheran Church. Hans Munk, ed., Love, Anordninger, Traktater, Resolutioner, Kundgjoerelser, Departementsskrivelser, Cirkulaerer m. m. for Kongeriget Norge, vol. 5: 1856-1860 (Christiania: Chr. Toensbergs Forlag, 1861), p. 104. 3 December 1858: Mormon children, whose parents would not allow them to participate in religious instruction at public schools, could not be refused admittance to public schools. Ibid., p. 424. 26 May 1866: No graveside ceremony was to accompany Mormon burials; Mormon deaths were to be registered in a separate section of the parish registers. Otto Mejlaender, ed., Love, Anordninger, Traktater, Resolutioner, Kundgjoerelser, Departementsskriveler, Cirkulaerer m. m. for Kongeriget Norge, vol. 7: 1866-1870 (Christiania: P. T. Mallings Forlagsboghandel, 1871), p. 129. 31 October 1874: No law prohibited Mormons from establishing schools for instruction of their children in secular disciplines, but government authorities were empowered to prohibit instruction at such schools of doctrines propounding polygamy or other doctrines deemed injurious to public morality. Religious instruction in Mormon schools was to be monitored by state officials. M. V. Malling and Otto Mejlaender, eds., Love, Anordninger, Traktater, Resolutioner, Kundgjoerelser, Departementsskrivelser, Cirkulaerer m. m. for Kongeriget Norge, vol. 8: 1871-1876 (Christiania: P. T. Mallings Boghandel, 1878), p. 754. 12 July 1875: If authorities of the School Commission discovered that secular instruction at Mormon schools was deficient, parents and/or guardians of children involved were to be fined in accordance with the Law of 12 July 1848, paragraphs 15-16, and the Law of 16 May 1860, paragraphs 50-51. Mormon children, on request, were exempted from religious instruction. Ibid., p. 913. 28 April 1881: Mormon children, and children of dissenters, could graduate from school when their general development and knowledge of secular subjects corresponded with that of their Lutheran peers who generally left school at age fourteen after participating in the Lutheran confirmation. Children of dissenters (including Mormon children) over age fourteen who had not advanced to the two upper levels of instruction in public schools, could still graduate after successful completion of an annual examination as per the Law of 12 July 1848, paragraph 20, or by meeting minimum requirements of similar examinations administered twice annually by the School Commission. Children of dissenters--including Mormon children-enrolled in Mormon or private schools could graduate after successfully completing any of the above-described examinations. Otto Mejlaender, ed., Love, Anordninger, Traktater, Resolutioner, Kundgjoerelser, Departementsskrivelser, Cirkulaerer m. m. for Kongeriget Norge, vol. 9: 1877-1882 (Christiania: P. T.

Mallings Boghandel, 1883), pp. 843-44. <u>3 September 1881</u>: With reference to an incident where a Mormon priest, despite warnings to the contrary by a Lutheran priest, prayed at the graveside of one deceased, the KUD, after correspondence with the JPD, concluded that the Dissenter Law did not entitle non-Christians, or their priests or leaders, to conduct any graveside ceremonies; the JPD felt the Mormon involved could be prosecuted under Norwegian Law 6-1-4, but agreed with the KUD that the accused would not be prosecuted. The KUD did feel it necessary to prevent similar occurrences by formulating preventive regulations, i.e., priests could rely on police support to prosecute offenders. Ibid., pp. 921-22. <u>31 August 1897</u>: With reference to the question from a parish priest as to what he should do about two children in his parish who were formerly baptized as Mormons, but who now desired Lutheran confirmation, the KUD emphasized that Mormon baptism was not Christian baptism, even if performed in the name of the Trinity; the children must be baptized in accordance with Lutheran ritual and according to rules established for the baptism of adults. <u>Norsk Lovtidende, 2den Afdeling: Samling af Love, Resolutioner m. m., 1897</u> (Kristiania: Groendahl & Soens Bogtrykkeri for E. R. Baetzmann efter offentlig Foranstaltning, n.d.), p. 453.

[32] KUD Skrivelse, 16 June 1853, in Otto Mejlaender, ed., <u>Love, Anordninger, Traktater, Resolutioner, Kundgjoerelser, Departementsskrivelser, Cirkulaerer m. m. for Kongeriget Norge</u>, vol. 4: <u>1851-1855</u> (Christiania: Chr. Toensbergs Forlag, 1857), p. 262.

[33] "Skrivelse fra Kirkedepartementet, at Departementet antager, at der ikke er Adgang for Mormoner til gjennem Vielse af Statskirkens Praester at indgaa Aegteskab." KUD Skrivelse, 6 August 1858, in Munk, <u>1856-1860</u>, p. 388. Scandinavian Mission President Jesse N. Smith gave the following account of problems with Norwegian marriage laws on 21 October 1862: "The clergy of Norway having ruled our Church outside the pale of Christianity, it was held that members of our Church could not be legally married, the Clergy solemnizing all the marriages. Under these circumstances a man who had been excommunicated at his own request had married, and now came before the Council, and asked to be taken into the Church again. I recommended that he wait awhile." Jesse Nathaniel Smith Journal, p. 106, 21 October 1862, typescript, LDS Church Archives.

[34] "Broder Brynild Isaksen og Soester Lovise Halvorsdatter, begge Medlemmer of Christi Kirke af de Sidste Dages Hellige, bleve, i en Forsamling som i den Anledning var ordnet, Aegteviede som Mand og Hustru, overeenstemmende med Kirkens Regler, af Aeldste Olsen, og erklaerede for lovlige Aegtefolk." Historical Record and Record of Members, 1852-1862, p. 14, Brevik Branch, Christiania Conference, Scandinavian Mission, LDS Church Archives. On 1 August 1853 at Flisvig--on the outskirts of Oester Risoer--

ex-Conference President Christian J. Larsen "performed the marriage ceremony to Jens Gundersen and Stine, that made them man and wife." Larsen Journal, vol. 3, p. 51, 1 August 1853.

[35] ". . . [Dorius] maatte . . . foelge paatraengende Noedvendighed, og efter instaendig Begjaering, sammenvie Broder Gunde og hans Kjaereste Ane. . . ." Dorius, "Dagbog," 6 November 1862. The last recorded "Mormon marriage" in Norway occurred on 9 May 1866 in Oslo when Lars Larson Olson (born in 1832) was married to Randine Gundersen by Conference President G. M. Brown. Olson and his new bride emigrated soon afterwards. Olson Journal, 9 May 1866. The practice of "blessing" couples after a civil marriage was especially common during the early 1900s. On 2 November 1911, Mission President Andrew Jenson attended a feast "on the occasion of the marriage of Sigbert Hoejem and Andrea Lillevik" in Bergen and "gave them a blessing before the eating was commenced." Andrew Jenson Diary, bk. J, p. 715, 2 November 1911, holograph and typescript, LDS Church Archives. Conference President Hans J. Christiansen "blessed two young persons [not named] who had recently entered the bonds of matrimony" ["velsignede to unge Folk, der nylig var indgaaet i Aegteskab"] at Oslo on 29 March 1916. Christiansen Journal, vol. 10, p. 172, 29 March 1916.

[36] ". . . mormonerne enten tillurte seg kirkelig vigsel eller ogsaa levde i konkubinat." Norway, Storting, Storthings Forhandlinger i Aarene 1862-1863, pt. 10, "Indstillinger og Beslutninger af Odelsthinget og Lagthinget: Syttende ordentlige Storthings Indstillinger og Beslutninger i Aarene 1862-1863," p. 539.

[37] N. Bonnevie, C. Collett, and A. Kjerulf, eds., Departements-Tidende for 1861 (Christiania: Chr. Schibsted, n.d.), pp. 80-84.

[38] C. C. N. Dorius described the funeral and burial of O. P. Christensen on 9 July 1861 in Oslo: "A large company of Brethren assembled. A song (duet in six verses) was sung by twelve brethren before the coffin was closed; after that was done, and under thunder, lightning and storm clouds, I held a short talk, related incidents from the deceased's life and comforted those standing nearby and the next of kin. [Christensen died at age thirty-seven, and was survived by his wife and four children.] The brethren carried him [Christensen] to the new churchyard, but enroute the coffin was placed in a mortuary where Priest Vexel [Lutheran priest] sprinkled earth on the coffin. We then went to the churchyard where a song was sung whilst the body was lowered into the ground." ["Een stor Skare af Broedre havde indfundet sig--En Sang (Duet paa 6 Vers) blev afsjunget, af 12 Broedre forend [sic] Laaget paa Kisten blev fastslaaet; Efter dette var gjordt, og midt under Torden Lynild og Regn, holdt jeg en kort Tale, og skildrede noget af den Afdoedes Liv og Levnet, samt trostede [sic], de omkringstaaende, og Forladte. Broedrene

bar ham til den nye Kirkegaard, men paa Veien blev han indsat i et Lighuus, hvor Praesten Vexel kastede Jord paa ham. Vi gik da til Kirkegaarden--hvor atter Sangen blev afsjunget medens Ligen saenkedes need."] Dorius, "Dagbog," 9 July 1861.

[39] Ferdinand Friis Hintze Diary, vol. 1, p. 432, 1 August 1885.

[40] Andrew M. Israelsen, Utah Pioneering: An Autobiography (Salt Lake City, Utah: Deseret News Press, 1938), p. 98.

[41] Ibid., p. 126.

[42] Christiansen Journal, vol. 3, pp. 48-50, 24 July 1894.

[43] Peter Olsen Diary, 9 July 1897, microfilm of holograph, LDS Church Archives.

[44] Storting, Storthingstidende 1883, "Odelsthinget," p. 609.

[45] Andrew Knudsen and C. B. Olsen to JPD, 26 August 1887, Mormonpakken, TS, JPD.

[46] Bergens Politikontor to Bergens Stift, 8 September 1887, Mormonpakken, TS, JPD.

[47] JPD to Bergens Stift, 29 September 1887, rough draft, Mormonpakken, TS, JPD.

[48] ". . . [p.g.a.] den stoerre Toleranse, der i den senere Tid gjoer sig gjaeldende m.H.t. disse Spoergsmaal." Document entitled "JN 1552-1887C foreslaaes Taget til Efterretning" and signed with the initials "GK," 23 November 1887, Mormonpakken, TS, JPD.

[49] H. S. Waaler to the Faculty of the University of Christiania, Norway, 11 February 1904, "Mormonerne," A, KUD, RA. On 20 February 1904, Waaler sent a second letter to the University of Christiania officials, and, among other things, stated: "I am perfectly willing to furnish you with a truthful history of the Mormon Church from its early begining [sic] to the pressent [sic] time, It reads like a romance, and is in many instances a history mingled with bloody deeds, the paralell [sic] to which can only be found in the days of the Spanish Inquisition." H. S. Waaler to the Faculty of the University of Christiania, Norway, 20 February 1904, "Mormonerne," A, KUD, RA. In May 1893, missionary Andrew Israelsen attended "a great feast held in a large hall by the Home Missionaries Society of the Lutheran Church, in honor of Pastor Skabo, who was to be sent to Utah to bring back to the Lutheran Church and faith, the deluded Mormons, who had been led astray." Israelsen, Utah, pp. 99-100. For an overview of Lutheran proselyting efforts in Utah, see Knut Rygnestad, Dissentarspoersmaalet i Noreg fraa 1845 til 1891: Lovgjeving

og Administrativ Praksis (Oslo: Lutherstiftelsens Forlag, 1955), pp. 372-73.

[50] Untitled loose page used by the KUD in preparing its letter of 4 January 1905 to the JPD, "Mormonerne," A, KUD, RA.

[51] "Den nye udgave af sekten og dennes 'nye' laere er nok som en ny lap paa et gammelt klaedebon; hensigten er at skaffe mormonismen--under nyt navn og ny form--indpas hos troskyldige sjaele." Document entitled "Om mormonerne," denoted "ad KD jno. 967 A04," and signed "sv. O." [Sven Owren?], 23 March [1904?], "Mormonerne," A, KUD, RA.

[52] "Efter det anfoerte kommer jeg til det resultat at der her i riget nu er fuld religions og forsamlingsfrihed, og at det ikke gaar an at hindre mormonerne i at udoeve sin religion og sin propaganda for den. Hvis de derimod giver sig at med at doebe, meddele alterens sakramente, aegtere eller jordfaeste-- hvad alene skatskirkens prester og de kristne dissenteres forstander og prester kan--kan de straffes efter . . . den nye straffelovs ff 328 no. 3. . . . Kommer Aeldste fra Utah hid og gjoer propaganda, kan de ikke udvises uden videre (kfr. den nye straffelovs ff 38 og lov no. 1 af 4/5 1901 ff 6)." Ibid. Paragraph 328, item 3, of the New Criminal Law of 1902 prescribed fines or up to three-months' imprisonment for anyone who "performs any rite appertaining to an official calling which he does not have." ["Med boeter eller med fengsel inntil 3 maaneder straffes den som foretar noen handling, som alene kan foretas i henhold til en offentlig tjenestestilling, som han ikke innehar."] Hilmar Freidel, "Historiske dokumentasjoner: Rettsstilling," p. 3, xerox of typescript, Norway Office, Translation Services Department, The Church of Jesus Christ of Latter-day Saints, Moss, Norway. Paragraph 38 of The New Criminal Law stated that foreigners who were sentenced to more than six months' imprisonment, or to restrictions (including probation) lasting more than three years, could be deported. (Native Norwegians and those who had enjoyed permanent residency status for three consecutive years immediately preceding prosecution were excluded.) *Norsk Lovtidende, 2den Afdeling: Samling af Love, Resolutioner m. m., 1902* (Kristiania: Groendahl & Soens Bogtrykkeri for E. R. Baetzmann efter offentlig Foranstaltning, n.d.), p. 294. Law Number One of 4 May 1901, paragraph 6, stated that aliens could be deported if they failed to register with police authorities, if they had no means of support, or if they were guilty of supporting themselves by illegal means. *Norsk Lovtidende, 2den Afdeling: Samling af Love, Resolutioner m. m., 1901* (Kristiania: Groendahl & Soens Bogtrykkeri for E. R. Baetzmann efter offentlig Foranstaltning, n.d.), pp. 195-96.

[53] KUD to JPD, 4 January 1905, "Mormonerne," A, KUD, RA. Members of the Salvation Army in Norway adopted a similar resolution on 22 January 1906 against "Mormon propaganda," and forwarded

it to the KUD on 12 February. KUD kopiboknr. 505 A06, A, KUD, RA. Mormon relations with dissenters in Norway were touch-and-go. In 1867, Svend Larsen visited a <u>Methodist</u> priest named Steensen in Sarpsborg and gave him several books and tracts on Mormonism. Larsen Diary, 27 February 1867. A group of friendly Methodists attended a Mormon meeting in Drammen in 1896. Christofer Iversen Diary, 9 April 1896, microfilm of holograph, LDS Church Archives. Methodists in Larvik allowed Mormons use of their meetinghouse in 1909. Jenson Diary, bk. J, 26 July 1909. Mormons at a <u>Baptist</u> meeting near Stavanger in 1876 were permitted to discuss Mormon doctrine. Schou Diary, vol. 1, p. 23, 31 Decemger 1876. But in Trondheim in 1894, a Mrs. Nielsen accused the Mormons of "criminal behavior, murder and plundering" before 250 persons in the Baptist chapel. <u>Skandinaviens Stjerne</u> 43 (1 July 1894):297-99. <u>Quakers</u> in Stavanger in 1854 refused Canute Peterson permission to speak at their meeting. Peterson Journal, 3 September 1854. But C. C. A. Christensen was well-received by Quakers near Kristiansand in 1855. Hansen, <u>Christensen</u>, p. 425. Sixteen Mormons in Trondheim joined with members of the <u>Salvation Army</u> and hired a steamboat for a Sunday excursion to Christiansund in 1905. Nils Evensen Autobiography, p. 20, microfilm of typescript, LDS Church Archives. Anti-Mormon lectures by a Salvation Army Captain Christoffersen at Aalesund in 1906 aroused interest in Mormon doctrines and increased attendance at Mormon meetings. Johann August Olsen Journal, p. 115, 13 February 1906, holograph, LDS Church Archives. E. C. Ekman, a Mormon missionary in Larvik, reported in 1906 that the Salvation Army "held a masmeeting [mass meeting] to night [26 February 1906] to see what thay [sic] could do in regard to geting [sic] us out [of town]." Ekman Diary, 26 February 1906. The Church Committee of The Free Church [<u>Frimenighedens Kirke</u>] in Droebak denied A. M. Nielsen, a Mormon missionary, permission to preach in their hall in 1892 althought they claimed their chapel was open to any preacher of religion. A. M. Nielsen to Scandinavian Mission Headquarters in Copenhagen, 16 July 1892, quoted in <u>Skandinaviens Stjerne</u> 41 (15 August 1892):347. Oslo Conference President Hans J. Christiansen preached to a large gathering of <u>Adventists</u> and members of <u>Kristi Menighed</u> [Campbellites] at Fredrikstad in 1893. Christiansen Journal, vol. 2, 27 September 1893. Groups of Adventists attended Mormon meetings in Oslo in 1895, and in Trondheim in 1896. Ibid., vol. 3, 15 April 1895; Johan L. George Johnson Diary, 23 February 1896, holograph, LDS Church Archives. Mormons in Bergen attended a <u>Pentecostal</u> meeting on 3 May 1909. Kjaer Diary, 3 May 1909. On 26 November 1909, Scandinavian Mission President Andrew Jenson personally shook hands with the famous apostle of Pentecostalism, Thomas Ball Barratt, in Copenhagen; Jenson described Barratt as "quite a gentleman and considerable of a speaker." Jenson Diary, bk. J, pp. 153-54, 26 November 1909. Near Tromsoe in 1897, a group of about three hundred persons called "Evangeliets Troende" [Gospel Believers] withdrew from the State Church and investigated Mormonism. D. K. Brown to C. N. Lund, 4 August 1897, quoted in <u>Skandinaviens Stjerne</u> 46 (15 August 1897):347-48.

A Campbellite [Kristi Menighed] reverend named Johnsen held "a very friendly talk" with Mormon missionaries in Halden in 1908; missionaries also visited Johnsen's associate, Reverend Linberg, who, with his family, "were very friendly," and treated the missionaries to refreshments. James Jensen Journal, p. 83, 9 November 1908, xerox of holograph, LDS Church Archives. Perhaps surprisingly, Mormon relations with members of <u>The Reorganized Church of Jesus Christ of Latter Day Saints</u> (sometimes called "Josephites") were little short of dreadful. Mormon shortsightedness was often to blame as witness Mission President Carlquist's comment in 1893 to a Josephite leader that "we would treat him no different from all the others who are doing all they could to hinder the work of the Lord!" "I told him," continued Carlquist, "that when he repented and came to us with humble and contrite feelings, asking for baptism we would be pleased to help him all we could to serve the Lord." Carl Arvid Carlquist, "Life of Carl Arvid Carlquist," trans. Myrtle Carlquist McDonald, pp. 34-35, typescript, Carl Arvid Carlquist Papers, LDS Church Archives. Mormon-Josephite debates in Larvik were especially bitter in 1906. Ekman Diary, 25 January, 12 March, 23 April 1906.

[54]". . . [Mormonsamfund], uagtet det ikke er anerkjendt som kristeligt dissentersamfund, fremdeles boer tolereres." Kristiania Politikammer to JPD, 15 December 1904, Mormonpakken, TS, JPD.

[55]"I borgerlig henseende synes mormonerne fremdeles gjennemgaaende at vaere aedruelige, lovlydige, arbeidsomme og i det hele skikkelige folk, saa at man forsaavidt kun maate oenske, at der var ret mange saa gode medborgere." Ibid.

[56]Trondhjems Politikammer to JPD, 31 January 1905; Stavanger Politikammer to JPD, 2 December 1904; Drammen Politimesterembede to JPD, 5 December 1904; Mormonpakken, TS, JPD.

[57]". . . [JPD] antager, at der ikke for Tiden er Opfordring for det offentlige til at skride ind mod Mormonernes Virksomhed." JPD to KUD, 11 November 1905, "Mormonerne," A, KUD, RA.

[58]KUD to JPD, 20 January 1906, carbon copy, KUD kopiboknr. 250 A06, A, KUD, RA. A letter from the Bishop of Tromsoe described "a veritable invasion" of Mormons. Peter Wilhelm Kreydal Boeckman to KUD, 9 February 1906, "Mormonerne," A, KUD, RA.

[59]"I tilslutning hertil skal dette departement [JPD] for sit vedkommende bemerke, at der ikke antages efter den nugjaeldende lovgivning at vaere adgang for det offentlige at gjennem politiforanstaltninger at soeke stanset, mormonernes virksomhet her i landet." JPD to KUD, 23 June 1908, MS copy, "Mormonerne," A, KUD, RA.

⁶⁰Ibid. The JPD forwarded results of a survey conducted by the Ministry of Foreign Affairs on laws relating to Mormons elsewhere in Europe. Authorities in <u>Berlin</u> reported there were no laws specifically aimed at controlling Mormon propaganda; Mormons in Germany, however, were under close surveillance, and any missionaries from Utah guilty of encouraging others to emigrate were summarily deported. Police authorities in <u>Denmark</u> were advised from time to time to keep tabs on Mormon preachers, but no laws had been passed to curb Mormon preaching or propaganda. The Norwegian Delegation in <u>Sweden</u> sent a memo from the Swedish Ecclesiastical Department stating that no arrangements had been made to control Mormon activities, and no laws passed regarding Mormons and/or Mormon propaganda; resolutions dated 11 December 1868 (concerning special devotional gatherings), 16 November 1869 (concerning restrictions on those who sought to convince other persons to renounce their Lutheran faith), and 31 October 1873 (concerning foreign religionists), meanwhile, contained regulations against such propaganda. Swedish Mormons had petitioned the King for the right to establish a special congregation in Stockholm which would be recognized by the State, but their petition had been denied. On the other hand, the King had determined that a recommendation from the Stockholm City Council [Stockholm bys konsistorium], that regulations be adopted to counteract Mormon activity, be dropped without further discussion.

⁶¹Evensen had baptized. Karlsen and Andresen had distributed the Lord's Supper in a Mormon meeting.

⁶²"Med boeter eller med fengsel inntil 3 Maaneder straffes den som . . . foretar noen handling, som alene kan foretas i henhold til en offentlig tjenestestilling, som han ikke innehar." Freidel, "Rettsstilling," p. 3.

⁶³"Det indsees imidlertid ikke, at de tiltalte kan straffes efter denne paragraf for den av dem utfoerte daabshandling eller nadverutdeling, aldenstund den sekt, hvortil de hoerer ikke henregnes til de kristne samfund. Det er den kristelige daab og den kristelige nadversutdeling, som er henlagt under de kristne prester (dissenterforstandere) og some det formentlig regelmaessig er forbudt andre at befatte sig med; . . . at et utenfor de kristnes troesbekjendelse staaende religionssamfund . . . benytter ceremonier, der i mere eller mindre grad ligner de kristnes sakramenter, kan dog ikke gjoere sekten til et kristent samfund og heller ikke disse ceremonier til kristelige symboler eller uttryk for den kristelige troesbekjendelse. Det kan, saalaenge der ikke handles om bespottelse av den kristne tro, formentlig intet vaere til hinder for, at et ikke kristent troessamfund benytter vandet -som overgydning eller neddypning- til betegnelse av den enkeltes indtraeden i samfundet, men derfor vil ingen bekjender av den kristne tro paastaa, at denne person nu i virkeligheten gjennem daaben er bleven medlem av det kristne

samfund; men i saafald er jo dermed ogsaa erkjendt, at det ikke er den kristelige daab, som er kommet til utoevelse, og da det kun er denne, som ingen anden end de kristne prester kan foreta, og at det samme maa gjaelde om nadverdutdelingen, saa foelger herav, at de tiltalte ikke har foretaget 'nogen handling, der alene kan foretages i henhold til en offentlig tjenestestilling, som han ikke indehar,' idet de alene har foretaget en i det kristne samfunds Oeine fuldstaendig betydningsloes handling, som med lige foeie og lige virkning maatte kunne foretages av hvemsomhelst. . . . De tiltalte vil saaledes blive at frifinde. Det siger sig selv, at retten er fuldt opmerksom paa, at dette resultat av mange maaske vil findes meget uheldigt, og at det navnlig kan ta sig ut som en synderlighet, at paa samme tid, som de kristne dissentere, der doeber en av statskirken ikke utmeldt person, skal straffes, saa vil den ikke kristne mormon der gjoer det samme, blive ladet straffefri; men herved boer dog erindres, dels at i det foerstnaevnte tilfaelde handles om en av loven truffen ordning mellom statskirken og de av staten anerkjendte kristne dissentersamfund, hvor staten . . . har maattet traekke en graense, medens det i sidstnaevnte tilfaelde gjaelder handlinger som staten fra sit standpunkt ikke anerkjender som vaerende av betydning for de kristne samfund, og dels at det her tilstedevaerende hul i lovgivningen . . . ikke kan rettes paa anden maate end ved ny lov. Dommen er ensstemmig." "Utdrag av praemisserne til Trondhjems meddomsrets dom av 19. april 1907," "Mormonerne," A, KUD, RA. Mormon commentary on the case included the following: "In the first place, it is strange, and remarkable, that a Church founded on the teachings of the New Testament, and belief in God and in Jesus Christ, and in revelations from them, should be considered a non-Christian sect; and in the second place, it is quite as remarkable that the opposition against them which was intended to fetter completely their freedom, has been so turned that they have more freedom than anybody else." Edward H. Anderson, "Events and Comments," Improvement Era, June 1906, p. 664. Nils Evensen, the protagonist in the case, gave this account: "A minister of the Seventh-Day Adventists stirred up a persecution against us again and as quite a few were baptized a complaint was again made to the police which resulted in that I and four of the Sisters were called to meet at the Police Station and explain in detail how baptism was performed. We did so (this was March 19, 1906). . . ." On 28 March 1906, a lower court fined Evensen five hundred crowns or forty-five days in prison on bread and water for baptizing; his fellow-defendants, Karlsen and Andresen, were each fined fifty crowns for distributing the Lord's Supper. The Mormons were given three days to appeal the lower court's verdict. Evensen's account continues: "On one of these three days the Chief of Police called me to his office where we had a long conversation and he advised me to appeal to the Higher Court. . . . [The Appellate Court decreed that] "being we [Mormons] were not recognized as Christians [sic] ministers, nothing could be in hindrance for us non-Christians to perform ceremonies as long as it was not done in blasphemy or ridicule. Therefore, we as non-Christians had the right to perform ordinances and worship according to our religion, If Not a new law had to be effected. . . . Just as soon as the decision was read, not guilty, extra papers and notices were sent all over town [Trondheim] and all the papers both in Sweden and Denmark as well as Norway took it up and commented on it." Evensen Autobiography, pp. 23-25.

[64]"Saker angaaende ovennaevnte forbud behandles paa hurtigste og enkleste maate bl. a. saaledes, at der blir adgang for retten til umiddelbart at erholde inappellabelt skjoen af theologisk uddannede maend om beskaffenheten af det laereindhold, som eventuelt anklagede maatte paaberaabe sig." KUD kopiboknrs. 3046-51 A08, A, KUD, RA. Those who looked to the Book of Mormon "and the revelations of their prophets as guideposts for doctrine and personal conduct" ["og sine profeters aabenbaring som rettesnor for sin laere og sit liv"] were to be denied every public practice of their religion. Under terms of the proposed law, police authorities could forbid or break up every public Mormon meeting, and participants in such meetings would be punished. Mormons would be prohibited from publicly or privately attempting to win converts, and offenders would be assessed stiff fines; second-time offenders would be sentenced to extended prison terms. In lieu of such punishments, defendants who were not Norwegian citizens or natives could be deported. All provisions would likewise apply to members of the Reorganized Church of Jesus Christ of Latter Day Saints. KUD to samtlige biskoper, 19 December 1908, rough draft, "Mormonerne," A, KUD, RA. The rough draft of KUD proposals contained a paragraph (subsequently deleted from the final draft sent to the Bishops) which one KUD official (probably a departmental lawyer) later described as "calling to mind medieval legal procedures which would no doubt never be accepted by Parliament" [". . . det minder lidt om den middelalderske rettergang og vil vistnok aldrig bli vedtat av stortinget"]: "In addition, a resolution should probably be adopted such that the Kingdom's [Lutheran] Bishops can summon persons suspected of [spreading] Mormon propaganda, and, in the presence of witnesses, examine them and, if necessary, issue them a warning." ["Endvidere boer der maaske tilfoeies en bestemmelse om at rikets biskoper skal ha adgang til at kalde personer, som mistaenkes for mormonsk propaganda, for sig for i vidners overvaer, at eksaminere dem og i tilfaelde gi dem en advarsel."] Ibid.

[65]Einar Skavlan to KUD, 14 January 1909; Johan Willoch Erichsen to KUD, 2 January 1909; "Mormonerne," A, KUD, RA.

[66]"Muligens det til sidst vil vise sig, at der kun er en eneste ting, som kan foere til maalet, det er et almindeligt forbud mod mormonernes ophold i riget. En saadan bestemmelse vilde vistnok vaere drakonisk, men kan haende den vilde vaere vel saa meget paa sin plads mod mormonerne som mod jesuiterne,

som dog vel nu maa ansees for alene at vaere religioese agitatorer, medens mormonerne er noget mere." Peter Wilhelm Kreydahl Boeckman to KUD, 18 January 1909, "Mormonerne," A, KUD, RA. The clause in the Norwegian Constitution prohibiting Jesuits from entering Norway was not repealed until 1956. James A. Storing, Norwegian Democracy (Boston: Houghton Mifflin Company, 1963), p. 5.

[67]"Efter min opfatning boer alle religioner ha fri offentlig religionsoevelse inden lovs og aerbarheds graenser. Dette er en konsekvens av det religionsfrihetens princip, som med rette haevdes saa sterkt i vor tid. Ogsaa ikke-kristelige, ogsaa hedenske religioner boer nyde godt av denne frihet. Ut fra dette synspunkt har det overfor spoersmaalet om fri religionsoevelse ingen interesse her at undersoeke, om mormonerne skal regnes til kristne dissentere eller ikke. Og hvis man som grund til at stille dem i en saeregen klasse vilde fremholde, at laeren om flerkoneriet utgjoer en integrerende del af deres system, saa maa det merkes, at de dog ikke, saavidt vites, har gjort noget forsoek paa her i vort land at omsaette denne laere i praksis." Christen Brun to KUD, 18 January 1909, "Mormonerne," A, KUD, RA.

[68]"Men midlet mot mormonernes fordaervelige virksomhet maa foerst og fremst soekes i en stoerre kristelig oplysning. Det er et vidnesbyrd om, at forholdet i denne henseende ikke er saa godt, som man gjerne forestiller sig, naar mormonerne kan fange i sine garn unge piker, som har gjennemgaat vor folkeskole og er blit konfirmert i vor kirke." Ibid.

[69]Ibid.

[70]"At beskytte et enkelt kirkesamfund gjennem bekjaempelse av avvikende religioese meninger og deres utbredelse med straf og politiforanstaltninger antages at ligge utenfor hvad der efter den i vor tid almindelige opfatning hoerer med til statens opgaver." JPD to KUD, 9 August 1910, "Mormonerne," A, KUD, RA.

[71]"Saerlig forekommer det departementet at vaere en i principiel henseende forkastelig ordning at rette straffebestemmelser mot medlemmerne av et specielt naevnte troessamfund uten angivelse av saklige kriterier." Ibid.

[72]"Departementet er imidlertid for sit vedkommende tilboeielig til at anta, at disse anker tildels er noget overdrevne og ikke altid er bygget paa et fuldt paalidelig kjendskap til mormonernes liv og laere nu for tiden." Ibid.

[73]Ibid. KUD efforts to restrict Mormon activity were largely ineffective in the years 1911-1916. In 1913, the KUD petitioned a committee appointed to discuss a new emigration law [Komiteen til behandling av spoersmaalet om en ny utvandringslov] asking for new, stricter controls on Mormon emigration (especially emigration

of young girls) and "Mormon emigration agents." KUD to Komiteen til behandling av spoersmaalet om en ny utvandringslov, 14 January 1913, KUD kopibok F, pp. 78-81, kontor F, KUD, RA. On 27 November 1913, Den norske Kirkes Presteforening [The Norwegian Association of Lutheran Priests] likewise appealed for state control of Mormon propaganda campaigns. KUD journalnr. 4,060 A1913, A, KUD, RA. The KUD again examined deportation and emigration laws in 1915 in an effort to formulate policy providing for deportation of Mormon missionaries. KUD to JPD, 2 July 1915, rough draft, "Mormonerne," A, KUD, RA; KUD kopiboknr. 1822 A15, A, KUD, RA. A KUD circular of 12 November 1915 informed priests of specific laws under which Mormons could conceivably be prosecuted, as also deportation laws, and advised priests "to inform police authorities of any violations thereof." KUD kopiboknr. 2770 A 1915, A, KUD, RA. On 23 March 1916, the KUD proposed that paragraphs 20 and 22 of the Dissenter Law (prescribing punishments for those who baptized a person who had not officially withdrawn from the State Church) be revised to include "non-Christians." Response was lukewarm, and Tromsoe Bishop Dietrichson rejected the proposal entirely since it could conceivably give non-Christians equal status with Jews and Unitarians already protected under the law. Jens Froelich Tandberg to KUD, 21 June 1916; Johan Willoch Erichsen to KUD, 1 April 1916; Peter Wilhelm Kreydahl Boeckman to KUD, 27 March 1916; Christen Brun to KUD, 29 March 1916; Bernt Andreas Stoeylen to KUD, 27 March 1916; Gustav Johan Fredrik Dietrichson to KUD, 11 April 1916; "Mormonerne," A, KUD, RA. A KUD lawyer (possibly Sigurd Oestrem) again reviewed laws which might be invoked against polygamists and "White Slave Traders" in 1918. "Foreloebig betaenkning angaaende sp. om statsforanstaltninger mot mormonerne," 9 November 1917; "PM. ang. sp. om forholdsregler mot mormonerne," 11 September 1918; "Mormonerne," A, KUD, RA. The JPD, meanwhile, refused to get involved with proposed legislation (or revision of prior legislation) aimed at Mormon activities. JPD to KUD, 26 February 1916; JPD to KUD, 31 July 1916; "Mormonerne," A, KUD, RA. During the final years of World War I, Utah missionaries and Mormon authorities in Scandinavia described increasing animosity toward foreigners; Mission President Hans J. Christiansen was refused permission to return to Denmark following his tour of Norwegian branches in October 1917, but Mormon MP Frederik Ferdinand Samuelsen forced a belated reconsideration which allowed Christiansen entrance. Christiansen Journal, vol. 12, pp. 98-109, 111, 3 October 1917. On 2 November 1917, Christiansen was informed of deportation proceedings against Mormon missionary, Hyrum P. Noekleby, in Stavanger, ostensibly for spying. Ibid., pp. 120, 130-31; 2, 12 November 1917. A severe food shortage in Norway in 1918 prompted new passport restrictions and additional deportation proceedings against aliens. Skandinaviens Stjerne 67 (14 January 1918):32. On 19 April 1918, the Norwegian Consulate in Copenhagen denied Mission President Christiansen's plea to visit Norway. Said Christiansen: "It [the refusal] reeks of animosity toward me because I am a Mormon." ["Den lugter af modfoelelser til mig fordi jeg er Mormon."] Christiansen Journal, vol. 12, p. 238, 19 April 1918. Six Utah missionaries were living in Norway early in 1918, but on 31 August 1918, Christiansen released Bergen Conference President Cephus E. Andersen who had been ordered to leave Norway, and Nephi Andreasen who faced imminent induction into the Norwegian Army. Hans J. Christiansen, "Missionsrejsen i Foraaret 1918," Skandinaviens Stjerne 67 (15 May 1918):152-53; Christiansen Journal, vol. 13, p. 38, 31 August 1918. Eight resident Norwegian Mormons petitioned Central Paskontoret i Christiania [The Central Passport Bureau in Christiania] in September 1918 asking that Mission President Christiansen be allowed to visit Norway, but permission was denied. Christiansen Journal, vol. 13, pp. 48-49, 18 September 1918. On 31 October 1919, Christiansen was released as Mission President and told he could return to America via Norway. Ibid., p. 224, 31 October 1919. Although police authorities in Bergen denied Christiansen's request for extension of his three-day visa, Christiansen stayed in Norway three additional weeks--until 11 December 1919. Ibid., vol. 14, 17-19 November, 11 December 1919. In light of a new law dated 13 July 1917 on passport restrictions for all American citizens seeking entrance into Norway, the Central Passport Bureau in Oslo adopted a blanket policy denying visas to all Mormon missionaries from America. In 1921, however, the Norwegian Legation in Washington, D.C., informed the Norwegian Department of Foreign Affairs that American Mormons could no longer be singled out in such a manner. On 12 April 1921, the American Legation in Oslo challenged the Norwegian Department of Foreign Affairs to state its reasons for denying visas to all Mormons; that department accordingly cited parliamentary debates on Mormon propaganda in 1912, and also a department circular dated 14 September 1915 informing police and other officials of provisions for deportation of aliens deemed undesireable. The Department further claimed that granting visas to Mormon missionaries "would imply official sanction" ["vilde indeholde en officiel tillatelse"] of an activity (Mormon door-to-door tracting or proselyting) harmful to public morality. Under JPD auspices, and as a result of action by the American Legation on 12 April 1921, the passport law was revised to allow all Norwegian-born American citizens entrance into Norway on production of a valid passport. The JPD further suggested to the KUD that all American-born Mormon missionaries be set on an equal footing with Norwegian-born American citizens (1922), i.e., all American citizens with a valid passport should be admitted to Norway. KUD authorities referred the question to the Lutheran Bishops; the Bishops decreed in 1923 that Mormon missionaries should be denied visas. Meanwhile, the American Legation in Oslo had petitioned the JPD asking that visa restrictions on American-born Mormons be dropped since the Mormon Church no longer countenanced polygamy, and Mormons in America had the same rights and duties as other American citizens. The JPD accordingly removed all passport restrictions on American-born Mormons, and informed the KUD on 1 October 1923 that Mormons could not be placed in a class by themselves, but must enjoy equal rights under provisions governing visas for aliens. Karl Sandvin, "Mormonisma i Noreg med utsyn over samfunnet si amerikanske historie" (Hovedoppgave, University of Oslo, 1946), pp. 83-85.

[74] Andreas Brandrud, Udsigt over religionsfrihedens historie i Norge og Danmark efter reformationen (Hamar: n.p., 1898), pp. 2-3.

[75] P. I. Paulsen, ed., Kong Christian den Femtes Norske Lov af 15de April 1687 (Kristiania: H. Aschehoug & Co., W. Nygaard, 1904), p. 225.

[76] Kong Christian den Siettes Allernaadigste Forordninger og Aabne Breve for Aar 1745 (Copenhagen: Hans Kongel. Majestets og Universitets Bogtrykkerie, n.d.), p. 158; Laurids Fogtman, ed., Kongelige Rescripter, Resolutioner og Collegialbreve for Danmark og Norge, udtogsviis udgivne i chronologisk Orden, vol. 2, pt. 4: 1740-1746 (Copenhagen: Gyldendals Forlag, 1788), pp. 644-45.

CHAPTER VI

[1] Ingrid Semmingsen, ed., <u>Husmannsminner</u> (Oslo: Tiden Norsk Forlag, 1961), pp. 2-3, 97; S. Skappel, <u>Om Husmandsvaesenet i Norge: Dets Oprindelse og Utvikling</u> (Kristiania: I Kommission hos Jacob Dybwad for Videnskapsselskapet, 1922), p. 157.

[2] Andreas Aarflot, <u>Norsk Kirkehistorie</u>, vol. 2 (Oslo: Lutherstiftelsen, 1967), p. 405.

[3] Einar Haugen, Introduction to <u>Norwegian-English Dictionary</u>, eds. Einar Haugen, et al. (Oslo: Universitetsforlaget, 1965; Madison, Wisconsin: University of Wisconsin Press, 1965), p. 24.

[4] "Beboerne var ligesaa haarde og uimodtagelige for Evangeliet som de stejle, noegne Klipper, der omgav dem paa alle Sider." John S. Hansen, ed., <u>Mindeudgave C. C. A. Christensen: Poetiske Arbejder, Artikler og Afhandlinger tilligemed hans Levnedsloeb</u> (Salt Lake City, Utah: Bikubens Bibliotek, 1921), p. 424.

[5] "Foroevrigt er Folket meget snevre af Hjertet baade i Bye og Bygd her paa Vestlandet." Carl C. N. Dorius, "Dagbog: Carl C. N. Dorius's Missionsforretninger i Skandinavia, samt en kort Beretning om det tidligere Levnetsloeb," 18 August 1862, holograph, Library-Archives, The Church of Jesus Christ of Latter-day Saints, Salt Lake City, Utah [hereinafter cited as LDS Church Archives].

[6] ". . . den mentalitets-forskjell og ulikhet i karakter og tenkemaate som bestod mellom de forskjellige befolkningsgrupper i vaart land." Aarflot, <u>Kirkehistorie</u>, p. 405. J. Kvistad divided Norway into three main areas--northern Norway, eastern Norway with Troendelag Province, and western and southern Norway-- for purposes of his characterization of Christian types in 1945. Kvistad especially probed the religious mentality of the "Vest- og Soerland" [western and southern] Christian types such as "the unassuming, reserved and taciturn farmer and fisherman" ["den stillfarende, beskjedne og faamaelte bonde og fisker"] who "shys away from the adiaphora, because he sees in them a great danger to his Christian life, whereas on the other hand he has abandoned the strict, pietistic outlook with regard to dress, hair style and serious facial expression etc." ["Hva den kristne livsfoersel angaar, tar han bestemt avstand fra adiafora, fordi han anser dem som en stor fare for sitt kristenliv, derimot har han forlatt det strengt pietistiske syn paa klesdrakt, haarfasong og alvorlig ansiktsuttrykk osv."] J. Kvistad, "Kirkeliv og kristentype paa Vest- og Soerlandet," <u>Luthersk Kirketidende</u> 80 (3 November 1945): 198, 209, 211. "They are a good people in the country

round, about Trondhjem," declared Oslo Conference President, George M. Brown, in 1865, "and will generally treat a man well if he observes their manners and customs." George Mortimer Brown Autobiography and Diary, p. 97, 3 June 1865, typescript, Library Services Division, Genealogical Department, The Church of Jesus Christ of Latter-day Saints, Salt Lake City, Utah.

[7]"Jo laengere mod Oest desto mere Bevaegelighed, desto mere Individualisme i Trosopfatningen og Uklarhed i Laeren, desto mere Indiferentisme og desto lettere Adgang for Sekter; derimod vestover en Ensartethed i Tro og Laere, som let slaa over i Bogstavtraeldom, en Frygt for ikke at gjaelde som Kristen, der frembringer meget Formvaesen og vistnok ogsaa Hykleri, og en naesten fuldstaendig Frihed for Sekter. . . ." Johan Christian Heuch, *Visitasberetninger 1889-1902* ([Oslo]: A. S. Lunde & Co's Forlag, [1965]), p. 118. Provinces such as Vestlandet and Oestlandet also comprised numerous pocket regions where typologies had little or no meaning as per Carl Kjaer's discovery in 1908 that people in Onarheim near Bergen "were favorable and wanted us to hold meeting." Carl Kjaer Diary, p. 70, 20 August 1908, holograph, LDS Church Archives. Oslo Conference President George M. Brown made the following observations while traveling in Hallingdal in 1865: "Nowhere were we treated with such kindness and consideration as in the Thellemarken and Numedal. Wherever we requested anything to eat or drink [in Hallingdal] they were very particular to know how much we wanted and on asking the price they were not long in fixing it at a high figure. . . . In Thellemarken and Numedal they never thought of setting a price but said give what you choose, and many places they did not wish to take anything." Brown Autobiography, p. 103, 9 July 1865.

[8]Over forty newspapers were operational by 1851, and the number increased to seventy-two by 1868. Jens Arup Seip, *Utsikt over Norges historie*, vol. 1: *Tidsrommet 1814-ca. 1860* (Oslo: Gyldendal Norsk Forlag, 1974), p. 163. Popular, inexpensive magazines were also proliferating: *Skilling Magazin* [Shilling Magazine] in 1835; *Almuevennen* [The Commoner's Friend] in 1849; *Folkevennen* [The People's Friend] in 1852--magazines which soon boasted a readership in the tens of thousands, and penetrated even remote districts where newspapers were not established. Arne Bergsgaard, *Norsk Historie 1814-1880* (Oslo: Det Norske Samlaget, 1964), p. 223. On 23 February 1861, C. C. N. Dorius reported "a frightful storm" ["en frygtelig Storm"] against the Mormons in the Oslo *Aftenbladet* where a series of articles accused Mormon missionaries of coming to Norway to collect "girls and wives, etc." ["Piger og Koner osv."]. Dorius, "Dagbog," pp. 97-98, 23 February 1861. "The Papers are full of Exciting news from Utah," wrote Scandinavian Mission President Canute Peterson on 28 December 1871. "Somtime [sic] the Mormons are going to leve [sic] the [Utah] Territory, som times thay are going to Fight, and at other tims [times] all the People are

going to be put in Prison, that is the Man, and the Wivs [Wives] of the Mormons given to the Miners. In one of the Papers give a Picture of Brigham [Brigham Young] and his Wivs and Children, and . . . Brigham had abig [sic] horn on the Top of his Head. som [sic] of his Wivs was as Raget [ragged] as . . . Rags could make them, some coutting [sic] ther [sic] Throats, some puting Raps on ther nak [necks]. The Childrin war [were] all raget Frisly and crying this kind of damn nonsense, this the People throw in our Face whare [where] we come for to talke to them." Canute Peterson to Ole Ellingson, 28 December 1871, pp. 3-4, Canute Peterson Collection, LDS Church Archives. Mission President Andrew Jenson reported "a scurrelous [sic] article" in the Oslo Social-Demokraten on 20 October 1909 accusing Mormons "of agitating for young women to emigrate to Utah." Andrew Jenson Diary, bk. J, p. 139, 20 October 1909, holograph and typescript, LDS Church Archives. Two days later, the editor promised "to publish an explanation" if Jenson would write one. Ibid., p. 140, 22 October 1909. In 1912, a second flood of articles appeared in Scandinavian newspapers labeling Mormon missionaries "agents of the White Slave Traffic" who sought to lure young girls to Utah and "consign them to destruction." Anti-Mormon agitation was especially strong in Oslo. Skandinaviens Stjerne 61 (1 October 1912):296-300. An article in Nordmands-Forbundet in 1911 by J. A. Jacobsen painted a lurid picture of Mormon rapine, skulduggery, and murder, and claimed: the Mormon prophet controlled votes for the United States Presidency in four states; Mormons taught "that it was not only legal, but also a holy act, to rob and steal from the Church's enemies" ["at det er ikke blot lovlig, men endog en hellig handling, at roeve og stjaele fra kirkens fiender"]; Brigham Young was responsible for the Mountain Meadows Massacre; Brigham Young had twenty polygamous wives at the same time; most Mormons were slaves trodden under the feet of their leaders; new converts to Mormonism were forced to swear an oath to avenge the deaths of Hyrum and Joseph Smith on the American people; Mormon missionaries came to Norway to lure away ignorant boys and girls to serve as slaves of the Great Prophet in Salt Lake City. "They [Mormons] do not refer to themselves as Americans," concluded Jacobsen; "they are Mormons. They have established a state within the state, a smaller state which is an enemy of the larger state and [which] plots the larger state's destruction." ["De kalder sig for det foerste ikke Amerikanere; de er mormoner. De har dannet en stat inden staten, en mindre stat som er fiendtlig mot den stoerre stat og planlegger den stoerre stats oedelaeggelse."] J. A. Jacobsen, "Mormonerne og deres mission: En advarsel," Nordmands-Forbundet 4 (October 1911):389-96.

[9]"Det var ikkje her eit baade 'pro et contra' . . . dei stilte seg alle fraa foerste stunda paa den same sida, dvs. mot mormonane og deira verksemd. Heller ikkje ser det ut som avisfolka trong lang tid for aa orientera seg i sitt syn daa mormonisma kom hit. Samstundes som dei kunne melde om dei foerste moeta

paa denne eller hin staden, hadde dei alt gjort seg opp si meining om det heile, at mormonisma var lite aa samle paa, og at folk difor burde halde seg undan." Karl Sandvin, "Mormonisma i Noreg med utsyn over samfunnet si amerikanske historie," (Hovedoppgave, University of Oslo, 1946), p. 39. "The people here generally believe that we [Mormons] are the worst blasphemers who have ever existed on the face of the earth," wrote Canute Peterson from Oslo in 1855. Referring to news accounts in the popular press, Peterson continued: "There are only two things here of any importance, that [sic] is the Mormons and the War [Crimean War]." ["Folket her i almendlighed [sic] troer at ve [sic] er de stoerste Gudsbespottere som nogen Tid har vaeret paa Jorden, her er kuns to ting som er af nogen vegtighed, det er Mormonerne og Krigen."] Canute Peterson to [Sarah Peterson?], [1855?], Canute Peterson Collection, LDS Church Archives. Mormon missionaries in Stavanger "lived in a garret room in the so-called Mormon Castle" in 1858. Newspaper accounts claimed that tenants of the Castle "were so numerous that it was necessary to write with chalk on the floor so each family might know its place in the rooms." Christopher Sigvarth Winge Autobiography, p. 3, microfilm of typescript, LDS Church Archives. There were some objective newspaper articles on Mormonism such as a series in Den norske Tilskuer edited by Ludvig Kr. Daa which presented a comparatively objective view of Mormon history and doctrine. Den norske Tilskuer, 13 December 1851, pp. 81-83, 108-11; 31 January 1852, pp. 137-40; 30 October 1852, pp. 449-51; 11 June 1853, pp. 710-11, 716. A few articles in the Oslo Morgenbladet during the 1850s urged government authorities to grant Mormons religious freedom. Knut Rygnestad, Dissentarspoersmaalet i Noreg fraa 1845 til 1891: Lovgjeving og Administrativ Praksis (Oslo: Lutherstiftelsens Forlag, 1955), pp. 368-70. C. C. N. Dorius reported publication of an article (23 February 1862) in Ilustreret Nyheds-Blad critical of anti-Mormon accounts by Pastor Lund in Morgenposten; the article called Lund "unmerciful" ["Ubarmhjertig"] and "barbaric" ["barbarisk"]. Dorius, "Dagbog," 23 February, 5 March 1862. Oslo Conference President George M. Brown summarized an editorial in Oslo's Morgenbladet on 20 March 1865 as follows: "The . . . editorial . . . spoke very favorably of us and desired that we should have freedom of religion as well as others who were not of the State Church. . . . The Mormons now existed here in large numbers and were regularly organized and held public meetings as well as performing all the ordinances of their religion, in spite of the law. The editor also wishes that we might, when the Storthing [Parliament] met again, be permitted to freedom of religion or at least the privilege of exercising our religious faith without being subject to persecution from the law, if not the privilege of proselyting." Brown Autobiography, 20 March 1865. On 22 October 1903, Oslo Conference President J. A. Hendricksen visited the editors of several newspapers including Verdens Gang and Nyhedsblad. "I was treated courteously," said Hendricksen, "and I think good will result." John Anthon Hendricksen Diary, vol. 2, p. 44, 22 October 1903, microfilm of holograph,

LDS Church Archives. On 26 October 1903, Hendricksen met with the editor of the Oslo Forposten who agreed to print an article by Hendricksen "refuting that '4,000' had been prosecuted in Utah in the year 1902 for poligamy [sic]." Ibid., p. 45, 26 October 1903. Tidens Gang (Oslo) printed a lengthy letter from Erling Bjoernson, son of the famous poet, decrying (25 June 1910) anti-Mormon agitation by various Norwegian newspapers, praising Mormons as true American patriots, describing them as "the happiest people I have ever met" ["de allerlykkeligste Mennesker, jeg har truffet"], and stating that their personal lives and morals were equally as good as any in Norway. Skandinaviens Stjerne 59 (1 August 1910):233-34. By the 1880s, newspaper editors allowed Mormons to advertise meetings and other Mormon events. Thus F. F. Hintze, Mormon branch president in Fredrikstad, "went to the Frederikstads Tilskuers [Fredrikstad Tilskuer] Office and had our meeting published" on 6 November 1885. "It [the advertisement] will in [sic] for 3 consecutive Saturdays commensing today [7 November 1885]," continued Hintze. "A few years ago one our [sic] Elders was jailed here in town for publishing our meetings; but let come what may I am bent on them knowing we are here. . . ." Ferdinand Friis Hintze Diary, vol. 1, p. 533, 6 November 1885, holograph, LDS Church Archives. J. G. Joergensen wrote from Bergen in December 1890 that Mormons had advertised meetings in Bergen newspapers for the first time. Skandinaviens Stjerne 40 (1 January 1891):105. Hans J. Christiansen, who returned to Norway in 1893 after a five-year absence, noted that in Oslo "it was now customary to advertise the topics which would be discussed on Sundays, something which I did not agree with and which I felt was contrary to Scripture, but I understood that this was the Spirit of the Age. . . ." ["En omordning var sket [sic] i flere henseende saavel med Forsamlingerne som i andre Henseende. Det var nu i brug at advetere om Emner at der skule tales over om Soendagene, noget som jeg fandt ei at stemme med mine Anskuelser, ei heller med Skriften, men jeg forstod at dette var Tidens Aand. . . ."] Hans Jacob Christiansen Journal, vol. 2, 15 June 1893, holograph, LDS Church Archives. Missionary C. Iversen described "a large advertisement in Drammens Blad . . . concerning our belief and doctrine" on 9 December 1894. Christofer Iversen Diary, 9 December 1894, microfilm of holograph, LDS Church Archives. Mormon missionaries in Aalesund placed the following advertisement in Aalesunds Tidende on 10 March 1895: "Lectures each Sunday at 6 P.M. and on Wednesday at 8 P.M. in Baard Falberg's old quadrangle Floor 3 on Keppervig Street on Latter-day Saint doctrine by Christofer Iversen from Drammen who has been in Utah for 12 years and [who] will impartially describe his experiences among the Mormons. Free admission for every peaceful person. C Iversen." ["Foredrag Holdes hvaer Soendag Kl 6 og Onstag [sic] Kl 8 Efterm. i Baard Falbergs forige Gaard 3die Etage i Kepperviggaden over de Siste Dages Helliges Laere af Christofer Iversen fra Drammen som haver vaeret i Utah en 12 Aar og vil fortaelle sine Erfaringer blant Mormonaerne upartiskt. Fri Adgang for endhvaer fredelig paerson C Iversen."]

Ibid., 10 March 1895. Mormons in Trondheim and Stavanger began advertising meetings about 1896. Johan L. George Johnson Diary, 7 March 1896, holograph, LDS Church Archives; Peter Olsen Diary, 20 November 1896, microfilm of holograph, LDS Church Archives.

[10] Theodore C. Blegen, <u>Norwegian Migration to America</u> (Northfield, Minnesota: The Norwegian-American Historical Association, 1940), pp. 113-14.

[11] Sandvin, "Mormonisma," p. 48.

[12] William Mulder, "Image of Zion: Mormonism as an American Influence in Scandinavia," <u>Mississippi Valley Historical Review</u> 43 (June 1956):30-31. Svend Larsen quoted from a book entitled <u>Laesebog for Folkeskolen og Folkehjemet</u> [Reader for the Grammar School and the Private Home], p. 250, in 1865: "It is not only a Mormon's right, but his duty to have several wives, since only that woman who has been married to a Mormon can live in Paradise. And the Mormon paradise is like that of the Mohammedan--full of carnal pleasures." ["Det er ikke blot en Mormons Ret, men hans Pligt at have flere Koner. Da kun den Qvinde som haver vaeret gift med en Mormon, kan faa deel i Paradiset. Og Mormones [sic] Paradis er ligesom Muhammedanens, fuld af kjoedelige Glaeder."] The same book also stated that "the Mormons are not much better than Mohammedans" ["Mormonerne er ikke stort bedre end Muhammedanerne"]. Svend Larsen Diary, 12 October 1865, holograph, LDS Church Archives. The historian, David Brion Davis, described anti-Mormon and anti-Catholic literature in America, and his observations help explain anti-Mormon campaigns in Norway: "Freemasons, it was said, could commit any cime and indulge any passion when 'upon the square,' and Catholics and Mormons were even less inhibited by internal moral restraints. Nativists expressed horror over this freedom from conscience and conventional morality, but they could not conceal a throbbing note of envy. What was it like to be a member of a cohesive brotherhood that casually abrogated the laws of God and man, enforcing unity with dark and mysterious powers? As nativists speculated on this question, they projected their own fears and desires into a fantasy of licentious orgies and fearful punishments. . . . Such a projection of forbidden desires can be seen in the exaggeration of the stereotyped enemy's powers, which made him appear at times as a virtual superman. Catholic and Mormon leaders, never hindered by conscience or respect for traditional morality, were curiously superior to ordinary Americans in cunning, in exercising power over others, and especially in captivating gullible women. . . . While nativists affirmed their faith in Protestant monogamy, they obviously took pleasure in imagining the variety of sexual experience supposedly available to their enemies. By picturing themselves exposed to similar temptations, they assumed they could know how priests and Mormons actually sinned. . . . We should recall that this literature was written in a period of increasing anxiety and uncertainty

over sexual values and the proper role of woman. As ministers and journalists pointed with alarm at the spread of prostitution, the incidence of divorce, and the lax and hypocritical morality of the growing cities, a discussion of licentious subversives offered a convenient means for the projection of guilt as well as desire. The sins of individuals, or of the nation as a whole, could be pushed off upon the shoulders of the enemy and there punished in righteous anger." David Brion Davis, "Some Themes of Counter-Subversion," in <u>Mormonism and American Culture</u>, eds. James B. Allen and Marvin S. Hill (New York: Harper & Row, 1972), pp. 67-69.

[13]"Det meste av denne literaturen er sterkt polemisk, sjoelvrettferdig, og ofte skjemd av meiningslause rykte og paastand. . . ." Sigmund Skard, <u>USA i Norsk Historie: 1000-1776-1976</u> (Oslo: Det Norske Samlaget, 1976), p. 122. Anti-Mormon pamphlets published in Norway before 1913 included the following: S. B. Hersleb Walnum, "Vogter Eder for de falske Propheter!" [Beware of the false Prophets!] in 1853; Caspar H. Jensenius, "Kort Begreb om den egentlige Mormonisme" [Short account of the real Mormonism] in 1855; E. P. Kjerkegaard, "Om og mod Mormonismen" [About and against Mormonism] n.d.; Joach. B. Lund, "Beretning om et Besoeg i Mormonernes Kapel" [Account of a visit in the Mormon Chapel] in 1862; Andreas Mortensen, "Fra mit besoeg blandt Mormonerne" [From my visit among the Mormons] in 1887; G. H. Stub, "Foredrag om den norsk-lutherske Misjon i Utah" [Lecture on the Norwegian-Lutheran Mission in Utah] in 1894; William E. Smythe, "Hvad vi kan laere af Mormonerne" [What we can learn from the Mormons] in 1896; O. A. Johnson, "Mormonismen Avsloeret" [Mormonism Exposed] in 1906; Rudolf Muus, "Mormonernes Pigefangst" [The Mormon White Slave Traffic] in 1906; Karl Schreiner, "Mormonerne" [The Mormons] in 1911; Karl Schreiner, "Foredrag" [Lecture] in 1912. Hilmar Freidel, <u>Jesu Kristi Kirke i Norge: Den norske misjons historie, 1851-1966</u> (Oslo: Jesu Kristi Kirke av Siste Dagers Hellige Misjonskontoret, 1966), p. 71.

[14]Popular songs which poked fun at the Mormons proliferated in Norway during the 1850s and 1860s such as the following verse and refrain which contains the response of an impoverished housewife to her husband's intention to travel to "Salte-Lake" in "Juta." (Subtleties of dialect and use of puns preclude a sensible translation--the wife gives her husband a good drubbing which destroys his desire to emigrate, afterwhich he seeks solace in cardplaying and strong drink.)
Naa, skal jeg saltelake deg, din liddelige fant.
Ja, jeg skal saltelake deg, din liddelige fant.
Dermed saa rauk jeg paa'n, skal si at han fikk stryk.
Jeg holdt jo paa aa klaa'm til han ble moer og myk.
Og dermed saa gjekk loesta til mormonismen vekk.

Men siden har'n troesta seg med kortspell og med drekk.
Men siden har'n troesta seg med kortspell og med drekk.
NRK, "Pipervika - Tankespill om en bydel: Med Rolf Soeder paa historisk vandring i et av Oslos gamle arbeiderstroek," 28 December 1977.

[15] Lectures by a lay preacher in Christiansund in 1901 included a "hate song" and claims that Mormons "believed in blood atonement, had Danites and murdering angels," forced their women to pull plows, i.e., "a Mormon bishop would stand with a long black snake whip and lash the women so they would go faster," and that "a Norwegian sea-captain sailing along the California coast had used his spy-glasses and had seen a Mormon murder his wife because she wouldn't consent to a second wife being taken." Milton Herman Knudsen Autobiography, pp. 16-17, xerox of typescript, LDS Church Archives. Female missionaries, Anna K. G. Widtsoe and Petroline J. P. Gaarden, lectured on "the condition of women and education of children in Utah" at Stavanger on 11 October 1906. Johan August Olsen Journal, p. 166, 11 October 1906, typescript, Special Collections, Harold B. Lee Library, Brigham Young University, Provo, Utah. Lectures in the larger Norwegian towns by the Norwegian Vice-Consul for Utah, C. M. Nielsen, in 1911, earned several favorable press reviews. Skandinaviens Stjerne 60 (15 August 1911):251.

[16] Hansen, Christensen, pp. 419-21.

[17] Hendricksen Diary, vol. 2, p. 50, 12 November 1903.

[18] Skandinaviens Stjerne 60 (1 August 1911):235-36.

[19] Jenson Diary, bk. J, p. 731, 5 December 1911. "People look at us as if we were criminals," complained missionary Carl P. Lind in describing the film's effect on public opinion in Toensberg, "and our young Sisters [female Mormons] are hard put to defend themselves and their faith before their fellow workers and acquaintances. . . . And wherever we or our members show ourselves on the street, [we] hear the expletive 'Mormon.'" ["(I Toensberg) ser man paa os, som om vi vare Misdaedere, og vore unge Soestre have fuldt op at gjoere med at forsvare sig selv og deres Tro overfor deres Arbejdskammerater og andre Omgangsfaeller. . . . Og hvorsomhelst vi eller vore Medlemmer vise sig paa Gaden, hoeres Skjaeldsordet 'Mormon.'"] Carl P. Lind to Andrew Jenson, 13 November 1911, quoted in Skandinaviens Stjerne 60 (1 December 1911):368.

[20] Skandinaviens Stjerne 61 (1 March 1912):72-73.

[21] Anthony Armstrong, The Church of England, the Methodists and Society 1700-1850 (Totowa, New Jersey: Rowman and Littlefield, 1973), p. 106.

[22] Residents of Holmen near Fredrikstad encouraged "street boys" to disturb Mormon meetings in 1856. Mons Pedersen Journal, 20 April 1856, holograph, LDS Church Archives. At Skudesnes in 1865, a group of three adults and a large flock of children followed missionaries Svend Larsen and companion yelling "hurrah for the Mormons," singing ribald songs about "Zion," and plastering the missionaries with garbage and gravel. Larsen Diary, 27 November 1865. Apprentices caused a disturbance at a Mormon meeting at Sagene near Drammen in 1866. August Severin Schou Diary, vol. 1, p. 8, 7 January 1866, trans. Lauritz G. Petersen, xerox of typescript, LDS Church Archives. C. J. Z. Hansen, a journeyman tailor in Bodoe, was told by a friend in 1903: "If you want fun go to the Mormon meeting. The boys throw snowballs through the windows." Mormon meetings throughout Norway were usually held in the poorer sections of town because Mormons could not afford high rent. Meetings in Bodoe, for example, were held in a basement at Sjoegaten [Harbor Street]--"the first street above the wharves and the harbor, and the roughest street in town." Conrad Johan Zahl Hansen, A Glance at my Life (Provo, Utah: Scott Printing Company, 1971), p. 29.

[23] Justice of the Peace Engebreth Finne reported to District Governor Iver Steen Thomle on 25 June 1853 that survey markers placed on various outlying islands led to rumors in Risoer "that these [markers] signaled the impending capture of the City by 100 to 200 Mormons who would supposedly come from Denmark" [". . . at disse varslede Mormonernes Overfald paa Byen, hvortil der fra Danmark skulde komme 100 til 200 Medlemmer"]. Engebreth Finne to Iver Steen Thomle, 25 June 1853, MS copy, pakke "Mormonerne 1851-1920," Kontor A, Det kongelige Kirke- og Undervisningsdepartement, Riksarkivet, Oslo, Norway. "It takes Utah Elders," declared Mission President Nils C. Flygare in 1878, "to preach the Gospel, none [sic] others can draw a house or congregation." Niels C. Flygare to Jos. F. Smith, 17 June 1878, carbon copy, "Letter Book of Niels C. Flygare, President of the Scandinavian Mission, 1878-1879," p. 26, LDS Church Archives. Native Mormons, however, often assisted missionaries with proselyting and distribution of tracts. Thus C. Fjeld, a resident of Oslo who was so weak he could not work at a regular full-time job, filled a ten-day proselyting mission in 1857. Hans Peter Lund Journal, vol. 1, pp. 61-62, 10 November 1857, holograph, LDS Church Archives. Two residents of Fredrikstad, a Brother Berthelsen and Jens Pedersen, traveled to Sarpsborg in 1857 where they preached Mormonism and avoided arrest by posting security for themselves at a court hearing in Edsberg. Pedersen Journal, pp. 47-48, 28 December 1857, 4 January 1858. At a special council meeting in Fredrikstad on 10 January 1858, the majority of the local Priesthood holders were called to go out and sell Mormon tracts. Ibid., pp. 49-50, 10 January 1858. L. S. Andersen reported from Oslo in 1874 that about sixteen male members had been called as missionaries in Oslo, "and I have encouraged them," he said, "to visit everyone, the rich as well as the poor" ["og jeg har opmuntret

dem til at besoege Alle, saavel den Rige som den Fattige"].
Skandinaviens Stjerne 23 (1 April 1874):202. "Sunday" or "home"
missionaries in Oslo in 1876 included several teenagers. Olaf
Henrik Nielsen Journal, vol. 2, p. 22, 29 October 1876, holograph,
LDS Church Archives. Mormon women preached and distributed tracts
in Oslo in 1877. Ibid., 24 April, 6 May 1877. On 7 November
1893, Oslo Conference President Hans J. Christiansen noted that
ten young men had been set apart to serve as Sunday missionaries,
with the added requirement that they report in Sunday branch
meetings the number of tracts sold, families they had visited, and
the number of gospel discussions held. Christiansen Journal,
vol. 2, 7 November 1893. On 24 January 1894, one "Sunday missionary"
reported visits to over fifty non-member families. Ibid., 24 January
1894. On 24 November 1903, Oslo Conference President J. A.
Hendricksen appointed "about 15 young brethren and sisters . . .
as missionaries to talk to the people who want conversations
after our regular meetings"; these missionaries were "prepared
with books and tracts to loan or sell to all who become interested."
Hendricksen Diary, vol. 2, p. 54, 24 November 1903. As early
as 1874, about sixteen members in Oslo established a "Tract
Society"; its name was changed in 1880 to Soendagsmisjonen [The
Sunday Mission]. Mormons in Oslo also organized the so-called
Skrifteforeningen [The Tract Association] in 1899 which merged with
the Mutual Improvement Association (MIA) in 1910. Norwegian
Mission, Jubileum aaret 1850-1950 (Oslo: Haraldssoen A.S., [1950]),
p. 26. "The Tract Association" was still operational as late
as 1927. Carl M. Hagberg, Den Norske Misjons Historie (Oslo:
Universal-trykkeriet, 1928), p. 39. On 20 October 1913, Sister
Fanny Gebhardt reported that members of "The Tract Association"
in Oslo had distributed 7,195 tracts and forty-six books, and
had held 169 Gospel conversations. Skandinaviens Stjerne 62
(1 December 1913):367. Another tract society was formed in
Bergen in 1919 to facilitate distribution of Mormon tracts.
Skandinaviens Stjerne 68 (1 August 1919):239.

[24] Drammens Tidende published a letter on 30 October 1891
from a Norwegian doctor in Hyrum, Utah, advising Norwegians
not to listen to two Mormon missionaries who were coming to
Drammen from Utah. The letter "termed the Mormon church as
the world's greatest murderers, liars, animals, and whoremongers
of the worst stripe; as a whole, a fearful, rotten set or community."
The letter claimed that Mormons "had murdered a whole train
of emigrants in Salt Lake City at midnight, and that they did
not even spare the engineer or fireman." Andrew M. Israelsen,
Utah Pioneering: An Autobiography (Salt Lake City, Utah: Deseret
News Press, 1938), p. 95. Missionaries often dressed differently
than Norwegians. Canute Peterson's wardrobe in 1853, for example,
included a buffalo robe "which I presume," he said, "gave us
away." Canute Peterson et al., "Story of the life of Canute
Peterson as given by himself and by some members of his family,"
p. 33, xerox of MS, LDS Church Archives. Or consider missionary
J. A. Hendricksen's comment in 1888 that "I have rec[d] today the

promise of a new silk stovepipe hat. Wont [sic] I be a dude when I get that on!" Hendricksen Diary, p. 61, 30 December 1888. Einar Strand, a Mormon who grew up in Drammen in the early 1900s, described missionaries who wore stove-pipe "floss" hats and "fine coats," "were well-turned-out," and "set themselves apart from the general public." "They were something to look at," and their arrival in town usually triggered cries of "here come the Mormons!" Interview with Einar Strand, Maurits Hansens Gate 4, Oslo 3, Norway, 7 March 1978. "We went thru the strit and the people de notised us wer ever we kam" ["We went through the street and the people they noticed us wherever we came"] reported missionary C. Iversen after visiting Namsos in 1896. Iversen Diary, 15 July 1896. In 1897, Mormon missionaries J. L. G. Johnson and an "Elder Gundersen" stopped to visit a tailor in Arendal, "and," said Johnson, "as we started to climb up the steps into his shop I look [sic] straight across the street and see all the people in the shop streaming to the door in order to look at us Mormons." [". . . og som at vi var iferd med at gaa op trapperne og ind i hans Butik saa ser jeg at lige over Gaden stroemmer alle Folk i Butikken hen til Doeren for at se paa os Mormoner."] Johnson Diary, 19 June 1897. Missionary E. C. Ekman reported little opposition in 1907 as he and other missionaries went around from door to door "for thay [the Norwegians] just stick ther heads out of the Dore and look at one like thay Expected to see a wild anamal." Edward C. Ekman Diary, 4 April 1907, holograph, LDS Church Archives. Missionaries Carl Kjaer and companion asked around for a night's lodging in the countryside near Haugesund in 1909, and finally found a place "after we'd asked 20 times. . . ." "We asked 2 places for [a] Barn to sleep in," said Kjaer, "but [were answered] no not that sort in my barn." Carl Kjaer Diary, p. 235, 9 August 1909, holograph, LDS Church Archives. An Oslo Conference report for 1887 noted that "it was said among the people that anyone, who purchased a tract from them [Mormon missionaries] or gave them lodging, committed an unforgivable sin." [". . . der var ogsaa bleven sagt blandt Folket, at den, som kjoebte Skrifter af dem eller gav dem Husly, begik en utilgivelig Synd."] Skandinaviens Stjerne 37 (15 October 1887):26. Some missionaries were hardly bashful about attracting attention. Christian Aslaksen, a merchant in Moss, described the visit of Mormon missionaries Jeppe Folkmann and Nils Hansen in 1852, who were teased and booed by other house guests when Hansen, "kneeling, offered up a prayer, whereas the other [missionary] stood upright with folded hands." [". . . de viste sig som stilfaerdige Mennesker, men blev der af nogle lystige Mennesker der i Huset drevet adskillig Kommers med dem, da En af dem, nemlig Nils Hansen, knaelende forrettede sin Andagt, medens den Anden stod opreist med sammenfoldede Haender."] Avskrift av "Extraret paa Raadhuset i Moss under ledelsen af Byfoged Lorentz Juhl Vogt," 25 October 1852, Mormonpakken, Trossamfunn Samling, Det kongelige Justis- og Politidepartement, Oslo, Norway. Mormon missionaries, "in advance of the tourists, the GI's, and the Point Four experts of more recent time," were also "evangels of American ways. . . ." Mulder, "Image," p. 18. Oslo Conference President George M. Brown, for example, visited Bakenrud Farm near Kjorven in Romerike in 1864, and related that: "The news flew around the country quicker than lightning that an American had come, and in the evening the house was crowded with strangers, all eager to catch a glimpse of me. After looking at me until I was almost tired of it, they began to ask questions about Utah, all of which I answered to the best of my knowledge. The more they heard, the more eager they were. . . ." Brown Autobiography, p. 51, 11 January 1864. A year later, Brown and a missionary surnamed Anderson arrived at Boertnes Station near Nes in Hallingdal "with the hope of obtaining a quiet and retired place to rest us in after our hard mountain journey of more than twenty-five miles. But our hopes of taking a supper to ourselves were soon frustrated as well as our hopes of rest. We had no more than entered when the stationkeeper, as is usual began to ask questions and after answering some time we at length got him to show us to a room after repeated requests. The room was as good as could be expected and we ordered supper and determined to have a little comfort when a large number of the neighboring men and boys who had seen us come entered the room much in the same style as the American Indians do, and began to talk, converse, and question until we gave them to understand that we wanted a little rest and then we would talk with them. They presently withdrew into another room and we ate supper and rested us a little after which we talked with the people and the Landlord considerably and they were much interested in us. It is not the badness of these people at all that makes them so troublesome when strangers arrive, but it is their curiosity. . . ." Ibid., p. 103, 8 July 1865.

[25] Canute Peterson to his wife and family in Utah, 7 December 1853, quoted in Peterson, "Story," pp. 90-91.

[26] Christian J. Larsen Journal, vol. 3, p. 35, holograph and MS, LDS Church Archives.

[27] "Folkets Stemning begyndte at blive mere og mere uhygelig og deres Raab var at de skulde spytte os i Ansigtet, jage os ud af Byen, slaebe os ned i Elven o.s.v." Saamund [Samuel] Gudmundsen Journal, 3, 10 February 1856, holograph, LDS Church Archives.

[28] Pedersen Journal, pp. 30-31, 13 February 1857. While staying at a house in Boerseskogen near Trondheim in 1857, missionary N. C. Poulsen was warned by neighbors that a mob planned to kidnap him after dark. Poulsen watched from a window, and about "2 or 3 A.M. -- what do I see. -- 10 or 12 men come down out of the forest and sneak into the adjoining farmyard; -- and I figured it was best to get myself out of there. . . . I saw the heads of these men and they all had on red stocking

caps." ["Da kl. var i mellem 2 a 3 -- hvad seer jeg. -- en 10 a 12 karle komme nede i fra Skogen og smaettede sig bort til en naerligede [sic] Gaard; -- og jeg tante [sic] at det var best at forfoeie sig bort. . . . Jeg saa Haavedet af disse Mennesker og de havde alle roede Luer paa."] Niels Christian Poulsen Journal, 18 October 1857, holograph, LDS Church Archives. At Brastein south of Stavanger (near Klepp) in 1866, Svend Larsen was chased out of town by Rasmus Braastei [sic] and eight other men who prodded him along with sticks. Larsen Diary, 24 January 1866.

[29] Hans Olsen Magleby Journal, 12 September 1858, trans. John A. Widtsoe, typescript, LDS Church Archives.

[30] Pedersen Journal, p. 83, Sankt Hans Aften 1860.

[31] Ekman Diary, 18 February 1906. "We cant [sic] Tract for fear of the mobe [sic]," said Ekman, "so we just visit among the saints and frends [sic] we are Expect [sic] araid [sic] at any time so we have prepared for it we have hid most of our books and the most valuable thing [sic] so if thay make a brake [sic] on us thay will have only the furniture to distroy. . . ." Ibid., 22 February 1906.

[32] Mormons in Fredrikstad were ordered out of a rented meeting hall in 1853 because the new owner, a Mr. Adamsen, "declared that he would not have such 'heathens' occupy it." Larsen Journal, vol. 3, p. 11, 20 April 1853.

[33] "Mine foreldre hoerte Evangeliet i og omkring Kristiania og annammede det fordi de foelte og forstod det var sandhed; da vare vi boernene alle smaa og jeg omtrendt 1 1/2 aar gammel. --Nu begynte Djevlen at rase; mine foreldre boede den gang i Maridalen 1 mil nord fra Hovedstaden; og nogle dage foerend de kom i Pagten, indfandt gaardmanden sig med svoeben i haanden med denne advarsel: at saafremt mine foreldre 'bleve Mormonere idag skulle de ud fra huset i morgen og fader opsiges af sit arbeide.' Foelgerne udebleve ikke: vi maatte forlade hus og arbeide for Evangeliets skyld; og min Fader gik arbeidsloes i lengre tid; ingen vilde have ham i arbeide 'fordi han var Mormon.'" Nielsen Journal, vol. 2, n.p.

[34] Schou Diary, vol. 1, p. 47, 6 May 1878.

[35] Peterson, "Story," pp. 45-46. When a man named Bent Frandsen in Risoer struck missionary Erik G. M. Hogan "such a blow that he fell" in 1853, Hogan picked himself up, "stretched out his arm, and with his finger close to the man's face said in English: 'I Curse you in the name of Jesus Christ for striking Me.'" Ibid., p. 46. A few missionaries occasionally talked back to those who treated them rudely as witness the case of C. Iversen who was invited into a parlor by the woman of one

house at Volden in 1895, "but as soon as the husband discovered I was a Mormon he commanded me to pack up my things and get out immediately and naturally I had to leave like a dog but not with my tail between my legs because I told him he was an ignorant and uncouth fellow." [". . . men saa snart manden fandt ud at jeg var mormon blev jeg af ham befalet at pakke mine sager sammen og i en fart se at komme mig ud af doeren og naturligvis jeg havede til at gaa som en hund men ikke med rumpen melem [sic] benene thi jeg fortalte ham at han var en uopdragen og raa fyr."] Iversen Diary, 5 June 1895.

36". . . jeg . . . gaged [sic] dem or Hauset og forfulget dem til dem for lod Stadet." Canute Peterson Journal, 16 July 1854, holograph, LDS Church Archives.

37Ekman Diary, 21 January 1906.

38Jenson Diary, bk. J, pp. 711-13, 29 October 1911.

39Theodore M. Samuelsen to George M. Brown, 23 February 1866, quoted in Brown Autobiography, p. 141. In 1878, missionary A. S. Schou came upon a "house raising" in the countryside near Trondheim. A Lutheran lay preacher conversed with those assembled during rest pauses, but when Schou got into a discussion with the preacher, he was immediately asked to leave. Schou Diary, vol. 1, p. 62, 10 June 1878.

40Winge Autobiography, pp. 5-6.

41Interview with Strand, 7 March 1978.

42Nielsen Journal, vol. 2, 13 July 1877.

43Schou Diary, vol. 1, p. 43, 13 April 1878. The president of the female Relief Society in Halden went out of her mind during childbirth in 1888. "A sorrowful case it is," lamented branch president, J. A. Hendricksen. "People says its [sic] through 'Mormonism.'" Hendricksen Diary, vol. 1, p. 194, 27-28 August 1888.

44Schou Diary, vol. 1, p. 43, 18 April 1878. "The people are very superstitious and preistridden [sic]," declared F. F. Hintze in 1885, "and they believe all manner of falshoods [sic] told about us, so that it seems at first almost imposible [sic] to approach them." Hintze Diary, vol. 1, pp. 550-51, 9 December 1885. "The prejudice against our Faith is so great among some," observed J. A. Hendricksen in 1889, "that they hardly know how bad to treat us." Hendricksen Diary, p. 66, 4 January 1889. After a Mormon meeting in Bergen in 1893, a man stood up, expressed thanks for the sermon, said that all that had been preached that day was true, and then told the people to watch out for the

Mormons. A. M. Nielson to C. A. Carlquist, 10 August 1893, quoted in <u>Skandinaviens Stjerne</u> 42 (1 September 1893):363.

[45]Ekman Diary, 27 April 1906. Even most of the troublemakers were hardly out after blood. In Aalesund in 1893, a noisy gang of about fifty men stormed, yelling and cursing, into a room occupied by two missionaries. The Mormons remained calm, and asked the mobsters to come in as Christians and not as a bloodthirsty mob. James Erickson, one of the missionaries, described Utah and freedom of religion in America, afterwhich the mobsters quietly dispersed. James Erickson to Joseph Christiansen, 4 January 1893, quoted in <u>Skandinaviens Stjerne</u> 42 (1 February 1893):142. Torkel Torkelson, a missionary working in the coastal town of Kjaerringvik east of Larvik, advertised in 1894 that he would speak to the townspeople on Sunday afternoon following the Haugian sermon. "This the good people could not tolerate," said Torkelson, "and they prepared themselves with stones, and their rifles were also readied; for that a Mormon should come with his frightful doctrine just couldn't be allowed; if he did come, he would not leave here alive." ["Dette kunde de gode Folk ikke taale, og de beredte sig med Sten, og deres Gevaerer sattes ogsaa istand; thi at en Mormon skall komme med sine forskraekkelige Laerdomme, det gaar ikke; kommer han, skal han ikke komme levende herfra."] Sunday arrived and the priest lectured for two hours. Torkelson asked to speak, but the priest said the people had sat long enough until the next time, and "then addressed a pair of old fogies, who sat by his side; these arose and declared themselves so richly fed with the bread of life that they had enough until the next time they should meet and sighed so [deeply], one could imagine their hearts would burst." ["Han vendte sig da til et Par Oldinger, som sad ved hans Side; disse reiste sig og sagde, at vaere saa regeligt [sic] bespiste med Livets Broed, at de havde nok til naeste Gang, de skulde moede og sukkede saa, man kunde taenke, at Hjaertet skulde briste."] Torkelson then went outside and told the people he had tried to reach them, but they felt themselves too good for a servant of the Lord; thus he would meet them at the judgment bar of God with his garments free of their blood forever. A crowd had gathered, and "doors and windows were opened," said Torkelson, "for I stood on the beach, and the houses were built in a semicircle fronting [the beach], where I stood, and there were certainly few who could not hear me, for I spoke as loudly and clearly as I could." ["Doere og Vinduer aabnedes thi jeg stod paa Strandbraedden, og Huse vare byggede i nesten en Sirkel rundt om, hvor jeg stod, og der var sikkerligen faa uden at de hoerte mig, thi jeg talede saa hoeit og tydeligt som jeg kunde."] The town magistrate then stepped forward and, putting his hand on Torkelson's shoulder, declared: "Do not consign us to such a fate, dear Brother. If one door closes, another opens up. . . ." ["Overlad oss ikke kjaere Broder, til en saadan Dom. Lukkes en Doer igjen, saa lades [sic] en Anden op. . . ."] Concluded Torkelson: "There was not a person [thereafter] who did not wish to speak with me, shake my hand

and invite me to his house." ["Der var ikke et Menneske, som ikke oendskede at tale til mig og faa roere ved min Hand [sic] og indvetere [sic] mig til sit Hus."] Torkel E. Torkelson, "En Kort Beskrivelse af Mit Livs Historie skrevet af mig selv," vol. 2, pp. 57-61, Summer 1894, holograph, LDS Church Archives. The people of Kjaerringvik were probably more touched by Torkelson's self-pity and hurt feelings than by any fear of the Judgment. Although highly melodramatic, the story does reveal some of the solicitude and basic honesty of the Norwegian people, and paints an interesting picture of small town society and Sunday life.

[46]". . . og han begynte at klappe i henderne at se op i mod skyerne og at le alt han orked og det samme jorde [sic] alle de omkringstaaende thi daer var en hel flok samlet fra de omligende gaarde." Iversen Diary, 17 July 1895.

[47]Kjaer Diary, p. 242, 27 August 1909. On 9 July 1909 at Haugesund, Kjaer "met an old cranky man, who was sitting on a bench outside of his house, together with another man and a woman who were more polite than the old man they'd listen to what I had to say, about Mormonism men [but] the old man kept interrupting me and telling me to go and at the same time the woman got up off the bench offering me her seat, so I did'nt know what to do, I finally accepted the old man's Kind invitation and went." Ibid., p. 222, 9 July 1909. Kjaer also had "quite a hot time with 3 old washwomen one isaer [especially] who tried to call me down and tell me all about Utah etc. But before I left 2 of them were on my side." Ibid., p. 199, 5 May 1909.

[48]Ibid., p. 246, 1 September 1909.

[49]"Mendene var ifoert hvid korte troeier og veste, lange sorte bukser eller knaebukser, roede topluer [sic]. qvindene [sic], lange sorte skjoerter som sidder helt op under armene, belter om livet sorte korte troeier, soeiler og ringe i brystet og store, broderede toerkler om hovedet. Det var et rigtig norsk nationalt skue og meget interesant at betragte. . . . Jeg . . . forklarede vor tro og laere stadfestet ved bibelske beviser og alle lyttede til min roest med stor opmaerksomhed. . . . Dette var saavidt mig mig [sic] bekjendt den foerste forsamling som var holdt paa disse kanter af 'de sidste dages hellige.'" Nielsen Journal, vol. 2, 6 December 1877. George M. Brown and another missionary stopped at a farmhouse enroute to Kongsberg from Drammen in 1863, and gave this description: "On entering we were invited to a seat near the table, and presently the lady of the house came and set before us what I called a young wash tub full [of] clabbered milk with the cream on, which is a very common dish in this country among the farming population. The inmates of the house were very kind, and had the appearance of being an honest family who lived on their own production. An air of comfort pervaded the apartment; the fire blazed brightly,

and the old man sat in the corner smoking his pipe, while the women-folk were busy spinning, and the children playing about the hearth. . . . Elder Berg kept up a conversation while we were eating and answered many questions which they were eager to ask as fast as opportunity presented itself." Brown Autobiography, p. 46, 9 December 1863. In Gulbrandsdalen in 1865, Anthon L. Skanchy preached before large crowds, "and many were of the most wealthy of the population [and] were so touched that they permitted me to hold meetings in their large farm houses. I was received everywhere as a gentl[e]man so much so that I was really astonished at the spirit and emotion which was among the people. . . . Many were very afraid of the priest [Honoratus Halling, Parish Priest of Lom and editor of the popular Sunday newspaper, For Fattig og Riig, established in 1848] while others were determined that he should not make them fear to examine what they desired in the way of religion." Anthon L. Skanchy to George M. Brown, 18 December 1865, quoted in Brown Autobiography, p. 127. On 8 October 1893, Torkel Torkelson preached at the farm of Eilert Mossige, a Norwegian Army officer who lived near Stavanger. Mossige personally asked Torkelson to preach, told all his hired servants to stop working, and gathered them all in the parlor of the farmhouse. Torkelson preached four and a half hours, and reported that many "wished that the day would come, that they could gather the strength to tear themselves loose, that they might soon see the day, when they could bear the testimony [which] I had borne for them." ["(Mange) oenskede at Dagen vilde komme, da de kunde faa Kraft til at rive sig loes, at det [sic] maatte snart see den dag, da De kunde baere det Vidnesbyrd, jeg havde baaret til dem."] Torkelson, "Historie," vol. 2, pp. 47-48, 8 October 1893. Carl Iversen, a native of Norway serving as a missionary, described a similar idyllic preaching scene at Sande near Drammen in January 1895: "I drank home-brewed mead there made from honey and ate [sic] and drank coffee I had a long discussion there with the people of the house together with the shoemaker and Jorgen Sjoel, the butcher, he sat over on the woodbox by the oven and huffed and puffed while I read from the Pearl of Great Price about Joseph's [Joseph Smith's] first visions and revelations I tarried there until 9 P.M. afterwhich I went back to Grandmother's." [". . . jeg drak hjaemlavet mjoe der af honing og spiste og drak kaffe jeg havde et langt diskusjons mode [sic] der af husets folk tiligemed skomageren og Jorgen Sjoel Slagteren han sad henne paa brenne kassen ved ovenen og suked og blaeste medens jeg leste af den kostelige paerle Josaefes foerste syner og aabenbarelser jeg stoped der til Kl 9 p.m. derefter gik jeg tilbage til Bestemor."] Iversen Diary, 21 January 1895.

[50]"Der gik jeg ind, at spoerge om Logi, men da jeg var saa medtagen of Mathed kunne jeg naesten ikke tale, Manden i Huset foerstod dette, ikke sagde noget til mig--men tog en en [sic] Stol satte mig ved den varme Ovn--og tog mine Stoevler af gik saa ned i sin Kjelder bragte op en Bolle med Hjemlavet

Malt Oel--og gav mig at drikke, bad mig at saette mig ved Bordet aa spise. Dette var gjort i al hast. Saa begyndte han at spoerge mig om jeg kom over Eidet, og hvorfor jeg ikke robte naar jeg kom til Stranden--saa skulle han har [sic] taget sin Baad og hentet mig, thi han havde jort [sic] det foer siger han, for dem som har gaaet over Edet [sic]. Dette var en fattig Fiskers Hjem, det eneste Hus paa den side af Oeen. Efter jeg har [sic] spist og var vederqvaeget begynte Konen at red [sic] Sengen som var i Huset (lagde rene Lagener og Pudevar i den tog saa in [sic] Straa Matter og gamle Badseil og loge i en Krog (Det var bare et Rom i Huset) Holdte saa Boen. De viste [sic] hvem jeg var. Jeg blev saa henvist til at sove i Saengen, som jeg ikke gjerne ville men var Taknemmelig til at sove paa det Straa som var boret in, men nei! det hjalp ikke. Jeg maatte ligge i Saengen, om Morgenen efter vi har [sic] haft vores tarvelig Frokost satte Manden mig over Sundet til Langoeen. Han ville ikke have nogen Betaling." Anthon L. Skanchy Autobiography, pp. 24-26, holograph, Anthon L. Skanchy Collection, LDS Church Archives.

[51]Brown Autobiography, p. 128, 2 January 1866. Canute Peterson preached at Maurset in Eidfjord in August 1854 to people "who were very much taken up with the talk, but none of them dared to join the church because they were too poor to emigrate, and depended upon others for employment, and they realized what pressure would be brought to bear against them." Peterson, "Story," p. 71. H. O. Magleby received two handkerchiefs in 1858 from a woman in Oslo who believed Mormonism was true, but was forbidden by her husband to be baptized. Hans Olsen Magleby Journal, 30 August 1858, holograph, LDS Church Archives. Anthon L. Skanchy reported from Bergen in 1887: "Fear of men is very strong [here], for they [the people] believe that if they should deviate from the doctrine of the [Lutheran] priests and that which is popular, they would lose their work and reputations." ["En stor Menneskefrygt hersker, thi Aanden er den, at om de skulle vige fra Praesternes Laerdomme og hvad som er populaer, ville de miste deres Arbejde og Ansaettelser."] Anthon L. Skanchy to N. C. Flygare, 16 March 1887, quoted in Skandinaviens Stjerne 36 (1 April 1887):203. At Christiansand in 1864, Oslo Conference President George M. Brown visited a "Herr Peter T. Landaas" whom he described as "the son of a wealthy family who live in this place." Landaas believed Mormon doctrine, but "his [social] position had detained him from receiving it." Brown Autobiography, p. 73, 21 June 1864. In 1894, missionary Torkel Torkelson often accompanied C. Th. Lund, a bank cashier in Larvik, on fishing trips. Lund even taught Torkelson to play the harp, but said he could not invite his family to Mormon meetings at the "hole" where Torkelson preached on Sundays, because "'my Family is my business [connection with] the finest ladies and gentlemen in the town'" ["'min Familie er mit Selskabs [Forbindelse med] de fineste Damer og Herrer i Byen'"]. Lund did rent the Good Templar Hall in Larvik so that Torkelson could preach there.

Torkelson, "Historie," vol. 2, p. 62. Because of heavy responsibilities, many missionaries were only able to stay at a place long enough to make "friends," but not long enough to win converts. Thus C. C. N. Dorius preached until midnight at Stokkesund on 14 July 1862 for a large group of so-called "seekers," joined them in singing "When will we meet again?" ["Naar skal vi vel sees igjen?"], and asked the Lord "to . . . bless and enlighten those present whose hearts were already very receptive to the truth" ["at . . . velsigne og oplyse de Tilstedevaerende hvis Hjerte allerede var meget opladte for Sandheden"]. "I have almost never seen a better spirit among strangers," said Dorius. "They accompanied me to the quay during the night, and tearfully bid me farewell. A fire was lighted, shame [sic] that I did not have time to enjoy it - but I must go many [sic] await me elsewhere." ["Jeg har naesten aldrig seet en bedre Aand blandt Fremmede - de fulgte mig med paa Bryggen om Natten og med Taarer boed mig Farvel. En Ild var taendt, skade at jeg ikke havde Tid at puste til Den - men jeg maae afsted Mange venter mig andre Steder."] Dorius, "Dagbog," 14 July 1862.

[52] Schou Diary, vol. 1, p. 63, 27 July 1878.

[53] ". . . i overvaer af hendes Moder og en Soester samt Manden i Huset som var troende." Ole Hendriksen Berg Diary, vol. 1, pp. 18-19, 29 February 1864, holograph, LDS Church Archives.

[54] ". . . at Aanden haver vaeret virksom til vores fordeel idet at flere haver fuld Tro paa Evangeliet." Christiansen Journal, vol. 3, p. 165, 17 April 1895.

[55] Poulsen Journal, 26 November 1857.

[56] Jenson Diary, bk. J, p. 892, 22 April 1912.

[57] Skandinaviens Stjerne 69 (15 June 1920):183.

[58] Ekman Diary, 22 May 1907.

[59] Jens Christian Andersen Weibye Diary, vol. 4, pp. 78-79, 11 February 1872, holograph, LDS Church Archives.

[60] Ibid., pp. 184-85, 29 December 1872. The Oslo Branch Choir also held open-air concerts such as one at Smedstad on 3 June 1895 where the choir serenaded the non-Mormon owner of a large farm. Christiansen Journal, vol. 4, 3 June 1895. On 7 July 1895, the Oslo Choir teamed up with members of the Mormon Choir in Drammen to sing on top of Bragernes Mountain, "to the great surprise of various strangers who were up there" [". . . til stor forundring for en deel Fremmede som her var tilstede"]. Ibid., 7 July 1895.

[61] Ekman Diary, 2 May 1907. The Oslo Branch Choir sang to a packed house on 6 April 1917 during one of the darkest periods of World War I. On 13 April 1917, the Mormon choir in Bergen held a public concert just a few days before the United States entered the War. Christiansen Journal, vol. 11, pp. 253-54, 260; 6, 13 April 1917.

[62] Israelsen, Utah, pp. 127-28.

[63] "Den stoerste deel af Byen er missionaeret og der er flere som haver tro paa Evangeliet af hvem er den ledende Politibetjendt." Christiansen Journal, vol. 3, 22-24 June 1894. Johann A. Olsen described a Mormon meeting in Aalesund "crowded full of honest listeners, mostly strangers," on 11 February 1906. Olsen Journal, 11 February 1906.

[64] Hendricksen Diary, vol. 2, p. 45, 25 October 1903.

[65] Skandinaviens Stjerne 55 (1 October 1906):294.

[66] Skandinaviens Stjerne 56 (1 June 1907):175. Bergen Branch Sunday School numbered 103 pupils in 1903, including thirty-nine non-Mormon children. Skandinaviens Stjerne 52 (1 December 1903): 366. There were 108 pupils in Bergen Conference Sunday schools in 1905, including seventy-three non-Mormons (sixty-eight percent of total enrollment). Skandinaviens Stjerne 54 (1 November 1905): 331.

[67] ". . . et glaedeligt Vidnesbyrd om den Tillid og Yndest som vore Laerdomme og vort Soendagsskolesystem vinder hos konservative og retttaenkende Foraeldre." Skandinaviens Stjerne 59 (15 May 1910):156. By 1910, the non-Mormon percentage had fallen to eighteen percent of total enrollment--86 of 475 pupils in six Oslo Conference Sunday schools. Skandinaviens Stjerne 59 (15 May 1910):156. Mission President Andrew Jenson attended Sunday school in Arendal on 6 November 1910 where "about 50 people (mostly children of non-members) were in attendance." "The Arendal branch is small," said Jenson, "but full of life, a number of young people having joined the Church lately." Jenson Diary, bk. J, p. 426, 6 November 1910.

[68] Skandinaviens Stjerne 51 (15 November 1902):350. The Mormon Sunday School in Trondheim shut down abruptly in 1911 after non-Mormons stopped sending their children in response to threats by Norwegian school authorities that children attending Mormon schools would be expelled from the public schools. Anti-Mormon campaigns raged in the daily press and thundered from Lutheran pulpits. Mission President Andrew Jenson characterized a proposal to prohibit children from attending Mormon Sunday schools as "incompatible with free and informed public opinion" ["uforenelig med et oplyst og frit Folks Opfattelse"]. Skandinaviens Stjerne 60 (1 December 1911):365-66.

[69] Christiansen Journal, vol. 12, pp. 94-95, 7 October 1917.

[70] Mormon relations with members of the Norwegian public were not totally confined to the lower classes. When missionaries H. O. Magleby and O. C. Larsen first went to Kongsberg in 1858, they "found well to do men with liberal views and succeeded in getting large halls in which to hold meetings . . . the congregations including men of wealth and education." Oluf Christian Larsen, "A Biographical Sketch of the life of Oluf Christian Larsen dictated by himself and written by his son Oluf Larsen dedicated to his posterity who might desire to read it," p. 16, xerox of typescript, LDS Church Archives. Oslo Conference President George M. Brown described "many strange faces and many who appeared to be among the wealthy and learned" at Mormon meetings in Oslo in 1865. Brown Autobiography, p. 105, 30 July 1865. Norwegian Mormons--especially those in Utah--hosted prominent Norwegians from time to time. On 7 March 1870, violinist Ole Bull performed at the Salt Lake Theatre for two concerts; the famous singer, Olivia Dahl, from Oslo, also visited Salt Lake City and performed in the Fourteenth Ward Meeting Hall on 2 April 1906; Erling Bjoernson, son of the famous national poet, Bjoernstjerne Bjoernson, lectured in Salt Lake City (7 September 1906), Provo, and Logan on "Norway's Independence Movement"; on 2 March 1907, Roald Amundsen, the Norwegian polar explorer, presented a slide lecture on "the Gjoea Journey" in Salt Lake City's Barratt Hall, and visited Salt Lake City again on 14 March 1913 to present a film lecture at the Salt Lake Theatre on his discovery of the South Pole. Josef Straaberg, "Nordmaend paa besoeg i Utah," in *Utah Fest Program for 17de mai: Hundredaars Jubilaeum for Norges Grundlov*, ed. [Arrangementskomiteen for festligholdelsen af den 17de mai 1914] ([Salt Lake City, Utah]: n.p., [1914]), p. 10. Missionary John A. Andersen visited "our Norwegian patriot Bjoernstjerne Bjoernson" ["vor norske Patriot Bjoernstjerne Bjoernson"] in January 1893 at Gausdalen; Bjoernson had a copy of the Book of Mormon, "and admitted, that he certainly believed that America had earlier been inhabited by civilized people" ["og tilstod, at han troede nok, at Amerika forhen havde vaeret befolket med civiliserede Mennesker"]. John A. Andersen to Joseph Christiansen, 26 February 1893, quoted in *Skandianviens Stjerne* 42 (15 March 1893):187. On 2 November 1910, Scandinavian Mission President Andrew Jenson and two missionaries visited "the great Norwegian Statesman, Christian Mikkelsen . . . at his town office in Bergen . . . and had quite a little chat. . . ." Jenson described Mikkelsen as "a man with a large nose and a commanding appearance who impresses at first sight and shows unmistakeable [sic] evidence of natural ability to lead." Jenson Diary, bk. J, p. 423, 2 November 1910.

[71] Schou Diary, vol. 1, p. 24, 1 January 1877.

[72] Hintze Diary, vol. 1, p. 402, 11 July 1885. "Drunkenness was common, and licentiousness rampant," said missionary A. H. Lund in describing conditions in Oslo in 1885. "I saw boys and girls walking embracing one another and some were laying in the grass in indecent postures. . . . Even students were girl hunting. Talk about Utah being immoral such [sic] sights cannot bee [sic] seen there, I know." Anthon Hendrik Lund Diary, 17 May 1885, microfilm of holograph, LDS Church Archives. Bergen Branch President J. A. Hendricksen wrote in 1888 about a young Norwegian couple living together unmarried for several months until they had enough money to pay for the marriage ceremony. Said Hendricksen: "But people think anything like that is all right as long as 'they intend to get married' and dont [sic] seem to think it at al [sic] out of the way. But Polygamy, among the Mormons is 'abhorent.'" Hendricksen Dairy, p. 83, 9 February 1888.

Chapter VII

[1] Edvard Bull, *Arbeiderklassen i Norsk Historie* ([Oslo]: Tiden Norsk Forlag, 1947), pp. 89-90. Oslo had 31,715 inhabitants according to the census of 1855; and in 1878, the population was 106,781; in 1887, 135,615; and by December 1900, over 227,000. S. C. Hammer, *Kristianias Historie*, vol. 5: *1878-1924* (Oslo: J. W. Cappelen for Hovedkommission, 1928), pp. 188, 276. The appearance of the city suffered accordingly: a newspaper account in 1880 described the "burnt-out" aspect of nearly every quarter plus "the many hovels, which stand side by side with stately buildings on the city's main streets" ["de mange roenner, som i byens hovedgater staar side om side med statelige bygninger"]. Ibid., p. 76. Press reports in 1890 complained about streets filled with all sorts of rubbish, "stale, fog-filled air permeated by a stinking black smoke" ["en stillestaaende luft opfyldt av taake og en stinkende sort roek"] during winter, and "a conspicuous lack of open, uncongested areas" ["en paafaldende mangel paa aapne utrafikerte pladse"]. Ibid., p. 174. Travelers approaching Oslo by sea during summer months could see ships "plying about the city and probibly [sic] a thousand or more [ships] lying on the Piers." John Anthon Hendricksen Diary, p. 157, 16 May 1889, microfilm of holograph, Library-Archives, The Church of Jesus Christ of Latter-day Saints, Salt Lake City, Utah [hereinafter cited as LDS Church Archives]. During winter months (December-April), the fjord was usually iced over, and Oslo was cut off from sea connections with the outside world. Harald Hals II, *Byen, Havnen og Sjoeen* (Oslo: Oslo Bymuseum, 1957), p. 30.

[2] "Det hele gir bildet av et samfunn i oppbrudd. Det gamle rotfestede fellesskapslivet ble brutt i stykker. Folk ble som Abraham rykket op fra 'sit land fra sin slekt og fra sin fars hus,' og mange begav seg som han inn i det ukjente. Blant alle disse rotloese mennesker vokste naa paa nytt trangen etter samfunn, etter aa kunne forene seg med likesinnede. Det gjaldt paa det sosiale og politiske omraade saavel som paa det religioese." Andreas Aarflot, *Norsk Kirkehistorie*, vol. 2 (Oslo: Lutherstiftelsen, 1967), p. 286. Approximately twelve thousand Norwegian industrial workers labored in cotton mills, machine shops and textile factories in 1850; twenty-five years later (1875), the number of industrial workers exceeded forty-eight thousand. Bull, *Arbeiderklassen*, pp. 89-90.

[3] Joseph Buckley, *Memoirs of Joseph Buckley*, ed. by his daughter (Glasgow: Robert Smeal, 1874; London: Samuel Harris & Co., 1874), p. 203.

[4] Eilert Sundt, *Om Piperviken og Ruseloekbakken: Undersoegelser om arbeidsklassens kaar og saeder i Christiania* (Oslo: Tiden Norsk Forlag, 1968), p. 7.

[5] "Det store flertall var altsaa kommet flyttende saa pass langt vei at de mistet den regelmessige kontakten med sitt opprinnelige miljoe; de hadde revet seg loes fra tradisjonens roetter." Edvard Bull, *Arbeidermiljoe under det Industrielle Gjennombrudd: Tre norske industristroek* (Oslo: Universitetsforlaget, 1958), pp. 116-17, 122-23, 127.

[6] Svend Larsen, "Extracts from my Autobiography," p. 9, typescript translation, LDS Church Archives.

[7] "I Saerdeleshed faengsledes min Opmaerksomhed ved Beretningen om Jaernstoeber H. P. Jensens kraftige Vidnesbyrd om 'Mormonismens' Sandhed. At en Jaernstoeber kunde tilintetgjoere Praesters og Politiembedsmaends Argumenter, foelte jeg som Fagmand mig stolt af, og jeg syntes nu, at Jaernstoeberne vare blevne til Noget." Carl J. E. Fjeld, "Aeldste Carl Fjelds Beretning," *Morgenstjernen* 3 (15 March 1884):91.

[8] "Her traf jeg mange gamle Bekjendte, og jeg lod nogle Smaaskrifter og min lille Salmebog, som jeg havde bragt med mig fra Danmark, samt det nye Testamente gaa rundt iblandt Stoeberne og Smedene, indtil disse Boeger vare ligesaa sorte som vi selv vare." Ibid., p. 92.

[9] Canute Peterson et al., "Story of the life of Canute Peterson as given by himself and by some members of his family," p. 52, xerox of MS, LDS Church Archives.

[10] Ibid., pp. 52, 56.

[11] ". . . de ere aldeles ukjendte Personer, og maelde sig, skjoent doebte Mormoner, ikke ud af Statskirken. . . . Foruden den Anledning, som den store samlede Arbejdsstyrke i Byen har tilbudt, er den betydelige Fabrikdrift ved Saugene, der ogsaa har Folk fra alle Steder og ikke mindst fra Xstiania, en beqvem Anledning til Paavirkning." Anton Wilhelm Fangen to Jens L. Arup, 5 July 1859, pakke "Mormonerne 1851-1920," Kontor A [hereinafter cited as "A"], Det kongelige Kirke- og Undervisningsdepartement [hereinafter cited as KUD], Riskarkivet, Oslo, Norway [hereinafter cited as RA]. Studies of convert birthplaces (Birthplaces are available for 78 percent of those baptized in Oslo Branch during the years 1853-1860 inclusive, and 75 percent of those baptized during the years 1895-1900 inclusive--see appendixes 4 and 5) show a surprising number of foreigners who converted to Mormonism in Norway (most of them Swedes from the border province of Vaermland). Oslo Branch membership in the years 1853-1860 included a sprinkling of Danes, one German, one Icelander, and fifty-four

Swedes (12 percent of those for whom birthplaces are available). Over 50 percent of the members were born outside the Oslo-Akershus Region with sizeable numbers from Hedmark County (12.79 percent); Buskerud County (11.08 percent); and Oppland County (6.82 percent). This correlates well with Eilert Sundt's investigations of residents in the Piperviken and Ruseloekbakken areas of Oslo in 1855-1856 which showed that 71 percent of the men and 51 percent of the women were born in country districts, and not in Oslo itself. Sundt, Piperviken, p. 56. Significantly, 74.46 percent of those interviewed by Sundt said they first came to Oslo as unmarried adults--strong indication they came in search of work. Ibid., p. 59. Oslo Branch membership in the years 1895-1900--the "second wave" of Mormon revivalism--included a percentage of Swedes (13 percent) nearly equal to the 12 percent in the 1853-1860 sample (see appendix 5). As in the earlier sample, over 50 percent of the converts were born in regions outside of Oslo and Akershus Counties, with sizeable numbers from Oestfold County (8.19 percent of the sample), Hedmark County (7.37 percent), and Buskerud County (6.96 percent). Most converts to Mormonism in Scandinavia joined in families, and the parents were generally in their "vigorous" thirties or forties according to Kenneth O. Bjork, West of the Great Divide: Norwegian Migration to the Pacific Coast, 1847-1893 (Northfield, Minnesota: Norwegian-American Historical Association, 1958), p. 131. There were, of course, wide age differentials among those who joined. Erik Gundersen accepted Mormon baptism on 19 September 1852 at Risoer when he was well into his nineties (born in April 1758 at "Gaarden Jaadal Giaerestad"). "Protocol for Oesterriisoeers Green i Jesu Christi Kirke af Siste Dages Hellige opretet i Oesterriisoeer i October 1851," microfilm of MS, Oester Risoer Branch, Brevik Conference, Scandinavian Mission, LDS Church Archives. The oldest members baptized in Brevik Branch during the years 1852-1853 were Olea Josephsdatter, born 9 March 1771 at Aker Parish, and Jens Hansen, born 23 December 1778 in "Bratsberg Amt." Historical Record and Record of Members, 1852-1862, Brevik Branch, Christiania Conference, Scandinavian Mission, LDS Church Archives. A majority of the converts baptized at Risoer, Brevik, and Fredrikstad in the years 1852-1853 were in their twenties. "Protocol"; Historical Record, Brevik Branch; Historical Record and Record of Members, 1852-1858, Fredrikstad Branch, Christiania Conference, Scandinavian Mission, LDS Church Archives. A sampling of adult members baptized at Bodoe in 1903 shows an average age of 29 years for males and 30 years for females. Record of Members, 1903-1913, Bodoe Branch, Trondheim Conference, Scandinavian Mission, LDS Church Archives. Years of birth are available for 85 percent of those baptized at Oslo from 1853-1860 inclusive. The average age at baptism during those years was 31 years (31.5 years for men and 30.8 years for women). For converts in Oslo Branch during the years 1895-1900 inclusive (Years of birth are available for 83 percent of those baptized at Oslo during the years 1895-1900 inclusive), the average age at conversion was 30 years (30.66 years for men and 30.33 years for women)--

(see table 6). These figures do not include those age fifteen or under who were probably children of members; branch records do not distinguish between children of Mormons and converts. If we include those baptized at age 15 and under, the average age at baptism would still be 31 years during the period 1853-1860 (31.12 years for males and 30.12 years for females--see table 5)--and for the years 1895-1900, it would be 24 years (23.33 for men and 25.5 for women) reflecting baptisms of second-generation Mormons (see table 6). The great majority of those baptized at Oslo in the 1850s were in their twenties and thirties (table 5), whereas in the 1890s, most adults joined the Mormons while in their twenties; a sizeable percentage (31.1 percent) of those baptized in Oslo Branch in the period 1895-1900 inclusive were "children" age 15 and under--probably children of Mormons born or reared in a Mormon household (table 6). Studies of Oslo Branch records from 1853-1907 (table 7) show that men comprised about 40 percent of total membership whereas women comprised 60 percent. This is in striking agreement with Seljaas's studies of Mormon emigration from Norway which showed a "very large" percentage of females (61.5 percent of total emigrants) during the years 1853-1970. Helge Seljaas, "The Mormon Migration from Norway" (M.A. thesis, University of Utah, 1972), p. 46. Mormon accounts often mention a female preponderance such as O. C. Larsen's observation in 1859 that "the branch of Fredrickhald [Fredrickshald] was composed mostly of sisters." Oluf Christian Larsen, "A Biographical Sketch of the life of Oluf Christian Larsen dictated by himself and written by his son Oluf Larsen dedicated to his posterity who might desire to read it," p. 20, xerox of typescript, LDS Church Archives. J. C. A. Weibye's figures for Oslo Conference showed a memberhip of 283 males (33.8 percent of total membership) and 552 females (66.1 percent) in 1872. Jens Christian Andersen Weibye Diary, vol. 4, p. 169, 24 November 1872, holograph, LDS Church Archives. According to Hans J. Christiansen, there were sixteen Mormons in Larvik in 1893, "but like other places, mostly sisters" ["men som andre Steder mest Soestre"]. Hans Jacob Christiansen Journal, vol. 2, 18 September 1893, holograph, LDS Church Archives. Missionary Carl Kjaer noted that most of those attending a Lutheran service in Bergen in 1909 were women, "as in our [Mormon] moeder [meetings] is always the case." Carl Kjaer Diary, p. 178, 11 April 1909, holograph, LDS Church Archives. A study of Mormon emigration from Norway during the years 1881-1903 conducted by the Swedish Government concluded that the high percentage of females emigrating "was due to the more religious nature of women." Helge Seljaas, "Polygamy among the Norwegian Mormons," Norwegian-American Studies 27 (1977):152-53. The general, non-Mormon emigration from Norway during the years 1869 to 1900 was 57 percent male according to William Mulder, "Utah's Ugly Ducklings: A Profile of the Scandinavian Immigrant," Utah Historical Quarterly 23 (July 1955):238. "Probably to a greater degree than in other Protestant countries and certainly more than in the United States, Norwegian culture encourages the men to leave religion to the women.

Religion is considered to be not very masculine." Seljaas, "Migration," p. 47. In addition, "the missionaries . . . were an attraction in a society short of men because many [men] were at sea and a large number had emigrated." Seljaas, "Polygamy," p. 153. Among Mormon emigrants from Norway, "there seems to have been an unusually high percentage of widowed, divorced or unmarried mothers" such that "the crisis caused by the death of a husband, divorce or the birth of an illegitimate child may well have been the deciding factor in baptism and emigration." Seljaas, "Migration," p. 48. A survey of the urban population in Norway in 1845 showed a total of 17,000 servants in the cities of which 14,000 (82 percent) were "servant girls." Oddvar Bjoerklund, <u>Marcus Thrane: Sosialistleder i et u-land</u> (Oslo: Tiden Norsk Forlag, 1970), p. 50. This accords well with Seljaas's comment that servant girls or "maids . . . were often newcomers, with few social ties, in the cities, where missionary activities were most intensive. They were also the ones who most often met the missionaries first as they went from door to door." Seljaas, "Migration," p. 34.

[12]"Langs Agers Elven og navnligen paa Spigervaerket er nok idelig holdt Forsamlinger." Alexander Lange to Jens L. Arup, 22 June 1859, "Mormonerne," A, KUD, RA.

[13]Paul Irgens Dybdal to KUD, 9 June 1859, "Mormonerne," A, KUD, RA.

[14]Larsen, "Biographical Sketch," p. 25.

[15]Seljaas, "Migration," p. 31.

[16]William Mulder's studies of Mormon emigration from Scandinavia showed that "small farmers, freeholders, tenants, or simply journeyman hands," acounted for about fifty percent of the emigrants in the 1850s, and comprised about one-third of the emigrants during the 1860s. Mulder, "Ducklings," pp. 238-39. Canute Peterson noted in July 1853 that the largest Mormon congregation was in Fredrikstad where "many of the Saints were well-to-do farmers." Peterson, "Story," p. 49. Names and addresses appended to Canute Peterson's missionary journal in 1854 reveal something about Mormon social circles: "C. Widerborg, Addr. Herr Skomager A. Nielsen, Theatergaden No 8, Christiania; T. Johansen, Hate mager, Bore, Stavanger; Oelbrygger Magnus i Bergen; Kjoebmand Ole Baade, Stavanger; Kjoebmand og Brygger Henrich Magnus; Peder Steksen Tommer man; Skeper [sic] Iver Beoern paa Kalhammer." Canute Peterson Journal, 1854, holograph, LDS Church Archives. Missionary Hans Olsen Magleby taught the following persons in Kongsberg in 1858 and 1859: a merchant named Traaen (28 July 1858); tailor's apprentice Nielsen who requested Mormon baptism (Nielsen was evidently apprenticed to a pro-Mormon tailor named Svane) (31 July 1858); master carpenter Smith, age 25 (18 December 1858); a carpenter named Simonsen (10 January 1859). Hans Olsen

Magleby Journal, 28, 31 July, 18 December 1858, 10 January 1859, holograph, LDS Church Archives. Magnus Brostrup Landstad, Lutheran priest in Halden, reported in 1859 that most of the traveling Mormon preachers "have supported themselves here as journeymen craftsmen, painters, shoemakers, tailors and chimney sweeps, and have tried to spread their poison in the factories and the houses" ["have her ernaeret sig som Haandvaerkssvende, Malere, Skomagere, Skraeddere og Skorsteensfeiere, og paa Verkstederne og i husene soegt at udbrede sin Giftaande"]. Magnus Brostrup Landstad to Jens L. Arup, 20 June 1859, "Mormonerne," A, KUD, RA. Hans Braanedalen in Fredrikstad Branch in 1855 was a seal hunter. Mons Pedersen Journal, p. 8, 26 February 1855, holograph, LDS Church Archives. A. Olsen in Arendal Branch in 1867 was a sail maker. Saamund [Samuel] Gudmundsen Journal, 8 October 1867, holograph, LDS Church Archives. Oslo Conference President George M. Brown visited Mormons at Nes in Hedemarken on 6 August 1864, and stayed at Konningrud Farm. "As all were busy in the hay fields and there was no chance for doing anything among strangers," said Brown, "both Grundvig [Brown's companion] and I went into the hay field with Elder L. Konningrud and the Saints who labored for him, and we worked very hard all day and rejoiced in it also as it was a chance for showing people that we were not afraid to work." George Mortimer Brown Autobiography and Diary, p. 76, 6 August 1864, typescript, Library Services Division, Genealogical Department, The Church of Jesus Christ of Latter-day Saints, Salt Lake City, Utah. Ole Harmon Olsen (born 1847), a Mormon in Oslo, got a job about 1863 in "the manufacture and sale of a patented device for the cure of rheumatism. The mechanisms of this apparatus [were] two flat, smooth wooden slats held together by a chain." Olsen got the job "through the influence of some L.D.S. friends," and described himself as "very busy filling orders, the rheumatic cure being very popular." Ole Harmon Olsen, "Ole Harmon Olsen - Pioneer 1868," in *Our Pioneer Heritage*, comp. Kate B. Carter, vol. 12 (Salt Lake City, Utah: Daughters of the Utah Pioneers, 1969), p. 115. Olsen's brother, Johann A. Olsen, worked for the same company: ". . . [1866] laerte jeg at forfaerdige Gigt-kjaeder som er til at baere paa Kroppen for Gigtsygdomme og hvis Forretning dreves af A. Arnesen og P. Christiansen jeg [sic] arbeidede for Dem i Forening med min Broder Ole for dagloen. Efterlidt emigrerede De Broedre [Arnesen and Christiansen who were evidently Mormons] og Firmaet overdroges min Fader, P. Christensen og min Broder Ole. min [sic] Fader & Christensen, begyndte at reise paa Handel paa Vestlandet i Bergens Stift, i Trondhjems [Stift], og paa Nordland. . . ." Olsen and his father "begyndte derpaa at reise paa Handel tilsammen dog aldrig vi reiste i Foelge men en reiste i 5-8 Dage i Forveien med Bekjendtgjoerelser (Plakater) og bekjendtgjorde da at en saadan handlende kommer efter paa den Dag-og time. jeg [sic] reiste fordet [sic] meste med disse Avertissementer." At Haavin in Telemarken on 7 June 1868, Olsen noted: "Venter nu paa Messen i Kirken for at faa bekjentgjort mine Affairer." Johann August Olsen, "Levnetsloeb eller Livsbegivenheder af

Johan [sic] A. Olsen nedskrevet i Februar 1873" and Journal, pp. 7, 9, 12, holograph, LDS Church Archives. Some Mormons worked at home industries such as Brother Iversen in Skudesnaeshavn in 1867 who "caried [sic] on the shoomaker [sic] trade with two hands beside himself." Gudmundsen Journal, 2 November 1867. A Mormon (unnamed) in Drammen made brooms in his home in 1897. Johan L. George Johnson Diary, 2 March 1897, holograph, LDS Church Archives. Gustaf Andersen and wife, Mormons in Halden Branch, were managing a farm for fifty-five crowns a month when two missionaries--James Jensen and companion--visited them in 1908: "When we got there he [Andersen] was hauling in potatoes, which were dug by an American machine. Sister Andersen was tending the cows that were tied up, in the stable. We gave our washing to her." James Jensen Journal, p. 73, 19 October 1908, xerox of holograph, LDS Church Archives. Oslo Conference President Andrew Israelsen described Mormons in Aalesund in July 1892: "Those who had received the Gospel were not of the poorer class, but were fairly well-to-do. . . . I have never in my life been so filled with good food. . . ." Andrew M. Israelsen, Utah Pioneering: An Autobiography (Salt Lake City, Utah: Deseret News Press, 1938), p. 141. Mormon emigrant companies in the late 1880s and 1890s included a few white-collar workers--salesclerks, office clerks, trade agents, and secretaries--but these never comprised more than one or two percent of the emigrants. Emigrating Mormons in the years 1886-1897 also included a piano tuner and a cigar maker. Emigrant Protokoll, no. 13, 2/3 1886-28/5 1897, fols. 2-21, Reisekontroll, Christiania Politikammer, Statsarkivet, Oslo, Norway [hereinafter cited as SA]. Mormons in Drammen about the year 1902 included a locomotive engineer, a whale harpooner, a baker, a painter, tailors, carpenters, sailors and many workers at the planing mills. Interview with Einar Strand, Maurits Hansens Gate 4, Oslo 3, Norway, 7 March 1978. The fact that most Mormons in the 1920s and 1930s belonged to the Norwegian Labor Party [Arbeiderpartiet] suggests strong Mormon ties to the urban working-class population. Ibid.; Interview with Ramm George Parley Arveseter et al., Jacob Aalls Gate 17c, Oslo 3, Norway, 24 February 1978.

[17]Seljaas's study established occupations for 669 emigrants-- "about 30 percent of the total for the period." Seljaas, "Migration," p. 34.

[18]Ibid., pp. 34-35. Although "day laborers" were generally considered a cut below "artisans" or craftsmen, artisans usually earned less than factory hands during the 1870s and 1880s. Bull, Arbeiderklassen, p. 104. Mormons also included significant numbers of merchants, skippers, master craftsmen, and well-to-do farmers, especially in the 1850s when the onus attached to polygamy was not quite so widespread. Mormons in Fredrikstad, for example, although mostly employed in the wood products industry, included several members of the borgerstand [bourgeoisie] or established middle class during the 1850s and 1860s such as skippers Svend

Petter Larsen and Johan Andreas Jensen; merchants Hans Larsen, Carl Widerborg and Rasmus Christian Bruun; master shoemakers Johan Johansen (first president of Fredrikstad Branch) and Christian Hansen Fleischer; blacksmith Hans Larsen, and dyer Niels Th. Emil Larsen. Haakon A. Veel, Fredrikstad Handels-, haandverks- og skipperborgere i aarene 1600-1900 (Sarpsborg: Frank Vardings Trykkeri, 1953), pp. 11, 14, 43-44, 66, 80, 90. Policemen raided a Mormon meeting at Fredrikstad on 5 March 1854 and found the following persons assembled in "ropemaker Andersen's room": "Ropemaker [Anders] Andersen [age 44] with his wife [Petrea Pettersdatter, age 54] and a grown child named Caroline Frederikke [Andersen, age 17], Ane Marie Loekeberg [Loekkeberg, age 34, a non-Mormon, married to cotter Ole Hansen], shoemaker [Christian] Fleischer [age 39] and wife [Oline Hansdatter, age 39], beam hewer Hans Amundsen [age 31], married woman Elen Jensen [Andersdatter?, age 46], Johanne Olsdatter from Gulbrandsen's Loekke [age 25, married to cotter Ole Jensen Gulbrandsen's Loekke], shoemaker [Johan Frederik] Johnsen [Johansen, age 31] and wife [Elisabeth Olsen, age 26], Oline Hansdatter Moella [age 37, married to beam hewer Torger Gundersen], [spinster] Randine Larsdatter [age 32], spinster Karen Andersdatter [age 28], spinster Anne Andersdatter [age 28], Marthe Olsdatter and Simen [Fredrik] Halvorsen Halvorsroed [age 25] of Onsoee as also Andersen's apprentices, [Elias] Levo [born in Helsingborg, age 36] and [Johan August] Halstroem [probably a Swede]" [Rebslager Andersen med Kone og et voxent barn ved Navn Caroline Frederikke, Anne Marie Loekeberg, Skomager Fleischer og Kone, bjelkehugger Hans Amundsen, Konen Elen Jensen, Johanne Olsdatter paa Gulbrandsens Loekke, Skomager Johnsen og Kone Oline [sic] Hansdatter Moella, Randine Larsdatter, Pigen Karen Andersdatter, Anne Andersdatter, Marthe Olsdatter og Simen Halvorsen Halvorsroed fra Onsoee samt Rebslagersvend [sic] hos Andersen, Levo og Halstroem"]. Forhoersprotokol, no. 5, 1852-1857, 14, 16 March 1854, Fredrikstad By, SA; Forhoersprotokol, no. 1, 1854-1866, 17 August 1854, Tune Sorenskriveri, SA.

[19] Seljaas, "Migration," p. 25.

[20] Ibid., p. 27. "Among the non-farm element, craftsmen outnumbered common laborers." Bjork, Divide, p. 132. Mulder's survey of thirty-one emigrant companies from Scandinavia before 1900 revealed that: "Among the artisans, carpenters and related craftsmen like cabinetmakers, coopers, wheelwrights, joiners, turners, and carriagemakers made up a considerable group, 11 per cent of the reported occupations. . . . The next largest group of artisans were the tailors, seamstresses, dyers and weavers (7 per cent). Smiths--blacksmiths, ironfounders, coppersmiths, tinsmiths, and an occasional machinist--followed these (6 per cent), with shoemakers, tanners, saddle- and harness-makers almost as large a group (5.6 per cent), not far outnumbering stonecutters, masons, and bricklayers (4.5 per cent)." Mulder, "Ducklings," p. 240. In 1882, the S. S. Nevada Company from Scandinavia

"counted 12 per cent farmers [including small farmers, tenants, or agricultural laborers], 37 per cent laborers, and 16 per cent servant girls, reflecting a shift from rural to urban membership" among Scandinavian Mormons. Ibid., pp. 238-39.

[21]Canute Peterson to wives and children in Utah, 13 June 1872, Canute Peterson Collection, LDS Church Archives. C. C. N. Dorius described "very oppressive" ["meget trykkende"] conditions among members in Trondheim in 1862: "Hansen [a Mormon] is very impoverished, both as regards food and lodgings, a little cot [sic] where a Brother Eriksen sat and sewed, and made the room even more unpleasant--they hardly have anything to sleep on, except rags. The congregation numbers over 50 members, poor and dispersed." ["Hansen har det meget kleint, baade med Spise og Logis, et lille Kot, hvor en Broder Eriksen, sat og syede, og gjorde Vaerelset en mere uhyggelig - knapt har dem noget at ligge i, uden Filler. Menighedens Antal er over 50, Fattige og Adspredte."] Carl C. N. Dorius, "Dagbog: Carl C. N. Dorius's Missionsforretninger i Skandinavia, samt en kort Beretning om det tidligere Levnetsloeb," ca. 18 September 1862, holograph, LDS Church Archives. As early as 28 September 1852, Mormons in Risoer established a fund "for the benefit of the Poor." Christian J. Larsen Journal, vol. 2, p. 121, 28 September 1852, holograph and MS, LDS Church Archives. Mormons in Norway also discussed a general poor fund for needy Norwegian Mormons at council meetings in 1854. Hilmar Freidel, "Raadsmoeter i 125 aar," p. 1, xerox of typescript, Norway Office, Translation Services Department, The Church of Jesus Christ of Latter-day Saints, Moss, Norway. Mormon poor relief in Norway was very sporadic, however; there was no consistent fund-raising effort, and leaders employed stopgap measures and spur-of-the-moment collections to help the most destitute. Pedersen Journal, p. 39, 7 June 1857. Mormon Relief Societies held so-called "work meetings" such as those held each Monday at Bergen during the 1890s; female members sewed and knitted articles of clothing which were sold to benefit the poor. Relief Society funds also helped with meetinghouse rent and other branch expenses. Israelsen, Utah, p. 139.

[22]August Severin Schou Diary, trans. Lauritz G. Petersen, vol. 1, p. 24, 3 January 1877, xerox of typescript, LDS Church Archives.

[23]Ferdinand Friis Hintze Diary, vol. 1, p. 432, 1 August 1885, holograph, LDS Church Archives.

[24]John Johnson, "Reminiscences, 1899-1935," p. 31, xerox of holograph, LDS Church Archives.

[25]Israelsen, Utah, p. 148.

[26]Anders Olsen returned home "til sin hustru og sine 8 barn og fant dem sittende paa gulvet og spise noget mat av en

gryte og de hadde blott 2 skjeer aa spise med som de vekselvis lot gaa rundt efter tur. Politiet hadde nemlig tatt moeblene og kjoert til auksjon for aa dekke mulkten paa 10 daler, som Olsen var doemt til at betale." Carl M. Hagberg, Den Norske Misjons Historie (Oslo: Universal-trykkeriet, 1928), p. 29.

[27] Magleby Journal, 10-11, 15 January, 23 February 1858. At Vang in 1864, Oslo Conference President George M. Brown assisted an Inge Dyrsven, evidently a widow, to retain custody over her children "who were to be taken to other people to bring up as she was not able to support them." Brown Autobiography, p. 89, 13 October 1864. Svend Larsen visited a Sister Ekmand in Oslo in 1865 whose husband, a Mormon, "had left her unprovided for, with 2 sons and 2 daughters 3 years ago because of her reservations [about Mormon doctrine]" ["Hvis Mand havde efterladt hende uforsoergede, med 2 Soenner og 2 Doetre for 3 Aar siden formedelst hendes Vantroe"]. Svend Larsen Diary, 15 August 1865, holograph, LDS Church Archives.

[28] Historical Record, bk. E, 1900-1905, p. 31, Raadsmoede 25 June 1901, Christiania Branch, Christiania Conference, Scandinavian Mission, LDS Church Archives.

[29] Ibid., p. 87.

[30] "Konen laa fremdeles i Sengen doed fra den foregaaende Dag, og da de kun havde det ene Rum foruden et meget lille Kjoekken, havde de sovet i samme Vaerelsen om Natten, hvor Moderen laa Lig." Christiansen Journal, vol. 10, p. 172, 30 March 1916. Although poverty was the lot of most Norwegian Mormons, there were exceptions. Many of the most well-to-do members emigrated in the 1850s and 1860s leaving behind the poor, the widowed, and the aged. Ivar Isaacksson, a mechanic who owned a large shop (machine works) in Oslo, joined the Mormons in 1865, and George M. Brown described him as "one of the most influential men of the place," and as one who "occupies a prominent place in the community." Brown Autobiography, pp. 93-95; 1, 20 March, 5 April 1865. Olaus Johnsen lived with his parents at Elnes Homestead near Roeyken in the 1860s, in "a nice home" with "enough land to raise the necessary things of life." Olaus Johnsen Autobiography, p. 1, typescript, LDS Church Archives. E. Olsen's wife sold their home in Oslo in 1872 for 6,600 dollars before immigrating to Utah to be with her husband. Weibye Diary, vol. 4, p. 148, 28 September 1872. A Mormon named Isaksen in Brevik was a naval offical who lived in a government-furnished house in 1861. Gudmundsen Journal, 13 March 1861. A Mormon named Gundersen in Halden lived "upon a hill, in a white house, called the moon" in 1908. Jensen Journal, p. 68, 8 October 1908. Johann A. Olsen visited a rich Mormon at "Schwejgaardsgade #72, III," Oslo, in 1895, ate fried trout and "all kind of other good things," and drank "home made wine." "The man of the house," said Olsen, "a prominent Foreman on a large blacksmith & Foundry

establishment has recently joined the church. . . . Their home was in one of the most stylish buildings in the street with a view from one side over Ekeberg and on the other side over a pleasure Park below. a [sic] large Piano and Furniture, oil paintings & c [sic] were all in keeping with the fine Building . . . . After meal we engaged in some select singing. Prest. Christiansen is a good Tenor Singer Morck [sic] also a good singer an [sic] he played the Piano. Bro. Andersen & I also helped to fill up the quartette then followed a long conversation." Johann August Olsen Journal, pp. 60-61, 2 July 1895, typescript, Special Collections, Harold B. Lee Library, Brigham Young University, Provo, Utah. Christofer Iversen lived with his parents on prosperous Eek Farm near Lier in 1896, and described the slaughtering of lambs, rides in a horsedrawn sleigh, the visit of a traveling tailor who mended torn clothes, the visit of the Lutheran priest, berry-picking excursions in the nearby forest, and boat rides in a large oaken boat. Christofer Iversen Diary, 19 September, 3, 16 October, 2, 4 November 1896; microfilm of holograph, LDS Church Archives. Oluf K. Karlsen, a Mormon in Bergen, employed one hundred or more persons at his shoe factory ["Nordens Skofabrik"] in 1919, and was probably the man who paid more tithing than anyone in the mission. Christiansen Journal, 17-18 November 1919.

[31]Bull, Arbeiderklassen, p. 104.

[32]Pedersen Journal, pp. 45-46, 14 December 1857.

[33]Olsen, "Levnetsloeb," p. 4; Christopher Sigvarth Winge Autobiography, p. 1, microfilm of typescript, LDS Church Archives.

[34]Olsen, "Pioneer," pp. 112-13.

[35]Conrad Johan Zahl Hansen, A Glance at My Life (Provo, Utah: Scott Printing Company, 1971), p. 22.

[36]Ole Harmon Olsen (born in 1847) was a young boy when a cholera epidemic hit Oslo in 1853. Olsen's father moved his family to a farm called Jefsen in Nannestad and remained there until the epidemic was over. The family returned to Oslo, and Olsen noted "that many of our neighbors had died." Olsen, "Pioneer," pp. 110-11. Several Mormon children in Oslo died of the measles in 1861. Dorius, "Dagbog," 17 July, 11 November 1861. Missionaries Kjaer and Keller visited the Totland Family in Bergen in 1908 to find the Totland's daughter "laying dead on the bed" after a bout with measles. Kjaer Diary, p. 132, 14, 16 December 1908. Brother Totland's "2 yr. old boy died of diptheria [sic] at 2 P.M." exactly a month later. Ibid., p. 142, 14 January 1909. Samuel Gudmundsen described outbreaks of scarlet fever and measles in Oslo in 1867 which claimed two of Brother A. Weihe's children and one of Brother P. Christensen's children. Gudmundsen Journal, December 1867. Dorthe Mathiesen's child contracted a mouth disease in 1877, and infected the mother's breasts. Olaf Henrik

Nielsen Journal, vol. 2, 4 July 1877, holograph, LDS Church Archives.

   ³⁷". . . under bordet eller senga." Bull, Arbeiderklassen, p. 36. Oslo Conference President George M. Brown and companion overnighted with a Mormon family at Slitte Gaard near Fetsund in 1865, and described "so many bugs and lice that we could not sleep." Brown Autobiography, p. 90, 28 January 1865. President Hans J. Christiansen put off a visit to an old Sister named Straaberg in Oslo as long as possible in 1894 because "one ran the risk of being plagued with lice and scabies which infested her place" ["man resikerede at blive befaenget med Lus og Skab som der var fuldt af"]. Christiansen Journal, vol. 3, p. 83, 23 October 1894. Andrew Amundsen described a Mormon household at Madland near Stavanger in 1883 as follows: "When we reached nearly the sumitt, I asked the way of some folks living in an old log cabin and here was the very man we was looking for, but he did not seem to like it very well and when we got to where he lived I had never seen such a mess as we did in this house. The old lady was glad to se os [us], but she was so durty [sic] she looked as though she had not washed for months and the children to [sic] - and the house was swept a little and some of the muck cleared away from the middle of the floor. We poled [sic] of [off] our wet duds and tried to dry them, but as this was all the cloths we had, we had to dry them on our backs and we was wet nearly through. After a few questions being answered we got something to eat and that was potatocake, with pealings [sic] on the potatoes, for had they been peeled there would [have] been nothing left of them - as they was about as large as small marbles and this was mixed with a little coarse rye-meal -- and after eating, and in fact while eating, I had to pick the tater peeling from between my teeth and then we had a little sour milk to drink. I tried to teach them to be cleen [sic] and lern [sic] them to serve the Lord and thus I was busy all the time talking to them about the gospel. Finely [sic] the old man streched [sic] out on an old laungh [lounge] and while I was talking commenced snoring and I began talking to the children. They was as ignorant as young Indians - uncultured, and in fact they seemed to know nothing." Andrew Amundsen Journal, p. 55, 27 September 1883, typescript, LDS Church Archives.

   ³⁸Hammer, Historie, p. 222. O. H. Nielsen described the attic room inhabited by his parents--Mormons in Oslo City--about 1859: "In the middle of the floor was an oven, and it rained so [hard] that it (the water) seeped down through the roof so that the oven was ready to explode; and my mother lay sick in bed and shook with the cold, and we had to set dishes and cups on the bed to catch the water which ran down through the roof." ["Paa midten af gulvet stod en komfur, og det regnede saa at det (vandet) trengte ned gjennem taget saa at ovnen var naer ved at sprekke; og moder laa syg til sengs og skjalv af kulde,

og vi maatte sette fade og koppe i sengen til at modtage vandet som floed ned gjennem taget."] Neilsen Journal, vol. 2, 1881, n.p.

[39] Bull, Arbeiderklassen, pp. 164-66. The diet of husmenn [tenant farmers] throughout Norway is described by Ingrid Semmingsen, ed., Husmannsminner (Oslo: Tiden Norsk Forlag, 1961). Prior to about 1890, a tenant or dependent farmer's diet in Troendelag included as many as three servings of herring each day--both salt and cooked herring. Ibid., p. 79. Soup and potatoes, fish, soup, and evening porridge were also common daily fare. Ibid., pp. 78, 85. Cottagers in Oestlandet ate mostly herring, potatoes, and porridge; meat was only served on special occasions, and vegetables, eggs, and butter were not common fare. Ibid., pp. 202-03, 209, 212. Farmowners had a somewhat better dinner diet including brown cheese and margarine on Sunday; blood sausage or pickled pork with potatoes and milk gruel on Monday; salt mackerel and potatoes or barley gruel with stew on Tuesday; peas, pork, and salted meat on Wednesday; pancakes and leftover peas on Thursday; rice pudding on Friday; and herring, sweet soup, and potatoes on Saturday. Ibid., p. 220.

[40] Larsen, "Biographical Sketch," p. 17. Children were hardest hit, and Mormon chroniclers often agonized over privations endured by "the little ones": Maren Nielsen had no food in the house in 1859, and her infant son sucked her breasts "until the milk was mixed with blood" ["indtil melken var blandet med blod"]. Neilsen Journal, vol. 2, 1881. Four-year-old Carl Nielsen asked his impoverished parents "for a crumb of bread as large as his fingernail one night as he got into bed [at Oslo in 1860], and when [his] mother answered that she didn't have it, . . . asked if he might have some salt to eat so that he could become thirsty and thus drink water." ["Min broder (Carl), bad kun om en smule broed saa stor som sin negel en aften da han gik iseng og da moder svarede hun intet havde, bad han om han maatte noget salt at spise saaat han kunde blive toerst og saa drikke vand."] Ibid., 1886. Oslo Conference President Hans J. Christiansen blessed a Sister Olsen's child at Oslo on 26 October 1885 and learned "that this poor woman, after giving birth, had lived on salt and bread" ["at denne Stakkels Kone efter sin Barselseng havde levet paa Salt og Broed"]. Christiansen Journal, vol. 1, 26 October 1885.

[41] Dorius, "Dagbog," 19 August 1862. Farm products indigenous to Norway, although not generally available, included "wheat, rye, barley, oats, potatoes, squash, beets [and] carrots." Brown Autobiography, p. 121, 7 October 1865.

[42] Ibid.

[43] Ibid., p. 84, 14 October 1864.

[44] Iversen Diary, 9 March 1895.

[45] Johnson Diary, 25 July 1897.

[46] Kjaer Diary, p. 143, 18 January 1909.

[47] Iversen Diary, 8 January 1895.

[48] Ibid., 14 July 1895.

[49] Ibid., 26 December 1895.

[50] Edward C. Ekman Diary, 14 November 1906, holograph, LDS Church Archives.

[51] Iversen Diary, 2 February 1895.

[52] Ekman Diary, 24 December 1905.

[53] Kjaer Diary, p. 81, 9 September 1908.

[54] Olsen Journal, pp. 141-42, 8 June 1906.

[55] Johnson Diary, 2 December 1895.

[56] Olsen Journal, pp. 56-57, 29 June 1895.

[57] Johnson Diary, 9 February 1896.

[58] Jensen Journal, p. 69, 11 October 1908.

[59] Brown Autobiography, p. 84, 15 October 1864.

[60] Bull, *Arbeiderklassen*, p. 166.

[61] Semmingsen, *Husmannsminner*, p. 213.

[62] Ibid., pp. 182, 213.

[63] Olsen, "Pioneer," p. 113.

[64] John Van Cott Diary, vol. 4, 3 May 1862, xerox of holograph, LDS Church Archives.

[65] Iversen Diary, 14 September 1894. C. J. Zahl Hansen, a thirteen-year-old boy on the Arctic Island of Kvitvaer, saw his first telephone at a hospital in 1896: "I noticed a nurse make a long-distance call over the telephone, and she was as much surprised to get an answer as was I. How words can travel along a wire has always been a mystery. . . ." Hansen, *Glance*, p. 19.

[66] *Skandinaviens Stjerne* 59 (1 March 1910):79.

[67] Jens Arup Seip, <u>Utsikt over Norges historie</u>, vol. 1: <u>Tidsrommet 1814-ca. 1860</u> (Oslo: Gyldendal Norsk Forlag, 1974), p. 139.

[68] Jens Arup Seip, <u>Tanke og handling i norsk historie</u> (Oslo: Gyldendal Norsk Forlag, 1968), p. 27. Christian Knudsen of Ringsaker was fifteen years old before he saw his first train in June 1872 at Eidsvold: "I was struck with wonder for I had never seen a trane [sic] befor [sic] I did not know wat [sic] to think of it seeing all them Tracks and how the Trane coul [could] get from one Track to another But we borded [sic] the Trane and way we went and was soon to Christiania. . . ." Christian Knudsen Autobiography, p. 14, holograph, LDS Church Archives.

[69] Larsen, "Extracts," p. 6.

[70] Ten Mormons in Drammen rented a sled for travel to Sunday meeting in Roervik in 1855. Niels Christian Poulsen Journal, 26 December 1855, holograph, LDS Church Archives. President J. C. A. Weibye described "the Thomsons Steam Road-Locomotive No. 2085" at the town of Lillehammer in 1871; the locomotive was "expected to run regular from Lille Hammer and about 50 mile up Gudbrands Valley." The locomotive "cost the owner between 4 and 5000$. bought from Amerika," but the owner was not completely satisfied because the locomotive had "to [sic] little steampower." Weibye Diary, vol. 4, p. 6, 31 July 1871. Bicycles greatly increased missionary and member mobility after about 1906. Ekman Diary, 4, 12 July 1906. Members and missionaries also enjoyed motorboat rides on Oslo Fjord in the summer of 1908. Jensen Journal, pp. 24-25; 19, 23 June 1908.

[71] Israelsen, <u>Utah</u>, p. 101.

[72] Gudmundsen Journal, 27 October 1867.

[73] Israelsen, <u>Utah</u>, p. 147.

[74] "Der kan dog fornemmeligt kun blive virket om Sommeren omkring i Fjordene, da det er nok saa vanskeligt at komme omkring i moerke og mulm som da om Vinteren hersker saavel Nat som Dag eller rettere Dag, som Nat." Christiansen Journal, vol. 3, p. 39, ca. 7 July 1894.

[75] Knudsen Autobiography, p. 34.

[76] Dorius, "Dagbog," 8 January 1862. Steamboat travel was slow and tedious, especially for those, like Oslo Conference President George M. Brown in 1864, who could not afford sleeping cabins. "I did not feel overly well as I was much fatigued," said Brown, "not having slept any for three nights, as I had deck passage and there was no chance for sleeping there being

so many drunken people on board." Brown Autobiography, p. 75, 8 July 1864.

[77] Gudmundsen Journal, 12 March 1868.

[78] "Den uendelige Maengde Fjorde, Bugter og Soeer gjoer Seilads noedvendig, og Broedrene ere i Almindelighed sjaelden forsynede med Reisepenge." Skandinaviens Stjerne 20 (15 June 1871): 284. O. C. Larsen, Fredrikstad Branch President, traveled from Moss to Fredrikstad in December 1859, and "waded through deep snow for twenty-one miles reaching Ole Gundersen's place in the evening nearly exhausted." Larsen, "Biographical Sketch," p. 26. Oslo Conference President George M. Brown and companion took a difficult journey on foot from Romerike to Hedemarken on 12 January 1864: "We had a very rough time as the snow was deep and the forest very thick and interspersed with hollows, canyons, and cliffs of rock. More than once Grundtvig fell enough to break his neck." Brown Autobiography, 12 January 1864. Brown gave the following account of a trip from Halden to Fredrikstad in 1865 by horse-drawn sled: "The wind blew and the snow was drifted up as high as the houses in many places. . . . The snow which had fallen to a considerable depth during the night and the previous day, now drifted on account of the wind and the road was so full that we could not pass and were obliged to drive around through the fields and often we plunged into snow banks which entirely concealed our view, horses and all as well." Ibid., p. 92, 20 February 1865. Samuel Gudmundsen described a journey on skis from Krageroe to Jernnaes in January 1861: ". . . saa gik je til Tobakmanden og fik mine Skie og saa tog dom paa Axla, gik saa ned paa Vandet, gik saa omkring Byen [Krageroe] paa Isen over en Raak, bortigjennem til en Oei og saa gik je ind i et Huus og spurgte Vegen da je inte var rigtig sikker. Og saa gik je mig ned paa Isen igjen, gik saa omkring et Fjel paa Isen bort over et langt Stykke til je kom imot Land og da kom je til 2. Veier, . . . og inte viste enten je skulde tage til hoegre eller til venstre; men saa tog je til venstre og det var naa rigtig au, saa kom je til en Gaard som Folk kalte Eiet. Saa var je inde i Huset der og kjoebte mig lidt Melk og den drak je op, og saa laante je en hamar og bankede en Bloeig i Skiet mit for Bandet i det var loest, gik saa derfra bort over et Vand, saa over en liten Skog, saa paa et Vand igjen som gik i mange Krokar og Svingar omkring Tjoeli, saa je taengte sometider at je aller [sic] kom til Folk meer. Moerkt var det, og Skog var der omkring mig og je taenkte sametier at den var ful af Skrubbar. Men ret som det var at je gik paa Skie i fullende Fart, saa begynte det at suse og dure, og je taenkte: naa kommer Skrubane, Men saa taenkte je de fik saa gjoera, og je gik mig laenger fram og med et stod der ligesom et stort Hugu af en Roese (Bjergetrol) med gloande Ougur i, men som eg gik mig laenger fram saa saa jeg at det var Qvaernhuset paa Jernnaes, og saa blev eg gla." Gudmundsen Journal, 22 January 1861.

Chapter VIII

[1]Helge Seljaas, "The Mormon Migration from Norway" (M.A. thesis, University of Utah, 1972), pp. 91-92. Despite the onus attached to polygamy, many Mormons were on excellent terms with non-Mormon relatives and friends. Canute Peterson, for example, spent several days "visiting with relatives and friends and with godfather's and God Mother's" at Maurset in Eidfjord in 1854. Canute Peterson et al., "Story of the life of Canute Peterson as given by himself and by some members of his family," p. 70, xerox of MS, Library-Archives, The Church of Jesus Christ of Latter-day Saints, Salt Lake City, Utah [hereinafter cited as LDS Church Archives]. Family ties were still going strong nearly twenty years later as witness Peterson's statement in December 1871 that "My Folks writs [sic] that if I can com and pay them a visit at Christmas it will be the happyest time thay everhad [sic] in their livs Cousin John says it was as a vois from the Dead to hear from me again. . . ." Canute Peterson to wives and children in Utah, 25 December 1871, Canute Peterson Collection, LDS Church Archives. Non-Mormon relatives frequently attended Mormon meetings. Mons Pedersen Journal, pp. 16-18, 3 February, 2 March 1856, holograph, LDS Church Archives. Non-Mormon relatives constituted the bulk of the congregation at Fredrikstad Branch on 4 December 1887 when thirty-five persons attended Mormon meeting, "of which," according to missionary J. A. Hendricksen, "about 10 or 12 were members and the balance my relatives." John Anthon Hendricksen Diary, vol. 1, p. 54, 4 December 1887, microfilm of holograph, LDS Church Archives. Hendricksen's relatives also gave him a good send-off a year later: "I went to the pier where there were present the following of my relatives: Cousins Eliza (who gave me a nice boquet & card) Hansine (with oranges and traveling danties [sic]) Gunborg (a nice card), Uncle Carl and wife (with K. 1,00 money) Auntie Nettie (eatables and 2 Krs in cash) (and K 1,00 from her daughter Augusta who could not come on the pier) . . . ." Ibid., p. 155, 15 May 1889. Andrew Israelsen returned to his native Kasfjord in 1892 after an absence of nearly thirty years to find that he was "very kindly received by the people in Kastfjorden. Because they held my parents in very high esteem, if for no other reason, the people treated me very courteously. At no time did they refuse to allow me to hold a [Mormon] meeting in a house if I asked that privilege." Andrew M. Israelsen, _Utah Pioneering: An Autobiography_ (Salt Lake City, Utah: Deseret News Press, 1938), p. 106. When Israelsen asked Ole Engebretsen, his mother's stepfather, for permission to hold a meeting, Engebretsen replied: "Yes, you may have it, and more than that, if you will send for your wife and children I will give you this house and farm. All I ask is that you

let me live here with you until I die, and that won't be long, as I am now nearly eighty years old." Ibid., pp. 115-16.

[2] Edward C. Ekman Diary, 15 August 1906, holograph, LDS Church Archives.

[3] Carl C. N. Dorius, "Dagbog: Carl C. N. Dorius's Missionsforretninger i Skandinavia, samt en kort Beretning om det tidligere Levnetsloeb," 3die Pindsedag 1861, holograph, LDS Church Archives.

[4] Torkel E. Torkelson, "En Kort Beskrivelse af Mit Livs Historie skrevet af mig selv," vol. 1, p. 42, ca. 1880, holograph, LDS Church Archives. Some Mormons soured relationships with relatives by displaying "preachiness," i.e., feeling it their duty "to testify to everybody" and condemn the general populace as "blind as far as religion was concerned." Oluf Christian Larsen, "A Biographical Sketch of the life of Oluf Christian Larsen dictated by himself and written by his son Oluf Larsen dedicated to his posterity who might desire to read it," p. 12, xerox of typescript, LDS Church Archives.

[5] ". . . jeg saa en Slange, omtrent 3 Alen lang, som vilde sprude Forgift paa mig, men jeg tog op min Follekniv og stak den igjennem Slangens Hode, og derpaa flaade jeg alt Skindet af den." Svend Larsen Diary, p. 39, 26 October 1853, holograph, LDS Church Archives.

[6] "[Jeg droemte] at jeg var paa et Norsk Fartoei og . . . forlod jeg Fartoeiet og begav mig ind i Landet, Efter at jeg havde besoegt adskillige Huse, begyndte Folk at forfoelge mig. fra alle Kanter, endeel kom roende og andre gik og loeb indtil en stor Skare var forsamlet, og jeg stod mig iblandt dem. . . . Herren gav mig Frimodighed og Kraft Og jeg Praediket for dem, alle stod stille og hoerte til min Tale, og da jeg havde slutet gik alle i Fred." Ibid., p. 40, 18 October 1853.

[7] Niels Christian Poulsen Journal, 28 November 1855, holograph, LDS Church Archives.

[8] Ibid., 16 October 1857.

[9] George Mortimer Brown Autobiography and Diary, p. 55, 6 March 1864, typescript, Library Services Division, Genealogical Department, The Church of Jesus Christ of Latter-day Saints, Salt Lake City, Utah. Torkel Torkelson dreamed of confronting the Devil himself: "Under denne Henrykkelse forekom det mig, at en Mand tog mig hen til en skjoen og hoei Plads og der talte denne man til mig, at jeg skulde forsoege og tage en ualmindelig smuk Fugl med Rede, som var ikke hoeiere fra Jorden, end jeg godt kunde raekke det. Jeg gjorde Forsoeg men fandt at jeg ikke kunde raekke Fuglen og Redet. Da jeg saa, at det flyttede sig, vilde jeg ikke have noget med denne Mand at skaffe, men da

jeg vilde undvige, saa var mandens Skikkelse forvandlet til en grum Bjoern. Jeg anstraengte alle mine Krafter [sic] for bleve [sic] fri dette Vaesen, men kunde ikke. I denne Stilling kom Herren mig til Hjaelp, idet disse Ord bleve lagde i min Mund- 'I Jesu af Nasarets Navn, og ved Praestedoemmets Fulmagt og Myndighed Byder jeg dig at fare hen.' --Og Fristeren maatte forsvinde og det vistes som en Straale af Ild og Roeg efter ham. Jeg kom ogsaa bort fra den Plads og kom til mit Legeme igjen, og da kunde min Hustru vaekke mig." Torkelson, "Beskrivelse," vol. 1, pp. 25-26.

[10] Baptismal candidates usually answered several questions: "Do you believe that God has restored His Gospel through revelation?"; "Is it your intention to be baptized by immersion and arise and enter into a new life?"; "Do you believe Mormon priests have full authority to baptize in the name of Christ?" Ole Hendriksen Berg Diary, vol. 1, pp. 18-19, 29 February 1864, holograph, LDS Church Archives. Mormons in Norway also practiced "rebaptism for renewal of convenants" as late as 1904 as per Hendricksen Diary, vol. 2, p. 79, 11 January 1904, and the practice was especially widespread on the heels of the "Utah Reformation" of 1856 and 1857. Canute Peterson Journal, 4 August 1853, holograph, LDS Church Archives; Hans Peter Lund Journal, vol. 1, p. 48, 4 April 1857, holograph, LDS Church Archives; Hans Olsen Magleby Journal, 15 February, 4 April 1857, 8 August 1858, 27 January 1859, holograph, LDS Church Archives; Pedersen Journal, pp. 35-38, 5, 12 April, 3, 10, 13 May 1857; Johan L. George Johnson Diary, 3 April 1897, holograph, LDS Church Archives.

[11] Hans Jacob Christiansen Journal, vol. 3, p. 86, 28 October 1894, holograph, LDS Church Archives; Andrew Jenson Diary, bk. J, p. 620, 24 April 1911, holograph and typescript, LDS Church Archives. The baptismal font room in the new building at Oesterhausgade 27, Oslo, in 1907, contained a painting depicting John the Baptist baptizing Jesus Christ, and various "paintings of land scaps [sic] and trees." Ekman Diary, 23 April 1907. An earlier font, located in the cellar of the older building on the same property, was dedicated on 28 October 1894. It was constructed of bricks and cement, was filled from a water pipe, and was equipped with a drain. Christiansen Journal, vol. 3, p. 86, 28 October 1894. Missionaries purchased "a beautiful baptismal font made of iron" for 185 crowns in 1911, and placed it in the Trondheim Branch meetinghouse. Jenson Diary, bk. J, p. 620, 24 April 1911.

[12] Carl Kjaer Diary, p. 314, 14 March 1910, holograph, LDS Church Archives.

[13] Peterson, "Story," p. 57.

[14] Poulsen Journal, 24 November 1857; Ferdinand Friis Hintze Diary, vol. 1, p. 401, 11 July 1885, holograph, LDS Church Archives;

Dorius, "Dagbog," 23 July 1862; Israelsen, Utah, p. 132. C. C. N. Dorius described an idyllic scene on 15 July 1862 near Stokkesund where he baptized Knud Simondsen and wife at 1:00 A.M.: "Under det behagelige Himmelblaae omgivet af den stille blanke Soee, i hvis Flade Maaned synes at bade sig, gjorende [sic] vort Nattetog til en Behagelighed, ankom vi til 'Siktesoee' hvor Kund og Kones lille Hytte kneisede frem bag det nagne Fjeld--Kl 1 om Natten, Efter Taksigelse for Dagen--gik jeg udenfor Huset steeg need i den klare Soee, og doebte dem begge i Jesu Christi Navn." Dorius, "Dagbog," 15 July 1862.

[15] Johnson Diary, 5 May 1896.

[16] Christofer Iversen Diary, 12 July 1895, microfilm of holograph, LDS Church Archives.

[17] Iversen rode "paa en syg Hest tilhoerende hans Huusbonde og under dette hoerte han, at der paa Krageroesiden i Fuglevigbugten var megen Tale som om der holdtes Praediken. Der var paa den Tid moerkt saaledes at Dpt ikke kunne see over til Stedet. Hvad der blev foretaget veed Dpt ikke at opgive. Omtrent kl. 2 til den anfoerte Nat kom der roende en Baad fra Fuglevigbugten der lagde i Land ved Vaterland hvori efter Udseende var en 5 a 6 Personer." Forhoersprotokol, no. 5, 1852-1857, fols. 18-19, Extraret 10 May 1853, Fredrikstad By, Statsarkivet, Oslo, Norway [hereinafter cited as SA].

[18] According to William Mulder: ". . . conversion answered a variety of needs rational and emotional felt by the dispossessed looking for a place to belong, the worldly ready for moral reformation, the dissenter unsatisfied by the established creed or piqued with the clergy, the scriptural literalist looking for fulfillment of prophecy. Many were ripe for a spiritual experience, so many Bunyans earnestly seeking their grace abounding." William Mulder, "Utah's Ugly Ducklings: A Profile of the Scandinavian Immigrant," Utah Historical Quarterly 23 (July 1955):249-50. Reasons for disaffection with the State Church included allegations that priests were not interested in common people and pandered only to the rich. O. C. Larsen, later a Mormon convert, was confirmed a Lutheran at Drammen about 1849, and recalled that "the priest seemed satisfied with the answers to his questions, which were not many to me. I sometimes thought he had other reasons for not asking me many questions, for being a poor man's son he could not consistently place me at the head of the class on the day of confirmation when there were so many sons of rich men to be confirmed." Larsen, "Biographical Sketch," p. 5. In 1874, three Lutheran priests visited a widow in Larvik and commanded her to stop allowing Mormon meetings in her home. Her reply was to the point: "When I was sick and poor, you never came to me; now I do not need you." ["Da jeg var syg og fattig, kom De aldrig til mig; nu behoever jeg Dem ikke."] Andrew Jenson, "Erindringer Fra Missionen i Skandinavien," Morgenstjernen 3

(1 October 1884):289-90. According to the Census of 1855, Oslo had a population of 31,715. The entire city comprised only one Lutheran parish staffed by five priests. Of these, one was the Cathedral Dean who largely concerned himself with administrative duties, a second was the military chaplain, and a third was assigned to the prison population. This left two priests to meet the needs, both spiritual and physical, of the population at large. Ola Rudvin, <u>Indremisjonsselskapets Historie</u>, vol. 1: <u>Den Norske Lutherstiftelse 1868-1891</u> (Oslo: Lutherstiftelsens Forlag, 1967), p. 215.

[19]"Dersom de folk i Piperviken og paa Ruseloekbakken, som have viist sig saa ligegyldige for verdslig laesning, havde viist en modsvarende iver for forstandig og betaenksom laesning af sine religioese skrifter, saa skulde visselig ikke netop Ruseloekbakken have vaeret det sted, hvor mormonerne have faaet mest indgang. Men jeg mener, det kan ansees som en kjendsgjerning for vort lands vedkommende, at mormonismens urimeligheder i det hele taget kun have fundet tiltro, hos saadanne, som ikke alene have vaeret lidet befaestede i religioes henseende, men som tillige have vaeret saare lidet oevede i laesning og taenkning og i hoei grad blottede for almindelig oplysning." Eilert Sundt, <u>Om Piperviken og Ruseloekbakken: Undersoegelser om arbeidsklassens kaar og saeder i Christiania</u> (Oslo: Tiden Norsk Forlag, 1968), p. 53.

[20]Seljaas, "Migration," p. 17. Whether by study at home or attendance at school, some Mormons obtained a comparatively wide-ranging education. Thus M. H. Knudsen described his grandfather, Hans Knudsen (1819-1891) of Loeiten in Hedemarken, as follows: "Grandfather was a lay-Preacher of the Lutheran Church before accepting the Gospel [Mormonism]. He was a well-read man, a student and a scholar. After he died . . . I came across some of his library books. Among them were books on Psychology, Phrenology, History, Astronomy and Political Science." Milton Herman Knudsen Autobiography, pp. 2-3, xerox of typescript, LDS Church Archives. Andrew Amundsen (born in Oslo on 17 May 1849) described his education as follows: "I started to read when very young. At four years olde I could read a little, and at seven I could read moste eney boock. In the class, I lerned to write very fast. At ten years olde I could write a better hand than I can today. I allways tried to tend my lessons, and this is how I made progress. Father sent me then to a better, a private School where I made good progress. . . . When I was ten and until I was twelve years olde, I was cept [kept] at a Private School -- and the Teacher was an olde graheaded clark of a Sertain Pastor in the Part of that Town. He had several of os [us] Boys in the Sunday Service to sing to the Organ, and then efter [after] services we had to sing for children's christenings and marriages likewise the beriels [burials]." Andrew Amundsen Journal, pp. 1-2, typescript, LDS Church Archives. Others, such as Torkel Torkelson in Stavanger, hired their own

teachers: "Vintermaanederne for 1870-71 og 72 gik jeg i Skole. Vi var omtrint [sic] 40 unge Maend, 20 a 22 Aar, som forenede os om at sende for og loenne 2 af de dygtigste Laerere, som vi kunde faae for Penge. De Fag, som vi tog, og som vi troede mest nyttig var. Lov. Geomotri [sic]. Geografi. Skrivning. Regning. Gramatik. lit Landmaaling. Det hjalp os saameget at vi kunde idet mindste se til vort eget Vel." Torkelson, "Beskrivelse," vol. 1, pp. 9-10. Most Mormons, however, were educated at home or in common grammar schools. Thus O. H. Nielsen (born in Oslo in 1858) learned to read the Bible at home, and had only twenty days of formal education. Olaf Henrik Nielsen Journal, vol. 2, 1870, holograph, LDS Church Archives. Olaus Johnson (born at Roeken in 1833) recorded that "until I was eight years old my time was spent with my mother at home. Mother used to spin fish nets for father, and while working at this, she taught us children, this being the only education we had." Olaus Johnson Autobiography, p. 1, typescript, LDS Church Archives. Born in Drammen about 1836, O. C. Larsen first attended school at age thirteen, being "obliged to attend school half a day and work the other half. The teacher being very partial took little notice of a poor man's son, but in a rough and unsympathetic manner demanded the lessons necessary for us to learn before we could be confirmed [in the Lutheran Church]. These lessons . . . were brief historical sketches from the Bible, selections from the Psalms and the Catechism. This was an easy task for me for by reading my lessons a couple of times I knew them by heart. I therefore had plenty [of] time to play." Larsen, "Biographical Sketch," p. 4. Born the son of a drayman in Oslo in 1849, Johann A. Olsen began attending school in 1855 "hos, A. Bjuge oestre Sagene Sandagerveien hvor jeg undervistes i almindelig Almues underviisning: Religion, Laesning, Skrivning og Regning." Johann August Olsen, "Levnetsloeb eller Livsbegivenheder af Johan [sic] A. Olsen nedskrevet i Februar 1873" and Journal, vol. 1, pp. 1-2, holograph, LDS Church Archives. Olsen's brother, Ole H. Olsen (born in Oslo in 1847), attended a common grammar school about 1855: "I mastered fractions that year, studied reading, writing, language, history, anatomy and religion. I memorized the prescribed Lutheran State Church questions and answers on the Ten Commandments, the Lord's Prayer, Sacrament of Baptism, Sacrament of the Lord's Supper and Bible History. Our lesson assignment for each day had to be committed to memory and recited orally." Later--about 1860--Olsen attended school only twice a week: "On school days, I worked from 5 a.m., until 7:30 a.m., then ran home, changed clothes and ran to school. I remained in school from 8 a.m. until 2:30, then ran home, changed clothes and went to work in the factory until 7:15 p.m. During this time I earned $1.25 per week, the factory docked us one-fourth day on each school day." Ole Harmon Olsen, "Ole Harmon Olsen - Pioneer 1868," in <u>Our Pioneer Heritage</u>, comp. Kate B. Carter, vol. 12 (Salt Lake City, Utah: Daughters of the Utah Pioneers, 1969), pp. 112-13. Many Mormons from rural areas, such as Christian Knudsen from Ringsaker (born on 24 September

1856), received only sporadic schooling: "At the Age of 7 sevn [sic] years old i [sic] was sent to school but that was only in the winter but I could only go Every forth week. I went that way thill [until] i was 14 years Old." Christian Knudsen Autobiography, p. 1, holograph, LDS Church Archives. Some Mormons, of course, had no formal education. Carl J. E. Fjeld (born in 1825 at Drammen), the first Mormon in Oslo, was entirely unschooled: "My parents being very poor, my opportunities for gaining even the rudiments of an education, were quite out of the question. My father, being given to drink, left the burden of providing for the family, which consisted of four children, almost entirely upon my Mother. Consequently, we were many times short of food." Andrew Fjeld, A Brief History of the Fjeld-Fields Family (Springville, Utah: Art City Publishing Co., 1946), p. 7.

[21] Mulder, "Ducklings," p. 237. That description would apply to Mormons such as Mons Pedersen Orli of Onsoe or Carl Widerborg, a Swede who joined the Mormons in Norway. Born on 9 May 1821, Orli became a schoolteacher in Onsoe when only sixteen years old (1838). Anton Fredrik Christian Stabell, parish priest in Onsoe, testified in 1852 that Orli had been a diligent teacher, and that his students had exhibited noteworthy progress. Extraret paa Kjoelbergbroe under Tunoee Sorenskriveri, 1 October 1852, MS copy, Mormonpakken, Trossamfunn Samling [hereinafter cited as TS], Det kongelige Justis- og Politidepartement, Oslo, Norway [hereinafter cited as JPD]. Widerborg taught at the Solie Sawmill School ["Brugets faste Skole paa Solie Brug"] near Fredrikstad for ten years during the 1840s. Forhoersprotokol, no. 9, 9/12 1852-16/12 1857, pp. 70-71, 6 March 1854, Drammen By, Politimesterensarkiv, Tinghuset, Drammen, Norway [hereinafter cited as PA]. Widerborg was described as "perhaps the ablest public speaker which the Scandinavian Mission has produced." Andrew Jenson, History of the Scandinavian Mission (Salt Lake City, Utah: Deseret News Press, 1927), p. 128.

[22] O. C. Larsen described Lutheran confirmation as a declaration of independence of sorts: "With great satisfaction mingled with anxiety, all looked forward to the day of confirmation as the time when we should be subject to nobody and entirely independant [sic] when parents, priests, teachers and masters had no right to order or command us. As a general thing at the age of confirmation [about age fifteen or sixteen] the young men had decided on their ideal occupation, some choosing the sea, some the army, some business and some one thing and some another." Larsen, "Biographical Sketch," p. 5.

[23] Torkelson, "Beskrivelse," vol. 1, p. 5.

[24] Anthon L. Skanchy, A Brief Autobiographical Sketch of the Missionary Labors of a Valiant Soldier for Christ, trans. and ed. John A. Widtsoe (n.p., 1915; reprint ed., n.p., 1966), p. 2.

[25] Larsen, "Biographical Sketch," pp. 1, 10.

[26] Fjeld, Brief History, p. 14.

[27] "[Ole Ellingsen] . . . forklarede, at han var tilstaede ved de Praedikener som bleve holdte paa Kjoelbergbroe og Kjaevelsroed; dette gav Anledning til at han laeste i Bibelen og fandt at det var stemmende med hvad der passerede i Christi Tid at Menneskene bleve doebte paa saadan Maade, hvorfor han besluttede sig til, at lade sig gjendoebe." Extraret, 1 October 1852, Mormonpakken, TS, JPD.

[28] "Dpt har ikke vaeret overtalt til at lade sig doebe eller meddele Nadveren, hvorimod hun ved at lese det ny [sic] Testemente er kommen til Overbeviisning om, at det var rigtig." Avskrift av Extraret paa Fredrikstads Raadstue, 11 October 1852, Mormonpakken, TS, JPD.

[29] "Dpt bragtes foerste Gang til at gaae over til Mormonernes Tro ved at hoere en Samtale i Arresten mellem Amtmanden og Olsen hvorunder Sidstnaevnte ytrede at det ikke var en Tyddel af Guds Ord overeenstemende med Daab og Nadveren i Bibelen, og fandt dette rigtig ved at anstille Undersoegelse i Bibelen." Forhoersprotokol, no. 5, 1852-1857, fol. 19, 11 May 1853, Fredrikstad By, SA. Johannes Johnsen Selvigen, age thirty-four, a Swede, was present when Hans Larsen from Oslo, the first Mormon to visit Hurum Clerical District, preached in the summer of 1854. Larsen discussed the Bible with Selvigen from the Mormon point of view, and Selvigen, who had previously "occupied himself a great deal with the reading of non-controversial writings" ["befattet sig meget med Laesning af rolig [sic] Skrifter"], began for the first time to entertain doubts about his Lutheran faith. These doubts increased, and he was baptized a Mormon in February 1855. Forhoersprotokol, no. 4, 1851-1861, 21 February 1855, Lier, Roeyken og Hurum sorenskriveri, SA. Olea Hansdatter, age thirty-two, a servant girl in Drammen, joined the Mormons in January 1858. She "was moved to accept Mormonism by participating in their meetings . . . as also by reading in the New Testament." ["Angl. er bevaeget til Overgang til Mormonerne ved Deeltagelse i deres Forsamlinger . . . samt ved Laesning i det nye Testamente."] Forhoersprotokol, no. 12, 13/2 1858-29/10 1861, fol. 11, 5 March 1858, Drammen By, PA.

[30] Karen Andrea Nielsdatter attended Mormon meetings at Kjoelbergbroe and Kjaevelsroed, "og ved de der holdte Foredrag opstod der en indre Trang hos hende til at lade sig doebe, uden hvilket hun antog ikke at kunde blive salig." Avskrift av Forhoeret paa Kjoelbergbroe under Tunoee Sorenskriveri, 29 September 1852, Mormonpakken, TS, JPD.

[31] ". . . i den Tanke at det skulde virke heldigt paa ham som Synder, var det at han lod sig doebe, hvortil han ikke af Nogen blev opmuntret." Ibid.

[32]"[Berthe Jacobsdatter] forklarede, at hun var forligt med sin Gud og derfor lod sig doebe for at erholde sine Synders Forladelse, hvorhos Deponentinden anfoerte at Bibelen [sic]: 'Uden at vaere foedt paany' kan man ikke erholde sine Synders Forladelse." Ibid.

[33]Ibid.

[34]". . . Alt er Skeed, fordi hun ikke paa anden Maade antog at kunne erholde Fred, da hun foelte sig urolig baade Nat og Dag." Avskrift av Extraret paa Fredrikstads Raadstue, 11 October 1852, Mormonpakken, TS, JPD. O. C. Larsen wrote about a nineteen-year-old woman from Onsoe who contracted typhoid fever in 1860: "She had attended nearly all our meetings and had heard enough to understand that if she died in her condition it would not be good for her. This so worked on her mind that she told her father and wanted to be baptized [a Mormon] immediately." Larsen, "Biographical Sketch," p. 27. Larsen himself first heard about the Mormons in 1854 from a friend in Drammen. The friend told him that one of the quotations used by Mormons in their sermons was: "They that believe and are baptized shall be saved and They that believeth not shall be damned." Said Larsen: "These words made such an impression on the man's mind that he could not forget. . . . I listened with great attention to what he had to say and when he quoted the words of the Savior a peculiar uneasy feeling fell upon me." Ibid., p. 8. Similar experiences were common among early converts to Mormonism in England according to Malcolm R. Thorp, "The Religious Background of Mormon Converts in Britain, 1837-52," *Journal of Mormon History* 4 (1977):55: "In addition to Biblical fundamentalism, the theological issue that was of major concern to many individuals was fear of eternal torment. . . . To many, the traditional view of the horrible punishment awaiting the wicked in a hell of fire and brimstone could not be reconciled with Biblical passages that emphasized universal salvation. But, while hell was brought into question, the doctrine created considerable anxiety and doubt."

[35]Christopher Sigvarth Winge Autobiography, p. 1, microfilm of typescript, LDS Church Archives.

[36]Fjeld, *Brief History*, p. 15. The first Norwegian to convert to Mormonism in Scandinavia, Svend Larsen of Risoer, was surprised that so few accepted his testimony of Mormonism in 1851, "thi jeg forstod ikke dengang at uden Herrens Aands paavirkning kan Menisket ikke fatte den himmel [sic] Sandhed. Det giver et levende Vidnesbyrd om at det er Guds Verk og ikke Menneskelig Opspind." Svend Larsen, "Uddrag af min Biographi (1816-1867)," pp. 9-10, holograph, LDS Church Archives.

[37]Larsen, "Biographical Sketch," pp. 10-11.

[38]Israelsen, *Utah*, p. 18.

[39] Nils Evensen Autobiography, p. 1, microfilm of typescript, LDS Church Archives.

[40] Conrad Johan Zahl Hansen, *A Glance at My Life* (Provo, Utah: Scott Printing Company, 1971), p. 31.

[41] Anna Helena Dyresen Johnson Autobiography, p. 1, xerox of typescript, LDS Church Archives.

[42] ". . . og den foerste Salme, som var sjunget satte det Stempel i mit Bryst, at de vare Guds Boern. Aanden ledsagede dem." Torkelson, "Beskrivelse," vol. 1, pp. 14-15.

[43] Robert W. Doherty, "Sociology, Religion, and Historians," *Historical Methods Newsletter* 6 (September 1973):162.

[44] Parley P. Pratt, *Key to the Science of Theology*, 9th ed. (Salt Lake City, Utah: Deseret Book Company, 1965), p. 133. Jedediah M. Grant, Brigham Young's counselor, put it another way: "I am fully aware that many people have been bred and raised in poor-pussyism all their days, both in America and in Europe, and when they hear doctrines and principles taught by men who speak as freedom permits them, and as freemen have a right to speak, those who are clothed with the garments of poor-pussyism get the grunts; well, grunt on until you grunt it all out. The Latter-day Saints who enjoy the light of the Lord, that power which loves the intelligence of heaven and imparts it to the faithful, thank the Lord that we expect that our elder brother, Jesus Christ, will give unto us according to our works. We expect that he will be rewarded according to his works, and that his associates will be rewarded according to theirs, and if our works are not good we ask for no good reward." Jedediah M. Grant, "Men Rewarded According to their Works: Remarks made by President J. M. Grant, in the Bowery, Great Salt Lake City, October 6, 1855," in *Journal of Discourses*, vol. 3 (Liverpool: Orson Pratt, 42, Islington, 1856; London: Latter-Day Saints' Book Depot, 1856; reprint ed., Los Angeles, California: General Printing & Lithograph Co., 1961), p. 126.

[45] "Jeg anmodede de Hellige om at opfylde Tiendeloven . . . at leve et respectabelt Levnet i enhver Henseende; ikke at bruge eller understoette Bagtalelse; at hjaelpe hvad de kunde med Bidrag til Huusleie. . . ." C. D. Fjeldsted to Jesse N. Smith, 23 October 1869, quoted in *Skandinaviens Stjerne* 19 (15 November 1869):58.

[46] Mulder, "Ducklings," p. 254.

[47] Hansen, *Glance*, p. 30.

[48] Parley P. Pratt, *Key to the Science of Theology*, 2nd ed. (Liverpool: George Q. Cannon, 1863), pp. 160-61; "Love for

Aegteskab og Menneskeslaegtens Formerelse," <u>Skandinaviens Stjerne</u> 9 (15 January 1860):119.

[49]". . . i Jesu Christi Kirke kan ikke det Aandelige og det saakaldte Timelige skilles ad, og det Ene forsoemmes paa det Andets Bekostning, men begge Dele maa varetages med lige stor Samvittighedsfuldhed." Carl Widerborg, Remarks at a council meeting in Copenhagen on 11 May 1858, quoted in <u>Skandinaviens Stjerne</u> 7 (1 June 1858):268.

[50]<u>Skandinaviens Stjerne</u> 8 (1 April 1859):202.

[51]An editorial in <u>Skandinaviens Stjerne</u> for 15 July 1856 intoned: "It is gross blasphemy to talk about the divine right of Kings or Czars whose title to their thrones is written with the blood of their subjects, and who require trained mercenaries to hold their subjects underfoot. . . . They have placed themselves above God, for He has never robbed men of their free agency. . . ." ["Det er hoeitidelig Gudsbespottelse at tale om Kongers og Keiseres hellige Rettigheder, hvis Hjemmel til deres Troner er skrevne med deres Undersaatteres Blod, og som behoever indoevede Krigerskarer for at holde deres Folk i Underkastelse. . . . De har ophoeiet sig over Gud, thi han har aldrig beroevet Mennesket deres frie Raadighed. . . ."] <u>Skandinaviens Stjerne</u> 20 (15 July 1856):315. "Consider Babylon," said Brigham Young's counselor George Q. Cannon in 1874, "and you will there observe a set of conditions the direct opposite of what should exist in Zion. The one class is in steady conflict with the other. There are the rich who desire only the good things of this world. . . . They are clad in the finest clothing which can be produced. . . . But what is the condition of the poor? Many of them do not have enough food to exist or clothes to cover their nakedness." ["Betragt Babylon, og I ville der se en Tingenes Tilstand, som er netop modsat af, hvad der skulde finde Sted i Zion. Den ene Klasse er i stadig Kamp med den anden. Der ere de Rige, som kun attraa denne Verdens gode Ting. . . . De er klaedte i de fineste Klaeder, som kunne tilvirkes. . . . Men hvilken er de Fattiges Stilling? Mange af dem have ikke Foede nok til deres Ophold eller Klaeder til at skjule deres Legemer i."] Geo. Q. Cannon, "Den forenede Orden," <u>Skandinaviens Stjerne</u> 24 (15 December 1874):87. Scandinavian Mission President Nils C. Flygare wrote (1879) that "Bismark [Bismarck] is trying to bring Germany back to the times of the allmighty knighs [knights] or the Spanish inquisition; after getting the law past [passed] there [that] has exiled all sosialister [socialist] leaders and supresed [sic] all liberal publication, he is now trying to get a law pased [sic] by which he can expell from the <u>Richsdag</u> [Parliament] and make them for all future iligable [ineligible] to be again elected, anyone who shoud [sic] dare to speak against his highnes [sic] ruls [sic] and regulations or who should dare to advance any liberal mesures [sic]." Nils C. Flygare to A. W. Carlson, 30 January 1879, carbon copy, "Letter Book of

Niels C. Flygare, President of the Scandinavian Mission, 1878-1879," p. 81, LDS Church Archives.

[52] Erastus Snow to Willard Snow, 25 September 1851, LDS Church Archives. "Things are conducted on such a principle here that it is hardly possible for the working class to live," reported Oslo Conference President George M. Brown in 1866. "Thousands are without employment all winter and it takes them all summer to pay up their debts again." Brown Autobiography, p. 143, 5 March 1866.

[53] John Van Cott Diary, vol. 1, pp. 111-12, xerox of holograph, LDS Church Archives.

[54] August Severin Schou Diary, trans. Lauritz G. Petersen, vol. 1, p. 61, 8 July 1878, xerox of typescript, LDS Church Archives. C. C. A. Christensen's poem, "Evangeliets Indflydelse" [The Gospel's Influence], written at Ephraim, Utah, in May 1872, equated Mormonism with freedom from spiritual and temporal bondage:

> "Mangen Sjael i mange Aar
> Har i Moerket sukket;
> Haabet om en Frihedsvaar
> Syntes vaere slukket.
> Livet var en oede Oerk
> Uden Laeskedraabe,
> Evigheden kold og moerk
> Intet gav at haabe.
>
> Lyset kom -- og Troest tilsidst
> Bragtes de fortrykte,
> Haabets himmelsendte Gnist
> Alles Hjerter soegte;
> Mangen Sjael, som foer var tom,
> Fyldtes da af Aanden;
> Mange Saa, at Babels Dom
> Netop var for Haanden."
> John S. Hansen, ed., Mindeudgave C. C. A. Christensen: Poetiske Arbejder, Artikler og Afhandlinger tilligemed hans Levnedsloeb (Salt Lake City, Utah: Bikubens Bibliotek, 1921), p. 23.

[55] William Mulder, Homeward to Zion: The Mormon Migration from Scandinavia (Minneapolis: University of Minnesota Press, 1957), pp. 18-19.

[56] ". . . eet af Oeiemedene med Indsamlingen er at frigjoere de Fattige og Traellende, som annamme Evangeliet, og derved give dem baade timelig og evig Frelse." Skandinaviens Stjerne 8 (15 May 1859):249. Church aid to needy immigrants was funneled

through the Perpetual Emigration Fund (P.E.F.). According to Mulder, "P.E.F. aid to the Scandinavians in the form of church wagon trains assumed significant proportions. Of 10,843 Scandinavian converts setting out for Zion by 1869, before the completion of the transcontinental railroad, at least 6810 were transported from the frontier to the Salt Lake Valley in church wagons, signing I.O.U.'s for $36 for a share of the wagon as one of eight passengers--though they more often walked. This was wholly in the 1860s; in the 1850s 1032 went through by handcarts, which they could either purchase outright or sign for at $18 a share, four shares to the handcart. The rest, or about 3000, went all the way as 'independents,' having been able to buy their own equipment and provisions." Mulder, Homeward, p. 144.

[57]". . . hvor aerligt Arbeide og Kunstflid moeder en passende Beloenning, hvor Livets hoeiere Stier er aabne for de Ringeste og Fattigste, og hvor de kan laegge en Grundvold til en uoploeselig Forening immelem dem og deres Boern i den fremadskridende Stigen af menneskelig Tilvaerelse. . . ." Jedediah M. Grant, Heber C. Kimball, and Brigham Young, "Trettende almindelige Epistel [dated Great Salt Lake City 29 October 1855]," Skandinaviens Stjerne 10 (15 February 1856):149. According to the Mormon scheme of hierarchy, women and children were duty bound to obey the husband, and he in turn was "to obey those who preside over him in the Church" ["at adlyde dem, som er i Myndighed over ham i Kirken"]. "Familieforholde," Skandinaviens Stjerne 5 (1 December 1855):78. Any woman, however, who obeyed a man "exercising unrighteous dominion," was guilty of sin, and children were not described as puppets: "In family affairs, the husband's decision should be considered as binding; and the wife should willingly support him in carrying out the same. If the children require reprimanding, it should be administered with understanding . . . . They [parents] should teach their children to be clean, orderly and diligent, while at the same time showing them by example that such things are necessary for health and happiness." ["I Familiebestyrelsen skulde Mandens Afgjoerelse eller Kjendelse vaere Lov, og Hustruen skulde staae ham villigen bi i Udfoerelsen af samme. Om Boernene behoeve Tugtelse, skulde den tildeles dem med Forstand. . . . De skulde laere deres Boern den Vane at vaere reenlige, ordentlige og flittige, og til samme Tid vise dem ved Exempel, at saadanne Ting ere noedvendige for Helbred og Lyksalighed."] "Boern ere en Velsignelse," Skandinaviens Stjerne 7 (1 September 1858):359. A child, furthermore, was "an eternal soul, a saintly, pure, undefiled being, brought forth from the Hand of God" ["en evig Sjael, et helligt, reent, ubesmittet Vaesen, udsprungen fra Skaberens Haand"], and entrusted to the care of righteous parents. Skandinaviens Stjerne 12 (15 November 1862):57.

[58]Brigham Young, "The Necessity of the Saints Having the Spirit of Revelation--Faith and Works--the Power of God and of the Devil: A Discourse, by President B. Young, Delivered

in the Tabernacle, Great Salt Lake City, May 6, 1855," in Journal of Discourses, vol. 3 (Liverpool: Orson Pratt, 42, Islington, 1856; London: Latter-Day Saints' Book Depot, 1856; reprint ed., Los Angeles, California: General Printing & Lithograph Co., 1961), p. 154.

[59] Mulder, Homeward, p. 23.

[60] Ibid.

[61] "Blant alle disse rotloese mennesker vokste naa paa nytt trangen etter samfunn, etter aa kunne forene seg med likesinnede." Andreas Aarflot, Norsk Kirkehistorie, vol. 2 (Oslo: Lutherstiftelsen, 1967), p. 286.

[62] "Ogsaa der samledes vi med de Hellige, vore aegte Slaegtninger i Aanden, med hvem vi kunde sammensmelte i Foelelser og Sympathier langt mere end med dem, der gjoere Krav paa Blodets Baand." P. O. Thomassen to W. W. Cluff, 16 October 1870, quoted in Skandinaviens Stjerne 20 (1 November 1870):35.

[63] Jonas Johansen Diary, p. 10, 10-13 October 1870, holograph, LDS Church Archives.

[64] ". . . at vi snart laerer at kjende hver andre, Formedelst at vi er i Besiddelse af den samme Aand, nemlig enighedens og Fredens Aand. . . ." Johnson Diary, 4 April 1896.

[65] "Engelbrecht Olsen talte om den Kamp, han havde bestaaet med Venner og Fraender dengang, han forlod Verdens Samfund, men han foelte, at de Venner han havde faaet i sine Broedre og Soestre fuldkommen erstatte ham Alt; han foelte sig saa lykkelig som han kunde vaere." Skandinaviens Stjerne 12 (15 November 1862):59.

[66] A Mormon petition to the King in 1853 named seven basic tenets of Mormonism: "Repentance from dead works, and faith in God, and baptism for the remission of sins, the laying on of hands for the Gift of the Holy Ghost, as also the doctrine of the Lord's Supper, the resurrection of the dead and an Eternal Judgment" ["Omvendelse fra doede Gjerninger, og Tro paa Gud, og Daab til Syndernes Forladelse, Haandspaalaeggelse for den Helligaands Gave, samt Laeren om Nadveren, de Doedes Opstandelse og en evig Dom"]. Petition by Mormons in Brevik, Fredrikstad and Risoer to the King of Sweden-Norway, p. 2, 19 April 1853, pakke "Mormonerne 1851-1920," Kontor A [hereinafter cited as "A"], Det kongelige Kirke- og Undervisningsdepartment [hereinafter cited as KUD], Riksarkivet, Oslo, Norway [hereinafter cited as RA]. Mormons usually attended their weekly religious meetings in the branch leader's home in the 1850s. John F. Ferdinand Dorius, "No. 1 Dagbog for J. F. Ferdinand Dorius tilligemed et kort Udtog af hans tidligere Levnetsloeb," pp. 77-78, 10 October 1852,

holograph, LDS Church Archives; Lund Journal, vol. 1, p. 51, 1 June 1857. By the 1870s, most meetings convened in rented halls. Sunday school became an integral part of Mormon Sunday worship during the 1870s, and a typical Mormon meeting program for larger branches in the 1880s included morning Sunday school, a general afternoon or evening meeting each Sunday, and one evening meeting during the week, usually on Thursday. Amundsen Journal, p. 54, 16 September 1883; Hintze Diary, vol. 1, pp. 526, 528. By 1895, general meetings (including investigator meetings) were held nearly every week night in Oslo as per Christiansen Journal, vol. 3, p. 123, 17-31 January 1895, whereas members in remoter congregations, such as those at Vaalerengen, attended only one meeting per week--an evening meeting on Thursday or Friday. Ekman Diary, 27 April 1907. Priesthood members, especially conference and branch leaders and missionaries, attended council meetings, beginning on 12 September 1852 when the first council meeting convened aboard Svend Larsen's boat <u>Zions Loeve</u> anchored in Oslo Fjord near Brevik. Hilmar Freidel, "Raadsmoeter i 125 Aar," p. 1, xerox of typescript, Norway Office, Translation Services Department, The Church of Jesus Christ of Latter-day Saints, Moss, Norway [hereinafter cited as Norway TSD]. Leaders discussed branch and conference finances, member affairs, statistical reports, and missionary assignments at council meetings; native Norwegians were often called as missionaries at council meetings, and worthy male members were ordained to their priesthood offices. Magleby Journal, 20 September 1857. At a council meeting in Drammen on 1 September 1858, for example, conference leaders divided Drammen Branch into the Hurum-Roeyken Branch under President J. Johnsen, and the Drammen Branch under President E. Torgersen. Ibid., 1 September 1858. At a council meeting in Oslo on Tuesday evening, 12 December 1882, Andrew Amundsen spoke "on the duties of the Priesthood and the Teachers as well." Amundsen Journal, p. 36, 12 December 1882. A similar meeting on 31 March 1906 in Larvik featured reports by teachers assigned to visit individual members in their homes. Ekman Diary, 31 March 1906. Members also attended regularly scheduled conferences twice each year. Mission leaders from Copenhagen conducted such conferences if at all possible; conferences included special priesthood sessions where missionaries and branch leaders reported on conversions and member activity in their districts. All members were invited to general sessions of the twice-yearly conferences where leaders imparted general advice and directives from The First Presidency in Utah, and preached gospel sermons. Anthon L. Skanchy convened a unique conference for members in Nordland during the early summer of 1865: "Jeg skrev saa Breve til alle de Hellige paa Nordland og Findmarken at Moede paa den historiske Bjarkoee [Bjarkoey] til en bestemt Tid. Alle de Hellige kom der ogsaa Fremmede Min Kjoedelige Soester Emilie kom ogsaa fra Kloeven Station. Vi var tilsamen [sic] der i 2 a 4 Dage Min Soester Emilie blev doebt der. Ve [sic] noed ogsaa Nadvaeren tilsammen og vi havde en meget behagelig Tid." Anthon L. Skanchy Autobiography, pp. 28a-29, holograph, Anthon L. Skanchy Collection,

LDS Church Archives. Outside of Oslo and Drammen, attendance at weekly Mormon meetings was never very great, especially before 1900. Arendal Branch, for example, comprised sixteen villages or towns in 1877 with a total membership of seventy, of whom only about fifteen bothered to attend Sunday and other meetings. Nielsen Journal, vol. 2, 27 May 1877. Other congregations, such as those at Roervik (1855), Kongsberg (1858), Jelsoe (1862), Stjoerdalen (1871), Boesseskogn (1871), and Egersund (1910), met for only a few years. Peterson Journal, 11 March 1855; Magleby Journal, 28 November 1858; Dorius, "Dagbog," 5, 18 August, 9 September 1862; Christiansen Journal, vol. 3, p. 15, June 1894; Jens Christian Andersen Weibye Diary, vol. 4, pp. 10-12; 14-15, 19 August 1871, holograph, LDS Church Archives; Nielsen Journal, vol. 2, 26 January, 23 June 1878; Nephi Hansen Diary, 3 April 1910, holograph, LDS Church Archives. Branches at Sarpsborg, Tistedalen, and Moss struggled along year after year with only a score of regular attenders. Weibye Diary, vol. 4, pp. 18-19, 10, 12 September 1871; James Jensen Journal, p. 30, 5 July 1908, xerox of holograph, LDS Church Archives. Branches at Fredrikstad, Trondheim and Halden experienced good and bad years with a high ranging between thirty and forty regular attenders at meetings in each branch. Christian J. Larsen Journal, vol. 3, p. 47, 18 July 1853, holograph and MS, LDS Church Archives; Hendricksen Diary, p. 122, 7 April 1889; Weibye Diary, vol. 4, pp. 10, 17, 6 August, 7 September 1871; Iversen Diary, 7 June 1896; Christiansen Journal, vol. 10, p. 41, 9 October 1915. Meeting attendance in newer branches such as those at Aalesund, Bergen, Larvik, and Toensberg began picking up around 1900. Iversen Diary, 1, 3 March 1895; Hendricksen Diary, p. 15, 15 December 1887; Johann August Olsen Journal, p. 134, 30 April 1906, typescript, Special Collections, Harold B. Lee Library, Brigham Young University, Provo, Utah; Jenson Diary, bk. J, p. 294, 18 January 1910; Christiansen Journal, vol. 11, p. 76, 16 July 1916. Attendance at Bergen seldom exceeded a hundred persons, however; a very high attendance figure for Larvik was seventy-five persons; and at Toensberg and Aalesund, attendance at meetings averaged well under twenty persons. Ibid. Attendance figures at Oslo meetings reached the four hundred mark several times during the 1870s, but average attendance was probably less than half that number, and dipped even more during the 1880s and early 1890s; average attendance at meetings in Drammen Branch fluctuated between forty and fifty regular attenders during the years 1875-1910. Weibye Diary, vol. 4, pp. 131-32; Lund Journal, p. 48, 12-13 April 1857; Weibye Diary, vol. 4, p. 35, 8 October 1871 and vol. 5, p. 2, 1 January 1873; <u>Skandinaviens Stjerne</u> 32 (15 June 1883):279. Active members in larger branches, such as Oslo, kept busy attending four regularly scheduled weekly meetings in 1855 including two preaching meetings on Sunday, and one each on Wednesday and Thursday evenings. Canute Peterson to wife Sarah and children, 28 March 1855, Canute Peterson Collection, LDS Church Archives. Members in smaller branches generally met on Sundays for purposes of group prayer, Bible reading, and sermonizing during the 1850s. Larsen, "Uddrag," p. 11.

[67] Nielsen Journal, vol. 2, 29 April 1877-28 July 1878; Interview with Einar Strand, Maurits Hansens Gate 4, Oslo 3, Norway, 7 March 1978.

[68] Mission leaders instructed members at a general conference in Oslo on 27 October 1872 to celebrate the Lord's Supper with bread and water, water being used in place of fruit juice or wine. That same evening, J. C. A. Weibye noted that "we had the Lord [sic] Supper . . . for [the] first time here in Norway with Bread and Watter [sic], as the use in Utah and in Copenhagen." Weibye Diary, vol. 4, p. 162, 27 October 1872. Beginning about 1907, sacrament meetings were generally combined with so-called fast meetings. Olsen Journal, p. 191, 3 March 1907.

[69] "Meddelelsen af Alterens Sacramente foregik saaledes, at de der skulde modtage samme faldt paa Knae tilligemed Praedikanten, der holdt en Boen, og derhos erklaerede, at forsaavidt at der var nogen af dem som havde imod nogen af sine Medmennesker, da var de ikke vaerdig til at modtage Sacramentet, hvorpaa han tog almindeligt Rugbroed som han efter Skriftens Ord broed og havde paa en Tallaerken, som gik omkring til dem, og hvoraf de hver tog et Stykke. Derefter gik ligeledes Kalken omkring, hvoraf de drak, og bestod denne af Viin." Avskrift av Forhoer under Tunoee Sorenskriverie, 15 October 1852, Mormonpakken, TS, JPD.

[70] "Dorius, der som Praest forrettede Sacramentet, tog et almindeligt Rugbroed som han broed istykker og lagde paa en Tallaerken, hvorpaa han faldt paa Knae tilligemed alle de der skulde modtage Sacramentet, samt velsignede Broedet og gik derefter omkring saa at Enhver tog et Stykke Broed af Tallaerkenen. Ligeledes foregik det med Uddelelsen af Kalken, der var Viin eller Saft blandet med Vand, og ved Meddelelsen saavel af Broedet som Vinen, blev benyttet de samme Ord som Christus da han meddeelte sine Desciple Sacramentet." Avskrift av Forhoer paa Lensmandsgaarden Marielyst i Onsoee Sogn under Tunoee Sorenskriverie, 19 October 1852, Mormonpakken, TS, JPD.

[71] Larsen Journal, vol. 3, p. 29, 2 June 1853.

[72] "Naar I opoffre Eder i Faste til Herren paa Eders regelmaessige Fastedag, forsoemmer ikke samvittighedsfuldt at betale Eders Fastepenge til Fattigkassen. . . ." Skandinaviens Stjerne 8 (15 July 1859):313.

[73] Poulsen Journal, 23 December 1855.

[74] Magleby Journal, 25 June, 10, 28 July 1858, 6 March 1859.

[75] Christiansen Journal, vol. 2, 18 April 1894.

[76] "Det var ret fornoeieligt at see, de mange unge Mennesker samlede, der udgjorde, et behageligt Selskab." Dorius, "Dagbog," 4 January 1862. See also Larsen Diary, pp. 7-8, 28 March 1853.

[77] ". . . de Tilstedevaerende falde ned og bede hoeit, een efter een. . . ." Forhoersprotokol, no. 12, 13/2 1858-29/10 1861, fols. 12-13, 5 March 1858, Drammen By, PA.

[78] Larsen Journal, vol. 2, p. 130, 13 October 1852.

[79] ". . . andre bad til Herren. . . ." Dorius, "Dagbog," 8 May 1861.

[80] Larsen Diary, 22 July 1866.

[81] Weibye Diary, vol. 4, p. 43.

[82] "Boennemoede paa Egeberg . . . var godt besoegt saavel af Fremmede som af Soedskende og flere Fremmede var meget bevaeget over Boennerne samt over Vidnesbyrd som aflagtes." Christiansen Journal, vol. 2, 20 November 1893.

[83] Larsen Diary, p. 16, 12 April 1853; Pedersen Journal, pp. 18-19, 43, 75, 81-82, 19 March 1856, 8 October 1857, 10 July 1859, 27 May 1860; Poulsen Journal, 28 September, 29 November 1855; Amundsen Journal, p. 37, 21 December 1882.

[84] Larsen Journal, vol. 3, p. 40, 29 June 1853; Larsen Diary, p. 21, 24 April 1853; Pedersen Journal, pp. 60, 88-89, 14 May 1858, 13 November 1860; Amundsen Journal, p. 36, 4 December 1882.

[85] Nielsen Journal, vol. 2, 13 January 1881.

[86] Iversen Diary, 13 June 1896.

[87] Poulsen Journal, 14 December 1855.

[88] Ibid., 15 December 1855.

[89] Samuel Lindsay Sprague Diary, 30 August 1865, holograph, LDS Church Archives.

[90] Magleby Journal, 30 May 1857.

[91] Ibid., 3 February 1858.

[92] Christiansen Journal, vol. 3, p. 81, 19 October 1894.

[93] Forhoersprotokol, no. 1, 15/7 1854-7/5 1866, fol. 12, 17 August 1854, Tune Sorenskriveri, SA.

[94] Larsen Diary, 30 January 1867.

[95] Schou Diary, vol. 1, p. 30, 21 January 1878.

[96] Goudy E. Hogan Journal, p. 57, microfilm of typescript, LDS Church Archives.

[97] Magleby Journal, 3 October 1858.

[98] "... spiste, drak, dandsede, sang og legede meget fornoeiligt [sic] til Kl 2 om Natten." Dorius, "Dagbog," p. 90, 16 December 1860.

[99] Larsen Diary, 4 November 1866.

[100] Schou Diary, vol. 1, p. 58, 23 June 1878.

[101] Iversen Diary, 8 September 1895.

[102] "... pilled Blaabaer Sang og legede spiste og Drak Kaffe alt under Skyggen af Traerne i den Herlige Frie Natur." Johnson Diary, 11 July 1897.

[103] "Der er een Ting, som jeg isaer finder Feil ved, ... det er disse Fornoeielses Gilder, med Dands, og andre Lege som fra Tid til anden foretages af Menigheden ... naturligviis til ikke lidet Anstoed for andre Folk som maaske en Dag, nei! om Soendag formiddag see os praedike me [sic] hoei Roest Omvendelse og Tro paa dette Vaerk, som en Forberedelse for Herrens Komme og Verdens Dom, og om Eftermiddagen see os Unge og Gamle; Praester og Aeldster hvirvle rundt paa Dandsebod=Maneer for Alles Oeine." C. C. A. Christensen to K. Pedersen [Canute Peterson], 7 November 1865, p. 4, LDS Church Archives.

[104] "... som endnu troe, at et helligt og gudfrygtigt Liv er uforeneligt med naevnte Forlystelser." Skandinaviens Stjerne 15 (1 December 1865):73.

[105] Weibye Diary, vol. 4, pp. 34-35.

[106] "Dans og andre uskyldige Fornoejelser kunne nydes af gudhengivne og oprigtige Mennesker, uden i nogensomhelst Maade at vaere syndigt eller have daarlige Foelger. Erfaring har imidlertid ogsaa laert de praesiderende Broedre i Skandinavien, at den de Helliges Samfund [sic] der tilhoerende Ungdom er udsat for stoerre Farer, og de unge Broedre og Soestre fristede til at tage upassende Friheder, mere en Ungdomen i Zion. Af den Aarsag har det til forskjellige Tider vaeret Noedvendigt at naegte de Hellige i Adspredelsen visse Fornoejelser, som vilde have vaeret aldeles tilladelige, hvis Deltagerne ikke, foerend de annammede Evangeliet, havde vaeret under en syndig og ugudelig

Verdens Indflydelse." Andrew Jenson, "Erindringer fra Missionen i Skandinavien," <u>Morgenstjernen</u> 3 (15 October 1884):308.

[107] Weibye Diary, vol. 5, pp. 26-27, 14 March 1873.

[108] Anthon Hendrik Lund Diary, 17 March 1884, microfilm of holograph, LDS Church Archives.

[109] Hintze Diary, vol. 1, p. 558, 7 February 1886.

[110] Christiansen Journal, vol. 2, 3 January 1894.

[111] Saamund [Samuel] Gudmundsen Journal, 12 May 1856, holograph, LDS Church Archives.

[112] "Det var blik stille soee og deilig vaeir og lyst som en dag." Iversen Diary, 20 June 1895.

[113] Pedersen Journal, p. 84, 29 July 1860.

[114] Johnson Diary, 28 December 1895.

[115] Pedersen Journal, pp. 80-81, 9 May 1860; Dorius, "Dagbog," 16 March, 5 April 1862; Iversen Diary, 7 February 1895.

[116] Ekman Diary, 26 December 1906. See also Brown Autobiography, 27 December 1862; Weibye Diary, vol. 4, p. 183, 26 December 1872; Hendricksen Diary, p. 58, 25 December 1888.

[117] Larsen Diary, 27 December 1866; Christiansen Journal, vol. 2, 28 August 1893.

[118] Dorius, "Dagbog," 8 December 1861; Hendricksen Diary, vol. 2, p. 67, 8 December 1903.

[119] Johnson Diary, 31 January 1896; Iversen Diary, 31 January 1895.

[120] Olsen Journal, pp. 54-55, 26 June 1895. Other activities included Bible discussion evenings, Relief Society lotteries, and fireside chats. Poulsen Journal, 21? February 1856; Hintze Diary, vol. 1, p. 394, 4 July 1885; <u>Skandinaviens Stjerne</u> 62 (1 September 1913):266-67. Oslo Conference President George M. Brown described a Mormon get-together at "Kunningrud" in Hedemarken on 13 January 1865 as follows: "In the evening we sat by the cheerful blazing fire and sang hymns and spoke a great deal about the land of America, the future home of the Saints. Sister Johanne Poulson related considerable of her experience in the Church and dwelt especially on the times when the Gospel was first introduced in this part. The many persecutions and trials which the Elders and Saints had to pass through. We felt quite comfortable and happy as the fire blazed brightly

and the cold wintry wind could be plainly heard without." Brown Autobiography, p. 89, 13 January 1865.

[121]Hintze Diary, vol. 1, p. 509, 19 September 1885.

[122]Ibid., pp. 514-15, 27 September 1885.

[123]"Redaktionens Bemaerkninger," Skandinaviens Stjerne 6 (15 February 1857):153-57.

[124]"En anden meget vigtig Ting er, at hun skulde uddanne sin Aand ved Laesning af gode og nyttige Boeger." Skandinaviens Stjerne 24 (15 October 1874):25.

[125]Lund Diary, 8 October 1884.

[126]"Denne 'Stjerne' er beregnet paa at give de Hellige Raad, Laerdomme og Veiledninger i baade timelig og aandelig Henseende. . . ." Skandinaviens Stjerne 22 (1 October 1872):8. Skandinaviens Stjerne was the true vehicle of assimilation, not only into the spiritual and cultural aspects of the latter-day faith, but as a publication which challenged the intellect by acquainting its readership with subjects as diversified as the phonograph (1878), the importance of oceans to world trade (1890), and the "transitory" qualities of the North Pole (1896). Skandinaviens Stjerne 27 (1 April 1878):221; G. Hartwig, "Oceanets Majestaet," Skandinaviens Stjerne 40 (1 October 1890):13-15; Skandinaviens Stjerne 45 (1 August 1896):334-35. "Stjerne was scripture, mission historical record, newssheet, emigrant guide, and . . . a serialized 'America Book.' As carrier of Zion's sermons and . . . letters from emigrants, excerpts from American newspapers, and reprints from the Millennial Star and Salt Lake City's Deseret News, it was a storehouse of information about a new world. . . . Scandinavian readers learned more of what was happening in Utah Territory than in their own community and, fascinated, followed the fortunes of Mormons in their conquest of the desert and their continuous conflict with the world, a drama in which apostate and gentile were the stock villains." Mulder, Homeward, p. 80. Mormon periodicals for young people such as Ungdommens Raadgiver [The Young People's Advisor] (from 1880 to 1887) and Kundskab og Lys [Knowledge and Light] (1919 to ?) further acquainted readers with a variety of secular and religious subjects. Skandinaviens Stjerne 43 (15 August 1894):344-45; Skandinaviens Stjerne 68 (15 June 1919):192.

[127]Young priesthood holders attended "preaching practice schools" ["prekeoevelsesskoler"] in 1859 aimed at acquainting young men with Mormon scriptures and tracts, and improving their ability to defend Mormonism in the debating or preaching arenas. The Norwegian Mission, Jubileum aaret 1850-1950 (Oslo: Haraldssoen A.S., [1950]), p. 27; Skandinaviens Stjerne 9 (15 October 1859):24. Oslo Conference President J. C. A. Weibye described "lotteries"

for the Mormon school of needlework in Oslo in 1871 and 1872. Between twelve and fifteen girls regularly attended the school. Weibye Diary, vol. 4, pp. 65, 88, 26 December 1871, 24 March 1872. Members of the Young Men's Association (YMMIA) established a lending library in Oslo in 1881. Nielsen Journal, vol. 2, 1881, n.p. Oslo YMMIA President Sigvart Christian Jensen wrote as follows about YMMIA meetings in 1883: "We have adopted a new method, viz. that I assign the brethren a certain subject to discuss in each meeting . . . and this I feel is a good procedure since the brethren are thereby encouraged to search the Scriptures & become more familiar with what they contain." ["Vi have forsamlinger i 'Unge Mends Forening,' som er opmuntrende og livlige. Vi har taget en ny methode nemlig at jeg giver broedrene et vist emne at predike over til hvert moede . . . og dette foeler jeg er en god fremgangmaade [sic]; thi da foeler broedrene til at undersoege skriften og bliver bekjendt med dens indhold."] Sigvart Christian Jensen to Olaf H. Nielsen, 24 March 1883, quoted in Nielsen Journal, vol. 2, 1886, n.p.

[128]Pedersen Journal, pp. 23, 25; 31 August, 2 November 1856.

[129]Dorius, "Dagbog," 2den Pinsedags Aften 1861.

[130]Brown Autobiography, p. 118, 3 October 1865. Anthon L. Skanchy and Christine Otterbeck taught the Mormon day or "accredited" school until 1867, and Oluf Josva Andersen taught the school during the years 1868 and 1869. Skanchy Autobiography, pp. 34-35; Gudmundsen Journal, 3 September 1867; Andrew Jenson, "Oluf Josva Andersen," Skandinaviens Stjerne 58 (15 March 1909):88-89. Oslo Conference President J. C. A. Weibye mentioned an "Industriel Schoole [sic] (for Children)" at Oslo in 1871 taught by "sister Elisa Haalter, and Caroline Halvorsen" according to Weibye Diary, vol. 4, p. 34, 5 October 1871. Johannes Groen, a Mormon lighthouse keeper "at Kjeoeen Lighthouse in Svolvaer" ["ved Kjeoeens Fyr i Svolvaer"] aroused widespread consternation in 1865 when KUD officials learned he was teaching "reading and writing" to resident children in direct competition with a government school. Bishop Essendrop in Tromsoe joined other Lutheran authorities in calling for Groen's dismissal as a State-employed lighthouse keeper, but naval commissioners [officials of "Den Kongelige norske Regjerings Marine-og Post-Departement"] felt Lutheran leaders had overreacted, and refused to implement dismissal proceedings. Priest Neumann of Kirkevaag to Tromsoe Bishop Essendrop, 4 November 1865, KUD jnr. 1917 A65, RA; Tromsoe Bishop Essendrop to KUD, 21 November 1865, KUD jnr. 1917 A65, RA; Provst Neumann to Tromsoe Bishop Essendrop, 13 April 1866, KUD jnr. 858 A66, RA; Stiftskappelan S. Weenaas to Tromsoe Bishop Essendrop, 18 April 1866, KUD jnr. 858 A66, RA; KUD to Marine-og Post-Departementet, 26 May 1866, KUD kopibok no. 411-A66, RA; Skolelaerer H. Petersen to Herr Pastor Neumann, 2 June 1866, KUD jnr. 1223 A66, RA. "Den Kongelige norske Regjerings Marine-og Post-Departement" to KUD, 28 November 1866, KUD jnr. 2265 A66, RA.

"J. L. Groenn [sic], an Elder, of Stavnes Fyr ved Christiansund [Stavnes Lighthouse adjoining Christiansund]," died on 21 July 1895. Historical Record, bk. C, 1880-1918, p. 269, Trondheim Branch, Trondheim Conference, Scandinavian Mission, LDS Church Archives.

[131]". . . ved at tilade Skolekommision Officerer en gang aarlig at komme og undersoege hvorvidt vi overholdte Udvikling og Orden--men Boernene skulle blive fritagen fra Religion og Bibelhistorie." Hilmar Freidel, "Historiske dokumentasjoner: Barnedaap og Skolegang," p. 3, xerox of typescript, Norway, TSD.

[132]Weibye Diary, vol. 5, p. 62.

[133]Ibid., vol. 4, pp. 74-75, 28, 30 January 1872.

[134]Iversen Diary, 28 October 1894; Skandinaviens Stjerne 51 (15 November 1903):348; Skandinaviens Stjerne 62 (15 February 1913): 56-57; Hendricksen Diary, vol. 2, pp. 33, 47, 20 September, 1 November 1903.

[135]John F. Dorius to Jesse N. Smith, 22 July 1862, quoted in Skandinaviens Stjerne 11 (15 August 1862):346-47; C. D. Fjeldsted to Jesse N. Smith, 9 October 1869, quoted in Skandinaviens Stjerne 19 (1 November 1869):44; Hendricksen Diary, vol. 2, p. 80, 16 January 1904. Oslo Conference President Christian D. Fjeldsted described two English schools in Oslo "divided into several classes" in 1869: "Vi have oprettet 2 engelske Skoler her i Byne [sic], hvoraf jeg bestyrer den ene, som holdes herpaa Contoiret. Den anden bliver holdt paa Salen, og er indeelt i flere Klasser og de fleste Hellige besoege den." C. D. Fjeldsted to Jesse N. Smith, 9 October 1869, quoted in Skandinaviens Stjerne 19 (1 November 1869):44. Johann A. Olsen summed up his progress after attending English school in Oslo during the 1860s: "I attended English School for several years under R. Johansen, Geo M. Brown & C.C.A. Christensen where I learned to read English quite well. . . ." ["Jeg gik i flere Aar paa Engelsskole [sic] hos R. Johansen Geo M. Brown & C.C.A. Christensen hvor jeg laerte temmelig godt at laese engelsk. . . ."] Olsen, "Levnetsloeb," vol. 1, p. 6. Conference President J. A. Hendricksen "started an English school in the small hall [Oesterhaugsgade 27, Oslo]" on 16 January 1904 "with Miss Clara Larsen of Salt Lake [City] as an instructor," and about "30 members to start in with." Hendricksen Diary, vol. 2, p. 80, 16 January 1904. English instruction in branches such as Bergen, Aalesund, Trondheim, and Larvik depended largely on the arrival or departure of qualified Elders from Utah. Hendricksen Diary, p. 17, 15 October 1888; Iversen Diary, 29 March, 2, 5 April, 3 May 1895; Johnson Diary, 10 January 1896; Ekman Diary, 12 December 1905. Enrollment in Mormon English schools was highest during the 1860s, 1870s, and early 1900s--decades of heavy Mormon immigration to America,

and indication prospective immigrants took the business of learning English seriously.

[136]Olsen, "Pioneer," p. 115.

[137]Norwegian Mission, Jubileum, p. 26.

[138]Larsen, "Biographical Sketch," p. 25. A. S. Schou started a "song school" in Drammen in 1879: "There were 22 that began, which had a desire to learn to sing. So the prospects were good for us singing praises to the name of the Lord, and to the uplifting of mankind." Schou Diary, vol. 2, p. 5, 18 March 1879. Mormons in Drammen used a portable organ beginning about 1880 according to Schou Diary, vol. 3, p. 2, 1 January 1880, and purchased a more permanent instrument in 1896 for thirty-three crowns. Iversen Diary, 16 March 1896. Members in Trondheim organized a choir with eighteen members under direction of Nephi Andersen in 1917. Christiansen Journal, vol. 11, p. 250, 2 April 1917. Mormon children's choirs sang from time to time at special holiday or anniversary ceremonies. Norwegian Mission, Jubileum, p. 26; Olsen, "Levnetsloeb," p. 31, 11 October 1868.

[139]". . . begynte vi en deel Broedre at at [sic] synge igjen og havde saa faaet en ny Laerer med Naven 'Johnsen' fra Bergen, hvem vi skulde betale 5 Spd pr Maaned for at synge een Gang ugentlig to Timer hver Gang." Gudmundsen Journal, 15 November 1860.

[140]Olsen, "Pioneer," p. 115; Mons Peterson, "Mons Petersens [sic] Beretning," Morgenstjernen 4 (June 1885):88; Gudmundsen Journal, December 1867.

[141]Olsen, "Pioneer," p. 115.

[142]The organ "bidrog betydelig til at stoette Choret og forhoeie den religioese Stemning." Skandinaviens Stjerne 20 (15 June 1871):285. Oslo Branch leader Weibye paid an organist named Petersen ten dollars in 1872 for playing "26 times in 13 Sundays." Weibye Diary, vol. 4, p. 167, 17 November 1872. The Oslo Branch Choir numbered forty-five members in 1903 according to Hendricksen Diary, vol. 2, p. 34, 27 September 1903, and approximately forty members in 1915. Christiansen Journal, vol. 9, p. 86, 16 April 1915.

[143]Skandinaviens Stjerne 27 (1 June 1878):280.

[144]Skandinaviens Stjerne 8 (1 August 1859):330.

[145]Larsen Journal, vol. 3, pp. 48, 51, 22, 31 July 1853; Weibye Diary, vol. 4, pp. 112, 115, 4, 11 June 1872; Pedersen Journal, pp. 37-39, 46-47, 70, 10, 29 May, 5, 7 August, 27 December 1857; Hendricksen Diary, vol. 1, p. 207, 16 September 1888; Christiansen Journal, vol. 3, p. 162, 9 April 1895.

[146]Jenson, *History*, p. 536. Excommunications proved highly disruptive at times. Mormons stopped meetings at Skien in 1861 after eight members were excommunicated. Dorius, "Dagbog," 16 July 1861. Leaders in Bergen in 1888 excommunicated five members--almost half the regular attenders. Hendricksen Diary, p. 52, 16 December 1888. For accounts of excommunicants who remained friendly to the Mormons see Larsen Diary, 27 May 1866; Hendricksen Diary, p. 88, 12 February 1889; Iversen Diary, 22 April 1896. An Article entitled "Barnedaab, Konfirmation og Jordpaakastelse," in *Skandinaviens Stjerne* 21 (1 August 1872): 328-30, condemned Mormons who allowed their young children to be baptized and confirmed in the Lutheran Church, and Mission President Canute Peterson told members in Oslo on 27 May 1872 "to work against that practice that some of the Saints let their Children be sprinklen [sic] when the [sic] have help of the Lutheran poorfond [sic], as well as that to let any one of the Saints children be confirmed, and take Lord [sic] supper in the Lutheran Church, etc, etc, which are not Doctrines of God but of men." Weibye Diary, vol. 4, pp. 109-10, 27 May 1872. Mormon Sunday school teacher James Jensen discovered he "was out of a job" on 4 October 1908 in Halden when the Mormon Sunday school was empty because "today the children get confirmed in the different churches, that is why there are so many absent." Jensen Journal, p. 66, 4 October 1908. For accounts of members excommunicated for participating in Lutheran ceremonies or allowing their infant children to be baptized by Lutheran priests see Weibye Diary, vol. 4, p. 69, 9 January 1872, and Christiansen Journal, vol. 3, p. 170, 23 April 1895.

[147]Jenson, *History*, p. 536.

[148]Larsen Journal, vol. 3, pp. 48, 51, 31 July 1853; Weibye Diary, vol. 4, pp. 112, 115, 4, 11 June 1872.

[149]Peterson Journal, 29 March 1855; *Skandinaviens Stjerne* 8 (1 August 1859):336.

[150]Larsen Diary, p. 20, 22 April 1853.

[151]Larsen Journal, vol. 3, pp. 40-41, 30 June 1853.

[152]Poulsen Journal, 6 November 1855.

[153]Petersen Journal, 10, 13, 26 April 1855; Pedersen Journal, p. 10, 13 April 1855.

[154]Dorius, "Dagbog," 30 August 1862.

[155]Weibye Diary, vol. 5, p. 77, 22 July 1873.

[156]Hendricksen Diary, vol. 1, p. 207, 16 September 1888.

[157] Johnson Diary, 14 January 1896.

[158] Christiansen Journal, vol. 8, pp. 160-61, 2 November 1914.

[159] Canute Peterson to J. C. A. Weibye, 18 November 1872, quoted in Weibye Diary, vol. 4, p. 171.

[160] Weibye Diary, vol. 5, pp. 4-5, 6 January 1873.

[161] Lund Diary, 5 November 1884.

[162] Ibid., 30 September 1885. See Jenson, **History**, pp. 287-88.

[163] Anthony Armstrong, **The Church of England, the Methodists and Society 1700-1850** (Totowa, New Jersey: Rowman and Littlefield, 1973), p. 216.

[164] "Mormonernes udvortes borgerlige Forhold har jeg al Grund til at ansee for godt. Vel er det saa, at Ingen er saaledes inderligen loesrevne fra det borgerlige Samfund, hvori de leve, som netop disse, og at de under vanskelige Omstaendigheder vel mindst af Alle er at Stole paa for Stad og Land, men dog har jeg hoert det Vidnesbyrd afgivet af trovaerdige Folk, at der i mange Huse er bleven stor Forandring, siden Manden eller Konen eller begge gik over til denne Sect." Sven Brun to KUD, 27 June 1859, "Mormonerne," A, KUD, RA.

[165] Frederik Ingier to Christiania Bishop Jens L. Arup, 12 June 1859, "Mormonerne," A, KUD, RA. Mormons in Norway were counseled to avoid strong drink, tobacco and other harmful substances in accordance with the "Word of Wisdom" contained in the Mormon Doctrine and Covenants, section 89. Oslo Conference President J. C. A. Weibye instructed members "not to use Thee [sic] Tobacco, coffee, and strong drinks, but keep the Word of Wisdom," in 1872 according to Weibye Diary, vol. 4, pp. 109-10, 27 May 1872--indication that the use of these products was rather widespread among the Saints. Most Mormons, however, abstained from strong drinks as a general rule, but were certainly not averse to "a flask of beer," a glass of "beer and lemonade," "a hot toddy," or "a glass of wine" at birthday parties, farewell banquets or other social gatherings. Magleby Journal, 4 July 1858; Larsen Diary, 31 October 1866; Hendricksen Diary, p. 151, 14 May 1889; Olsen Journal, p. 153, 30 July 1906; Gudmundsen Journal, 20 December 1860; Berg Diary, vol. 1, p. 28, 24 March 1864. Mormon accounts of drinking coffee or tea are also numerous. Sprague Diary, 25 September 1865; Amundsen Journal, p. 36, 30 November 1882; Kjaer Diary, p. 198, 23 May 1909. Indication that Scandinavian Saints were somewhat lax in Word of Wisdom observance is provided by Andrew Jenson's account of a meeting with Apostles John Henry Smith and Anthony W. Ivins, "who," said Jenson, "instructed me to enforce the word of wisdom strictly

in the Scandinavian Mission." Jenson Diary, bk. J, p. 8, 12 January 1909.

[166]". . . han har virkelig i flere Henseende forbedret sit Levnet, og laegger klarligen for dagen, at han ledes af en god Maning." Paul Irgens Dybdahl to KUD, 9 June 1859, "Mormonerne," A, KUD, RA.

[167]"I Borgerlig henseende synes mormonerne fremdeles gjennemgaaende at vaere aedruelige, lovlydige, arbeidsomme og i det hele skikkelige folk, saa at man forsaavidt kun maate oenske, at der var ret mange saa gode medborgere." Kristiania Politikammer to JPD expeditions schef Hallager, 15 December 1904, Mormonpakken, TS, JPD.

[168]Mulder, "Ducklings," p. 254.

[169]Kenneth O. Bjork, *West of the Great Divide: Norwegian Migration to the Pacific Coast, 1847-1893* (Northfield, Minnesota: Norwegian-American Historical Association, 1958), pp. 133-34.

[170]Canute Peterson to wives and children in Utah, 24 July 1871, Canute Peterson Collection, LDS Church Archives. Mission President Canute Peterson described "emigration fever" among Scandinavian Mormons on 3 May 1872: "A. H. L. [Anthon H. Lund] rad [read] about 30 letters for me this morning be for [sic] I was out of bed, heep [sic] of letters all wants to go home to Zion. I tell them if I git [sic] money enough you will go. I hope that good many will have the chans [sic] to go home this year, for some have ben [sic] here for 20 years, and evre [every] one says that thay [sic] cant standit annylonger [sic], if I had awagonlod [sic] of mony [sic] I could find good jus [use] for it, wher ever [sic] I come thay have letters from ther folks in Utah telling them to ask me for mony to come or help them come home. And they have so much to talk about that I never can come to bed befor 1 or 2 o C. [o'clock] in the Morning. . . ." Canute Peterson to family in Utah, 3 May 1872, pp. 1-2, Canute Peterson Collection, LDS Church Archives.

[171]Amundsen Journal, p. 3.

[172]Brown Autobiography, p. 95, 25 April 1865. J. A. Hendricksen, a missionary in Bergen, accompanied a member girl named Inger on a walk "to the Ocean" on 10 January 1889 where they both "looked toward Zion." Hendricksen Diary, p. 87, 10 January 1889. C. C. N. Dorius described the departure of a ship with three hundred emigrating Mormons from Copenhagen in December 1852: "Ved Afreisen havde nogle Tusinde Mennesker forsamlet sig paa Toldboden, og der hoertes mangen Slags Snak, men da Skibet gleed forbii, frembragtes en almindelig Taushed, og Alle forstummede ved Lyden af den fra Skibet saa herlig klingende Sang, 'til Babylon til Babylon vi sige Farvel, i Ephrahims [sic]

Land, vi vil fryde vor Sjael.'" Dorius, "Dagbog," 29 December 1852.

[173] Brown Autobiography, p. 65, 16 May 1865.

[174] ". . . jeg gik op i en Aas, holdt Boen og sang nogle Sange, og glaedede mig meget over Guds Godhed til Menneskene." Gudmundsen Journal, 5 March 1856.

[175] ". . . vi gik ned til stranden for at Udfoere denne Ordenance [sic] til ham, og udfoerte ve [sic] det paa hans eget Land, ved Strandbredden af Laurviks-Fjord, Et meget smukt Sted, Og Gundersen udfoerte Daaben og Gav jeg ham Haanspaaleggelse [sic]. . . . Mandens kat fulgte ogsaa med os ned til Strandbredden, som er et godt Stykke Vei ifra hans hus, og sad den paa en sten der, til ve var ferdig, og saa fulgte den hjem med os. . . ." Johnson Diary, 24 April 1897.

[176] ". . . en Flok Boern bestaaende af 5 fra 4 1/2 til 15 Aar. Deres Fader rejste til Utah for ca. to Aar siden, og siden den Tid er deres Moder doed i Frederikstad, og nu rejser de til deres Fader." Christiansen Journal, vol. 11, pp. 141-42, 6 October 1916.

[177] Hintze Diary, vol. 1, pp. 465-66, 468-69, 21, 25 August 1885.

[178] Canute Peterson to his family in Utah, 13 August 1856, quoted in Peterson, "Story," p. 141.

[179] Christiansen Journal, vol. 14, 1919.

[180] Hilmar Freidel, <u>Jesu Kristi Kirke i Norge: Den norske misjons historie, 1851-1966</u> (Oslo: Jesu Kristi Kirke av Siste Dagers Hellige Misjonskontoret, 1966), p. 122.

[181] Jenson, <u>Scandinavian Mission</u>, pp. 501-04.

[182] "Da der ingen misjonaerer var, maatte jeg overta bestyrelsen av Kristiania konferanse, hvor der dog finnes mange gode broedre og soestre, og gode levende organisasjoner; saa der var ingen mangel paa aandelig foede." August S. Schow, quoted in Freidel, <u>historie</u>, p. 124.

[183] Jenson, <u>Scandinavian Mission</u>, p. 536.

[184] "President August S. Schow gjorde meget for aa trekke ungdommen til Kirken, hans arbeide besto primaert i aa befeste det vaerende, styrke den indre arbeidsfront og utvide en selvstendig virksomhet. Han trengte ungdommelig paagangsmot og arbeidsiver og ga dem derfor ansvar og oppgaver." Freidel, <u>historie</u>, p. 196.

SELECTED BIBLIOGRAPHY

Primary and Manuscript Sources

Drammen, Norway. Tinghuset. Politimesterensarkiv. Drammen By. Forhoersprotokol, no. 9, 1852-1857.

_____. Tinghuset. Politimesterensarkiv. Drammen By. Forhoersprotokol, no. 12, 13/2 1858-29/10 1861.

Moss, Norway. The Church of Jesus Christ of Latter-day Saints. Translation Services Department. Norway Office. Ole Podhorny and Petter Svanevik, "Noen Kommentarer Omkring Et 'Ikke-Kristent' Trossamfunn." Oslo, 1977. (Typescript.)

Oslo, Norway. Hoeiesteretsarkiv. Dom-protocol for Hoeiesteret.

_____. Det kongelige Justis- og Politidepartement [hereinafter listed as JPD]. Trossamfunn Samling. Mormonpakken.

_____. Metodisme-historisk Selskap Archives. Ole Peter Petersen, "Nogle Erindringer om mine Oplevelser og Religions Erfaringer." (Holograph.)

_____. Metodisme-historisk Selskap Archives. Ole Peter Petersen, "Short and imperfect sketches of my expiriance [sic]. and labor." (Holograph.)

_____. Riksarkivet [hereinafter listed as RA]. Hoeiesteret. Extractprotokol for Hoeiesteret.

_____. RA. Hoeiesteret. Utdrag i muntlige saker for Hoeiesteret.

_____. RA. Hoeiesteret. Voteringsprotokol for Hoeiesteret.

_____. RA. JPD. pakke Thrane-saken. Medlemsfortegnelser.

_____. RA. JPD. pakke Thrane-saken. Petisjoner.

_____. RA. Det kongelige Kirke- og Undervisningsdepartement [hereinafter listed as KUD]. Kontor A. pakke "Mormonerne 1851-1920."

_____. RA. KUD. Kontor A. Bergen Stift. Visitasberetninger, 1851-1857; 1881-1900.

_____. RA. KUD. Kontor A. Kristiania Stift. Visitasberetninger, 1850-1924.

_____. RA. KUD. Kontor A. Kristiansand Stift. Visitasberetninger, 1851-1870.

_____. RA. KUD. Kontor A. Tromsoe Stift. Visitasberetninger, 1851-1872.

_____. RA. KUD. Kontor A. Trondheim Stift. Visitasberetninger, 1851-1927.

_____. RA. Private arkiv. Chr. Birch-Reichenwald arkiv.

_____. RA. Private arkiv. Det Motzfeldtske familie-arkiv.

_____. Statsarkivet [hereinafter listed as SA]. Bamble Sorenskriveri. Forhoersprotokol, nos. 5-6, 1851-1857.

_____. SA. Christiania Politikammer. Reisekontroll. Emigrant Protokoll, no. 13, 2/3 1886-28/5 1897.

_____. SA. Fredrikstad By. Forhoersprotokol, no. 5, 1852-1857.

_____. SA. Fredrikstad By. Forhoersprotokol, no. 6, 1857-1862.

_____. SA. Kongsberg By. Ekstrarettsprotokol, no. 4, 1857-1862.

_____. SA. Kongsberg By. Forhoersrettsprotokoller, no. 9, 1858-1864.

_____. SA. Krageroe By. Ekstrarettsprotokol, no. 1, 1851-1858.

_____. SA. Lier, Roeyken og Hurum sorenskriveri. Forhoersprotokol, no. 4, 1851-1861.

_____. SA. Lier, Roeyken og Hurum sorenskriveri. Forhoersprotokol, no. 5, 1861-1868.

_____. SA. Porsgrunn By. Ekstrarettsprotokol, vol. B, 1851-1852.

_____. SA. Smaalenenes Amt. "Inkomme brev fra JPD 1853-1857."

_____. SA. Smaalenenes Amt. "Kopibok 1851-1854."

_____. SA. Tune Sorenskriveri. Forhoersprotokol, no. 1, 15/7 1854-7/5 1866.

_____. Universitetsbiblioteket. Brevsamling. Berhard Dunker til Conradine Dunker.

_____. Universitetsbiblioteket. Brevsamling. Conradine Dunker til Bernhard Dunker, 1850-1857.

Provo, Utah. Brigham Young University. Harold B. Lee Library. Special Collections. Johann August Olsen Journal, 1891-1920. (Typescript.)

Salt Lake City, Utah. The Church of Jesus Christ of Latter-day Saints. Library-Archives [hereinafter listed as LDS Church Archives]. Josephine H. Adair and Goudy E. Hogan, "Biography of Goudy E. Hogan by himself and daughter, Mrs. Josephine H. Adair." (Microfilm of typescript.)

_____. LDS Church Archives. Andrew Amundsen Journal, 1849-1882. (Typescript.)

_____. LDS Church Archives. Ole Hendriksen Berg Diary, 1864-1865. 3 vols. (Holograph.)

_____. LDS Church Archives. M. F. Brovn [sic] and Svend Larsen, "Journal of Navigation," 1833. (Holograph and MS).

_____. LDS Church Archives. Carl Arvid Carlquist Papers. Carl Arvid Carlquist, "Life of Carl Arvid Carlquist." Translated by Myrtle Carlquist McDonald. (Typescript.)

_____. LDS Church Archives. Carl Christian Anthon Christensen to Canute Peterson, 7 November 1865.

_____. LDS Church Archives. Hans Jacob Christiansen Journal, 1848-1919. 14 vols. (Holograph.)

_____. LDS Church Archives. "Church Emigration," 1831-1881. 3 vols. (Xerox of typescript.)

_____. LDS Church Archives. Carl C. N. Dorius, "Dagbog: Carl C. N. Dorius's Missionsforretninger i Skandinavia, samt en kort Beretning om det tidligere Levnetsloeb," 1830-1893. (Holograph.)

_____. LDS Church Archives. John F. Ferdinand Dorius, "No. 1 Dagbog for J. F. Ferdinand Dorius tilligemed et kort Udtog af hans tidligere Levnetsloeb," 1832-1853. (Holograph.)

_____. LDS Church Archives. George Parker Dykes Diary, 1849-1851. (Holograph.)

_____. LDS Church Archives. George Parker Dykes to Mrs. King, 8 August 1864.

_____. LDS Church Archives. Edward C. Ekman Diary, 1905-1907. (Holograph.)

_____. LDS Church Archives. Nils Evensen Autobiography, ca. 1871- ca. 1910. (Microfilm of typescript.)

_____. LDS Church Archives. Nils C. Flygare, "Letter Book of Niels [sic] C. Flygare, President of the Scandinavian Mission, 1878-1879."

_____. LDS Church Archives. Frants Christian Grundvig Autobiography, 1836- ca. 1898. (Holograph.)

_____. LDS Church Archives. Saamund [Samuel] Gudmundsen Journal, 1855-1900. 4 vols. (Holograph.)

_____. LDS Church Archives. Hector C. Haight Journal, 1813-1862. (Typescript.)

_____. LDS Church Archives. Nephi Hansen Diary, 1909-1910. (Holograph.)

_____. LDS Church Archives. Peter Olsen Hansen Collection. Peter Olsen Hansen Autobiography and Journal, 1818-1876. (Holograph.)

_____. LDS Church Archives. Peter Olsen Hansen Collection. Peter Olsen Hansen, "Elder P. O. Hanson's account of his mission to Denmark," 29 September 1855. (Holograph.)

_____. LDS Church Archives. Peter Olsen Hansen Collection. Peter Olsen Hansen, "How the Danish translation of the Book of Mormon originated." (Holograph.)

_____. LDS Church Archives. John Anthon Hendricksen Autobiography, 1860-1935. (Microfilm of typescript.)

_____. LDS Church Archives. John Anthon Hendricksen Diary, 1887-1902. 3 vols. (Microfilm of holograph.)

_____. LDS Church Archives. Ferdinand Friis Hintze Diary, 1884-1904. 6 vols. (Holograph.)

_____. LDS Church Archives. Goudy E. Hogan Journal, 1829-1881. (Microfilm of typescript.)

_____. LDS Church Archives. Christofer Iversen Diary, 1894-1896. (Microfilm of holograph.)

_____. LDS Church Archives. Hans Peter Jensen Autobiography and Journal, 1834-1854. (Holograph.)

_____. LDS Church Archives. James Jensen Journal, 1908-1909. (Xerox of holograph.)

_____. LDS Church Archives. James Christian Jensen, "Record Book," 1904-1906. (Holograph.)

_____. LDS Church Archives. Andrew Jenson Diary, 1850-1941. 18 vols. (Holograph and typescript.)

_____. LDS Church Archives. Andrew Jenson, "Scandinavian Mission General History, 1850-1926." 8 vols. (MS and typescript.)

_____. LDS Church Archives. Jonas Johansen Diary, 1870-1871. (Holograph.)

_____. LDS Church Archives. Anna Helena Dyresen Johnson Autobiography, 1844-1915. (Xerox of typescript.)

_____. LDS Church Archives. Johan L. George Johnson Diary, 1895-1897. (Holograph.)

_____. LDS Church Archives. John Johnson, "Reminiscences, 1899-1935." (Xerox of holograph.)

_____. LDS Church Archives. Olaus Johnson Autobiography, 1833-1922. (Typescript.)

_____. LDS Church Archives. Journal History of the Church. (Typescript, scrapbook and MS.)

_____. LDS Church Archives. Christopher Jensen Kempe Autobiography, 1837-1899. (Microfilm of typescript.)

_____. LDS Church Archives. Carl Kjaer Diary, 1908-1910. (Holograph.)

_____. LDS Church Archives. Christian Knudsen Autobiography, 1856-1914. (Holograph.)

_____. LDS Church Archives. Milton Herman Knudsen Autobiography, 1881-1969. (Xerox of typescript.)

_____. LDS Church Archives. Christian J. Larsen Journal, 1831-1914. 5 vols. (Holograph and MS.)

_____. LDS Church Archives. Oluf Christian Larsen, "A Biographical Sketch of the life of Oluf Christian Larsen dictated by himself and written by his son Oluf Larsen dedicated to his posterity who might desire to read it." (Xerox of typescript.)

_____. LDS Church Archives. Svend Larsen Diary, 1852-1868. (Holograph.)

_____. LDS Church Archives. Svend Larsen, "Extracts from my Autobiography." (Typescript translation.)

_____. LDS Church Archives. Svend Larsen, "Uddrag af min Biographi (1816-1867)." (Holograph.)

_____. LDS Church Archives. Carl P. Lind Journal, 1910-1935. (Holograph.)

_____. LDS Church Archives. Anthon Hendrik Lund Diary, 1860-1921. 42 vols. (Microfilm of holograph.)

_____. LDS Church Archives. Christian N. Lund, "Diary of Christian N. Lund, 1846-1921." (Xerox of typescript.)

_____. LDS Church Archives. Hans Peter Lund Journal, 1821-1880. 2 vols. (Holograph.)

_____. LDS Church Archives. Hans Olsen Magleby Journal, 1835-1875. 2 vols. (Holograph.)

_____. LDS Church Archives. Hans Olsen Magleby Journal, 1835-1875. 2 vols. Translated by John A. Widtsoe. (Typescript.)

_____. LDS Church Archives. Olaf Henrik Nielsen Journal, 1858-1896. 3 vols. (Holograph.)

_____. LDS Church Archives. Johann August Olsen, "Levnetsloeb eller Livsbegivenheder af Johan [sic] A. Olsen nedskrevet i Februar 1873" and Journal, 1868-1895. (Holograph.)

_____. LDS Church Archives. Peter Olsen Diary, 1896-1898. (Microfilm of holograph.)

_____. LDS Church Archives. Lars Larson Olson Journal and Notebook, 1865-1870. (Holograph.)

_____. LDS Church Archives. Mons Pedersen Journal, 1854-1861. (Holograph.)

_____. LDS Church Archives. Perpetual Emigrating Fund Company General Files. (Microfilm of MS.)

_____. LDS Church Archives. Canute Peterson Collection. (MS.)

_____. LDS Church Archives. Canute Peterson Collection. Johan F. F. Dorius to John Frantsen, 3 September 1876.

_____. LDS Church Archives. Canute Peterson Journal, 1852-1856. 3 vols. (Holograph.)

_____. LDS Church Archives. Canute Peterson et al., "Story of the life of Canute Peterson as given by himself and by some members of his family." (Xerox of MS.)

_____. LDS Church Archives. Niels Christian Poulsen Journal, 1855-1858. (Holograph.)

_____. LDS Church Archives. Scandinavian Mission. Brevik Conference. Oester Risoer Branch. "Protocol for Oesterriisoeers Green i Jesu Christi Kirke af Siste Dages Hellige opretet i Oesterriisoeer i October 1851." (Microfilm of MS.)

_____. LDS Church Archives. Scandinavian Mission. Christiania Conference. Historical Record, bk. B, 1873-1895. (MS.)

_____. LDS Church Archives. Scandinavian Mission. Christiania Conference. Historical Record, bk. C, 1896-1919. (MS.)

_____. LDS Church Archives. Scandinavian Mission. Christiania Conference. Letter-Copy-Book, bk. B, 1880-1905. (MS.)

_____. LDS Church Archives. Scandinavian Mission. Christiania Conference. Letter-Copy-Book, bk. C, 1905-1906. (MS.)

_____. LDS Church Archives. Scandinavian Mission. Christiania Conference. Brevik Branch. Historical Record and Record of Members, 1852-1862. (MS.)

_____. LDS Church Archives. Scandinavian Mission. Christiania Conference. Christiania Branch. Historical Record, bk. E, 1900-1905. (MS.)

_____. LDS Church Archives. Scandinavian Mission. Christiania Conference. Christiania Branch. Record of Members, 1853-1867. (Microfilm of MS.)

_____. LDS Church Archives. Scandinavian Mission. Christiania Conference. Christiania Branch. Record of Members, 1853-1900. (Microfilm of MS.)

_____. LDS Church Archives. Scandinavian Mission. Christiania Conference. Christiania Branch. Record of Members, 1853-1907. (Microfilm of MS.)

_____. LDS Church Archives. Scandinavian Mission. Christiania Conference. Drammen Branch. Minute Book and Record of Members, bk. A, 1854-1873. (MS.)

_____. LDS Church Archives. Scandinavian Mission. Christiania Conference. Fredrikstad Branch. Historical Record and Record of Members, 1852-1858. (Microfilm of MS.)

_____. LDS Church Archives. Scandinavian Mission. Trondheim Conference. Historical Record, bk. C, 1901-1917. (MS.)

_____. LDS Church Archives. Scandinavian Mission. Trondheim Conference. Bodoe Branch. Record of Members, 1903-1913. (Microfilm of MS.)

_____. LDS Church Archives. Scandinavian Mission. Trondheim Conference. Tromsoe Branch. Historical Record, bk. A, 1886-1908. (MS.)

_____. LDS Church Archives. Scandinavian Mission. Trondheim Conference. Tromsoe Branch. Historical Record, bk. A, 1890-1905. (MS.)

_____. LDS Church Archives. Scandinavian Mission. Trondheim Conference. Trondheim Branch. Historical Record, bk. C, 1880-1919. (MS.)

_____. LDS Church Archives. August Severin Schou Diary, 1857-1880. 3 vols. Translated by Lauritz G. Petersen. (Xerox of typescript.)

_____. LDS Church Archives. Anthon L. Skanchy Collection.

_____. LDS Church Archives. Anthon L. Skanchy Collection. Anthon L. Skanchy Autobiography, 1839-1914. (Holograph.)

_____. LDS Church Archives. Jesse Nathaniel Smith Journal, 1834-1906. (Typescript.)

_____. LDS Church Archives. Erastus Snow Collection. Erastus Snow, "A Summary of the Danish Mission by Erastus Snow to the Presidency of the Church of Jesus Christ of Latter-day Saints." (Microfilm of holograph.)

_____. LDS Church Archives. Erastus Snow Collection. Erastus Snow Letter File, 1848-1887. (Xeroxes of holographs.)

_____. LDS Church Archives. Erastus Snow Collection. Erastus Snow Letter File, 1848-1887. Willard Snow to Erastus Snow, 9 July 1852.

_____. LDS Church Archives. Erastus Snow Journal, 1818-1857. 7 vols. (Microfilm of holograph.)

_____. LDS Church Archives. Erastus Snow Reminiscences, 1818-1854. (Holograph.)

_____. LDS Church Archives. Willard Snow Diary, 1851-1853. (Holograph.)

_____. LDS Church Archives. Samuel Lindsay Sprague Diary, 1865-1866. (Holograph.)

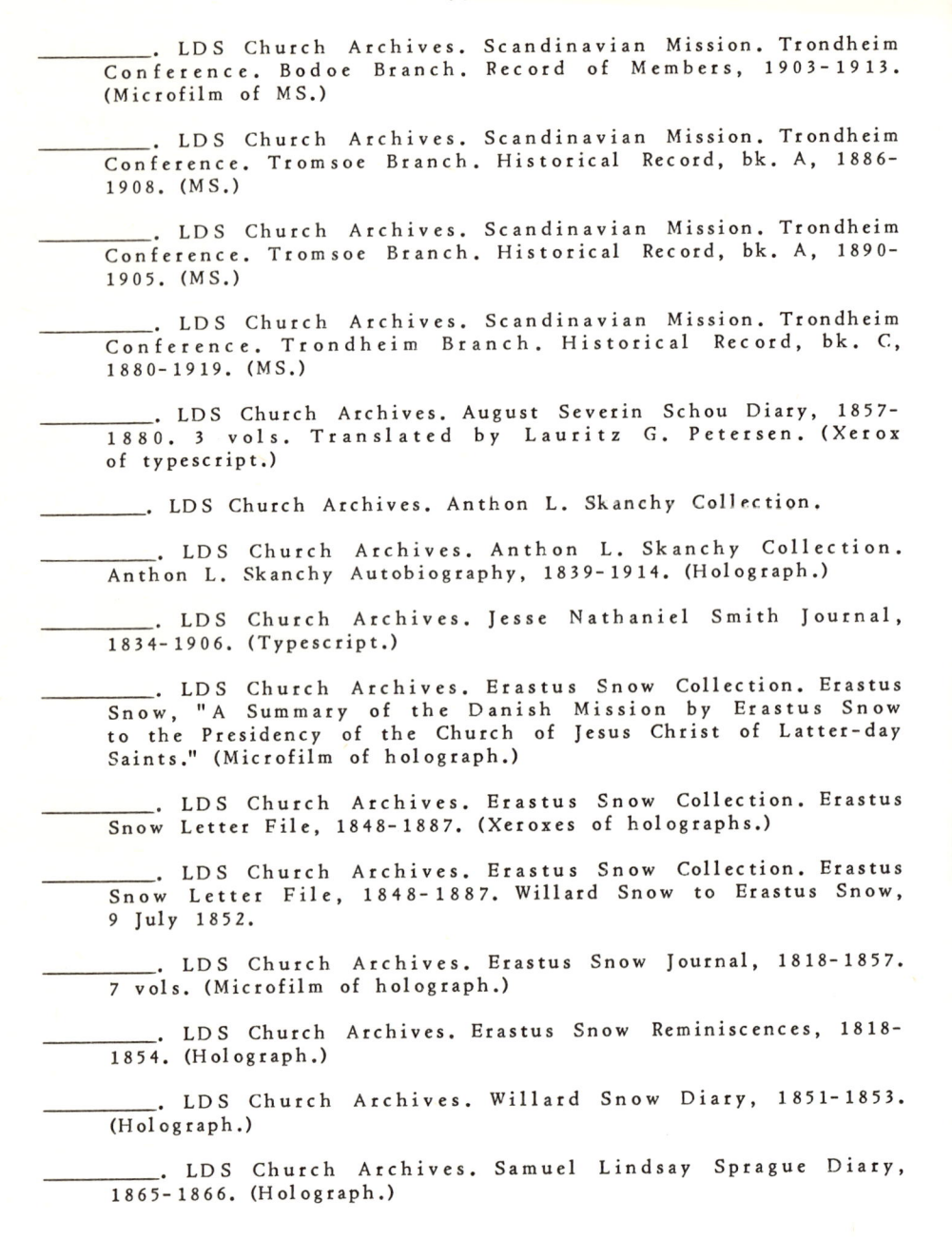

_____. LDS Church Archives. Supplement to Journal History of the Church, 1849. (Typescript, scrapbook and MS.)

_____. LDS Church Archives. Peter Olaff Thomassen Journal, 1853-1891. (Holograph.)

_____. LDS Church Archives. Ingwald Conrad Thoresen Diary excerpts, 1876-1877. (Holograph.)

_____. LDS Church Archives. Torkel E. Torkelson, "En Kort Beskrivelse af Mit Livs Historie skrevet af mig selv." 3 vols. (Holograph.)

_____. LDS Church Archives. John Van Cott Diary, 1852-1862. 4 vols. (Xerox of holograph.)

_____. LDS Church Archives. Jens Christian Andersen Weibye Diary, 1861-1892. 13 vols. (Holograph.)

_____. LDS Church Archives. Christopher Sigvarth Winge Autobiography, 1835-1880. (Microfilm of typescript.)

_____. The Church of Jesus Christ of Latter-day Saints. Genealogical Department. Library Services Division [hereinafter listed as GS]. George Mortimer Brown Autobiography and Diary, 1863-1866. (Typescript.)

_____. GS. Early Church Information File.

_____. GS. Family Group Record Archives.

_____. GS. International Genealogical Index [IGI].

_____. GS. Nauvoo Temple Endowment Register.

Dissertations, Theses, Papers and Interviews

Arveseter, Ramm George Parley; Arveseter, Rosa Baldani; Freidel, Paula Pedersen; Johansen, Alvilde Kristiansen; and Johansen, Erik. Members of the Church of Jesus Christ of Latter-day Saints, Oslo, Norway. Interview, 24 February 1978.

Cushman, Robert Brookman. "American Religious Societies in Norway." Ph.D. dissertation, Northwestern University, 1942.

Ellingsen, A., ed. "Kyrkjebok for Hoele og Fossand 1702-1854." Transcript prepared for Rogaland Historie og Aettesogelag, [Stavanger], 1965. (Mimeographed.)

Engoey, Einar. "Kirkeforfatningsdebaten i 1850-aarene: Om bakgrunnen for kirkekommisjonen av 1859." Hovedoppgave, University of Oslo, 1968.

Hassing, Arne. "Methodism and Society in Norway: 1853-1918." Ph.D. dissertation, Northwestern University, 1974.

Henriksen, R. Lasse. "Synopsis til Spillefilm '<u>Christian</u>'." MS proposal for a feature film, Oslo, Norway, 1978.

Hov, Helge. "Bakgrunnen for og Nedsettelsen av Kirkekommisjonen av 1908." Hovedoppgave, University of Oslo, 1973.

Hunsaker, Curtis B. "History of the Norwegian Mission from 1851 to 1960." M.A. thesis, Brigham Young University, 1965.

Joergensen, Bent Raymond. "Mormonsamfundet i Danmark, 1850-1900: Fra dansk folkelig bevaegelse til amerikansk styret institution." Konferens-opgave, University of Copenhagen, 1978.

Langeland, John. President of the Norway Mission of the Church of Jesus Christ of Latter-day Saints, Oslo, Norway. Interview, 16 February 1978.

Marthins, Ragnhild. "Synet paa religionsfrihet i Norge i foerste halvdel av det 19. aarhundre slik det kommer fram i debatten om paragraf 2 i grunnloven." Hovedoppgave, University of Oslo, 1963.

Mulder, William. "Utah's Nordic-Language Press: Aspect and Instrument of Immigrant Culture." M.A. thesis, University of Utah, 1947.

Podhorny, Ole. "Christian Nephi Anderson: Popular 'Mormon' Author of Norwegian Origin." M.A. thesis, University of Oslo, 1980.

Sandvin, Karl. "Mormonisma i Noreg med utsyn over samfunnet si amerikanske historie." Hovedoppgave, University of Oslo, 1946.

Seljaas, Helge. "The Mormon Migration from Norway." M.A. thesis, University of Utah, 1972.

Strand, Einar. Member of the Church of Jesus Christ of Latter-day Saints, Mauritz Hansens Gate 4, Oslo 3, Norway. Interview, 7 March 1978.

Periodicals and Articles

<u>Adresse-Tidende for Brevig, Stathelle og Langesund</u>, 1851-1853.

Andersen, John A. "John A. Andersen to Joseph Christiansen, 26 February 1893." Skandinaviens Stjerne 42 (15 March 1893): 187-88.

Andersen, L. S. "L. S. Andersen to C. G. Larsen, 9 March 1874." Skandinaviens Stjerne 23 (1 April 1874):202-03.

Andersen, Mons. "Mons Andersen to W. W. Cluff, 3 December 1870." Skandinaviens Stjerne 20 (1 January 1871):108-09.

Andersen, Nephi, and Christensen, Heber C. "Nephi Andersen and Heber C. Christensen to Peter Sundwall, 5 June 1895." Skandinaviens Stjerne 44 (15 July 1895):314-15.

Andersen, Oluf. "Konferencemoedet i Kristiania den 25de og 26de mai 1872." Skandinaviens Stjerne 21 (15 June 1872): 279-80.

Anderson, Edward H. "Events and Comments." Improvement Era, June 1906, pp. 663-64.

"Arbeide er Gudsdyrkelse." Skandinaviens Stjerne 13 (1 June 1864):257-60.

Berge, Olav, ed. "Manntal for Ryfylke 1801." Rogaland Aettesogelag 3 (1943):3-67.

Bitton, Davis. "Mormon Polygamy: A Review Article." Journal of Mormon History 4 (1977):101-18.

Bolling, Reidar. "Biskop Andreas Grimelund." In Aarbok for Nidaros Bispedoemme, 1949, pp. 57-66. Trondheim: F. Bruns Bokhandels Forlag for Nidaros Bispedoemmeraad, 1949.

Borg, L. P. "L. P. Borg to Jesse N. Smith, 29 December 1869." Skandinaviens Stjerne 19 (15 January 1870):122-23.

Breistein, Dagfinn. "Bakgrunnen for Lov om Menighetsraad og Mennighetsmoeter av 3. Desember 1920." Tidsskrift for Teologi og Kirke 29 (1958):34-48.

Brown, D. K. "D. K. Brown to C. N. Lund, 4 August 1897." Skandinaviens Stjerne 46 (15 August 1897):347-49.

_____. "D. K. Brown to C. N. Lund, 31 January 1898." Skandinaviens Stjerne 47 (15 February 1898):58-60.

Brown, George M. "George M. Brown to Samuel L. Sprague, 14 June 1864." Skandinaviens Stjerne 13 (1 July 1864):300-02.

"Boern ere en Velsignelse." Skandinaviens Stjerne 7 (1 September 1858):355-59.

Cannon, Geo. Q. "Den forenede Orden." Skandinaviens Stjerne 24 (15 December 1873):86-87.

Christensen, C. C. A. "C. C. A. Christensens Beretning." Morgenstjernen 3 (1 July 1884):203-07.

_____. "C. C. A. Christensens Levnedsloeb udarbejded efter hans egne optegnelser og dagboeger." In Mindeudgave C. C. A. Christensen: Poetiske Arbejder, Artikler og Afhandlinger tilligemed hans Levnedsloeb, pp. 329-81. Edited by John S. Hansen, Salt Lake City, Utah: Bikubens Bibliotek, 1921.

_____. "Lidt om Missionens Begyndelse i Norge." Skandinaviens Stjerne 51 (1 February 1902):42-45.

Christiansen, Chr. "Chr. Christiansen to Andrew Jenson, 15 February 1882." Morgenstjernen 1 (February 1882):26-27.

Christiansen, H. J. "H. J. Christiansen to Anthon H. Lund, 27 July 1885." Skandinaviens Stjerne 34 (15 August 1885): 346-47.

_____. "H. J. Christiansen to N. C. Flygare, 6 January 1886." Skandinaviens Stjerne 35 (15 January 1886):121-22.

_____. "H. J. Christiansen to N. C. Flygare, 14 July 1886." Skandinaviens Stjerne 35 (1 August 1886):330-31.

_____. "H. J. Christiansen to N. C. Flygare, 24 September 1886." Skandinaviens Stjerne 36 (15 October 1886):26-27.

_____. "H. J. Christiansen to P. Sundwall, 26 July 1894." Skandinaviens Stjerne 43 (1 August 1894):329-31.

Christiansen, Hans J. "Den Spanske Syge." Skandinaviens Stjerne 67 (1 November 1918): 332-33.

_____. "Midsommer - Missionsrejsen i Norge og Danmark." Skandinaviens Stjerne 65 (15 August 1916):249-50.

_____. "Min Foraarsrejse i Missionen." Skandinaviens Stjerne 65 (1 June 1916):168-70.

_____. "Min Rundrejse til Efteraarskonferencerne." Skandinaviens Stjerne 65 (1 December 1916):360-62.

_____. "Misjonsrejsen i Efteraaret 1917." Skandinaviens Stjerne 66 (1 December 1917):362-63.

_____. "Missionsrejsen i Foraaret 1918." *Skandinaviens Stjerne* 67 (15 May 1918):152-53.

_____. "Naervaerende vanskelige Tider." *Skandinaviens Stjerne* 66 (15 February 1917):56-57.

Christiansen, John E. "H. F. Petersens Biografi." *Morgenstjernen* 3 (1 September 1884):267-72.

Christophersen, M. "M. Christophersen to Anthon H. Lund, 5 December 1884." *Skandinaviens Stjerne* 34 (15 December 1884):86.

_____. "M. Christophersen to Anthon H. Lund, 31 January 1885." *Skandinaviens Stjerne* 34 (15 February 1885):154-55.

_____. "M. Christophersen to Anthon H. Lund, 5 March 1885." *Skandinaviens Stjerne* 34 (15 March 1885):189.

Davis, David Brion. "Some Themes of Counter-Subversion." In *Mormonism and American Culture*, pp. 59-73. Edited by James B. Allen and Marvin S. Hill. New York: Harper & Row, 1972.

De Pillis, Mario S. "Cleng Peerson and the Communitarian Background of Norwegian Immigration." *Norwegian-American Studies* 21 (1962):136-57.

Doherty, Robert W. "Sociology, Religion, and Historians." *Historical Methods Newsletter* 6 (September 1973):161-69.

Dorius, C. N. "C. N. Dorius to Jesse N. Smith, 13 January 1863." *Skandinaviens Stjerne* 12 (15 February 1863):155-57.

Dorius, John F. "John F. Dorius to Jesse N. Smith, 22 July 1862." *Skandinaviens Stjerne* 11 (15 August 1862):346-47.

Dorius, John F. F. "John F. F. Dorius to O. N. Liljenqvist, [?] December 1876." *Skandinaviens Stjerne* 26 (1 February 1877):140-41.

Dykes, Geo. P. "Geo. P. Dykes to the Editor of *Times and Seasons*, 19 May 1843." *Times and Seasons* 4 (15 May 1843):195.

Erickson, James. "James Erickson to Joseph Christiansen, 4 January 1893." *Skandinaviens Stjerne* 42 (1 February 1893):141-42.

"Familieforholde." *Skandinaviens Stjerne* 5 (1 December 1855):75-80.

Farr, Lorin. "Lorin Farr to H. S. Eldredge, 17 April 1871." *Skandinaviens Stjerne* 20 (1 May 1871):236-37.

First Presidency of the Church of Jesus Christ of Latter-day Saints. "Sjette almindelige Epistel." Skandinaviens Stjerne 1 (1 March 1852):81-85.

Fjeld, Carl J. E. "Autobiography of Carl Johan Ellefsen Fjeld." In A Brief History of the Fjeld-Fields Family, pp. 7-27. By Andrew Fjeld. Springville, Utah: Art City Publishing Co., 1946.

_____. "Aeldste Carl Fjelds Beretning." Morgenstjernen 3 (15 March 1884):90-93.

Fjeldsted, C. D. "C. D. Fjeldsted to Jesse N. Smith, 9 October 1869." Skandinaviens Stjerne 19 (1 November 1869):43-44.

_____. "C. D. Fjeldsted to Jesse N. Smith, 23 October 1869." Skandinaviens Stjerne 19 (15 November 1869):58-59.

"Forfoelgelserne i Trondhjem." Skandinaviens Stjerne 61 (1 July 1912):200-02.

Grant, Jedediah M. "Men Rewarded According to their Works: Remarks made by President J. M. Grant, in the Bowery, Great Salt Lake City, October 6, 1855." In Journal of Discourses. Vol. 3, pp. 125-27. Liverpool: Orson Pratt, 42, Islington; London: Latter-Day Saints' Book Depot, 1856; reprint ed., Los Angeles, California: General Printing & Lithograph Co., 1961.

Grant, Jedediah M.; Kimball, Heber C.; and Young, Brigham. "Trettende Almindelige Epistel." Skandinaviens Stjerne 10 (15 February 1856):145-54.

Grue, A. C. "A. C. Grue to W. W. Cluff, 16 October 1870." Skandinaviens Stjerne 20 (1 December 1870):75-76.

Gulbranson, Johannes. "Hans Nielsen Hauge og Christiania." St. Hallvard 49 (1971):142-79.

Hagen, Albert. "I Midnatssolens Land." Skandinaviens Stjerne 53 (1 September 1904):270-72.

Halvorsen, John. "An Interview with King Haakon VII of Norway." Improvement Era, December 1911, pp. 146-48.

_____. "John Halvorsen to Andrew Jensen, 17 July 1911." Skandinaviens Stjerne 60 (15 August 1911):251-52.

Hansen, H. C. "H. C. Hansens Beretning." Morgenstjernen 2 (1 January 1883):9.

Hansen, Peter O. "Evangeliets Indfoerelse i disse Lande." Skandinaviens Stjerne 32 (1 October 1882):11-15.

_____. "Peter O. Hansens Autobiografi." *Morgenstjernen* 3 (1 November 1884):330-36.

Hartwig, G. "Oceanets Majestaet." *Skandinaviens Stjerne* 40 (1 October 1890):13-15.

Haugen, Einar. Introduction to *Norwegian-English Dictionary*, edited by Einar Haugen et al. Oslo: Universitetsforlaget, 1965; Madison, Wisconsin: University of Wisconsin Press, 1965.

Hogensen, Chr. "Chr. Hogensen to C. D. Fjeldsted, 28 November 1881." *Skandinaviens Stjerne* 31 (15 December 1881):91-92.

Hougan, Gaudy. "Gaudy Hougan to N. Wilhelmsen, 29 November 1879." *Skandinaviens Stjerne* 29 (1 January 1880):106-07.

"Hvad er Hensigten af Evangeliet?" *Skandinaviens Stjerne* 14 (1 June 1865):260-61.

Jacobsen, J. A. "Mormonerne og deres mission: En advarsel." *Nordmands-Forbundet* 4 (October 1911):389-96.

Jenson, Andrew. "Biografiske Skizzer: Hans Peter Jensen." *Morgenstjernen* 1 (July 1882):101-10.

_____. "De sidste-Dages Helliges Forsamlingslokaler i Christiania." *Skandinaviens Stjerne* 52 (15 November 1903):345-48.

_____. "Erindringer fra missionen i Skandinavien." *Morgenstjernen* 1 (January 1882):1-7; 1 (April 1882):49-55; 1 (November 1882):161-67; 2 (January 1883):1-7; 2 (February 1883):17-23; 2 (April 1883):49-55; 2 (May 1883):65-71; 3 (February 1884):49-55; 3 (1 March 1884):65-71; 3 (1 October 1884):289-95; 3 (15 October 1884):305-11.

_____. "For tredsinstyve Aar siden." *Skandinaviens Stjerne* 59 (1 August 1910):225-31.

_____. "Oluf Josva Andersen." *Skandinaviens Stjerne* 58 (15 March 1909):88-89.

_____. "Praesident Andrew Jensons Afskedshilsen." *Skandinaviens Stjerne* 61 (15 May 1912):152-55.

_____. "Scandinavian Reminiscences." *Contributor*, March 1895, pp. 297-305; May 1895, pp. 417-21.

Jaeger, Gunnar. "Kirken, dissenterne og lekmannsbevegelsen i Bergen 1850-1880." In Bergens Historiske Forening: Skrifter, pp. 33-126. Bergen: J. D. Beyer A. S. Boktrykkeri, 1971.

"Joergen Jansen-Fuhr." Skandinaviens Stjerne 60 (1 August 1911): 235-37.

Karlsen, Oluf K. "Oluf K. Karlsen to A. Schou, 28 May 1920." Skandinaviens Stjerne 69 (15 June 1920):183.

Kirkhusmo, Anders. "Trondheim fra ca. 1800 til i dag: Noen trekk av byens historie." In Trondheim i 1000 Aar: Historisk Guide, pp. 157-86. Edited by Anders Kirkhusmo. Trondheim: F. Bruns Bokhandels Forlag A/S, 1972.

Knudsen, Milton H. "Milton H. Knudsen to Anthon L. Skanchy, 24 February 1903." Skandinaviens Stjerne 52 (15 March 1903):93.

Koht, Halvdan, and Schreiner, Johan. "Aarsakene til at Regjeringen grep inn mot Hans Nielsen Hauge." Historisk Tidsskrift 30 (1934-1936):53-63.

Kvistad, J. "Kirkeliv og kristentype paa Vest- og Soerlandet." Luthersk Kirketidende 80 (3 November 1945):198-212.

Larsen, C. G. "C. G. Larsen to John Frantzen, 21 April 1874." Skandinaviens Stjerne 23 (1 May 1874):236-37.

Larsen, John E., and Monson, Laurence C. "John E. Larsen and Laurence C. Monson to Andrew Jenson, 30 January 1912." Skandinaviens Stjerne 61 (1 March 1912):76-77.

Lind, Carl P. "Carl P. Lind to Andrew Jenson, 13 November 1911." Skandinaviens Stjerne 60 (1 December 1911):368.

"Love for Aegteskab og Menneskeslaegtens Formerelse." Skandinaviens Stjerne 9 (15 January 1860):118-21.

Lund, H. P. "H. P. Lund to Jesse N. Smith, 18 June 1862." Skandinaviens Stjerne 11 (1 July 1862):296-97.

Mamen, H. Chr. "Amerikas Bidrag til Norsk Kirkeliv." Kirke og Kultur 65 (1960):45-54.

Moe, Olaf. "Caspari og Johnsons Theologiske Tidsskrift." Tidsskrift for Teologi og Kirke 29 (1958):1-9.

Molland, Einar. "Kristen Tro og Oekonomisk Aktivitet hos Hans Nielsen Hauge." Norsk Teologisk Tidsskrift 59 (1958):193-208.

Molland, Einar, and Skrondal, Anders. "Dissentarspoersmaalet i Noreg 1845-1891: Opposisjonsinnlegg ved stiftskapellan

Knut Rygnestads disputas for den teologiske doktorgrad 22. september 1956." *Norsk Teologisk Tidsskrift* 57 (1956): 193-217.

"Mormonernes 'Pigejagt.'" *Skandinaviens Stjerne* 61 (1 October 1912):296-300.

Mortinsen, Hans J. Quoted in "Messages from the Missions." *Improvement Era*, February 1912, pp. 330-31.

Mulder, William. "Image of Zion: Mormonism as an American Influence in Scandinavia." *Mississippi Valley Historical Review* 43 (June 1956):18-38.

_____. "Mormons from Scandinavia, 1850-1900: A Shepherded Migration." *Pacific Historical Review* 23 (August 1954):227-46.

_____. "Norwegian Forerunners Among the Early Mormons." *Norwegian-American Studies and Records* 19 (1956):46-61.

_____. "Scandinavian Saga." In *The Peoples of Utah*, pp. 141-85. Edited by Helen Z. Papanikolas. Salt Lake City, Utah: Utah State Historical Society, 1976.

_____. "Utah's Ugly Ducklings: A Profile of the Scandinavian Immigrant." *Utah Historical Quarterly* 23 (July 1955):233-59.

Nielsen, A. M. "A. M. Nielsen to J. M. Christensen, 15 July 1906." *Skandinaviens Stjerne* 55 (15 August 1906):246-47.

Nielsen, Adolph M. "Adolph M. Nielsen to Hans J. Christiansen, 26 March 1917." *Skandinaviens Stjerne* 66 (15 April 1917):124-25.

Nielsen, Peter. "Peter Nielsen to C. A. Carlquist, 13 September 1893." *Skandinaviens Stjerne* 43 (1 October 1893):11.

Nielson, A. M. "A. M. Nielson to Joseph Christiansen, 21 December 1892." *Skandinaviens Stjerne* 42 (15 January 1893):122-23.

_____. "A. M. Nielson to C. A. Carlquist, 10 August 1893." *Skandinaviens Stjerne* 42 (1 September 1893):363-64.

Nissen, Kristian. "Frederik Rode 1800-1883: En Hoeireist Presteskikkelse i den Norske Kirke: En biografisk Skisse." *Norsk Teologisk Tidsskrift* 52 (1951):227-50.

Norske Tilskuer, 1851-1852.

"Noedvendigheden af at opfylde givne Loefter." *Skandinaviens Stjerne* 16 (1 July 1867):291-93.

Olsen, John A. "Et Besoeg i Kristiania." *Skandinaviens Stjerne* 44 (15 July 1895):316-17.

Olsen, Ole Harmon. "Ole Harmon Olsen - Pioneer 1868." In *Our Pioneer Heritage*, pp. 110-16. Compiled by Kate B. Carter. Vol. 12. Salt Lake City, Utah: Daughters of the Utah Pioneers, 1969.

"Passing Events." *Improvement Era*, August 1910, pp. 957-58.

Pedersen, H. A. "H. A. Pedersen to Joseph Christiansen, 27 December 1892." *Skandinaviens Stjerne* 42 (15 January 1893):123-25.

Penrose, Charles W. "En mindevaerdig og betydningsfuld Rejse." *Skandinaviens Stjerne* 58 (1 September 1909):260-63.

Petersen, Mons. "Aeldste Mons Petersens Beretning." *Morgenstjernen* 4 (March 1885):46-48; 4 (June 1885):88-89.

Peterson, Canute. "Barnedaab, Konfirmation og Jordpaakastelse." *Skandinaviens Stjerne* 21 (1 August 1872):328-30.

Richards, Geo. F. "Geo. F. Richards to Hans J. Christiansen, 15 November 1918." *Skandinaviens Stjerne* 67 (1 December 1918):362-63.

"Sager, paakjendte i Hoeiesterets 2den Session 1853." *Norsk Retstidende* 46 (14 November 1853):735-36.

Seierstad, Andr. "H. N. Hauge og Kvekarane." *Tidsskrift for Teologi og Kirke* 14 (1943):145-59.

Seljaas, Helge. "Polygamy among the Norwegian Mormons." *Norwegian-American Studies* 27 (1977):151-62.

Skanchy, A. L. "A. L. Skanchy to N. C. Flygare, 16 March 1887." *Skandinaviens Stjerne* 36 (1 April 1887):202-03.

Skandinaviens Stjerne. 1851-1920.

Skrondal, A. "Chr. Bruun: Folkelige Grundtanker." *Syn og Segn* 39 (1933):442-56.

Steene, Hans Toennesen. "Beretning om en tre aars reise i Amerika 1849-1852." *Aett og Heim* (1974):46-56.

Steffensen, C. H. "C. H. Steffensen to Anthon H. Lund, 14 June 1884." *Skandinaviens Stjerne* 33 (1 July 1884):298-99.

Straaberg, Josef. "Nordmaend paa besoeg i Utah." In *Utah Fest Program for 17de mai: Hundredaars Jubilaeum for Norges Grundlov*, p. 10. Edited by [Arrangementskomiteen for festligholdelsen af den 17de mai 1914]. [Salt Lake City, Utah]: n.p., [1914].

Stoeren, Wilhelm K. "Trondheim og industrien: Fabrikker og Anlegg." In <u>Trondheim i 1000 Aar: Historisk Guide</u>, pp. 185-90. Edited by Anders Kirkhusmo. Trondheim: F. Bruns Bokhandels Forlag A/S, 1972.

Sundwall, Peter. "Peter Sundwall to John A. Olsen et al., 25 September 1894." <u>Skandinaviens Stjerne</u> 44 (1 October 1894):10-11.

Soerensen, Anton J. T. "Anton J. T. Soerensen to Andrew Jenson, 30 June 1911." <u>Skandinaviens Stjerne</u> 60 (1 July 1911):206-08.

Tanga, Gunnar. "Lekmannsforkynning i nokre austlandsbygder i foerre hundreaaret." <u>Heimen</u> 9 (1952-1954):10-16.

Thomassen, P. O. "P. O. Thomassen to W. W. Cluff, 16 October 1870." <u>Skandinaviens Stjerne</u> 20 (1 November 1870):35-36.

Thorp, Malcolm R. "The Religious Background of Mormon Converts in Britain, 1837-52." <u>Journal of Mormon History</u> 4 (1977):51-66.

Walker, Ronald W. "Crisis in Zion: Heber J. Grant and the Panic of 1893." <u>Sunstone</u> 5 (January-February 1980):26-34.

Weibye, J. C. A. "J. C. A. Weibye to K. Peterson, 24 July 1871." <u>Skandinaviens Stjerne</u> 20 (1 August 1871):335-36.

_____. "J. C. A. Weibye to K. Peterson, 28 December 1871." <u>Skandinaviens Stjerne</u> 21 (15 January 1872):124.

_____. "J. C. A. Weibye to K. Peterson, 30 October 1872." <u>Skandinaviens Stjerne</u> 22 (15 November 1872):58.

_____. "J. C. A. Weibye to C. G. Larsen, 24 August 1873." <u>Skandinaviens Stjerne</u> 23 (1 October 1873):11-13.

Wisloeff, Carl Fr. "Det Geistlige Embete og det Alminnelige Prestedoemme i Norsk Pastoralteologi fra W. A. Wexels til Gustav Jensen." <u>Tidsskrift for Teologi og Kirke</u> 29 (1958): 49-68.

Young, Brigham. "Brigham Young to John Van Cott, 9 August 1860." <u>Skandinaviens Stjerne</u> 10 (1 October 1860):8-10.

_____. "The Necessity of the Saints Having the Spirit of Revelation--Faith and Works--the Power of God and of the Devil: A Discourse, by President B. Young, Delivered in the Tabernacle, Great Salt Lake City, May 6, 1855." In <u>Journal of Discourses</u>. Vol. 3, pp. 153-60. Liverpool: Orson Pratt, 42, Islington; London: Latter-Day Saints Book Depot,

1856; reprint ed., Los Angeles, California: General Printing and Lithograph Co., 1961.

Books and other Published Materials

Aarflot, Andreas. *Hans Nielsen Hauge: Liv og budskap*. Oslo, Bergen, and Tromsoe: Universitetsforlaget, 1971.

_____. *Norsk Kirkehistorie*. Vol. 2. Oslo: Lutherstiftelsen, 1967.

_____. *Tro og Lydighet: Hans Nielsen Hauges kristendomsforstaaelse*. Oslo, Bergen, and Tromsoe: Universitetsforlaget, 1969.

Ahmanson, John. *Vor Tids Muhamed: En historisk og kritisk fremstilling af mormonismens fremkomst og udbredelse, samt skildringer af Utahs hemmelige historie*. Omaha, Nebraska: Den Danske Pioneer's Trykkeri, 1876.

Allen, James B., and Leonard, Glen M. *The Story of the Latter-day Saints*. Salt Lake City, Utah: Deseret Book Company, 1976.

Andersen, Arlow W. *The Norwegian-Americans*. Boston: Twayne Publishers, 1975.

Anderson, Rasmus B. *The First Chapter of Norwegian Immigration, (1821-1840): Its Causes and Results*. Madison, Wisconsin: By the Author, 1906.

Armstrong, Anthony. *The Church of England, the Methodists and Society 1700-1850*. Totowa, New Jersey: Rowman and Littlefield, 1973.

Arnholm, Carl Jacob, and Bahr, Henrik, eds. *Norges Lover 1685-1971*. Oslo: Groendahl & Soen Boktrykkeri for Det Juridiske Fakultet, 1972.

[Arrangementskomiteen for festligholdelsen af den 17de mai 1914], eds. *Utah Fest Program for 17de mai: Hundredaars Jubilaeum for Norges Grundlov*. [Salt Lake City, Utah]: n.p., [1914].

Arrington, Leonard J., and Bitton, Davis. *The Mormon Experience: A History of the Latter-day Saints*. New York: Alfred A. Knopf, 1979.

Balling, J. L., and Lindhardt, P. G. *Den Nordiske Kirkes Historie*. Copenhagen: Nyt Nordisk Forlag, Arnold Busck, 1973.

Bergsgaard, Arne. *Norsk Historie 1814-1880*. Oslo: Det Norske Samlaget, 1964.

Birch-Reichenwald, [Christian]; Collett, J. C.; and Kyhn, L.; eds. Departements-Tidende for 1844. Christiania: Krohn & Schibsted, n.d.

Bitton, Davis, comp. Guide to Mormon Diaries & Autobiographies. Provo, Utah: Brigham Young University Press, 1977.

Bjork, Kenneth O. West of the Great Divide: Norwegian Migration to the Pacific Coast, 1847-1893. Northfield, Minnesota: Norwegian-American Historical Association, 1958.

Bjoerklund, Oddvar. Marcus Thrane: sosialistleder i et u-land. Oslo: Tiden Norsk Forlag, 1970.

Blegen, Theodore C. Norwegian Migration to America. Northfield, Minnesota: The Norwegian-American Historical Association, 1940.

Bloch-Hoell, Nils. Pinsebevegelsen: En undersoekelse av pinsebevegelsens tilblivelse, utvikling og saerpreg med saerlig henblikk paa bevegelsens utforming i Norge. Oslo: Universitetsforlaget, 1956.

Bonnevie, N.; Collett, C.; and Kjerulf, A.; eds. Departements-Tidende for 1861. Christiania: Chr. Schibsted, n.d.

Brandrud, Andreas. Udsigt over religionsfrihedens historie i Norge og Danmark efter reformationen. Hamar: n.p., 1898.

Buckley, Joseph. Memoirs of Joseph Buckley. Edited by his daughter. Glasgow: Robert Smeal; London: Samuel Harris & Co., 1874.

Bull, Edv.; Krogvig, Anders; Gran, Gerhard; Jansen, Jonas; Andersen, Oeyvind; and Kaldhol, Bjarte; eds. Norsk Biografisk Leksikon. 18 vols. Oslo: H. Aschehoug & Co. (W. Nygaard), 1923-1977.

Bull, Edvard. Arbeiderklassen i Norsk Historie. [Oslo]: Tiden Norsk Forlag, 1947.

_____. Arbeidermiljoe under det Industrielle Gjennombrudd: Tre norske industristroek. Oslo: Universitetsforlaget, 1958.

Burns, Annie Walker, and Miller, J. Emerson, eds. First Families of Utah as Taken from the 1850 Census of Utah. Washington, D.C.: By the Editors, 1949.

Castberg, Frede. Rett og revolusjon i Norge. Oslo, Bergen, and Tromsoe: Universitetsforlaget, 1974.

Collett, J. C.; Kyhn, L.; and Motzfeldt, C.; eds. Departements-Tidende for 1853. Christiania: Chr. Schibsted, n.d.

Danbolt, Erling. Presten G. A. Lammers for og mot frimenighetstanken. [Oslo]: Universitetsforlaget, 1963.

Dehli, Martin. Fredrikstad bys historie. Vol. 2: Fra festningsby til trelastsentrum, 1767-1860. Fredrikstad: Fredrikstad Kommune, 1964.

Dunker, Bernhard. Breve til A. F. Krieger. Edited by Oeyvind Anker. Oslo: J. W. Cappelens Forlag, 1957.

_____. Breve til Julie Winther. Edited by Solveig Tunold. Oslo: J. W. Cappelens Forlag, 1954.

_____. Reise til Tellemarken og til Arendal Sommeren 1852. Kristiania, Copenhagen, London, and Berlin: Gyldendalske Bokhandel, 1922.

Dykes, G. Parker. Mindeblad efter Aeldste Parker Dykes til Jesu Christi Kirke af Sidste Dages Hellige i Aalborg. [Aalborg?]: n.p., 1851.

Einung, H. H. Tinn Soga. Vol. 2. Krageroe: Eigi Forlag, 1953.

Ellingsen, Terje. Kirkestyre i Historisk Lys. n.p.: Nomi Forlag, 1969.

Eltzholtz, Carl F. Et Vaaben mod Mormonismen. Copenhagen: Andr. Fred. Hoest & Soen, [1884].

Enger, Knut. Statskirke eller frikirke? Oslo: Elingaard Forlag, 1968.

Erlandsen, Andreas. Biographiske Efterretninger om Geistligheden i Throndhjems Stift. Christiania og Levanger: n.p., 1844-1855.

_____. Biographiske Efterretninger om Geistligheden i Tromsoe Stift. Christiania: Chr. Toensbergs Forlag, 1857.

Faye, Andreas. Christianssands Stifts Bispe- og Stiftshistorie. Christiania: Broegger & Christie's Bogtrykkeri, 1867.

Finne-Groenn, S. H. Norges Prokuratorer, Sakfoerere og Advokater 1660-1905: Biografiske Oplysninger. Vol. 2: De Embedsmaessig Utnaevnte Advokater 1814-1860 og Prokuratorer 1814-1848. Oslo: Fabritius & Soenner for Den Norske Sakfoererforening, n.d.

Fjeld, Andrew. A Brief History of the Fjeld-Fields Family. Springville, Utah: Art City Publishing Co., 1946.

Fladby, Rolf; Imsen, Steinar; and Winge, Harald; eds. Norsk Historisk Leksikon: Naeringsliv, rettsvesen, administrasjon, mynt, maal og vekt, militaere forhold, byggeskikk m. m. 1500-1850. [Oslo:] J. W. Cappelens Forlag A/S, 1974.

Fogtman, Laurids, ed. Kongelige Rescripter, Resolutioner og Collegialbreve for Danmark og Norge, udtogsviis udgivne i chronologisk Orden. Vol. 2 pt. 4: 1740-1746. Copenhagen: Gyldendals Forlag, 1788.

Freidel, Hilmar. Gren og Misjon: Jesu Kristi Kirke av Siste dagers hellige Norske misjon. Oslo: Skrivestua A/S, 1971.

_____. Jesu Kristi Kirke i Norge: Den norske misjons historie, 1851-1966. Oslo: Jesu Kristi Kirke av Siste Dagers Hellige Misjonskontoret, 1966.

Hagberg, Carl M. Den Norske Misjons Historie. Oslo: Universaltrykkeriet, 1928.

Hallager, G. Norges Hoeiesteret 1815-1915. Vol. 1: 1815-1863. Kristiania: H. Aschehoug & Co., W. Nygaard, 1915.

_____. Norges Hoeiesteret 1815-1915. Vol. 2: 1864-1915. Kristiania: H. Aschehoug & Co., W. Nygaard, 1916.

Hals, Harald II. Byen, Havnen og Sjoeen. Oslo: Oslo Bymuseum, 1957.

Hammer, S. C. Kristianias Historie. Vol. 4: 1814-1877. Kristiania: J. W. Cappelen for Hovedkommission, 1928.

_____. Kristianias Historie. Vol. 5: 1878-1924. Oslo: J. W. Cappelen for Hovedkommission, 1928.

Hansen, Conrad Johan Zahl. A Glance At My Life. Provo, Utah: Scott Printing Company, 1971.

Hansen, John S., ed. Mindeudgave C. C. A. Christensen: Poetiske Arbejder, Artikler og Afhandlinger tilligemed hans Levnedsloeb. Salt Lake City, Utah: Bikubens Bibliotek, 1921.

Hansson, Kristian. Norsk Kirkerett. Oslo: H. Aschehoug & Co., W. Nygaard, 1935.

Hardy, Aage. O. P. Petersen: Metodistkirkens Grunnlegger i Norge (En livsskildring). Oslo: Norsk Forlagsselskap, 1953.

Heidel, Norvald. Gamle Fredrikstad: Festningsbyen. Fredrikstad: Naesgaards Boktrykkeri for Reisetrafikkforeningen for Fredrikstad og Omegn, 1968.

Heuch, Johan Christian. *Visitasberetninger 1889-1902*. [Oslo]: A. S. Lunde & Co's Forlag, [1965].

Hjelm, Andreas. *Christian Birch-Reichenwald: En Studie i Norsk Konservatisme*. Oslo: Gyldendal Norsk Forlag, 1950.

Hjelm, [Claus Winther]. *Betaenkning og Forslag til Lov om Graendserne for Religionsfriheden, og navnlig om Separastister og gudelige Forsamlinger Afgivne af Professor Hjelm til Kirkedepartementet under 21de Mai 1840*. Christiania: Chr. Groendahl, [1840].

Holm-Hansen, Bjoern. *Vaare Trossamfunn*. Oslo: Forlaget Magne, 1970.

Holt, Lars Jakob. *Norges historie med hovedlinjer i de andre nordiske lands historie*. [Oslo:] H. Aschehoug & Co., 1974.

Hoeigaard, Einar, and Ruge, Herman. *Den Norske Skoles Historie: En Oversikt*. Oslo: J. W. Cappelens Forlag, [1947].

Israelsen, Andrew M. *Utah Pioneering: An Autobiography*. Salt Lake City, Utah: Deseret News Press, 1938.

Iversen, Frithjov. *Norges Baptister: 100 Aar*. Oslo: Norsk Litteraturselskap, 1960.

Jenson, Andrew. *History of the Scandinavian Mission*. Salt Lake City, Utah: Deseret News Press, 1927.

_____. *Latter-day Saint Biographical Encyclopedia: A Compilation of Biographical Sketches of Prominent Men and Women in the Church of Jesus Christ of Latter-day Saints*. 4 vols. Salt Lake City, Utah: Andrew Jenson History Company, et al., 1901-36; reprint ed., Salt Lake City: Western Epics, 1971.

Johnsen, Oscar Albert. *Norges Boender: Utsyn over den norske bondestands historie*. 2nd ed. Oslo: H. Aschehoug & Co., 1936.

Kemp, Annie Hyer. *What We Know About the Hayer (Hyer) Family*. Logan, Utah: By the Author, 1954.

Kiil, Alf, *Arkivkunnskap: Statsarkiva*. [Oslo]: Universitetsforlaget, 1969.

Kirkhusmo, Anders, ed. *Trondheim i 1000 Aar: Historisk Guide*. Trondheim: F. Bruns Bokhandels Forlag A/S, 1972.

Kolltveit, Olav. *Granvin, Ulvik og Eidfjord i gamal og ny tid: Bygdesoga*. Vol. 2. Granvin, Norway: Granvin, Ulvik og Eidfjord Bygdeboknemnd, 1977.

Kong Christian den Siettes Allernaadigste Forordninger og Aabne
Breve for Aar 1745. Copenhagen: Hans Kongel. Majestets
og Universitets Bogtrykkerie, n.d.

Kong Friderich den Fierdes Allernaadigste Forordninger og Aabne
Breve for Aar 1701 til 1702. Copenhagen: Hans Kongel. Majests.
Privilegerede Bogtrykkeri, n.d.

Lampe, Johan Fredrik. Bergens Stifts Biskoper og Praester efter
Reformationen: Biografiske Efterretninger. Vol. 1. Kristiania:
Cammermeyers Boghandel, 1895.

_____. Bergens Stifts Biskoper og Praester efter Reformationen:
Biografiske Efterretninger. Vol. 2. Kristiania: Cammermeyers
Boghandel, 1896.

Larson, Andrew Karl. Erastus Snow: The Life of a Missionary
and Pioneer for the Early Mormon Church. Dugway, Utah: Pioneer
Press, 1971.

Larson, Gustive O. Prelude to the Kingdom: Mormon Deseret Conquest:
A Chapter in American Cooperative Experience. Francestown,
New Hampshire: Marshall Jones Company, 1947.

Lavik, Johs. Spenningen i Norsk Kirkeliv: Kirkehistoriske konturtegninger. Oslo: Gyldendal Norsk Forlag, 1946,

Lieberman, Sima. The Industrialization of Norway 1800-1920. Oslo,
Bergen, and Tromsoe: Universitetsforlaget, 1970.

Lindstoel, Tallak. Risoer gjennem 200 Aar: 1723-1923. Risoer: I
Hovedkommission hos Erik Gunleikson for Risoer kommune,
1923.

Malling, M. V., and Mejlaender, Otto, eds. Love, Anordninger,
Traktater, Resolutioner, Kundgjoerelser, Departementsskrivelser,
Cirkulaerer m. m. for Kongeriget Norge. Vol. 8: 1871-1876.
Christiania: P. T. Mallings Boghandel, 1878.

Malmin, Gunnar J., trans. and ed. America in the Forties: The
Letters of Ole Munch Raeder. Minneapolis: University of
Minnesota Press, 1929.

Mannsaaker, Dagfinn. Det Norske Presteskapet i det 19. Hundreaaret.
Oslo: Det Norske Samlaget, 1954.

Mejlaender, Otto, ed. Love, Anordninger, Traktater, Resolutioner,
Kundgjoerelser, Departementsskrivelser, Cirkulaerer m. m. for
Kongeriget Norge. Vol. 4: 1851-1855. Christiania: Chr.
Toensbergs Forlag, 1857.

_____, ed. Love, Anordninger, Traktater, Resolutioner, Kundgjoerelser, Departementsskrivelser, Cirkulaerer m. m. for Kongeriget Norge. Vol. 7: 1866-1870. Christiania: P. T. Mallings Forlagsboghandel, 1871.

_____, ed. Love, Anordninger, Traktater, Resolutioner, Kundgjoerelser, Departementsskrivelser, Cirkulaerer m. m. for Kongeriget Norge. Vol. 9: 1877-1882. Christiania: P. T. Mallings Boghandel, 1883.

Mejlaender, Otto, and Munk, Hans, eds. Love, Anordninger, Traktater, Resolutioner, Kundgjoerelser, Departementsskrivelser, Cirkulaerer m. m. for Kongeriget Norge. Vol. 6: 1861-1865. Christiania: P. T. Mallings Forlagsboghandel, 1867.

Molland, Einar. Fra Hans Nielsen Hauge til Eivind Berggrav: Hovedlinjer i Norges Kirkehistorie i det 19. og 20. aarhundre. Oslo: Gyldendal Norsk Forlag, 1972.

Mulder, William. Homeward to Zion: The Mormon Migration from Scandinavia. Minneapolis: University of Minnesota Press, 1957.

Munk, Hans, ed. Love, Anordninger, Traktater, Resolutioner, Kundgjoerelser, Departementsskrivelser, Cirkulaerer m. m. for Kongeriget Norge. Vol. 5: 1856-1860. Christiania: Chr. Toensbergs Forlag, 1861.

Mustorp, H. Haugianere i Oestfold. Olso: Lutherstiftelsens Forlag, 1930.

NRK. "Pipervika - Tankespill om en bydel: Med Rolf Soeder paa historisk vandring i et av Oslos gamle arbeiderstroek." 28 December 1977.

Nerboevik, Jostein. Norsk Historie 1870-1905. Oslo: Det Norske Samlaget, 1973.

Norsk Lovtidende: Samling af Love, Resolutioner m. m., 2den Afdeling, 1887. Kristiania: Groendahl & Soens Bogtrykkeri for E. R. Baetzmann efter oftentlig Foranstaltning, n.d.

Norsk Lovtidende, 2den Afdeling: Samling af Love, Resolutioner m. m., 1895. Kristiania: Groendahl & Soens Bogtrykkeri for E. R. Baetzmann efter offentlig Foranstaltning, n.d.

Norsk Lovtidende, 2den Afdeling: Samling af Love, Resolutioner m. m., 1896. Kristiania: Groendahl & Soens Bogtrykkeri for E. R. Baetzmann efter offentlig Foranstaltning, n.d.

Norsk Lovtidende, 2den afdeling: Samling af Love, Resolutioner m. m., 1897. Kristiania: Groendahl & Soens Bogtrykkeri for E. R. Baetzmann efter offentlig Foranstaltning, n.d.

Norsk Lovtidende, 2den Afdeling: Samling af Love, Resolutioner m. m., 1899. Kristiania: Groendahl & Soens Bogtrykkeri for E. R. Baetzmann efter offentlig Foranstaltning, n.d.

Norsk Lovtidende, 2den Afdeling: Samling af Love, Resolutioner m. m., 1901. Kristiania: Groendahl & Soens Bogtrykkeri for E. R. Baetzmann efter offentlig Foranstaltning, n.d.

Norsk Lovtidende, 2den Afdeling: Samling af Love, Resolutioner m. m., 1902. Kristiania: Groendahl & Soens Bogtrykkeri for E. R. Baetzmann efter offentlig Foranstaltning, n.d.

Norsk Lovtidende, 2den Afdeling: Samling af Love, Resolutioner m. m., 1903. Kristiania: Groendahl & Soens Bogtrykkeri for E. R. Baetzmann og Einar Hansen efter offentlig Foranstaltning, n.d.

Norsk Lovtidende, 2den avdeling: Samling av lover, resolusjoner m. m., 1918. Kristiania: Groendahl & Soens boktrykkeri for Byraachef Young efter offentlig foranstaltning, n.d.

Norway. Storting. Storthings Forhandlinger i Aaret 1854. pt. 9. "Stortingets Forhandlings- Protocoller."

_____. Storthings Forhandlinger i Aarene 1862-1863. pt. 6. "Kongelige Propositioner og Meddelelser fremsatte paa syttende ordentlige Storthing i 1862-1863: indeholdende de Kongelige Propositioner O. No. 13 til og med 40, fremsatte for Odelsthinget."

_____. Storthings Forhandlinger i Aarene 1862-1863. pt. 10. "Indstillinger og Beslutninger af Odelsthinget og Lagthinget: Syttende ordentlige Storthings Indstillinger og Beslutninger i Aarene 1862-1863."

_____. Storthings Forhandlinger i Aaret 1883. pt. 5. "Dokumenter, indgivne til Storthinget og dets Afdelinger."

_____. Storthings Forhandlinger i Aaret 1891. pt. 8. "Forhandlinger i Odelsthinget."

_____. Storthings Forhandlinger i Aaret 1891. B. "Indstillinger til og Beslutninger af Odelsthinget og Lagthinget."

_____. Storthings Forhandlinger 1912. pt. 7. "Forhandlinger i Stortinget B. (Side 1705-3318)."

_____. Storthings Indstillinger og Beslutninger 1883. B. "Odelsthingets og Lagthingets Indstillinger og Beslutninger."

_____. Storthingstidende. "[Det] syttende ordentlige Storthings Forhandlinger: Forhandlinger i Odelsthinget." (ca. 1863.)

_____. Storthingstidende. "[Det] syttende ordentlige Storthings forhandlinger: Forhandlinger i Lagthinget." (ca. 1863.)

_____. Storthingstidende indeholdende to og tredivte ordentlige Storthings Forhandlinger, (Odelsthinget) 1883. "Forhandlinger i Odelsthinget."

_____. Storthingstidende indeholdende sex og tredivte ordentlige Storthings Forhandlinger, 1887. "Forhandlinger i Odelsthinget."

Norwegian Mission. Jubileum aaret 1850-1950. Oslo: Haraldssoen A.S., [1950].

Olafsen, Arnet. Vaare Sorenskrivere: Sorenskriverinstitusjonen og Sorenskrivere i Norge (Et Bidrag til den Norske Dommerstands Historie). Vol. 2: 1814-1927. [Oslo]: A/S O. Fredr. Arnesen Bok og Akcidenstrykkeri, 1945.

Ousland, Godvin. En Kirkehoevding: Professor Gisle Johnson som Teolog og Kirkemann. Oslo: Lutherstiftelsens Forlag, 1950.

Paulsen, P. I., ed. Kong Kristian den Femtes Norske Lov af 15de April 1687. Kristiania: H. Aschehoug & Co., W. Nygaard, 1904.

Pratt, Parley P. Key to the Science of Theology. 2nd ed. Liverpool: George Q. Cannon, 1863.

_____. Key to the Science of Theology. 9th ed. Salt Lake City, Utah: Deseret Book Company, 1965.

Qualey, Carlton C. Norwegian Settlement in the United States. Northfield, Minnesota: Norwegian-American Historical Association, 1938.

Quamme, O. A., and Tjoennaas, Ketil. Gransheradsoga. Vol. 1: Aettar, Gardar og Plasser. Notodden, Norway: Notodden Kommune, 1977.

Rosdail, J. Hart. The Sloopers--Their Ancestry and Posterity: The Story of the People on the Norwegian Mayflower--The Sloop, "Restoration". Broadview, Illinois: Norwegian Slooper Society of America, 1961.

Rudvin, Ola. Indremisjonsselskapets Historie. Vol. 1: Den Norske Lutherstiftelse 1868-1891. Oslo: Lutherstiftelsens Forlag, 1967.

Rygnestad, Knut. Dissentarspoersmaalet i Noreg fraa 1845 til 1891: Lovgjeving og Administrativ Praksis. Oslo: Lutherstiftelsens Forlag, 1955.

Schmidt, Julius August S., ed. Love, Anordninger, Tractater, Resolutioner, Kundgjoerelser, Departementsskrivelser, Circulaerer m. m. for Kongeriget Norge i Tidsrummet fra 1814-1848. Vol. 2: 1832-1848. Christiania: Chr. Toensbergs Forlag, 1850.

Seierstad, Andreas. Kyrkjelegt Reformarbeid i Norig i Nittande Hundreaaret. Vol. 1. Bergen: A/S Lunde & Co.s Forlag, 1923.

Seip, Jens Arup. Et regime foran undergangen. Oslo: Gyldendal Norsk Forlag, 1965.

_____. Fra Embedsmannsstat til Ettpartistat og Andre Essays. [Oslo]: Universitets Forlaget, 1963.

_____. Tanke og handling i norsk historie. Oslo: Gyldendal Norsk Forlag, 1968.

_____. Utsikt over Norges historie. Vol. 1: Tidsrommet 1814-ca. 1860. Oslo: Gyldendal Norsk Forlag, 1974.

Semmingsen, Ingrid, ed. Husmannsminner. Oslo: Tiden Norsk Forlag, 1961.

Skanchy, Anthon L. A Brief Autobiographical Sketch of the Missionary Labors of a Valiant Soldier for Christ. Translated and edited by John A. Widtsoe. n.p., 1915; reprint ed., n.p., 1966.

Skappel, S. Om Husmandsvaesenet i Norge: Dets Oprindelse og Utvikling. Kristiania: I Kommission hos Jacob Dybwad for Videnskapsselskapet, 1922.

Skard, Sigmund. USA i Norsk Historie: 1000-1776-1976. Oslo: Det Norske Samlaget, 1976.

Skullerud, Aage. Bondeopposisjonen og religionsfriheten i 1840-aarene. Bergen, Oslo, and Tromsoe: Universitetsforlaget, 1971.

Smith, Joseph. History of the Church of Jesus Christ of Latter-day Saints. Vol. 5: Period I: History of Joseph Smith, the Prophet, 1842-43. 2nd ed. Salt Lake City, Utah: Deseret Book Company, 1973.

_____. History of the Church of Jesus Christ of Latter-day Saints. Vol. 6: Period I: History of Joseph Smith, the

Prophet, 1843-44. 2nd ed. Salt Lake City, Utah: Deseret Book Company, 1971.

Snow, Erastus. En Sandheds - Roest til de Oprigtige af Hjertet. [Copenhagen]: F. E. Bording, [1850].

_____. One Year in Scandinavia: Results of the Gospel in Denmark and Sweden - Sketches and Observations on the Country and People - Remarkable Events - Late Persecutions and Present Aspect of Affairs. Liverpool: F. D. Richards, 1851; reprint ed., Dallas, Texas: S. K. Taylor Publishing Co., 1973.

Steen, Sverre, gen. ed. Norges Historie. 2 vols. Oslo: Gyldendal Norsk Forlag, 1938. Vol. 2: Fra 1660 til Vaare Dager, by Magnus Jensen.

Steffens, Haagen Krog. Den Norske Central-administrations Historie 1814-1914. Kristiania: I. M. Stenersens Forlag, 1914.

Steiro, Birger. marcus thranes politiske agitasjon 1849-1855. Melhus, Norway: snoefugl forlag, 1974.

Storing, James A. Norwegian Democracy. Boston: Houghton Mifflin Company, 1963.

Stoeylen, Bernt, ed. Register over Lover, Retterboeter, Resolusjoner og Skrivelser m. v. for den Norske Kirke. Oslo: Groendahl & Soens Boktrykkeri, 1934.

Sundt, Eilert. Om Piperviken og Ruseloekbakken: Undersoegelser om arbeidsklassens kaar og saeder i Christiania. Oslo: Tiden Norsk Forlag, 1968.

Sunnanaa, Vilhelm, and Vetrhus, Haavard. Rennesoey Gards og Aettesoge. Rennesoey, Norway: Rennesoey Kommune, 1974.

Svalestuen, Andres A. Tinns Emigrasjons Historie 1837-1907: En undersoekelse med saerlig vekt paa den demografiske, oekonomiske og sosiale bakgrunn for Amerikafarten, og en statistisk analyse av selve utvandringen. Oslo: Universitetsforlaget, 1972.

Taranger, Absalon. Utsikt over den Norske Retts Historie. Vol. 1: Innledning: Rettskildenes Historie. 2nd ed. Oslo: Nationaltrykkeriet for Knut Robberstad, 1935.

Taylor, P. A. M. Expectations Westward: The Mormons and the Emigration of their British Converts in the Nineteenth Century. Ithaca, New York: Cornell University Press, 1966.

Ulvestad, Martin. <u>Nordmaendene i Amerika, deres Historie og Rekord</u>. Minneapolis, Minnesota: History Book Company's Forlag, 1907.

Valton, Fridtjof O. <u>De Norske Vekkelsers Historie: Et Kortfattet Overblikk over det Kristelige Liv i Norge fra Begynnelsen inntil vaare Dager</u>. Oslo: Filadelfiaforlaget A/S, 1942.

Veel, Haakon A. <u>Fredrikstad Handels-, haandverks- og skipperborgere i aarene 1600-1900</u>. Sarpsborg, Norway: Frank Vardings Trykkeri, 1953.

West, Orson B. <u>Den Danske Missions Historie</u>. [Copenhagen?]: Jesu Kristi Kirke af Sidste Dages Hellige, 1965.

Wisloeff, Carl Fr. <u>Norsk Kirkehistorie</u>. Vol. 3. Oslo: Lutherstiftelsens Forlag, 1971.

Woxholth, Yngve, comp. <u>KNA Kart- og Reisehaandbok</u>. Oslo: KNA-Forlaget A/S, 1971.

Zobell, Albert L., Jr. <u>Under the Midnight Sun: Centennial History of Scandinavian Missions</u>. Salt Lake City, Utah: Deseret Book Company, 1950.